Kon Yang

¹⁰/1

960

The Ministers Manual for 1992

By the same editor

Best Sermons 1
Best Sermons 2
Best Sermons 3
Best Sermons 4
Biblical Preaching: An Expositor's Treasury
God's Inescapable Nearness (coauthor with Eduard
  Schweizer)
A Guide to Biblical Preaching
Learning to Speak Effectively
Minister's Worship Manual (coeditor with Ernest A.
  Payne and Stephen F. Winward)
Preaching
Surprised by God
The Twentieth Century Pulpit, Volumes I and II

SIXTY-SEVENTH ANNUAL ISSUE

THE MINISTERS MANUAL

(Doran's)

1992 EDITION

Edited by

JAMES W. COX

HarperSanFrancisco

A Division of HarperCollins*Publishers*

Editors of THE MINISTERS MANUAL

G. B. F. Hallock, D.D., 1926–1958
M. K. W. Heicher, Ph.D., 1943–1968
Charles L. Wallis, M.A., M.Div., 1969–1983
James W. Cox, M.Div., Ph.D.

Translations of the Bible referred to and quoted from in this book are indicated by their standard abbreviations, such as NRSV (New Revised Standard Version) and NIV (New International Version). In addition, some contributors have made their own translations and others have used a mixed text.

Other acknowledgments are on page 321.

THE MINISTERS MANUAL FOR 1992.

FIRST EDITION

Library of Congress Catalog Card Number
25–21658
ISSN 0738–5323

90 91 92 93 94 HC 10 9 8 7 6 5 4 3 2 1

This edition is printed on acid-free paper that meets the American National Standards Institute Z39.48 Standard.

CONTENTS

PREFACE

What is *The Ministers Manual* for? Who uses it? Ministers, of course, use it, but there are many laypeople who find this annual volume a source of personal inspiration, a help in making talks, and a guide for devotional programs.

All preachers of the Word welcome the insights and testimonies of other preachers, scholars, teachers, and authors. Such insights and testimonies stimulate creative ideas and help in the production of many excellent, original sermons. Moreover, they provide quotable materials that confirm and supplement the preacher's own thoughts and enrich the preacher's messages.

Many pastors preach each week from a lectionary text, believing that this offers the best way of covering all of the most important teaching of the Scriptures over a period of three years. So, in addition to the topical sermon and related worship materials for every Sunday, *The Ministers Manual* has a sermon on the Common Lectionary gospel text for each Sunday of the Christian year; also, outlines on Old Testament and epistle texts for each Sunday. In addition, there are special sections with a selection of sermons for communion services, funeral services, Lent and Easter, Advent and Christmas, and Evangelism and World Missions.

Also, each year two different features are presented: homiletical studies on a particular part of the Bible and homiletical studies on a particular theme. Sermons for children and copious illustrations offer widely welcomed materials.

We receive letters from all parts of the world telling us of how *The Ministers Manual* contributes to readers' personal lives and to their service in the church. Through the years these reassuring words have encouraged us greatly.

I wish personally to express gratitude for the practical encouragement given by the trustees of The Southern Baptist Theological Seminary and President Roy Honeycutt and to thank the many individuals and publishers for permission to quote from their material. Alicia Gardner, office services supervisor, and Keitha Brasler, who typed the manuscript, also have my profound gratitude for their careful attention to the production of this volume. In addition, I am most appreciative of the faithful work of the editorial staff at Harper/San Francisco.

James W. Cox
The Southern Baptist Theological Seminary
2825 Lexington Road
Louisville, Kentucky 40280

SECTION I.
General Aids and Resources
Civil Year Calendars

1992

JANUARY

S	M	T	W	T	F	S
			1	2	3	4
5	6	7	8	9	10	11
12	13	14	15	16	17	18
19	20	21	22	23	24	25
26	27	28	29	30	31	

FEBRUARY

S	M	T	W	T	F	S
						1
2	3	4	5	6	7	8
9	10	11	12	13	14	15
16	17	18	19	20	21	22
23	24	25	26	27	28	29

MARCH

S	M	T	W	T	F	S
1	2	3	4	5	6	7
8	9	10	11	12	13	14
15	16	17	18	19	20	21
22	23	24	25	26	27	28
29	30	31				

APRIL

S	M	T	W	T	F	S
			1	2	3	4
5	6	7	8	9	10	11
12	13	14	15	16	17	18
19	20	21	22	23	24	25
26	27	28	29	30		

MAY

S	M	T	W	T	F	S
					1	2
3	4	5	6	7	8	9
10	11	12	13	14	15	16
17	18	19	20	21	22	23
24	25	26	27	28	29	30
31						

JUNE

S	M	T	W	T	F	S
	1	2	3	4	5	6
7	8	9	10	11	12	13
14	15	16	17	18	19	20
21	22	23	24	25	26	27
28	29	30				

JULY

S	M	T	W	T	F	S
			1	2	3	4
5	6	7	8	9	10	11
12	13	14	15	16	17	18
19	20	21	22	23	24	25
26	27	28	29	30	31	

AUGUST

S	M	T	W	T	F	S
						1
2	3	4	5	6	7	8
9	10	11	12	13	14	15
16	17	18	19	20	21	22
23	24	25	26	27	28	29
30	31					

SEPTEMBER

S	M	T	W	T	F	S
		1	2	3	4	5
6	7	8	9	10	11	12
13	14	15	16	17	18	19
20	21	22	23	24	25	26
27	28	29	30			

OCTOBER

S	M	T	W	T	F	S
				1	2	3
4	5	6	7	8	9	10
11	12	13	14	15	16	17
18	19	20	21	22	23	24
25	26	27	28	29	30	31

NOVEMBER

S	M	T	W	T	F	S
1	2	3	4	5	6	7
8	9	10	11	12	13	14
15	16	17	18	19	20	21
22	23	24256		26	27	28
29	30					

DECEMBER

S	M	T	W	T	F	S
		1	2	3	4	5
6	7	8	9	10	11	12
13	14	15	16	17	18	19
20	21	22	23	24	25	26
27	28	29	30	31		

1993

JANUARY

S	M	T	W	T	F	S
					1	2
3	4	5	6	7	8	9
10	11	12	13	14	15	16
17	18	19	20	21	22	23
24	25	26	27	28	29	30
31						

FEBRUARY

S	M	T	W	T	F	S
	1	2	3	4	5	6
7	8	9	10	11	12	13
14	15	16	17	18	19	20
21	22	23	24	25	26	27
28						

MARCH

S	M	T	W	T	F	S
	1	2	3	4	5	6
7	8	9	10	11	12	13
14	15	16	17	18	19	20
21	22	23	24	25	26	27
28	29	30	31			

APRIL

S	M	T	W	T	F	S
				1	2	3
4	5	6	7	8	9	10
11	12	13	14	15	16	17
18	19	20	21	22	23	24
25	26	27	28	29	30	

MAY

S	M	T	W	T	F	S
						1
2	3	4	5	6	7	8
9	10	11	12	13	14	15
16	17	18	19	20	21	22
23	24	25	26	27	28	29
30	31					

JUNE

S	M	T	W	T	F	S
		1	2	3	4	5
6	7	8	9	10	11	12
13	14	15	16	17	18	19
20	21	22	23	24	25	26
27	28	29	30			

JULY

S	M	T	W	T	F	S
				1	2	3
4	5	6	7	8	9	10
11	12	13	14	15	16	17
18	19	20	21	22	23	24
25	26	27	28	29	30	31

AUGUST

S	M	T	W	T	F	S
1	2	3	4	5	6	7
8	9	10	11	12	13	14
15	16	17	18	19	20	21
22	23	24	25	26	27	28
29	30	31				

SEPTEMBER

S	M	T	W	T	F	S
			1	2	3	4
5	6	7	8	9	10	11
12	13	14	15	16	17	18
19	20	21	22	23	24	25
26	27	28	29	30		

OCTOBER

S	M	T	W	T	F	S
					1	2
3	4	5	6	7	8	9
10	11	12	13	14	15	16
17	18	19	20	21	22	23
24	25	26	27	28	29	30
31						

NOVEMBER

S	M	T	W	T	F	S
	1	2	3	4	5	6
7	8	9	10	11	12	13
14	15	16	17	18	19	20
21	22	23	24	25	26	27
28	29	30				

DECEMBER

S	M	T	W	T	F	S
			1	2	3	4
5	6	7	8	9	10	11
12	13	14	15	16	17	18
19	20	21	22	23	24	25
26	27	28	29	30	31	

Church and Civic Calendar for 1992

JANUARY

1 New Year's Day
   The Name of Jesus
5 Twelfth Night
6 Epiphany
18 Confession of St. Peter
19 Robert E. Lee's Birthday
20 Martin Luther King Day
25 Conversion of St. Paul

FEBRUARY

1 National Freedom Day
2 Presentation of Jesus in
   the Temple
   Groundhog Day
   Boy Scout Sunday
3 Four Chaplains Memorial
   Day
9 Race Relations Sunday
12 Lincoln's Birthday
14 St. Valentine's Day
15 Susan B. Anthony Day
17 Presidents' Day
22 Washington's Birthday
23–Mar. 1 Brotherhood Week

MARCH

3 Mardi Gras
4 Ash Wednesday
6 World Day of Prayer
8 First Sunday of Lent
9 Orthodox Lent Begins
15 Second Sunday of Lent
17 St. Patrick's Day
19 Purim
22 Third Sunday of Lent
29 Fourth Sunday of Lent

APRIL

5 Fifth Sunday of Lent
   Daylight Saving Time
   Begins
12 Palm/Passion Sunday
   Sixth Sunday of Lent
12–18 Holy Week
16 Maundy Thursday
17 Good Friday

18 Passover Begins
19 Easter
24 Arbor Day
25 St. Mark, Evangelist
26 Orthodox Easter

MAY

1 May Day
   St. Philip and St. James,
   Apostles
3–10 Festival of the Christian
   Home
5 National Teacher Day
10 Mother's Day
16 Armed Forces Day
20 Victoria Day (Canada)
22 National Maritime Day
24 Memorial Sunday
25 Memorial Day
28 Ascension Day

JUNE

7 Pentecost
   Shavuot
11 St. Barnabas, Apostle
14 Trinity Sunday
   Flag Day
21 Father's Day
29 St. Peter and St. Paul,
   Apostles

JULY

1 Canada Day (Canada)
4 Independence Day
25 St. James, Apostle

AUGUST

6 The Transfiguration
15 Mary, the Mother of Jesus
24 St. Bartholomew, Apostle

SEPTEMBER

7 Labor Day
8 Birth of the Virgin Mary
17 Citizenship Day

21 St. Matthew, Apostle and
   Evangelist
28 Frances Willard Day
   First Day of Rosh
   Hashanah
29 St. Michael and All Angels

OCTOBER

 4 World Communion
   Sunday
   St. Francis of Assisi
 7 Yom Kippur (Day of
   Atonement)
12 First Day of Sukkoth
   Columbus Day
   Thanksgiving Day
   (Canada)
18 St. Luke, Evangelist
24 United Nations Day
25 Daylight Saving Time Ends
28 St. Simon and St. Jude,
   Apostles
31 Reformation Day
   Halloween

NOVEMBER

 1 All Saints' Day
 2 All Souls' Day
 3 Election Day

 8 Stewardship Day
11 Veterans' Day
   Remembrance Day
   (Canada)
12 Elizabeth Cady Stanton
   Day
15 Bible Sunday
22 Christ the King
26 Thanksgiving Day
29 First Sunday of Advent
30 St. Andrew, Apostle

DECEMBER

 6 Second Sunday of Advent
13 Third Sunday of Advent
15 Bill of Rights Day
20 Fourth Sunday of Advent
   First Day of Hanukkah
21 St. Thomas, Apostle
   Forefathers' Day
24 Christmas Eve
25 Christmas Day
26 St. Stephen, Deacon and
   Martyr
   Boxing Day (Canada)
27 St. John, Apostle and
   Evangelist
28 The Holy Innocents,
   Martyrs
31 New Year's Eve
   Watch Night

Common Lectionary for 1992

The following Scripture lessons are commended for use in public worship, with some modifications, by various Protestant churches and the Roman Catholic church and include first, second, Gospel readings, and Psalms according to Cycle C from January 5 to November 22 and according to Cycle A from November 29 to December 27.

January 5: Jer. 31:7–14 or Ecclus. 24:1–4, 12–16; Eph. 1:3–6, 15–18; John 1:1–18.

EPIPHANY SEASON

January 6 (Epiphany): Isa. 60:1–6; Ps. 72:1–14; Eph. 3:1–12; Matt. 2:1–12.

January 12 (Baptism of the Lord): Isa. 61:1–4; Ps. 29; Acts 8:14–17; Luke 3:15–17, 21–22.

January 19: Isa. 62:1–5; Ps. 36:5–10; 1 Cor. 12:1–11; John 2:1–11.

January 26: Neh. 8:1–4a, 5–6, 8–10; Ps. 19:7–14; 1 Cor. 12:12–30; Luke 4:14–21.

February 2: Jer. 1:4–10; Ps. 71:1–6; 1 Cor. 13:1–13; Luke 4:21–30.

February 9: Isa. 6:1–8 (9–13); Ps. 138; 1 Cor. 15:1–11; Luke 5:1–11.

February 16: Jer. 17:5–10; Ps. 1; 1 Cor. 15:12–20; Luke 6:17–26.

February 23: Gen. 45:3–11, 15; Ps. 37:1–11; 1 Cor. 15:35–38, 42–50; Luke 6:27–38.

March 1 (Transfiguration): Isa. 55:10–13; Ps. 92:1–4, 12–15; 1 Cor. 15:51–

58; Luke 6:39–49; or Exod. 34:29–35; Ps. 99; 2 Cor. 3:12–4:2; Luke 9:28–36.

LENT

March 4 (Ash Wednesday): Joel 2:1–2, 12–17a; Ps. 51:1–12; 2 Cor. 5:20b–6:2 (3–10); Matt. 6:1–6, 16–21.

March 8: Deut. 26:1–11; Ps. 91:9–16; Rom. 10:8b–13; Luke 4:1–13.

March 15: Gen. 15:1–12, 17–18; Ps. 127; Phil. 3:17–4:1; Luke 13:31–35; or Luke 9:28–36.

March 22: Exod. 3:1–15; Ps. 103:1–13; 1 Cor. 10:1–13; Luke 13:1–9.

March 29: Josh. 5:9–12; Ps. 34:1–8; 2 Cor. 5:16–21; Luke 15:1–3, 11–32.

April 5: Isa. 43:16–21; Ps. 126; Phil. 3: 8–14; John 12:1–8.

April 12 (Palm Sunday): Isa. 50:4–9a; Ps. 118:19–29; Phil. 2:5–11; Luke 19:28–40; or (Passion Sunday): Isa. 50:4–9a; Ps. 31:9–16; Phil. 2:5–11; Luke 22:14–23:56 or Luke 23:1–49.

(Monday): Isa. 42:1–9; Ps. 36:5–10; Heb. 9:11–15; John 12:1–11.

(Tuesday): Isa. 49:1–7; Ps. 71:1–12; 1 Cor. 1:18–31; John 12:20–36.

(Wednesday): Isa. 50:4–9a; Ps. 70; Heb. 12:1–3; John 13:21–30.

(Thursday): Jer. 31:31–34; Ps. 116:12–19; Heb. 10:16–25; Luke 22:7–20.

April 17 (Good Friday): Isa. 52:13–53:12; Ps. 22:1–18; Heb. 4:14–16; 5:7–9; John 18:1–19:42; or John 19:17–30.

SEASON OF EASTER

(Easter Vigil): Gen. 1:1–2:2; Ps. 33; Gen. 7:1–5, 11–18; 8:6–18; 9:8–13; Ps. 46; Gen. 22:1–18; Ps. 16; Exod. 14:10–15:1; Exod. 15:1–6, 11–13, 17–18; Isa. 54:5–14; Ps. 30; Isa. 55:1–11; Isa. 12:2–6; Bar. 3:9–15, 32–4:4; Ps. 19; Ezek. 36:24–38; Ps. 42; Ezek. 37:1–14; Ps. 143; Zeph. 3:14–20; Ps. 98; Rom. 6:3–11, Ps. 114; Luke 24:1–11.

April 19 (Easter): Acts 10:34–43; or Isa. 65:17–25; Ps. 118:14–24; 1 Cor. 15:19–26; or Acts 10:34–43; John 20:1–18; or Luke 24:1–12.

April 19 (Easter Evening): Acts 5:29–32; or Dan. 12:1–3; Ps. 150; 1 Cor. 5:6–8; or Acts 5:29–32; Luke 24:13–49.

April 26: Acts 5:27–32; Ps. 2; Rev. 1:4–8; John 20:19–31.

May 3: Acts 9:1–20; Ps. 30:4–12; Rev. 5:11–14; John 21:1–19; or John 21:15–19.

May 10: Acts 13:15–16, 26–33; Ps. 23; Rev. 7:9–17; John 10:22–30.

May 17: Acts 14:8–18; Ps. 145:13b–21; Rev. 21:1–6; John 13:31–35.

May 24: Acts 15:1–2, 22–29; Ps. 67; Rev. 21:10, 22–27; John 14:23–29.

May 28 (Ascension): Acts 1:1–11; Ps. 47; Eph. 1:15–23; Luke 24:46–53; or Mark 16:9–16, 19–20.

May 31: Acts 16:16–34; Ps. 97; Rev. 22:12–14, 16–17, 20; John 17:20–26.

SEASON OF PENTECOST

June 7 (Pentecost): Acts 2:1–21; or Gen. 11:1–9; Ps. 104:24–34; Rom. 8:14–17; or Acts 2:1–21; John 14:8–17, 25–27.

June 14 (Trinity Sunday): Prov. 8:22–31; Ps. 8; Rom. 5:1–5; John 16:12–15.

June 21: 1 Kings 19:9–14; Ps. 43; Gal. 3:23–29; Luke 9:18–24.

June 28: 1 Kings 19:15–21; Ps. 44:1–8; Gal. 5:1, 13–25; Luke 9:51–62.

July 5: 1 Kings 21:1–3, 17–21; Ps. 5:1–8; Gal. 6:7–18; Luke 10:1–12, 17–20.

July 12: 2 Kings 2:1, 6–14; Ps. 139:1–12; Col. 1:1–14; Luke 10:25–37.

July 19: 2 Kings 4:8–17; Ps. 139:13–18; Col. 1:21–29; Luke 10:38–42.

July 26: 2 Kings 5:1–5ab (". . . in Israel"); Ps. 21:1–7; Col. 2:6–15; Luke 11:1–13.

August 2: 2 Kings 13:14–20a; Ps. 28; Col. 3:1–11; Luke 12:13–21.

August 9: Jer. 18:1–11; Ps. 14; Heb. 11:1–3, 8–19; Luke 12:32–40.

August 16: Jer. 20:7–13; Ps. 10:12–18; Heb. 12:1–2, 12–17; Luke 12:49–56.

August 23: Jer. 28:1–9; Ps. 84; Heb. 12:18–29; Luke 13:22–30.

August 30: Ezek. 18:1–9, 25–29; Ps. 15; Heb. 13:1–8; Luke 14:1, 7–14.

September 6: Ezek. 33:1–11; Ps. 94:12–22; Philem. 1–12; Luke 14:25–33.

September 13: Hos. 4:1–3, 5:15–6:6; Ps. 77:11–20; 1 Tim. 1:12–17; Luke 15:1–10.

September 20: Hos. 11:1–11; Ps. 107:1–9; 1 Tim. 2:1–7; Luke 16:1–13.

September 27: Joel 2:23–30; Ps. 107:1, 33–43; 1 Tim. 6:6–19; Luke 16:19–31.

October 4: Amos 5:6–7, 10–15; Ps. 101; 2 Tim. 1:1–14; Luke 17:5–10.

October 11: Mic. 1:2; 2:1–10; Ps. 26; 2 Tim. 2:8–15; Luke 17:11–19.

October 18: Hab. 1:1–3; 2:1–4; Ps. 119:137–44; 2 Tim. 3:15–4:5; Luke 18:1–8.

October 25: Zeph. 3:1–9; Ps. 3; 2 Tim. 4:6–8, 16–18; Luke 18:9–14.

November 1 (All Saints' Day): Hag. 2:1–9; Ps. 65:1–8; 2 Thess. 1:5–12; Luke 19:1–10; or Dan. 7:1–3, 15–18; Ps. 149; Eph. 1:11–23; Luke 6:20–36.

November 8: Zech. 7:1–10; Ps. 9:11–20; 2 Thess. 2:13–3:5; Luke 20:27–38.

November 15: Mal. 4:1–6 (3:19–24 in Heb.); Ps. 82; 2 Thess. 3:6–13; Luke 21:5–19.

November 22 (Christ the King): 2 Sam. 5: 1–5; Ps. 95; Col. 1:11–20; John 12:9–19.

November 26 (Thanksgiving Day): Deut. 26:1–11; Ps. 100; Phil. 4:4–9; John 6:25–35.

ADVENT

November 29: Isa. 2:1–5; Ps. 122; Rom. 13:11–14; Matt. 24:36–44.

December 6: Isa. 11:1–10; Ps. 72:1–8; Rom. 15:4–13; Matt. 3:1–12.

December 13: Isa. 35:1–10; Ps. 146:5–10; James 5:7–10; Matt. 11:2–11.

December 20: Isa. 7:10–16; Ps. 24; Rom. 1:1–7; Matt. 1:18–25

CHRISTMAS SEASON.

December 24/25 (Christmas Eve/Day): Isa. 9:2–7; Ps. 96; Titus 2:11–14; Luke 2:1–20; (also): Isa. 62:6–7, 10–12; Ps. 97; Isa. 52:7–10; Ps. 98; Titus 3:4–7; Heb. 1:1–12; Luke 2:8–20; John 1:1–14.

December 27: Isa. 63:7–9; Ps. 111; Heb. 2:10–18; Matt. 2:13–15, 19–23.

Four-Year Church Calendar

	1992	1993	1994	1995
Ash Wednesday	March 4	February 24	February 16	March 1
Palm Sunday	April 12	April 4	March 27	April 9
Good Friday	April 17	April 9	April 1	April 14
Easter	April 19	April 11	April 3	April 16
Ascension Day	May 28	May 20	May 12	May 25
Pentecost	June 7	May 30	May 22	June 4
Trinity Sunday	June 14	June 6	May 29	June 11
Thanksgiving	November 26	November 25	November 24	November 23
Advent Sunday	November 29	November 28	November 27	December 3

Forty-Year Easter Calendar

1992 April 19	2002 March 31	2012 April 8	2022 April 17
1993 April 11	2003 April 20	2013 March 31	2023 April 9
1994 April 3	2004 April 11	2014 April 20	2024 March 31
1995 April 16	2005 March 27	2015 April 5	2025 April 20
1996 April 7	2006 April 16	2016 March 27	2026 April 5
1997 March 30	2007 April 8	2017 April 16	2027 March 28
1998 April 12	2008 March 23	2018 April 1	2028 April 16
1999 April 4	2009 April 12	2019 April 21	2029 April 1
2000 April 23	2010 April 4	2020 April 12	2030 April 21
2001 April 15	2011 April 24	2021 April 4	2031 April 13

Traditional Wedding Anniversary Identifications

1 Paper	7 Wool	13 Lace	35 Coral
2 Cotton	8 Bronze	14 Ivory	40 Ruby
3 Leather	9 Pottery	15 Crystal	45 Sapphire
4 Linen	10 Tin	20 China	50 Gold
5 Wood	11 Steel	25 Silver	55 Emerald
6 Iron	12 Silk	30 Pearl	60 Diamond

Colors Appropriate for Days and Seasons

White. Symbolizes purity, perfection, and joy and identifies festivals marking events, except Good Friday, in the life of Jesus: Christmas, Epiphany, Easter, Eastertide, Ascension Day; also Trinity Sunday, All Saints' Day, weddings, funerals. Gold may also be used.

Red. Symbolizes the Holy Spirit, martyrdom, and the love of God: Good Friday, Pentecost, and Sundays following.

Violet. Symbolizes penitence: Advent, Lent.

Green. Symbolizes mission to the world, hope, regeneration, nurture, and growth: Epiphany season, Kingdomtide, Rural Life Sunday, Labor Sunday, Thanksgiving Sunday.

Blue. Advent, in some churches.

Flowers in Season Appropriate for Church Use

January. Carnation or snowdrop.
February. Violet or primrose.
March. Jonquil or daffodil.
April. Lily, sweet pea, or daisy.
May. Lily of the valley or hawthorn.
June. Rose or honeysuckle.

July. Larkspur or water lily.
August. Gladiolus or poppy.
September. Aster or morning glory.
October. Calendula or cosmos.
November. Chrysanthemum.
December. Narcissus, holly, or poinsettia.

Historical, Cultural, and Religious Anniversaries in 1992

Compiled by Kenneth M. Cox

10 years (1982). *April 25*: Egypt ceremonially regains control of the Sinai, restoring the line of demarcation between Egypt and Israel essentially to the pre-1967 location. *June 21*: A Washington, D.C., federal court jury finds John Hinckley not guilty by reason of insanity of shooting President Reagan and three others on March 30, 1981. *July 16*: Unification Church founder Sun Myung Moon is sentenced to prison for tax fraud and conspiracy to obstruct justice. *November 10*: Soviet Communist party general secretary Leonid Brezhnev dies in Moscow. *December 2*: Barney Clark receives the world's first permanent artificial heart transplant.

25 years (1967). *April 28*: Heavyweight boxing champion Muhammad Ali is arrested, following denial of conscientious objector status and his refusal of induction into the U.S. Army. *June 5*: The Six-Day Arab-Israeli War begins, following months of conflict between Israel and Syria. *October 2*: Thurgood Marshall is sworn in as the first black U.S. Supreme Court justice. *October 9*: Revolutionary leader Che Guevara is killed by Bolivian troops in the Andes. *December 2*: The first human heart transplant is performed in Capetown, South Africa. *Debut: Rolling Stone* magazine.

50 years (1942). *April 9*: U.S. troops surrender to the Japanese on the Bataan peninsula in the Philippines. *June 25*: General Dwight D. Eisenhower is appointed commander-in-chief of U.S. forces in Europe. *August 22*: The Battle

of Stalingrad begins and, until the Germans surrender the following February, hundreds of thousands will die. *November 11*: "Unoccupied France" is occupied by the Germans. *December 2*: The world's first controlled, self-sustaining nuclear reaction is achieved by a team including Enrico Fermi and Edward Teller. *Debuts*: Kellogg's Raisin Bran; napalm; the Office of Strategic Services.

75 years (1917). *March 2*: Congress passes the Jones Act, making Puerto Rico a U.S. territory. *April 6*: The U.S. declares war on Germany, following the German sinking of eight U.S. vessels. *May 29*: John F. Kennedy is born in Brookline, Massachusetts. *November 6*: The Russian Bolshevik revolution begins at Petrograd, as Lenin and Trotsky come to power; New York becomes the first state to grant equal voting rights to women. *Debuts*: Uncle Sam "I want you" posters; term *surrealism*; *World Book* encyclopedia; National Hockey League.

100 years (1892). *September 7*: Gentleman Jim Corbett defeats John C. Sullivan in the first title prizefight fought by Marquis of Queensberry rules. *October 12*: Former clergyman Francis Bellamy's "pledge of allegiance" is first recited to commemorate the 400th anniversary of the discovery of America. *Debuts*: Book matches; cold cream; Sierra Club.

125 years (1867). *March 29*: The British North America Act unites Ontario, Quebec, New Brunswick, and Nova Scotia into the Dominion of Canada. *March 30*: Russian czar Alexander II signs a treaty ceding Alaska to the United States for the price of $7 million. The First Vatican Council is summoned by Pope Pius IX. *Debuts*: The curveball pitch; Karl Marx's *Das Kapital*.

150 years (1842). *March 1*: U.S. Supreme Court rules in *Prigg* v. *Pennsylvania* that the owner of a fugitive slave may recover the slave under the Fugitive Slave Act of 1793. Georgia physician Crawford Williamson performs the first recorded operation using general anesthesia (ether). *Debut*: Wire suspension bridge in United States.

200 years (1792). *March 16*: Swedish assassin shoots King Gustavus III of Sweden in Stockholm. *April 2*: U.S. Mint is established, begins decimal coinage of silver, gold, and copper at Philadelphia. *September 21*: French National Convention meets and abolishes the monarchy. *Debut*: Eli Whitney's cotton gin.

250 years (1742). Jews are expelled from Russia. *Debuts*: Franklin stove, Sheffield silverplate.

350 years (1642). *March 4*: France's Cardinal Richelieu dies. *Debut*: Calculating machine.

400 years (1592). University of Pisa mathematician Galileo Galilei quits after having defied the accepted belief that objects fall to the ground at speeds proportionate to their weight. The Congregation for Affairs of Faith is established, beginning modern missionary activity.

500 years (1492). *October 12*: Christopher Columbus sights land in what will be called North America and sets foot on San Salvador (now Watling Island).

Anniversaries of Hymn Writers and Hymn-Tune Composers in 1992

Compiled by Hugh T. McElrath

25 years (1967). *Death* of Donald Wynn Hughes (b. 1911), author of "Creator of the earth and skies," "Lord God, we see thy power displayed"; John Masefield (b. 1875), author of "O Christ who holds the open gate," "Sing, men and angels, sing," "By weary stages the old world ages"; Thomas Tiplady (b. 1882), author of "Above the hills of time the cross is gleaming," "From Nazareth the Lord has come," "Beyond the wheeling worlds of light," and many others; John W. Work III (b. 1901), arranger of "Go, tell it on the mountain" and other African-American spirituals.

50 years (1942). *Birth* of Michael Dawney, composer of BAYHALL ("Reap me the earth as a harvest of God"), FE-

LINFOEL ("See Christ the wounded for our sake"); Gloria Gaither, author (with William J. Gaither) of "Because he lives," "Jesus, Jesus, Jesus," and others; Stephen Charles Orchard, author of "Lord, you give to us the precious gift of life"; Michael A. Perry, author of "The God of heaven," "Blest be the God of Israel," and other texts. *Death* of Frederick Arthur Jackson (b. 1867), author of "Master, we thy footsteps follow," "Down the mines for hidden treasure"; Frederick J. Work (b. 1879), adapter of the words of "Were you there," "Lord, I want to be a Christian," "New born again," and other spirituals.

75 years (1917). *Birth* of George B. Caird (d. 1884), author of "Not far beyond the sea nor high," "Almighty Father, who for us thy Son didst give"; Ian M. Fraser, author of "Lord, bring the day to pass," "Lord, look upon our working days," and others; John Gardner, composer of WIDERSMOUTH ("When Christ was born of Mary free"), ILFRACOMBE ("Glorious the day when Christ was born"); Francis Alan Jackson, composer of EAST ACKLAM ("For the fruits of his creation"); Erik Routley (d. 1982), author of "All who love and serve your city," "New songs of celebration render," and others; composer of SHARPTHORNE ("What does the Lord require"), CHALFONT PARK ("Eternal light, eternal light"), ABINGDON ("Lord God, whose love has called us here"), and others. *Death* of William Stevenson Hoyte (b. 1844), composer of ST. COLOMB ("From glory unto glory!"), ST. EDMUND ("Lord, when we bend before thy throne"), ST. NICOLAS ("Herald in the wilderness"); John Hunter (b. 1848), author of "Dear Master, in whose life I see"; William DeWitt Hyde (b. 1858), author of "Creation's Lord, we give thee thanks"; Folliott Sandford Pierpoint (b. 1835), author of "For the beauty of the earth"; Ernest W. Shurtleff (b. 1862), author of "Lead on, O King eternal"; Samuel Smith (b. 1821), composer of RUTH ("Summer suns are glowing"); Alfred Henry Vine (b. 1845), author of "O breath of God, breathe on us now" and others; Harry Ellis Wooldridge (b. 1845), composer of YATTENDON 46 ("Breathe on

me, breath of God") and arranger/harmonizer of many more.

100 years (1892). *Birth* of Katherine K. Davis (d. 1980), composer of MASSACHUSETTS ("Make room within my heart, O God"), arranger of ASH GROVE ("Let all things now living"); Harry Dixon Loes (d. 1965), composer of REDEEMER ("Up Calvary's mountain one dreadful morn"), BOUNDLESS PRAISE ("We sing the boundless praise"), and others; Wendell P. Loveless (d. 1987), composer of LOVELESS ("Trust in the Lord with all your heart"); John Jacob Niles (d. 1980), author and composer of "I wonder as I wander" and other folk hymns; Herbert Howells (d. 1983), composer of MICHAEL ("All my hope on God is founded"), NEWNHAM ("Lord Christ, when first you came").

100 years (1892). *Death* of Fenton John Anthony Hort (b. 1828), translator of "O strength and stay upholding all creation," "O joy, because the circling year"; Samuel Longfellow (b. 1819), author of "Holy Spirit, truth divine," "Now on land and sea descending," and others; Basil Manly, Jr. (b. 1825), author of "Soldiers of Christ in truth arrayed"; Alfred Lord Tennyson (b. 1809), author of "Ring out, wild bells, to the wild sky," "Strong Son of God, immortal love," "Sunset and evening star"; John Greenleaf Whittier (b. 1807), author of "Dear Lord and Father of mankind," "Immortal love, forever full" and others.

125 years (1867). *Birth* of Percy Dearmer (d. 1936), author of "Draw us in the Spirit's tether," "Sing praise to God who spoke through man," "To the name that is salvation," and many more; C. Winfred Douglas (d. 1944), composer of ST. DUNSTAN'S ("He who would valiant be") and arranger/harmonizer of numerous others; Carl Doving (d. 1937), translator of "Built on the rock, the church doth stand"; F. A. Jackson (d. 1942), author of "Down the mines for buried treasure," "Master, we thy footsteps follow"; William P. Merrill (d. 1954), author of "Rise up, O men of God," "Not alone for mighty empire," and others; Edward Woodall Naylor (d. 1934), composer of FROM STRENGTH TO STRENGTH ("Soldiers of Christ, arise"); Thomas Tertius Noble

(d. 1953), composer of ORA LABORA ("Come, labor on"), EASTWICK ("O Lord most high, eternal king"); Frederick George Russell (d. 1929), composer of LOMBARD STREET ("When through the whirl of wheels"). Death of Ithamar Conkey (b. 1815), composer of RATHBUN ("In the cross of Christ I glory"); John James Cummins (b. 1795), author of "Jesus, Lord of life and glory"; James Edmeston (b. 1791), author of "Savior, breathe an evening blessing," "Lead us, Heavenly Father, lead us"; John Fawcett (b. 1789), composer of MELLING ("Come, Lord, to our souls come down") and other tunes; Edward Hodges (b. 1796), composer of GLOUCESTER ("Look down upon us, God of grace"), adapter of HYMN TO JOY ("Joyful, joyful we adore thee" and others); William Letton Viner (b. 1790), composer of DISMISSAL ("Lord, dismiss us with thy blessing").

150 years (1842). *Birth* of Sidney Lanier (d. 1881), author of "Into the woods my master went"; George Matheson (d. 1906), author of "O love that wilt not let me go," "Make me a captive, Lord," and others; Henry Williams Mozley (d. 1919), author of "Lord who fulfillest thus anew," "Lord, who while yet a boy"; Sir Arthur S. Sullivan (d. 1900), composer of ST. KEVIN ("Come, ye faithful, raise the strain," ST. GERTRUDE ("Onward Christians soldiers"), and others; Thomas Vincent Tymms (d. 1921), author of "Our day of praise has ended," "Lord, I read of tender mercy." *Death* of John Henley (b. 1800), author of "Children of Jerusalem."

175 years (1817). *Birth* of Jane Montgomery Campbell (d. 1878), translator of "We plow the fields and scatter"; Henry Mayo Gunn (d. 1886), author of "Our fathers were high-minded men"; George Herbert (d. 1916), composer of SUNSET ("O Saviour, bless us ere we go") and others; Carolyn M. Noel (d. 1877), author of "At the name of Jesus." Death of Timothy Dwight (b. 1752), author of "I love thy kingdom, Lord"; John Fawcett (b. 1939/40), author of "Blest be the tie that binds," "How precious is the book divine," "Lord, dismiss us with thy blessing"; Justin Henrich Knecht (b. 1752),

composer of VIENNA ("Children of the heavenly father"), ST. HILDA ("O Jesus, Thou art standing").

200 years (1792). *Birth* of John Bowring (d. 1872), author of "In the cross of Christ I glory," "God is love, his mercy brightens," "Watchman, tell us of the night"; John Keble (d. 1866), author of "Sun of my soul, thou Saviour dear," "New every morning is the love," "The voice that breathed o'er Eden," "God, our Lord, a King remaining," and others; Lowell Mason (d. 1872), composer of OLIVET ("My faith looks up to thee"), BETHANY ("Nearer, my God, to thee"), MISSIONARY HYMN ("From Greenland's icy mountains"), and many other tunes; Joseph Mohr (d. 1848), author of "Silent night, holy night." Death of Edward Perronet (b. 1726), author of "All hail the power of Jesus' name."

250 years (1742). Publication of *The Foundery Collection,* famous tune-book used by the Wesleys in mass singing; source of AMSTERDAM ("Praise the Lord who reigns above"), SAVANNAH ("Jesus, Lord, we look to thee"), and others.

275 years (1717). *Birth* of Benjamin Beddome (d. 1795), author of "God, in the gospel of his son," "Did Christ o'er sinners weep," "Father of mercies, bow thine year," "My times of sorrow and of joy," and others; William Williams (d. 1791), author of "Guide me, O thou great Jehovah," "O'er the gloomy hills of darkness," and others.

300 years (1692). *Birth* of John Byrom (d. 1763), author of "Christians, awake, salute the happy morn."

325 years (1667). *Death* of Johann Rist (b. 1607), author of "Break forth, O beauteous heavenly light"; George Wither (b. 1588), author of "Behold the son, that seemed but now," "To God with heart and cheerful voice," and others.

400 years (1592). Publication of Thomas Est's *The Whole Booke of Psalmes,* source of WINCHESTER OLD ("While shepherds watched their flocks by night"), OLD 120TH ("O thou not made with hands"), and others.

750 years (1242). *Death* of Peter Abelard (b. 1079), author of "O what their joy and their glory will be."

Quotable Quotations

1. A man possesses only what he gives away.—Elie Wiesel

2. When religion comes in the front door, mirth and laughter will not go out the back door.—Billy Sunday

3. Injustice is relatively easy to bear; what stings is justice.—H. L. Mencken

4. First you take a drink. Then the drink takes a drink. Then the drink takes you.—F. Scott Fitzgerald

5. Most of the trouble in the world is caused by people wanting to be important.—T. S. Eliot

6. Of all forms of tyranny the least attractive and the most vulgar is the tyranny of wealth; the tyranny of plutocracy.—J. P. Morgan

7. Humility is the first of the virtues—for other people.—Oliver Wendell Holmes

8. Example is the best precept.—Aesop

9. Children have never been very good at listening to their elders, but they have never failed to imitate them.—James Baldwin

10. The penalty of success is to be bored by the people who used to snub you.—Lady Astor

11. He who lives without quarreling is a bachelor.—St. Jerome

12. Keep your eyes wide open before marriage, half shut afterwards.—Benjamin Franklin

13. War is sweet to those who have not experienced it.—Erasmus

14. Everything that irritates us about others can lead to an understanding of ourselves.—Carl G. Jung

15. The hell to be endured hereafter, of which theology tells, is no worse than the hell we make for ourselves in this world by habitually fashioning our characters in the wrong way.—William James

16. The future is something which everyone reaches at the rate of sixty minutes one hour, whatever he does, whoever he be.—C. S. Lewis

17. A failure is a man who has blundered but is not able to cash in on the experience.—Elbert Hubbard

18. Sin is poison poured into the stream of time.—George A. Buttrick

19. Love must be learned and learned again and again; there is no end of it. Hate needs no instruction, but waits only to be provoked.—Katherine Anne Porter

20. You can never do a kindness too soon, for you never know how soon it will be too late.—Ralph Waldo Emerson

21. The Christian faith, which we believe is the hope of our troubled world, is a revolutionary faith. It is rooted in inward experience, but, wherever it is genuine, it leads to radical changes in the ways in which men live and act.—Society of Friends, Oxford, 1952

22. There is nothing so bad but it can masquerade as moral.—Walter Lippmann

23. Courage is doing what you're afraid to do. There can be no courage unless you're scared.—Eddie Rickenbacker

24. Problems are only opportunities in work clothes.—Henry J. Kaiser

25. The holy passion of Friendship is of so sweet and steady and loyal and enduring a nature that it will last through a whole lifetime, if not asked to lend money.—Mark Twain

26. Many a man thinks he is buying pleasure, when he is really selling himself a slave to it.—Benjamin Franklin

27. No one can worship God or love his neighbor on an empty stomach.—Woodrow Wilson

28. To know Christ is not to speculate about the mode of his incarnation, but to know his saving benefits.—Philip Melanchthon

29. This is certain, that a man that studieth revenge keeps his wounds green, which otherwise would heal and do well.—Francis Bacon

30. Make the best use of what is in your power, and take the rest as it happens.—Epictetus

31. They also serve who only stand and wait.—John Milton

32. In his holy flirtation with the world, God occasionally drops a handker-

chief. These handkerchiefs are called saints.—Frederick Buechner

33. Love is an act of endless forgiveness, a tender look which becomes a habit.—Peter Ustinov

34. Character consists of what you do on the third and fourth tries.—James A. Michener

35. The trouble with the world is that the stupid are cocksure and the intelligent full of doubt.—Bertrand Russell

36. The value of life lies not in the length of days but in the use we make of them; a man may live long yet live very little.—Montaigne

37. It is the heart that is not sure of its God that is afraid to laugh in His presence.—George Macdonald

38. Even before you knew his name, before you were born, before you were a thought in your parents' mind, God loved you.—Raymond Bailey

39. To get an idea of our fellow countrymen's miseries we have only to look at their pleasures.—George Eliot

40. He who sees the Infinite in all things, sees God.—Richard Hooker

41. Wherever law ends, tyranny begins.—John Locke

42. There are a thousand hacking at the branches of evil to one who is striking at the root.—Henry David Thoreau

43. Every artist was first an amateur.—Ralph Waldo Emerson

44. We must believe in luck. For how else can we explain the success of those we don't like?—Jean Cocteau

45. What does it matter what men think a man to be if God thinks him to be a saint?—Raymond Bailey

46. When you enjoy loving your neighbor it ceases to be a virtue.—Kahlil Gibran

47. So live that you wouldn't be ashamed to sell the family parrot to the town gossip.—Will Rogers

48. No man does anything from a single motive.—Samuel Taylor Coleridge

49. I never did anything worth doing by accident, nor did any of my inventions come by accident; they came by plain work.—Thomas A. Edison

50. Every calling is great when greatly pursued.—Oliver Wendell Holmes

51. The strongest man in the world is he who stands alone.—Henrik Ibsen

52. By obeying one learns how to obey.—George Macdonald

53. The greatest waste of money is to keep it.—Jackie Gleason

54. Enthusiasm for a cause sometimes warps judgment.—William Howard Taft

55. Never wait for fitter time or place to talk to Him. To wait till thou go to church or to thy closet is to make Him wait. He will listen as thou walkest.—George Macdonald

56. Everybody ought to do at least two things each day that he hates to do, just for practice.—William James

57. Integrity needs no rules.—Albert Camus

58. The courage to be is rooted in the God who appears when God has disappeared in the anxiety of doubt.—Paul Tillich

59. Sin is not hurtful because it is forbidden, but it is forbidden because it's hurtful.—Benjamin Franklin

60. The Bible will always be full of things you cannot understand, as long as you will not live according to those you can understand.—Billy Sunday

61. Take care of the minutes, for the hours will take care of themselves.—Lord Chesterfield

62. You send your child to the schoolmaster, but 'tis the schoolboys who educate him.—Ralph Waldo Emerson

63. Happiness is the result of discovering that you do not have to have what you want.—James K. Feibleman

64. If you can keep your head when all about you are losing theirs, it is just possible that you haven't grasped the situation.—Jean Kerr

65. We are not punished for our sins but by them.—Leon Harrison

66. Courage is grace under pressure.—Ernest Hemingway

67. Friendship makes prosperity more shining and lessens adversity by dividing and sharing it.—Cicero

68. If I were to give the liberty of the press, my power would not last three days.—Napoleon Bonaparte

69. In the last resort, a love of God without love of man is no love at all.—Hans Küng

70. Ingratitude is always a form of weakness. I have never known a man of real ability to be ungrateful.—Goethe

71. As soon as any man says of the affairs of the State *What does it matter to me?* the State may be given up for lost.—Jean-Jacques Rousseau

72. As sure as God ever puts his children in the furnace, he will be in the furnace with them.—Charles Haddon Spurgeon

73. A man is a god in ruin.—Ralph Waldo Emerson

74. If you have nothing to cry about, you really have something to cry about.—Peter Kreeft

75. When the final judgment is passed on me, it will rest on one four-letter word: Did you really love?—Walter J. Burghardt

76. Enmity is anger waiting for a chance for revenge.—Cicero

77. The butterfly counts not months but moments and has time enough.—Rabindranath Tagore

78. Home is the place where, when you have to go there, they have to take you in.—Robert Frost

79. It is the heart which experiences God and not the reason. This, then, is faith: God felt by the heart, not by the reason.—Blaise Pascal

80. You cannot step twice into the same river, for other waters are continually flowing on.—Heraclitus

81. No one wants advice—only corroboration.—John Steinbeck

82. If we will take the first few steps in God's direction, he will help us the rest of the way.—William F. Evans

83. We don't love qualities, we love a person; sometimes by reason of their defects as well as their qualities.—Jacques Maritain

84. The very best and utmost of attainment in this life is to remain still and let God act and speak in thee.—Meister Eckhart

85. Tart words make no Friends; a spoonful of honey will catch more flies than a Gallon of Vinegar.—Benjamin Franklin

86. A fellow that doesn't have any tears doesn't have any heart.—Hubert Humphrey

87. The side that wins is not always the best side.—James K. Feibleman

88. A fanatic is a man who does what he thinks the Lord would do if He knew the facts of the case.—Finley Peter Dunne

89. Forget injuries, never forget kindnesses.—Confucius

90. A good scare is worth more to a man than good advice.—E. W. Howe

91. Fortunately, truth does not cease just because people give up believing it.—Edward Norman

92. The national anthem of hell is "I Did It My Way."—Peter Kreeft

93. No virtue is ever so strong that it is beyond temptation.—Immanuel Kant

94. Going to church doesn't make a man a Christian any more than going to a garage makes him an automobile.—Billy Sunday

95. Do good by stealth, and blush to find it fame.—Alexander Pope

96. A civilization without culture and art is no civilization.—Nelson Rockefeller

97. No pleasure is unalloyed: some trouble ever intrudes upon our happiness.—Ovid

98. The most eloquent prayer is the prayer through hands that heal and bless. The highest form of worship is the worship of unselfish Christian service. The greatest form of praise is the sound of consecrated feet seeking out the lost and helpless.—Billy Sunday

99. Man's capacity for evil makes democracy necessary and man's capacity for good makes democracy possible.—Reinhold Niebuhr

100. There is no folly of the beasts of the earth which is not infinitely outdone by the madness of men.—Herman Melville

Questions of Life and Religion

These questions may be useful to prime homiletic pumps, as discussion starters, or for study and youth groups.

1. How can spiritual health affect physical health?

2. What is the role of hope in the human pilgrimage?

3. Is there value in reviewing our personal moral history?

4. Are there yearnings within every individual that can lead him or her to God?

5. Which is more appropriate to an experience of conversion—joy or remorse?

6. What did Jesus Christ come to do?

7. Can Jesus Christ bless us unless we consciously and personally accept him as our Lord and Savior?

8. How can we make the best use of our time without being paralyzed by its swift passing?

9. Are we to believe that the majority is always right?

10. Does God somehow use even our mistakes and wasted years to do his work and glorify him?

11. How are we to interpret the apparent silence of God?

12. What is the obligation of the person who hears God's message, as to listening, understanding, and obeying?

13. How does a Christian maintain faithfulness to his or her Lord?

14. Why do we often prefer not to know of injustice and suffering in our world?

15. Why do some people quit trying to live a Christian life?

16. What is or will be the basis of church unity?

17. What is the meaning of "resurrection" as it applies to the Christian's living today?

18. How does the Bible describe the life to come?

19. How does our confidence in and anticipation of the life to come affect our present living?

20. What does faith do with evil?

21. Do angels play a role in our lives today?

22. In what ways are we to determine authentic prophetic voices in our time?

23. How can we individually be Christ to the world?

24. Who on earth could we consider expendable—anybody?

25. What does it mean to take God seriously?

26. Does love require that we give people everything they want from us?

27. What can we do individually to preserve the earth from depletion and pollution?

28. What, for you, is the hardest commandment in the Bible?

29. Are we in danger of changing the gospel "to fit" our inadequacies?

30. How important is a sense of God's presence in struggle and suffering?

31. Is forgiveness of others significant in our relationship to God?

32. What is the role of commitment in the continuing success of a marriage?

33. How does God become our ultimate security?

34. What difference did and does Jesus make in the way people think or should think of women?

35. How good is the gift of life?

36. Does wealth add to or subtract from the quality of life?

37. How does our faith help us in the testing times of life?

38. Why is it important for the family to have a table blessing?

39. Is the sense of the absence of God sometimes a "normal" experience in a believer's life?

40. What role can worship play in a life active in the modern world?

41. How is baptism related to the life of a Christian?

42. How is communion related to the life of a Christian?

43. Do the hymns we sing establish our understanding of the Christian faith?

44. Does affluence help or hurt our spiritual formation?

45. Are there constructive uses of anger?

46. In what ways is our faith made stronger?

47. Can we prove the existence of God?

48. What is the meaning of the Atonement?
49. How is the Bible a human book?
50. How is the Bible a divine book?
51. How do the lives of heroes of the faith affect our lives?
52. How far should we go in bearing the burdens of other people?
53. What are the common and special *charismata* (gifts) of believers?
54. If we are not saved by works, are works important at all?
55. What and where is the church?
56. Is good citizenship a mark of the Christian life?
57. Does confession promote Christian growth?
58. When is conformity good and when is it bad?
59. Is worry ever productive?
60. How can parents instill values in their children?
61. Is doubt a sin?
62. "What is truth?" (Pontius Pilate)
63. How does the Trinity function in our understanding of God?
64. What is conversion?
65. Is tithing a Christian duty?
66. What are the standards for Christian stewardship?
67. Does suffering draw us closer to God?
68. What is "the social gospel" and how is it related to "the gospel"?
69. How can silence relate to worship?
70. Is Satan alive and well today?
71. What and who is a saint?
72. When is conscience a reliable guide?
73. Is the prevailing culture an enemy of the Christian life?

74. How can we make good decisions?
75. How can failure contribute to success?
76. What can we do about our personal enemies?
77. Is evangelism the duty of every Christian?
78. How can we resolve the problem of guilt?
79. Can we know the will of God?
80. Is ecology a Christian issue?
81. What is greatness?
82. What is happiness?
83. Is judgment one expression of God's love?
84. What is justification by faith?
85. How is knowledge related to faith?
86. What constitutes a "call" to professional ministry?
87. What is true peace?
88. How does prayer "work"?
89. What is providence?
90. How can we gain self-control?
91. What is the difference between happiness and joy?
92. Is there an appropriate simplicity for the Christian life?
93. What is salvation?
94. Is service demeaning?
95. How does prejudice operate in an individual or a group?
96. Why do we call Jesus Christ "Lord"?
97. Does laughter contribute to physical and spiritual health?
98. Is honesty more than a good policy?
99. How should we think about death?
100. Why is the gospel "good news"?

Biblical Benedictions and Blessings

The Lord watch between me and thee, when we are absent from one another.—Gen. 31:49.

The Lord bless thee, and keep thee; the Lord make his face to shine upon thee, and be gracious unto thee; the Lord lift up his countenance upon thee, and give thee peace.—Num. 6:24–26.

The Lord our God be with us, as he was with our fathers; let him not leave us, nor forsake us; that he may incline our hearts unto him, to walk in all his ways, and to keep his commandments, and his statutes, and his judgments, which he commanded our fathers.—1 Kings 8:57–58.

Let the words of my mouth, and the meditation of my heart, be acceptable in thy sight, O Lord, my strength, and my redeemer.—Ps. 19:14.

Now the God of patience and consolation grant you to be likeminded one toward another according to Christ Jesus; that ye may with one mind and one mouth glorify God, even the Father of our Lord Jesus Christ. Now the God of hope fill you with all joy and peace in believing, that ye may abound in hope, through the power of the Holy Ghost. Now the God of peace be with you.—Rom. 15:5–6, 13, 33.

Now to him that is of power to establish you according to my gospel and the preaching of Jesus Christ, according to the revelation of the mystery, which was kept secret since the world began, but now is manifest, and by the scriptures of the prophets, according to the commandment of the everlasting God, made known to all nations for the obedience of faith: to God only wise, be glory through Jesus Christ for ever.—Rom. 16:25–27.

Grace be unto you, and peace, from God our Father, and from the Lord Jesus Christ.—1 Cor. 1:3.

The grace of the Lord Jesus Christ and the love of God, and the communion of the Holy Ghost, be with you all.—2 Cor. 13:14.

Peace be to the brethren, and love with faith, from God the Father and the Lord Jesus Christ. Grace be with all them that love our Lord Jesus Christ in sincerity.—Eph. 6:23–24.

And the peace of God, which passeth all understanding, shall keep your hearts and minds through Christ Jesus. Finally, brethren, whatsoever things are true, whatsoever things are honest, whatsoever things are just; whatsoever things are pure, whatsoever things are lovely, whatsoever things are of good report; if there be any virtue, and if there be any praise, think on these things. Those things, which ye have both learned and received, and heard, and seen in me, do; and the

God of peace shall be with you.—Phil. 4:7–9.

Wherefore also we pray always for you, that our God would count you worthy of this calling, and fulfill all the good pleasure of his goodness, and the work of faith with power; that the name of our Lord Jesus Christ may be glorified in you, and ye in him, according to the grace of our God and the Lord Jesus Christ.—2 Thess. 1:11–12.

Now the Lord of peace himself give you peace always by all means. The Lord be with you all. The grace of our Lord Jesus Christ be with you all.—2 Thess. 3:16–18.

Grace, mercy, and peace, from God our Father and Jesus Christ our Lord.—1 Tim. 1:2.

Now the God of peace, that brought again from the dead our Lord Jesus, that great shepherd of the sheep, through the blood of the everlasting covenant, make you perfect in every good work to do his will, working in you that which is wellpleasing in his sight, through Jesus Christ, to whom be glory for ever and ever.—Heb. 13:20–21.

The God of all grace, who hath called us unto his eternal glory by Christ Jesus, after that ye have suffered a while, make you perfect, establish, strengthen, settle you. To him be glory and dominion for ever and ever. Greet ye one another with a kiss of charity. Peace be with you all that are in Christ Jesus.—1 Pet. 5:10–11, 14.

Grace be with you, mercy, and peace, from God the Father, and from the Lord Jesus Christ, the Son of the Father, in truth and love.—2 John 3.

Now unto him that is able to keep you from falling, and to present you faultless before the presence of his glory with exceeding joy, to the only wise God our Savior, be glory and majesty, dominion and power, both now and ever.—Jude 24–25.

Grace be unto you, and peace, from him which was, and which is to come; and from the seven Spirits which are before his throne; and from Jesus Christ, who is the faithful witness, and the first begotten of the dead, and the prince of the kings of the earth. Unto him that loved us, and washed us from our sins in his own blood, and hath made us kings and priests unto God and his Father; to him be glory and dominion for ever and ever.—Rev. 1:4–6.

SECTION II.
Sermons and Homiletic and Worship Aids for Fifty-two Sundays

SUNDAY: JANUARY FIFTH

SERVICE OF WORSHIP

Sermon: The Word and the World

TEXT: John 1:1–5

I. Some folks make things out of wood or brick or ceramic tile or fabric. I make things out of words: lectures, sermons, articles, etc. Words don't seem as real as bricks, maybe; you can't touch them or hold them; but they have a power and a life of their own sometimes. Think of the word *bird*; the word creates a picture in your mind that may be a little vague; think of the words *blue jay* and a more specific picture comes up. Words give life; words create.

Ancient people were very impressed by the power of words. They thought words and ideas were more real than objects. Think about it—before there was a telephone, there had to be an idea for it in the mind of Alexander Graham Bell. First he had the idea, and then he wrestled with it until he could make an object like the thought in his head. This power of ideas to create objects the Greeks called *Logos*, which means "word," "idea," "concept," "story"—a very powerful image, this Logos.

The Bible also testifies to the power of words. Do you remember the story of Isaac intending to give a blessing to Esau, his older son, and being tricked into giving it to Jacob instead? The thing was that once the blessing was spoken, even

in error, it had a life of its own and could not be brought back. Words create; words live; words are power.

II. I wanted you to have those ideas in your minds as we think about this scripture today. This Gospel does not begin, as Mark did, with Jesus as an adult, entering into his ministry. It does not start with the story of Jesus' birth, as did Matthew and Luke. Instead, the Gospel of John begins with the time before the world came into being, before there were people or plants or animals or stars or planets; before all this, in the very beginning, there was the Logos, the Word.

"In the beginning"—John begins where Genesis begins, with the same phrase, and you really can't read this passage without thinking of the first creation story. You'll remember that in Genesis God spoke to bring the world into being; in the beginning, then, before there was a world, there was the creative Word, which brought it all about.

Who is this Word? Was John speaking of just the blueprints for the cosmos, the mental image God had before he created it all? Was he speaking of a separate divine being, a lesser god who was entrusted with creation? The second half of verse 1 answers that: The Word was with God (that is, something alongside God— not just an idea in God's head) and the Word was God (that is, fully identical with God and not some lesser divinity).

17

How can something be the same as something else and yet be different from it? How can the Logos be God and yet be separate from God? That, of course, is the mystery of the Trinity, and it is a real can of worms. When we think of the words *God the Father* and *God the Son*, and *God the Holy Spirit*, we probably either get a picture in our mind of three separate beings standing close together to show their unity or of one being who does three separate functions. Neither picture will do, I think; the first one makes us worship three gods, the second one makes it impossible to distinguish the human Jesus from the eternal God.

Instead, think with me a moment about how words create. When Bell thought of the telephone and worked out the theory in his head, that was his idea. It was a product of his own study and imagination and creativity; while it was in his head, you could not have separated the idea from the man, so close was the identity. Yet once he spoke it—once he made it known—it had a life of its own. Others could think about it, too. Maybe that helps—maybe that is a way to think about how the Word could both be God and be different from God. In the end, though, we have to say that the Trinity is a mystery that cannot be fully explained.

In the end, too, we have to say that the Trinity, important as it is to us, is not the most important thing for the text. What is vital is this: the world-that-was-God was in the beginning, before all else. Before there were human ears to hear, before there were human words to say, God was the Word, itching for the chance to communicate with us. We parents understand this feeling. When your baby is born it cannot speak or understand your speech, and there are countless times when it cries when you say, "I wish you could only tell me what you need." We long to communicate, long before they are ready. God's desire, though, is greater. Before there was a you, God was the Word, already positioned, poised to speak to you. You have been on God's mind, in God's plans, for all eternity.

III. Then one day it happened. So long ago, in the midst of darkness

"darker than a thousand midnights down in a cypress swamp," God spoke and said, "I'm lonely—I'll make me a world." Through the Word, infinitely more powerful than ours, God created; and without the Word there was not anything made that was made.

God's creation, then, was a self-revelation. Every year I get a new crop of freshmen in my classes, and they take four tests during the semester. By the third test, I could tell you who wrote which test just by the way it was written—not the handwriting, but the way the words are put together. Words—the words we use—reveal something about ourselves. When I say "turnip greens" instead of "turnip salad," I show that I'm not native to these parts. God's creative act—the world that came from the Word—shows us things about God: power, wisdom, love for diversity, sense of order, the gift of free will.

God's creation, too, shows us something about us. The pointers to God within creation have always been here—the light has been shining in the darkness since the first day of creation until the present. And yet it is still a struggle to get people to see it. The fact that there is still darkness after so many eons, that people still stubbornly refuse to see the light, is a mystery even greater than the Trinity. God lets us look for him; he calls to us and lets us respond; but he will not insist that we look, and there are plenty who don't.

A friend found a bird in his basement the other day. He tried to coax him out the only exit with all sorts of ploys—bird seed trails, etc.—but the bird couldn't understand and continued to fly about aimlessly, crashing into things, until it dazed itself, and Mike took it outside. So, too, with the dark things of this world. Verse 5 says that the darkness has never overcome the light, and the verb there has the double meaning of "conquer" and "understand." The world, on the whole, is flying blind in God's creation, never comprehending, continuing to lash out at the light that it hates irrationally.

But, thanks be to God, there is a victory promised. The darkness, though it has endured, has never quenched the light. "The sun will come out tomorrow," says Little Orphan Annie, and for those of us who live for the light, that's a great comfort. This great wicked world still has the sunshine of people who live for God and do his will and speak the gospel, and you are this world's promise of victory. Believe it, brothers and sisters: Before there was a world or ears to hear, there was the Word, and he was poised to speak to you of his love and his will an eternity ago. Now you are in this world that he made, helping poor, blinded people to see their maker. You can speak the gospel that can give them Life.

Those are words, but they aren't just words; they're as real and true as the bricks in this building. Believe it, brothers and sisters, believe it and say it.—Richard B. Vinson

Illustrations

THE LIGHT UNDIMMED. Imagine yourself standing alone on some headland in a dark night. At the foot of the headland is a lighthouse or beacon, not casting rays on every side, but throwing one bar of light through the darkness. It is some such image that St. John had before his mind. The divine light shines through the darkness of the world, cleaving it, but neither dispelling it nor quenched by it. The word translated in the Authorized Version "comprehended," in the text of the Revised Version "apprehended," and in its margin "overcame," is a word of two meanings; literally, it is "to take down or under" and may thus mean "to take right into the mind" (apprehend) or "to take under control" (overcome). In this context the two meanings are direct opposites, for to apprehend light is to be enlightened by it, and to overcome light is to put it out. Yet the word truly means both of these. The darkness in no sense at all received the light; yet the light shone still undimmed. So strange is the relation of the light of God's revelation to the world which exists to be the medium of that revelation.—William Temple

DIVINE IN THE HUMAN. The splendor of the prologue to the Gospel must never be lost in exegetical details. It inaugurates the message of the Gospel on a level unparalleled in the gospel tradition. In the human, the limited experience of humans, the evangelist sees the divine presence, and perhaps this is his major insight into the story of Jesus. The unfolding of the story will tell.—George W. MacRae

Sermon Suggestions

HOMECOMING.   TEXT: Jer. 31:7–14. (1) A stirring hope, verses 7–9. (2) A solid certainty, verses 10–11. (3) A joyous celebration, verses 12–14.

A TWOFOLD PRAYER.   TEXT: Eph. 1:3–6, 15–18. (1) Thanksgiving for God's choice of us to be his special people, verses 3–6. (2) Petition for a profound knowledge of what God has given us in Jesus Christ, verses 15–18.

Worship Aids

CALL TO WORSHIP.   "Praise the Lord, O Jerusalem; praise thy God, O Zion. For he hath strengthened the bars of thy gates; he hath blessed thy children within thee. He maketh peace in thy borders, and filleth thee with the finest wheat. He sendeth forth his commandment upon earth; his word runneth very swiftly" (Ps. 147:12–15).

INVOCATION.   Speak, Lord, for thy servants listen. Move, Lord, for thy servants see. Stir, Lord, for thy servants await thy every bidding this day and every day of every year it is thy pleasure for us to know.—E. Lee Phillips

OFFERTORY SENTENCE.   "Blessed be the God and Father of our Lord Jesus Christ, who hath blessed us with all spiritual blessings in heavenly places in Christ" (Eph. 1:3).

OFFERTORY PRAYER.   Your lovingkindness never fails us, Father. May our gratitude never fail you. On this altar this morning we place our offerings as a mere token of our thanksgiving for all the immense blessings that come from you. Help us to follow the offering with service like that which Christ gave as he walked among people in that long-ago day. Truly, whatsoever we do may it be done to the honor and glory of Christ in whose name we pray.—Henry Fields

PRAYER.   Brood over us, O Holy Spirit of God, that we may receive serenity in our hearts and a quiet calmness in our fevered spirits. Infill us with some high and holy purposes for our lives and give us a determined steadfastness to follow those purposes to their fulfillment. This morning let us hear again the creative words spoken in the infancy of time, "Let there be light," and let us determine that we will make ourselves available to be the instruments through which your light shines into the darkness of the world. Fulfill in us this morning the truth spoken of Jesus that we are the light of the world.

Show us how to be light to those who are lost in the darkness of sin, Father. Give us the inspiration and the words to share that will guide them into the light of your salvation.

Show us how to be light to those who are lost in the depths of suffering. Grant us the compassion and sympathetic spirits that exemplify the healing caring of Christ for the wounded of life.

Show us how to be light to those who are lonely this morning, we pray. Endow us with a bright spirit that is contagious with friendliness to such a degree that others will find sympathetic companionship in our presence.

Show us how to be light to those with some overshadowing burden, Father. Instill in us the strength of body, mind, and spirit to join them under the load and exert a lifting power that will lighten the burden thus setting them somewhat free.

Show us how to be light to the desperately depressed, we pray. Generate in us an understanding heart and a vision of what yet can be for those who see no light

in their hard circumstances, that we may guide them from the desperate darkness into the light of hope.

Let there be light, Father. Let it come through us as we commit ourselves to him who was altogether light and who taught all his followers to pray, [the Lord's Prayer].—Henry Fields

LECTIONARY MESSAGE

Topic: Grace Upon Grace
TEXTS: John 1:1–18; Jer. 31:7–14

Advent has come and gone. Do we then forget God's gift in the form of a baby—born in Judea at a particular time, under a certain temporal ruler? The genius of the passage of Scripture is its eternal perspective. Away from the shepherds' field when Caesar Augustus was emperor we move to the very beginning and to eternity beyond that. It's grace from the beginning—unmerited favor—undeserved mercy. It's God's self-revelation. Persons did not discover God. God made persons and then revealed himself.

I. *God revealed himself as life and light.* In the beginning was the Word—in the beginning was a word, a word of revelation. God spoke a word. In the beginning God spoke a word creating life . . . "Live," he said. And in that word all life began—"all things were made through him." In the darkness God caused the light to shine . . . "Shine," he said. "And God said, Let there be light, and there was light" (Gen. 1:3). And the light overcame the darkness—it always does. And there were living witnesses to the light. John came as such a witness—a live person. He was not the light, but he bore witness to the light. And the true light was coming.

II. *God revealed himself as love.* He had always been love—from the beginning. There is a perspective of eternity in the simple statement, "God is love." Unfortunately it was unrequited love. That was the story of his dealings with Israel. He was in the world—this great God—and he had made the world and the world would not acknowledge him. He came unto his own—people or things—and his own folks would not receive him. And we know that the cross was the clearest image of that rejection. But there were some who received him. To them he gave the right to become his children . . . born not of flesh and blood but born of God.

Grace is unmerited favor—undeserved love. The eternal Word of God became flesh and dwelt among us. This is the eternal truth—down on the plains of human history—"We beheld him." God revealed himself in a manner clear and unmistakable. And there were witnesses to the Incarnation. John bore witness and we bear witness.

III. *God's grace overflows in our time.* He was all filled with grace and truth. Of that fullness we all received, and grace upon grace. This has been our experience with God in Christ—grace upon grace. No law compares with it . . . undeserved love . . . unmerited mercy . . . unexcelled abundance . . . forgiveness, reconciliation. This is God's clearest revelation: The Word become flesh.

From the beginning to the present—grace upon grace. "Sing with gladness . . . My people shall be satisfied with my goodness, saith the Lord" (Jer. 31:7, 14).—J. Estill Jones

SUNDAY: JANUARY TWELFTH

SERVICE OF WORSHIP

Sermon: If Winter Comes
TEXT: Rom. 5:1–9

Despite the rightful insistence which we hear calling us to live in the present, the fact remains that often we must look to the future to find hope. When cold weather and snow begin to weary us, we can hardly be faulted for looking to a warmer and better time. Let us think of the wintry cold and also of the wintry soul.

No one could argue against the reality of winter, but we need more than present reality. We need to have hope for and in the future. The English poet Shelley penned these words to express the present reality and future hope: "If winter comes, can spring be far behind?"

I. Shelley knew what we know: There is no "if"; winter comes! This fact was made even more unpleasant by the dampness of the England Shelley knew more than a century and a half ago. Another Englishman, Rudyard Kipling, living about a century after Shelley but still in a time when homes lacked central heating, wrote, "Never again will I spend another winter in this accursed bucketshop of a refrigerator called England."

The winter which comes to the soul is hardly to be desired. Yet it comes. If it can be said, "Into every life a little rain must fall," it can also be said, "Into every life winter comes." This is not a condition unique to our contemporaries. Job complained, "I am allotted months of emptiness, and nights of misery are apportioned to me. . . . The night is long, and I am full of tossing till the dawn" (7:3–4). What Job called "nights," I call "winter."

Every person faces unhappiness, disappointment, and grief if he lives for at least several decades. Perhaps you find it hard to believe, but Jesus shared the wintry feelings. The gospels do not portray Jesus as always the pleasant man with little children nor the peaceful man so often pictured. If we think of winter as unhappiness and disappointment, then Jesus had his share and more. To think that Jesus was untouched by such events as the death of John the Baptist and the betrayal by Judas is to miss what the gospels want us to know. When Jesus was confronted by the death of Lazarus, Jesus wept. The gospel writers did not intend for us to think that Jesus was somehow above such emotions. In fact, just the opposite is true. How little his family and friends, his disciples, and his enemies understood what he was doing. To say that this did not affect Jesus would be nonsense.

II. Having accepted the fact of the coming of the wintry cold and the wintry soul, let us think of what brings winter.

William Cowper, who wrote, "God moves in mysterious ways his wonders to perform," called "Winter [the] ruler of the inverted year."

Winter cold comes because we are not long enough in the warmth of the sun's rays and not close enough. Our souls need warmth and closeness in fellowship with God and other humans. Let's not cause winter to come to anyone because we do not open our fellowship.

What do we or don't do to someone might cause winter to come. One such way is to give someone the "cold shoulder." Another way we bring winter is by dampening a person's enthusiasm unjustly. Many years ago Colonel Low, a professor at St. Joseph's College in Bardstown, Kentucky, was fired by the trustees of the college. Why? Because he wrote a pamphlet advocating a railroad to the West Coast. You will know that he wrote a long time ago and that the trustees were short-sighted men when I tell you that Low was fired "on the ground of insanity." The trustees knew that anyone who wrote about the possibility of a train going to the West Coast had to be insane.

Let's not overlook what we do to ourselves. One of the church's prayers includes these words, "Deliver us, when we draw nigh to thee, from coldness of heart and wanderings of mind." It may be that we consciously turn our minds from God. A cartoon showed a man and his wife looking into the next yard where their neighbors were on their knees and bowing before a huge, cold-looking black figure. The man, surprised at the actions of his neighbors, says to his wife, "I thought the Saunders were agnostics." The fact is that the only time some people get on their knees is to work in the garden or lawn. The fact is that many so-called agnostics really worship. They worship status or money or popularity or their lawns. Worshiping something other than God can bring winter to us and to others.

III. Let us also realize that not every wintry condition is our fault. To say that disappointment and grief come to a man because he has done wrong is but to echo the so-called friends of Job, whose views have long been repudiated by Jews and Christians. Let there be no such people here. It may be that a person's troubles are brought on by his or her actions but not necessarily. Certainly we should not let winter or the threat of winter freeze us into inaction.

Job was told by his "friends" that he suffered bad health and the loss of his goods because he had sinned. We can thank God that he does not treat us so severely. Though not God's fault, sometimes the innocent suffer and sometimes life treats us harshly, and unexpectedly something bad happens. This does not mean that we are overcome. Even in the bad time, generally we can do something. William and Mary College was damaged and closed during the Civil War. After the Civil War it opened but was closed again for seven years. The president of William and Mary daily acted in hopes of a better future. Despite the fact that there were no students or faculty and that the buildings had fallen into disrepair, the president every morning went out to ring the bell. We can be thankful for the examples of persons who remain unvanquished.

IV. Christians are called to be harbingers of hope. Though the chill of winter is a present reality, we do not forget that spring will come. We affirm that by being faithful and obedient to God, we can bring in the hope and the warmth of spring. Paul, who knew this truth from personal experience, wrote, "Let us rejoice in our troubles, for we know that trouble produces endurance, endurance brings God's approval, and his approval creates hope" (Rom. 5:3–4, TEV).

Let us think of the winter and spring sequence and find hope through some of the Beatitudes. For example, the winter of feeling poor in spirit is followed by the spring of the kingdom of heaven, the winter of mourning is followed by the spring of being comforted by God, and the winter of hungering and thirsting for righteousness is followed by the spring of being satisfied.

A popular song of some time ago contained the words "Love turns winter to spring." If you feel cold in your heart, hear again the words "God has shown how much he loves us: It was while we were still sinners that Christ died for us!" (Rom. 5:8, REV). *Today's English Version* has an exclamation point after that statement and rightly so! I would not want to be impervious to anyone's suffering or troubles, but I want to affirm what the assurance of God's love can do and has done for many people.

In the winter a man has an unusual occupation, one that can be helpful to our thinking. During the winter this man goes into various areas of the northwest and measures the amount of snow in order to tell how much water will be in the rivers in springtime. It is in the winter that he tells of what will happen in the springtime.

Our mission is to go to those people who are locked in wintry conditions to tell them that spring will come and to tell them of the sufficient water of eternal life. What we do, even though little, makes a difference. Those who have shoveled snow know the cumulative effect of one little flake falling after another. By themselves these small flakes are insignificant. When they are joined by others, they have quite an effect.

You can have a good effect. So don't give up hope. Bring hope to others. Shelley knew what we know: "If winter comes, can spring be far behind?"—David W. Richardson, PULPIT DIGEST

Illustrations

HOPE.   Of all the galleries I have visited, among all the masterpieces I have viewed, the picture that stands out most clearly now is one which I went to see again in the Tate Gallery in London—Frederic Watts's "Hope." All that one sees is a beautiful female figure seated upon a globe—and yet he can never forget that figure. She is blindfolded, and in her hand she holds a lute, of which all the strings but one are broken. The blindfolded girl is touching that one string with her hand, and her lovely head is bent toward it in the closest attention, earnestly waiting to catch the note of that one wire. So it was that Frederic Watts conceived of hope, triumphant over the world's sin and sorrow, surviving its pain and disaster. In this simple and yet profound study there is infinite pathos and tenderness. Eternal hope! Perhaps one reason why I remember that painting more clearly than many of the descents from the cross or transfigurations or entombments is that I came back with a deep impression that our world today stands in sore need of a revival of hope.—Clarence E. Macartney

HOW TO HAVE HOPE.   As William James pointed out, if we are indeed part and parcel of a meaningless universe, the kind in which Jesus could be murdered on a cross with no Resurrection, then being depressed only makes good sense. Under these conditions the sensitive and sensible person will be depressed. I have discovered only one event in history that redeemed all this evil for me and gave me hope: the Resurrection of Jesus. Allowing the resurrected One to be constantly present, I can deal with all the evil suffered by Jesus, by my friends, and by me. I can face all the rape, pillage, war, and hatred that I hear about daily and still have hope. The Resurrection reveals the ultimate nature of the universe, and the risen Christ continues to give victory over the power of evil.—Morton Kelsey

Sermon Suggestions

A PREACHER'S MAIN BUSINESS.   TEXT: Isa. 61:1–4. Like the ideal prophet, especially Jesus Christ, the faithful preacher (1) receives anointing for service, verse 1a; (2) brings good news to all classes of the disadvantaged, verses 1b–3a; (3) who, in turn, make their own constructive contribution to the work of God, verses 3b–4.

THE GIFT OF THE HOLY SPIRIT.   TEXT: Acts 8:14–17. (1) Promised to all believers (see Acts 3:38–39). (2) Received in relationship to the church.

Worship Aids

CALL TO WORSHIP.   "Blessed be the God and Father of our Lord Jesus Christ, which according to his abundant mercy hath begotten us again unto a lively hope by the resurrection of Jesus Christ from the dead . . . to an inheritance incorruptible, and undefiled, and that fadeth not away, reserved in heaven for you" (1 Pet. 1:3–4).

INVOCATION. For your unconditional love that goes out to all the world and embraces all persons as your children, we worship and adore you, O Father. That your love has found me—us—in some far country of our own willfulness—trying to be free, but enslaved by our own passions—and has drawn us back home where there is real freedom to be and become, we are grateful.

May the coming of your grace and truth in Christ be heralded on this occasion with such commanding insight and persuasive power that we may be awakened to a vision of freedom that unlocks every door, breaks down every wall, tears down every fence that we may live with all peoples as your children.

Praise be to you—Father, Son, and Holy Spirit!—John Thompson

OFFERTORY SENTENCE. "So then every one of us shall give account of himself to God" (Rom. 14:12).

OFFERTORY PRAYER. Holy God, help us to use our money as opportunity not as an insulator, to do good where good is needed, to spread the gospel where hope is needed, to give privately in our Savior's name, generously in thy economy, and joyfully in thy will.—E. Lee Phillips

PRAYER. Let us pray for persons who work with the chronically ill and for their families: that they find the strength necessary; that they not ask of themselves to be superman, superwoman; that they be wise as serpents as well as harmless as doves; that, when recovery is despaired of, they respect the mystery of the timing of death's coming; that motives be reasonably clean; that they not be embarrassed to be "behind" or "down" or depressed; that they not always be depressed; that they not be embarrassed

when the house is what they call a "sight," when it is, in fact, a war zone of caring; that they not shut out friends; that they turn the prose of hard-won understanding—of soiled linen and ghastly sights, of armories of pills and unanswered prayers and hospital vigils—into a kind of poetry, a psalm of lament. That their lamentations be acceptable to you and to themselves. That their tears be turned to joy, their night to day.—Peter Fribley

LECTIONARY MESSAGE

Topic: **Who Are You?**
TEXTS: Luke 3:15–17, 21–22; Isa. 61:1–4

The problem of identity is serious. Few of us forget our names. Some of us forget what we are doing. Many of us forget who we are—and whose we are. The search for identity goes beyond name and title. It goes to the bedrock of being.

John the Baptist hurtled on the scene of history. It had been centuries since a real live prophet had been seen in Judea. Then he came, filled with the prophetic consciousness, sent to baptize. Could he stand the popularity, the confidence of his people? Did he know who he was and where he fit into God's purpose?

I. *Many wondered.* The Gospel according to John describes the dialogue (1:19ff). "Who are you?" they asked. He resorted to an earlier prophetic message: "A voice in the wilderness." What a voice! What a wilderness! Was it a sign of humility? I don't matter. I'm a nobody. Hardly! His was a ministry of the word. God's Word used a human voice. His word was to prepare the way for the Word—the Word become flesh.

"Who are you?" they asked. Are you the Messiah? His message challenged repentance and caught their imagination. He spoke directly to the needs of ordinary folks with two coats, of tax collectors prone to cheating, of soldiers on service. He was not satisfied to merely say, "Repent"; he told them what repentance involved. Is this the Messiah?

The act of baptism was a typical prophetic symbol. Prophets had traditionally worn a yoke about their necks or had lain on one side for months. Oh, he's a prophet all right. But ... are you the Messiah?

II. *John knew.* "True, I baptize," he said. But John knew that it was only water that he used. There was no magical formula in the water. And he knew that it symbolized repentance and forgiveness, but forgiveness was God's business, not John's. He knew his limitations.

I am weak in comparison with the coming One. You think because I thunder forth God's judgment on sin that I may be the Messiah. Not so! John knew that he could not match the power of the Spirit-filled One. His message of judgment could not compare with the action of judgment in God's hand.

I am unworthy to even untie his shoes. This was the task of the lowliest servant. John knew who he was. But a prophet,

even a humble one, was doomed. Herod could not stand the truth and imprisoned him. John's problem is described differently in Matthew (3:12–15). Jesus offered him assurance and identity.

III. *God identified.* For Jesus came in commitment to God's will and to God's purpose and to God's people. There was no question in the confirmation of the voice that came from heaven, a confirmation of the voice crying in the wilderness as well as of the commitment that Jesus made.

"My beloved." That's who he was. "My Son." That's who he was. "My pleasure." That's who he was. And is! Perhaps John had not seen clearly, but he saw enough—a voice and the confirmation of the Holy Spirit.

Later Jesus expressed it clearly: "The Spirit of the Lord God is upon me ..." (Isa. 61:1).—J. Estill Jones

SUNDAY: JANUARY NINETEENTH

SERVICE OF WORSHIP

Sermon: Vocation and Vision
TEXT: 1 Sam. 3:1

There is something both fascinating and frightening about the story of the boy Samuel, and there is enough of each for everybody. We all know the fascinating parts: his setting apart at his birth, his being "lent to the Lord," in the words of his mother, Hannah. And when we encounter him, we find him serving in the Temple as a sort of secretary and administrative assistant to the high priest Eli: "Now the boy Samuel was ministering to the Lord under Eli." He was there, we discover, doing his work, and well, we may suppose not necessarily because he wanted to be there or even because he knew he should be there. His service in the Temple was not in response to some sense of his own vocation, his own special relationship with God. The text tells us, "Now Samuel did not yet know the Lord, and the word of the Lord had not yet been revealed to him" (3:7). No, he was where he was because somebody placed

him there, and he was doing what he did because he was told to do it. He was fulfilling the obligations of his mother and the expectations of the high priest: an altogether normal and unexciting profile in habit and piety.

I. And here is where the fascination begins, for God chooses to interrupt this ordinary and uninspired routine with his own invitation to service. It is God, we discover, who calls for the boy, God who introduces him to a whole new vocation, and God who visits him in the midst of the ordinary, routine, predictable circumstances of his life and work. This is no mountainside epiphany, no manifestation in the middle of the sea or in the desert. It is all the more spectacular because it happens in the last place one would expect to find God: in church. Surely, we look for God, when we care to find him, "where cross the crowded ways of life," in the high places of nature and the low places of life, in the exotic, and in the serene. But how odd to find God where we are, and even odder to find God where we are, in church. But like the prophet Isaiah, Samuel's vocation is made real by a vision of the holy, in the midst of holy things.

That, too, is frightening: For if God can invade our space in church, he can come anywhere at any time. He can intrude upon our best efforts to keep him at arm's length: We discover that there are no limits to the day and the way of his appearing. Visions of God are not the comfortable things we, in their absence, imagine them to be. They interrupt, they summon, they are unexpected and inconvenient, and they are demanding and tiresome.

II. The call of God, for that is what vocation is, both fascinates and frightens because there is inherent in it the most fascinating and frightening of all human experiences: change. And here in our text is where the focus of interest must move from the boy Samuel to the aged priest Eli, for it is Eli who understands the implications of change. He knew what the boy Samuel cannot possibly know: that things, including Samuel himself, will never, ever be the same again. The changes for Eli and his house were enormous; the priesthood was to be taken away from him and his family forever; his sons would die miserable deaths, and he himself would break his neck and die at the news. Power was to pass from him to Samuel, and God was to pass him by. And Samuel too would know profound change: He would know the Lord as an intimate and would be forced to witness the Lord's swift justice against his old boss and benefactor Eli. Samuel would become a man of great expectations. His life and his sleep no longer would be his. His vocation, his calling was the will of God. (Perhaps it would have been better for all had he remained asleep!) And yet, he did not.

Vocation has taken on so guarded and guided a personality, that change is the last thing one wishes to contemplate: It might interrupt the program. And yet if we understand change to be no accident or error, human or otherwise, but transformation that is a reforming toward a new purpose, we may begin to understand the dangers and the opportunities

of responding to God's initiative in our lives. Our text reminds us that the Word of the Lord was rare in those days; there was no frequent vision. Things moved on at their sad and predictable pace; lives, including the life of God's servant Eli, were lived in quiet desperation. God was heard about, perhaps, but was not frequently heard. And yet, where he was neither expected nor invited, God speaks, and his servant listens. The vision, so infrequent, so difficult for the dim eyesight of Eli to see, was not a vision to be seen as we ordinarily understand sight: It was not sight but knowledge that was the point, inner-sight or insight, the quality of seeing not with the eyes but with the eyes of the heart, the capacity to be enlightened, to at last, at first, understand what is going on—who calls and to what?

III. Vision is not ecstasy, rapturous sight; it is understanding. It is not truth; it is meaning. It is not simply perception; it is experience. One's vocation in God is a call to self-understanding that means I understand, I "see" who and whose I am. Our vocation of God is to see, not God, but ourselves for what God intends us to be and do. That is what the seers saw; that is what Eli's failing sight, his lack of insight, could no longer see; and that is the vision God gives to the boy Samuel: vocation and vision, the call to understanding, of self, of God, and of oneself in God.

This then is an epiphany story: a story of how God manifests himself in the midst of human life, how God is made real both to Eli and to Samuel. It is God who initiates. God who gives the light, and God who gives the understanding. The Epiphany is an invitation to vocation and vision: to an openness to change and a new understanding of who we are and what we are to do and be. And at the Epiphany, the manifestation of Christ to the world, while we may marvel at the phenomena, the exotic kings at the manger, the baptism of our Lord in the Jordan, the miracle of the wine at Cana, and even at the mysterious voice calling to Samuel, we miss the point if we do not see (that is, understand) that what is to be seen is God at work in and through us: The light shines both that we may see and be seen.

The work of the church in this season of light is vocation and vision: openness to the will of God and understanding as to who and what we are in response to the will of God. The Word of the Lord is rare these days, and there is no frequent vision. It is just at such times as this, the darkest and coldest of times, that we need to look for the initiative of God and be prepared to respond to it with all that we are and would be: And if it happened once, before the altar of God, it could happen again, even here, even now, even to you. Pray God that it may be so.—Peter J. Gomes

Illustrations

CRISES. At any time, from infancy to old age, crises may arise in the individual life. In any one of a myriad combinations of outward and inward events, one finds himself in circumstances where he feels the propulsion to pass over some sort of Jordan and enter upon some new level of responsibility and recompense. And yet this new step forward is a step into the unknown, peopled with dangerous creatures of fact, as truly as with menacing creations of fancy. The stage one has already reached in growth is good, though not yet fully satisfying. In that case is it better to bear the ills we know or fly to others that we know not of? So the motive of growth is met by the motive of shrinking back. In that time of conflict, we have come to crisis, whether we are one year old or three score years and ten.—Lewis J. Sherrill

LOVE AND ADVENTURE. Love is also, in my view, the meaning of all human adventure. The instinct of adventure which God gave man in creating him in his own image is in fact, I believe, an instinct of love, a need to give himself, to dedicate himself, to pursue a worthwhile goal, accepting every sacrifice in order to attain it. This is the source of the joy of adventure, the joy of doing something, and of doing it for someone—for God who has

called him to do, if he is a believer, and in any case for mankind, to procure for mankind the benefits he is striving for. One is reminded of St. Ignatius Loyola's beautiful words: "We must make no important decision without opening our hearts to love."—Paul Tournier

Sermon Suggestions

RESULTS WORTH PREACHING FOR. TEXT: Isa. 62:1–5. (1) The coming of justice. (2) The glory of God. (3) The joy of belonging.

THE WORK OF THE SPIRIT. TEXT: 1 Cor. 12:1–11. (1) Basically: the confession of Jesus as Lord, verses 2–3. (2) But also: varieties of service, verses 4–11.

Worship Aids

CALL TO WORSHIP. "How precious is thy steadfast love, O God! The children of men take refuge in the shadow of thy wings" (Ps. 36:7).

INVOCATION. Lord, give our thoughts to thy bidding, our wills to thy leading, and our voices to thy praise, as we worship and adore the Lord, our God.—E. Lee Phillips

OFFERTORY SENTENCE. "There are varieties of working, but it is the same God who inspires them all in every one" (1 Cor. 12:6, RSV).

OFFERTORY PRAYER. Lord, from whom all good comes and all joy emanates, allow us to spend and be spent for that which upholds life and outlives it, through Jesus Christ our Redeemer.—E. Lee Phillips

PRAYER. In unhurried silence, heavy with wonder, deep in mystery, we venture into your inviting and glad presence, Holy God, seeking to worship you as Creator, Sustainer, Redeemer, and Lord of all. Receive our willing presence and sincere praise as offerings of our worship.

In the beginning of time, Creator God, you called the earth out of darkness into light. And it was called good. In the passing of time, Sustaining God, you sent faithful servants to declare your words of life and light. And in the fullness of time, Redeemer God, you gave the best gift, for in Christ you called the world from darkness and death to marvelous light and eternal life. Thanks be to God.

Accepting and Forgiving God, we confess the shadows of our public lives and private selves. Forgive the darkness of our hearts, closed and cold, leaning hard against the warmth and wealth of love's pure light. Pardon the darkness of our minds, shaping and harboring evil that sabotages our relationships and injures our commitment to you. Forgive the darkness of our deeds: all that hurts and harms your children and brings tears to your eyes and brokenness to your heart. Cleanse our lives and shine the light of forgiveness upon us all.

God of wholeness, we offer prayers of thanksgiving for healing experienced by many this week past. God of comfort, cradle tenderly those for whom healing has not come and for those for whom it will not come in this life. God of all faithfulness, lead us to be faithful, too. Breathe your Spirit on us and stir us to places of service for the kingdom to come and your will to be done.—William M. Johnson

LECTIONARY MESSAGE

Topic: Water and Wine and Glory
    Texts: John 2:1–11; Isa. 62:1–5
    I suppose every pastor has a favorite wedding story. There have been times when the minister feels like a chandelier and about as useful amid flowers and candles and finery of dress. I remember, for example, driving to the church a half hour before the ceremony was to begin and finding two police cars there—the wedding was anything but peaceful! But a wedding ought to be an occasion of happiness. The one in Cana of Galilee began in that fashion.

I. *An occasion of joy and frustration.* Jesus enjoyed simple things, and he would certainly have enjoyed a simple wedding. He told parables about seeds and fish and sons. It sounds most natural that he should have been invited to a wedding. Perhaps the family members were friends to Mary, and she engineered the invitation. His disciples were there, too. You can almost imagine the conversation between family and friends.

Even simple joys have disappointments. It may have been a conversation piece: "Son, they have run out of wine." Jesus heard the tone of her voice. She thought him sufficient for the occasion. If the wedding family were close friends she would have shared their shame: The failure of the wine supply was a major tragedy for the host.

Note the conversations in what must have been a short span of time: Mary spoke with Jesus. Jesus spoke with Mary: "That doesn't concern us." Mary spoke to the servants: "Whatever he says, do it." Jesus spoke to the servants: "Fill the waterpots with water."

II. *An opportunity of miracle and ministry.* There were six waterpots set there near the entrance, each holding from twenty to thirty gallons. Everything was set for the law's fulfillment. John rarely wastes numerical symbolism. Seven was the perfect number for Jews, and there were only six pots. We note that beginning with 1:19 this was the seventh day of John's Gospel. They were provided as wash pots—to ceremonially cleanse the guests.

The servants filled the pots with water—all six of them. Then they drew again—the seventh drawing—and they served the toastmaster. It was wine, delicious wine, better than the first. The joy was preserved and enhanced. Now while you contrast the wash water and the wine, be careful to contrast the Law and his glory.

III. *A sign of his glory.* What seemed like a miracle performed merely to perpetuate the joy of a wedding had a deep meaning for John. He described it as a sign, a symbol, an indication, a manifestation. John describes several such events as signs, signs pointing to his glory.

His glory was his real self—who he really was. He was to be seen as much more than a miracle worker. Already Nathaniel had confessed him as Son of God, as King of Israel (1:49). This is who he is. Look at the sign!

Faith followed: "His disciples believed on him." They did not have full knowl-edge, but they had seen enough to pro-voke their faith.

Isaiah had dreamed long before: "And the nations shall see . . . thy glory . . ." (Isa. 62:2).—J. Estill Jones

SUNDAY: JANUARY TWENTY-SIXTH

SERVICE OF WORSHIP

Sermon: Called or Hauled Off the Job
TEXT: Mark 1:16–18

Let me tell you what amazes me about this story. Jesus was looking for disciples, right? So. Did he go to the local syna-gogue? Did he recruit followers from the best of Galilee's rabbinical schools? Was he combing the corridors of the Temple for some pious hot prospects?

Jesus began his search for disciples by heading down to the docks! The folks with weathered skin and dirt under their fingernails were his prime picks. People who knew something about hard labor with little or no rewards. The kind of folks who will never win any awards for their religious awareness. Surprised? If so, I wouldn't understand why.

I. After all, Paul himself wrote the church: "Think of what you were when you were called. Not many of you were wise by human standards; not many were influential; not many were of noble birth." Jesus began his campaign for fol-lowers by choosing some very common folk.

Why should God choose such common stock for sainthood? According to Paul it was to "shame the wise and the strong of this world—to make things that seem im-portant look unimportant." But mostly it was "so that no one could boast before God!"

Boasting is a big problem in the church. Well, actually, it didn't begin with the church. It started with the dis-ciples. They argued about who was the greatest, to the point of taking potshots at one another! And Jesus said what? "Whoever wants to become great among you must be your servant, and whoever wants to be first must be slave of all."

After all, we have little reason to boast. In the words of Paul, "It's because of God that you are in Christ Jesus." In other words, as Jesus once said, "You did not choose me; I chose you!" One day Jesus took a stroll by the docks and said to some common laborers, "Follow me."

So often I've heard persons in the church say, "I can't serve in that way. I'm just not cut out for it!" Well, maybe not. But then again, who is—really? Do you honestly believe that old salty-dog Peter thought for one minute that his name and fame would be remembered for over two thousand years? And Lord knows the other disciples were anything but cut from the fabric of saintly silk! We're not talking here about theological whiz kids, you know. These guys were former hard hats and hand-to-mouth workers. Yet de-spite all that, Jesus said, "Follow me."

Housewives and home builders. Teachers and truck drivers. The stuff of which the church is made up!

II. Discipleship is not about our poten-tial or power. It is, however, about Christ's promise and presence. And we don't qualify for the position by padding our resume with exaggerated attributes. Common folk become Christ's followers. And that by an act of sheer grace. It's not about us. It's about Christ in us!

Still, we sometimes worry, don't we? I mean, we fret about the ambition that burns within our breast. We want to be something. We desire to become some-body. Perhaps we dream of the day when we'll make our mark on this world. And sometimes while eating our lunch from a brown paper bag, we dream of corporate deals and black-tie dinners. We want to be remembered for something more than our dedication to the drudgery of a nine-to-five!

And somehow this desire gets under our Christian skin as well. We want to do something striking for the Lord. We hope our contribution will be significant. We yearn for our devotion to be more dynamic. But Jesus seems to be unimpressed by all that. I suppose he's not searching for superstars. Looks to me like Jesus is scanning the crowds of common people, looking only for some faithful followers.

Whenever Jesus calls us to follow, there's this element of the unknown. We never know in advance where following Jesus will take us.

The hospital room, where a respirator pumps life into a loved one or friend. The kitchen table, where a neighbor's tears belie a marriage torn by a certain madness. The lunch room, where a fellow employee lays her heart in your hands. Whenever Jesus says, "Follow me," we are drawn into a world of dark uncertainties and deep passion.

Perhaps that's why it requires faith to be a follower of Jesus. Faith assures us that, no matter where we are called to serve, Christ is always one step ahead!

Even more important, because Christ is always there before us, we needn't rely on our own strength or ability or character alone to see us through. Just remember what Jesus promised those first followers. He said, "I will make you fishers of men."

III. Faith empowers us to enter the most unlikely—sometimes the most ungodly—circumstances with confidence. But only because we follow him who said, and says, "I will make you." I will make you a powerful pray-er. I will make you a talented teacher. I will make you a competent spiritual counselor. I will make you a committed Christian. Because we follow Christ, Christ makes us what we need to be, when we need to be it.

When Christ comes to us with his call to serve, it is rarely in those moments we might consider convenient. Maybe Christ will suddenly call you to minister to the fellow who sits opposite you at the board meeting. Perhaps he'll ask you to reach out to some troubled teenager in your classroom. Maybe the woman who works beside you will one day confide in you that her heart is aching and her marriage breaking up. Then Christ will call on you to show her compassion.

IV. And whenever we follow, we must leave something—sometimes someone—behind. Seldom is that easy. Because the call of Christ is never ending. We are time and again asked to relinquish one thing so that we can more effectively embrace another. It could be the comfort of the familiar, the security of family, or a promising future. It could be something as major as a promotion. Or it might be something as minor as a much-needed lunch break.

Maybe that's why he once said, "Whoever does not take up the cross of compassionate commitment and follow me is not worthy of me." You think, perhaps, denial of self has something to do with discipleship? Those four followers from the shores of Lake Galilee were quite content tossing and mending their nets. Then along came Jesus, and the four became followers simply by being distracted—"I will make you fishers of men." They were promised nothing more than a lifetime of distractions! And why not? After all, the life of Christ was one great drama of distraction! Time after time, he denied himself while distracted by some other person's need. I guess you could say Jesus was distracted to death. Even death on a cross!

Because the call—"Follow me"—will come. And when it does, it really makes little difference what we were doing five minutes prior to Christ's plea. But believe me, it makes all the difference in this world—and maybe even more so in the next—what we are found doing five minutes after that call of Christ comes!—Albert J. D. Walsh

Illustrations

THE KIND HE CALLED. As far as posterity is concerned, the twelve of course as individuals are faceless men. Even their names are not absolutely certain: The lists differ from each other, particularly with reference to Thaddaeus or Simon. The evangelists do not seem interested in the prehistory and the characters of individuals. Obviously, there are some very unimportant people among them: fishermen; a tax collector (Matthew, presumably identical with Levi) and a Zealot (Simon, the Canaanite), as such, deadly enemies; perhaps also some peasants or workmen. Only two stand out (the two "Sons of Thunder," John and James, remain very sketchy figures): Judas Iscariot and Simon, with the nickname—perhaps given by Jesus himself—of "Cephas" or "Petros" (rock). The latter, a fisherman from Bethsaida, married in Capernaum, passionately devoted to Jesus but wavering at the end, was indisputably spokesman for the other disciples—even if his role was subsequently stylized—and was later important as the first witness of the risen Christ and leader of the primitive community. The ambivalent figure of Peter in particular clearly shows that the two first Gospels at least do not attempt to idealize the disciples: They are normal, erring and sinful men, not heroes or geniuses.—Hans Küng

THE ATONING LIFE.   Christ is not our vicarious substitute in the sense that to be saved we have only now to accept the dogma that he is our vicarious substitute. Christ is our vicarious substitute as doing what we could not and cannot do of ourselves. He is, however, inclusively our representative, offering in perfect form an obedience which each one of us is required to offer and which by his help we can begin to offer even though imperfectly.—William J. Wolf

Sermon Suggestions

WHEN GOD'S WORD GOES FORTH.   TEXT: Neh. 8:1–4a, 5–6, 8–10. (1) It must be heard. (2) It must be given attention. (3) It must be explained. (4) It should be an occasion of celebration.

A PLACE FOR EVERYONE.   TEXT: 1 Cor. 12:12–30. (1) *Situation*: People tend to separate themselves into exclusive groups. (2) *Complication*: Natural exclusiveness often leads to envy, rivalry, hatred, slander, and even violent acts; at

best, to misunderstanding and loneliness. (3) *Resolution*: Our problem can be resolved when we follow the unifying lead of the Spirit and recognize the importance of every part of "the Body of Christ" to the whole.

Worship Aids

CALL TO WORSHIP.   "Let the words of my mouth and the meditation of my heart be acceptable in thy sight, O Lord, my rock and my redeemer" (Ps. 19:14).

INVOCATION.   O God, forever and ever our Lord, be the Lord of our thoughts and feelings and hopes, our joys, this morning, and our griefs always. Very many of us have come together here, O God, with nothing sufficiently interesting to hold us in times of sorrow and disappointment, in the storm. Wilt Thou interest us this morning in Thyself! Deliver us from ourselves by taking us into thyself. We bring to thee such a variety of experience of the human thought that the endeavoring to circumscribe it staggers and hesitates and fails. Thou shalt not fail with us. Thou shalt take us all in. Thou wilt take all of us; every side of us. We can leave it all to thee. Give us this hour of peace and strength and progress, through our Lord and Savior, Jesus Christ. Amen.—Frank W. Gunsaulus

OFFERTORY SENTENCE.   "Now you are the body of Christ and individually members of it" (1 Cor. 12:27, RSV).

OFFERTORY PRAYER.   Allow, O Lord, that we might walk in thy way, live in thy will, and achieve thy purposes. And let this offering be a bright reflection of our commitment, through Christ our Savior.—E. Lee Phillips

PRAYER.   "Lord, thou has been our dwelling place in all generations. Before the mountains were brought forth, or ever thou hadst formed the earth and the world, from everlasting to everlasting thou art God."

You *are* the great God and the great King above all gods, but yet you are present to each one of us as though there were no other person in the world to love. You uniquely love us even down to the tips of our fingers. You *are* immanent among us, but yet you are always present as the Stranger—for your thoughts are not our thoughts and your ways are not our ways. Your coming is always so low key—so unspectacular—that most of the time we miss you. You don't act like God. Your appearances are so unobtrusive.

To reveal yourself to all the world you come as a helpless baby born in a cattle stall, and our redemption draws nigh in a peasant hanging on a cross. Are such antics becoming to the God of all gods—to the King above all kings? You *are* such a stranger!

To be the Messiah, you called one from among *us*—Jesus of Nazareth. He did not spend a ministry talking about religion but about life—he calls us not to be more *religious* but to be more *human*—more brotherly and sisterly—to be *your* children. He proclaimed a strange order or re-ordering of things: "The first shall be last and the last shall be first." "And, inasmuch as you have done it unto one of the least of these—my brother, my sister—you have done it unto me."

We praise you that there is a grace at work among *us* quietly, subtly, but yet surely—bringing the light where there has only been darkness, or so it has seemed; bringing hope out of despair, houses out of shacks, gardens out of weed patches, joy out of sorrow, wholeness out of brokenness, life out of death—the grace of our Lord Jesus Christ!

How strange that we should be channels of this grace—coworkers in the building of your kingdom. To this end let us pray and live, [the Lord's Prayer].—John Thompson

LECTIONARY MESSAGE

Topic: Anointed and Sent
TEXTS: Luke 4:14–21; Ps. 19:7–14
The act of anointment for a special task is quite ancient. Two familiar Old Testament examples stand out. Saul was anointed by Samuel to be king of Israel. Later Samuel anointed David to be king of Israel. The men were anointed but did not immediately undertake the task. Later they were sent to accomplish it.

The Holy Spirit had come upon Jesus at his baptism. In the Spirit he was led to the wilderness of temptation. In the power of the Spirit he returned to Galilee.

I. *In the power of the Spirit.* There's a neat phrase. All of his ministry would be exercised in the power of the Spirit. Now, having resisted the winsome wiles of Satan, he returned to Galilee. Galilee was as attractive as the wilderness had been foreboding . . . beautiful Galilee. The modern traveler has little difficulty in marking the contrast. Judea itself is rough and rocky, not to mention the proposed site of the temptation. Galilee is a broad expanse of field and flower. Isaiah (9:1) described it as "Galilee of the Gentiles." There is an openness, a free spirit about it.

Galilee was home for most of the disciples and for Jesus. Perhaps only Judas Iscariot was a native of Judea. In the power of the Spirit, Jesus and his friends went home. All over the towns of Galilee Jesus taught in their synagogues. He was well received by all, and then he came to Nazareth.

II. *He came to Nazareth.* The atmosphere was different. Nazareth was "where he had been brought up." He was a prophet at home. Do you remember the attitude of your home church to you and your ministry? Perhaps they called you their "preacher boy." Perhaps they dignified it as our "ministerial student." He was in the home church.

As his custom was, he went to the synagogue on the Sabbath. As their custom was, he was enlisted as reader of the day. He stood, and the attendant gave him the roll of the prophet Isaiah. He found the passage in Isa. 61:1ff. and read, The Spirit of the Lord anointed me. His mind must have gone back to the descent of the Spirit at his baptism. It might not have been evident then, but now in the words of the prophet, "he anointed me to preach good tidings."

And "he sent me." His was to be no static ministry, with chapel built at the site of baptism. He was sent to proclaim release of the captives and recovering of sight to the blind. He was sent to set at liberty the oppressed and to proclaim the Year of Jubilee.

III. *The Word fulfilled.* He closed the book and sat down, and all eyes were upon him. How much did they know or think they knew about him? Did they know that he was the Anointed, their Messiah? He began to say "Today . . ." The word from Isaiah was fulfilled at his baptism and now in his ministry. In the power of the Spirit he moved through their villages preaching the good news and exemplifying the good news in healings, kindness, and courage.

Anointed and sent! So are we. The prayer of the psalmist then becomes our petition: "Let the words of my mouth and the meditation of my heart be acceptable in thy sight, O Lord, my rock and my redeemer" (Ps. 19:14).

Or hear the words of the risen Lord: "As the Father hath sent me, so send I you" (John 20:21).—J. Estill Jones

SUNDAY: FEBRUARY SECOND

SERVICE OF WORSHIP

Sermon: What Christianity Is All About
TEXT: Acts 25:19

Can we quote a single sentence from the Bible that will tell us what Christianity is all about?

There is such a sentence in the twenty-fifth chapter of the Book of Acts, and we make it our text now. It occurs in the description of an incident that took place in Caesarea where the Apostle Paul was in prison at the close of his missionary career. If he had been willing to bribe Felix, the Roman governor, he might have been set free, but Paul knew that he was safer in prison than out of it, because his enemies were waiting outside to assassinate him. After a while Felix was recalled to Rome and his place taken by Festus, who asked Paul if he would go to Jerusalem and stand trial in the presence of his accusers. For the sake of his own safety, Paul refused. Also, he invoked his right as a Roman citizen to be taken to Rome and tried before the emperor. At this point, Festus received some distinguished visitors, the Jewish king Herod Agrippa and his wife Bernice. The story begins. [Read Acts 25:13–19, NEB.]

That's the sentence I have in mind— "someone called Jesus, a dead man whom Paul alleged to be alive." In twelve words, without knowing it, Festus informed the Jewish king exactly what Christianity is all about, and no one could do better. If we were asked to explain the Christian faith to an unbeliever, especially to explain how it differs from other religious faiths, we might very well quote Festus and tell him that Christianity is all about "someone called Jesus, a dead man whom Paul alleged to be alive." We should not speak as patronizingly as Festus did but rather with the same reverence that we recite the creeds. On our lips those words are, in fact, a creed, a confession of faith, a statement of the great doctrines of our religion, and we might well memorize and recite them over and over again to remind ourselves what Christianity is all about.

I. First, it is about someone called Jesus. It is not about someone called Moses or Mohammed or Buddha or Billy Graham or Martin Luther King, not about the Golden Rule or liberation theology or speaking with tongues, but about someone called Jesus. Other world religions may have begun with the ideas, the visions and the practices of people, but Christianity began with the birth of a baby named Jesus who grew up to be a very special person and lived a unique life upon this earth.

The unbeliever might well ask how those simple facts grew into the greatest of world religions. Surely we don't build churches and create theologies in memory of an itinerant teacher and faith healer. No indeed! It was not Jesus alone who created Christianity. It was Jesus plus what the New Testament writers believed and said about him. See how Mark opens his biography of Jesus: "Here begins the Gospel of Jesus Christ the Son of God." See how John concludes his account: "These are written that you may believe that Jesus is the Christ, the Son of God, and that believing, you may have life in his name."

That is the foundation belief of the New Testament, especially Paul's letters. After I had preached a sermon on one of them, someone made an interesting observation. He said, "I understand that Paul never knew the historic Jesus, yet we have all his wonderful writings in the New Testament. How much more wonderful they would be if he and Jesus had actually met." I replied, "But they did meet on the Damascus Road." That's what Paul said when he was permitted to make his defense before Festus and Agrippa. In that royal presence of pomp and splendor, Paul, the prisoner in chains, told the story of Jesus whose followers he had persecuted to the death but who came to him in a vision, turned his life around, and claimed his eternal obedience. "And so, King Agrippa," he declared, "I did not disobey the heavenly vision." How could he? For it was no mere memory that arrested him, no fantasy of his own mind, but a living encounter with one whom he later described as "the image of the invisible God."

Karl Barth's great system of church dogmatics begins with Christ as the way to God, the truth about God and the very life of God made visible and brought within our experience. Just before his death he said, "The last word which I have to say as a theologian is not a term like 'grace' but a name 'Jesus Christ.' *He* is grace, and he *is* the last, beyond the world and the church and even theology. . . ." That's what Christianity is all about.

II. So Festus spoke the truth when he said that Paul was on trial because of a dispute about someone called Jesus. He spoke the truth also when he said that Jesus was "a dead man." Jesus did die physically, because his enemies put him to a violent death on a cross. There was no doubt about that. His friends saw his mangled corpse taken down from the cross and buried in a borrowed tomb.

Yes, Jesus was a dead man, but the wonder of it is that he saw his dying and the writers of the New Testament saw it not as defeat but as victory, not as the frustration but as the completion of his saving work. Paul made the cross central in his proclamation of the gospel. It dominates his New Testament letters to the churches, especially First Corinthians, where he specifically states, "We preach Christ crucified, a stumbling block to Jews and folly to Gentiles, but to those who are called, both Jews and Greeks, Christ the power of God and the wisdom of God." Again: "When I came to you, brethren, I did not come proclaiming to you the testimony of God in lofty words of wisdom. For I decided to know nothing among you except Jesus Christ and him crucified."

Why is that so? Why is the cross central to Christianity? It is central because, as Paul said, it is "the power of God and the wisdom of God." There is power in the cross of Christ, magnetic power that draws people to God when all else fails. We could resist a God who roars at us and frightens us and simply punishes us for our sins. But how can we resist a gracious God who suffers for our sins and allows them to nail him to a cross? The cross draws us to God because it is the supreme demonstration of his stubborn love for us, his refusal to be compromised by our sins, to let our friendship with him be broken. We defy God, but the cross of Christ is God's superior act of defiance. Through it he seems to say, "You can do with me what you like. You can break my bones and bruise my flesh and drain my blood, but you cannot stop me from being what I am, the Father who loves you and will not let you go."

We can go deeper than that and say that the cross is central because it makes Christianity a gospel, the good news that God has done for us what we cannot do for ourselves and what must be done for our eternal salvation.

III. Again Festus spoke the truth when he referred to Jesus as "a dead man whom Paul alleged to be alive." Festus himself did not allege Jesus to be alive, nor did Paul's accusers, nor do many people today, even some who claim to be Christian teachers.

Say what they will, however, the truth is that not only Paul but all the writers of the New Testament allege Jesus to be alive. Indeed, the supreme fact about Jesus to which they bear witness and try to interpret is not his birth, life, teaching, ministry, or death but the fact that God raised him from the dead. They begin with the Resurrection and from there look back and find significance in the events of his life and death. Even the disciples, who were with Jesus during his earthly ministry, think of him not in terms of past memories but in terms of present experience. If we stopped one of them on a Jerusalem street and asked, "Where is your Lord?" he would not reply, "My Lord is in a sepulchre." He would say, "My Lord is everywhere, in Judea, in Galilee, wherever we go. He is here now."

The church for nineteen centuries has alleged Jesus to be alive. In fact, the church is founded on the faith that God raised Jesus from the dead, and if that faith were shown to be false, the whole structure of Christianity would collapse. In fact, however, we base our belief not on a tomb that was empty but on hearts that are full of the presence of the risen, living Christ. We don't prove the Resurrection. We experience it. We allege Jesus Christ to be alive.

Malcolm Muggeridge believed that Jesus Christ is alive. So he alleged in his book *Jesus Rediscovered*, describing his return to the faith after many long years of doubt and unbelief. He explains what happened to him not as conversion but as recognition—recognition of the Christ who has never been away from him, recognition that Christ is the goal of all his seeking and the meaning of his life. It came to him most vividly on the road to Emmaus in the Holy Land where he had been preparing some films for television. Walking along that road with a friend, as

two others did on the evening of the first Easter Day, he felt a presence that convinced him that Christ is eternally alive. Later when he was asked in a television interview, "Are you sure that there was a Resurrection?" he replied, "I am sure there was . . . but I don't in the least care whether the stone was moved or not moved or what anybody said or anything like that. . . . There must have been a Resurrection because Jesus Christ is alive now, two thousands years later. . . . He is alive as a person who can be reached."

That's the Bible definition of what Christianity is all about—"someone called Jesus, a dead man whom Paul alleged to be alive." That single sentence, spoken by a pagan diplomat, contains the great central doctrines of our faith, God's mighty works of Incarnation, Atonement, and Resurrection. Our own lives as Christians proclaim the truth even more eloquently. Let those outside the faith see our personal obedience to Christ, our worship before his cross, our joy in his living presence. Then they will know what Christianity is all about.—Leonard Griffith

Illustrations

FAITH'S CENTER OF GRAVITY.   We have moved our faith's center of gravity, and we have detached it too far from the experiences that gather specially about the Cross and the Resurrection. We cultivate the pieties, and we are strange to the hells and heavens that open about that historic moment, which was the crisis both of our souls and of human destiny. We have a religion whose keynote is evolution rather than crisis, education rather than conversion, good form rather than great power.—P. T. Forsyth

MISSION   AND   PERSONAL   FULFILLMENT.   I trust those witnesses who tell me about the person of Jesus (and who had no "interest" in doing so). I trust the person of Jesus, and I enter the world of faith in the words that he spoke. The mission of the "good news" has been accomplished, and yet it still remains to be accomplished, because Jesus is who he is and nobody else. I don't offer any proofs or rational justifications. But the one who suffered, who was crucified and raised in his glorified body, he still speaks to me today with words that burn, that start me off and push me into being something other than what I am, even while fulfilling every particle of myself as I am.—Jacques Ellul

Sermon Suggestions

THE MAKING OF A PROPHET.   TEXT: Jer. 1:4–10. (1) Through a call, verses 4–5. (2) Through God's compensating help, verses 6–8. (3) Through the transcendent power of God's Word, verses 9–10.

WHAT CAN WE SAY ABOUT CHRISTIAN LOVE?   TEXT: 1 Cor. 13:1–13. (1) Without it we are nothing. (2) With it life achieves its fullest potential.

Worship Aids

CALL TO WORSHIP.   "In thee, O Lord, do I put my trust; let me never be put to confusion" (Ps. 71:1).

INVOCATION.   Father, still our busyness that we may gather our fragmented selves together. Focus our attention that we may be attuned to your special speaking. Silence our noisiness that we may be able to hear your still small voice. Make us courageous that we may even endure your silence. Grant that we may exemplify Christ in all things. Visit us now with your Spirit and power that we may understand that we are in the presence of the Eternal Father of us all.—Henry Fields

OFFERTORY SENTENCE.   "I may have the gift of inspired preaching; I may have all knowledge and understand all secrets; I may have all the faith needed to move mountains—but if I have no love, I am nothing" (1 Cor. 13:3, TEV).

OFFERTORY PRAYER.   Give us to know, O Lord, the joy of sharing, the depths of sacrifice, the rewards of generosity, for thy love is wrapped up in giving as must be our living.—E. Lee Phillips

PRAYER.   O Lord, our God, this is thy unspeakable glory that we may call out for thee, "O Lord, our God, our Creator, our Savior"—that thou knowest and lovest us all and desirest to be known and loved by each one of us—that thou seest and governest all our ways—that we all come from thee and go to thee.

We spread out everything before thee—our cares, that thou wouldst care for them—our anxiety, that thou wouldst still it—our hopes and desires, that thy will be done and not our own—our sins, that thou wouldst forgive them—our thoughts and longings, that thou wouldst purify them—our whole life in this our time, that thou wouldst lead it to the resurrection of the body and the life everlasting.

[We remember before thee all the inmates of this house and all the other captives around the world.] Be thou with our loved ones at home, with all the poor, the sick, the distressed, and the afflicted. Enlighten the thoughts and govern the actions of all those in our land and in all other lands who are responsible for justice and order and peace. Let the day break through Jesus Christ, our Lord, in whose name we pray, "Our Father. . . ." —Karl Barth

LECTIONARY MESSAGE

Topic: A Prophet at Home

TEXTS: Luke 4:21–30; Jer. 1:4–10

Nothing so troubles us as to suppose that God loves another nation, another people, so much as he loves us. A prophet is to be enjoyed at home—where we can control him. These concepts are not foreign to our experience.

I. *Stirs up pride.* That's what a prophet does. How many in the synagogue at Nazareth must have swelled with pride when Jesus declared that Scripture had been fulfilled in their midst . . . "in your ears."

"What a fine man!" They marveled at the way he read the passage from Isaiah. They were amazed at his bearing. He was one of theirs. He could do no wrong. "Words of grace" came from his mouth.

We know his father, what a fine person Joseph was. What a hard worker. Why, that plowshare he worked on is yet in good shape. That chair he repaired is still strong.

He'll favor us with a miracle. We know he will. We've heard about his powers. Both Matthew and Mark place this appearance in Nazareth after an extensive preaching and healing ministry. He'll upgrade our reputation. We can hardly wait to inform Capernaum that Nazareth is the home of Jesus ... Jesus of Nazareth. It was said "that he did not many mighty works there because of their unbelief" (Matt. 13:58).

II. *Stirs up prejudice.* He continued to speak. A negative statement split the air: "No prophet is acceptable in his own country." They did not hear him at first. They were basking in their pride. This is the center of the universe, they said. God lives here, they claimed.

And Jesus said, "But of a truth ..." Now why should he muddy the waters? Why should he not accept their praise? That there were many widows in Israel had always been true. That they suffered from famine and disease had always been true. And then he split the air again. God sent the prophet Elijah outside the Prom-

ised Land to Sidon to minister to a foreign widow. Could the prophet not work a miracle in Israel? Did not God love Israel's widows best?

And there were many lepers in Israel. Always the scourge of leprosy stirred fear and sympathy. And they remained untreated. But God healed only Naaman, the Syrian soldier. Could the prophet Elisha not work a miracle in Israel? Did not God love Israel's lepers best?

Both Elijah and Elisha worked miracles of God's grace on foreigners!

III. *Stirs up wrath.* And it wasn't "righteous indignation"! Is he suggesting that we ought to share God with the Gentiles? We want to keep God and his prophets at home.

And the wrath filled the synagogue. And the wrath filled the city. And the wrath filled the countryside. They were about to stone him to death. They were mad enough to throw rocks. They were mad enough to eat nails.

But he was calm enough to walk away from them without calling down a bolt of lightning from the eternal God. Perhaps he remembered the commitment of Jeremiah: "I have appointed thee a prophet unto the nations" (Jer. 1:5).—J. Estill Jones

SUNDAY: FEBRUARY NINTH

SERVICE OF WORSHIP

Sermon: A City Set on a Hill
TEXT: Matt. 5:14–16

Combine the clear air and brilliant sunshine of a desert climate with a whitewashed, gleaming city and you have a thrilling sight! Come into San Francisco from the Pacific and pass through the Golden Gate at sunset. The great bridge gleams through its coat of Rustoleum, and houses climbing up the slopes of Telegraph Hill and Nob Hill will win your heart with their rosy blushes. Ride up from the deep sink of the Great Salt Lake to Salt Lake City, made brilliant by the setting sun against the dark backdrop of the Wasatch Mountains, and you'll

think it as majestic as the New Jerusalem that it was built to be.

I have not seen enough of the cities of the world to know which one is absolutely the most dramatic on account of its being set on a hill, but I have seen one that Jesus also knew—and it is stunning. Approach Jerusalem for the first time from the west at evening. When you pass the village of Abu Ghosh, go to the top of the hills beyond. Turn and face east, and there it is! About nine miles away the city sits on the hill of Zion and its other hills, shining brilliantly in the golden light, four thousand feet above the Dead Sea, which can be seen sulking deep in the Jordan Valley beyond it. Surely this is the very city of which Jesus was thinking when he said, "A city set on a hill cannot be hid." It is a city for all to see, so brilliant that, as the prophet put it, "Nations shall come to your light, and kings to the brightness of your rising" (Isa. 60:3).

A city set on a hill. A city for all to see.

I. Our Puritan ancestors came to this continent to build a New Jerusalem and here to set a city on a hill—yes, Beacon Hill—that would shine so brightly that it would draw all the world unto itself, if not into its political domain, at least into the realm of its spirit. The vision of America as such a city, as brilliant at dawn as Jerusalem is at close of day, warmed the imaginations of our parents and grandparents. Until recently at least, it has been a vision dear to American self-understanding, educational strategy, and political rhetoric.

But metaphors will get mixed, and good visions will get into quarrels with each other. In our case, the image of the exposed and open city on the hill has had to struggle with another image, that of the fortress, the walled city of refuge!

The historical Jerusalem got caught in the same struggle between images. When one finally arrives at the city that provided Jesus with his metaphor, one makes an interesting discovery. The mirror that reflected the light of the setting sun back to the west is primarily its wall. The great, beautifully constructed limestone fortification that surrounds the entire Old City of Jerusalem was built in A.D. 1538 by the Turkish sultan Suleyman the Magnificent. As one prepares to enter one of the massive gates that give access to the Old City, one really cannot see the city at all but only its armor plate! What a surprise! Must a city set on a hill have walls then? Must the gleaming city of God also be a fortress?

II. Now if we move out of the mode of a metaphor to talk about real walls around real human communities—and more modern things like nuclear deterrents and peace shields—we become involved in the practical consideration of whether any human community has the right to defend itself against its enemies or not. Certainly from time immemorial the people of Jerusalem found it necessary to surround their city with walls in order to keep any light burning there at all. Nor were they the first to do so. In fact, the walls of Jebusite Jerusalem impeded the progress of the conquering Israelites until David sent his men worming up the watershaft (2 Sam. 5:8). In the days of Hezekiah, the walls of Jerusalem held off the Assyrian army of Sennacherib until the angel of the Lord could finish the job of getting rid of 185,000 of them (2 Kings 19:35). The most important job undertaken by Nehemiah during his governorship of Judah after the Babylonian exile of the Jews was the rebuilding of the walls of Jerusalem. And even after the threat of the terrible Crusaders had abated, Suleyman cried, "More walls!"

It's a dangerous world out there, especially in the neighborhood of Jerusalem. Unknown menaces howl in the wilderness outside. The city or even the nation that wants to take care of its children and its culture may well decide on walls.

But does the community of the light need walls? Must the Christian commonwealth be compassed about?

The metaphors that follow his teaching about the city make clear Jesus' attitude on this. You don't light a lamp and cover it with a hood or hurricane lantern. You lift it on high. You shower everyone within reach with the blessing of light. You radiate. Now we are near the point of Jesus' teaching, and the point really has nothing to do with cities or bushels or even lamps. The headline of the passage says it all: "You are the light of the world." *You* ... That's who you really are—not hot shots but hot spots in the world, sources of illumination, thousands of points of light. And well aware that if you don't use it you lose it, this metaphor culminates in the very practical admonition "Let your light so shine before others, that they may see and understand what God's works are like because they see them in you."

Jesus thinks we're good enough to shine! Jesus tells us that we are sources of radiance and energy in the world. They were right in Sunday school all along: Jesus wants us for sunbeams. The purpose of these analogies in the Sermon on the Mount is to make clear that a Christian life-style is one lived outside any shrouding, probably outside any walls. It is a life visibly radiant with love.

III. But now comes a big problem. How can our light shine without fuel? After all, light has to be fed with something, right? The light from a candle emanates from a solid base of wax. The light of a Chesapeake Bay lighthouse, which used to guide endangered ships to safety, could shine only because it drew upon a deep reservoir of whale oil solidly encased in a stone tower. So the question that these metaphors raise for the community of Christian disciples goes something like this: What is the relation of our safe home base, from which we are refueled, to our vocation of shining? Or to put it superpragmatically: What percentage of the time should we expect to spend being nurtured, consorting with our kind of people, drawing on the lore of the community of disciples and learning its language—and what percentage should we expect to be radiating light? Pick a ratio, any ratio: 1:3 or 1:10 or 1:20. Should it be 5 percent drawing energy within the walls and 95 percent radiating light in and outside them?

Now a sect will answer the percentage question somewhat differently than a church will. The gathered community of saints traditionally has recourse to *itself* for guidance and support. Be they residents of cloistered convents in our time or of the Qumran community of old, the saints of the sect will look inward to the good of their own group and will devotedly take care of the needs of their fellow saints first. Theirs may even be an underground community that cannot afford to radiate the words of the gospel except in very shielded circumstances. Fueling: 99 percent, radiating 1 percent may be all you can expect from a sect.

But you can expect more from a church. And we're church people not sectarians. Just the other evening I asked an active laywoman how she enjoyed her job as chair of a church committee. She said quietly that she was shocked at just how much time and energy went into the church structure simply perpetuating itself! Yet the fueling that the light of our spirits draws from its infinitely renewable energy source, the power of God's Spirit, conveyed through the Word of God rightly divided in the midst of the fellowship of believers, ought to have an absolutely exponential effect. For every ten units of energy that that light draws from the deep reservoirs of the Christian community, perhaps we can hope for ninety units of new illumination and new hope awakened among those tender human creatures on which that light shines! I am not speaking primarily about the ratio of R & R to action in individuals, of course, though God knows we individuals often need rest and refreshment to our souls. I am speaking about the church as a whole. Fortress, no. Light source for the human community, yes!

Of course we need our fortresslike buildings and a few gargoyles and lancets just for fun. Of course we need our in-house organs and our presbyteries and our conventions and conferences. Of course we need a few good old boys and girls, because we need to be catechized in the lore of Christian covenant. Of course we need to practice the art of Christian love starting with those who are closest at hand, our mentors and comrades in the movement, even with those who have gone on before.

IV. But the *vocation* of the Christian community is to radiate upon the world the light that Jesus assures us that we are. Radiation is our *raison d'etre*. Our business is to shine out there.

You know, all Christian confession about human nature is rooted in our confession about God. All anthropology is theology. That is true of the notion of the shining light, as well. As far as we creatures are concerned, *God's* only meaning is in God's going forth. What the Creator does apart from creating is unknown to us, nor does it matter. God may be omnipotent, omniscient, perfectly just, etc., etc. But those absolute qualities of God are hard for us meaningfully to assess. And how God refuels within the ineffable fellowship of the Trinity we can only guess. But the Creator *does* express the divine vocation by radiating light outside the godhead. In John 1 we are told, "In the beginning was the Word, and the Word was with God, and the Word was God. He was in the beginning with God; all things were made through him, and without him was not anything made that was made. In him was life, and the life was the light of humankind. The light shines in the darkness, and the darkness has not overcome it" (John 1:1–5).

God's vocation is Jesus' vocation, too. He was always reaching out to touch someone. Does the gospel suggest what Jesus' ratio of refueling to radiating was? There had to be some of both, of course, for he was a human being. One to ten? One to fifty? I don't know. I only know that if God and Christ find their vocation in radiating light upon the darkness and in creating being and order where there was nothing, surely our more modest vocation is to shine forth.

Whatever we may need as we draw together in the safety of our heavy stone church buildings and our theological schools we need only as a means to the end that we exercise our vocation. As to the exercise itself, we do that by walking out of the gates and down the slopes of the hill on which the sacred city is built. We step out from under the peace shield and all the other human provisions vainly designed to enable us to carry on our work in total safety. There is not total safety. There is a movement, and the movement won't stay put inside the walls. It beams on out. The movement seeks more ecumenism not less; more globalization not less; more effective speaking of the gospel among its detractors not less; more fraternal workers and evangelists not fewer; more intimacy with the saints of the inner city not less; more understanding of and fellowship with AIDS victims not less; more new theologies forged in the crucible of the experience of the marginals not fewer.

I'm not sure *exactly* what the Russian word *glasnost* means, but I know I'm trying to describe a Christian *glasnost* right now as that life-style most likely to lift the light on high and to let it shine. I'm talking about human communities not hedged about with sectarian rules and blue laws but true churches, their windows thrown open to let the radiance stream out, their doors thrown open as wide as are the gates of the New Jerusalem in through which the nations stream (Rev. 21:24–26). All retrenchment; all long-range planning; all management by objectives; all overweening concern with the institution itself; all wall-building—practically necessary as these things may be from time to time—have to take a back seat to the freedom of the Christian conscience to show forth the light wherever it will.—W. Sibley Towner

Illustrations

EXPOSING GOD.   To light a lamp only to place it at once under a bowl (in other words, to extinguish it) is absurd. The lamp is there to give light to "everyone in the house"—the house in Palestine, as a rule, consisting of a single room. Once more the mission of the disciples to "all" is underlined.

In the context of Jesus' parables, the lampstand refers to Jesus' preaching (Mark 4:21 = Luke 8:16); in the context of Jesus' glorification and the saying about the sign of Jonah (Luke 11:33) it refers to Jesus himself (or possibly, if taken with v. 34, the inner light of men). Matthew can hardly have had another meaning in mind, although he makes the saying refer to the disciples. To him they are, as it were, transparent, and reveal the light of the one who stands above them and gives all that they are. So of course the saying means something different from the cliché about not hiding your light under a bushel. What is rendered visible is not the man himself but only the "Father in heaven." If works are truly good and not evil, they reveal their true agent. But even this does not suffice; such works are to be done within the purview of "people," not within the seclusion of a brotherhood—so that all people may encounter God.   —Eduard Schweizer

OUR TRUE CAPACITY.   It is a common impression with persons who hear, but do not accept, the calls of Christ and his salvation that they are required to be somewhat less in order to be Christian. They must be diminished in quantity, taken down, shortened, made feeble and little, and then, by the time they have let go their manhood, they will possibly come into the way of salvation. They hear it declared that, in becoming little children, humble, meek, poor in spirit; in ceasing from our will and reason; and in giving up ourselves, our eagerness, revenge, and passion—thus, and thus only, can we be accepted; but instead of taking all these as so many figures antagonistic to our pride, our ambition, and the determined self-pleasing of our sin, they take them absolutely, as requiring a real surrender and loss of our proper manhood itself. Exactly contrary to this, the gospel requires them to be more than they are—greater, higher, nobler, stronger—all of which they were made to be in the power of their endless life. These expressions, just referred to, have no other aim than simply to cut off weaknesses, break down infirmities, tear away boundaries, and let the soul out into liberty and power and greatness. What is weaker than pride, self-will, revenge, the puffing of conceit and rationality, the constraining littleness of all selfish passion? And in just these things it is that human souls are so fatally shrunk in all their conceptions of themselves; so that Christ encounters, in all men, this first and most insurmountable difficulty; to make them apprised of their real value to themselves. For no sooner do they wake to the sense of their great immortality than they are even oppressed by it. Everything else shrinks to nothingness, and they go to him for life. And then, when they receive him, it is even a bursting forth into magnitude. A new inspiration is upon them, all their powers are exalted, a wondrous inconceivable energy is felt, and, having come into the sense of God, which is the element of all real greatness, they discover as it were in amazement, what it is to be in the true capacity.—Horace Bushnell

Sermon Suggestions

WHEN A PROPHET FAILS. TEXT: Isa. 6:1–8 (9–13). (1) Is it because he has not met God? Sometimes, but not always, v. 1–5. (2) Is it because he has not been called? Sometimes, but not always, v. 6–8. (3) Is it because the message is wrong? Sometimes, but not always, v. 9–10. (4) It is the prophet's duty to preach faithfully despite every discouragement, v. 11–13.

THE BLESSINGS OF THE GOOD NEWS. TEXT: 1 Cor. 15:1–11. (1) Opportunity—"I preached to you the gospel." (2) Status—"which you received, in which you stand." (3) Salvation—"by which you are saved, if you hold it fast."

Worship Aids

CALL TO WORSHIP. "I thank you, Lord, with all my heart. . . . You answered me when I called to you; with your strength you strengthened me" (Ps. 138:1, 3, TEV).

INVOCATION. Holy, holy, holy, Lord, God of hosts, great is thy name and greatly to be praised. Give us to know today a praise worthy of thy glory and fitting of our faith, that what thou dost deserve and what we need might merge in worship's exaltation.—E. Lee Phillips

OFFERTORY SENTENCE. "You are saved by the gospel if you hold firmly to it— unless it was for nothing that you believed" (1 Cor. 15:2b, TEV).

OFFERTORY PRAYER. Help us to realize that it isn't ours, Father, but rather has been entrusted to us for a short while that we might use it wisely for creature comforts and meeting need about us. Call us again this morning to understand that we are but temporary stewards of it, not permanent owners. Make us realize that we will all too soon lay it aside and leave this world where it is so important. Give us to understand that its only real value resides in using it to benefit your kingdom now and across the future. Lead us this morning to rightly understand the meaning of money, Father, and how to use it to the best advantage of your purpose and will for all mankind as we give it in Christ's name.—Henry Fields

PRAYER. For your presence in the light *and* in the darkness—for the light of your countenance upon us as seen in the face of Jesus of Nazareth, we worship and adore you, O Father of us all. For your call that awakened us to the glorious light of this Lord's Day morning, we praise you. For this privilege to celebrate together the meaning of family in this household of faith, we give thanks. For your Word present in the beginning, and in our beginning, that has created church and sacrament as means of grace for our salvation and the salvation of all, we are grateful. Praise be to you—Father, Son, and Holy Spirit.—John Thompson

LECTIONARY MESSAGE

Topic: A Fisher of Men

TEXTS: Luke 5:1–11; Isa. 6:1–8

A prospective seminary student came by my office to talk about his call to the ministry. When a teenager, he had felt God wanted him. He resisted and had become successful in another profession. Yet he felt God was calling. Should he bring his wife and two children away from the known to the unknown? I think they will come.

Jesus was attracting attention and followers. He was popular. Crowds were pressing in upon him and almost forcing him to wade into the waters of the Seas of Galilee. He saw two boats "standing by" as he was "standing by." Almost made for one another!

I. *A comfortable vocation.* Simon and John and James liked to fish. They appear to be among those who enjoyed the work they did to earn a living. The Gospel according to John describes a post-resurrection scene in which six disciples followed Simon's suggestion that they go fishing. It's an enjoyable activity.

They appear to have been successful. Two boats were involved, one apparently Simon's and one belonging to James and John. Stories in the Gospels about their fishing indicate that they made a living at it. . . . Simon, for example, was married and cared for his wife's mother.

The three men, along with Andrew and others, were willing friends. The assistance offered to Simon by James and John was naturally sought and comfortably offered. All of this is to say that the three men were comfortable in their vocation.

II. *A challenge from a nonprofessional.* It was one thing for them to allow Jesus to use their boat. He needed their help, and they were willing to give it. It was quite another for this landlubber to tell them how to fish! When the teaching concluded, Jesus said simply, "The fish are out there, Simon." "No, sir, we have fished all night and have caught nothing . . . we did that while you were sleeping . . . see, our nets were dirty."

"But at thy word . . ." Simon let down the nets, and the fish swarmed into them. He called to James and John for help. So many fish were in the nets that both boats were filled. Simon, the vocational fisherman, was overwhelmed by the nonprofessional. He reacted in fear, "Master, go away from me!"

III. *A commitment made.* They were all amazed at the number of fish caught in their net. There must have been more than three fishing that day. Jesus responded to their amazement with a challenge to commitment: You have been successful fishermen; now you will become fishers of men. And they did—Simon at Pentecost, James faithful to death by martyrdom, and John exiled for his faith.

They left all and followed him. It's the same sort of response the prophet Isaiah made to the Lord's call, "Who will go for us?" The prophet answered, "Here I am, send me" (Isa. 6:8). And we who have been caught hear the words: "From henceforth thou shalt catch men."—J. Estill Jones

SUNDAY: FEBRUARY SIXTEENTH

SERVICE OF WORSHIP

Sermon: What Do You Say When You Don't Have Anything to Say?

TEXTS: Hab. 1:2–4, 2:20; 2 Cor. 4:6–7

"Have you ever felt that you did not have a recent, fresh word from God to proclaim? If so, did you refuse to preach?" Neither question was new to me. However, both questions gripped me with new strength when a student raised them at the end of a lecture.

I. My answer to the first question is yes. For those of us who preach, situations arise in which it is time for us to say something, and we have nothing to say. No doubt numerous factors contribute to this condition.

Do I refuse to preach? My answer to the second question is no. I have come to this pulpit and to others feeling ill-prepared within myself, devoid of the kind of fresh word that I like to speak, preoccupied because of personal problems, tired to the point of not functioning at my best. I have to preach, however, because of convictions about God's Word and God's power to work in and through the lives of persons who are weak. Far more is involved in sharing a word from God or doing the work of God than merely what I am thinking or feeling at any one moment. The same is true with you. People are far more interested in what God says than in what we think.

II. Actually, questions about speaking on behalf of God when we don't know what to say or acting on behalf of God when we don't know what to do are based upon the false assumption that saying and doing are more important than being. Sometimes our best response to persons in need and to situations of need is a silent presence. Being there is more important than saying something or doing anything.

Why are we so afraid of silence? Jesus did not always speak or act. Recall his response to the crowd that had decided to stone a woman caught in the act of adul-tery. Look at the contrast. All of those who stood in judgment of the woman knew what to say and what to do on behalf of God. However, the response of the Son of God was a loving silence. He knelt down and made markings in the dust before forgiving the woman and sending her on her way.

Being is more important than doing. Is it not significant that the identity of God was established by the verb "to be"? In the Old Testament, we are told that God's name is " I AM." God is to be worshiped and served not because "he said" or "he did" but because "he was, he is, he will be." Often God's most redemptive response to his people is his presence—not his speaking or his doing but his divine being. You may not know what to say or to do in defense of God with a family in crisis but being there communicates volumes about God's love and yours.

III. The false assumption needs to be challenged. However, that does not do away completely with situations that require a response of words or deeds of which we feel incapable. The Word of God and the works of God are bigger than any one person. God's message is mightier than I am. God's work is greater than my work.

Paul observed that the gospel is contained in earthen vessels. A trustworthy message can be delivered by an unworthy messenger.

If every word of Scripture could be proclaimed or commended only when a person had perfectly incarnated that word, what a dearth of helpfulness we would know. Some texts would be silenced forever.

Henri Nouwen is correct in his observation that "our worth is not the same as our usefulness." More than once it has been proven that even through our individual weaknesses, God can convey his almighty strength.

Carlyle Marney once said that if we find ourselves in a situation in which God seems to be silent, in which there seems to be no word from God, we will do well to act on the last word from God that we heard.

IV. Let me tell you what I know for sure. First, God loves us—individually and corporately. That means God is for us. Second, the gospel is about grace. Both the first word and the last word of the gospel are words of grace. And that grace—free but not cheap—is available to everyone of us.

Here, now, is where we discover the amazing economy of faith. In staying silent when there is not anything to say, we eventually discover words. In not doing anything when we do not know anything to do, eventually we discover something to do. In saying all that we can say, we find more to say. In doing all that we can do we find more to do. In faithfulness to what we know and have, to what we can say and to what we can do, we discover faith.

God expects no more from us than we can give. God expects us to say and do no more than we are capable of saying and doing. However, he does expect that much. When in such situations of demand, we offer to him our very best, he supplies our needs for being, speaking, and doing. Paul promises that "the spirit helps us in our weakness."—C. Welton Gaddy

Illustrations

WITNESS. Evangelism is witness. It is one beggar telling another beggar where to get food. The Christian does not offer out of his bounty. He has no bounty. He is simply guest at his Master's table and, as evangelist, he calls others, too.—Daniel T. Niles

WOUNDED HEALERS. Even when we know that we are called to be wounded healers, it is still very difficult to acknowledge that healing has to take place today. Because we are living in days when our wounds have become all too visible. Our loneliness and isolation has become so much a part of our daily experience that we cry out for a Liberator who will take us away from our misery and bring us justice and peace.

To announce, however, that the Liberator is sitting among the poor and that the wounds are signs of hope and that today is the day of liberation is a step very few can take. But this is exactly the announcement of the wounded healer: "The master is coming—not tomorrow but today, not next year but this year, not after all our misery is passed but in the middle of it, not in another place but right here where we are standing."—Henri J. M. Nouwen

Sermon Suggestions

TOWARD TRUE SUCCESS. TEXT: Jer. 17:5–10. (1) It is easy but tragic to trust and worship our natural desires and to go the way of human pride and presumption. (2) But it is wise and blessed to fix our faith and affection on the Lord, who gives us strength, security, and a fruitful life.

IF THERE IS NO RESURRECTION. TEXT: 1 Cor. 15:12–20. (1) Is the preaching of the gospel in vain? Often it is, for various reasons, but it would be definitely so if Christ has not been raised. (2) Is our faith in vain? Many of our expectations of God may come to disappointment, but our faith in God would amount to nothing if Christ has not been raised. (3) Are our sins forgiven? Acknowledgment of our wrongdoing may bring relief to our conscience, but our guilt remains if Christ has not been raised.

Worship Aids

CALL TO WORSHIP. "How lovely is your dwelling place, O Lord of hosts! My soul longs, indeed it faints for the courts of the Lord; my heart and my flesh sing for joy to the living God" (Ps. 84:1–2, NRSV).

INVOCATION. O God, for this privilege to be in this place among your people, we worship and adore you. As together we celebrate your Word present in the beginning and coming to us in these days in the life, ministry, Passion, and living again of Christ, we pray that the seed faithfully sown may fall upon good ground and grow to a beautiful harvest of faith, joy, peace, love, and hope through Christ our Lord.—John Thompson

OFFERTORY SENTENCE. "First they gave their own selves to the Lord and to us through the will of God" (2 Cor. 8:5).

OFFERTORY PRAYER. Creator of all, help us to be good sisters and brothers in the community of faith, so that we may reach those outside the fold and enlarge that family for whom heaven is home and faith in Christ Jesus is joy.—E. Lee Phillips

PRAYER. God of all time, place, and memory, let us never forget you have made us and not we ourselves. From lowly dust of the good earth, you blew holy breath into our being and called us forth to life.

We who had not shape were formed grandly in the gentle cradle of your master hands. We who had no image were made in your very likeness, eternal goodness beyond our best knowing. We who had no name were chosen, set apart, blessed and called your children, your people. We who had no hope of salvation were given the matchless gift of Jesus the Christ, our redeemer and Lord. God of bold expectation and boundless grace, we pause in time and place and remember and voice our thanksgiving and praise.

Receiving God, Lord of holiness, forgive our taking lightly your creation, overlooking the grandeur and wonder of it all; for belittling the sacred gift of life; for tarnishing your image within us; for forgetting our name and lineage, which comes surely from you even in Jesus Christ. Forgive our begrudging the joy and claim of our salvation.

We pray, God of mercy and light, for deeper understanding and experience of the sufficiency of your grace; for fresh indwelling of your power in our weakness; for wisdom and passion to know and follow the way that leads to life and wholeness. O Love that calls us, names us, blesses us, and will not let us go, we

give our lives freely and gladly to you, even in Jesus Christ our Lord, in whom we pray.—William M. Johnson

LECTIONARY MESSAGE

Topic: Words of a Deeper Wisdom
TEXTS: Luke 6:17–26; Psalm 1

The most familiar beatitudes are to be found in the Sermon on the Mount. They are not, however, the only ones. A familiar psalm begins, "Blessed is the man that walketh not in the counsel of the wicked . . ." (Ps. 1:1). Similarly the prophet Jeremiah has written, "Blessed is the man that trusteth in the Lord and whose trust the Lord is . . ." (Jer. 17:7). Another, from Paul quoting Jesus, reads, "It is more blessed to give than to receive" (Acts 20:35). Hence the form was ready-made for Jesus to offer as "Words of a Deeper Wisdom."

I. *Ministry prepares for a message.* The effectiveness of Jesus' wise words was sharply heightened by his ministry. Early in his ministry his reputation as a healer had grown until many came to be healed. Many were healed. Indeed Luke sums up this early period with the simple statement, he "healed them all" (6:10). Great variety characterized their needs . . . diseases, demons . . . and he ministered to them. They were ready to hear him.

II. *A message of affirmation.* The message is reported differently in this Gospel from Matthew . . . small differences: here the pulpit was a level place, there the mountain; here the direct address is used . . . "ye poor," "ye that hunger now," there the indirect address . . . "the poor," "the hungry."

Yet both Gospels major on the affirmative . . . "Blessed!" The genius of these wise words is their paradox. They are addressed to the down-and-out. Significantly, much of the gospel's appeal has been to this crowd, and it was in the days of Jesus.

"Blessed are the poor" Jesus said. These are not only the economically depressed. The word translated "poor" may well be understood as "beggarly." These are asking for something, and their quest has been rewarded, "For yours is the kingdom of heaven." They are blessed because they have something.

"Blessed are ye that hunger now." Jesus did not speak nonsense. They are blessed because they have something, because "ye shall be filled."

"Blessed are ye that weep now." Weeping is not a desirable condition. They are blessed because "ye shall laugh."

"Blessed are ye when men shall hate you." That doesn't make sense—apart from Jesus' wisdom. They are blessed because "your reward is great in heaven."

You are blessed because you are in both a position and a condition to receive and appreciate God's blessing.

III. *A message of negation.* Unlike Matthew, Luke includes four woes that are the opposites of the four blessings. To the rich, "Woe" for you have already had it. To the full, "Woe" for you will hunger. To the laughing, "Woe" for you will weep. To the well liked, "Woe" for you will be persecuted.

How can this be? Those whom God does not appear to be blessing—the poor, the hungry, the weeping, and the despised—will receive God's blessing. Those whom God appears to be blessing—the rich, the full, the laughing, the well liked—will be cursed. Does it sound like "the last shall be first, and the first last?"

Read the very first psalm. Hear the beatitude, "words of a deeper wisdom." 'Blessed is the person who walketh not in the counsel of the wicked. . . ."—J. Estill Jones

SUNDAY: FEBRUARY TWENTY-THIRD

SERVICE OF WORSHIP

Sermon: Nourishment for Aging

TEXT: Ruth 4:15

The story of Ruth is also the story of Naomi, her mother-in-law. In the opening scene, Naomi has lost everything: her husband, her sons. As an aging widow in a patriarchal society, she has nothing to offer and justly says she should be called *mara*, which means "bitter." At the close of the Book of Ruth, Naomi rejoices in a daughter-in-law, who is better than seven sons, and Ruth's son, who is like a grandson to her. Indeed, the Scripture says, "He shall be to you a restorer of life and a nourisher of old age."

"A nourisher of old age"; that was too inviting a phrase to be resisted. What does nourish us as we grow older? That's not a trifling question, for I find that many Christians are more afraid of growing old than of dying.

There is a temptation to avoid the issue. In reading the sermon title, we may decide to "tune out" because we are too young to think about aging. Yet all are caught up in this relentless process. The girl of ten, seeing a cute little boy, says, "When I get to the age of not hating boys, I'm going to not hate him first." That was a statement about aging. The columnist Nancy Stahl writes, "When I was fifteen, I was given to spending half an hour in front of the bathroom mirror experimenting with makeup in an effort to look twenty-one. I do the same thing at thirty-nine." Ten, fifteen, thirty-nine . . . aging is a part of our life. We will have to deal with greater numbers because we are living longer. I was a part of the "baby boom." When I turn sixty-five, it will be a sexagenarian boom. Between 2010 and 2030, our population of older Americans will explode by a million a year (Landon Jones, *Great Expectations*, 370).

We can't wait until then. Now we see more and more people living into their eighties and nineties. How do we see traditional retirement in that light? What about social securities? As Christians who believe Jesus is not only the savior from sin and death but the giver of life, can we face our later years with hope?

I. Obed and Ruth, who were not old, were seen as restorers of life and nourishers of Naomi's old age. Our first question is, then, how can we (every person, regardless of age) be a part of a church, a society, that nourishes and restores dignity to people who are older? If that is to happen, "age" must not be a dirty word. I want to use those three letters, a-g-e, to suggest what our role might be.

(a) First, we are called to be *advocates.* Taking that word literally, we have "a case to argue, a cause to support." The needs of older citizens must be addressed not for the sake of a few but for the well-being of a society under God. Ruth did not abandon her mother-in-law. She went against cultural norms and showed to Naomi loyal love (*chesed*) that would not give up or let go. That's where our advocacy should begin, with steadfast love. This is the kind of love that was in Christ. Being in the press of the cross's cruelty, he turned to his mother and commended her to the care of a disciple and commended him to her: "Woman, behold your son. . . . Behold your mother" (John 19:21, 27).

Compare this with a culture that is youth obsessed and fixed on the present moment. When we live in a disposable society, can people be seen as valuable rather than expendable? The answer, regardless of age, must be "This is a person created in God's image, a person for whom Christ died." We are called to be advocates.

(b) Yet we are called to be more than a voice; we are to be *givers.* Ruth did not care for Naomi from a distance. She gave of her self. Increasing age can mean isolation unless we who are younger give of our time, our talk (with listening), and our touch. Richard Cromie, pastor of First Presbyterian in Ft. Lauderdale, tells of a friend of his who is eighty and lives in a nursing home. She says it's not so bad: Her worries have become narrower, her aches and pains more commonplace are more accepted. But she added, "the worst thing of all—the saddest—is that nobody hugs me anymore."

Giving is not sympathy, much less condescension. It is touching another person. In Plato's *Republic,* Socrates says there is nothing he likes better than conversing with aged men, "for they are travelers who have gone on a journey which I, too, may have to go." Yes, it is a journey, and we prepare for our own as well as helping another when we become more giving at our present age. We are called to be givers.

(c) Still, this emphasis on giving may unfortunately obscure the fact that the older among us are not just receivers but have *much* to give and contribute. So if we are to be nourishers, we must *employ* those who are older. I don't mean just to hire; employ means to put into service. A sociologist listed, as one of the primary difficulties that comes with aging, the lack of creative and active roles. If that is true, we all lose. The biblical view has always been that the oldest in the community have much to offer in leadership, wisdom, service. A couple in our church lived for a while in Korea. They were showing me recently one of their mementos of that sojourn. It is a Hwan-Gap worn by the elders in the Korean community. This lacquered stovepipe hat is made of a horsehair mesh material; symbolically, the holes in the mesh provide openings for the wisdom of the elders to pass to the young. Such a tradition is a reminder of the importance of older people in a society. We need to be reminded and to "employ" those who are older.

II. Now we have been talking about what all of us can do to nourish the aging, yet this will not really help unless those of us who are "older" can ask, "How do *we* cope with our aging? Where does our nourishment come from?" Again, let's not run from the word a-g-e. The beginning point is a tough one for many of us but, nonetheless, necessary.

(a) It is *acceptance* of loss . . . saying good-bye to parts of ourselves and our world. We experience loss in giving up our children to adult responsibilities. There is loss in terms of physical strength, jobs, places, even close friends. A friend of mine said, "Life may begin at forty, but everything else begins to wear out, fall out, and spread out." Some loss and change can be controlled or modified; some must be accepted.

The key is to be able to let go without losing our self. By faith we know that nothing in life or death or any other thing can separate us from the love of God (Romans 8). Naomi lost her sons and husband, her financial security, yet she did not lose her self. Often our response is "I admire people that go on, but she or he doesn't have my problems, my ill health." Yet even as we say it, we know we are running from life and the possibilities that God has in store for us despite the losses. First, we must accept the losses.

(b) That is not the end, however. The great good news of the gospel is that no matter what losses have been sustained, no matter how old we are, if we are living, God enables us to grow. *Growing* is that pivotal next step after accepting the losses that come. Naomi continued to grow because she was able to begin a new chapter of her life. Can you begin a new chapter of your life at fifty, sixty, seventy, or eighty? Thomas Robb, who works with the church's office on aging, gives the biblical example of Caleb, who at eighty-five said, "I am as strong as when Moses sent me out." We can also view old age as a victim, like Barzillai, who at eighty said to David, "I am already eighty, nothing gives me pleasure any more." God has blessed me with Calebs as examples. Do I have to mention a "retired" minister and his wife, both in their seventies, who live by a lake? Smiling, zipping around on a motor scooter, their love as strong as when they were first sent out. Dr. Sweazey, here from Princeton to lead our evangelism seminar, at seventy-nine took his first flying lessons. I visited a member of our congregation last week. At ninety-three, her eyesight has been dimmed but she is "reading" by audio cassette, Hawthorne's *Marble Fawn*. She is still growing.

(c) Nourishment in aging means *acceptance*, continued *growing*, but perhaps most importantly, it means *enthusiasm*. Not just existing, numbing times, but living with enthusiasm. That word comes from *en theos*, "God in us." This is the difference the Holy Spirit makes: God alive in us all the days we live on earth and beyond. It is this Spirit that changed Naomi from *mara* (bitter) to one who rejoiced in God's blessing. We can face life with hope. Someone told of a lady eighty-five who went out to greet an older man who was moving to her retirement village. She said, "You look just like my third husband." He asked her how many times she had been married. She said, "Twice!" That's hope. Our hope is even greater. "Christ in you the hope of glory." Yes, the glory of heaven after this life but also, as St. Ireneaus reminds us, "The glory of God is a person fully alive." That's not feigned or artificial enthusiasm. *En theos*—Christ in you the hope of glory.—Gary D. Stratman

Illustrations

RESURGENCE.   To share with Jesus some measure of his heroic suffering because of trying to help in his task of moving life forward makes one's hurts seem small and the reward so great there is no agony left. When such conversion has come to pass, when discipleship, not self-protection, dominates one's spirit, a sense of persecution from life or from others has vanished. Nor is this all. For when we accept sorrow as an integral part of life, when we cease to ask immunity from pain, by some strange paradox, we begin to know the meaning of joy. Resurgence is the greatest of all personal miracles, for there is magic in discovering the kingdom within and its guiding power.—David Seabury

EARNED RESPECT.   Deference simply because of advanced age is not an inborn right. Honor and esteem are not gifts to which a man by sheer reason of hoary age is entitled but rewards which are merited by character and service. The fretful and gloomy, the sordid and avaricious do not win regard and esteem at any period of life. The cheerful and obliging, the understanding and tactful, the considerate and thoughtful regardless of age are the recipients of the respect of those who know them. In fact, the aged who have won the admiration of others may become the guides and counselors of young people. Indeed, a chief reward of the aged wise is the confidence which youth reposes in them.—Karl Ruf Stolz

Sermon Suggestions

BEST OF THE WORST. TEXT: Gen. 45:3–11, 15. (1) What would you do with the worst possible situation in which you could imagine yourself? (2) Rather than complaining about the turn of uncontrollable events in our lives, we should attempt to find the positive elements. (3) This does not mean that we should like what has happened to us or that we should approve the ethics of contributors to our situation but rather that we should affirm God's providence and his transcendent, creative power. (4) This attitude can give us hope in even the most unpromising situations. (5) Resolve to put yourself more into God's hands and live with victory.

OUR BODY IN THE LIFE TO COME. TEXT: 1 Cor. 15:35–38. (1) *Situation*: We are confronted with the puzzle of the nature of our resurrection body. (2) *Complication*: Our present human body is adapted to the material, physical world and its requirements, and we find it difficult to imagine it beyond this life. (3) *Resolution*: God our Creator will give us a new body continuous with the old, suitable to our new place of existence.

Worship Aids

CALL TO WORSHIP. "O come, let us sing unto the Lord; let us make a joyful noise to the rock of salvation" (Ps. 95:1).

INVOCATION. O Lord, grant that we might praise thy name, ponder thy precepts, and behold thy glory. Then fit us through worship to serve those who know none of these things and whose emptiness cries out for the Lord their God.—E. Lee Phillips

OFFERTORY SENTENCE. "The Lord said to Moses: Tell the Israelites to take for me an offering; from all whose hearts prompt them to give you shall receive the offering for me" (Exod. 25:1, NRSV).

OFFERTORY PRAYER. Lord, forgive our blindness in the face of need and our approval in the face of greed. Turn us from that which turns us from thee and bring us to a generous offering and a holy dedication, through Christ our Lord.—E. Lee Phillips

PRAYER. We thank you, God, for the common everyday things that we often take for granted but in which we can discover the miracle of your life. We thank you for a world with all its variety of climate, terrain, vegetation. We thank you that you have not just made a world but that you have peopled it and given to us loved ones, family, and friends.

We thank you that you have not just made a single flower of one color but that you have made many flowers in a panorama of colors. We are grateful, too, that you have not created but one bird with a single song but many birds that fill the morning air with a symphony of music.

For the love of family, for opportunities of education, for a church that encourages us to grow in the ways of Jesus, we give you thanks.

Our Father, to all of our relationships may we bring the spirit of love, forgiveness, and understanding. May we learn to celebrate the *you* in each other. In the home may we be responsible as father or mother, son or daughter. In these days may we learn to be faithful stewards of this world, of life, and all of its resources.

Give us faith, love, and courage to follow him who teaches us to pray together, saying, "Our Father. . . ."—John Thompson

LECTIONARY MESSAGE

Topic: Good for Evil

TEXTS: Luke 6:27–38; Gen. 45:3–11, 15

In a sense this passage is the second movement in Jesus' sermon. It is interesting that words in the sermon should be illustrated in a familiar Old Testament story. Joseph and his brothers had never been on friendly terms. His dreams put them down. He was his father's favorite.

They sold him into slavery and, after many difficulties, he rose to a high position in Egypt. Famine devastated Canaan and they went to Egypt for food. Joseph, unrecognized, helped them. When he finally revealed his identity they were ashamed. They had sent him to Egypt. Not so, said Joseph, God sent me, not you. He exchanged good for evil.

I. *The exchange is made possible by faith in God.* God sent me! You must be doing something right if you are able to make the exchange. You must recognize the difference between good and evil. You must believe that God is on the side of the right. You must be a member of the human race if you are able to make the exchange. The exchange will not be made in the spiritual stratosphere. It will be made down on the plains of human history—between human beings. If you are unjustly mistreated, your faith in God will enable you to exchange good for evil. But remember—"faith without works is dead."

II. *The exchange is made possible by love of God.* It is not only that God loves you but that you love God as well. Yet God loved us first. God loves you. In that confidence you can afford to love—even your enemies. Only a confident person can love his enemies. You can do good to them that hate you. You can pray for those who mistreat you. You can turn your other cheek to one who strikes you. How can you do that? Because you know that God loves you.

You can even afford to give good things to those who may not be your friends, who would take from you by force. In the assurance that God is good to you, you can afford to be good to another. You know that God loves you.

You can afford to forgive, regardless of the offense. God has forgiven you. He is kind to you and gentle with you. When asked to set a limit on the number of times we ought to forgive a person, Jesus left it unlimited. Forgive as you are forgiven. You know that God loves you.

You can afford to be merciful then because God is merciful with you. And this to a person who despitefully uses you. It takes little grace to be nice to a friend or colleague. To an enemy it takes mercy. You know that God loves you.

III. *The exchange is made possible by hope in God's mercy.* God isn't through with you. His mercy is everlasting. So love your enemies, "never despairing." Look to the future. Here is the promise of God: "Your reward will be great."

Do not harshly judge another, and you will not be judged by another. Do not harshly condemn another, and you will not be condemned by another. Pardon another, and you will be pardoned by another. Give to another, and you will be given to by another . . . and God will make it bountiful!

The summary statement in Romans is certainly a challenge: "Be not overcome by evil, but overcome evil by good" (Rom. 12:21).—J. Estill Jones

SUNDAY: MARCH FIRST

SERVICE OF WORSHIP

Sermon: Have You Got Religion?

TEXT: Matt. 6:1–18

What makes people cynical about Christians and churches? Fraudulent Christianity.

Our Lord is clear about our problem. He warns against worship leaving ethics at the narthex door. He cautions against philanthropy done for the society pages or the admiring eye of our neighbor. He castigates piety practiced with an eye to enhancing our reputations. Follow those routes and you will be properly rewarded, he says. Others will duly recognize your good works and offer you their praise and honor. If that's what you want, that's what you'll get.

But is that what really counts in life: admiration from others, even for good works? Oh, certainly it's better to be recognized for good works than for bad. But our Lord knows us well. He knows about our complicated and mixed motives. He wants to bring authenticity to our piety, sincerity to our service, integrity to our commitment.

And our Lord provides a resource for us. He gives us the Lord's Prayer. The Lord's Prayer is not simply a string of words on our lips, a ritual incantation repeated Sunday after Sunday, a desperate plea in time of trouble. The Lord's Prayer is a way of life.

I. The prayer begins "Our Father." "*Our*." Not "My," not "Me," not "Mine," but "*Our*." We converse with, we share, we root ourselves in One who is socially engaged. We confess mutuality, solidarity, interdependence with nation, tribe, gender, race. We recognize one another as sisters and brothers in a universal human family.

II. "Our Father," we continue. "Father"? Our Lord opens the door here to personal address. Jesus himself used the Aramaic word *abba*, the equivalent of one of our own infants saying, "da-da" or "daddy." Our God is *Someone* with whom we commune, who sheds mercy, offers forgiveness, sends us, receives us, waits for us, runs to meet us. We pray to no abstract divine principle, no mystic ether hidden in the depths of a bottomless cosmic hole. Communion, intimacy, tenderness, says Jesus, enables us to address our God as "Father."

When we say "Our Father," the last thing we want to do is to perpetrate and encourage injustice by using language or images excluding, displacing, or relegating to submissive positions any of God's children. That blasphemes our God! If we must use human analogies in our understanding of God, surely we know that many of the things we love most about this God of Jesus are virtues we stereotypically tend to associate with women: tenderness, compassion, connectedness, nurture, tenacious and enduring love amid all that would do injury to or crush love. In One whom Jesus dared call "Father," we know the motherliness of God.

Through Jesus we know One whose love suffers for others; whose care probes, seeks, searches until the lost child is found and carried securely home. We address this God intimately, trustingly, like a gurgling child: "abba," "da-da," "our Father."

III. "Who art in heaven." "Heaven!" A place? A celestial address: hardly. We recognize God's distance from us. We do not say, "O God, who art our chum." Intimate we may be with our God, but there yet remains distance, difference, over-againstness between us. Our God is yet the Creator; we, the creatures. We address God as parent and remain the children.

And yes, heaven signifies the dynamic source of God's activity. God acts on the creation, on our world, on you and me, from a context of healing and reconciliation. Heaven is God's home. From there, God seeks to make all of creation an extension of that home. Finally, to that home, God calls us.

IV. "Hallowed be thy name." We've trivialized God's holiness, abused it, employed it for our own self-interest. We've tried to get God on our side at basketball games, presidential inaugurations, beauty pageants, locker-room pep talks, military escapades. We use God's name to bless partisan platforms, class interests, cultural chauvinism. What a travesty!

We hallow God's name by illuminating God's character as seen through Jesus. We hallow God's name by treating others with grace and compassion, by joining the pilgrimage for peace with justice.

V. "Thy kingdom come." Can you imagine the passion lying behind this petition? Here our Lord's presence among us and his hope for our future converge. Here we find a plea for the uprooting and the transformation of our makeshift, tenuous human institutions. We live for a new constellation of communal relationships grounded in mutuality, grace, and service.

VI. "Thy will be done on earth as it is in heaven." In this petition we do not accede with the words "God's will be done" to some numbing fate grinding us down or breaking our hearts. We seek harmonization of our will with God's. This is a plea that we may in truth be ourselves instruments of what we see of heaven in Jesus Christ: consecration to the well-being of others, a reaching out to those who have injured us, a gracious embrace of this diverse, ornery, glorious body we call the human family.

VII. "Give us this day our daily bread." We pray for bread not only for our own survival but so we might be enabled to offer others bread. We pray for bread in a hungry world anticipating and working toward the kingdom where bread exists for everyone in abundance.

VIII. "And forgive us our debts as we forgive our debtors." We know the damage we do one another: the slights, the wounds, the betrayals, the words of encouragement kept to ourselves, the kindnesses left undone, the personal concern lost in the "thousand and one things I have to do before noon." All of this bespeaks a rupture in creation yearning for healing, for restoration, for reconciliation; and a rupture dividing us. The alienation cannot be closed by hard work, by peace offerings, by therapy, by self-help books, by barter. It can be restored only by the mystery of forgiveness, the move toward a fresh beginning, the bearing of a wound, the embracing of one who has let us down or done us in.

And because we know forgiveness like that, because we are loved when we deserve it least, we discover ourselves enabled to forgive others like that, too.

IX. "And lead us not into temptation." Our Lord does not flag our petty vices here. He's putting his finger on those things diverting our loyalty, those sidetracks placing our obedience in jeopardy. God knows we are tempted to grasp for our full humanity in status, titles, income, or achievement. Our ambition for ourselves, our families, our children, our vocation puts at risk our readiness to witness to what God wants for human life. We need protection from the weakness and frailty blunting us from making the joys of the kingdom available to a desperate and yearning world.

X. "And deliver us from evil." Finally, we pray for deliverance from the powers diminishing and truncating human life. These familiar powers finally succeeded in nailing our Lord to the cross; they haunt us, they confront us, they co-opt us

no less so today. We need assurance that God never abandons us to them; that nothing, finally, separates us from the love of God in Christ Jesus our Lord. Nothing! "Deliver us from evil."—James W. Crawford

Illustrations

FOR DISCIPLES ONLY.   The first thing to remember about the Lord's Prayer is that it is a prayer which only a disciple can pray; it is a prayer which only one who is pledged and committed to Jesus Christ can take upon his lips with any meaning. The Lord's Prayer is not a child's prayer, as it is so often regarded; it is, in fact, not meaningful for a child. The Lord's Prayer is not the Family Prayer as it is sometimes called, unless by the word *family* we mean *the family of the Church*. The Lord's Prayer is specifically and definitely stated to be the *disciple's* prayer; and only on the lips of a disciple has the prayer its full meaning.—William Barclay

IN THE SPIRIT OF JESUS.   If one wants really to pray "through Jesus Christ our Lord," the best preparation is to sit down and read, thoughtfully and prayerfully, the Sermon on the Mount. Or one may, if he prefers, think through the words of the Lord's Prayer, and note what its few great phrases tell us of the spirit of our Lord. A great American preacher has told me that he never preaches on Sunday morning without taking time the evening before to go through the Lord's Prayer slowly and thoughtfully to discover its bearing on his message to his people.

There is no blueprint for the art of praying, and there is no exact picture of Jesus in the New Testament. Yet these facts need not stop us from praying in his spirit. To the degree that one lets himself be captured by the portrait of Jesus' personality and spirit that we have, un-Christian praying will be purged and Christian prayer will take its place.—Georgia Harkness

Sermon Suggestions

GOD UNDAUNTED. TEXT: Isa. 55:10–13. God's Word accomplishes God's purpose: (1) In God's good time. (2) According to God's sometimes mysterious ways of working. (3) Often through those who continue to believe in God despite many difficulties. (4) For God's honor and for the joy of his people.

THE SECRET IS OUT! TEXT: 1 Cor. 15:51–58. We who belong to Christ will be changed to immortal life. This means (1) death will be defeated in the future, (2) sin is defeated now, (3) we have work to do for Christ, which is sure to achieve God's purpose.

Worship Aids

CALL TO WORSHIP. "Oh, come, let us worship and bow down; let us kneel before the Lord our Maker" (Ps. 95:6).

INVOCATION. O God, for your Word that creates, sustains and redeems life—your Word of grace, we praise and adore you. For this occasion to congregate as the church, to celebrate your Word, we give you thanks. That you so love the world that you give to the uttermost—your only Son, we worship and adore you. That your own Spirit dwells in and among us to quicken our minds to recall your mighty deeds for our salvation, we are grateful. Praise to you Father, Son, and Holy Spirit.—John Thompson

OFFERTORY SENTENCE. "And to whomsoever much is given, of him shall much be required; and to whom they commit much, of him will they ask the more" (Luke 12:48).

OFFERTORY PRAYER. We would praise you, O Father, not only in word but in deed, for all your love in our creation and re-creation. As your children may we share with our brothers and sisters here and everywhere. And through your consecration may these gifts of monies become the bread and water of life for many. Through him who gave all.—John Thompson

PRAYER. O God of constant newness in whom all renewal abides and all hope originates, bless us as we worship thee and pause again to ponder the possibilities of a new week.

Lead us, Lord, to hear the voices of anguish that call out to us, overtly or disguised. Let us be stilled, quiet enough to hear and courageous enough to act. Enable us to look beneath the surface of events to human hearts and to address the needs of the soul.

Help us, O Lord, to confront the good and evil in the world and to encourage the good and shun the evil. Grant us the firmness and poise born of the Holy Spirit to confront prejudice and littleness. Attune us to truth and light. Draw us to the mind of Christ: Jesus' way of thinking, Jesus' kind of love, Jesus' illuminating light, so that our actions may radiate the presence no darkness can overcome, which saves to the uttermost.—E. Lee Phillips

LECTIONARY MESSAGE

Topic: Hearing and Doing
TEXTS: Luke 6:39–49; Ps. 92:1–4, 12–15

Engraved in stone above the doors leading out of the sanctuary of the church where I am a member is the familiar admonition from James, "Be ye doers of the Word and not hearers only." It seems especially fitting to read the words immediately after hearing the Word. Pretense, like pride, is a deadly sin. Jesus sought to get folks to see and avoid hypocrisy. Much of his teaching revolves around this problem. This is, in a sense, the third movement of the sermon as Luke records it.

I. *Prelude to parable.* The prelude to the well-known parable is itself a brief parable. Actually it is introduced by a series of brief parables, several in the form of questions. "Can the blind guide the blind?" The clearly anticipated answer is negative. They would both fall into trouble because one of them pretended to see. He pretended to be what he was not.

"And why do you see the speck in your brother's eye and offer to remove it when you do not admit to the logjam in your own?" It would be dangerous for you to work on another's eye. First you must cleanse your own eye. Do not pretend to be clear-sighted when you see dimly.

A tree is known by its fruit. A good tree bears good fruit. A bad tree bears bad fruit. How simple the equation! A tree is not known by its appearance—a fruit tree, that is. You do not identify its goodness or badness by its leaves or by its trunk. Even a novice can tell the difference between good and bad fruit. A pastor friend said, The Lord did not call us as judges but as fruit inspectors.

II. *Foundations of faith.* The larger parable serves as commentary on the briefer ones. It suggests three levels of spiritual experience.

(a) Confession is important. To acknowledge "Jesus is Lord" is a significant beginning to the relationship. Jesus accepted Simon's confession, "You are the Christ, the Son of the living God." Then he admonished him to work out the confession in terms of ministry.

(b) Hearing is more important. In the parable both persons heard Jesus' words. Hearing is an art. There are so many sounds that to hear one voice above all the rest is progress. It is important to be able to listen and understand. It is possible that this is the end result of much of our preaching—the congregation heard and understood and perhaps enjoyed it.

(c) The point of the parable is at the doing of it. Doing is most important of all. You may confess and not do the will of God. You may hear and not do the will of God. That which distinguished the two persons was neither the confession nor the hearing. The difference was in the doing . . . and we may add, the being!

"Hearing and doing" insures stability. The one house withstood the rain and the flood. It was founded upon hearing and doing. The second house could not stand up against the rain and the flood. It was founded upon hearing only. Hypocrisy is like that. When the going gets rough, the pretender runs for cover. His foundations are weak.

And all of this "to show that the Lord is upright. He is my rock, and there is no unrighteousness in him" (Ps. 92:15).—J. Estill Jones

SUNDAY: MARCH EIGHTH

SERVICE OF WORSHIP

Sermon: What Is Freedom?

TEXT: John 8:31–32

Sam is an eighteen-year-old girl from the novel *In Country.* Her father was killed in Vietnam, and she is struggling to learn more about him and what the war was like. She lives with her mother's brother, also a Vietnam vet, who lets her do pretty much as she pleases. Sam smokes marijuana occasionally, is "sexually active," eats junk food, stays out all night if she feels like it. I suppose my feelings toward her character reflect my age, but it seems to me she's ruining her life. Yet I'll bet the average eighteen-year-old will think Sam is in the best of all worlds because she's free—free to make her own rules and decisions with no parental interference.

What is freedom? That's what this passage is all about. The Jews confronting Jesus are convinced that they are free, and slaves to no man, but Jesus disputes that point. He shows them a source of freedom, a symptom of freedom, and a sequel to freedom.

I. Source: Where does freedom come from? Jesus says that it comes from knowing the truth, which may seem only to trade one abstraction for another, for truth is even harder to define than freedom. "What is truth?" asked Pilate at Jesus' trial, and our world asks the same question. We have so much information thrown at us every day, and much of it is designed to sell something: manufacturers want to sell their products; politicians want to sell themselves; TV programs want to sell time—what's truth amid all the hype and glitz?

There have been two theories down through the ages that have been more important than the rest. The first says that truth is an absolute standard up in heaven somewhere, and things down here may approximate it but never reach it. Somewhere up there, there is the perfect desk, the perfect flower, the perfect man or woman. We can see them with our mind's eye, but we can see with our physical eyes that nothing ever measures up exactly to perfection. The second theory says that truth is what we see with our eyes and touch with our hands. This is the truth theory behind science: If you can do it in a laboratory, it's true.

The problem with the first theory is that it is always entirely abstract. Truth is always beyond the reach of humans. The problem with the second theory, the truth theory of science, is that truth changes. It used to be "true" that the sun revolved around the earth; then that was disproven. It used to be "true" that the smallest particles of matter were called "atoms"; now we know that inside the nucleus of an atom there are different kinds of particles, most of them not made of matter at all. What will be true in thirty years? We don't know, because science constantly changes; and so scientific truth is always changing.

The truth that Jesus spoke of, however, is consistent and constant. It is constant because truth comes from God: "When you have lifted up the Son of man, you will know that I do nothing on my own authority but speak thus as the Father taught me." God will never leave us in the lurch or abandon us; Jesus said that God's constancy would be evident even when his enemies had crucified him. He is true because he is constant. God's truth is also consistent—it isn't one thing in heaven and another on earth, but he demonstrated it in the real world by sending Jesus as a human. When we know Jesus and his words, when he lives in our hearts, then we have known the only constant, consistent truth that there

is in the universe, and that is the source of freedom.

II. Jesus also points out a symptom of freedom (v. 34–36): Freedom is demonstrated by sin-free living. Not everyone will agree, of course. In *Wall Street* the hero says that freedom is being rich enough so that other people can't waste your time—freedom to fly whenever you get ready because you own your own plane, for example. Sam of *In Country* would say "freedom from restrictions," I expect, and when I was a teenager I'd probably have said the same. More and more people are defining freedom as finding yourself—discovering that you had a past life as Cleopatra, discovering that you can do time travel in your mind, discovering that pyramids give you special powers.

The last is getting closer to the truth. The man in *Wall Street* was trapped in the end by the wealth he thought set him free—in his struggle to protect it, he broke the law and went to prison. Sam is trapped, if statistics prove true, to an unsatisfactory life of chemical dependency, divorce, etc. "Finding yourself" comes closer to freedom, but the question is what you do with yourself when you find it.

When we examine ourselves truly and in the light of God's Word, we find we are sinners—can anyone deny it? And yet people find all sorts of ways to escape responsibility for what they are: My past lives have made me this way; the stars control my destiny; etc. The only way to be free is to face yourself and your own sinfulness and turn it over to God, asking for help. It isn't a one-time-takes-care-of-all event either but a lifelong struggle to face the facts and to draw on God's power to improve.

III. That's a struggle that lasts a lifetime, but when this life is over, freedom has a sequel. For those who persevere, freedom here brings freedom hereafter—a life beyond life, where we will be truly free from death and sin. We struggle to free ourselves from anger here, from hatred, from prejudice, from greed, sloth, lust, all the other dismal parts of our own natures. But Jesus promises that we will be free from the struggle and from the temptations to sin. There is a victory celebration already planned in the Christian conflict against sin. Someday we shall overcome.

So what is freedom? Freedom comes from knowing the truth, and you know the truth about yourself and the world when you have a personal, living relationship with Jesus Christ. You are set free from sin—given the power to overcome your own weaknesses through Christ, and some day, in God's plan and by his grace, you'll be given an eternal victory over sin in heaven. That's freedom—anything else is a poor imitation, and anyone whom Jesus sets free can never be truly a slave to anyone else.—Richard Vinson

Illustrations

THE GOAL OF FREEDOM.   As a teacher and writer, I value books. I would not do so if I did not believe in truth. But fundamentally, when we have learned everything we can from books and theory and discussion, truth will never create in us the way of salvation until Christ becomes in us the hope of glory, until God's presence quickens our spirit and we know in our spirit that we are children of God. Christ is the truth, but he is the truth *on the way to life*. Ponder this relation: "I am the *way*, the *truth*, and the *life*." As we honestly and openly dare to reach out in all fullness for life, we shall find that Christ is the secret to the finding of it.—Nels F. S. Ferré

THE NEW CREATION.   Most of us envisage the Last Supper through the eyes of Leonardo da Vinci. The ages have looked upon his painting and loved it. But there is one modern painting which, for me, ranks with it and sometimes even impresses me more. It is one by Ford Madox Brown, which you can see in the Tate Gallery in London. The artist has painted Jesus kneeling before a surly, half-ashamed Peter to wash his feet. This painting of the stooping Christ will in time, I think, stamp itself upon the imagination of the world.—W. D. Davies

Sermon Suggestions

WHEN GOD HAS BLESSED YOU.   TEXT: Deut. 26:1–11. (1) Present an offering to the Lord. (2) Worship the Lord. (3) Rejoice. (Ponder the sequence of these three actions.)

OUR GENEROUS LORD.   TEXT: Rom. 10:8a–13, NRSV. (1) The way of salvation: (a) faith in the heart; (b) Confession with the mouth. (2) The Lord of salvation: rich toward all who call on him.

Worship Aids

CALL TO WORSHIP.   "Because he hath set his love upon me, therefore will I deliver him: I will set him on high, because he hath known my name" (Ps. 91:14).

INVOCATION.   Holy God, who calls out to us; oh, that we might listen! Holy God, who speaks to us; oh, that we might hear! Holy God, who keeps appealing to us; oh, that we might see and in seeing comprehend the quiet purposes of unfettered love! In Jesus' name.—E. Lee Phillips

OFFERTORY SENTENCE.   "All belong to the same Lord who is rich enough, however many ask his help, for everyone who calls on the name of the Lord will be saved" (Rom. 10:12–13, JB).

OFFERTORY PRAYER.   O Giver of every good and perfect gift, in our more perceptive thoughts we know that you have need of nothing, for "the earth is yours and the fullness thereof, the world and those who dwell therein." But we have need, the need to be saved from our own selfishness—to express your love not only in word but also in *deed*. Consecrate these gifts, that through your consecration they may be translated into the Word of life for us who dwell here, for those in distant places, and for the healing of the nations, so that all peoples may know Shalom, the health of your coming. —John Thompson

PRAYER. Father, you have demonstrated your love for us and for all humankind by invading this planet in person. We praise you for your Spirit let loose in the world through Jesus of Nazareth.

Grant that the spirit of his life lived on this common earth under these ordinary skies may be with us in all the tasks and possibilities of this week before us. Help *us* to show forth his eagerness, not to be ministered unto but to minister; his sympathy with suffering of every kind; his courage in the face of his own suffering; his joy in doing your work even when it meant the discipline of a cross; his simplicity; his poise at all times even when threatened by his enemies; his complete trust in you as Father. Grant us grace, grant us courage to follow *him*.

O Father, whoever else you are in the mystery and greatness of your being, you *are* love. You are the fountain of *all* love. "We love because you *first* loved us." To what radical love you keep calling us: to be forgiving to the uttermost, to return good for evil, to pray for those who spite us, to persevere through every estrangement; to be available, vulnerable, even to dying on a cross. Who among us is equal to such challenge? Only in the meaning and experience of your love in Christ crucified can we ever respond to such a high calling.

As we sense your love reaching out to us and to all others, may we reach out to one another. We pray for our family and friends with whom we work and play, for those who give leadership to our church in its various ministries, for those who are lonely because they are bereft of loved ones or rejected by others, for those broken with pain and discouraged by illness and for family and friends who faithfully keep vigil and pray for their wholeness, for those who are perplexed by difficult decisions, for those who have the great responsibility of governing others in our nation and in all nations. With them, may we hear your call to the righteousness that alone exalts.

In all things draw us to yourself, O God, that our work may not be for us a burden but a delight. Let us not serve in the spirit of bondage as slaves, but in the cheerfulness and gladness of children rejoicing in the doing of your will through the grace of our Lord Jesus Christ, who, present among us as your eternal Word, teaches us to pray together, "Our Father . . ."—John Thompson

LECTIONARY MESSAGE

Topic: If You Are God's Son

TEXTS: Luke 4:1–13; Ps. 91:9–16

"Thou art my beloved Son"—that was the substance of the voice out of heaven that greeted Jesus' baptism. The Holy Spirit was in evidence at his baptism. The Holy Spirit was with him when he returned from the Jordan. The Holy Spirit led him to the wilderness site of the temptation experience. The temptations were designed personally for him as Son of God. Every person's temptations are designed personally.

This is the first Sunday of Lent, a Christian season preceding the Passion and closely related to the temptation of Jesus. This is not the complete account of Jesus' temptation. The word in verse 13 is significant: "He departed from him for a season." Here are three representative temptations.

I. *Satisfy your appetites by using your God-given powers.* "If you are God's Son . . ." The devil was quite devilish. This was the confession at the height of his spiritual experience. And the temptation to make bread came at the height of a physical experience—he had not eaten for forty days.

Yet his physical hunger was symbolic. That he could have made the stones into bread is usually conceded. Later, on the cross, they mocked him, "Come down from the cross." It was a recurrence of this temptation—save yourself with your God-given powers. But God's Son was obedient to God's will. The quotation from Deuteronomy was a part of his defense against temptation—"Man shall not live by bread alone." The following clause, "but by every word proceeding from the mouth of God," is included in Matthew.

II. *Direct your attention to worldly success.* "If therefore you will worship me, I will give it all to you." All the kingdoms of the world—that's the promise. To yield to this temptation first involved the acknowledgment that Satan had all power. To finally confess that he possesses the world is to admit defeat. He lied when he said that it had been delivered to him and that it was all his. Little wonder that Jesus described him as the father of liars (John 8:44).

But to yield also meant that Jesus would deny the sovereignty of God. You cannot worship God and mammon. To worship the devil would have been to deny God. God's Son would not do that. Again he reached into the treasury of the Law and came out with "Thou shalt worship the Lord thy God."

III. *Presume upon God's love and win a following.* Perhaps this was the most devilish of all. The conversation may have gone like this, "Oh, you are God's Son, are you—and you trust him and you worship him? Well, go your way. God will take care of you. His angels will protect you wherever you go, whatever you do. And when the world sees this powerful protection, the world will follow." And all of this atop the Temple with the milling crowds below.

His response was quick, "Thou shalt not make trial of the Lord thy God." He is to be trusted and obeyed. And the promise of the Father, "Because he hath set his love upon me, therefore will I deliver him. I will set him on high, because he hath known my name" (Ps. 91:14).

Since you are God's Son, you will not yield!—J. Estill Jones

SUNDAY: MARCH FIFTEENTH

SERVICE OF WORSHIP

Sermon: Seeing Jesus
Text: John 4

In a certain church there used to be a picture hanging in the baptistry just behind the preacher's head, a picture of Jesus praying in the Garden of Gethsemane. He's kneeling down next to a rock, his hands folded, his face raised toward heaven; he has on a white tunic with a red cloak draped over one shoulder. His eyes are blue; his hair is long and brown, as is his beard, and the expression on his face is one of extreme sorrow. Now, I know there isn't one chance in a million Jesus really looked that way, but I saw him that way so many times as a boy that I can't put that picture out of my mind's eye.

How do you see Jesus? When you shut your eyes and think of him, what comes to mind? At the beginning of the day, this woman had no picture of him. He was a total stranger to her. He sat on the ground beside the hole in the ground called Jacob's well, sitting there in the sun at high noon, tired out with his thirty-mile hike from Jerusalem north to Sychar. He was a Jew, she noticed—probably could tell by the tasseled undergarment called the *talith* that hung down below the edge of his outer cloak. She expected him to ignore her, a Samaritan woman, since Jews normally did, but he surprised her. "Give me a drink." He confounded her confusion, when she pointed out the difference in their race, by telling her that he could give her "living water."

I. Here she draws her first conclusion about Jesus—he's an interesting man. She allows herself to be drawn into a conversation with him. "Living water," see, is a way to say "running water"—a stream or spring, in other words. She wants to find out where it is. Maybe he means the spring at the bottom of the well, but the man has no bucket, no rope—maybe he's joking. No, says the man, if you drink from Jacob's well, you'll be thirsty again; if you drink what I give you, you'll never thirst again, because you'll have a spring of water inside you.

What an interesting thing to say—what an interesting figure of speech—what an interesting man! I know folks who, like the woman at this point, have that sort of notion about Jesus. Jesus was a good teacher, a great storyteller; sort of a first-century Will Rogers, doing tricks with bread and fish and telling jokes and never meeting anyone he didn't like. But look at this story: The woman thinks he's talking about real water, when he really means salvation, eternal life. He means that he can cause it so that she'll never die. C. S. Lewis said that a man who claims that is either a liar, a lunatic, or the Lord of heaven and earth, but he's not just an interesting teacher . . . as the woman is about to discover.

The man, who still hasn't volunteered his name, now takes a different approach: "Go tell your husband." Why did he bring that up? wondered the woman, but she answered, "I have no husband." "Yep," said the man, "married five times, living with a sixth, I guess you could say that you've never had a real husband."

II. Now the woman draws a new conclusion about this stranger. He's never met her, yet he knows her—he can read a person's mind. He must be a prophet if he can do miracles like that. A prophet—so she puts on her religious face and her religious voice and says, "Well, brother prophet, should people worship God in the Samaritan temple or in the Jerusalem Temple?" Because if this man is a prophet he'll be interested in religious things, and I'd better act religious around him; then I can be myself later when I get home.

Do you know folks like that? Jesus is a person you meet at church. He's a prophet and a powerful fellow, and he cares about tithing and baptism, and I like him OK, but I wouldn't want to have him on the job around me all the time because then I'd have to be too nice all the time. Jesus loves everybody, even his enemies, but he's a little too serious about religion.

There are lots of good Christian people who shake Jesus' hand at the door of the church on Sunday morning on their way out, and he never crosses their minds until they cross the threshold again. I know a lady who is as active as she can be in a church in Danville—one of those who really carries a lot of the work of the church. But she is as prejudiced toward blacks as anyone I have ever met. It never crossed her mind that Jesus would actually want her to love everybody, including blacks—that's just preacher-talk, church-talk.

I think if you press hard enough, we're all hypocrites to some degree. We all know better than we do. But it's the attitude I'm thinking of here—the attitude that says that Jesus and his teachings are for 10–12 A.M. on Sunday, safely hedged away inside the church. He's more than just a prophet, brothers and sisters . . . as he led the woman to see.

She wanted to peg him "religious" and keep him on religious matters, but he wouldn't have it. "God doesn't care whether you worship in Samaria or Jerusalem. He's looking for people to worship him truly, by worshiping him in Spirit." What he meant was that we worship him best by giving ourselves over to the Holy Spirit, by turning over our whole lives to God's control. The woman began to understand, because she said, "When Messiah comes, he'll teach us how to do what you're suggesting—he'll teach us the truth in everything." At this point, Jesus smiled, I think: "I'm he." And she believed, so strongly overcome by her new picture of Jesus that she began to tell her whole town about him.

A very famous biblical scholar once came to lecture on Jesus, and his lecture made clear that Jesus was, to him, an interesting teacher and a fascinating field of study and no more. At a reception afterwards he asked me a question he said he asked lots of people at parties: "Would you rather be stranded on a boat with Jesus or with Rabbi Akiba?" "Jesus," I said. Then he told me about asking another famous scholar who had replied, "There are some of us who believe that if one were stranded with Jesus one would not be stranded any longer." To the one, Jesus was just an interesting man; to the other, Jesus was the one who makes life meaningful.

How do you see Jesus? May he be as meaningful to you as he was to this Samaritan woman one hot noon, when she thought she met an interesting man or a prophet but found that she had met the Lord of all.—Richard Vinson

Illustrations

GOD INCARNATE.   Every good scientist feels a tremendous sense of awe and wonder as he discovers more and more of this amazing universe. But I don't believe that he discovers God as a person, not only infinite in His greatness but infinite in His concern for the individual, unless he accepts Jesus Christ as what He claimed to be. You may be moved to wonder and awe at the infinite Mind behind all those things that we can observe, but you cannot easily love, worship, and adore what is practically an abstraction. It is only when we see God expressed, as it were, in a human being, living under human conditions and limitations, that the springs of worship begin to flow.—J. B. Phillips

AN AWE-INSPIRING JESUS.   If there is one thing missing in most of our contemporary pictures of Jesus—the popular paintings, the folksongs, the movies, and the books—it is this note of awe. We seem to want a Jesus we can fully understand, one about whom there is no ultimate mystery, a "regular guy." But he was an "irregular guy"; totally one of us, yet uniquely one with the "immortal, invisible God only wise." That is why I turn from the shimmering pictures of modern church publications, not to the theatricality of Dali but to the dark splendor of a Rouault or an icon. The Jesus we find in Mark's Gospel is intensely human, but there is something about him that evokes our wonder, our awe, and even at times our fear.—David H. C. Read

Sermon Suggestions

WHEN DARKNESS DEEPENS   TEXT: Gen. 15:1–12, 17–18, especially verse 12. (1) Fear, anxiety, and depression may follow a significant encounter with God, verses 1–12. (2) God returns with the under-girding power of his word of promise, verses 17–18.

STANDING FIRM.   TEXT: Phil. 3:17–4:1 REB. (1) The peril of those whose minds are set on earthly things. (2) The hope of those who are citizens of heaven.

Worship Aids

CALL TO WORSHIP.   "Except the Lord build the house, they labor in vain that build it; except the Lord keep the city, the watchman waketh but in vain" (Ps. 127:1).

INVOCATION.   To come into your presence, Father, is truly life's highest privilege. To be able to bring the burdens of our hearts, souls, and lives with us as we enter your presence and speak with the creator of the universe, the Father of all mankind, about them is life's greatest healing balm. To discover solutions for much that hampers us in our daily walk is one of life's greatest needs. To be able to confess failures and faults and sins and experience forgiveness, understanding, and guidance for future living is life's greatest joy. This morning we come just as we are with all the baggage of life weighing heavy upon us, Father. Some of us enter your presence weighed down with sorrow, others with doubt, others with guilt, others with pain, others in loneliness but all with needs that cannot be met in our own power and knowledge. Here in this sacred place as we enter your presence in all humility, help us, we pray, whatever our need. For only you have the words of life. Only you can take away the sin of our hearts. Only you can grant the gift of forgiveness and restoration. Only you can bind up our deep wounds and heal our land. Only you can inject hope where all seems hopeless. Only you can replace our loneliness with complete, caring friendship. Only you can ultimately save us and set us free from all our encumbering fetters and oppressions. Only you in Christ Jesus can make us whole. Oh, come even now Lord Jesus and make us whole and refreshingly new, even as you did when you walked among those of Galilee long ago.—Henry Fields

OFFERTORY SENTENCE. "For many—as I have often told you and tell you now with tears—many live as enemies of the cross of Christ. Destruction is their fate, the belly is their god, they glory in their shame, these men of earthly mind! But we are a colony of heaven, and we wait for the Savior who comes from heaven, the Lord Jesus Christ, who will transform the body that belongs to our low estate till it resembles the body of his glory, by the same power that enables him to make everything subject to himself" (Phil. 3:18–21, Moffatt).

OFFERTORY PRAYER. That we are called to be instruments of yours in your love purpose for all humankind is incredible. It is of your *amazing* grace. May we be courageous to so let our light shine before men that they may see our good works and glorify you. May we give our monies *and* ourself in such self-forgetfulness that our giving and our living may proclaim the coming of your kingdom in Christ.—John Thompson

PRAYER. Attending God, through the dark and quiet of night you have kept us and brought us safely to this glad hour. Inviting God, who bids us to come into your presence with praise and singing, we seek to rightly worship you and worthily glorify your name.

Creating God, author of all beauty and truth, you have surrounded us with a grand symphony of sight and sound, of melody and movement, of shape and color. "All nature sings and around us rings, the music of the spheres." In joyful response, we raise our hymn of grateful praise.

Redeeming God, who in the cross has shown us the full face of grace and forgiveness, we bow before you in repentance and confession of our sin. Forgive our misuse of the gift of speech. By your Spirit, teach us to speak in thoughtful, measured manner, addressing the truth in love, graciously and closely following your kind voice in our heart of hearts.

Forgive our misuse of power and wealth. Evidence of ill use crowds our every path and seeds destruction. Forgive our harboring thoughts of evil against those who trouble us. Cleanse us from the temptation of striking back, getting even. Loving God, soften our hearts, remove the stones from our hands, embrace and warm our cool spirits, calm and resolve our inner quarrel.

Abiding and presiding God, cradle gently those grieving the death of a loved one, struggling with the painful absence in their life. Sustain those whose loved one is critically ill, swaying to and fro on words of better then worse. For all who are weary and heavy laden, cumbered with a load of care, we pray your tender mercies and healing touch.

We pray for ourselves, a family of faith. Grant us wisdom and courage, vision and will for the right living of these days. Old wineskins, safe and comfortable as they are, will not hold any more. So lead us and teach us as we seek the new wineskins and pour out the gospel on a dry and thirsty world waiting for good news. May we be kind to one another, tenderhearted, forgiving, affirming, faithful all, to the call and to the journey.—William M. Johnson

LECTIONARY MESSAGE

Topic: Success in Failure
TEXT: Luke 13:31–35

The ancient Romans often built statues of their Caesars with removable heads. It saved a lot of expense when a new Caesar came to power. The heads would be changed to reflect the new Caesar, and everything would be in order. Society treats its great men, kings, and prophets in strange ways. A king who is disliked in his lifetime may become popular after his death.

Jesus realized that Jerusalem had often hated the prophets before him, only to end up whitewashing their tombs. He knew that Herod Antipas sought his death. Yet he sent the message back to Herod that he would continue to do his ministry—nothing could stop him.

I. By the modern criterion of Madison Avenue, one would think that ministers of the Lord must always be successful. Sometimes in ministry failures speak louder than successes. In Mark's Gospel, Jesus is presented as a failure from the world's point of view. Yet in his very failure he was a success. Very few people would have interpreted the cross as a success—it was a gigantic failure to end one's life in such horrible torture. Yet Jesus made it into the essence of salvation for mankind.

If one has made no enemies in one's ministry, then one has not really done much. Anytime a person has made everyone happy, then not too many programs have been achieved. It did not take Jesus long to draw the anger of Herod Antipas, the tetrarch of Galilee. Like John the Baptist before him, Jesus' message soon began to shake the "powers that be." When warned of Herod's ire, Jesus replied that he simply must do the work that God has set before him. He could not spend all of his time looking over his shoulder to see the reaction that Herod might have to his ministry.

II. Christian ministry of any kind always involves a risk to the person involved. There is no ministerial insurance policy that can really protect one from all the risks and dangers involved. In ministry one must venture out and declare the message given to one by God. The minister must always be resourceful and aware of the situation but not fearful of "stepping on someone's toes."

III. A person doing forthright ministry always stands as a beacon of comfort for others. He or she stands as a gathering point for other less courageous people. Jesus indicated that he would have loved to gather the people of Jerusalem around him as a mother hen does her chicks. However, the people were too afraid of the power of the political leaders of the day. Jesus had to stand alone and ended up on a cross. Sometimes ministry can be a lonely position. The person standing "tall" also can act as a lightning rod attracting the ire of the opposition.

The ultimate picture will be gained at the end of the day. Failures will be judged successes. Successes of political powers will be seen as failures. Those who stood alone for just causes will be in the company of others who throughout the generations were committed to truth.—James L. Blevins

SUNDAY: MARCH TWENTY-SECOND

SERVICE OF WORSHIP

Sermon: Religious Life under Changed Conditions

TEXT: Ps. 137:4

Here in a familiar psalm was a group of men who refused to sing. They were Jews who had been carried away captive to the city of Babylon. They were homesick, bitter, rebellious. When they were asked by those who had carried them away to sing one of the songs of Zion for the entertainment of Babylon, they refused. "How can we? How can we sing the Lord's song in a strange land?"

What a picture! How modern it is! People who feel that they cannot be religious now because conditions have changed! Let me speak of just two such groups!

I. The Lord's song has been silenced in certain quarters by a change of belief. People feel that they cannot be religious anymore because they have come to think so differently about many things. Times have changed.

(a) There has come a new and more modern method of interpreting the Bible and of viewing the whole subject of religion. When people generally believed in an infallible Church or in an infallible book or in some well-made system of doctrine which seemed to answer all their queries, they could sing. They felt sure. It is hard to tell now what is what and which is which. How can we sing the song of confidence in this strange land of religious uncertainty?

Behavioristic psychology, moral determinism, the economic interpretation of history have frightened a lot of people out of their wits. They no longer feel sure that they are living souls; perhaps they are merely a more intricate sort of two-legged animal or machine. Gloomy, pessimistic notions like these are not confined to a few sad-eyed highbrows shut up in a library. They are preached at the street corners and proclaimed from the housetops. How can people who have swallowed all that sing the Lord's song! It is ever so much worse than Babylon.

(b) What shall we say? The modern method of interpreting the Bible, the finer discriminations in religious belief, the greater sense of mystery attached to human personality are here to stay. But all that need not silence the song of aspiration.

Are we any less sure that at the center and foundation of everything, there is Being, Personality, Intelligent Purpose, a Benign Will? How could a universe without that at the foundation of it produce all this being, personality, intelligent purpose, benign will which we find about us on every side?

Therefore, let us bravely hold fast to those experiences and sing the song of courage, aspiration, and high resolve, for the deeper diapason tones in it will sound forth as clear and as strong as they did when the morning stars sang together and all the sons of God shouted for joy. The Lord's song is not to be silenced by some change of weather in the current thinking.

II. The Lord's song has been silenced in some places by a changed feeling regarding the world of industry.

(a) Men are saying that it is impossible to square Christian ethics with the economic conditions under which millions of our fellow beings are living and must apparently continue to live. Men are claiming that those old songs of peace on earth and goodwill toward men which were heard around Bethlehem in the long ago have no place whatever in this modern world where we find ourselves.

(b) What shall we say to that? We are living these days in the presence of much more exacting ideals in the workaday world. They impinge upon us constantly from every side. There is no escape from it. We have no desire to escape from it, because it has become an essential element in our general scheme of aspiration.

(c) But all that need not, it must not, silence the song of courage and high resolve. Let us thank God that there has come into the teaching of our pulpits and into the aspiration of the pews a much more inclusive grasp of Christian purpose. It is to those men who have the mind of Christ that we shall have to look for counsel, for guidance, for leadership in the bringing in of a better social order throughout the land. When we take that broader view of the matter and gain that more inclusive grasp of the forces which make for human well-being, we can sing the song of courage, aspiration, high resolve with the social note sounding through it.

III. The hour is coming for every one of us when we shall have to go forward into a strange land, into a region which we have not explored as yet, into that Unknown Country from which travelers do not return. In that hour it will be Jesus Christ or nothing. All the wealth of the world, however evenly it might have been divided up by that time, cannot make it otherwise. Therefore, let's take our Christian faith with us and sing the song of confidence and courage.— Charles R. Brown

Illustrations

NEED AND ANSWER. John Fiske in a very noble argument whose clear finality sums up a world of dusty controversy, maintains that any function is at once the creation and the revelation of some encompassing reality. The air made wings and the ocean fins; light has made the eye and sensible reality the fact-seeking, fact-answering mind. It is incredible that what is finest and far-reaching in human nature, the spirit of man, should find in the universe no conspiring reality, out of which it has issued and to which it is akin. We have come so far and by so arduous a road—is it empty at the top? Religion assumes that it is not empty. The confidences in which the human enterprise has found support are themselves the evidence of a supporting reality.—Glen Atkins

THE FLAT PLACES OF LIFE.   A remarkable illustration is found in the story of Jean Baptiste Lamarck, the distinguished French naturalist. Coming originally from a military family, he followed the traditions of his family and when seventeen years of age enlisted in the army. At twenty-one he suffered illness and went to Paris for a year of treatment. Poor and alone he lived in a small attic room, where he lay for hours at a time, flat upon his back. The only window in the room was a skylight, and through it he looked up and watched the clouds as they drifted over. He began to note the characteristic forms of the clouds and the kind of weather with which they were associated. He learned to recognize the nimbus that brings the storm, the cumulus that comes at the end of a fine summer afternoon, the cirrus that betokens good weather. When the year was over and he was well, Lamarck was a cloud expert, and instead of returning to the army he began, although still without funds, the scientific career in which he attained eminence.—Jack Finegan

Sermon Suggestions

THE GOD OF MOSES AND YOUR GOD.
    TEXT: Exod. 3:1–15. (1) A God who comes to his people, verses 1–6. (2) A God who cares, verses 7–12. (3) A God who reveals himself, verses 13–15.

NEEDED: A WAY OUT.   TEXT: 1 Cor. 10:1–13. (1) Temptation to embrace the present age and its debased values is real and timeless. (2) Falling to such temptation can happen to anyone. (3) Nevertheless, God knows our weakness and provides a way of escape from our potential destroyers.

Worship Aids

CALL TO WORSHIP.   "Bless the Lord, O my soul; and all that is within me, bless his holy name. Bless the Lord, O my soul,

and forget not all his benefits" (Ps. 103:1–2).

INVOCATION.   Lord, help us to be honest and open and genuine in our worship today, to desire what thou dost desire, to act in accordance with thy word and live to do thy will.—E.Lee Phillips

OFFERTORY SENTENCE.   "Shun idolatry, then, my beloved. I am speaking to sensible people; weigh my words for yourselves" (1 Cor. 10:14–15, Moffatt).

OFFERTORY PRAYER.   Father, you have given us such wealth of blessing and such wonders of grace. Lead us to respond to all you have given with gratitude and love. Here before you we bring the gift of money, calling it tithes and offerings. Inspire us to give amounts that signify the depths of our response to all that you have done for us. Bless what is given, we pray, that it might be scattered across the earth and used for your glory.—Henry Fields

PRAYER.   Almighty God, we would praise and honor thee in this time of worship. We must be honest for we have been greatly blessed and truly find ourselves when most we find thee.
    Hear our cry, O Lord, in distress. Many of us begin the day in prayer and go through its routine, and when sunset beckons we are tired and want to escape and shed the pressures of the day. We often find ourselves in such hours the heirs of the weaknesses of flesh and mind. Faith wavers, we know what it is to become victims to our imaginations. Often our vulnerability leads us to desire actions that in stronger moments we would avoid.
    Lord, God, thou knowest our weaknesses and those temptations that try us more than all others. Grant us thy sustenance in the hour of need. Lead us to be true to the faith that holds us safe in thy hand, to be loyal to our families, and to hide thy Word on our hearts that we might not sin against thee.
    In the name of Jesus, we pray, who bore the burden of all sin yet sinned not,

and in the power of the Holy Spirit, strong to deliver, mighty to save.—E. Lee Phillips

LECTIONARY MESSAGE

Topic: Hope in the Midst of Hopelessness

TEXT: Luke 13:1–9

Luke colors the beginning of the passage with harshness and a legalistic outlook. Sin inevitably brings about judgment. Here in Luke, Jesus spoke of some of the "hot" news items of his day—the Galileans killed by Pilate and those who were killed by the falling tower of Siloam. Many in his audience would have made the assumption that those killed must have sinned in some terrible way to have died that kind of death. Jesus heated the fire of the discussion by going on to say that, unless the audience repented, they too would perish

I. Yet the harsh statements in verses 1–5 are a foil for the parable related by Jesus in verses 6–9. The subject of the parable is the endless mercy of God available to those who would repent. Many people want to hear only a "hellfire-and-damnation" style of preaching. Such persons want to be made to feel guilty at the end of the worship service. They find it so hard to accept the forgiveness of God. Many carry a burden of guilt around their whole lives because they cannot accept the fact that they can be forgiven.

The fig tree was given another chance. The three years of waiting for fruit is even more remarkable when you consider that for the first three years of the tree's life, the farmer would have viewed the tree as unclean according to Lev. 19:23. Thus, as Jeremias indicated, probably the farmer had in reality waited six years! He would not have sought fruit during the three-year-period of uncleanness.

II. On face value there seems to be no hope at all. After six years of waiting for fruit, what farmer would possibly expect one day to come to the tree and find some fruit? There is always a fishhook in the parables of Jesus to capture the attention of the audience. There is something said so unusual that it makes the people standing around say, "What?" What farmer would continue to waste precious time and money on caring for an unfruitful tree? However, the vinedresser in the story suggested that very thing.

III. The most surprising thing of all about the story, as B. S. Scott has suggested, is that the final act of the parable is missing. Hearers would like to know what happened to the tree. One cannot have a story without an ending. Did the tree come back to life? Jesus left the story open-ended. The mercy of God is like that. Just at the time that everything looks hopeless, hope blossoms forth. Just at the time that everyone else was talking about judgment and damnation, Jesus mentioned the endless mercy of God.

The task of the Christian in view of the parable is to keep on trying—keep on with the care and nurture of the tree—never give up. Unfortunately, as humans we cannot see if we are going to be successful. We just have to trust in the ultimate and endless mercy of God to save sinners.—James L. Blevins

SUNDAY: MARCH TWENTY-NINTH

SERVICE OF WORSHIP

Sermon: The Principle of the Spiritual Harvest

TEXT: Gal. 6:7–8

I. There is a close analogy between the world of nature and the world of spirit.

They bear the impress of the same hand, and hence the principles of nature and its laws are the types and shadows of the Invisible.

(a) It was upon this principle that Christ taught. Truths come forth from his lips, not stated simply on authority, but based on the analogy of the universe.

His human mind, in perfect harmony with the divine mind with which it is mixed, discerned the connection of things and read the Eternal Will in the simplest laws of nature. For instance, if it were a question whether God would give his Spirit to them that asked, it was not replied to by a truth revealed on his *authority*; the answer was derived from facts lying open to all men's observation. "Behold the fowls of the air"—"behold the lilies of the field"—learn from them the answer to your question. A principle was there. God supplies the wants which he has created. He feeds the ravens; he clothes the lilies; he will feed with his Spirit the craving spirits of his children.

(b) It was on this principle of analogy that St. Paul taught in this text. He tells us that there is a law in nature according to which success is proportioned to the labor spent upon the work. In almost all departments it is "the diligent hand which maketh rich."

The keen eye of Paul discerned this principle reaching far beyond what is seen, into the spiritual realm which is unseen. As tare seed comes up tares, and wheat seed, wheat—and as the crop in both cases is in proportion to two conditions, the labor and the quantity committed to the ground—so in things spiritual, too, whatsoever a man soweth, that shall he also reap. Not something else, but "*that*." The proportion holds in kind—it holds, too, in degree, in spiritual things as in natural. "He which soweth sparingly shall reap also sparingly; and he which soweth bountifully shall reap also bountifully." If we could understand and rightly expound that principle, we should be saved from much of the disappointment and surprise which come from extravagant and unreasonable expectations.

II. The principle is this: "God is not mocked: for whatsoever a man soweth, that shall he also reap."

(a) We will not depreciate the advantages of this world. It is foolish and unreal to do so. Comfort, affluence, success, freedom from care, rank, station—these are in their real way goods; only the labor bestowed upon them does not procure one single blessing that is spiritual.

On the other hand, the seed which is sown for a spiritual harvest has no tendency whatever to procure temporal well-being. It is not said that the pure in heart shall be made rich, nor that they who hunger after goodness shall be filled with bread, nor that they who mourn shall rise in life and obtain distinction. Each department has its own appropriate harvest—reserved exclusively to its own method of sowing.

Everything in this world has its price, and the price buys *that*, not something else. Every harvest demands its own preparation, and that preparation will not produce another sort of harvest. You cannot enjoy the statesman's influence together with freedom from public notoriety. If you sensitively shrink from that, you must give up influence or else pay his price—the price of a thorny pillow, unrest, the chance of being today a nation's idol, tomorrow the people's execration.

(b) Now the mistakes men make, and the extravagant expectations in which they indulge, are these: They sow for earth, and expect to win spiritual blessings, or they sow to the Spirit and then wonder that they have not a harvest of the good things of earth. In each case they complain, What have I done to be treated so?

But if you look into it, the balance is perfectly adjusted even here. God has made his world much better than you and I could make it. Everything reaps its own harvest, every act has its own reward. And before you covet the enjoyment which another possesses, you must first calculate the cost at which it was procured.

It is all fair. Count the cost. "He that saveth his life shall lose it." Save your life if you like but do not complain if you lose your nobler life—yourself; win the whole world, but remember you do it by losing your own soul. Every sin must be paid for; every sensual indulgence is a harvest, the price for which is so much rain for the soul. "*God is not mocked.*"

Popularity is one of the things of an earthly harvest for which quite earthly qualifications are required. I say not always dishonorable qualifications but a certain flexibility of disposition, a certain courtly willingness to sink obnoxious truths and adapt ourselves to the prejudices of the minds of others, a certain adroitness at catching the tone of those with whom we are. Without some of these things no man can be popular in any profession.

Now, your price: Your price is dislike. The price of being true is the cross. The warrior of the truth must not expect success. What have you to do with popularity? Sow for it, and you will have it.

This is the mistake men make. They expect both harvests, paying only one price. They would be blessed with goodness and prosperity at once. They would have that on which they bestowed no labor. They take sinful pleasures and think it very hard that they must pay for it in agony and worse than agony, souls deteriorated. They would monopolize heaven in their souls, and the world's prizes at the same time. This is to expect to come back, like Joseph's brethren from the land of plenty, with the corn in their sacks and the money returned, too, in their sacks' mouths. No, no; it will not do. "Be not deceived; God is not mocked." Reap *what* you have sown. If you sow the wind, do not complain if your harvest is the whirlwind. If you sow to the Spirit, be content with a spiritual reward: invisible—within: "more life and higher life."—Frederick W. Robertson

Illustrations

GOD'S LAW.   G. K. Chesterton said that there was once a man who disbelieved in the law of gravity, and to prove his disbelief, he walked off the edge of a cliff. He did not prove his disbelief. He proved the law of gravity.

The moral law of God is not the same as a law of nature. The laws of nature are both unchangeable and inviolable, while the moral laws of God, though unchangeable, are not, of course, inviolable. You can break them. That is the tragedy of our world. Millions do!

But they cannot be broken with impunity. Sooner or later they will break you.

Where his moral laws are disregarded, the bill is bound to come in. He has made a world which will only work his way. When the consequences of wrongdoing come down upon us, we raise piteous protests to heaven, but it is no use saying, "I didn't profess to believe." For our own good the law works on independently of our unimportant opinions, and what a man sows, that shall he also reap.—W. E. Sangster

THE COST.   Surely George Washington lived a sacrificial life, but so did Benedict Arnold, heaven have mercy on him! God said to both of them, Take what you want; take it and pay for it! Surely Christ lived a sacrificial life, but so did Judas Iscariot, poor fellow—with one of the greatest chances a man ever had, giving it all up for thirty pieces of silver and a rotting memory.—Harry Emerson Fosdick

Sermon Suggestions

GOD STILL CARES.   TEXT: Josh. 5:9–12. (1) When God blesses us in a special way, we might like for this way of blessing to go on forever. (2) But time and new conditions bring change. (3) Still, the God who is forever the same has different and even better ways of blessing us.

THE POWER OF THE RISEN CHRIST. TEXT: 2 Cor. 5:16–21. (1) To make a sinner a new creation. (2) To enable this reconciled sinner to be his ambassador.

Worship Aids

CALL TO WORSHIP.   "O magnify the Lord with me, and let us exalt his name together" (Ps. 34:3).

INVOCATION.   I was glad when they said unto me, let us go into the house of the Lord. What a privilege, O Father, to be in this place and once again look upon those symbols that recall your mighty deeds for our salvation. What a joy to unite mind, heart, and voice in songs of praise and thanksgiving. To celebrate your Word as it is read, proclaimed, and heard, we are grateful. To sense the depth of your Presence in the fellowship of prayer—what a blessing! Praise be to you—Father, Son, and Holy Spirit.—John Thompson

OFFERTORY SENTENCE.   "God was making all mankind his friends through Christ. God did not keep an account of their sins, and he has given us the message which tells how he makes them his friends" (2 Cor. 5:19, TEV).

OFFERTORY PRAYER.   Lord, if our outward giving does not match our inward intent, or our daily witness does not match our private prayers, then forgive our sins, heal our divisions, and align us inside and out with the Savior whom we can never outgive and in whose life our purpose and peace is complete.—E. Lee Phillips

PRAYER.   Gracious Lord, we pray for persons with loved ones who are ill or aged and infirm: that they honor them, loving them well and doing all that they can; that they live out the ministry of mourning and consolation and receive the beatitude of comfort; that they hold the sick appropriately accountable; that they have a proper regard for their own health, keeping the twofold commandment to love neighbor and themselves.

We pray for the staff of nursing homes: that they find strength; that they be of good cheer; that they be truly respectful of the vulnerable people entrusted them; that we lobby for their welfare and at price—better conditions, better schedules, better wages, better benefits, more respect; that we uphold their lives as role models; that we thank them; that we hear what their world has to say to our own.

We give you thanks for the community's stalwarts in well-doing: for volunteers; persons who tutor, work in libraries, coach, deliver meals, visit the sick, work in shelters and soup kitchens, read, advise and counsel, serve on boards and committees, are nurses' aids, teachers' aides. Remind us to say thanks and that we may genuinely share their dream, open our hearts and clear our calendars.—Peter Fribley

LECTIONARY MESSAGE

Topic: The Elder Brother Syndrome

TEXT: Luke 15:1–3, 11–32

Jesus was faced with a charge of eating with tax collectors and sinners. In answering this charge Jesus told of an angry older brother who looked with scorn on the return home of his younger prodigal brother. In fact, over against the image of the self-righteous older brother stands not only the parable of the lost son but also the lost sheep and lost coin in Luke, chapter 15. They key to interpreting these last things is the attitude of the elder brother who stayed home.

I. It would have been very easy for Jesus' audience to have said, "Amen, Jesus, preach on," when he told of the unbelievable activity of the younger son. What teenage boy would demand his part of the inheritance while the father was still on the land? In essence, it would treat him as if he were already dead. The parable describes in some detail the riotous, wild living of the prodigal. Certainly he deserved all that came to be his lot. The audience hearing Jesus must have agreed that his proper due was to end up in a pig pen.

How easy it is for Christians to rail against juvenile delinquency or the divorced person. Many preachers find it much easier to preach against the people not at church rather than the ones there on a given Sunday. The sinners are always an easy target for criticism and judgment. No wonder preachers have for years preached on the prodigal son but never quite reached the main character of the chapter—the elder brother.

II. Jesus wanted his audience to identify with that very figure. It is there that we find the answer to the charge of the Pharisees and scribes in Luke 15:1. Jesus wanted them to look deep into the eyes of the elder brother and see their own faces reflected back in his eyes. In fact, it was the elder brother more than the prodigal who had taken his father for granted. One can tell by the harsh discourse between the elder brother and his father that their relationship has been filled with hostility and greed. It was the elder son's role to greet his father's guests at a banquet. He refused not only to do that but even to call the prodigal "brother." He spoke of his brother spending money on prostitutes when nothing had been said of prostitutes in the whole parable.

III. How hard it is for us to identify with the elder brother. How easy it is to adopt his self-righteous attitude. We find it much easier to condemn sinners rather than share the love and mercy of God

with them. Some quickly list the faults of others and point out the error of their ways. How many more obstacles stand in the way of welcoming the prodigals back home.

Over both figures—the prodigal and the elder brother—stands the figure of God. He bestows his love on both—the runaway son and the embittered self-righteous one. It is no wonder that Jesus in his earthly ministry ate with tax collectors and sinners.—James L. Blevins

SUNDAY: APRIL FIFTH

SERVICE OF WORSHIP

Sermon: Can Dry Bones Live?
Texts: Ezek. 37:1–14, reb; Rom. 8:5–11, reb

When the prophet Ezekiel arrived to begin his ministry among the Jewish exiles, he found a sorry and hopeless lot. Feeling broken in separation from their homeland, still horror-stricken at having seen their beloved Jerusalem destroyed, now in the cruel control of Babylon, they—worst of all—felt separated and alienated from God; they were certain that the "divine-human relationship . . . had been broken . . ."[1] That is devastating, isn't it—to sense, for whatever reason, that we are cut off from God?

I. And Ezekiel, who had come to give a word of hope in God's name, was having a terrible time doing so. Even an off-the-wall kind of guy like Ezekiel was in touch enough with reality to know that morsels of hope would be hard to swallow for these who felt so abused and cut off from all that was essential to them. So Ezekiel had it rough in knowing what to say, and he had an even tougher time not buying into the perspective of those who felt that they were dying individually and as a people. In fact, he thought they were onto something; he was all but convinced

[1] Robert R. Wilson, "Ezekiel," *Harper's Bible Commentary* (San Francisco: Harper & Row, 1988), 691.

that they were right and that God had given him a sermon for another group of people whom he just hadn't yet found. But God said, "No, Ezekiel, this is the right group: your sisters and brothers in the Babylonian exile. They are the ones who are to hear your word of hope."

And Ezekiel retorted, "Oh, sure God. It's easy for you to talk about hope and what needs to be said to these people because you don't have to face them! I'm the one they'll laugh at when I talk about hope, and in their state of mind, they could do a lot worse than laugh at me!"

God said, "Ezekiel, if you get laughed at, that's just part of the job. Your prophetic responsibility isn't to establish or control the response of the people to what you say; your job is simply to tell them what I lead you to say. I'll take responsibility for the validity of the message."

II. Well, Ezekiel didn't do anything rash or rushed. He pondered the matter further and tried to imagine how in the world things could ever be right again for these poor captives. And while he was trying to reason this out, he had a prophetic vision in which God showed him how hopeless situations can become hopeful in the power of God.

Suddenly he is aware of the presence of God enfolding him, and he is transported right out in the middle of a huge plain that was covered—as far as he could see in every direction—with bones. And he didn't have to look all that closely to see that they were human skeletal remains, parched by long exposure to the relentless sun. What a feeling of despair. He might very well have been standing on the site of some battle where hundreds had been slain. This is certainly how such a scene would be left, but that was not where these bones came from.

While Ezekiel was pondering the sadness and loss of whatever could have caused such a tragedy, God asked him one of those divine trick questions, or else God was having a hard time trying to make conversation: "O man, can these bones live?" (Ezek. 37:3a, REB).

Ezekiel wanted to say, "*Right.* Bones come back to life all the time!" But he didn't. Instead Ezekiel gave an appropriate and respectful answer: "Only you, Lord God, know that" (Ezek. 37:3–8, REB). Remember Ezekiel's answer. If God ever asks you one of those surprising and open-ended questions, don't bite; just answer as Ezekiel did. It's always the right answer about what can and cannot be: "Only you, Lord God, know that."

Ezekiel had been having a tough time trying to mutter encouragement to his people on the basis of divine hope. Now, in his vision, God is telling him to prophesy to the dry bones. He at first wondered if this were some kind of punishment in which God was saying, "If you think the exiles are a tough crowd, let me show you something." From an audience that is emotionally and spiritually dead, Ezekiel is to move to an audience that is physically dead.

Again, God is giving Ezekiel his message; the prophet doesn't have to dream up something. And what God tells him to say to the dry bones is this: The Lord God is "going to put breath in you, and you will live. . . . Then you will know that I am the Lord" (Ezek. 37:5, 6c, REB).

In his vision, Ezekiel tells those bones exactly what God had told him to say, and an eerie, unsettling thing began to happen. There "was a rattling sound and the bones all fitted themselves together" (Ezek. 37:7b, REB). And you know the rest—probably from the old rhythmic spiritual that sings of bones connected to bones—all obeying the Spirit of the Lord. The bones were reconnected and restruc-

tured from the inside out until they were flesh-and-blood human beings again—amazing to behold, but they weren't yet living. They had "no breath in them" (Ezek. 37:8b). There was more prophesying to do, and when Ezekiel uttered forth the divinely inspired words, breath entered those lifeless bodies, and "they came to life and rose to their feet" (Ezek. 37:10b, REB).

God had asked Ezekiel, "Can these bones live?" And Ezekiel hadn't known that they could live. Now he did, and standing out there in the middle of that plain surrounded by new life created from what had been dead and dusty, Ezekiel knew how powerful the hand of God could be. And in that sense of awe that comes over us all when we have seen God at work, the identity of the people was made known to the prophet. They were the people of Israel.

From his vision, from his reminder of the power of God, he was to go back to his hopeless-feeling sisters and brothers and give to them the Word from the Lord: "You, my people, will know that I am the Lord when I open your graves and bring you up from them. Then I shall put my spirit into you and you will come to life, and I shall settle you on your own soil, and you will know that I the Lord have spoken and I shall act" (Ezek. 37:13–14c, REB). Part of coming back to life for the Israelites was a promise that they could return to their homeland, and that was a part of what God promised in their restoration.

III. Now I want you to notice here that there are two powers that make dry bones live: the Spirit of God alive and at work *and* the healing Word of God that calls us to wholeness. And what we need to hear today is that both of these powers are still at work in our world and in our lives and that, because of these, dry bones are still coming to life. We know a whole lot more about dry bones than we know about the life-giving power of God's Word and God's Spirit, but God is still giving new life where there has been death.

Can dry bones live? You tell me. Tell me about your ability to love, which you thought was gone—impossible to reactivate, you were quite sure, long years after a loss or a disappointment or a divorce. However, in communion with God and with the fellowship of God's people and maybe in the presence of a caring person who invited your love, you knew one day that love and the ability to love were still alive inside you. What a glorious discovery.

Can dry bones live? Have you ever been overtaken and destroyed by one of the life-draining emotions like grief or depression—beyond hope of recovery? I mean, have you ever felt so overcome with such a loneliness or despair that you were quite certain you could never get past it? And then something happened. Somehow you knew that God wasn't dead or standing idly by in the time of your pain. You heard the word of hope, and before long the Spirit of God was stirring in your soul, and you found that you could not only cope, but also you could live—really live! Grief and depression could not steal your life from you permanently. You could laugh again. You could celebrate your independence again. You could face and pull all the way through a crisis without giving in to the bleak and deadly grip of emotional illness. You could hope again.

Can dry bones live? What about it? Haven't we all been wiped out spiritually and known in the depths of who we are that the spiritual dimension of us is as dead as dusty, dry bones? We stay with church attendance; we stay with Bible study. We stay with some attempts to pray, but we know that our spirits are making no contact with the living God. A part of us has died, and we know it. Haven't you been in such a position only to discover, to your absolute amazement, that your longing for the presence of the living God began to be satisfied once again, that your spiritual self began to be rebuilt? What could be more thrilling than that!

Paul proclaimed to the Romans in resurrection power, "If the Spirit of [the One] who raised Jesus from the dead dwells in you, the God who raised Christ Jesus from the dead will also give new life to your mortal bodies through [God's] indwelling Spirit" (Rom. 8:10–11, REB).—David Albert Farmer

Illustrations

THE POWER OF GOD.   So the power of God stands in violent contrast with the power of man. It is not external like man's power but internal. By applying external pressure, I can make a person do what I want him to do. This is man's power. But as for making him be what I want him to be, without at the same time destroying his freedom, only love can make this happen. And love makes it happen not coercively but by creating a situation in which, of our own free will, we want to be what love wants us to be. And because God's love is uncoercive and treasures our freedom—if above all he wants us to love him, then we must be left free not to love him—we are free to resist it, deny it, crucify it finally, which we do again and again. This is our terrible freedom, which love refuses to overpower so that, in this, the greatest of all powers, God's power, is itself powerless.—Frederick Buechner

LIFE FOR THE CHURCH.   *The gates of hell shall not prevail against it.* The Christian fellowship is an eternal kingdom. Whosoever belongs to Jesus the Risen Lord is sealed for eternal life. And the promise of God in Jesus Christ is that always even unto the end of the world there will be a Christian community believing in Jesus as the Christ and delivered by Him not only from sin but also from the fear of death.—Emil Brunner

Sermon Suggestions

WHEN GOD DOES A NEW THING.   TEXT: Isa. 43:16–21. (1) We should avoid fixation on the past when we are dealing with the living God. (2) We can rely on God's resourcefulness to meet every crisis as the future unfolds.

WHAT YOU CAN GIVE UP EVERYTHING ELSE FOR.   TEXT: Phil. 3:8–14. (1) Knowing Christ Jesus as Lord. (2) Sharing in

Christ's sufferings. (3) Winning the heavenly prize to which God has called us.

Worship Aids

CALL TO WORSHIP. "The Lord hath done great things for us; whereof we are glad" (Ps. 126:3).

INVOCATION. Holy God, give to our earth-bound eyes a heavenly vision and give to our sin-burdened hearts divine forgiveness. Then use us to redeem this planet through the saving power of the gospel.—E. Lee Phillips

OFFERTORY SENTENCE. "In the very truth I count all things but loss compared to the excellence of the knowledge of Christ Jesus my Lord. For his sake I have suffered the loss of all things, and esteem them but refuse that I may gain Christ, and be found in him" (Phil. 3:8–9a, Montgomery).

OFFERTORY PRAYER. Bring us closer to the goal, O Lord, of giving as generously as we have received and allow that we may get all the closer to that goal today.—E. Lee Phillips

PRAYER. O Father, for this privilege to celebrate the gifts of your Word to the world in the person of your only Son, we give you thanks. Through the Word sung, read, and preached in this hour we have heard your call to the Church to be faithful stewards of your Word, which breathes life. We thank you for congregations so faithful in proclaiming and living out your Word that men and women at all ages hear your call to the ministry. We are grateful for those who give responsible and responsive leadership to our seminaries that the church may have a well-trained and committed leadership now and in the future.

With your Holy Spirit quicken *us* in mind and empower us in purpose that through us the Church may be the harbinger of that new order that your coming in Christ portends for all humankind. Grant to us such a sense of destiny to believe that we have been born to the kingdom for such times as this.

Whatever else your Word is, may we know and receive it as your Word of grace for us and for all others. We are grateful for the healing of your grace among us and pray for your healing where there is still brokenness of body, of mind, of heart. Through him in whom your grace becomes real and is present among us as your perennial Word teaching us to pray as one family, [The Lord's Prayer].—John Thompson

LECTIONARY MESSAGE

Topic: A Politician, First-Century Style
TEXT: John 12:1–8
Judas Iscariot certainly might fit well into a modern-day political election. In our present day of television ads, negative images appear on our television screens of the opposing politician who loves taxes, hates babies, and is out "to sock it to the poor." Of course, the politician running the ad is one who kisses babies, hates taxes, and supports the poor. Throughout the centuries, the poor have been used by politicians and others with less than altruistic causes.

Judas certainly fits the modern pictures. John related that his grave concern for the poor was a mask for his own selfish greed—"he used to take what was put into the money box." The major concern was not the three hundred denarii (about $1,500) for the poor but rather the three hundred denarii destined for his own money bag.

I. Many Christians as well as politicians often use the poor of the world for selfish and less than holy ways. We have all heard of charities that spend a large percentage of their collections on administrative costs, and the poor end up receiving little. Even more etched on our consciences are the faces of a few television evangelists who under various pretexts robbed the widows and the poor from selfish, greedy motives. For some religious organizations the poor are among the other freaks in the sideshow tent to attract the large audience and yet larger donations.

II. Jesus in his own ministry identified with the poor—he praised poor Lazarus the beggar and placed rich Dives in hell. In the sermon on the plain in Luke he said, "Blessed are the poor people." Jesus, because of a lifelong true identity with the poor, could accept the sacrificial act of Mary in pouring costly perfume over his feet. His response of "the poor you have with you" (v. 8) was not callous nor harsh when measured over against his whole earthly ministry.

III. In the midst of carrying out the ministry of Jesus to the poor and oppressed of our world, the Christian must pause occasionally and look into the face of Christ. In the swirl of modern poverty and Third World despair, it is easier for the disciple of Christ to become hopeless and discouraged. Like Mary, each Christian must at times stop the feverish pace of activity and attempt to view the face of Christ. There is something beyond the maze of hungry faces and pot-bellied hungry children. There is the Master who came to our world to show a better way—of love and concern for the "little people." Feeding the poor is always a worthwhile cause. However, in Christ it is even more—the evidence of a God who sent his Son into the world to identify himself with "the least of these" and to deliver them into a kingdom of justice and love. In Mary's act we see the total picture—cross, burial, self-giving—Jesus' mission in this world. This represents just one second, a short pause in the ongoing reaching out to the poor and outcasts of the world.—James L. Blevins

SUNDAY: APRIL TWELFTH

SERVICE OF WORSHIP

Sermon: Not Turning Back
TEXTS: Isa. 50:4–9a, REB; Matt. 21:1–11, REB

To face adversity when the cause is worthy enough and—in every instance—to learn from adversity, especially to learn to trust God in adversity: this is the challenge, the inescapable pattern for living among people of faith. It is the way the prophetic Suffering Servant lived; it is the way Jesus lived and—in this spirit—the way he died.

Well, that's just fine for Jesus, we think, and that Suffering Servant about whom Isaiah wrote—whoever *he* was. But it's an unreasonable perspective for "average folks" like us. And with our way of looking at life, maybe that is true. Perspective, after all, is practically everything. So what we are called to think through here is our perspective.

When adversity pops up in our path, we forget about everything else. We forget about the path, why we are on the path, where we are headed, and often those who are traveling with us. Once adversity makes itself known, we become utterly preoccupied with it; that is all we can think about. It is as if we begin living merely to confront what has interfered with the way things were for us. I'm not suggesting that adversity either can or should be ignored, but I am wondering with you about the value and the propriety of giving threat and attack sudden and permanent centrality in our lives. I'm wondering about our tendency not to look through or past some turbulence in our way.

You see, people of grit and insight have—all along—given themselves to some kind of endurance on their way to the realization of their goal. On many occasions, the pain is a surprise that comes unexpectedly and very much against their will. At times, the adversity has been taken up voluntarily. Not infrequently the sacrifice for these people of courage has been great.

Whether to be grappled with head on, whether to be dulled when possible, or whether to grit one's teeth for endurance when we face it, adversity need not keep us from our path, from the goal of serving and sharing life with the God who created us and who has a positive pur pose for us. Almost assuredly—and more than once—adversity will appear while we are on our way. Without tenacity and without healthy perspective, it can destroy us. It can negate—in our thinking and, sometimes, in fact—all that we have stood for, all that we have longed and worked for. Perspective, a sense of mission, a sense of what we are about in God's plan can keep this from happening.

I. In order for a defiant attitude toward adversity to be reality, we must get past the too typical reflex theology we have that God is the one who put the obstacle in our way. It is hard not to give up when you think that God is the one who inflicts the pain. If that is how you feel, I don't see a way to move into a redemptive frame of mind; indeed, the burden of divinely appointed adversary is too great. If you can, however, look to God as always a part of deliverance and meaning and *not* a part of arbitrary punishment and useless tragedy, then there is hope for making life valuable *in spite of* adversity.

The testimony of the Suffering Servant—as recorded by the prophet Isaiah—was uttered from this point of view. In fact, it is astounding that, over against his own pain and abuse by enemies, the Servant—whose experiences so closely paralleled the experience of Jesus—could view his mission and ministry so redemptively.

"I offered my back to the lash, and let my beard be plucked from my chin. I did not hide my face from insult and spitting" (Isa. 50:6, REB).

Now, against such humiliation and sore abuse, God's Servant could see both his ongoing ministry and his source of help in his time of trial. We need a dose of his perspective.

This is a man in pain who says,

The Lord God has given me the tongue of one who has been instructed to console the weary with a timely word; [God] made my hearing sharp every morning, that I might listen like one under instruction. The Lord God opened my ears and I did not disobey or turn back in defiance. (Isa. 50:4–5, REB).

He followed God's path for him. He owned God's will for him as a person of God, as a minister of God, and that realization was too great to be torn down by godless adversity. He would keep trying to serve, and he would keep trying to learn in the midst of the trial. He would keep trying to listen for God's Word of comfort and God's Word of leadership; these would keep him on the path when turning away would appear to be both the simplest and the most logical response. His cause was greater than his pain, and—thus—he would go on as God's person, *not turning back.*

II. How could he do it? Well, as the Suffering Servant explained it,

. . . the Lord God is my helper; therefore no insult can wound me; I know that I shall not be put to shame, therefore I have set my face like flint. One who will clear my name is at my side. Who dare argue against me? Let us confront one another. Who will dispute my cause? Let him come forward. The Lord God is my helper; who then can declare me guilty? (Isa. 50:7–9a, REB).

The ability not to be overcome with pain and abuse is not an innate characteristic though some of us learn to be survivors. Adversity can be cruel, and it has the capacity for destruction. We come at it, faces set hard and stern like a stone, with a confidence that God and God's love and God's plan are greater. Walking assuredly through the crisis, the Suffering Servant—head held high—testifies to all who will hear him: ". . . the Lord God is my helper. . . . The Lord God is my helper." And God helps not only with the pain, but also with the changing perspective of those who move ahead with their eyes fixed on God's plan and with the audacity not to bow down before the enemy that disrupts and that seeks to destroy life itself.

How could Jesus have returned to Jerusalem under those life-threatening circumstances? Why would he do it? So much was at stake for him and for those sympathetic to his cause. Jesus didn't like the pain that he suspected was awaiting him sometime during the week of what we now call his "Passion." Maybe he didn't know how bad it would get—finally deserted by those who claimed to be most loyal to him; rejected, beaten, scoffed at for who he said he was and how he looked at things: The convictions of his heart made matters for laughter.

When Jesus rode the colt through the crowd and their shouts of praise, he was riding into adversity, and he knew it. His followers begged him not to go. This was pain he didn't *have to* bear, they tried to tell him. But Jesus believed that, somehow, he could ride through it; he could live through it to the glory of God. And God honored his sacrifice.

Jesus' cause was a great cause, and all the opposition in the world could not alter that. Whatever pain there was to endure for his convictions could not tear away what he knew in his heart about the devotion of God to humanity and the need of people—even his people who thought they knew it all about matters of religion—to find their way into the love of God. To avoid the pain—in this instance—would be to deny his understanding of God and the dimensions of his ministry in God's name to hurting people about which others objected. That Jesus could not do. For him there was not any turning back.

His pain was great—culminating with his agony on the cross. But for Jesus, it could not obscure the dominant reality of his life and thought: the God of love and grace and compassion and peace reaching out for all people.

Adversity might bring forgetfulness for a season—forgetfulness about our course and our cause. But it cannot rob us of the reason for our living. It is to be acknowledged and dealt with as possible. But adversity is to be ridden through or walked past on the path of faithful service to God, for God draws us to the abundant life even with adversity, even on this side of resurrection, greater and more glorious than we can imagine. So let us go forward with courage and determination—eyes fixed on God, even when there is adversity in our way. Adversity is not our life, not the sum total of who we are, and never—in God's intent—the last word about us. To face adversity when the cause is worthy enough, and—in every instance—to learn from adversity, especially to learn to trust God in adversity, that is our calling. And so we press on with confidence knowing all the while that there may be a cross ahead.—David Albert Farmer

Illustrations

OUR PARTNERSHIP. You and I are in that crowd wishing desperately God would step in and provide an easy, simple, dramatic answer for our world. But he won't. He has too much respect for us. Way back at the beginning of things God took man into partnership and gave him dominion over all of this created world of ours. He will not go back on that. But he will and does show us the way of creative obedience and suffering. And if you and I respond in love and trust, and if, consequently, peace in our world begins to take root and grow, it will be because a man rode into Jerusalem one day, not to set himself upon a throne, but to enthrone his cross in the hearts of me like you and me.—Edmund A. Steimle

A WAY THROUGH. When Jesus loved guilt-ridden persons and helped them, he saw in them straying children of God. He saw in them human beings whom his Father loved and whose straying caused him sadness. At the same time he saw them as God had originally intended them to be, and therefore he saw through the layers of dirt to the genuine article beneath. Jesus did not *identify* human beings with their guilt; he saw that guilt as foreign, as not really belonging to them, but as binding and mastering them. He wanted to free them again, to take them away from the powers and make this his own. Jesus could love people because he loved through the layers of dirt, so to speak.—Helmut Thielicke

Sermon Suggestions

THE WAYS OF A CHRISTLIKE LIFE. TEXT: Isa. 50:4–9a. (1) Listening to God. (2) Obeying God. (3) Suffering for God. (4) Trusting in God's vindication.

A GLORY TO SING ABOUT.   TEXT: Phil. 2:5–11. (1) Glory possessed. (2) Glory relinquished. (3) Glory earned. (4) Glory acclaimed.

Worship Aids

CALL TO WORSHIP.   "This is the day which the Lord hath made; we will rejoice and be glad in it" (Ps. 118:24).

INVOCATION.   Holy God, we greet again the Savior Son who comes riding our way and pray that we might be open and receptive and faithful in our worship and adoration, because Jesus keeps coming to us, and this is the truth that never leaves us.—E. Lee Phillips

OFFERTORY SENTENCE.   "God has chosen the weak things of the world to confound the things which are mighty" (1 Cor. 1:27b).

OFFERTORY PRAYER.   Because of your amazing resourcefulness, O Lord, we believe that even the smallest of our gifts can do astonishing things. So we give boldly, trusting in your providence and power.

PRAYER.   O Father of us all who is above all, yet in us all, make us grateful for the sense of seeing, of hearing, of smelling, of feeling, of tasting. Make us ever sensitive to all expressions of your grace in the world about us: the glory of the morning hour; the refreshment of the cool breeze that invigorates; the technicolor of life—in the tree, the shrub, the flower, the sky, the sea. May the matter-of-fact orientation of this scientific age never blind us to the glamour, the romance, the wonder, the mystery of life.

If in the midst of all the excitement, color, variety of nature about us we find ourselves yawning at life, take the dimness of our soul away. Provoke us from conforming ways that we may be transformed from within by the renewing of our minds to all the uniqueness of our creation as persons.

You have called us into being through the creative power of your love and call us again and again to be. Grant us such attentiveness in these moments of worship that we may hear your call again. May we respond in faith according to our unique opportunity.

In our love and concern for one another, may we discover that we are made whole—"No man lives and no man dies unto himself." For those who anxiously toss on beds of pain, we pray health; but if death be more merciful, we must pray, your will be done. May we who have our work, our families, our friends not be insensitive to the needs of others for a sense of usefulness and belonging. May we not turn from the pain, the hurt, the tragic among us but seek those inexhaustible resources of your love by which we may be the Church to the sick, the lonely, the bereaved, the discouraged, the estranged. With them may we not just survive or merely cope but win the victory that is present for all of us in Christ.

You are at work in this world—you so love the *world* and all peoples in it that you have come in person, not to condemn to death but to offer the gift of life. What the years ahead can be in the liberation of all humankind from the fears of war and threat of war, from disease, from starvation, from illiteracy if we have the vision to grasp the new thing that you are seeking to do in these tremendous times! We pray for the leaders of nations. We pray for our leaders that they may not just act or react with outmoded clichés of another day but respond to the living Word that you are speaking today.—John Thompson

LECTIONARY MESSAGE

Topic: Celebration in Despair
TEXT: Luke 19:28–40

It was like being at a football game in the closing minutes of action. The score is 75–0 and little hope is left for victory. Yet the home team's cheerleaders do not give up. They get the home crowd chanting, "Go team, go team." Jesus and his disciples were approaching Jerusalem for the last days and hours of his ministry. Three times along the way he had told them of his need to suffer and die on a cross. What despair must have fallen over the group as they neared the city of Jerusalem.

I. Suddenly someone started shouting, "Blessed is the king who comes in the name of the Lord. Peace in heaven and glory in the highest." Others began to shout the same phrases over and over again. Some people threw their clothing down on the road for Jesus to ride upon. It was as if suddenly the utter despair of the moment had been lifted and the rays of sunshine beamed through—if only briefly. Soon they would be at Jerusalem where no one would meet them and silence would prevail. The only noise would be the footsteps of those plotting to kill Jesus.

II. We all need our Palm Sunday experiences. We need to see the veil of despair lifted for just a few brief seconds. We all need to shout out our acclaim of Jesus and his mighty works. Yet we cannot close our eyes from seeing the cross in the background. Our despair needs to be breached momentarily by hope and the realization of the meaning of the ultimate message of Jesus. The only danger is that one is tempted to remain at the "pep rally" and not venture on into the city of tribunals and crosses.

III. Perhaps the danger in the past has been that the church has celebrated Palm Sunday without a close association with Good Friday. The bright sunshine of that afternoon on the road to Jerusalem might blind our eyes to the hours of darkness on the very next Friday. Some might even dare to think that this young messiah figure might have a chance in Jerusalem. His message might be heard after all. In the exitement of the moment even the celebrating Galilean followers failed to notice that Jesus had selected a donkey on which to ride. The Jews believed the Messiah would arrive on a donkey only if he was bringing judgment for unrepentant people.

For those Galileans with clear eyes, the great celebration outside the gates of Jerusalem was surrounded by ominous clouds. Many knew that the Messiah who dared bring judgment to Jerusalem would end up on a cross. Yet for a moment the clouds lifted, and in excitment they celebrated, and their shouts rang out over the hills and valleys.—James L. Blevins

SUNDAY: APRIL NINETEENTH (EASTER)

SERVICE OF WORSHIP

Sermon: Joy in the Morning
TEXTS: Psalm 30; Matt. 28:1–10

I. Mary Magdalene loved Jesus. She loved him very much. As she watched him die on the cross, her heart was broken. She was devastated. The burial had been rushed. She still needed to say good-bye. So she went to the tomb at dawn on Sunday. The Gospels of Mark and Luke tell us that she and the other women brought spices to anoint his body. That was the last tender act of caring that anyone could do for a loved one who died. There were no funeral homes then. Instead, the family washed and prepared the body. It wasn't a happy task, but it was necessary; more for those left behind to grieve than for the one who died. As Mary walked to the garden with the spices, her arms were laden, but her heart was the heaviest load. She had led a tormented life, feeling guilty for the way she had to live but unable to change until Jesus believed in her. He had turned her life around. He had been her joy, and now that he was gone, what would she do? How could she go on living?

If she had seen his body that morning, it would have reminded her of events from the few years they spent together. Placing coins on his eyelids, she might have remembered the first time their eyes met; the way he looked deep inside her, right to her very soul. It was as if he saw the person she really was; the one she wanted to be. He saw the reasons for her shame, but he loved her anyway. That kind of look, that kind of love, was terrifying at first. She had worked hard to keep her secrets. She couldn't let anyone know them or she'd lose the last shred of tattered self-respect she'd managed to clutch around her. But Jesus knew. He knew her as no one else did. It was strange. He was so attractive and so frightening all at the same time. She didn't want to go near him, and she couldn't stay away. Somehow he brought into focus all the mixed-up feelings she had about herself. She felt so ugly; but he saw something beautiful in her. It made her feel good! She had stopped hating her life. And now he was dead.

If she had spread the aloes on his arms, she might have recalled how strong they were from years of working with lumber and stone but how gentle they could be as he embraced the children. She would remember how his hands gestured when he taught and how they blessed one boy's lunch and fed a crowd. She would remember how his finger wrote in the sand when he refused to condemn the one caught in adultery and shamed all her accusers.

Anointing his feet, she would remember how many miles she followed him around Galilee. There was always one more town to walk to so he could preach the good news of the kingdom of God there. He said a time was coming soon, even now, when people would worship God in spirit and truth and care for one another in love. It was so different from what she had been taught before. She smiled behind her veil when he punctured the pretensions of the chief priests and Pharisees. They were supposed to be so religious, but they would have nothing to do with her. Jesus was different. It was so exciting to be with him. It felt like the earth moved under his feet. She believed what he said. She believed in him. And

she loved him very much.

It had all seemed too good to be true, and maybe it was. His enemies had killed him. His disciples were in hiding. Only a few, mostly women like her, had dared to stand near the cross or come to the tomb. What would become of them now? Would life return to the drudgery and shame it was before he came? What about the kingdom of God? Was it just a beautiful dream, a fairy tale? Even if it did come true, it wouldn't be the same without him.

II. We know that Mary never anointed Jesus' body. As the silent, grieving women approached the tomb, their hearts sank further. Not only had he died, but it seemed someone had taken his body away. As they stared in shock and disbelief, something more astounding happened. An angel told them Jesus was not dead. He had risen and was going to meet them in Galilee. As they ran to tell the other disciples, they met Jesus himself and fell at his feet in adoration. Can you even imagine how they felt? It's a long, long way from the valley of despair to the mountain of elation. Their tears of grief turned to tears of joy as they hurried away. It turned out to be a beautiful morning, one like the psalmist sang about: "Weeping may remain for a night, but rejoicing comes in the morning."

Even so, I wonder if Mary might have looked back over her shoulder to see if he was really there. And in the days that followed she still had something to grieve. Jesus was risen. Hallelujah! But he would no longer walk the dusty roads of Galilee. No more would she be able to sit at his feet or prepare him a meal or embrace him. That physical Jesus was part of her history. Life would be different than it was and different from her hopes and dreams. She had felt good about herself in his presence; now she needed to live as a new person in her own right.

Once, when the disciples were complaining about Jesus' prophecy of his death, he told a parable about a seed. He reminded them that in order for a new plant to grow, its seed must be buried in the ground and die. That's not always easy. Sometimes we're so hungry we'd rather eat our seed corn than trust that we can have more in the future by planting it. Mary, like all the disciples, had to let the dream of earthly companionship with Jesus die before she experienced the full joy of relationship with him. In the days that followed Easter, she began a whole new adventure with her friend and Lord.

III. I'm wondering what needs to die in you and me this morning so that we can fully live. What needs to be crucified so we can be resurrected? What pain will we have to endure in order to be free of pain? Some of us need to say good-bye to someone we loved early. Some of us are clinging to a dream for our lives that isn't coming true and is making us treat ourselves and others as if this life were a bad dream. For others of us, there are old, destructive patterns that die hard. We all have something to let go and grieve.

It's important to realize that the faith that comes from the Resurrection is not one that makes everything turn out perfectly rosy, but one that transforms the lost things of our lives. Instead of bringing back our loved ones, it enables us to live with them. Resurrection faith empowers us to rise from the ashes of defeat, older and wiser, to reclaim our lives. It finds us in the pit of despair and shines a ray of hope. Sometimes that hope is just a faint glimmer in the distance until we climb toward it and discover that it grows brighter and warmer. Resurrection faith claims the promise of God to be near us and help us heal. Mary was willing to go to the garden tomb at the break of dawn to say good-bye. There are "tombs" that many of us need to visit so we can pay our last respects to what we've lost and go on with the rest of our lives.

There was a quotation in one of the nurses' stations last week that caught my eye. It said, "It's never too late to become what you might have been." Did you hear? "It's never too late to become what you might have been." I believe that. That's what Mary learned from Jesus. That's what the whole cowering bunch of disciples discovered on Easter morning.

The joy they felt has echoed down to us Easter morning after Easter morning through the ages. My prayer for you today is that you, too, will pass through the night of weeping and shout for joy in the morning, even this very morning.—Alan Hoskins

Illustrations

THE GROUND OF HOPE.   Our world is dark and frantic, and it would appear that if history continues, it will be in spite of human leaders, not because of them. There are few gleams of political hope. But then, hope never was political. Its only ground is God, who raised Christ from the dead, "the first fruits of those who have fallen asleep." We would never have learned the vastness of the universe if night had not come. Perhaps our present darkness will reveal providences and powers in God which otherwise we could not have known. Bombs may fall, but God does not fall. History may end, but God never ends. So we choose now a faith for our times. We choose Jesus and the Resurrection, and thus we shall know that "everything matters, nothing matters." "Everything matters," in glad obedience; "nothing matters," because nothing can thwart the love and power of God.—George A. Buttrick

SUPERNATURAL POWER.   We are so slow to take it in. "Our lives," we say, "are not the stuff out of which God's Easter victories are made. And as for hoping to live on Christ's level, with that new risen quality of life, why, what's the use? Our problems are too many, our thwarting frailties too baffling, our chains of defeat too firmly shackled on our souls. We have toiled all night and taken nothing."

In this respect, we are like our forefathers who lived all their days in a world containing the marvel of electricity and never guessed it was there. Or we are like the man with the rake in Bunyan's dream, gazing permanently downwards, so obsessed with his task of gathering sticks and straws and dust off the floor that he never noticed, standing behind him, a shining figure with a celestial crown held forth in his hand. We are so apt to be obsessed with the sticks and straws of our own weak efforts of will, ineffectual resolves, and insubstantial longings; never dreaming that the Lord God who resurrected Christ is standing there beside us, with that gift of supernatural power—ours, if we would but take it!—James S. Stewart

Sermon Suggestions

THE GOSPEL IN A NUTSHELL.   TEXT: Acts 10:34–43. (1) God has no favorites. (2) Jesus went about doing good to all. (3) Jesus was put to death. (4) God raised Jesus from the dead. (5) Everyone who trusts in this Jesus receives forgiveness of sins.

THE WORLD'S GREATEST CONTRAST. TEXT: 1 Cor. 15:19–26. (1) Adam brought death. (2) Christ brings life.

Worship Aids

CALL TO WORSHIP.   "The Lord is my strength and song and is become my salvation" (Ps. 118:14).

INVOCATION.   O holy God, whose power in the life of the Son did loose the bonds of sin and death and give to all children of faith eternal hope, open us this day to deeper meanings of resurrection, so that our trust might be made secure and our joy full, through Christ, our Lord.—E. Lee Phillips

OFFERTORY SENTENCE.   "And he commanded us to preach unto the people, and to testify that it is he which was ordained of God to be the Judge of quick and dead. To him give all the prophets witness, that through his name whosoever believeth in him shall receive remission of sins" (Acts 10:42–43).

OFFERTORY PRAYER.   God of the Resurrection, we pray that the offerings that we bring will help to tell the glad message everywhere that Christ is risen and that because of him life for everyone can be new and different. Grant that we may find the joy of sharing that good news.

PRAYER.   O Lord, our God! Here we are, celebrating Easter together in thy presence. This is the day when thou hast revealed thy beloved Son, our Lord Jesus Christ, to be the living Savior. He has taken upon himself all our sins, our human misery and death and in our place expiated, suffered, and once for all, conquered and dismissed them.

We know well our plight, and thou knowest it even better. Yet now we approach thee with thanksgiving for the freedom we have to look away from ourselves and to thee who hast wrought this mighty work for the world and for us also.

Grant sincerity to our speaking and our listening—that thy true word may govern, move, and replenish us in this hour—that it may comfort, encourage and admonish us all by its power—that our poor praise may be pleasing to thee! Let this come to pass among us and everywhere in town and country, nearby and afar, wherever people are gathered today to hear and to grasp thy promise of resurrection and life! Shed thy mercy upon thy people!—Karl Barth

LECTIONARY MESSAGE

Topic: Surprise or Confirmation
TEXT: Luke 24:1–12

The women on the way to the tomb thought that it would be a very ordinary first day of the week. After all, Sunday for them was more like our Monday. Yet an unfinished job lay before them. They must finish anointing the body of Jesus. In ancient Palestine, the Jews did not practice embalming. The body was prepared for the tomb by cleansing it and anointing it with perfumes. On Friday as the Sabbath began, the women did not have enough time to complete the work. Thus they were headed to the tomb early on Sunday morning after the end of the Sabbath observance.

I. One might have expected them to be prepared for what they found—an empty tomb. In his life Jesus had often spoken of his Resurrection to them. Somehow they had all been somewhat dense and dull students. The empty tomb should have been the ultimate confirmation of what Jesus had said to them. Instead it became for them a gigantic surprise.

There is so much about the Christian life that brings with it unusual surprises. Just when you think you understand it all, you encounter something that you had never thought of before. How shocked the peasants of Bethlehem must have been to learn that the baby born in one of their barns would turn out to be the longed-for Messiah, even though signs abounded that that would be the very case. The believer should always be ready for these surprises from God. Suddenly the heavens are opened, and we receive a direct revelation from God.

The reason one is surprised is that the revelation of God often comes in the everyday and in the commonplace. The women did not expect that commonplace first day of the week to take on such important meaning for the history of the Christian faith. Who of them would have thought that their trip to the tomb that early morning would shatter the history of the world? What a surprise!

II. Is it not strange how hard it is to turn from surprise to the realization of what has really happened? The women looked into the empty tomb, saw two men in dazzling apparel, and then they finally remembered Jesus' words to them. It took them a long time to overcome their initial surprise. Then the empty tomb was no longer perplexing to them. They saw the very revelation of God in the very emptiness of the tomb. Jesus was indeed alive. His message and mission were not over and dead. What should not have been a surprise in the first place suddenly became a confirmation of all that he had said and done.

III. As one comes to Easter, one can stand back in shock and surprise and say, "How can it be that the tomb is empty?" Even Easter can become dull and commonplace. Christians arrive to worship expecting just another worship service. Suddenly one is overwhelmed by the surprise—the tomb is still empty! Why, I knew that all the time! In the moments of surprise, however, one receives the revelation of God—he is alive and his kingdom has come.—James L. Blevins

SUNDAY: APRIL TWENTY-SIXTH

SERVICE OF WORSHIP

Sermon: My Son Died for You?
    TEXT: Rom. 8:31–39

Tony Campolo, in his lectures and book titled *Who Switched the Price Tags?* tells the story of a West Point graduate sent to Vietnam. He led his group of new recruits into the combat zones. He did his job well and tried his best to keep his men out of booby traps and ambushes. They were surprised, though, one night by a battalion of Viet Cong. All the men except one were able to get to cover and fight from a safer position. The one soldier left behind was severely wounded. From their positions, the young lieutenant and his men could hear the agonized cries of their wounded comrade. They wanted to reach him and tend to him, but leaving cover meant being subjected to the vicious cross fire of the enemy.

Finally, though, the young officer could stand it no more and went himself into the deadly area. He reached his wounded man and managed to drag him back toward safety. But just as he pushed his man into the trench, the lieutenant was fired upon, hit, and killed instantly.

Months later, the rescued soldier returned to the states. The parents of the dead officer, the young hero, learned that this man was in their vicinity, and they invited him over for dinner. They wanted to get to know this young man whose life was spared at such a great cost to them.

On the night of the dinner, their guest arrived—drunk. He was loud and boisterous and obnoxious. He told off-color jokes, was rude, and showed no concern for his suffering hosts. The parents of the dead hero were also brave, and they did the best they could to salvage the evening—to make it worthwhile. Their efforts went unrewarded.

The torturous visit did finally end, and the obscene guest left. As her husband closed the door, the mother collapsed in tears and cried, "To think that our precious son had to die for somebody like that."

Tony Campolo concludes, "But, before we go too far in our criticism of that ungrateful soldier, shouldn't we consider how much like him most of us are? Jesus died for us, yet we continue to sin. Jesus paid a terrible price to give us life eternal, yet we continue to behave obscenely. We owe him something better, but we fail to deliver what we should. We fail to reflect upon the cost of our salvation. If we did our lives would be radically different. The suffering of God did not end with Calvary. The sins we commit here and now bring pain to Jesus here and now."[1] In a similar way, might not God, our Father, be watching us this day and asking, like those distraught parents, "My Son died for you?"

I. "What, then, shall we say in response to this? If God is for us, who can be against us? He who did not spare his own Son, but gave him up for us all—how will he not also, along with him, graciously give us all things?" In his own way, Paul is restating what Jesus told his disciples: "Therefore, I tell you, do not worry about your life, what you will eat or drink; or about your body, what you will wear. . . . But seek first [God's] kingdom and his righteousness, and all these things will be given to you as well."

This is what God wants for us, has promised us, has provided us in the sacrifice of Jesus Christ. So what's the problem? At what point do we break down?

What causes us to seek other sources for security and pleasure? Why do we turn our backs and our hearts and our souls away from our Father? Why is it that having been invited to the meal, we show up drunk in our own pride, telling God obscene stories of our self-sufficiency, boasting about how we mistreat others in our midst? "My Son died for you?"

II. One of the primary contributors to our disregard for God's sacrifice—the price paid by Jesus on the cross—is our immature way of dealing with sin. We'll do almost anything to rationalize away our sins; to explain and justify them; to make them trivial. We "grade" different sins. Take that deranged man who recently raped and tortured some women, killed some others, and then shot himself. I'm certainly better than he is. Now there's a sinner. I haven't done anything like that.

But I wonder. Am I better than he is? Do I recognize anymore than he did the price of Christ on the cross? Do I hear any better the agonized cries of my Father in heaven when I turn away from Him in a fit of temper? or when I fail to worship? or when I am too busy—all legitimate, of course—to pray and receive His ministry? or when I've accepted the invitation to God's dinner and have shown up too drunk with myself to pay attention to my host? Gustaf Aulen has written this about sins:

> From the viewpoint of Christian faith it would be meaningless to divide "sins" into two classes: sins against God and sins against the neighbor. There is no sin against the neighbor which is not sin against God. The sin against the neighbor becomes sin just because it is against God."[2]

"My Son died for you?" Whenever we downplay or rationalize away sin, we are, at the same time, downplaying the sacrifice of Jesus Christ. In other words, if we don't think we're wounded or in danger, then we don't think that we need a lieu-

---

[1] Tony Campolo, *Who Switched the Price Tags?* (Waco: Word Books, 1986), 33–35.

[2] Gustaf Aulen, *The Faith of the Christian Church* (Philadelphia: Fortress Press, 1960), 232

tenant to come and drag us into the trench. Was Jesus just some poor fool, then, who happened to get caught between Jewish and Roman law? Hardly, for the warning from God is clear: ". . . for all have sinned and fall short of the glory of God . . ." We are wounded and trapped in no man's land and moaning for help.

III. Or maybe we have already been dragged to safety and have escaped death through the cross. Does that mean, then, that we forget about the sacrifice? The price paid? I don't think so. Were we offended by the actions of the obscene guest? Yes, I believe that we were. So listen to these words of Paul in Romans 6:

What shall we say, then? Shall we go on sinning so that grace may increase? By no means! We died to sin; how can we live in it any longer? Or don't you know that all of us who were baptized into Christ Jesus were baptized into his death? We were therefore buried with him through baptism into death in order that, just as Christ was raised from the dead through the glory of the Father, we too may live a new life.

"My Son died for you?" the Father asks. And then the Father himself answers, "Yes, my Son died for you. You were wounded and bleeding and dying, and my Son left his safety and went out into the cross fire for you and dragged you back. His reward? He was nailed to a cross." Philippians 2, in part, reads, "Your attitude should be the same as that of Christ Jesus. Who . . . made himself nothing, taking the very nature of a servant, being made in human likeness. And being found in appearance as a man, he humbled himself and became obedient to death—even death on a cross!"

The Father answers: "Yes, my Son died for you. Even when you fail to recognize that you are injured and dying, my Son still came and saved you from death." Perhaps the full force of the work of Christ should impact us here. Gustaf Aulen wrote that

if we listen to the testimony of Christian faith where it is given in its deepest

and clearest form, it is abundantly evident that the essential element is this: God's forgiveness is given, not to one who is sufficiently qualified to receive it, but to one who is entirely unworthy.[3]

You and I have been injured and have lain helpless, moving closer to death. But someone came and pulled us away from danger and into safety. For his efforts, though, he was killed. He was beaten. He was mocked. He was crucified. He was buried. You and I, are we sorry? Does this cause us sorrow, that our life should cause someone else's death? Yes, it should.

But wait—this is still the season of Easter. Our sorrow, like the disciples', turns to joy, because, as the angel told the women, "He is not here; he has risen just as he said." The Father invites us to his meal. He wants to know who it is that his Son died for. How will you come? How will I come? Drunk? Cursing? Foul? Hateful?

No, don't be that way. Let us come, instead, like one who is grateful for life. Let us come as one who reflects upon the cost of salvation. Let us come as one who rejoices with the Father for the love of the Father. "What, then, shall we say in response to this? . . . He who did not spare his own Son, but gave him up for us all— how will he not also, along with him, graciously give us all things? . . . For I am convinced that neither death nor life, neither angels nor demons, neither the present nor the future, nor any powers, nor anything else in all creation, will be able to separate us from the love of God that is in Christ Jesus our Lord."— Charles A. Layne

Illustration

LIKE HIM WE RISE. True loyalty to the Risen Lord is surely that displayed by Peter, who finally went the second half, who became ten times the person he was before Jesus' death; the loyalty of St. Stephen, who wasn't afraid of confrontation, and who under the rain of death-dealing

[3] Aulen, *Faith of the Christian Church*, 259.

stones cried out, Christlike, "Father, forgive"; the loyalty of so many early Christian men and women who, like Peter and Stephen, watered with their blood the seed of the church until it became the acorn that broke the mighty boulder that was the Roman Empire.—William Sloane Coffin

Sermon Suggestions

WHEN OUR RELIGION GETS US INTO TROUBLE.   TEXT: Acts 5:27–32, especially verse 29. (1) God has purposed an orderly and law-abiding society (see Rom. 13:1–6). (2) However, the specific purpose of God may transcend the human institution that ordinarily serves his will.

THE SOURCES OF GRACE AND PEACE. TEXT: Rev. 1:4–8. (1) Our grateful praise, verses 5b–6. (2) Our glorious hope, verse 7. (3) Our solid security, verse 8.

Worship Aids

CALL TO WORSHIP.   "Why do the nations conspire, and the peoples plot in vain? The kings of the earth set themselves, and the rulers take counsel together, against the Lord and his anointed, saying, 'Let us burst their bonds asunder, and cast their cords from us.' He who sits in the heavens laughs; the Lord has them in derision. Then he will speak to them in his wrath, and terrify them in his fury, saying, 'I have set my king on Zion, my holy hill' " (Ps. 2:1–6, RSV).

INVOCATION.   Teach us the secret of thy ways, O Lord, that listening we may hear quiet things and singing we may utter joyous things and witnessing we may speak holy things, as the Scripture speaks to us, and we behold the Christ.—E. Lee Phillips

OFFERTORY SENTENCE.   "I am Alpha and Omega, the beginning and the ending, saith the Lord, which is, and which was, and which is to come, the Almighty" (Rev. 1:8).

OFFERTORY PRAYER.   Lord, build thy kingdom with these gifts. Touch lives long hardened by rebellion, undergird missions in difficult places, and bring the peace of God to sinners saved by faith in the very Lamb of God.—E. Lee Phillips

PRAYER.   Lord, you have been our dwelling place in all generations. Before the mountains were brought forth or ever you had formed the earth and the world, from everlasting to everlasting you are God.

As we seek your presence in the meaning of prayer, we praise you for your faithfulness in spite of our faithlessness. We come affirming that though heaven and earth shall pass away, your Word shall not pass away. We know that you are steadfast in love and bountiful in mercy to every generation. With what love you love us that we are your children so created in your image that we know the blessing of prayer. What a joy to realize that we are not orphans but that we can pray, "Abba," which is to say, "Father."

But with the apostles we come confessing that we do not know how to pray as we ought—often we use prayer, even abuse prayer. There are times when we need no greater salvation than to be saved from our unwise prayers. We pray for we know not what. We pray selfishly, indulgently,   even   self-destructively. Many times your no is a far kinder answer than yes. Teach us the patience of unanswered prayer that we may learn to pray, really.

As Father, you are turned toward us in the eternity of your love. As the apostle concluded, "He who spared not his own Son but delivered him up for us all, how shall he not with him freely give us all things." If there is reluctance, it is in us. "You are more willing to give many times than we are to receive." Often, it seems, we are so anxious to make you hear us that we miss the most important part of prayer—hearing you—listening for your still small voice calling us to be and become.

Drop thy still dews of quietness till all our strivings cease; take from our souls the strain and stress, and let our ordered lives confess the beauty of thy peace. Through him who is our peace when he is our prayer. As he taught the apostles, so he is here now teaching us to pray, [The Lord's Prayer].—John Thompson

LECTIONARY MESSAGE

Topic: The Eternal Pessimist

TEXT: John 20:19–31

For centuries, Thomas has been called the doubter. One seldom hears his name in a church building without the subsequent adjective of description. The reading of the Gospel of John, however, presents a Thomas who was more a pessimist than a doubter. Every group needs one eternal pessimist to just keep the group's feet on the ground.

I. In John 14:3, Jesus gave to his disciples those famous words that ministers so often use in funeral sermons: "And when I go and prepare a place for you, I will come again and take you to myself . . ." In response to those beautiful words of Jesus, Thomas in essence said, "If you go away, how in the world will we ever find you!" (14:4). Once Jesus and the Twelve were east of the Jordan, they heard that Lazarus was ill unto death. The Jews in Jerusalem were involved in plotting death for Jesus. It would be dangerous to return to Bethany. After much debate among the Twelve about the implied danger, Thomas said, "Well, let us all go back and die together" (11:16).

II. Revelations of God often come to us in the midst of somberness and despair. At the very moment when pessimism seems to flourish, suddenly a note of optimism flows in. Someone has defined an optimist and a pessimist in the following way: The optimist gets up in the morning and says, "Good morning, dear Lord," while the pessimist says, "Good lord, it's morning." Some disciples seem to demand more proof that God is out there and at work. We can think of Gideon and his fleece or a Moses going before Pharaoh with a stick that turned into a snake.

In any case, Thomas has always been in good biblical company. He had always to be convinced of God's declaration and intentions. The church has always found it so easy at Easter to condemn Thomas's desire to touch the wounds in Jesus' hands and side. Yet somewhere deep down at Easter, many would desire to do the same. It would be so much easier to believe if we had some physical proof.

III. Yet at Easter the words of Jesus keep coming to us, "Blessed are those who have not seen and yet believe" (20:29). Jesus revealed himself at the very moment of Thomas's greatest despair. The other disciples were so filled with optimism because they had seen the resurrected Jesus. Thomas could not trust himself to leave his pessimism and receive the good news. Finally Jesus stood before him and showed him his wounds.

Not all disciples of Jesus are full of faith and optimism. At Easter time, the preacher must remember those standing in the shadows full of pessimism about God's role in the world. How joyful it is, however, when the pessimistic Thomases of the world also receive the Easter message and celebrate the Resurrection of the Lord. The pessimists should know that even in their darkest moment, God will seek to reveal himself to them. Perhaps the revelation will not be so dramatic as that given to Thomas, but we know by faith that in our darkest hour, he will be there.—James L. Blevins

SUNDAY: MAY THIRD

SERVICE OF WORSHIP

Sermon: Is Love Ever Really Enough?
TEXT: Gen. 24:62–66

I. This message addresses the myth that states, So long as you genuinely love each other, everything will always work out. One of the most tender scenes in *Fiddler on the Roof* occurs when, on the night of his daughter's marriage, Tevye asks his own wife of twenty-five years, "Do you love me?" Their marriage had been arranged and, as Tevye explained to his wife, "My father and mother said that we would learn to love each other. And now I'm asking, Golde, do you love me?"

After reciting some of the ways her love for him has been expressed over those twenty-five years, Golde replies, "I suppose I do." Then Tevye responds in a chorus, which she takes up with him, "After twenty-five years, it's nice to know."

And it is! It is nice to know that you are loved. In fact, it is absolutely essential to the survival of the human spirit to know and experience love! And yet it is nothing more than a myth to believe that love is all you need to build and maintain a durable relationship of any kind—especially a marital and family relationship.

One of the most fascinating love stories in all the Bible clearly illustrates that love is not always enough to sustain a deep and enduring relationship. If there was ever a marriage made in heaven, this was it—the marriage between Isaac and Rebekah! It was a marriage that got off to a wonderful start. But then, as this couple neared their golden wedding anniversary, the marriage was threatened by disillusionment, misunderstanding, deceit, and miscommunication. Only by the grace of God is love strong enough to resist those self-destructive forces.

According to the biblical record, Isaac was forty years old when he was married (Gen. 25:20). It was his father who even-tually took the initiative in finding Isaac a wife. In keeping with the customs of that time, Abraham appointed his most reliable servant as matchmaker. He was to go back to Chaldea to find a wife for Isaac.

The servant was given very specific instructions. This father wanted a bride for his son who, in character, personality, background, and religious faith, was a good match for Isaac. He believed that a proper matching was an essential foundation for a successful marriage. He knew that who a person marries does make a difference.

Every couple who is about to be married harbors dreams of life together. They envision a life filled with shared interests, common goals and values, mutual cares and concerns. Many newlyweds feel lucky on their wedding day—lucky to have met someone who understands them, shares their likes and dislikes, someone who is so obviously right for them!

But no matter how ideally suited they are, at some point every husband and wife realize that theirs is not a perfect match. They realize that they do not always agree. They do not think, feel, and behave the same way. The merging of their two personalities, preferences, and backgrounds is much harder than they ever imagined. Many are shocked and devastated when the bubble bursts. Some secretly confide in some friend or counselor: This is not the same person I married.

Someone once said that while love is blind, marriage is not! It's not always that marriage partners do not see certain truths about their spouse before the wedding. Many times, they simply choose not to see them. Swept up in the surge of passion, they do not want to focus on anything but the positive.

Love does not always conquer all. Most couples who get divorced were in love when they first were married. Just being in love is never the primary reason for marriage.

II. The Bible consistently stresses the importance of compatibility in relationships. The Apostle Paul specifically urged the Corinthian Christians to avoid marriage with non-Christians (2 Cor. 6:7). Recent statistics indicate that the odds are not in favor of so-called mixed marriages. The rate of divorce, separation, or annulment for these marriages is almost four times greater than for marriage between those of the same faith.

There should also be common interests with your spouse. With both partners working in most cases today, the only time a couple has together is in their leisure. If you do not marry someone with whom you can be a friend as well as a roommate and financial partner, you are headed for trouble.

I do not mean that you must be identical to your mate at every point. Nothing would be so boring as a relationship between two people who are exactly alike. It simply means, as Abraham realized, that the more similarities there are, the more common ground there is. The more perfectly matched you are, the less traumatic will be the adjustments that have to be made and the better chance you have for a successful marriage.

Even a successful marriage will encounter problems, as the biblical record illustrates. Isaac and Rebekah married and their love for each other continued to grow (v. 67). You may find that difficult to believe in light of the fact that their marriage was arranged for them by their families.

But you may also find it interesting to note this. This is the first time in Scripture that love is even linked with marriage. Apparently, the idea of love as the basis for a lifelong union between a man and a woman was a rather late development.

Neither Isaac nor Rebekah had ever laid eyes on the other until after all the arrangements had been made and Rebekah came to Canaan for the actual wedding. But the love that developed between them was genuine and enduring, even in light of the problems that developed.

III. Their twin sons, Esau and Jacob, were at least forty years old when the marriage faced its most serious threat (Gen. 26:34). The biblical record describes the problem in simple and concrete terms (Genesis 27).

It was over the children. Isaac had always been more drawn to Esau, the firstborn of the twins. He was a rugged outdoorsman, extroverted and liked by everyone. On the other hand, Rebekah found it easier to be close to Jacob. To complicate matters, the brothers had always been extremely competitive with each other. The nature of their relationship had been determined from birth. Esau came first, but Jacob was right behind, prophetically holding his brother's foot as if to hold him back so that he could get ahead of Esau.

In the Old Testament era, it was common for the father to give a blessing to the son who would succeed him as head of the family at the father's death. The blessing always went to the firstborn son. The blessing conveyed a tangible and legal power to the one to whom it was given. And once it was given, it could never be rescinded.

One day, Rebekah overheard Isaac tell Esau that it was time for him to pass on the blessing. But since Isaac was blind, Rebekah and Jacob seized the opportunity to deceive the old man and steal the blessing from Esau. Through a clever series of manipulative acts and disguises, they succeeded in taking what was not rightfully theirs.

What this woman and her son did was a blatant and intentional act of deception and fraud. It broke the sacred trust that is essential to an honest relationship between a husband and wife. And above all else, it demonstrated a basic contempt for the family.

Whether you are aware of it or not, everything you do, say, think, or feel reveals whether you see the world in terms of "I, me, and mine" or in terms of "we, us, and ours." And it is your chosen point of view—that is, whether you think in terms of family or self—and without regard to the number of people living under the same roof—that makes a family a family.

Families are failing because we are failing to see the world from a family perspective. We have believed the world's lies and concluded that it's every man for himself, and if I don't take care of me, nobody else will! That's the idea that Rebekah and Isaac seem to have adopted and that they apparently passed down to their children.

It did not matter to Rebekah and Jacob what family tradition dictated. It did not matter how heartbroken Isaac would be if he ever learned of the fraud. It did not matter how severe and painful would be the negative impact upon Esau to have this precious, irrevocable, paternal blessing stolen from him The only thing that mattered was to get what they wanted for themselves!

Listen! Reverence, respect, and love for the family requires the decision to value the family over everything else in the world, including your individual personhood. A family is dedicated to the primacy of a family point of view.

The reason we are so committed to the family is that we know that the family nurtures and encourages the development of each family member. As each individual is dedicated to family welfare, the family is committed to individual development and security. The primary goal of the family is to make sure that everyone is given the chance to live and love happily within the family system!

I warn you: If your family does not come first—if the needs of any individual family member come before the needs of the whole family—your family will not last! It is not merely an issue of setting priorities. The issue is one of making difficult choices for your family. There can only be one number one. Is it your family?—Gary C. Redding

Illustrations

SHARING LIFE.   "We ought to acquaint ourselves with the beautiful," said Goethe. "We ought to contemplate it with rapture and attempt to raise ourselves up to the height of it.

"In order to gain strength for that, we must keep ourselves thoroughly unselfish. We must not make it our own but rather seek to communicate it, indeed, to make a sacrifice of it to those who are dear and precious to us."

Here are lovely and wise words. If we are selfish with beauty, if we try to keep it for ourselves exclusively, we may even suffer the loss of a capacity for it. Selfishness defeats itself.

It is selfishness that spoils everything. In trying to exclude others we shut ourselves out. To be snobbish in our enjoyment of the higher things of life is to lose the power of enjoying.

All divine things can be kept only by sharing them, giving them away, and the more we give the more we have. Pleasure may be selfish, but joy dies when we try to fence it in and keep it.—Joseph Fort Newton

FRIENDSHIP EVANGELISM.   A friend of mine says, "I just make as many deep friendships with people as I can. Then when life perks some big problem to the surface in their lives, I'm ready and available to stand with them. And somewhere along the way I get my chance to share what my Friend Christ can make out of the raw material of problems." Dozens of people have become alive in Christ and will live forever because of his friendship evangelism.—Lloyd J. Ogilvie

Sermon Suggestions

ARRESTED!   TEXT: Acts 9:1–20. (1) Situation: Saul's murderous purpose. (2) Complication: Interruption on the road to Damascus. (3) Resolution: (a) the appearing of the Living Christ, (b) the ministry of Ananias, (c) calling and conversion.

THE WORSHIP OF JESUS CHRIST, THE LAMB OF GOD.   TEXT: Rev. 5:11–14. (1) Its extent—universal, verses 11 and 13. (2) Its nature—perfect (sevenfold), verse 12b. (3) Its appropriateness—manifesting the redemptive heart of God, verse 12a.

Worship Aids

CALL TO WORSHIP. "Thou hast turned for me my mourning into dancing; thou hast put off my sackcloth and girded me with gladness; to the end that my glory may sing praise to thee and not be silent. O Lord my God, I will give thanks unto thee forever" (Ps. 30:11–12).

INVOCATION. O God, in you we live and move and have our being. We come here not only to affirm and celebrate your presence in this holy place but also to affirm and celebrate your presence in all of life. In the beginning you created the heavens and the earth; in the fullness of time, you sent forth your only Son. For all generations you speak and manifest a Word, so that though heaven and earth shall pass away, your Word shall persevere. In this privilege of worship may we so contemplate your Word in its majesty, its power, its mystery, its saving grace that we discover ourselves lost in wonder, love, and praise. Praise be to you: Father, Son, and Holy Spirit.—John Thompson

OFFERTORY SENTENCE. "And I beheld, and heard the voice of many angels round about the throne and the beasts and the elders; and the number of them ten thousand times ten thousand, and thousands of thousands; saying with a loud voice, Worthy is the Lamb that was slain to receive power, and riches, and wisdom, and strength, and honour, and glory, and blessing" (Rev. 5:11–12).

OFFERTORY PRAYER. O God, may our gifts of time, abilities, and money be worthy of the sacrifice of Jesus Christ for us all. Receive and bless these offerings such as they are, to your glory and honor.

PRAYER. Holy Sculptor, the dance of your fingerprints molds and colors the landscape of our springtime. Bare trees have silently and quickly put on grand coats of heavy green. Tulips and daffodils voice their praise in nodding full blooms. Dogwoods, loaded with quiet pure colors, grace noble the yards and streets of our community. There is a mystery and smile about it all, Master Creator, and we see your face and delight at every turn. Yet all the glory and might of spring creation is but brief prelude to our Lord's victorious Resurrection and eternal reign over defeated death and new, eternal life. We, like your faithful creation, leap forth from the winter of our spirits to rejoice in the good news of Easter. All glory, laud, and honor to thee, Redeemer King.

Generous and gentle Redeemer, Lord of the cross, your death reminds us squarely of the cost and consequence of our sin. We long to confess our sin and know again the cleansing and release of forgiveness. Accept our confessions . . .

God of all providence and unity, we voice prayers for our neighbors, for the family of faith that meets next door; for our friends across the street who are about being family and home to those without either.

Holy God of resurrection hope and life, grant us all will to choose life and to be about giving life in your name and Spirit. In Christ we offer our worship and prayer.—William M. Johnson

LECTIONARY MESSAGE

Topic: Asking More Than Once
TEXT: John 21:15–19

Parents find no more grating task than having to tell their children over and over again to do certain tasks. Teachers often encounter the same kind of situation in the classroom. One might have explained the problem ten different ways, only to encounter students who are still dumbfounded because they have not listened.

I. Jesus often became frustrated with his disciples as students. Mark's Gospel, in particular, portrays the disciples as dull and dense. Jesus exclaimed on one occasion to the disciples, "Do you not yet perceive or understand? Are your hearts hardened?" (Mark 8:17). In John's Gospel (14:9), Jesus said to Philip, "Have I been with you so long, and yet you do not know me, Philip?" Thus, we should not be surprised that even after the Resurrection, Jesus had to ask Peter the leader of the Twelve three times, "Do you love me?"

II. Peter, of course, had always been the brash disciple. His words often got "way down the road ahead of his actions." We often remember Peter most for his denial of Jesus as the cock crowed. Yet he was the only one to take up the sword to defend Jesus from the temple guards. He was bold enough to follow Jesus to the place of the actual Jewish trial at the house of Caiaphas the high priest. However, he seemed unprepared for the soft words of a teenage maid whispered to others around the fire. Yes, Peter would have fought to his death for Jesus, but often evil comes to us in unexpected ways. Peter did end up that fateful night denying his Lord.

Jesus wanted to be certain of Peter's commitment. Much of his mission would be depending upon it. Peter, like so many of us, grew a bit angry because of being asked the same question over and over again. Remember how as a child you hated to be told over and over again to clean your room up or do some other tiresome task? Jesus wanted Peter to know that discipleship now would involve even greater demands and sacrifices. Was Peter ready for that task?

III. Often one must hear a question several times before it finally sinks in. Peter must have finally been grateful that Jesus kept asking the question. The Christian today also must be glad that Christ comes to us over and over again. He does not give up on the first try. There would be many not sitting in the church pews if certain faithful Christians had not kept asking the question even when they received a *no* answer. Christ never gives up on the unbelieving or even a weak disciple. The question comes over and over again, "Do you love me?" That question is one that makes you stop and ponder and not answer too quickly. For ultimately a *yes* answer will involve demands and sacrifices.

Peter's later life, as recorded in Acts, shows that his *yes* answer carried weight for him. He demonstrated his love for Christ in deed and action. Perhaps he realized how important that day was in his life when he answered Jesus' same question three times with affirmation instead of denying him three times.—James L. Blevins

SUNDAY: MAY TENTH

SERVICE OF WORSHIP

Sermon: And This Is Love

TEXT: Song of Solomon 2:2–4, TEV

What is love? One man defined it as a four-letter word consisting of two consonants (*L* and *V*), two vowels (*O* and *E*), and two fools—you and me! Another man said that if life is one crazy thing after another, love must be two crazy things after each other. A cartoon depicts two people, a man and a woman, on a dogsled in Alaska. The man said to the woman, "I'd drive my dog team one hundred miles to say 'I love you,' " to which the woman responded, "That's a lot of mush!"

Is that what love is? Two fools, you and me; two crazy things after each other; a lot of mush? What is love? One of the most beautiful biblical answers to that question is the Song of Solomon.

Much controversy has swirled around this unique Old Testament book. Some see the story to be an allegory about the love of God for his chosen people. Others feel the story is an actual depiction of human love between a man and a woman. I believe that it is both. The Song of Solomon is first of all a collection of love songs describing the love of a man for a women. This human love story becomes an allegory describing God's love for his people.

The inclusion of the book in the Old Testament canon demonstrates the sanctity of human love and the sacredness of the relationship between a man and a woman. And it provides some insight into the key ingredients of genuine love.

I. *In true love, there is appeal.* In verse 2 the man, addressing the woman, declared, "Like a lily among thorns is my darling among women" (TEV). She had an unusual appeal to him. Psychologists use the term *halo effect* to speak of this phenomenon. According to the halo effect, your general feeling about someone else influences your evaluation of his or her specific attributes or abilities. If you love a woman, you will probably think that she is smarter and better looking than you would if you didn't like her. If you love a man, you will probably believe him to be more intelligent and more handsome than if you didn't like him. In real love, the other person has a unique appeal to you.

Judith Viorst, writing in *Redbook*, humorously illustrated this quality of love. She defined the difference between infatuation and love like this: "Infatuation is when you think he's as sexy as Robert Redford, as smart as Henry Kissinger, as noble as Ralph Nader, as funny as Woody Allen, and as athletic as Jimmy Connors. Love is when you realize he's as sexy as Woody Allen, as smart as Jimmy Connors, as funny as Ralph Nader, as athletic as Henry Kissinger, and nothing like Robert Redford — but you'll take him anyway."

When you love someone, you see the best in that person. There is an appeal about that person that causes you to say, "Like a lily among the thorns is my darling among woman."

II. *In real love, there is attention.* The woman in the Song of Solomon said of her sweetheart, "Like an apple tree among the trees of the forest, so is my dearest compared to other men. I love to sit in its shadow" (v. 3, TEV). When you love someone, you want to be with him/her, and your thoughts are often tuned in to that person. As one modern sage put it, "She loves him if, when she's not thinking about him, she's thinking about him."

A popular comedian once told the story of a young man in Java who spotted a beautiful young lady walking down the road. He fell in right behind her and followed her for over a mile. Finally, the young lady wheeled around and demands, "Why do you dog my footsteps?" With fervent emotion he replied, "Because you are the loveliest thing I have ever seen, and I have fallen madly in love with you at first sight. Please be mine." The young lady responded, "You only have to look behind you and you will see my younger sister who is ten times more beautiful than I." He turned quickly to see as ugly a girl as he had ever seen. "What a mockery!" he said to the beautiful maiden, "You lied to me!" "So did you," she replied. "If you were so madly in love with me, why did you turn around?"

When love is real, you won't turn around. Your attention will be on the one you love, for you will enjoy sitting in the shadow of her presence.

III. *In real love, there is action.* The lover in the Song of Solomon did not simply talk about his concern. He showed it. For his sweetheart declared of him, "He brought me to his banquet hall and raised the banner of love over me" (v. 4, TEV). Genuine love not only thinks about the other person. Love acts out that concern in providing for the person's needs.

This is the chief contrast between real love and reel love, between genuine love and the Hollywood version. Reel love asks, "What can I get?" Real love asks, "What can I give?" Reel love asks, "How does it feel?" Real love asks, "What can I do?"

What is love? Three plain evidences of love are appeal, attention, and action. And that's no mush!—Brian L. Harbour

Illustrations

WALLS. I suppose that until the Kingdom comes in our imperfect society, prisons will be necessary. What disturbs me most are not the walls described above but the walls which have so often brought these persons to committing offenses against society and which confine many others. These are walls of poverty, with all its limiting circumstances; walls of prejudice whether racial, religious, or economic; walls of substandard education and early dropouts; walls of dismal and overcrowded housing and slum surroundings; walls of oversized families with neither material goods nor loving attention enough to go around; walls where alcohol and drunkenness do their disastrous work; walls of tension and bickering in both poor families and those of the well-to-do; walls of too great sternness without understanding; walls of too great leniency without discipline. Such walls, found throughout the land, are more confining than any prison.—Georgia Harkness

IMAGINATIVE SYMPATHY.   Acquire and cultivate the power to put yourself in the other person's place. That imaginative sympathy is the key to life, in fact, is life itself, for life is sensitiveness. One of the secrets of Jesus' power over us is just this quality of imaginative sympathy. But it is not just sympathy in imagination—it is sympathy in fact, or, literally, "suffering with." Our hunger becomes his; our bondages are his very own—"I was hungered, and ye gave me meat: . . . in prison, and ye came unto me." To the degree that we acquire and cultivate this spirit of imaginative sympathy are we Christian and can get along with other people.—E. Stanley Jones

Sermon Suggestions

PROVING   THE   WRONG   PROPHECY.
TEXT: Acts 13:15–16, 26–33, especially verse 27, RSV. (1) We may unwittingly or by choice fulfill prophecies that are against us, like "the residents of Jerusalem and their leaders" (e.g., "The wages of sin is death," or, "If you sow to your own flesh, you will reap corruption from the flesh"). (2) We may by choice reap the benefits of prophecies that are for us, like those receiving "the good news that what God promised to our ancestors he has fulfilled for us, their children" (e.g., "The free gift of God is eternal life in Jesus Christ our Lord," or, "If you sow to the Spirit, you will reap eternal life from the Spirit").

A VISION OF HEAVEN.   TEXT: Rev. 7:9–17. The redeemed are (1) many in number, (2) from all nations, (3) victorious and full of praise, (4) those who owe their salvation to Jesus Christ, (5) active in heaven, (6) totally and forever secure.

Worship Aids

CALL TO WORSHIP.   "The Lord is my shepherd, I shall not want" (Ps. 23:1).

INVOCATION.   O Lord, who art present to help us in every way, help us now. O Lord, who dost guide us by the Spirit and the Word and in prayer's soft measured step, make us aware of the Savior beside us and pour out thy wisdom upon us, our Maker and our God.—E. Lee Phillips

OFFERTORY SENTENCE.   "And all the angels stood around the throne and round the elders and the four living creatures, and they fell on their faces before the throne and worshiped God, saying, 'Amen! Blessing and glory and wisdom and thanksgiving and honor and power and might be to our God for ever and ever! Amen' " (Rev. 7:11–12, RSV).

OFFERTORY PRAYER.   Merciful God, bless the gifts, the givers, and all who channel this offering into the kingdom's work that those who are the recipients may sense the love of God and recognize the stamp of eternal worth through the cross of Jesus.

PRAYER.   Father God, who walks with us through the desert places of life and makes them to be fruitful as the fertile fields, we come before you with thankful hearts. You have blessed us with the riches of human life and tenderness that our hearts might rise in gratitude to you. Sorrow and troubles have come to us, but you have turned them to our spiritual good. Indeed through them we have seen again and again the ministering hands of your people extended in help and concern like those of angels ministering to the needs that would otherwise destroy us. Death has made our hearts desolate, but you have wiped away the tears from our eyes and have brought us again unto living hope by the Resurrection of Jesus Christ from the dead. In moments of reflection when we realize how much you have done for us, we declare that we will never again mistrust you or doubt your willingness and power to bless us. Whatever the future may have in store for us, whether our days be few or many, full of joy or sorrow, of pleasure or pain, we hold fast to the remembrance of what you have done in our lives and the promise of your presence with us in all things. There will be times when the bright truth of the morning will fade in the midday struggle. Yet in the deepest disasters of life, in the midst of our daily failures enable us to keep hold on the grand truth that our lives are hid with Christ in you.

In these moments of thought and worship this morning, move us to fresh ambition. Assure us of the Father's love and lead some soul here this morning to the wonder and joy of your forgiving grace. Lift all our hearts to new levels of wonder. Strengthen our resolves to do your will as children of obedience. Send us back into the world with a new vision of our purpose under Christ; a new understanding of your word of guidance and salvation; and a new hope in Christ that will enable us to bravely face the mystery of unknown tomorrows and a commitment to let Christ be Lord of all and in all.— Henry Fields

LECTIONARY MESSAGE

Topic: Revelation in Blasphemy?

TEXT: John 10:22–30

It was December, and Jesus was walking on Solomon's porch in the Temple with his disciples. They were there to celebrate the cleansing of the Temple as accomplished years before by Judas Maccabeus. The Jewish opponents of Jesus were trying to plot to find some charge to condemn him to death. To date, there was little to charge him with. He was highly popular with the people because of the mighty work he had accomplished. However, so far they had not believed even his signs and wonders. The Mes-

siah, when he came, would confirm his authority through signs and wonders. One would then expect revelation to come in this traditional form. Yet the Jewish leaders had not perceived it.

I. Jesus, however, chose to reveal himself in what the Jews considered blasphemous words—"I and the Father are one." Throughout their history the Jews had set forth monotheism—there is but one God. Thus, blasphemy was any human being claiming God's power for himself. On hearing blasphemy, the pious Jew was to rip his clothing in protest. The penalty for such a crime was death by stoning. By claiming to be one with the Father, Jesus had committed this terrible crime. Yet even in these so-called blasphemous words, he was revealing himself to the Jews.

We often catch a revelation of God in times and places where we least expect it. What Jew would have considered meeting Jesus face to face in such obvious blasphemous words? Yet where they least expected it, they met the unique claims of Jesus. They had missed the obvious revelation in his signs and wonders. Now perhaps in this so-called blasphemy, they realized for the first time who he claimed to be.

II. Sometimes, like Moses, we have to approach God from the backside. His radiance is too great to look upon his face. At least, we must put on a veil to protect us from the brightness of his presence. Some people seem to have to back into the kingdom of God. For some of the Jews, Jesus' words were too harsh, and they could only turn away. Perhaps others, once they got over the shock of hearing blasphemy, responded to the revelation of Christ as Son of God.

III. It is much easier to believe when one is in the fold and knows the friendly voice of the shepherd. The Jews had difficulty because they were on the outside of the fold looking in. Thus, the words of Jesus for most of them were just blasphemous expressions deserving of death. However, even those on the inside, such as the disciples, had their difficulties as well. Yet Jesus kept coming over and over again both to the insiders and the outsiders. He had a special relationship with his sheep that even death could not harm.

It was hard for the Jews to realize all the truths that day in the Temple. They could not see the special relationship that Jesus had with his own. They could hear only words of blasphemy. They were duly shocked! Yet perhaps for some the revelation of Christ filtered through to their minds, and some of the outsiders became insiders.—James L. Blevins

SUNDAY: MAY SEVENTEENTH

SERVICE OF WORSHIP

Sermon: Hearing the Call of the Shepherd

Text: John 10

Who was Jesus? *Time* magazine, in the wake of the furor over *The Last Temptation of Christ*, asked that question. They polled lots of New Testament scholars and got lots of answers, as you might expect. He was a wandering teacher, compassionate toward the poor—a first-century Gandhi. Others think he was a cynic, questioning all authority; others, a prophet predicting the end of the world; others, a fairly orthodox Jewish rabbi. *The Last Temptation* (the novel, that is) shows Jesus to be a mentally disturbed romantic who later becomes an apocalypticist and then a martyr.

I do not condemn those who study the New Testament sincerely and come up with ideas different from my own. All I can say is that the Christ who appears in these Scriptures making such radical claims for himself is real to me and has influenced my life immeasurably. Who is Jesus? Let's hear him speak for himself.

Jesus begins by telling a parable about a sheepfold. Palestinians who kept sheep often had a wall around their front yard, sometimes with hedges on the top of it and a strong gate in the front. The sheep could be herded in at night and guarded easily that way, both from two- and four-footed predators. A robber would have to climb over the wall to get in, but every morning the shepherd would enter the gate. Palestinian shepherds, with small flocks for the most part, often named each sheep and knew them individually. They would come out of the gate at the sound of his voice but then would group up and follow him as he led them to the day's pasture.

I. Jesus made two applications of this true-to-life description. I am the gate or the door, he said, and he meant this in two ways.

(a) Jesus meant that he was the only legitimate way into the sheep. Any legitimate person could enter through the gate of the sheepfold, but a burglar would have to climb over the wall. Just so, anyone who desires true knowledge of the sheep must go by way of Jesus; he is the only door. All other avenues to the hearts of men and women, all other remedies for the human condition, are false.

How can you say that? says the world—how can Jesus be the only way? Aren't there good people and good ideas in any religion? Yes, we reply—all that God has created is good. His world is filled with good things, good people, good ideas. Yet we misuse them and turn them into something evil. Just as a child's toy, built for thirty-pound bodies, will buckle and break if I sit on it, so God's created things won't bear the weight we try to put on them. Money can't replace God; job security can't replace God; other people can't replace God; yet we try to make these things carry the load in our lives that he would carry. A young man has never come to Christ because he doesn't think he needs it. His life is fulfilling, he says; he has a good job, plenty of friends, a very fulfilling commitment to the volunteer fire department—why does he need Jesus?

(b) Jesus provides the reason (verse 10)—he is the door to the truly abundant life. Not to wealth, fame, ease, or ecstasy, necessarily, but to true life. The reason is, of course, that he made us in his image, and until we fulfill that image we are less than we could be. It's as if life were a hall filled with doors, one marked fame, one money, etc.; if we open the one marked Jesus, what we find inside is our true self—not Richard the scholar or Richard the athlete or Richard the rich man or any of the things I think I am or I wish I could be—we don't find any of those false selves. I find Richard as Jesus created me, and you find yourself as God made you. That's true life, and only the one who drew up the blueprint for your particular self can show you how you really could be happy.

II. Jesus makes another application of his parable (verse 11). Not only the gate but also the shepherd—the one all of us ought to follow wherever he leads. He gives us two qualifications for the job, two reasons why we should follow him.

(a) He is willing to give his all for us. You all know how important that is in the business world. When I get the feeling that someone isn't really trying or doesn't really care, I usually take my business elsewhere. But when you find someone who loves his/her craft and seems to care more about doing a quality job than about emptying your pockets, you should stick with them.

Jesus gave his life up for us, knowing that most of the world would reject him. He promised that he would never leave us or forsake us and that no power on earth could snatch us from his care. Self-help fads come and go; new religions are born and fall by the wayside; fame is fickle, money is unstable—but Jesus is our savior for eternity.

(b) He also says that we should follow him because he knows each of us. It is incomprehensible how this could be, but it is true. H. E. Fosdick compares Christ to the mechanic in the electric plant at Niagara Falls. Fosdick talks about walking through and wondering at how anyone could keep up with so much machinery. "Ah, it's nothing," said the chief mechanic. "I know every bolt in here by name." Because he made us, because he loved us, and because he laid down his life for each of us, he knows us all by name—240 million Americans, 1 billion Chinese, or the number gathered here. He knows us all and he loves each of us dearly. A shepherd like that is certainly the one to follow wherever he leads.

Jesus the Door, Jesus the Good Shepherd—no, I can't prove any of that; but I would not follow Jesus the cynic or Jesus the schizophrenic prophet from *The Last Temptation*. No, faith depends upon a Jesus who could support that claim by his death and Resurrection, and faith in that Jesus cannot be proven; it can only be awakened in us as we answer the call of the Great Shepherd of the sheep.—Richard Vinson

Illustrations

DEFENDING THE FLOCK. Dr. W. M. Thomson in *The Land and the Book* writes, "I have listened with intense interest to their graphic descriptions of downright and desperate fights with these savage beasts. And when the thief and the robber come (and come they do), the faithful shepherd has often to put his life in his hand to defend his flock. I have known more than one case where he had literally to lay it down in the contest. A poor faithful fellow last spring, between Tiberias and Tabor, instead of fleeing, actually fought three Bedawin robbers until he was hacked to pieces with their khanjars, and died among the sheep he was defending." The true shepherd never hesitated to risk and even to lay down his life for his sheep.—William Barclay

JESUS AS PASTOR. When one recalls the pressures and dangers confronting the church addressed by this Gospel (John 15:18–25; 16:1–4), the model of Jesus as the pastor who will stay with the flock, whatever the cost, is a most appropriate one, as is the warning about pastors-for-pay who cut and run when problems pile up. In fact, there has never been a time when the images were not appropriate, and there has never been a time when there were not pastors who remembered. Before Roman sword or Nazi boot, burning crosses or threat of exile, economic reversal or police brutality, these have refused to abandon the flock.

And then there are the hirelings. — Fred B. Craddock

Sermon Suggestions

THE GODS HAVE COME DOWN TO US. TEXT: Acts 14:8–18. (1) *The story*: Because something miraculous happened through the agency of the bringers of the good news, the people who witnessed this event thought Barnabas and Paul were gods and tried to worship them, despite all protests. (2) *The meaning*: When good and unusual things happen through the ministry of God's servants, people often ascribe to these agents of God powers they do not possess and thus tempt these servants of God to pride and presumption. (3) *The application*: God's representatives must never forget who they are, their vulnerability, and the perennial temptation of people to pervert truth to personal ends.

THE GOD WHO MAKES ALL THINGS NEW. TEXT: Rev. 21:1–6. (1) God renews all creation. (2) God makes the Church, the new Jerusalem, beautiful and holy. (3) God, by his presence, removes all sorrows, threats, and pain from his people. (4) God pours into the lives of those who thirst for him eternally refreshing springs of the water of life.

Worship Aids

CALL TO WORSHIP. "The Lord is nigh unto all them that call upon him, to all that call upon him in truth" (Ps. 145:18).

INVOCATION. Father, as we come this morning to worship and praise your name, we ask that you defend us in all ways as we live in the world and face its demands. Defend our minds and hearts from thoughts and feelings unworthy of children of God. Defend our hands from deeds that would diminish the structure of your kingdom and place stumbling blocks in the pathway of others. Defend our tongues from utterances that would destroy reputations and bring half-truths to the surface that only confuse situations. May we ever speak the truth in love and use our speech to glorify you even as we uplift our fellow man through what we say. Defend eyes from dwelling on the unsavory sights that abound in life and from seeing only what is ugly and evil. Help us to focus on beauty and goodness so that seeing them we might follow their pathway and become more like the Lord. Defend our loves from focusing their power on what is base and corrupting and destructive and that ultimately destroy us. Lead us to love what is noble and clean, what is high and good, what will enhance life for the betterment of others rather than make it harder for all. Indeed, this day and every day may we focus on Jesus, the mighty defender of us all, and follow him as we do life, even as did those whom long ago he taught to pray ... [the Lord's Prayer]. — Henry Fields

OFFERTORY SENTENCE. "And I heard a great voice out of heaven saying, Behold, the tabernacle of God is with men, and he will dwell with them, and they shall be his people, and God himself shall be with them, and be their God" (Rev. 21:3).

OFFERTORY PRAYER. O God, our Redeemer, we know you are here with us in all that is happening, present with us when times are good or bad. May we be as much with you, pouring our hearts into your work, even as you pour your grace into our lives.

PRAYER. Gracious and glorious God, we praise and magnify thy holy name. More has been given us than ever we can acknowledge, thus do our prayers of gratitude rise continually unto thee.

We are so aware of our failures, Lord. In holy justice and tender mercy hear our prayer of contrition as in confession we bow before thee. Forgive those times we asked for more than we needed, wanting more than we could use; said what we didn't mean, meant less than we claimed, and vowed more than we intended; listened to all the words of the day before studying the Word of God; let comfort outweigh the demands of thy will; saw poverty and pain and passed by on the other side, thus failing to meet Christ where Christ is always to be found.

Have mercy upon us, Lord, for we have strayed from thy precepts, turning to self-centeredness rather than to divine directives. Restore our vision, renew our faith, and plant in us a new resolve that takes Jesus as its companion and the cross as its banner and marches forth in service of that kingdom no force can vanquish. In the name of the Nazarene.—E. Lee Phillips

LECTIONARY MESSAGE

Topic: Can Love Be a Commandment?

TEXT: John 13:31–35

One certainly does not expect to hear a law or commandment to love. Commandments usually deal with things that are forbidden or things to avoid. Jesus was most surprising here in giving a positive commandment to love. People are always writing advice columnists in the newspaper asking for a list of ten commandments for teenagers, drivers, or senior citizens. It seems that if we can just get life down into ten commandments on paper, then everything will be so much easier. Then one will know exactly what to do to be considered a righteous person.

I. The way of legalism has always been easier than the way of freedom as proposed by Jesus. The new commandment is simply to love one another. Even here, one might wish that Jesus had given us ten commandments telling us exactly how we are to accomplish this love. Jesus, however, left the door open so that believers can attempt such behavior on their own. He told us that loving behavior was expected of his disciples. Yet believers individually are to write their own program for accomplishing it.

II. The word *love* is used in so many ways in our modern culture that it is difficult to give to it a distinctive Christian meaning. We love to eat, and we love to go to football games. What makes love of a another person so different in the context of Jesus Christ? Perhaps one should begin with the concept that such love cannot be legalistic or legislated. We have all often heard it said that you cannot legislate morality.

Thus the reader is surprised to find Jesus putting the concept of love into a new commandment. How can you order someone else to love the neighbor? Jesus did not go on to spell out ten ways of doing this or establish a system of ethics for accomplishing it. Rather, love is what is expected of children of the Father. We must love out of obedience to him. It is not some humanitarian program but has its origins in the very demands of God upon us.

III. To love our fellow human beings means that in some way we have to overcome the basic human desire to love ourselves. It is not difficult to start a program of self love. Much of what we encounter in our world is based on that very principle. Jesus himself set the example by giving up his own life for that of the world. He demonstrated love in action. Again, we do not find this love expressed in a series of ten commandments. Yet we do encounter this very love in the mission and ministry of Jesus. He demonstrated the great love that he had for the people of the world.

On reading these verses in John 13, one might then be surprised to read about a new commandment. Yet one should realize how Jesus has radically reinterpreted the commandments and hear his radical call to obedience.—James L. Blevins

SUNDAY: MAY TWENTY-FOURTH

SERVICE OF WORSHIP

Sermon: Faith and the Fiery Ordeals
TEXTS: 1 Pet. 4:12–16; Dan. 3:16–18

This sermon is based upon a biblical text that simply acknowledges that life is full of problems. Appropriately, the writer refers to these difficult times "as fiery ordeals." Peter told the people to whom this letter was initially addressed that the first step toward dealing with life is to stop thinking that difficulties are strange and unusual. In fact, Christians sometimes suffer simply for doing what is good and right. The only guarantee is that tough times will come. If you haven't already, you will eventually go through the fire.

The Bible tells the story of three men who went through the most famous "fiery trial" of all time—and all because they were committed to worshiping God. But in spite of it all, they never lost their faith.

They were Shadrach, Meshach, and Abednego, three young Jewish men who were living in Babylon (Daniel 3). The king had become obsessed with a dream he had about a huge statue (Dan. 2:1–13). It was ninety feet high, nine feet wide, and made of pure gold. He ordered that a statue be manufactured in those exact dimensions. Once it was made, the king set it up on a raised platform and required the citizens of the kingdom to worship it.

Shadrach, Meshach, and Abednego refused to obey the king's order.

When he heard about their defiance, the king was outraged. He questioned them personally. And then he gave them one more opportunity to prove their loyalty to him. If they would only bow down and worship the statue, they could go free. But if they remained obstinate in their resistance, they would be thrown into a fiery furnace before the hour was up.

But quietly and without arrogance one of them spoke for all of them. "If there is a God who is able to save us from the blazing furnace, it is our God whom we serve; he will deliver us from your majesty's power. But if not, be it known to your majesty that we shall neither serve your gods nor worship the gold image you have set up" (Dan. 3:17–18). How did their faith become so strong?

Fortunately for us, their statement reveals three stages in the development of a growing faith.

I. The first stage affirms belief that God is powerful. One of the first faith affirmations we express is that God is the Creator of all that exists—a clear demonstration of his power. The word we use to describe God's power is *omnipotent*—meaning, of course, that in God is concentrated power that, in both quality and quantity, exceeds all other combined power in the universe.

Shadrach, Meshach, and Abednego believed that God had the power necessary to deliver them. 'If we are thrown into the blazing furnace," they said, "the God we serve is able to save us from it!" (Dan. 3:17).

As far as the Bible is concerned, God's power is unrivaled. Furthermore, the power of God has practical applications. It is not merely some abstract principle. Some people simply want to argue about God's power. Can God make a rock so big that he can't pick it up? Can he make $2 + 2 = 5$? Can God make a square circle? If we suggest that God can't do these things, then it implies that God's power is limited.

The Bible is not concerned with abstract questions nor with winning an argument. The biblical concern solely focuses upon God's practical ability to rescue his people from whatever oppresses or threatens to overwhelm them. God's power is not a matter of debate. It is a matter of concrete rescue and deliverance.

II. The second stage of faith development goes beyond the first. Not only is God capable of rescuing us, but he is also willing to do so. "If we are thrown into the blazing furnace, the God we serve is able to save us from it, and he will rescue us from your hand, O King" (Dan. 3:17).

To say that God is omnipotent does not guarantee that he will be concerned about our suffering. Power can be used for good or evil purposes. The same power that sheds light across an entire region or focuses microscopic treatment upon a cancerous tumor can also be used to destroy civilization.

Obviously, there is little comfort and security in brute strength only. The question is never whether God's muscles are bigger than anyone else's. The real issue is right here: Is God willing to use his strength to help me in my hour of need?

Shadrach, Meshach, and Abednego believed that God knew about their plight and was concerned about them.

This conviction that God cares about his people and will help them in their suffering is one of the most prominent themes in the Bible. In the Old Testament, the Hebrew word *hesed* is translated "everlasting mercy" or "steadfast love."

In the New Testament that everlasting mercy and steadfast love became incarnate in the life of God's Son. He gave Peter the confidence to tell the first-century Christians, who were preparing to face their own fiery ordeal, "Cast all your anxiety upon him because he cares for you" (1 Pet. 5:7).

When the doctors can do no more; when the counselor's advice makes little or no difference; when the months stretch into years since you last heard from your prodigal son or daughter; when your begging and pleading has no impact at all; it's this confidence in God's love that keeps you from giving up altogether.

But what if your faith is not rewarded in the way you expect? What if healing does not come? What if reconciliation never takes place? What if your prayers are never answered the way you expected? What if the king throws the three men into the fire and nothing miraculous happens? What then?

III. Here's how Shadrach, Meshach, and Abednego responded to that: "But if not [i.e., if he chooses not to rescue us],

be it known to your majesty that we shall neither serve your gods nor worship the gold image you have set up" (Dan. 3:18).

That's pure faith! It represents the third and final stage of faith development. When life gets whittled down, faith doesn't. It begins by trusting God, and it ends the same way. It says, "God is worthy of my trust, no matter what!"

Faith doesn't require you to simply and passively accept whatever happens. Most of us are not built like that anyway. If we had been the ones thrown into that fiery furnace, we would have gone kicking and screaming all the way. And that's all right.

But faith does say that no matter what happens, I'm still going to trust God! Why? Simply because I believe that no matter how much out of my control my life gets—even if it kills me—God lives, and nothing can happen to me that is beyond his control!

The Apostle Paul encouraged the Roman Christians when he wrote, "We know that in everything God is working for good with those who love him and who are called according to his purpose" (Rom. 8:28). He also wrote, "I am convinced that there is nothing in death or life, in the realm of the spirits or superhuman powers, in the world as it is or the world as it shall be, in the forces of the universe, in heights or depths—nothing in all creation that can separate us from the love of God in Christ Jesus our Lord" (Rom. 8:38–39, REB).

Do you remember what happened to Shadrach, Meshach, and Abednego? When the king looked into the furnace, he saw Shadrach, Meshach, and Abednego, along with a fourth person who appeared to be the Son of God. God was there, in the midst of the fire, taking care of his own!—Gary C. Redding

Illustrations

SPIRITUAL PRESENCE. One can compare the Spiritual Presence with the air we breathe, surrounding us, nearest to us, and working life within us. This comparison has a deep justification: in most languages, the word "spirit" means breath or wind. Sometimes the wind becomes storm, grand and devastating. Mostly it is moving air, always present, not always noticed. In the same way the Spirit is always present, a moving power, sometimes in stormy ecstasies of individuals and groups, but mostly quiet, entering our human spirit and keeping it alive; sometimes manifest in great moments of history or a personal life, but mostly working hiddenly through the media of our daily encounters with men and world; sometimes using its creation, the religious communities and their Spiritual means, and often making itself felt in spheres far removed from what is usually called religious.—Paul Tillich

PROVIDENCE.   Three men were treading over the inhospitable mountains and treacherous glaciers of South Georgia in the Antarctic, in an attempt to rescue the rest of the South Polar party. Later Sir Ernest Shackelton wrote in his diary, "When I look back at those days, I have no doubt that Providence guided us. . . . During that long and racing march of thirty-six hours over the unnamed mountains and glaciers of South Georgia it seemed to me that we were four, not three. I said nothing to my companions at this point, but afterwards Worsley said to me, 'Boss, I had a curious feeling on the march that there was another person with us.' Crean confessed the same idea. One feels the dearth of human words, the roughness of mortal speech, in trying to describe things intangible, but a record of our journeys would not be complete without a reference to a subject so very near to our hearts."—Charles L. Wallis

Sermon Suggestions

A PATTERN FOR WISE DECISION MAKING. TEXT: Acts 15:1–2, 22–29. (1) Consider the opinions of those who have a real stake in the issues, verse 26. (2) Consider the will of the Holy Spirit, verse 8. (3) Consider the value of unanimity, verses 25 and 28.

THE CHURCH TRIUMPHANT. TEXT: Rev. 21:10, 22–27. (1) Filled with God's

presence. (2) Illuminated by Jesus Christ, the redeeming Lamb of God. (3) Exemplary of the best in human government. (4) Universally accessible. (5) The home of those redeemed by the Lamb of God.

Worship Aids

CALL TO WORSHIP.   "Let the people praise thee, O God; let all the people praise thee" (Ps. 67:5).

INVOCATION.   Lord, thou hast bid us come to worship, and we have responded. May we find what thou hast for us, so that forever after we may serve thee in the needs of others with a stronger faith and deeper joy, through Christ our Lord.—E. Lee Phillips

OFFERTORY SENTENCE.   "Let the people praise thee, O God; let all the people praise thee. Then shall all the earth yield her increase; and God, even our own God, shall bless us" (Ps. 67:5–6).

OFFERTORY PRAYER.   We pray for people whose work is hazardous—farmers, miners, loggers, firemen, police, rescue teams. We pray for people who breathe a lot of bad stuff. We pray for workers in the Third World—low paid, unprotected: if injured or killed on the job, poorly compensated; workers whose goods we gladly buy.

We thank you for all agencies mandated to protect us from the hazards of our own perspective—from short cuts; from sloppiness; from the sated torpor of living well; from the spinning compass of trivial lives; from anxiety about being competitive; from poor excuses incorporated. Forgive us our cheap shots of agencies we so clearly need, our readiness to find fault with them, and our lack of zeal in their reform.

Comfort the bereaved of deaths at the workplace. Straighten our hearts that they not have died in vain. For they are not nobodies to you. You know them by name and always treat them with respect.—Peter Fribley

PRAYER.   O God, guide us through the dark places of life. Grant that we may not fear the loss of thee, knowing that thou art always by our side and that life will renew itself in us if we give it time and are willing to wait. And as we rise out of the low places through which we sometimes must walk, help us to be thankful for them and by them we may be able to help someone else through the darkness into light.—Theodore Parker Ferris

LECTIONARY MESSAGE

Topic: The Secret of the Indwelling Christ

TEXT: John 14:23–29

I. *The love that leads to the indwelling God.*

(a) *What love alone can do.* In answer to Judas (also known as Thaddaeus or Lebbaeus), Jesus declares that "keeping" his word flows only from love for him and will always be the fruit of that love. It also insures that both Jesus and God will indwell the believer's life.

Jesus declared that love for him is the key to his "manifestation." He could not show himself to the world more than he had already; but, if anyone saw Jesus' love in the life he lived and loved him in return, that one should receive the indwelling presence of Jesus and his Father.

(b) *What the absence of love assures.* Jesus emphasizes his truth by the negative of what he has already taught positively. He reminds them that his words are indeed the words of the Father, making sure that what he now says will be taken seriously. The force of telling them that the person who does not love him will not keep his words is that, with no place for Christ in the heart, God will not dwell there.

Such a life will be without God. That is our understanding of what hell is—the effort to exist where God is not, where there is no comfort, comradeship, good health, understanding, renewal, or ease. There can be no more frightening existence. If one could have an indwelt life by loving Jesus and keeping his word but does not, that one is most to be pitied. This is a choice each of us is offered. It is

like that given by Moses when he spoke to all the people of Israel (Deut. 30:14–20).

(c) *The way of sound judgment.* Loving God, walking in his way, and keeping his words are the ways to blessings abundant, life, and joy. The other way—the way of seeking and serving other "gods"—is the way of constant failure. People speak of the buffeting of fate. But their trouble is not fate. Their lives are the inevitable result of the concatenation of their choices. They do not control the world or its other inhabitants. But they can choose to love Jesus, keep his words, and find God dwelling within.

II. *The love that rejoices in greater life.*

(a) *How love can rejoice in a departure.* The message for the believers is in the apodosis of the conditional statement: "If you loved me, you would be happy that I go to the Father, for the Father is greater than I." There can be no question of the apostles' love for Jesus, hence, no question of their joy that he is going to the Father. Their love is a result of his words, deeds, and treatment of them. But they are saddened by seeing those opportunities about to end. It is necessary for their love to stretch to encompass the "greater" love of the Father, to rejoice in greater work and service, which will accompany the transformation of Jesus into the eternal greatness of the Father. For this reason, joy should exceed and remove any sadness of parting.

This passage specifies the indwelling of Father and Son promised in verse 23. Human love is an affinity of one spirit with the spirit of another. The spirits of both are apprehended through infinite nuances of look, gesture, and facial expression; voice in all its modulations, qualities, emphases, dictions, and accents; and deeds of action. This love can continue through temporary alterations, which are insignificant in the relationship of person to person.

But let the beloved change too much of the "personality" or "character" that originally inspired the love—and human love, in its inherent fragility, can be destroyed. What was seen as an inward similarity can be reinterpreted till it becomes inward repugnance. This kind of change can never happen with Jesus.

Because Jesus goes to the Father, he can forever inspire a believer with love and joy. The love does not depend on physical nearness. It becomes stronger, for God's love lives forever in the heart of the believer.

(b) *How love is strengthened.* Jesus, knowing that his disciples would experience a sense of abandonment after his death, prepared them by assurance of his continued presence. He has given them "inside information" on which to base confidence. He has loved them enough to write an agenda for their postresurrection fears, one that can be used to renew their faith and revive their courage. They are inoculated against desperation by his reassurance—"I have told you how it will be, so you need have no doubts."
—John R. Rodman

SUNDAY: MAY THIRTY-FIRST

SERVICE OF WORSHIP

Sermon: The Potter and the Preacher
TEXT: Jer. 18:1–6

The parable of the potter shop may provide an answer, or at least point a direction, for a very troublesome question. The question might be put something like this: How does God speak? If he were to speak to me, how would I know it? Would I hear an actual voice as Saul did? or Isaiah? or Moses?

Jeremiah in perfect candor tells us how he "heard" this Word of the Lord. He tells it without dissimulation or fancy footwork. He is plain and clear. In essence, the details are these: One day while out for a walk he happened by a potter shop. He stopped to watch, preoccupied. While the top of his mind was observing the potter at his work, the bottom of his mind was turning over a problem of the utmost gravity. It concerned the character of God.

Jeremiah was an astute observer of the times. He had risked his own personal safety to warn that the nation was fast drifting toward disaster. He had used all kinds of dramatic devices to make his sense of impending doom clear. He had taken some of his underclothing all the way over to the Euphrates in Babylon, left it there in a rock, and then later made a return trip to retrieve it. This was to symbolize the captivity. He had filled vessels with choicest wine and then broken the vessels only to let the wine splatter out on the ground. This pictured the fate of Jerusalem's kings and princes. In the Valley of Hinnom, Jeremiah had summoned the priests and community leaders, there to break treasured urns and vessels as a dramatic symbol of the broken treasures of Jerusalem.

But while Jeremiah was very sure of the imminent collapse of his beloved Jerusalem, he was not so sure of the morality of a God who would permit a blatant, arrogant heathenism to overrun this people of the covenant. True, Judah had sinned. She had broken the covenant. But Judah with all her sin was worlds better than heathen Babylon who made no pretense toward faith or morality at all.

In short, Jeremiah wondered at the ways of God.

While Jeremiah watched the potter at work, suddenly he "heard the Word of the Lord." That may be an awkward phrase for us. It was not so much what Jeremiah *heard* as what he *saw*. For as he watched the potter at work, Jeremiah *saw* a new truth; he caught glimpses of a new insight he had never seen before. What did he see?

Jeremiah observed the potter take his clay and mold a vessel. The vessel was defective, so he remolded it. Another did not work out as the potter originally intended it, so he adapted it to a modified form. Thought Jeremiah, "Is this not how God deals with Jerusalem?"

In that moment, God communicated with his prophet, and the prophet could speak his new truth in a way that we today can understand it.

What was the Word of the Lord that day to Jeremiah?

I. *Inescapable relatedness.* As Jeremiah watched the potter at work with his clay, one of the earliest thoughts to come was that the clay and the potter were vitally interrelated. The potter was not entire without the clay; the clay was only clay without the potter. Each needed the other.

It is easy for us to imagine that we can do very well without the Father. Particularly is this true in our air-conditioned, push-button age. Content, insured, possessed of a sometime security, we fall under the illusion that we can make it very well on our own. In these moments of self-sufficiency we comfort ourselves with the thought that if worse comes to worst, the family will be taken care of by a combination of insurance, social security, and good luck. But the thought we cannot bear to face is this: What of us? What about this one, personal, indestructible cell of life called *me*? What happens to *me* when I am beyond the reach of money or medicine?

This question drives us back to an admission the Bible makes without any embarrassment at all, namely, that the *me* all of us is concerned with would be nothing but a lump of clay without the heavenly Father. Beautifully, the Bible says, "And the Lord God formed man of the dust of the ground and breathed into his nostrils the breath of life; and man became a living soul" (Gen. 2:7).

Now we can deny this truth; we can run from it; we can ignore it. But all the while it is there, staring us in the face. Sooner or later we must come to grips with it: There is no escaping our relatedness to the Father. The psalmist describes the inescapableness of our relatedness to the Father with a passage that many of us remember (Ps. 139:3–12).

Perhaps our trouble is that we know this to be true but cannot afford to admit it. The dilemma of our restless, driven, neurotic age is the dilemma of a bad conscience. We are vitally related, inescapably related, totally related to the Father, even as the clay is related to the potter. But we may never really know this until we have nothing left but the Father. Only then are we aware that to have the Father is to have enough.

II. *The Father's freedom.* The second part of this Word of the Lord came a little slower. Jeremiah had to watch the potter work awhile, and even then the dawn came gradually. But eventually Jeremiah saw that the potter was not bound in his art; he could improvise as he went. If one form would not take shape, never mind; he could make another.

Then Jeremiah saw this fact in relation to Judah. The Master Potter was not bound by Judah and her Temple with its sacrifices and ritual. In fact, God had a kind of sovereign indifference toward the whole business, as Jeremiah had come to see (cf. 7:21–23).

What God wanted was obedience; he wanted the sacrifice of the heart (Ps. 40:6–8). And unless this is the form our faith takes, he will pass it by! Only a consummate conceit would dare think that our forms and our procedures are the only ones God can use. God is not bound to us nor to what may be congenial to us. He is as free as a potter at his wheel. What God looks for is not form; it is function. He may want to fashion a new form.

Now what does all this have to do with me? you ask. I would answer quite simply that if any of us would have the fullest possible kind of life we must concede our relationship of dependency and then ask, "What wouldst thou have me to do?"

God is utterly free, and in his freedom he uses the vessels at his disposal.

III. *The Father's patience.* The impassive patience of the potter of Hinnom spoke to Jeremiah of the patience of the Lord. But from here on the parable of the potter is not altogether true. For clay is *impersonal*; it has no will of its own. Any gap between design and product is a deficiency finally of the potter. So here we must take leave of Jeremiah and his rustic potter shop. Although he had truth, he did not have it all. It takes more than patience to make us pliable to the Master Potter; it takes conversion. For *we are personal*; we do have wills of our own; we can wreck the magnificent, wondrous design of the Father. And I should add, not only can, but do.

As we step outside the shop, we see a wondrous shadow cast upon it. It has the form of a cross. We turn from the shadow to face the cross itself. Can it be? Is the Potter also the crucified? What strange business is this? Here is a patience that no potter ever had. Here is an impliability that no potter ever found in his clay. What is it that will gently soften this hardness? It is not a threat; it is not harshness. If anything can reach through the hardness and make it pliable it is this strange sign, the cross, and what it signifies.

Then we remember a line from the New Testament that tells us just how infinite is the patience of the Master Potter: "God was in Christ, reconciling the world unto himself, not imputing their trespasses unto them; . . . For he hath made him to be sin for us, who knew no sin; that we might be made the righteousness of God in him" (2 Cor. 5:19, 21).

If that wondrous truth cannot reach us, nothing can. There is nothing left except the judgment the Master Potter reserves for those who rebel to the very end.—Ralph L. Murray

Illustrations

THE TRUE WAY OUT.   A man was brought in to see me. I say "was brought in" because he was on the verge of desperation and was accompanied by a friend. He had earned distinction in the service of his nation but had been utterly defeated within. There wasn't a thing that I could say to him that gave him encouragement. Invariably he replied, "There is no use—I am through. I am a beaten man, and I know it. Death is the only way out."

There was nothing I could do for him, nothing—until I began to tell him about the cross and of One who loved man enough to die for him, of One who believed in the redeemability of every human soul. When I finished that story, I saw hope light up his face with a glory greater than that of an Alpine sunrise.—John Sutherland Bonnell

THE PERSON REBORN.   I have received a visit from an elderly colleague. After a long career at the head of a hospital, he had been brusquely dismissed by the governing body, which had a young protégé to put in his place. I thought of the bitterness into which he might have sunk, of the solitude and inaction into which it would have led him, if he had not found in his faith the strength to forgive, and the confidence which lit up his face with a magnificent smile. He had at once asked himself into what new adventure God was now going to lead him, and it was not long before he was called to be superintendent of a more important hospital than the one he had left. In his new post his Christian message to those suffering from nervous diseases would be capable of bearing still more fruit than before.—Paul Tournier

Sermon Suggestions

A DEFEAT TURNED TO VICTORY.   TEXT: Acts 16:16–34. (1) *A promising situation:* The healing of an exploited slave girl, verses 16–18. (2) *A painful complication:* The arrest, flogging, and imprisonment of Paul and Silas, verses 19–24. (3) *A surprising resolution:* The miraculous deliverance of Paul and Silas and the conversion of the jailer and his family, verses 25–34.

FAMOUS LAST WORDS.   TEXT: Rev. 22:12–14, 16–17, 20. (1) A word of promise. (2) A word of judgment. (3) A word of reassurance. (4) A word of invitation and welcome.

Worship Aids

CALL TO WORSHIP.   "The Lord is king! Earth, be glad! Rejoice, you islands of the seas! Clouds and darkness surround him; he rules with righteousness and justice" (Ps. 97:1–2, TEV).

INVOCATION.   O God, the King of glory, who hast exalted thine only Son Jesus Christ with great triumph unto thy kingdom in heaven: We beseech thee, leave us not comfortless, but send to us thine Holy Ghost to comfort us, and exalt us unto the same place whither our Savior Christ is gone before; who liveth and reigneth with thee and the same Holy Ghost, one God, world without end. — *The Book of Common Prayer*

OFFERTORY SENTENCE. "Behold, I am coming soon, bringing my recompense, to repay every one for what he has done. I am the Alpha and the Omega, the first and the last, the beginning and the end" (Rev. 22:12–13, RSV).

OFFERTORY PRAYER. We thank thee, O God, that you do not overlook the widow's mite offered in love and dedication, nor do you forget the little kindnesses offered in concern and caring. Open our hearts more and more to your heart and to the needs of our neighbors and even of our unknown brothers and sisters in distant lands.

PRAYER. There are times when we cry out, How long, O Lord, how long— how long in a world where you have created plenty for all must a third of the human family go to bed hungry every night? To a world that you have brought order out of chaos—where you have ordained a balance in nature that breathes life—how disruptive are the selfish ways of man seeking his own aggrandizement rather than the good of all. Help us to comprehend that the violence of these times is not only the hate that kills but the love withheld.

Who among us, confronted with the suffering of others or our own, has not cried out against the seeming God-forsakenness of life? But how often in these times when we feel we have been abandoned to the forces of evil, the ravages of disease, or the unpredictable storms that blow we discover that the god we have been serving is no God but some machination of our little mind or perverted heart. In your seeming absence, we discover your Real Presence. We come to realize that you are "the great God and the great King above all gods." We experience the strength of the everlasting arms and know that we are held by a love that will not let us go.

We are so grateful that in this place we have caught a vision of your glory that we have never seen before. We pray now that we may not be disobedient to this vision but live it out in our every relationship. May we no longer try to hide our doubts, but may we confess them to you who can do something about them! "I believe, help my unbelief." —John Thompson

LECTIONARY MESSAGE

Topic: Christ's Prayer for Unity

TEXT: John 17:20–26

We are living in times of change and political reorganization. There is one hope for improvement, and that is the unity of the Church of Jesus Christ. The failure of international communism was and is an inescapable effect of its heartless, faithless, Christless core of atheism. It has failed as a system because it fails in its humanity. Any opponent of humanity and community must also fail, not only outwardly by conquest but inwardly when it foments hatred and cruelty based on its denial of God in Christ. God will bring unity to the people of the world in God's own time, sooner than we may expect, because Christians everywhere love one another in the unity of Christ's indwelling glory.

I. *The perfection of unity.* There is accepted to be an inherent difference of great magnitude between the number one and the numbers two and beyond. One is a different kind of number than any other. In order to understand how there can be any thought of all believers being "one" in Christ, we need to consider some of the qualities of "essential" and "accidental" properties described by Plato in *The Republic*: "Whenever a number of individuals have a common name, we assume them to have a corresponding idea or form." When we talk about the unity of the Church, we are saying that there is only one "Churchness" and that all who are believers in Christ possess the common essential attributes of faith in him, love for God, fellowship in faith and hope, and belief in the benefits of righteousness.

II. *Perfection of fellowship.* That identity of all believers in the one Church allows for incidental diversity of individuals (varying in what Plato called "accidental" qualities) and of groups who share certain emphases in worship and work (Eph. 4:11–13). It is the power of Jesus Christ to mold an individual in his likeness, and, to use a familiar figure, the closer anyone is to him, the closer that one will be to the fellow believer.

Charles H. Brent, senior chaplain of the American Expeditionary Forces in World War I, told a conference on faith and order, "It is thus that, by practicing unity, we shall gain unity." Paul applied the principle in his letter to the Ephesians (4:1–6)—the unity begins with God and extends to each believer, bringing with it personal qualities of divine origin so that no believer may have separatist feelings toward others.

III. *Perfection of evangelism.* The purpose of Jesus is clear in this prayer for all who should believe in him: First, the perfection of the believers that comes with recognized unity; next, the pulling, redeeming power of that singleness of faith over all the world. How else is the world to know that God sent him to show his love for them? "O just and holy Father, the world has not known thee, but I have, and these believers know that thou has sent me." Knowing is an obligation as well as a privilege, carrying its own duties with its blessings.

Elmer G. Homrighausen said, "The Christian community exists and survives; . . . It is the symbol of a redeemed humanity through the power of the living Gospel. The Church is an infinite potential for the redemption of mankind." How can the true communion of believers in Christ succeed in its tremendous task? By being a true communion of believers in Christ.— John R. Rodman

SUNDAY: JUNE SEVENTH (PENTECOST)

SERVICE OF WORSHIP

Sermon: Our Universal Mission

TEXTS: Isa. 61:1–4; 2:2–5; Matt. 9:35–10:7

I. The great light of revelation in my concept of missions came when I made the discovery of a new term. That word is *mission.* The two words sound alike, but the new word is singular. Rather than describing what "they" do in a faraway place, *mission portrays the idea that every Christian must be on mission.* The Christian faith does not have a missionary arm. *It is a missionary movement*! The paradox of the Christian faith is that relationship with Christ involves both an individual concern and a fellowship—in which we serve with others and through which we serve others. The great Quaker Christian Elton Trueblood reminds us that we cannot be Christians alone! What we do alone means our fellowship with others is richer because we can contribute. What we do together enriches what we experience alone.

The Gospels record that Jesus had been teaching and preaching in the synagogue. Mark recorded that, because of their unbelief, Jesus left the synagogue and began teaching elsewhere (Mark 6:1–12). Matthew noted that Jesus had compassion on the crowds because they were "harassed and helpless, like sheep without a shepherd. Then he said to his disciples, 'The harvest is plentiful, but the laborers are few; pray therefore the Lord of the harvest to send out laborers into his harvest' " (Matt. 9:36–38). Christ called out the twelve disciples. Do not make a mistake of thinking we have to convince God through our prayers to call laborers into his harvest. No, we need to *help both ourselves and others to be open to his call to us!* From the beginning the church was on mission. Christ told them they were on mission, and he sent them out— not initially to foreign lands but to their own land, saying, "Go rather to the lost sheep of the house of Israel" (Matt. 10:6). While the Temple and synagogues had the concept of "coming in," the church gathered on the first day of the week to "go out." The Christians came in for power to go out for service the rest of the week.

II. *Christians have difficulty being on mission seven days a week.* Dr. Trueblood once declared in a conference that there are three legs on which one's Christian faith must stand and grow. These are prayer, thought, and service. Few Christians accomplish simultaneous development of all three of these areas. But if you have ever tried to milk a cow on a two-legged stool or a one-legged stool, you can better understand the need for having all three of these legs! Mere activism without the spirit of Christ becomes harsh, judgmental, and destructive. Intellectualism alone becomes dry and spiritless. Prayer by itself becomes introverted and distorted.

Religious experience grows stale if it is isolated, and the man who worships in continual isolation soon begins to worship himself! In the long run the greatest detriment to vital religion can come more from an introverted religious feeling than from the avowed enemies of the world. The missionary movement demonstrates concern and service for the total person.

There have been numerous criticisms launched on the Christian missionary enterprise. Some have criticized foreign mission work because they feel our missionaries are offering solutions to the rest of the world when we are filled with problems here at home. Others have been critical of the manner in which missionaries have sought to superimpose a white Anglo-Saxon Protestant outlook on life to people whose culture is different than ours. And still others have questioned why we should bother, since people throughout the world have their own religious systems, and the missionaries might only tend to disrupt an existing pattern of belief.

These criticisms come apart under close examination. We must recognize, accept, and deal with our failures—in our lives, in our church, and in our nation,

without letting our mistakes become our scapegoats for neglecting to attempt anything positive elsewhere. Our missionaries abroad do need to encourage the nationals to develop their own Christian context instead of trying to persuade them to conform to American concepts. Christ knew the Jews worshiped God, but they had confusion and error mixed into their worship. He came that all men might know the Father with perception and realize the purpose of the abundant life one can live now. Indeed, "unless there is real validity in the idea of mission, Christians may as well accept with resignation the frequently repeated conclusion that we are finally living in the post-Christian age."

So Dr. Trueblood reminds us. The foreign mission enterprise has always led the way in caring for people—in schools and hospitals. Only later have the emerging governments assumed some of these tasks.

III. Christ gave us some graphic clues to the concept of our universal missions when he used the metaphors of penetration. He said his followers were to be like salt, light, and leaven. These things are worth nothing unless, and until, they penetrate something else—the salt flavoring the meat, the light melting the darkness, and the leaven causing the bread to rise. This was a reversal of the Jewish concept since the Exile. They had grasped the introverted, withdrawn concept of remnant. Jesus said not withdrawal, not saving yourself, but *reaching out into the world is the point of his discipleship.* The church, then, must not become a storm shelter to save us from the flood of the world's problems but a launching pad to put us into the midst of the world.

The proper question to raise among church members is not merely, "Are you saved?" but more specifically, "Are you on mission?" We have failed to ask the right question in the past. Unfortunately, many people in our churches today do not realize what is required of them as followers of Christ and how they can give expression to his expectation.

I feel it is a mistake to overemphasize either the gathered or the scattered church. We must have both. We cannot exist always on the cutting edge of the world; neither can we penetrate unless we go forth with good news. Some of us need insight; some need maturity; some need challenge; and others need encouragement. I heard of the man who went back to the used-car salesman with the car he had purchased. The salesman became uncomfortable and defensive, thinking he was going to be fussed at and accused of dishonesty. But the customer declared, "I have become a little discouraged; I simply wanted to hear the sales pitch again!"

In all of life we have the paradox of success and failure, whether we speak of our lives, our church, or the universal Christian mission. As Charles Dickens expressed in the beginning of his monumental work *A Tale of Two Cities*, the best and worst are so close together! The simple answer is always wrong, for truth is always complex! The fellowship of Christ is the richest thing we know, but too often it also becomes the most damaging thing. The church has been aptly described as both the hope and the despair of man.

There is a universal mission for every Christian. It is an equipping ministry of enabling others to know God in Christ and to know the fullness of life. This equipping is done on the job, in the home, and throughout the community. It involves being equipped both inwardly and outwardly on your part and mine so we can proclaim more ably what it is Christ calls all persons unto. Gauged on the basis of performance, one of the major contemporary mission fields remains the local church membership, which has so many inactive, indifferent, and un-Christlike people! Our universal mission involves money—but more than that! Our universal mission entails *prayer*—but even more than prayer. Our universal mission consists of *intellect* and *emotion*—but more than these. Our universal mission involves *service*—but even more than this alone. Our universal mission involves *all we are and have*—giving, praying, feeling, thinking, and going—not only on the other side of the world but where we are

now! In the name of Christ and on behalf of his church, I call you to commit yourself to your mission for Christ as expressed in the fellowship of this church. You see, our mission is corporate, but your participation in it involves your personal commitment. It is never easy to be on mission, but this is Christ's invitation to you. And this is how we tell the world that he cares, why he cares, and that he comes anew today.—Robert W. Bailey

Illustrations

SALT AND LIGHT.   "*You* are the salt of the earth . . . *you* are the light of the world." Read it with the right emphasis. Jesus was setting his disciples over against the old Israel, over against Judaism, over against Mosaic religion. He wanted them to see that it was *they*, not the priests and keepers of the old Law, for whom the world was waiting. *They*, not the scribes and Pharisees, would be heralds of the kingdom. *They*, not the old rabbis, would bring spice and light to the people of the earth. . . .

This is no theology of good works Jesus was recommending but a theology of the glory of God. We bring seasoning and light to the world, not that the world may praise us, but that it may see and fall down before the presence of God in our midst. Salt is lost in the flavoring of food; we do not praise the salt but the taste of the food. Light is overlooked when it reveals the contents of a room; we do not praise the light but the items on display.—John Killinger

THE CHRISTIAN IN THE WORLD.   The life-giving power at the heart of the gospel is not something the disciple is to hug to himself, to nourish for his own good alone. Rather, that life is to be shared with others and with all the world around.

There is, indeed, in the change of metaphor from "salt" to "light" the suggestion that, if life is indeed present in the disciple, it cannot be other than shared with those whom he contacts in the world. For it is indigenous to life that it gives life to others. As this is law in the natural world, so it is a law in the spiritual world. "Good works," therefore, are by no means the cause of salvation but rather its fruit. Those who have within themselves the character of saltness or of life produced by the righteous redemptive activity of God in their lives can do no other than to share it in saving activity. It should be obvious then to all the world, as the disciples themselves, that the praise for such good works goes not to the disciples but to the Father who is himself the life-giving agent at work within the disciples' lives (Eph. 2:10).—John Wick Bowman and Roland W. Tapp

Sermon Suggestions

MARKS OF THE MESSIANIC AGE.   TEXT: Acts 2:1–21. (1) The universal experience of the Spirit. (2) The universal availability of salvation.

WHAT THE SPIRIT OF GOD DOES TO US. TEXT: Rom. 8:14–17. The Spirit (1) provides leadership; (2) gives assurance of belonging; (3) promises future reward; (4) requires suffering with Christ.

Worship Aids

CALL TO WORSHIP.   "Play music in Yahweh's honour, you devout, remember his holiness and praise him. His anger lasts a moment, his favour a lifetime; in the evening a spell of tears, in the morning shouts of joy" (Ps. 30:4–5, JB).

INVOCATION.   Lord, allow thy precious Holy Spirit to open us to truth and anoint us unto good works, because we tarry now and wait in prayer and believe unto the uttermost, through Christ our Savior.—E. Lee Phillips

OFFERTORY SENTENCE.   "To be controlled by human nature results in death; to be controlled by the Spirit results in life and peace" (Rom. 8:6, TEV).

OFFERTORY PRAYER.   Spirit of the Living God, bring all our urges and energies under your loving and gracious control, that we may not only know abundant life and peace but that we may also share the fruits of these blessings with a needy world.

PRAYERS.   Almighty God, on this day you opened the way of eternal life to every race and nation by the promised gift of your Holy Spirit: Shed abroad this gift throughout the world by the preaching of the Gospel, that it may reach to the ends of the earth; through Jesus Christ our Lord, who lives and reigns with you, in the unity of the Holy Spirit, one God, for ever and ever.—*The Book of Common Prayer*

O God, you move in mysterious ways your wonders to perform. Forgive us our scientific orientation that would seek explanation of the inexplicable and miss the miracle of your grace that is everywhere about us and in us. In your house there is bread enough and to spare. You are such a spendthrift—lavishing your providence upon us not only with the gift of life but with all of life's extras. You have not only peopled this planet, but you have given us family and friends. You have not only created a single flower with but one hue, but you have made flowers without number in all kinds of intricate designs and clothed in myriads of colors. You have not given to us one bird with a single song, but you have created these little feathered troubadours without number to fill every morning with a beautiful symphony. You have not only given us a garden in which to live, but you have given the gift of true light—your love in your only Son—that we may see the grace-fullness of all of life and be glad.

What more could you do than what you have done and are doing, but how often we look for some other sign. We look to another time, some other place when salvation is present in the gifts that we hold in our hands. With what judgment the Word of this hour confronts the church that today is so impotent in the face of the world's great need. The quid pro quo of our calculating ways stands under the judgment of your abounding grace that causes the sun to shine on the evil and on the good and sends rain on the just and the unjust. Oh, to be channels of such a grace! Committing the gifts in our hands to the power of your love that so generously multiplies and feeds the multitudes.

You question, "If someone comes asking for bread, will you turn him away with a stone?" We do. There are those crying for bread, and we proffer them the hardware of war. How long, O Lord, how long will we continue to squander the resources of this planet on implements of destruction that even to use would be suicide when there are so many dying for the necessities of food, clothing, housing? Your haunting Word in Christ reminds us: "To whom much is given, of him is much required." Confirm and bless those efforts in the world today where leaders persevere to overcome estrangement and mistrust with communication and understanding.

In this household of faith we are privileged to share, there are those among us, our brothers and sisters, for whom we pray the healing of your grace. Where illness or infirmity must remain, we pray the healing of mind and spirit with that victory of faith that overcomes the world, through him who is our faith and teaches us to pray together, "Our Father. . . ."— John Thompson

LECTIONARY MESSAGE

Topic: Jesus' Gifts to His Disciples

TEXT: John 14:8–17; 25–27

It is the hunger of soul possessing all humans everywhere, the desire to know the Father—to see him, get truly acquainted with him. No wonder Philip expressed this longing. We want to really know! It has tantalized us since Adam and Eve ate the fruit of the tree of knowledge. Now Jesus removes the scales from our eyes and shows us how blind we have been.

I. *Finding the person of God in Christ.*

(a) *Believe what your senses tell you.* With a slight rebuke of his lack of realization, Jesus tells Philip what he seeks has been with him from the start. Jesus is showing him the Father in the puzzle picture of all he has done. The God of the universe is revealed to understanding in what Jesus has said already. See—in the blind eyes made to see again, there is the light of the Father shining forth; in the joy of the dead girl raised and the gratitude of the father, there is the breath of the Almighty. Only look at me, listen to me, says Jesus—these are indeed the deeds and words of the Father, in living presence among you.

(b) *Believe for the sake of greater works.* "Now, seeing the Father, you are ready to do what I no longer can do," Jesus tells us. You are more in number, longer in life, with the Father in you as well. He is to be gone so that he can work in more places for a longer time through them and us. We can work more works of love and care, right more wrongs of political aid and civil injustice, teach truth to more ignorant lost souls, heal more hurts, bear more burdens—because he goes to the Father.

II. *Finding the power of God in prayer.*

(a) *The need for Christ's presence.* The disciples can do Jesus' work only with his presence among them. Their whole motive is to obey him. They cannot keep him with them. But they can keep themselves with him! Whatsoever they ask in his name, he will do. His name is his presence.

(b) *Qualifications of the promise.* Jesus does not say, "Whatsoever you shall ask, that will I do." He says that what he will do is whatsoever is asked in his name. A believer is on dangerous ground if he prays for self-serving ends. The request is to be for the kind of soul-healing words; the kind of indefatigable, unselfish ministry; the lifting of unbearable burdens; the feeding of the hungry, in body and soul, that Jesus himself could not longer do except through their belief in him. These are the secret weapons of the human soul against its secret demons, of the church in its defense of love and justice and its attack on evil, these requests sought in the name of Jesus.

(c) *Jesus' purpose in his promise.* All this promise is for the sake of glorifying the Father. The unity of the Father and Son with the believer is the hope of glory for the believer. The King of kings and Lord of lords grants his special power so that all the world may see and realize the glory of the Lord of life. Yes, he will do whatsoever we ask in his name, for the glory of the Father.

III. *Finding peace in the Holy Spirit.*

(a) *The person of the Comforter.* Several times and in several ways, Jesus promises that his disciples will not be left alone to do his work. The third person of the Godhead is a real person, not an emanation, an influence, or an attribute. He is known in baptism "in the name of the Father and of the Son and of the Holy Ghost." We know him in the benediction as we say "the communion of the Holy Spirit." He has appeared as the dove at Jesus' baptism, the tongues of flame at Pentecost, the sound of the wind, and the still small voice, the pillar of cloud by day and of fire by night. He is a Comforter because he gives strength in trial, solace in suffering, and hope in discouragement. He teaches us to remember whatsoever Jesus has said to us and is our other comforter in his absence.

(b) *Knowledge through love.* Those with hearts and lives obedient to Jesus' commandments have them because they love him. This love—not science or philosophy—is the key to understanding and knowledge. Whoever knows the world only never knows the world. Only one who knows and loves Jesus Christ can truly know with understanding.

(c) *The peace of Christ.* Jesus gives his only possible bequest—his peace. He won it through all his works, and he gives it to us, in every infinite variety of our ways in this unquieting, deluding, seductive, and betraying world. He gives the inexhaustible peace of ultimate resource, of orderly living, purity of life, and constant companionship with God the Father. The world cannot give such peace. He gives the peace of the secret well in the besieged castle or of the gyroscope-steadied ship on the stormy sea.—John R. Rodman

SUNDAY: JUNE FOURTEENTH (TRINITY SUNDAY)

SERVICE OF WORSHIP

Sermon: Nicodemus

TEXT: John 3:1–15

Ah, Nicodemus! A good man, by anyone's standards. He was a Pharisee—not just a religious man, then, but a devotedly religious man, dedicated to obeying God's Law. He was a "ruler of the Jews"—that is, a member of their Supreme Court and thus a political as well as religious authority. Jesus called him the teacher of Israel, so he must have been more than just a local star but a nationally known celebrity. Wealthy, too; at the end of the Gospel he brings thousands of dollars' worth of burial spices to bury Christ. And to top it off, he was open-minded, willing to listen to him. Such a great man—why is he still in the dark?

Let me ask you a riddle: What do a birth, a bath, and a kite have in common? Nothing, except that they are images from the text—well, maybe the kite isn't actually in the text, but it almost is—images from the text to explain why Nicodemus is in the dark.

I. The story you know from end to end. Nicodemus came, by night, to talk to Jesus and began politely: "We know you are from God because of the wonders you perform." We who? Who else stands behind this good man sharing his point of view? Many suggest that Nicodemus perhaps was not alone among Jewish leaders of Jesus' day and that many of them shared his cautious affirmation of Jesus' good intent. Maybe Nicodemus even came that night to ask some questions on behalf of the group: "What are your future plans, Jesus? What are your political leanings? Do you think you'll stay in Galilee?"

We'll never know, because Jesus cut by Nicodemus-the-official-representative to put his finger on the real question deep down in the heart of Nicodemus-the-man. "You're in the dark, Nicodemus, because you're the wrong sort of person. You'll continue to be in the dark, never seeing the light of God's truth, until you become something other than what you are."

II. (a) Nicodemus, you need a new birth. Jesus told a riddle of his own here, using a word with two meanings. Jesus' phrase could have meant, "You have to be born twice," and that's how Nicodemus heard it. He objects, "That's impossible." Jesus, of course, meant not so much a second birth as a birth of a different sort—a birth from above.

What do giraffes have that no other animal has? Baby giraffes. Not so much a riddle as a simple law of nature; we all bring forth "each after our own kind." Try as you and I will, we will only have mortal children, and we might as well issue a death certificate with the birth certificate because they will all die some day. For life in eternity, we need to be born by an eternal power. God must be both father and mother to us, giving us everlasting life just as our parents gave us mortality. You need a new birth.

(b) Nicodemus, you need a new beginning. "I tell you the truth, unless one is born of water and the Spirit, one will never enter God's kingdom." Nicodemus would have caught the point here, but you and I may need a little refreshing to get it. Water and Spirit are both lifegiving forces in the Old Testament, and when they are combined, the effect is to recreate creation.

Let me ask you, How do you draw a picture of nothing? Does an empty white page of the black depths of a night sky covered with clouds signify nothing to you? To the ancient Hebrews, "nothing" was an ocean without borders—restless, undisciplined, untamed—nothing. In the beginning, then, there was only the vast deep—a universe-sized ocean—and the Spirit of God hovering over the waters. And God said . . . and the world was born. The prophets used water and Spirit to speak of a new beginning for the world in the future. Listen to Ezekiel: ". . . and I will sprinkle clean water on you, and you shall be clean . . . and I will

put my Spirit within you and cause you to walk in my statutes (36:25–27). Nicodemus needs a new beginning—he needs a bath.

Not a soap-and-water bath but a Spirit-and-water bath, which we symbolize in baptism. We Christians see baptism as a symbol of our entrance into God's kingdom, as our death to an old life and our pledge to live life anew. Nicodemus the Pharisee, the pillar of his community, the teacher of Israel, just isn't yet willing to take that step, that plunge into faith that baptism symbolizes. He is still in the dark.

(c) Nicodemus, you need a new motivation. From water and the Spirit, Jesus turns to focus on Spirit alone: "So is every one who is born of the Spirit." Think again of creation, this time from Genesis 2. God created people, the text says, by taking dirt and shaping it like a potter makes a jar out of red clay. Then he breathed into the person—only one word for breath, wind, and spirit in Hebrew and Greek—so that God's breath, God's Spirit, is what made that dirt live.

God once asked Ezekiel a riddle. He took him to a valley full of dead, dry bones and asked, "Can these bones live?" He answered his own question by blowing his Spirit over them, clicking and clattering those dead bones into living beings.

Nicodemus, like all living things, had God's breath within him, or else he'd not have been alive. Yet he did not have within him the power of God's Spirit such as fell upon the disciples at Pentecost. Nicodemus was still driven by his goodness, by his ambitions, by the sorts of things that all respectable people are driven by. He needed a new motivation, the wind of God's Spirit.

A kite is built for the sky. It has a large curved surface for lift, a tail for stability, and a string for guidance. Without the wind, though, it is grounded and uninteresting. Humans are built for the wind of God's Spirit, which blows across our consciences, asking us to surrender ourselves. Nicodemus still had his feet on the ground, unwilling to let go, still in the dark.

Nicodemus was a good man; why was he still in the dark at the end of this story? It was because he was not willing to be something else besides a good man. Good people are still people, still mortal, sinful, destined to die. We have to become something else, children of God, and that's something we can't do for ourselves no matter how good we are or how hard we try.

Instead, we must open up to the reality behind these symbols of birth, bath, and kite. Exactly how it will happen or has happened to you is something of a mystery; the light fell on St. Paul all at once on the road to Damascus, but it seems to have caught up with St. Peter little by little and only after several false starts. I know how it happened to me over the years, but no one can predict how God will come to you. Listen for it: the blowing, tugging, whistling, urging, insisting, inviting of God's Spirit. Listen for it, and let it make you something more than you are.—Richard Vinson

Illustrations

BY GOD'S GRACE. Nicodemus had to learn and we must learn, with him, that our religious opinions, views, feelings, and experiences matter nothing. All this is "flesh." And "the flesh profiteth nothing." The Spirit alone availeth. "That which is born of the Spirit, that is spirit." The Spirit, however, is not at hand. The Spirit is a part of life out of the other world, out of eternity. "The Spirit bloweth, where it will." We stand before God when we say "Spirit"; we are and remain cast upon him, upon him alone. We live by his grace. He gives us what we cannot give ourselves access to him. We can come to God only through God himself. He is the new man who knows that he comes *to* him because he comes *from* him. That is the mystery in the life of Jesus. Therefore he gave men no recipe about ways and means of coming to God, as all the other religious "masters" do. But he was himself the new man born of God and lived wholly by God's incomprehensible strength. We may continue to converse ingeniously about these things; we

may spin again our religious dreams about Jesus. It has been done repeatedly in Christianity. It may happen, also, that by God's grace we will awake and understand Jesus Christ as he wills to be understood. With him there is no room for religious dreams; no ways are prescribed how we, without God, can come to God. But he said of himself, "I am the Way! He that hath ears to hear let him hear"!—Eduard Thurneysen

POWER UNTO SALVATION. His limitless resources roll in on the shores of human life like the waves of the sea, ceaseless and unnumbered, terrible in wrath, majestic in their encompassing might, mysterious by their far horizon. Yet for all the immensity of that "sea of the Spirit" (a better metaphor than the wind for an island-race), it does not disdain to enter into our little lives, shaping itself to our pattern, rippling its way into the tiny pools, lifting the pink shells and floating the fronds of weed; nothing is too small for the dynamic activities of the Spirit, as nothing is too great. When the Christian truths are baptized into the consciousness of this, they become what the gospel is meant to be: the *dunamis* of God unto salvation (Rom. 1:16).—H. Wheeler Robinson

Sermon Suggestions

THE FIRST OF GOD'S WORKS. TEXT: Prov. 8:22–31. (1) The work of God identified, Prov. 8:22–31. (2) The God who works described, John 1:1–5, 10–14.

OUR SPECIAL HOPE. TEXT: Rom. 5:1–5. (1) Its owners, verses 1–2. (2) Its basis, verses 3–4. (3) Its evidence, verse 5.

Worship Aids

CALL TO WORSHIP. "Yahweh, our Lord, how great your name throughout the earth! Above the heavens is your majesty chanted by the mouths of children, babes in arms. You set your stronghold firm against your foes to subdue enemies and rebels" (Ps. 8:1–2, JB).

INVOCATION. Here in this sacred place, O God, shed abroad your light in our hearts. Let the words of Scripture so move us that through the sermon we may be filled with the comfort and challenge of a God who never stops calling us. Through the hymns we sing, let us truly praise you and receive the blessing as we wait before you.—Henry Fields

OFFERTORY SENTENCE. "We have access by faith into this grace wherein we stand and rejoice in hope of the glory of God" (Rom. 5:2).

OFFERTORY PRAYER. We thank you, O God, for the undeserved favor that we experience through faith in our Lord Jesus Christ. As we are aware of where this is pointing and leading, help us to bring our stewardship in line with our destiny with you, when we shall share in your glory.

PRAYER. O God, most holy and most gracious, never could we climb up to you by any ladder of our own making; therefore, in pity you have sent your Son into the world to show us the way to you. You have set the glory of your omnipotence in heaven and earth. And yet if you were only an infinitude of might, our hearts would faint within us. But now in Jesus Christ you have veiled your power, have come forth in the strength of your gentleness to live our life and die our death, that you might win us to sonship and eternal life. O God, we know not the meaning of Gethsemane and the cross. If we seek to grasp it, too often we but darken counsel with words of ignorance. We can only praise you for your grace and lift up a cry of penitence and of trust.

Living Father! We thank you for our life with its unspeakable privilege and dread responsibility. You have given it to us that through it may throb the mighty tide of your life, that in it may be revealed some aspect of your being and beauty. You have beset us behind and before. You make us to sorrow for our sins. You stir us with a divine discontent, and we forget the things that are behind and

reach forth unto the things that are before. We rejoice that you have set our life amid gracious opportunities, whereby you would train us to truer vision and larger understanding of you and of ourselves.—adapted from Samuel McComb

LECTIONARY MESSAGE

Topic: Infinite Spiritual Resources for Us
TEXT: John 16:12–15
I. *Our need for the Holy Spirit.*

Jesus assures believers in verse 12 that there are many things Christians ought to know that he himself did not teach. How can they learn what they could not then bear? This continued teaching is the ministry of God's Holy Spirit. Jesus, though hundreds and thousands did hear him, could not reach all the places and people of the world, nor all the future decades of the earth's history. And because his disciples were not ready, he could not teach all he wanted them to know. To reach other times and other places and to meet the growing capacity of believers is the work of the Spirit, who can go everywhere and at all times. We are not limited, since Christ's Resurrection, to one holy time or one holy place.

How blessed we are to learn what Christ has for us because his Spirit is with us in every communion service, every worship hour, wherever we may be.

II. *The marvelous wisdom of God.*

(a) *How we can learn Christ's further truths.* In the writings of the apostles to the churches, we have seen the beginning of the enlarged revelation brought by the Spirit to the believers. The truths they utter were revealed to them by the Spirit as experience exposed their need. They became willing recipients as new occasions exposed their ignorance, as new believers shared ministry with them, and as, seeking larger faith, they became abler to receive new truths. They became, as we shall continually become, abler to bear the truth. How long we have taken to learn the basic lessons of loving all God's children! When shall we be able to bear the greater truths, to hear the rest of

Christ's gifts of insight? When we earnestly recognize our inadequacy and make adequate use of present knowledge, we can bear to hear more.

(b) *How the Spirit teaches believers.* Can anyone learn algebra who does not have a mastery of arithmetic? Can anyone master medicine without thorough knowledge of human anatomy? We as Christians have propaedeutic lessons to be learned. Because we are human, subject to limitations of our tasks and our physical needs and dangers, we are limited in our capacity to apply ourselves to spiritual truth. We may feel overwhelmed by our needs, but as we are ready the Spirit reveals more to us. As we proceed through the fundamentals of faith, we hear again in time of need the Word of Christ, and the Spirit expounds it to us afresh.

III. *The Spirit's infinite access to truth.*

(a) *The work of preparing for truth.* Jesus says, "All the Father's things are mine." And the Spirit shows us what Christ has for us. Through a faithful quest we can have larger shares of truth. No one can ever say, "That's it! Now I know all there is to know." One can feel that one's knowledge is enough for the time, but it would be erroneously presumptuous for anyone to say, "There is no more to be learned," for the Spirit draws on an inexhaustible supply.

An archaeologist goes on from one clue to the next, digging, sifting, measuring, piecing, and studying to find and interpret his great discovery. All truth is disclosed to those who show they are ready for it. Truth about playing a certain position on a football team is never complete but is revealed to the player who practices and searches the films with a good coach.

(b) *Reception of spiritual truth.* A Christian learns by spiritual preparation, by allowing one's spirit to commune with God's Spirit, for "spiritual truth is spiritually discerned." Only then can one "bear it." Just as the disciples were promised the ability to learn of things to come in the days following Christ's Resurrection, we are promised equivalent revelations for today and tomorrow.—John R. Rodman

SUNDAY: JUNE TWENTY-FIRST

SERVICE OF WORSHIP

Sermon: My Father, My Teacher

Texts: Deut. 6:1–13; Eph. 6:1–4; Luke 15:11–32

One of my favorite biographies is of G. K. Chesterton. Chesterton's early childhood play revolved around a cardboard castle with cardboard figures. His favorite cardboard figure in this imaginary world was one that held a golden key. He said something like this, "I always thought that the cardboard figure with the golden key was my father because he was always unlocking for me mysteries and wonders." We are constantly teaching, and it has an influence on our children and our children's children. So you say then, "What can we teach? What do we teach that is enduring, that makes a difference, that will stand the test of time?" We will find no better curriculum than the one that is here in Deuteronomy 6. We give a lot of lip service in our country to the Judeo-Christian heritage, but we had better give more than lip service for it is the basis of our entire society and every institution in it.

At the heart of that tradition is Deuteronomy 6. The sum of Moses' address to the Jewish people is "Now if you go into the Promised Land you must teach your children and your children's children." According to Deuteronomy 6 there are three things that we must teach our sons and daughters: The first is that we teach about God. Second, we teach about grace. Third, we teach guts. That's right, I said it, guts. Some of you parents will have to straighten your children out later. The preacher should have chosen another word, but nonetheless it will probably stay in your mind. Guts, grace, God.

I. This passage begins by saying that we are to love the Lord our God with *all* of our heart and soul and strength. "Shema, O Israel": Hear, O Israel. It is saying, "Listen, this is all that will make a difference when your children come to you and are worried about death, destruction, disease, and other enigmas." At those moments, easy answers and pat responses do not suffice. Have you taught them that there is a God beyond yourself? One of the greatest pits that we fall into as parents is the preening and posturing that suggests we've done it on our own and there is no one beyond us. When we point beyond ourselves we have given our children a greater gift than any formed by loom or lathe. We either teach that we are the center of the universe or that there is One who has called us into being and will be with us each step of the journey.

Douglas MacArthur said that he was probably best known as a soldier, but it was not his most important work. His most important work was as a father because as a soldier he dealt in destruction, but as a father he dealt in building up. And the most important time he ever spent as a father was when his son would kneel with him to pray daily: "Our Father, which art in Heaven. . . ." The most important thing as mothers, fathers, grandparents, aunts, uncles, neighbors we ever teach our children is that *God is*, and God is to be worshiped, enjoyed, and served forever.

II. The second truth that we have to teach is grace. Did you notice that in this passage from the sixth chapter of Deuteronomy Moses says to the people, "You will go into a land that I will give you." *I will give you.* "You will then come into houses that you did not build. You will drink out of cisterns that you did not dig out of the ground. You will, indeed, enjoy vineyards that you did not plant." The most important thing we can give our children is a sense of grace. I didn't earn it, possess it, build it myself. The very fabric of the universe is a gift. God has given us health, opportunity, and salvation in and through Jesus Christ. What we are called to do is respond; for the only response to grace is gratitude. The lives that are strong and enduring beyond time are those that have learned that grace begets gratitude, and gratitude is a way of living that cannot fail.

One of my fathers in the faith, Elton Trueblood, has said that we come to a new understanding of living when we begin to plant trees under whose shade we will not sit. It is gratitude for God having given us so much that impels us to plant trees that we will never sit under. I think we have gotten ourselves into such an ecological mess because we have not taken the biblical injunction seriously to be caretakers of the earth, not just for ourselves but for our children and our children's children. Grace leads to gratitude and gratitude leads to a responsible stewardship of the earth's resources.

III. Then finally there is a need to teach "guts." In verse 12 it says when you get into the land you must fear the Lord. It sounds harsh to us. Yet if we fear the Lord, we will fear no one else. If we fear and love the Lord, we can stand up to all others who say, "You must do it our way or perish." To stand up against all the conventional wisdom of this "present age" takes guts. He goes on to say, "And you shall serve the Lord." It takes courage to serve the Lord instead of ourselves or the despots of this present age. You may call it gumption, but what we need to communicate to our children more than anything else is that there are a few important principles on which we will stand and on which we must continue to give all of our life's energy. We stand here, God help us, we can do no other. We can communicate to our children that there is a God who loves us and calls us in Jesus Christ. To stand against the "go with the flow" materialism is to bear witness that life is grace and we are given so much so that we may be a channel of God's blessing to others. Think of "guts" as the fortitude to stand when others would easily sit down. We have found that which is worth standing for and passing on to future generations. When we do it we are teaching "guts."

Like a good textbook, this passage not only gives us three subjects that we should teach our children, but it also tells us how. It says, "Teach your children diligently." First of all, when you sit in your house. Second, when you walk on the road, and third, in your rising up and your lying down.

(a) The first suggests that the most important ways in which we teach our children are not in teaching Sunday school or sending our children to Sunday school. I watch my children, and you know what I discover? They are watching me. They are watching me all of the time. The times they seem most open to learn are not when I have on my preacher hat. Oh, no, it's when I'm trying to get them to bed. Then all of the "great" questions come up; yet some of these questions are important ones. This is a reminder of the importance of what we teach when we are sitting in our houses. Indeed, if we're sitting at home but thinking about work we're not fully there when our children talk to us. We are teaching them something then when we are half listening to them. Yet when we overcome other pulls on our time and are fully present for our children, we are preparing the way for all we might teach them of the one who commands us to listen, "Hear, O Israel."

(b) We're also teaching when we're on the road. How we live our lives outside the home is so important. Believe me, our children will pick it up. Arthur Miller, the playwright, has given us in several plays the truth that what we do in our life outside the home will influence our children. In the play "All My Sons," a wartime industrialist wanted his children to respect him more than anything else, but in his work he cut corners. Because of cutting those corners in his industry his own son was killed. What he said he wanted most was lost. In another of Miller's plays, "Death of a Salesman," Willie Loman wanted his sons to respect him and honor him. Yet his self-esteem was so low that he thought he needed an affair to bolster it. His son found out about that affair, and the one thing he wanted more than anything else, the respect of his son, he lost. We do teach our children "when we walk on the road," for what we truly honor and value is often seen in our life outside the home.

(c) We are given the opportunity to teach our families about God, about amazing grace, about the guts it takes to stand and live. We do it in our sitting, in our walking out on the roads of our vocation, and also in our rising up and in our lying down. Think for a minute how you teach in that way. If you begin the day by saying in a horrified tone, "Good God! It's morning!" instead of "Good! God, it's morning!" you've already begun to set the mood. We begin in our rising up and then also in our lying down. I think about how we end the day some days. Last night was one of those times when the best way you can end the day is in the forgiveness of sins. It is saying, "I blew it, I didn't do the best as a father." It is hearing the confession of our children and believing that God forgives us, builds us up, and gives us a renewed vocation. God calls us in and through the family.—Gary D. Stratman

Illustrations

OUR BEST? How reluctantly we sometimes give our talents to the building of his kingdom. We put forth the best of our energy in the building of our own kingdom. Businessmen will go to their labors on Monday morning and give the best of their minds and bodies to the tasks before them. But in the service of the Church they suppose any haphazard contribution of talent will be acceptable. Many expect the best possible religious instruction for their children in the church school yet never stop to consider their own responsibility in instructing the children of other parents. They are quite sure even God will be pleased if they drag their tired bodies to a cushioned pew a half dozen times a year when the weather is good and there is nothing else to do.—Gaston Foote

THE LAST WORD. When Robert Louis Stevenson was a little boy, he one day locked himself in a closet. He became panicky and began to scream. His father heard his cries and tried to open the door, but the lock was jammed. A locksmith was sent for, but during the wait the father kept talking quietly to his son. Thereby he quieted his son's fears and kept up his courage. This experience remained a parable in Stevenson's mind. We may sometimes be locked in darkness, but the Father will have the last word, for he is the keeper of a door that no man shutteth.—H. Eugene Peacock

Sermon Suggestions

"WHY ARE YOU HERE?"   TEXT: 1 Kings 19:9–14, REB. (1) *Then*: The story of Elijah hiding in a case from the wrath of Jezebel. (2) *Always*: Those believing in the living God are accountable at all times for their whereabouts and their "whatabouts." Examples in Scripture and in history since. (3) *Now*: Ask these pertinent questions about your behavior: Am I unworthy? unprepared for my task? afraid of opposition? burned out? looking for an excuse? feeling self-pity?

CHRIST'S   LOOK-ALIKE.   TEXT: Gal. 3:23–29. (1) Our justification by faith, verses 23–25. (2) Our being clothed with Christ by baptism, verses 26–27. (3) The practical consequences, verse 28. (4) The rationale, verse 29.

Worship Aids

CALL TO WORSHIP.   "O send out thy light and thy truth: let them lead me unto thy holy hill, and to thy tabernacles. Then will I go unto the altar of God, unto God my exceeding joy" (Ps. 43:3–4a).

INVOCATION.   When we know the truth about you, O God, your goodness and your love, your justice and your forgiveness, we are drawn to worship you. And so we are here to lift our praise to you and to seek your will for our lives. Speak to us, that your will may be done in us.

OFFERTORY SENTENCE.   "There is neither Jew nor Greek, there is neither bond nor free, there is neither male nor female: for ye are all one in Christ Jesus" (Gal. 3:38).

OFFERTORY PRAYER.   Our Father, free us from the last bit of our prejudice toward other people, so that we may be constrained only by the demands of need and love, as we surrender to you the material means by which your love for all may be made known to all.

PRAYER.   Eternal God, who without our asking it hast set us in this strange scheme of circumstance, guide us in the same, we beseech thee, that we fail not ourselves, our fellows, or thee. Teach us to look upon our life as a high trust. Remind us of the great souls of the past through whom thou hast shined gloriously to make the face of this earth more beautiful, the saints, apostles, and martyrs, servants of the common good, whom thou hast given to mankind. May we see them committing to our charge the stewardship of their high calling and saying to us, Life is a trust.

To this end teach us to see more vividly the faces of our friends, the loved ones in our family circle who have cared for us as they cared not for themselves, and all true spirits who have given us their affection and confidence. Let them say to us today, Life is a trust.

To this end make real to us the sacrifices of the past, the martyrdoms where with vicarious outpouring of life the world was uplifted, and those simpler, humbler services of heavy cost that plain men and women have contributed to make this earth more decent for thy human family. As thus we stand before the universal cross, may it say to us, Life is a trust.

Especially to this end may we see today the Christ of God. Thanks be to thee for him! For the loveliness of his childhood, the beauty of his home, the integrity of his youth, for the greatness of his teaching, the grandeur of his life, the courage of his cross, his glorious victory, and for his undying, undefeated influence, thanks be to thee! As he passes to us the high heritage of his memory, let his voice say to us, Life is a trust.

We pray for our families. No lovely thing has ever come to earth save as behind it was a lovely home. Hast thou not called thyself Father and us sons and in our mutual relations called us brothers? Since we cannot understand thee except in family terms, God keep us from despoiling the family. Let thy benediction rest upon our households. Let no root of misunderstanding spring up among us. Let our homes grow beautiful that in their beauty we may see the likeness of thy Fatherhood and our sonship.— Harry Emerson Fosdick

LECTIONARY MESSAGE

Topic: A Promise Based on Recognition

Text: Luke 9:18–24

These verses in Luke essentially duplicate those in Matt. 16:13–25 and Mark 8:27–35, omitting the words particularly addressed to Peter. It is a straightforward account, especially suitable, as Origen says, for the Greeks, those not from birth acquainted with Jewish matters, as Matthew is for the Jews, Mark for the Romans, and John for the later Church.

I. *Results of Jesus' survey.*

(a) *Erroneous responses.* This is a section especially pertinent to today's culture, as the leader asks his aides for the results of the most recent survey of popular opinion. He learns what prejudice and general error he must overcome with truth in order to promote his program. The errors are those of assumption based on knowing the expectations of Jews but on insufficient insight. Speculation was bound to be rife, given Jesus' work and ministry.

(b) *Partial truths.* (1) Some said Jesus was John the Baptist. Herod even heard and accepted this, though he had killed John. They knew only that Jesus was a preacher and teacher, preparing people's hearts to receive God, as John had prepared them to receive Christ.

(2) Some said he was Elijah, for God had promised, through Malachi (4:5), to raise up the prophet Elijah to prepare the coming of the Lord's kingdom. They knew only that Jesus spoke of judgment and promise, as Elijah had done.

(3) Some said he was one of the old prophets come again, for God had promised through Moses (Deut. 18:15) to raise up a special spokesman for God. The people knew only that Jesus quoted from the second law book freely and spoke of God's commands.

(c) *Today's erroneous survey answers.* We find that in our time large portions of the earth's people limit Christ erroneously as a teacher; a great, even the greatest, prophet; or as a social worker without peer. But education, even moral education; Islam, with its stern monotheistic denial that Jesus is God; and psychology and welfare work, even with the good they do, fall far short of recognizing God in Jesus. There are many refinements of partial truth but only one total Truth for all people.

II. *A life-saving and life-shaping discovery.*

(a) *The universally required human question.* By the time you read this or hear this, millions more of the world's people will have come to their final tests, the question on which their eternities will rest. This is the question that divided all time and eternity to come from all the past: "Who do you say that I am?"

(b) *The advantage of acquaintance.* The disciples, being closest to Jesus of all people, had heard in his words the Word of God, had seen in his love the love of God, had known in his prophecy the way all things should be, and they confessed through Peter the true confession: "[Thou art] the Christ of God."

III. *The one-sentence gospel and its effects.*

(a) *The way of salvation.* Jesus described his life's work to them in one sentence, for the first time foretelling what the next weeks would hold. He told them to be prepared for his suffering, rejection, death, and Resurrection, and he set them a course of both danger and promise.

(b) *Affirming Christ by denying self.* There were then and there are now no two ways about it—if one chooses to follow Christ, one must surrender the control of one's life, even accepting the bearing of exhausting burdens. There can be only one overmastering aim and goal of one's life, responding with breath, heart, hands, and mind to the answer of Christ's question.

(c) *The world's most glorious promise.* "Whosoever will lose one's life for my sake, the same shall save it." If anyone misses the point of Jesus' glorious prom-ise of the saving of one's life, one has missed the whole purpose of life, that it should be lost to self-centered, ego-fulfilling, soul-destroying efforts to aggrandize oneself, for the sake of following Jesus into his glory.—John R. Rodman

SUNDAY: JUNE TWENTY-EIGHTH

SERVICE OF WORSHIP

Sermon: The Final Goal of Ill
TEXT: Luke 11:21–22

Jesus once said, "When a strong man armed keepeth his palace"—and mind you, he was talking about the devil!—"his goods are in peace: but when a stronger than he shall come upon him"—here he's talking about God!—"when a stronger than he shall come upon him, and overcome him, he taketh from him all his armour wherein he trusted, and divideth his spoils."

It was just another manner of saying that God is stronger than the devil. Or to put another *o* in God and take the *d* out of devil, that good is a sturdier customer than evil! Some people seem to like it that way better. They don't want to be too personal! It wasn't a guess with Jesus; it was a certainty. It was the deepest conviction he had. In fact, there was no *maybe* about it: no *perhaps*, no *peradventure*, no *if*. It was *when*! "When a stronger than he shall come upon him!"

So our theme is God's ultimate victory. It isn't much more than a frail hope with most of us, a pathetic sort of faith, as human faith usually is: groping around in the dark, half a doubt, making a stab at some final decency in the universe; wanting to believe that it would all add up to something sometime, that in the end everything would turn out for the best; but never quite able to get any farther along than supposing!

I. There's so much that seems to be set dead against any possibility even that the good will triumph. You look at the sky and the stars and the world and all that goes on; and there doesn't seem to be any noticeable prejudice anywhere in favor of the righteous! Most of it appears to be terrifyingly indifferent to your life and mine, whether we live or die or have our hearts broken. They say it's the best imaginable place for growing character; with plenty of hard knocks for everybody to keep us from getting soft and no shock-absorbers for the undefiled in the way that walk in the law of the Lord—none worth talking about. But that isn't the point. For pity's sake, in such a place, how can you ever even hope that the good will come out on top, much less be sure enough to stake on it everything you've got? Half the time all that virtue does, besides being its own reward, is to make things tougher!

II. Then you take a good look at human nature, and that doesn't improve matters much! There aren't many brutes that can contrive to pack as much cruelty into a few short years as mankind has done. It isn't a pretty picture—history never is!—against which to paint any very radiant future for the race.

Perhaps that's why—granted a universe like this, with all its apparent indifference to moral values, and such dwellers in it as we are, capable as Pascal says of being its glory but so often content to be its only shame!—perhaps that's why, over such wide areas of human life, we have lost a good deal of our interest in morals. It's craftiness that will get us through, we are sure of it. And force. We've got to strike and strike now, like the lightning! Conscience is a plain hindrance. If there are any devices that can be used to make things look better, all right; but in an un-ideal situation like this, un-ideal methods may be necessary; and one can't be too squeamish.

III. Something seems to be wrong with that, and I think I know what it is! It's this troublesome Christ! You can't wash your hands of him! He still insists on standing between us and chaos! He keeps wanting us to believe that no matter how it seems, no matter what happens, God even in our world is stronger than the devil! "When," not if, "a stronger than he shall come upon him, and overcome him, he taketh from him all his armour wherein he trusted, and divideth his spoils." That wasn't written for easy times. Hardly a page in the Bible. It was written for the times that "try men's souls"!

I'm glad that all this talk about modifying our ethics to meet something called reality, shaping our conduct so that it will fit more comfortably into a greed-torn, war-torn world—I'm glad it doesn't occupy much space in either the Old Testament or the New! There would have been no prophets if it had, and there would have been no recognizable Christ if that had been the burden of his Sermon on the Mount! To him the will of God was the will of God, whatever it cost, and the one thing you could hold to in a confused world was that right was eternally right and wrong eternally wrong and the odds altogether with him!

The Temple would be gone, not one stone left on another. The heavens would be gone. And the earth would be gone. His words would be left! You could relax, inside anyhow, and be of good cheer. He had overcome the world; whipped it to a standstill! And the next day they killed him! No matter. You couldn't fool him. He knew what would come of it!

Nobody ever felt the deep awe that Jesus felt for the human soul—not twaddle about its fundamental decencies, but breathless amazement at how far down it could fall and at the sheer glory to which he could lift it. Nobody ever rated it so high or asked so much of it; but he talked no petty nonsense, thank God! He didn't try to deny the ugly things about it that he didn't like. The last he saw of it when

he died was a mob of grinning faces, telling him to help himself now if he could! The last he heard of it was a curse. And he went on believing in it!

IV. And I'm not basing my confidence in the final triumph of good on any discoverable average in the long upward swing of the years either! It's an impressive fact that love does seem to get the better of hate, if you give it time enough. And honesty does fare farther than greed, and purity doesn't tire out so quickly as lust, and meekness has its way over force. Not right off, but in the end! Say what you please, something like that does go in this world: life driving out death, good driving out evil! All anybody needs is a little perspective. For all the apparent indifference of nature, there is a mighty drift somewhere at the very heart of things that sets itself slowly and with resistless determination against brutality and tyranny and injustice and oppression. But I'm not counting on that!

V. I'm counting on the same thing that Jesus counted on and the whole New Testament with him! I'm counting on this: that there's a holy God!

Look through the Gospels, in the Acts, in the letters of Paul: Every time they caught sight of the cross, they turned round with a shout. The world kept pulling at them. Old habits kept creeping up. Sin kept tugging them by the sleeve. But yonder were those two beams of wood. That showed them how God hated these things in the human heart, which had done such a dark day's work. It showed them how far God was ready to go with his love and his brave face. Calvary was like a flag fluttering against the black sky, with one ray of light shining on it through the only rift there was in the clouds. And they turned round and ran back to the hopeless task of winning, and they won! Fools that they were, with nothing but the kind of song we sing: "All hail the power of Jesus' Name!" And they won!

"Somehow good will be the final goal of ill." I read that Michelangelo used to get sick of the art that saw only the Suffering Savior, and I hold no brief for the religion that sees no more! "Why," he demanded hotly, "why is it always, always the Crucified? Hanging there for only six short hours on the cross? And never, never the Christ Triumphant? For that's what he is to all Eternity, with the keys of death and hell in his hands." "When a strong man armed keepeth his palace, his goods are in peace." That's the devil. "But when a stronger than he shall come upon him . . ." That's God! And I'm counting on him! I'm counting on him for the grace to count on him when there isn't anything else left!—Paul Scherer

Illustrations

THE BELIEVING HOPE.   In the contradiction between the word of promise and the experiential reality of suffering and death, faith takes its stand on hope and "hastens beyond this world," said Calvin. He did not mean by this that Christian faith flees the world, but he did mean that it strains after the future. To believe does in fact mean to cross and transcend bounds, to be engaged in an exodus. Yet this happens in a way that does not suppress or skip the unpleasant realities. Death is real death, and decay is putrefying decay. Guilt remains guilt and suffering remains, even for the believer, a cry to which there is no ready-made answer. Faith does not overstep these realities into a heavenly utopia, does not dream itself into a reality of a different kind. It can overstep the bounds of life, with their closed wall of suffering, guilt and death, only at the point where they have in actual fact been broken through. It is only in following the Christ who was raised from suffering, from a godforsaken death and from the grave that it gains an open prospect in which there is nothing more to oppress us, a view of the realm of freedom and of joy. Where the bounds that mark the end of all human hopes are broken through in the raising of the crucified one, there faith can and must expand into hope.—Jürgen Moltmann

WHY GOD SHAKES US UP.   There is just so much true and lasting community in our nation as there is Christian fellowship, the church of Jesus Christ, in it. The ruin of the church is the ruin of the nation; the decline of the churches is also the decline of real national unity. It is not civilization and culture, nor blood and soil, that can really unite us but only love, disinterested, sacrificing, selfless love—that love which Jesus Christ alone gives us. That is what will teach and show us God in these stormy times. He shakes everything so we will see what will really stand forever. He takes many things away from us so we will at last grasp what has eternal worth. He shakes even our nation so it will find its way back to the community that will never cease to be because it rests upon rocky ground, because it is descended from the Spirit of God himself.—Emil Brunner

Sermon Suggestions

OUR UNKNOWN ALLIES.   TEXT: 1 Kings 19:15–21, especially verse 18. (1) *Problem*: feelings of isolation and loneliness. (2) *Solution*: (a) The Lord's sometimes too-secret disciples and their coming forward in time of crisis, (b) the cloud of unseen witnesses urging us on, (c) the presence of the living God, who will never leave us nor forsake us.

A PARADOX OF CHRISTIAN EXPERIENCE.   TEXT: Gal. 5:1, 13–25. (1) We are free from the rigors of Law. (2) We are bound by the constraints of love.

Worship Aids

CALL TO WORSHIP.   "For they got not the land in possession by their own sword, neither did their own arm save them; but by thy hand, and thine arm, and the light of thy countenance, because thou hadst a favour unto them" (Ps. 44:3).

INVOCATION.   Lord, we come to tarry a while, to sit quietly, sing joyfully, pray sincerely, listen intently, and lean upon the everlasting arms. Thou who hast met us at every turn, we seek thy holy will as we meet again.—E. Lee Phillips

OFFERTORY SENTENCE. "By love serve one another. For all the law is fulfilled in one word, even in this; thou shalt love thy neighbor as thyself" (Gal. 5:13b–14).

OFFERTORY PRAYER. Lord, may the law of love woo us into every good work, every kind word, and every gracious thought. Let this and every other offering of our lives be guided by that pure grace.

PRAYER. Standing in the midst of time's quick-flowing flood, we reach out toward thee, O God, who art the Lord of eternity. Our days are as grass, and our years as a tale that is told; yet our hearts hold dreams that time cannot quench and cherish in the fading flesh treasures beyond change and decay. Although our life is but a span and our understanding limited on all sides, yet we have felt the intimations of a vaster world than any we have seen with mortal eyes. Even these days so rounded with a little darkness, these frail souls embarked on so great a sea of mystery, shine with the splendor of distant destinations. In the daring of our humblest yearning we set our sails across these tumbling seas of time for a port we shall not reach except through death's darkness and the light of thy guiding love.—Samuel H. Miller

LECTIONARY MESSAGE

Topic: The Cost of Discipleship

TEXT: Luke 9:51–62

In this passage, Jesus makes clear that those who want to follow him must realize their ultimate destination, must know the conditions of the journey, and must concentrate their whole being on it.

I. *Recognizing the goal.*

(a) *Jesus' anticipation of his Ascension.* Jesus, feeling that the time had come near for him to depart earthly life and ascend to his Father, began to travel the way he knew he had to go—to Jerusalem. For him, this is the beginning of the end. The expression "steadfastly set his face" is a Jewish reference, as in Jer. 21:10, representing a sternly determined course, here also expressing judgment and destruction for those who will not receive him and his salvation.

(b) *The goal defines the journey.* It was about seventy miles from Bethsaida, the region north of the Sea of Galilee, to Jerusalem, and as Josephus notes in *The Antiquities* (20:6:1), most travelers went through Samaria. The group needed a place to rest overnight, but when Jesus' messengers looked for accommodations, they were refused, leading Jesus to say later that he had no place to lay his head.

But Jesus' goal was not only Jerusalem. He was on an eternal journey, and he wanted those who would go all the way to the end with him. Rejected in one place, he went to another. He was not deterred, but those who rejected him would face eternal shame. There was long-lasting enmity between Jews and Samaritans because of supposed racial mixture. If Jesus was going to Jerusalem, the Samaritans would see his intent and take it as a Jewish matter.

(c) *The journey is no time for signs and miracles.* Jesus was willing to allow his message and his truth to make their way without miraculous intervention. He was patient, countering the bad attitude of James and John toward the Samaritans with a rebuke, when they wanted to call down fire from heaven to consume them. In words not in all the ancient texts, Jesus told them they did not know the spirit they were showing; that is, it was not his purpose to destroy but to save lives. He took them to a different place. We can all call down imprecations on those who reject us, too, but in so doing we are showing a far different spirit than that of Jesus. Instead, we ought to follow him in helping, not hurting.

II. *Conditions of the journey.*

(a) *Its privations.* Jesus' words with some who would follow him revealed that the would-be followers had no idea of the requirements. They needed to know that they would have no easy life, no comfortable, restful home in which to retreat from care and strife. Others, even the foxes and birds, had places of safety and rest, but those who follow Jesus have only one home, and it is not of this earth. We are always cautioned against worldliness, against attachment to places and things instead of to spirit and works of love. All the world recognizes and ridicules the false testimony of self-proclaimed holy persons, of whatever religion, who live in palatial and expensively furnished homes, who revel in gold and jewelry, or who ostentatiously dress themselves in rare finery. The one on the journey of following Jesus, while never in need, must recognize the purity of purpose Jesus calls for.

(b) *Its concentration on spirituality.* To another would-be follower who would delay for the funeral of his father, Jesus said he should leave nonspiritual tasks to nonspiritual people. He called them "the dead." The disciples were chosen, called, and dedicated, and they could not postpone allegiance to the Son of the Living God. Others must be left to care for the ordinary affairs of life. It is not that to-

day Christ's followers do not have to do many burdensome or routine tasks but that in service to him these tasks take on radiance and personal glory in his presence.

(c) *Its necessary changing of human bonds.* Jesus sought followers without distractions and other primary loyalties. He told the prospective follower who wanted to say farewell to those at home that he could not plough a straight furrow on a farm by looking anywhere but straight ahead—it is very difficult even then—and that he was not fitted for service in God's kingdom if he could not free himself from the distractions of lesser human ties. These stringent requirements are Jesus' method of attracting the ablest and most dedicated followers. The best are drawn to the highest challenge, and it is there for us today.—John R. Rodman

SUNDAY: JULY FIFTH

SERVICE OF WORSHIP

Sermon: Breaking the Alabaster Flask of Love and Forgiveness
Text: Luke 7:36–50
She really had the nerve. Why would a prostitute be found anywhere near a Pharisee's house? Her immoral life-style was humiliating enough without having to face the condemnation of a self-righteous Pharisee.

Yet she had heard that Jesus, the forgiver of sins, was a guest for dinner at Simon the Pharisee's house. Probably without knocking, she opened the door and fell at the feet of Jesus, and with her hair she washed his feet with a mixture of her tears and expensive perfume.

Perhaps no greater picture of love, except that of Jesus himself, could be painted from the New Testament. Jesus said of the sinful prostitute, "Her sins, which are many, are forgiven; for she loved much . . ." (v. 47a).

I. *Self-giving love.* Forgiven people best know how to love in a self-giving way (vv. 37–38). The prostitute gave Jesus her

tears, symbolic of repentance and sorrow over her past sins, as well as an alabaster flask of very expensive perfume. She felt forgiven by Jesus even before he pronounced it.

The more we realize how much Jesus Christ has forgiven each of us, the more we are motivated to love God and other people in tangible ways. Jesus always viewed love as active, not passive.

William Penn said,
"Love is a gift, take it, let it grow,
Love is a sign we should wear, let it show,
Love is an act, do it, let it go.
Love is indeed heaven upon earth;
Since heaven above would not be heaven without it."

To act our love is warmth in a cold world, light in a dark world, and joy to a sad world. I agree with the words of a well-known song, "What the world needs now is love, sweet love." Especially the world needs agape love, which has experienced the forgiving grace of God.

I imagine, too, that this former prostitute was unrestrained as she probably poured out not just a few drops, but the whole container of expensive perfume. Jesus had forgiven her of much, and she wanted to express her love by giving Jesus the best she had to give.

True love based on the forgiveness of sins never calculates how little it can get by with. True love's one desire is to give to the uttermost limits, and when it thinks it has given all there is to be given, wants to give even more.

This forgiven woman's gift of love was, as Luke the apostle reported, in "good measure, pressed down, shaken together, running over" (Luke 6:38).

II. *Misunderstood love.* Realize, though, that the forgiven person who actively shows God's love takes the risk of being misunderstood. Simon the Pharisee ridiculed Jesus for allowing such scum to touch him, let alone wash his feet with tears and perfume (v. 39).

It is difficult to continue with acts of love when you are misunderstood, even when your intentions are good.

A little boy saw a puppy he desperately wanted in the pet shop window. He went home and broke out the savings in his piggy bank. The determined lad walked into the store and caught the attention of the store owner.

"What can I do for you?" asked the owner.

The boy dropped the change on the counter and said, "I want to buy that puppy over there."

"Son, you don't understand," replied the man. "That puppy is sick. He's got a broken leg."

The boy wouldn't give up. "But I want him, I love him. I want to take him home and take care of him and fix him back."

"But son, you don't understand; that puppy's leg is broken. We're going to have to put him to sleep."

The boy stood back from the counter and pulled his pants legs up to his knees. He was wearing braces because he was crippled. The boy with tears in his eyes responded, "No, mister, you're the one that don't understand." (*Proclaim*)

A Christian who has genuinely been forgiven of his or her sins understands what it means to want to love other persons who need to experience the same forgiveness of sins. Yet that same person may know what it feels like to face misunderstanding, which may lead to opposition, suffering, ridicule, and rejection.

The Pharisees and scribes all through Jesus' ministry were filled with hatred and tried to stop Jesus. Why? Because he gave too much love and forgave too many people of their sins.

Yet Jesus calls his disciples to spread God's message of love and forgiveness even when misunderstood. Jesus understands the significance of active love, even when we don't fully realize what will be its results.

Don't carry God's love and forgiveness through life in an unbroken alabaster flask. Just as the fragrance of the perfume spread from one end of the room to the other, so also should we spread Christ's love and forgiveness.—Ron E. Blankenship

Illustrations

OUT OF THE WRECKAGE. It's at the end that she comes into focus most clearly. She was one of the women who was there in the background when he was being crucified—she had more guts than most of them had—and she was also one of the ones who was there when they put what was left of him in the tomb. But the time that you see her best was on that first Sunday morning after his death . . . he spoke her name—Mary—and then she recognized who he was, and though from that instant forward the whole course of human history was changed in so many profound and complex ways that it's impossible to imagine how it would have been different otherwise, for Mary Magdalene the only thing that had changed was that for reasons she was in no state to consider, her old friend and teacher and strong right arm was alive again, and RABBONI! she shouted and was about to throw her arms around him for sheer joy and astonishment when he stopped her.

"Noli me tangere," he said. "Touch me not. Don't hold on to me," (John 20:17), thus making her not only the first person in the world to have her heart stop beating for a second to find him alive again when she'd thought he was dead as a doornail but the first person also to have her heart break a little to realize that he couldn't be touched any more, wasn't there any more as a hand to hold onto when the going got tough, a shoulder to weep on, because the life in him was no longer a life she could know by touching it, with her here and him there, but a life she could know only by living it: with her here—old tart and retread, old brokenheart and last, best friend—and with him here, too, alive inside her life, to raise her up also out of the wreckage of all that was wrecked in her and dead.—Frederick Buechner

STEWARDSHIP OF INTENT.   Take the story about the woman who placed the two pennies in the temple-treasury, but let us poetise a little variation. The two pennies were for her a great sum, which she had not quickly accumulated. She had saved for a long time in order to get them saved up, and then she had hidden them wrapped in a little cloth in order to bring them when she herself went up to the temple. But a swindler had detected that she possessed this money, had tricked her out of it, and had exchanged the cloth for an identical piece which was utterly empty—something which the widow did not know. Thereupon she went up to the temple, placed, as she intended, the two pennies that is, nothing, in the temple-treasury: I wonder if Christ would not still have said what he said of her, that "she gave more than all the rich?"—Sören Kierkegaard

Sermon Suggestions

ON SELLING ONE'S SOUL.   TEXT: 1 Kings 21:1–3, 17–21. (1) Beginning in greed. (2) Advancing with intrigue (see verses 4–16). (3) Finishing with retribution.

WHAT COUNTS.   TEXT: Gal. 6:7–18. In living the Christian life, what is crucial? (1) Is it peace at any price? No. (2) Is it strict observance of arbitrary rules and timid assent to rigid creeds? No. (3) Is it self-denying, even reckless, commitment to the Lord Jesus Christ? Yes.

Worship Aids

CALL TO WORSHIP.   "Lead me, O Lord, in thy righteousness because of mine enemies; make thy way straight before my face" (Ps. 5:8).

INVOCATION.   Holy God through whom we find liberty in salvation, we pray for our nation today and ask that we be renewed to protect her freedoms and liberties in ways that are wise and prudent and informed by this hour of holy worship.—E. Lee Phillips

OFFERTORY SENTENCE.   "As we have therefore opportunity, let us do good unto all men, especially unto them who are of the household of faith" (Gal. 6:10).

OFFERTORY PRAYER.   Lord, make us willing to pray for and forgive those who would do us wrong, and let our loving words and deeds show them your love. To that end, bless these offerings, so that even those farthest from us in love and understanding, as well as our own dear Christian friends, may receive your grace.

PRAYER.   Great and merciful God, bless us as we enter again into thy presence, that our souls may lift their wings in prayer and praise and find their freedom in the sky of thy great and gracious will. Let there be light for those who are perplexed, forgiveness for those who suffer guilt, peace for those who strive against themselves, strength for the weary, and patience for those who suffer. Bless those who feel the strain of life's widening mystery; abide with those who stand in hard places, ruthlessly cornered by unyielding circumstance; manifest thyself to those who are alone, that they may find a glory in the long day or the quiet night; walk with those whose paths wind upward to perilous heights that they may not falter; let thy Holy Spirit move in the hands and hearts of all who by their artistry and skill fashion beauty or recover truth for us who are blinder and duller; and in thy fatherly compassion stand beside all humble men and women who have borne the tasks life demanded of them with faithfulness, sharing the world's injustice with patience and compassion.—Samuel H. Miller

LECTIONARY MESSAGE

Topic: Messengers of God's Kingdom

Text: Luke 10:1–12; 17–20

In these verses, Jesus tells seventy messengers to assure those that are healed that the kingdom of God has come near them. He tells them to warn those who reject them and his truth, that the kingdom of God has come near them.

I. *The kingdom brings blessing.*

(a) It brings peace. The very first thing that the messengers are to say is that peace is coming in with them. It should be a lasting peace, a personal peace, a household peace. The kingdom here spoken of is the eternal rule of God. Much more than the vaunted *Pax Romana*, God's rule will blend the harmony of the eternal ages of his loving care into every moment of every life it touches. It is personal. We do not need to understand eternity, although the frontispiece of Hendrik Willem Van Loon's *Story of Mankind* gives a good hint. What we need to know is that each one who has peace really has a well of calmness to draw upon in each needy hour. Wherever such a person of peace lives, the lives of those with that one will be drawn to God and be, with that one, touched with the serenity of action in the harmony of God.

(b) It brings healing. When a pair of these seventy messengers came to a house that received them, they were empowered to heal the sick living there, as a blessing of the kingdom of God. The healing was the true panacea of God. Everything we buy of a kind that can run down, wear out, or get broken must be returned to the manufacturer for repairs, or at least it must be taken only to a factory-authorized service center. If it is not, all warranties are terminated. This coming near of the kingdom of God, brought by Jesus' special team of representatives, is the presence of the One who made us. In his kingdom, we are in the hands of our Maker. What better place of healing could we find for our sicknesses of body, mind, or spirit?

II. *The kingdom brings judgment.*

(a) It brings a critical chance for choice. The seventy came to every house in every city or town with the same message— "Peace be to this house." Some would receive them. Some would not. The offer of the presence of the kingdom of God is a matter for decision. Perhaps refusing hospitality is a sign that there was no one at home for God's kingdom at all. Eternity for them hangs on receiving or rejecting God's team of two and thus receiving or rejecting Jesus and God (verse 16). We all make minor choices, some of which are predisposing as well as revealing. They lead to major choices that together determine life or death.

(b) It brings condemnation for rejection. The refusal to receive the king's messengers is tantamount to refusal to receive the king. Such rejection will cause the messengers to leave and take the message of peace and healing away with them. The last-minute opportunity, lest the person or house or city act on error, is clearly given—"Be sure of this, that the kingdom of God is near you."

If the answer is still no, then the promise to them is that they have less chance for eternity than those of the city of Sodom, who deliberately violated God's will for them. The term *that day* referred to the great and terrible day of the Lord, the day of final judgment by God of all living creatures. Jesus had recognized the dangers of sending his messengers out to all the Jews and to the Gentiles of the area. He likened them to lambs going among wolves, but he was bringing the opportunity spoken of in Isa. 11:6 for the "wolves" to join in peace with the "lambs."

III. *The kingdom brings glory.*

(a) It brings success. The seventy returned with joy. They had found in their message the way to success in overcoming evil spirits of all kinds and the way to avoid every kind of evil in the world.

ritual exaltation. No
n be as precious to a
ow that God has re-
at the messenger has

given to God. Even earthly peace, health,
and influence must yield in importance
and glory to personal godliness and
salvation.—John R. Rodman

SUNDAY: JULY TWELFTH

SERVICE OF WORSHIP

Sermon: Your God Is Too Small
TEXT: Ps. 139:1–6

J. B. Phillips in *Your God Is Too Small* observes, "No one is ever really at ease in facing what we call life and death without a religious faith. The trouble with many people is that they have not found a God big enough for modern needs." Many of us may be carrying about a nine-year-old child's conception of God along with our adult understanding of history, science, and ourselves.

Two men were seated aboard a jet as it lifted skyward and moved toward the west. A neatly dressed young man turned his gaze from the window to the older passenger sitting beside him and introduced himself. Upon learning that his companion was a minister, the young man, who had stated that his occupation was an astronomer, asked the minister if he would like to know his views on religion. Hesitating for a moment, the minister responded, "Well, sure." The astronomer replied that all that man needed to know about religion was the Golden Rule: "Do unto others as you would have them do unto you." The minister was silent for a while, and then he asked the astronomer if he would like to hear his views on astronomy. With a puzzled look the astronomer said, "Yes." "I think astronomy," the minister stated, "can be summed up in the phrase, 'Twinkle, twinkle, little star, how I wonder what you are.'"

I. If you and I are going to live in the modern world with a strong and relevant faith, it means that we shall need an adequate concept of God. We must discover a God who can demand and capture our minds, our hearts, and our lives! Many

men and women are living without a faith in God at all. This is not because they are wicked or selfish or arrogant. It is because they have not discovered an adult God with whom they can live. We work hard to acquire an education, to find a good job, to keep the family together, but for some reason we naively expect a casual yet adequate pilgrimage with God. It does not work that way! Will you dust off your spiritual antennas and begin a search for an adequate, adult God who can command your devotion and your commitment? How shall we visualize him?

(a) Some people see God as a help in times of trouble. That sounds helpful! A helpful God is certainly a hopeful view of him, isn't it? Not if we use him as a spare tire only in times of emergencies.

(b) You may worship a God who is the way to heaven. Sounds hopeful! But if God is not involved in the here and now, how can we believe that he is on the other side of the door of death?

(c) Perhaps we can find an adequate God when we see him as a badge of moral respectability. Sounds ethical! But such a god is always molded with clay hands, and he is no more than that.

(d) How about the God of our fathers? Sounds safe! But a hand-me-down religion may become an impersonal one based upon creeds or family habit. Many of us worship someone else's god. The living God of our fathers may be only a dead god for us if we merely receive him as a family heirloom.

(e) Some of us will desire to hold high a view of God that sees him only as the giver of all good gifts. Sounds biblical! But there is the great danger that we shall pervert a humble trust in God into a selfish effort to use him as a heavenly Santa Claus or a Cosmic Bellhop.

II. You are perhaps wondering if there is really an adequate view of God. Can man with his limited knowledge and spiritual blindness even look through "a glass darkly"? Let's not give up too soon.

(a) What about the God who is the sovereign creator of the universe? Sounds theological! Scholars of theology tell us that God is the mighty, majestic creator of the universe. And, of course, he is. The psalmist exclaims, "O Lord, our Lord, how majestic is thy name in all the earth!" (Ps. 8:1). Perhaps we have finally found an adequate God. Or have we? Aren't we tempted to transform him into a stained-glass saint? We make him into a theological abstraction or a musical phantom. God is launched into a distant, impersonal wild blue yonder. Such a vision of God is totally inadequate. The Bible says, "The Word became flesh." Jesus Christ is God himself coping with life on the very terms that he imposed upon his creatures. God was willing to get his hands dusty when he stepped down from heaven.

(b) For some people God is viewed as a perennial disappointment. Sounds realistic! Prayers go unanswered. Disasters fall upon the undeserved. Haven't we all whispered at least once or twice, "I trusted him, and he has let me down." Here is a family that is disintegrating. There is a man who has lost his job. And over there is a teenager who is pregnant. All have one thing in common—they are blaming God for letting this happen to them. Is it his fault? Or are they simply evading personal responsibility for their ills? We often expect things from God that he cannot deliver; we "set ourselves up" for disappointments. We wish to determine our destinies and to have a world in which good is rewarded and evil is punished like a well-run kindergarten. He didn't create a grade school when he made earth. He wanted mature adults, not childish adolescents. His school is based on one dominant principle, human freedom. To give us real freedom, God risks our failures and our sins. He must allow folly and failure to exist so that genuine faith may develop in the laboratory of life. They both flourish in the same soil. Those who are perennially disappointed in God's response to their plights view God as a giant Mr. Fix-It. They want this overindulgent parent to walk into their playrooms and repair the toys that they and their friends have carelessly demolished. But God is more like a Waiting Father, who allows his prodigal children to drift into the far country in hopes that they will grow up there and eventually return to him. I don't know about you, but I would rather be a prodigal son who has the *possibilities of becoming a real son* than a puppet on a string!

(c) Allow me to confess that I don't have all the pieces of the puzzle to explain God. I do know that you will be able to know God by looking at him in Jesus Christ. Christ is more than a grand teacher or a great prophet. He is more than a perceptive mystic who walked with God. He is more than the only sinless man ever to walk on the face of the earth. He is God in human furnishings, come down to the battlefield of life. He cannot be the *full* expression of all that God is for there is neither time nor space enough to hold God. But there is God enough in human paraphernalia to afford us all the knowledge of God that we need. A teenager fell into one of the comfortable chairs in her father's study at the church and asked, "Dad, you are minister; tell me what you know about God." He responded, "Helen, I don't know much, but I do know enough." To know Jesus and the power of his Resurrection is enough. He is where an authentic knowledge of God begins and ends.

Jesus said, "He that has seen me has seen the Father," and, "I am the way, the truth, and the life: no person comes to the Father but by way of me" (John 14:9, 6).—James E. Sorrell

Illustrations

EXPERIENCING GOD. There is an experience of the love of God which, when it comes upon us and enfolds us and bathes us and warms us is so utterly new that we can hardly identify it with the old phrase God is love. Can this be the love of God, this burning, tender, wooing, wounding pain of love that pierces the marrow of my bones and burns out old loves and ambitions? God experienced is a vast surprise.—Thomas R. Kelly

THE PART AND THE WHOLE.   The little that we know of God seems so precious that we grasp it as if it were the whole. We set up our narrow standards and build our protecting bulwarks to guard what we have won against the mutations of the years. And we forget that God is the living God, everywhere present, in the changing as in the permanent; in the future as in the past and in the present.—William Adams Brown

Sermon Suggestions

ULTIMATE POWER.   TEXT: 2 Kings 2:1, 6–14, especially verse 12. (1) Not in impressive military might. (2) Rather in unimpressive spiritual sources.

WHEN PRAYER FOR US IS ANSWERED. TEXT: Col. 1:1–14. (1) We will have spiritual insight. (2) We will live a fruitful life. (3) We will have enough strength for every need. (4) We will be thankful for the blessing of salvation that makes the former blessings possible.

Worship Aids

CALL TO WORSHIP.   "Lord, you have examined me and you know me. You know everything I do; from far away you understand all my thoughts. You see me, whether I am working or resting; you know all my actions. Even before I speak, you already know what I will say. You are all around me on every side; you protect me with your power" (Ps. 139:1–5).

INVOCATION.   Infinite and Eternal God, high above us yet appearing to us in your Son, who has shown us your face, we come to you asking that our hearts and minds may be open to all that you are. Stretch our capacities for faith, knowledge, and obedience as we worship you, we pray.

OFFERTORY SENTENCE.   "We pray that you will be ever grateful to the Father who has made you fit to receive a share in the possession which he promised to his dedicated people in the realm of light" (Col. 1:12, Barclay).

OFFERTORY PRAYER.   Our Father, we thank you for the blessings from you that we have seen and known and for the blessings that we do not see and know. Grant that your goodness may so penetrate our hearts and minds that all our decisions and actions may express our gratitude and love.

PRAYER.   "O the depth of the riches and wisdom and knowledge of God! How unsearchable his judgments—how inscrutable his ways!" As we contemplate your being—your presence, your absence—we marvel at your transcendence—your beyondness, at your immanence—your nearness. We are amazed at your timelessness—"before the mountains were brought forth or ever you had formed the earth and the world, even from everlasting to everlasting you are God." We marvel at your timeliness—"in the fullness of time you sent forth your only Son" for our salvation and the salvation of the world. You are "the great God and the great King above all gods," yet you are the Word becoming flesh dwelling among us.

As in this place we are awakened to a new vision of your glory, who among us does not discover himself exclaiming, "This is none other than the house of God—this is the gate of heaven." We praise you that your Spirit is at work among us, and we have been awakened at depths and to heights we have never known before. What a new vision, or renewed vision, of your grace in the gift of this new day and in the gift of your Word perennially fresh as the living Bread. For your Word of grace present from the beginning but now fully manifest in Christ creating and nurturing the Church among us and in us, we praise you. What a privilege is ours this morning to celebrate the greater Church with our Presbyter, your Presbyter, among us.

Your Word of grace in Christ is here in this his body in the world. We pray that we may be present in such love and trust, in such faith and openness that we may each receive this grace according to personal need in all of its power to make whole whatever our brokenness.

Your Word in Christ is not only for our health but for the healing of the nations. We pray for leaders and citizens who have humility and wisdom to know and act that wealth and power are a stewardship from you that all peoples may enjoy their inalienable right to freedom and the blessed bounty of the good earth.

We pray through him who is your Word from the beginning and is now present in resurrection power and glory, calling persons in every time and place to pray and live: "Our Father. . . ."—John Thompson

LECTIONARY MESSAGE

Topic: A Personal Answer for Crime
Text: Luke 10:25–37
I. *The reality of crime.*

(a) The crucial question. After Jesus rejoiced with his disciples over the return of the seventy messengers, he continued teaching them. One of the crowd who was skilled in Jewish Law quoted Lev. 19:18, "Thou shalt love thy neighbor as thyself," and has put to Jesus the question, "And who is my neighbor?" Jesus told the story in verses 30 to 35 and then answered the lawyer's question with the centrally important question, "Which, thinkest thou, was neighbor unto him that fell among the thieves?"

(b) Going beyond justice. The two who passed by the victim probably thought he was beyond what help they could give and that the criminals were also beyond their reach. But a despised Samaritan went the limit to help. Man's inhumanity to man can be answered only by man's godliness to man. We see repeated real and fictional accounts of the bestial, brutal, cruel, inhumane, and inhuman treatment of people by others. We are caught up in the solution of the mystery to identify the perpetrator of the crime, to isolate the criminal and bring him to "jus-

tice," but we are frustrated in restoring the victim to the sense of safety and sanity. We have carried Christian compassion to ridiculous extremes on behalf of the "rights" of the criminal but have almost totally abandoned the victims to face terrible personal disasters, bear all the exorbitant expense of their own care and recovery, and still accept the taunting mockery of a society that cares more for the criminal than for the victim and releases the criminal to go at large and brutalize still other helpless human beings. We must face the fact that *we* are *not* neighbors to those who fall among the thieves in our communities. The shocking result is that one out of four of us will sooner or later replace the victim.

II. *The penchant for self-justification.*

(a) The worried questioner. The lawyer betrayed himself by asking his question. He was willing to justify himself and therefore demanded a specific identity or at least an inerrant description of who it was to whom he owed the duty of a love equal to his feeling for himself. He, like us, thought it couldn't happen to him.

(b) A shared worry. He is not the only person who seeks objective and dependable means of reassurance. Most of humanity has difficulty assuring itself that all is well, but it is secure and unassailable in its own righteousness. We all constantly worry about our acceptability, not only in society but in heaven also. And there are many causes for doubting concern. The mores of society establish standards of conduct that people violate at their peril. These standards change somewhat from place to place and from time to time. Each one must attempt to keep alert and keep in compliance. But it can be managed acceptably. Our bigger worry by far is eternity.

(c) The snare of morality. The error of the lawyer is one that, unfortunately, many of us duplicate. We try, along with him, to put the question of our eternal salvation into terms that can be dealt with, whose requirements can be met with a little credit to spare, and that will leave us then to enjoy our lives. We should like to be able to love God by being acceptable to men and women among whom we live. We may have some hope of fitting into a certain social circle, of becoming working parts of human organizations or keeping ourselves from violating laws or, at least, from being caught doing so. But love God? With *all* our hearts, *all* our *souls*, *all* our *strength*, and *all* our *minds*? Let's rather get an authority to approve, to sign off on what we are already doing. It is better, we think, to be pleasing to God by being good husbands and wives, good citizens, good taxpayers, and good providers—and then let these things speak for us.

III. *The greater blessing of life.*

(a) The testing situation. Even with the pervasiveness of crime, it is possible one may never know a real victim. But the good Samaritan neighbor went where life was active and open and, in effect, dangerous—where a victim is as likely as not to be found. But he was ready for the emergent opportunity. Our tests may not be the same kind, but they will come. Somewhere each one will have occasion to prove the depth to which one's love for God has prepared one to be a neighbor.

(b) The command of Jesus. Paul tells us it is good "to remember the words of the Lord Jesus, how he said, "'It is more blessed to give than to receive'" (Acts 20:35). Jesus was showing this lawyer that it is better to *be* a neighbor than to *have* one. In his story he shows that the acute desire to define a neighbor gives way completely before the unselfish act of mercy shown to a fellow mortal. Self-justification goes out the window when one loses oneself in self-forgetting demonstration of a love thus shown to be learned from God. If you do love God, "Go, and do thou likewise." One may thus attack the problem of crime at least on behalf of the victim.—John R. Rodman

SUNDAY: JULY NINETEENTH

SERVICE OF WORSHIP

Sermon: A Father's Faith

TEXT: John 4:46–54

Suppose you could have anything you wanted. What would it be? A tie, some socks, some aftershave, or maybe a trip to Tahiti? Suppose one of your children were critically ill, at the point of death, and you could have anything you wanted. What would it be? No contest. You'd wish to be a father still when the day was over.

I. So we understand the man in our story as he hurries along the fifteen miles from Capernaum to Cana. We don't know who he was, but we do know what he was. He was a *basilikos*, an employee of Herod Antipas, a Gentile who must have heard of Jesus' miraculous deeds around Galilee. He was also on that day a distraught father whose child, the text says, was at the point of death. He was perfectly willing to beg Jesus to come fifteen miles to his home—a long day's journey by foot on those roads—in the hopes that maybe he'd get there in time to do something.

That's faith of a sort, it seems to me, faith in the powers of Jesus the wonder-working rabbi from Galilee but desperate faith that was born out of a father's love for his son more than any knowledge of Christ. Maybe we can call it faith, but it was a very weak, tremulous sort of faith that would have been dashed immediately had Jesus not provided the miracle.

Notice that Jesus comments on this: "Unless you all see signs and wonders, you all won't believe." Why the plural? Most commentators think that Jesus was, in a way, speaking over the man's head to a larger body of people whose faith depends on the miraculous. You've known folks like that, perhaps. They become religious at crisis time, hoping for a cure, or they have a religious conversion that doesn't take. A man like that was converted once. This man had no use for the church until a certain evangelist came who struck his fancy, and he got into the church in a big way. The teenagers loved

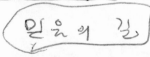

him and flocked to church because he was their hero. Then one day it was discovered that he was leaving his wife and children to marry one of the teenagers, and the whole experience came apart.

Faith needs more grounding than the miraculous or the emotional. One of my favorite preachers, Frederick Buechner, has a sermon in which he imagines God writing his name in the stars. Suddenly there would be worldwide reform, for about six months, he predicts, and then the world would return to normal. So what if God exists? I still have to make a living.

So Jesus rejects the miracle-faith of this distraught father. "Please come heal my boy," the man begs, but Jesus only replies, "Go—the boy is alive." The RSV translates it as if it were a promise—"your son will live"—but it more likely is a simple declaration, "The boy is alive." What, no lightning? No magic? Not even a few moments of fervent prayer? No, just the bare, bald statement, "the boy is alive," and that's all the father has to hold.

II. Now the man shows a sort of real faith, stronger than the miracle faith just before. His faith is now in Jesus' word. He has an obedient faith, born of the contact between him and the Living Word of God, faith enough to drop his hold on Jesus the miracle worker.

That's a hard step to take, to move from miracle-faith to faith in the word. To make it, you have to give up what you have and reach for something else. It's like walking out into the ocean and getting to the point that if you take one more step, you'll be over your head and you'll have to swim, and you hesitate: Am I strong enough to battle the waves? Do I really want to swim badly enough?

Each of us, I think, faces that sort of faith-trial if we stay with Christianity long enough. We wonder why God allows some people to suffer, or we come upon passages in the Scripture that are confusing, or we come to a decision for which there seems to be no clear and easy answers from God; I don't know what it might be for you. At those times we have to reach beyond simple faith. This man

had to leave Jesus, the man he knew could heal his son, and walk away without knowing for certain, as when you try and try but just can't feel certain about your direction and so you just go on in the way you believe you ought to go. That's faith: faith not to sit down in the road and demand certainty; faith to keep walking; faith that you can't fall in a hole too deep for God's rescuing arm.

III. So the man begins his fifteen-mile walk back to Cana, apparently walking through the night in his desperation to see his son alive, wondering all the time if he's done the right thing, wondering if he should have insisted that Jesus come with him. Halfway home, some servants meet him: "Your son is alive," they say, repeating word for word what Jesus has said to him. "When did he start to recover?" "Oh, about 1:00 P.M. yesterday," which was about the same time Jesus and the man had been talking. And now the text says, "Then the man himself believed along with all his household." This is faith in Jesus the life-giver, converting faith, faith that would lead a man and all his family and employees to commit themselves to Christ as Lord. This is faith that goes beyond obedience. This sort of faith recognizes in Jesus the power of life itself and will not let go. Jesus is what kept that man a father throughout that long, tension-filled day. Jesus gave his son life. Do you think that man would ever abandon Jesus?

One day in the life of a first-century father, a day's journey that took him through three of faith's stages, that took him from his son's deathbed on a thirty-mile hike to meet Jesus and find his faith and his son again. Our faith moves through some of the same stages, though not so quickly, but perhaps this father's story can help us to stick with the walk of faith. That's what stories do for us: This man's story shows us what's possible for us, how we may grow in our faith if we just keep walking and don't sit down in the road.—Richard Vinson

Illustrations

FAITH IN GOD.   Christian faith, when really tried, will not give up the conviction that somehow "all things are of God." Its desire is not merely for the friendship and help of a great Comrade in the battle against evil; its desire is for the Eternal God, our Everlasting Refuge and Home, the Perfection of Joy and Peace and Love. It is not enough for me to believe that as each situation arises God will help me to play the man in it, accepting the pain as part of the price of mankind's upward struggle, and so becoming a willing fellow-worker and fellow-sufferer with God himself. That is indeed a great and beautiful belief. But it is not the whole truth. Full Christian faith claims something else too—the complementary truth which is signified (however imperfectly) by the old notion of the Impassibility of God. Underneath all the suffering there is a divine perfection of joy and peace, a reconciliation in which all suffering is overcome and transfigured and finds its place in God's "Immemorial Plan," an eternal reality of God's Kingdom raised far above the changing fortunes of the great campaign, so that even while the tide of battle ebbs and flows in this world, souls can be conceived as passing into a perfect fruition of God. There is here something which we cannot give up if God is to be God for us at all, and if religion is to do the real work of religion.—D. M. Baillie

PATHS IN SPIRITUALITY.   There are no shortcuts from faith (the conviction that Christ is Lord and his love sovereign) to life (the acting out of this faith in daily deeds of self-giving love). On the contrary, this is for most people a long and arduous way. All kinds of obstructions have to be surmounted. There are unloving passions, which may be difficult to control. There are self-regarding and self-indulgent habits, sometimes built up over years and firmly entrenched. Even if we begin to overcome these obstacles, there is a long way to go before we begin to grasp in an affirmative sense the amazing height and breadth and length and depth of the love to which Christians are called. Worship, both in its corporate exercise and in whatever other acts may be appropriate to each individual, is the discipline leading from faith to action. It is the process by which the disciple is formed and becomes increasingly mature in the Christian religion.

St. Paul is one of the earliest and best guides on these matters, a true spiritual counselor. He himself underwent one of the most dramatic conversion experiences in all Christian history. But it seems that the first thing he did after his conversion was to retire for a time to the deserts of Arabia—he went on retreat, as we would say nowadays. He let three years pass before he went up to Jerusalem, and who can doubt that this time was spent in prayer and preparation for the tasks to which he believed himself called by God?—John Macquarrie

Sermon Suggestions

HOSPITALITY TO GOD'S WORD.   TEXT: 2 Kings 4:8–17. (1) *The story*: A Shunamite woman and her husband offer continuing hospitality to God's prophet. (2) *A significant truth*: God has special blessings for those who seek ways to honor his Word. (3) *Practical application*: (a) through family Bible reading and prayer, (b) through family public worship, (c) through family activities in service to God and community.

THE GOSPEL ALIVE.   TEXT: Col. 1:21–29. (1) The gospel described, verses 21–23. (2) The gospel lived out, verses 24–25. (3) The ultimate purpose of the revelation in the gospel, verses 26–27. (4) The immediate purpose, verses 28–29.

Worship Aids

CALL TO WORSHIP.   "Search me, O God, and know my heart; try me, and know my thoughts; and see if there be any wicked way in me, and lead me in the way everlasting" (Ps. 139:23–24).

INVOCATION.   God of might, call forth from us in this hour all that is highest and best, because we met the Savior and followed where he led. Then let us keep doing this till time shall end.—E. Lee Phillips

OFFERTORY SENTENCE. "This is the Christ we proclaim; we train everyone and teach everyone the full scope of this knowledge, in order to set everyone before God mature in Christ; I labour for that end, striving for it with the divine energy which is a power within me" (Col. 1:28–29, Moffatt).

OFFERTORY PRAYER. Help us, O God, to reach our full spiritual stature in Christ, deepening our sense of stewardship of all that we have and are, by the power of your Spirit within us.

PRAYER. Eternal God, who without asking it hast set us in this mysterious scheme of circumstance, widely we would open the doors and windows of our souls to thee. We crave the experience of thy people who have so felt thy nearness that they have cried, Whither shall we flee from thy presence? Whither shall we go from thy Spirit? In the beauty of nature, in the revealing relationships of friendship and family, in all that is excellent and worthy, courageous and full of hope in human life, in victories of light over darkness, love over hate, good over evil, become thou real to us and in the silence of our souls speak to us quietly that we may be sure of thy presence.

Through another week we have been tempted to be careless and ungrateful. Like streams flowing through our common days, goodness has been richly given and we have been thoughtless of the fountain. O God, today we thankfully acknowledge thee as the friend behind all friendship, the spring of all beauty, the source of all goodness.

Save us from dishonesty and every crooked way as we worship here. Let us not come before thee in court garments to appear as we think thou wouldst like to see us. Let us stand before thee as we are. If today our spirits are full of rebellion, make us candid with thee. Let us bring our lamentations and resentments into thy presence and speak them out frankly before thy face, complaining that life has not been just to us and that we have been ill-treated. But, O God, help us to stay long enough in thy presence for thy healing hand to be laid upon us. Like storm-tossed seas when the wind goes down, growing quiet, so bring thou us to peace.

If we stand before thee with sins in our lives for which we are not penitent but which we dearly love, help us to be frank with thee. Save us from the futility of pretending penitence when we have it not. Grant us the grace of honesty to stand before thee, saying, O God, behold! What thou hatest we love. Nevertheless, give us grace to stay long enough in thy presence for thee to throw thy light upon the loveliness of Christlike living until we are drawn to that. Let not Satan beguile us by fashioning himself as an angel of light.

We come with our need for courage. Thou living Spirit, walk through this congregation and lay thy hand on men and women outwardly placid and comfortable, inwardly dismayed and beaten. For life has laid a heavy weight on some of us; death has come into our households; we have been disappointed in our friends, discouragements have met us in our practical affairs and some of us are torn by anxiety. O God, we need the spirit of our fighting sires, who revealed the splendor of their souls when days were difficult. Speak to us, saying, Be not afraid.—Harry Emerson Fosdick

LECTIONARY MESSAGE

Topic: Choosing the Good Part

TEXT: Luke 10:38–42

This text follows that in which Jesus has shown the inspired application of love for one's needy neighbor. This one gives the emphasis to the intake side of faith, the other essential side of following Jesus, the spiritual side.

I. *Life a succession of choices.*

(a) Children must make choices. Human beings are not automata, not programmed machines. The essence of the human condition is the right, the liberty, of making choices. But choosing is not only a privilege; it is an essential part of life. The young child is not without power to choose and, thus, to influence the entire family. The child must choose whether to be happy or sad, whether to obey or disobey, whether to give joy to other people or to grieve them by misbehavior. Everything from birth onward is a selection.

(b) Youthful choices are life-determining. The time of growth from childhood to adulthood determines largely the major course of one's life. Oh, if we could only help young people gain knowledge to choose wisely *before* errors result in lifelong handicaps! Choice of school or college is not nearly as important as *choosing to study*. Choice of a career is not nearly as important as *choosing to work*. Choice of a mate, as important as it is, is not nearly as important as *choosing to love* whomever one chooses.

(c) Adult choices contribute to success. Grown-up people must choose many things also, but the difficulty occurs in choosing to live with one's choices. Adult choices bring continuing meaning to one's life. Job, spouse, car, house, hobby, military service, friends, music, art, insurance, clubs, and charities all offer almost infinite choices, and every choice brings its own rewards. A person does not need to be aged to know the necessity of choosing between time and eternity, but aging makes the choice more poignant.

II. *Choosing the lesser part.*

(a) Martha chose to be hospitable. In thinking about Martha, let us remember that it was she who invited Jesus into her house. She chose hospitality to offer the traveler. Her tasks must have been lovingly intended, but she was not willing to prepare and serve the food and drink without her sister's help. She was distracted from the one important element, the presence of Jesus. It is possible to be so engaged in a program of good deeds and constructive accomplishment that one's soul is lost.

(b) Martha chose the lesser part. In all her good intentions, Martha failed to give priority to the irreplaceable opportunity. She was so involved in helping sustain life or making it more pleasant that she ignored the significance of finding meaning in it.

III. *Choosing the good part.*

(a) Mary's choice earned approval. What would the millions of Christians, Jews, or even Muslims give to have only a few seconds in the presence of Jesus, to hear only a few words from him? There is only one good part in all of life, and Mary chose it. Mary saw the Word of God in the words of Jesus. By giving him rapt attention, she gained insight. Martha was hospitable, but Mary gave to Jesus what is the heart of hospitality: an attentive and lowly heart. Mary adopted the attitude of a learner, of a receptive mind and a devoted spirit, sitting at Jesus' feet. And Jesus gave his high approval: "Mary has chosen the good part."

(b) Choosing Jesus is everything. Of all life's choices, this is the one essential choice. All of life is lost without making the choice to give one's life to Jesus Christ. The child, in the words of Charles H. Spurgeon, is "often fascinated with the flaunting flowers of fortune and fashion," but that child must steer clear of them and choose Jesus. Paul said, "This one thing I do . . . I press toward the mark for the prize . . . in Christ Jesus" (Phil. 3:13). But no one is ready to "do," to engage in action or ministry as Paul did, without having been instructed at Jesus' feet. Even one who may be socially subordinate in the home, of lesser importance there, can become the spiritual heroine of any story, be the more important in the kingdom of God. A pianist, if he is to be great, must concentrate on his instrument until the keys take the shape of spoons. May Jesus be given any less importance in a Christian's life?—John R. Rodman

SUNDAY: JULY TWENTY-SIXTH

SERVICE OF WORSHIP

Sermon: God Opens the Doors

TEXT: 2 Cor. 2:12–17

For a number of years, the Apostle Paul had endured strained relationships with Christian friends in a church in Corinth. Although he had helped establish the church, some serious misunderstandings had developed between Paul and his friends.

A visit by Paul that was intended to repair the broken relationship only made things worse. He returned to Ephesus and decided to deal with the matter by writing a letter.

Titus delivered the letter. He was scheduled to meet Paul in Troas where the apostle was fulfilling a preaching engagement (v. 12). However, Titus did not arrive in Troas when Paul had expected him. So the apostle grew anxious about his friend's welfare and about the situation in Corinth.

Apparently, God had opened a wonderful "door" of ministry for Paul. But his spirit was so troubled about Titus and the Corinthians that he bypassed this open door and went instead to look for Titus in Macedonia (v. 12).

The sermon text recounts Paul's excitement when he and Titus were reunited. But even more, his joy is expressed because of the obvious reconciliation that had taken place between the Corinthians and himself. It was Paul's conviction that God had led every step of the way (v. 14).

These are days of unusual and incredible opportunity. And I believe God's Word provides insight and encouragement to help his people face the opportunities of living in the most exciting times that our world has ever seen! Out of God's Word, then, let me show you what you can do when faced with an open door.

I. The first thing you can do is to risk accepting the challenge. Jesus told a parable once about three men who were suddenly faced with an unbelievable chance to do something magnificent. We call it the parable of the talents (Matt. 25:14–30). A more contemporary name might be the parable of the investments.

A businessman decided to take an extended trip. He left portions of his investment portfolio in the trust of three brokers. When he returned from his travels, he called each one in order to audit his accounts.

The first two men who had invested his wealth were commended for a job well done. Apparently, they earned the right to keep his accounts as well as a handsome bonus. But the third man had been afraid to risk what was left in his custodianship. So he had done nothing with the funds. Consequently, he lost the account and also his job. He was the consummate picture of missed opportunity.

One consistent characteristic of people who make progress in life is that they are decisive. Sure, they are bound to make mistakes. But most of all, they make decisions and move on.

Someone suggested that God has given us two incredible things: absolutely awesome potential and the freedom of choice. However, the tragedy is that for the most part, many of us have refused them both.

If the story Jesus told truly represents God's relationship to man—and it does—then it ought to make us sit up straight. The businessman told his broker that he would have accepted anything—even rock-bottom savings account interest (v. 27). In other words, he really was not so much concerned with how much the broker made but whether the broker would take advantage of an opportunity given him by a gracious benefactor. What he condemned was not the broker's failure to earn a sizable return. What he condemned was the broker's decision to do nothing at all. Because of that, he lost everything!

II. A second way to respond to opportunity is to learn to recognize it even when it's disguised as difficulty.

In a famous study by Victor and Mildred Goertzel, the home backgrounds of three hundred highly successful people were investigated. All three hundred had made it to the top. They were men and women whose names everyone would recognize: Franklin D. Roosevelt, Helen Keller, Albert Schweitzer, Clara Barton, Albert Einstein, Sigmund Freud, Ghandi.

Here's what the study revealed. Three-fourths of these people were troubled in childhood either by poverty, broken homes, rejection, overpossessive or dominating parents. Seventy-four of the eighty-five writers of fiction or drama, and sixteen of the twenty poets came from homes where, as children, they saw or experienced physical, emotional, or spiritual abuse. More than seventy-five were victims of physical handicaps such as blindness, deafness, or crippled limbs. And yet every one of them somehow recognized the advantage of disadvantage and became the people God called them to be.

Some people automatically conclude that difficulty, adversity, obstacles, and objections are signs that God is closing the door of opportunity. And God does close doors as well as open them.

Paul was "kept by the Holy Spirit from preaching the Word in the province of Asia" (Acts 16:6). Apparently, he had decided to go to Ephesus, but the Holy Spirit hindered him. Some people think that the Holy Spirit spoke in an audible voice, "Don't go that way, Paul." Others think he may have gotten sick. Some suggest that the boat trip was canceled. An obstacle could have been placed in his way by the Jews who were determined to stop him.

Whatever it was, one time after another he tried to go in the direction of Ephesus, and he was prevented. Whether it was inner feeling or outer frustration, we simply do not know. But Paul was not allowed to do what he intended to do.

So he went in another direction, toward Bithynia. But the Spirit would not allow that either. Can you imagine the frustration ... the disappointment ... how discouraging this all must have been? God was not telling Paul where he did want him to go. He was simply telling Paul where he didn't want him to go.

In the meantime, Paul simply had to wait and to work. He determined not to just sit back and fold his arms when a door closed. He went to another door, and another. He kept pushing on doors to see which one would open.

Sometimes it's hard work to find the door that God has opened. The key, however, is your determination to magnify God and not the problems nor the obstacles you encounter along the way. In fact, I believe that those obstacles hold the key to your greatest opportunities, if you will only discipline yourself to see opportunities everywhere!

I understand that the Tartar tribes of Central Asia once had a curse against their enemies. They said, "May you stay in one place forever." Don't you agree that it would indeed be a curse to remain the way we are, where we are—forever?

And that's how I want to close this message: with a reminder that you don't have to stay the way you are forever. Right now, God is giving you an opportunity to experience his saving grace and life-transforming power.

Paul was once arrested and charged with desecrating the Temple in Jerusalem. His enemies said that he had brought a Gentile into the court of the Jews. They plotted to kill him while he was a prisoner in the Jerusalem jail. But the Romans heard about the conspiracy and with five hundred soldiers they escorted Paul to Caesarea where they thought he could get a fair trial.

The judge knew that Paul was innocent. But he didn't want to antagonize the hostile Jews. So he delayed the trial for two years. But during those two years, he postponed an even more crucial decision.

Felix and his wife Drusilla often listened to Paul preach the gospel. The Holy Spirit convicted this couple and impressed upon them their need to trust Jesus for the forgiveness of their sins. But they refused to take advantage of the opportunity.

It must have been a tormenting experience for this judge and his wife. In the middle of one of Paul's sermons, he even interrupted Paul. He said, "I've heard enough for now! Leave me alone. When it's convenient, I will send for you. We'll talk more about it then" (Acts 24:25).

But the refusal of that opportunity to trust Jesus as his personal Savior may have cost Felix eternity. He faded off the scene before two more years passed.

One day every one of us will stand before God as he audits the opportunities that have come our way. His primary concern will be how we handled the opportunity to accept Jesus as our personal Savior and Lord.

But he will also be concerned to know what we did with all the other opportunities he gave us to serve him.—Gary C. Redding

Illustrations

OPPORTUNITY.   Had the Russians remained another seven years, until the discovery of gold in 1848, they would have been in position to reach the richest lodes first. Had Mexico bought the cannons and livestock, it could have armed and fed its army and put down the Bear Flag Revolt in 1846 in Sonoma, only a day's march from Fort Ross. Had the Hudson's Bay Company bought Fort Ross and Bodega Bay, the British could have been so solidly entrenched by the time the Californio government dissolved that California might have fallen quite easily into their hands. —Irving Stone, *Men to Match My Mountains*

ASSERTIVENESS.   I would like to amend the idea of being in the right place at the right time. There are many people who were in the right place at the right time but didn't know it. You have to recognize when the right place and the right time fuse and take advantage of that opportunity. There are plenty of opportunities out there. You can't sit back and wait.— Ellen Metcalf

Sermon Suggestion (Old Testament and Epistle)

YES, . . . BUT!   TEXTS: 2 Kings 5:1–5ab, especially verse 1; Col. 2:6–15, especially verse 12. (1) Even the most able people may be haunted by some form of inadequacy, 2 Kings 5:1b. (2) Yet God's grace and power can transform and bring life and hope to our most desperate circumstance, Col. 2:12.

Worship Aids

CALL TO WORSHIP.   "Be thou exalted, Lord, in thine own strength; so will we sing and praise thy power" (Ps. 21:13).

INVOCATION.   Almighty God, our Father, we look to you for your strength and power to undergird our lives. Without you we fail; with you we succeed despite all appearances. Help us to sing and rejoice and pray and commit ourselves to you, knowing that you will never fail us nor forsake us.

OFFERTORY SENTENCE.   "As ye have therefore received Christ Jesus the Lord, so walk ye in him: rooted and built up in him, and established in the faith, as ye have been taught, abounding therein with thanksgiving" (Col. 2:6–7).

OFFERTORY PRAYER.   Father of eternal generosity, lead us to be generous with the gifts entrusted to us in the course of your providence. Help us to be generous in the giving of friendship that the friendless may escape loneliness. Help us to be generous in the giving of encouragement that the discouraged may find hope. Help us to be generous in giving physical help that the burdened may have their burdens lifted. Help us to be generous in the giving of our wealth that mighty needs may be met in the community and abroad throughout the world. Take these offerings we bring before you this morning and bless them to bring help and hope to the world after the fashion of Christ, in whose name we pray.—Henry Fields

PRAYER.   As you were present, O Father, with the Apostle Paul through dungeon, fire, and sword, so we claim your presence in all the untoward circumstances that try our faith. We praise you for your persevering and pursuing love that does not let us go. As one of our poets has written, you are "the Hound of Heaven" not willing that one should perish.

O Father, we have come here hungering and thirsting for the Bread and Water of Life, and we have not been turned away disappointed. We praise you for your Word—not the glib word that appeals to our conceit, complacency, and self-righteousness, but the strong Word that comes from the cross calling us to that faith that defies every enemy even death itself and proclaims in the face of every contradiction, "The Lord God omnipotent reigns." Not to success, but to faithfulness, you are calling us; but how often we are duped by the values of this present age and miss the verities of the eternal kingdom. Grant to us the wisdom, the faith, the courage to take the long look. Such vision can yield true perspective for the trauma of this present order.

In the embrace of your love so genuinely experienced in this fellowship, we realize we are all family. No person lives or dies unto himself or herself, therefore we would pray for one another and for all others. We pray for those shaken among us because of life-threatening news: Grant to them the poise of faith to handle creatively whatever life holds for them. Where the ache of loneliness persists, may you minister the balm of Gilead—the sense of your presence. May those walking through the valley of the shadow have the faith to pray, "I will not fear, for thou art with me." Free those who are ill from fear and anxiety to be trusting and open to receive the health of your healing grace. We pray for the healing of the nations, that swords may be beaten into plowshares and spears into pruning hooks—that weaponry may be translated into bread, clothes, housing, and medicine for so many desperately in need. We pray through him in whom word and deed are one and who teaches us to pray and live, "Our Father. . . ."
—John Thompson

LECTIONARY MESSAGE

Topic: Learning to Pray
Text: Luke 11:1–13

There are two meanings in the title of this sermon. First, learning to pray means learning *how* to pray and *what* to pray for; second, learning to pray means learning that we must continually engage in prayer. Christians must ask God for his good gifts, which he is willing that we should have.

I. *The substance of the prayer.*

The basic element in prayer is that prayer must have an object, a purpose, a petition. Jesus here suggests what suitable atmosphere and what suitable objects may enter into our prayers.

(a) Recognition of the One to whom we pray.

(1) "Our Father, who art in heaven" indicates that Christians are declared by Jesus to be children of God, as he develops later.

(2) "Hallowed be thy name," along with the phrase "who art in heaven" (omitted by some ancient texts), is part of the recognition of the holiness and glory of God, who, even though we call him Father, is still the Almighty, the Creator, the King of the universe.

(3) "Thy kingdom come; thy will be done, as in heaven, so in earth" recognizes God's authority and his supreme right, let alone his power, to do whatever he had in his eternal plan, not only in his own abode but in every part of his creation. But we need to show, if only to remind ourselves, that we also desire what he desires, that we submit ourselves to him. This petition should have the force of leading us to examine *our* wills, *our* wants, and *our* hopes and to test them by their congruity with the will of God, as we understand it, before we have the temerity to present them to God.

(b) Petition for the needs of life. "Give us daily our bread for the day" mentions only food and asks for only a day's supply at a time. This petition recognizes two things: That God is the source of everything that sustains human life—air, water, and rest, as well as food; and that the dependence we have on God is moment-by-moment and can never be forgotten. Each one of us is only one breath away from oblivion at any second, and we recognize by our prayers at mealtime and at bedtime that all life comes from God and is pointless without God's instant care.

(c) Petition for restoration in grace and righteousness. This reading in Luke changes the terms, calling the object of our petition for forgiveness *sins*, whereas Matthew's term is *debts*. Luke's word for sins is derived from a verb meaning "to miss the mark," to fall short of our rightfully required performance and thus to be guilty of an offense to God. Luke recognizes that while we can forgive another a debt, God alone can forgive sins. For our future protection, we are to put ourselves in the hand of God for each moment and allow him to keep us from sinning by keeping us from temptation. Inasmuch as sins are destructive blots on our spiritual lives, the spiritual ruler is the one we must allow to help us avoid sin.

II. *The importance of importunity.*

(a) The unwilling friend. Jesus adds this parable of a friend unwilling to rise after bedtime and disturb his house to help a neighbor in need. The friend will respond to importunity if not to friendship. This implies that fulfillment of petitions may take even a longer time. It teaches us directly that we should never give up. Buttrick has suggested that the friend is testing the neighbor's need, to be sure the desire is real and not merely a whim. Although God is not unwilling but rather eager to help us, he may welcome our importunity to sharpen our determination. This parable teaches us to keep on praying. It convinces us that our confirmed need is in fellowship with God's love.

(b) The required diligence. "Ask; seek; knock," for you are asking with assured success. Jesus uses a simple analogy between an earthly father and our heavenly Father to illustrate how ridiculous it is to lose faith in prayer. We who pray in faith shall find heaven waiting to open for us. God is not an unwilling neighbor or an evil father.—John R. Rodman

SUNDAY: AUGUST SECOND

SERVICE OF WORSHIP

Sermon: Freedom to Walk in the Spirit
TEXTS: Gal. 5:1, NEB; Gal. 5:25, KJV

Paul wrote to the Galatian Christians in words which pronounced the Magna Carta of spiritual freedom for all men: "Christ set us free, to be free men. Stand firm, then, and refuse to be tied to the yoke of slavery again" (Gal. 5:1, NEB). Here is a *declaration of independence* from all human controls, from all arbitrary legalisms. Christ has set us free! Free from what? Free to be and do what?

I. *Christ frees us from the bondage of false security.* Where does your security rest? What are the props that shore up your personal confidence? What is the structure of your own inner assurance?

Christ frees us from bondage of false securities because our ultimate security is in him and in no one else. He has accepted us; therefore, it does not ultimately matter if everyone else rejects us. His judgment is the only one that finally counts. He is our Lord, and we have no other. Therefore, we need neither fear nor favor any man. "The fear of the Lord is the beginning of wisdom" (Ps. 111:10). We look to him for our signals. We put down the pilings of our confidence deep within him, for he gives inner assurance which the world can neither give nor take away.

II. *Christ frees us from false evaluations of personal worth.* If mercy is a thing twice blessed, then false estimates of the worth of a man are twice cursed. Cursed are those who set the standards of measurement, and cursed are those who accept such standards for themselves. I think of a fine family of modest income living in a community of great wealth where the measure of personal worth is success, defined in terms of wealth and social position. In these terms this family definitely has not made the grade. The sad fact is that the family itself accepts the community's evaluation of their personal worth, and its members suffer from a kind of hangdog shame. They cannot get into the "right" club or any club; they can never get into the "right" social circles. Christ delivers us from this false yardstick. When we understand that God measures our personal worth, not in terms of what we have in the bank or where we live or whom we know, but in terms of the integrity of our personal response to his love, then we are free, gloriously free to cooperate with Christ, unhindered by the gimmicks of social snobbery. If God accepts us, who are we to condemn ourselves or to condemn another whom God has also accepted?

III. *Christ frees us from a false concept of progress.* We want to feel that we are making progress, climbing ever a little higher on the ladder of life. We feel confident if we manage to get ahead in terms of material prosperity and social popularity. Consider the progress Jesus made: from poverty to nothing; from relative popularity to a criminal's death. The symbol of his "progress" was not a promotion or a fat bonus check but a cross. He did not make progress in the terms by which we are accustomed to evaluate our lives. He was not successful by worldly standards. Yet he made progress in terms of faithful obedience to the Father.

Christ delivers us from the slavery of feeling that we have to be making progress in worldly terms. The question each Christian can ask himself is, "Am I making progress on the way of the cross marked out for me?"

IV. *Christ delivers us from a false longing.* Most of us find ourselves living for the future when we shall "have all things we want" and "be able to do all the things we want." Such fruitless longing makes us discontented with our present circumstances and prevents real fulfillment in the present or the future. For the world, anticipation may be 50 percent of realization, but for the Christian there is fulfillment already in this present time because our controlling desire is only to serve Christ, and in single-minded loyalty to him we are given a freedom to "sit loose in the saddle" to what the world calls progress, accepting both favor and scorn with equanimity.

V. *Christ delivers us from a false righteousness.* A man once said to me, "I don't swear; I don't smoke; I don't drink; I don't tell dirty stories." I felt like asking him, "Brother, what *do* you do?" Is there anything more repelling than a smug, self-righteous pharisee who neatly divides life into "dos" and "don'ts" and then separates people into sheep and goats, depending on whether they do or don't do these things? Christ sets us free from false righteousness, preparing us for the major surrenders and the decisive prunings, the merciless cleansing which opens the way to purity and humility.

VI. *Christ delivers us from a false freedom.* The man who has thrown off the bonds of legalistic moralism is tempted into an easy acceptance of his own imperfection. To acknowledge that one is a sinner is one thing; to shrug one's shoulders and say, "I'm only human; I'm not a saint after all," is another. We are sinners-called-to-be-saints and summoned to perfection. We are not free to be content with any lesser goal. Christ delivers us from pseudofreedom to a responsible liberty, drawing us out of ourselves with transforming power to serve others.

Paul wrote to the Galatians, "You, my friends, were called to be free men; only do not turn your freedom into license for your lower nature, but be servants to one another in love. For the whole law can be summed up in a single commandment: 'Love your neighbor as yourself' " (Gal. 5:13, 14, NEB). Here is a *declaration of interdependence.* We are free to become a voluntary slave to the neighbor. Luther puts this paradox in these words, "A Christian man is perfectly free lord of all, subject to none. A Christian man is a perfectly dutiful servant of all, subject to all."

This is freedom to do what I please only as it serves my neighbor. It is freedom, not to indulge my own appetites and desires, but to become responsibly involved in the sufferings and needs of the neighbor.

The content of Christian life together is an interdependent priesthood. Each Christian is called to mediate Christ's love to the other in a mutual ministry of forgiveness and burden-bearing. The church is called to prefigure and embody the ministry of reconciliation, which is God's purpose for the world.—Robert A. Raines

Illustrations

THE HOLY SPIRIT TODAY. Nowhere is the work of the Spirit more apparent today than in Christians' rediscovery of one another across centuries-old barriers of confessional difference. Windows and doors of communication, fellowship, worship, study, and ministry have been opened, and it is not likely that they will be soon shut, even though some would seem to want to do so. There are reassessments of their own positions within many major religious bodies today. The Scriptures are receiving intensive study in churches which long neglected them. Ministers and laymen in confessional groups which had been out of touch with one another or engaged in actual hostilities are now finding that they have more in common than they have that divides them. There is a deep longing to understand the other, to know one another, to enter into a *koinonia* of giving and receiving.

This does not mean that "convictions" have weakened or zeal has lessened. It does not mean that "denominations" are about to merge into one superstructure. In truth, there is little attention to that today. The concern is not so much with changing these outward structures but with rediscovering our brotherhood within and across these lines. Is not this the work of God's Spirit today?—Frank Stagg

THE VOICE OF GOD. Listen to Augustine speaking of his saintly mother, Monica. Monica had been praying about a certain matter and seemed not to get the answer, and Augustine says:

She saw, indeed, certain vain and imaginary things, such as the vehement desire of the human heart might conjure up; and these she told me about,

not with her usual confidence, when Thou hadst shown her anything, but slighting them. *For she could, she declared, through some feeling which she could not express in words, discern the difference between Thy revelations and the dreams of her own spirit.*

W. E. Sangster

Sermon Suggestions

WHEN HISTORY REPEATS ITSELF. TEXT: 2 Kings 13:14–20a. Compare 2:12. (1) Some truths remain the same (e.g., ultimate power lies not in military might but in unimpressive spiritual resources). (2) We are from generation to generation tempted to rely on our limited vision despite what we know deep down to be true. (3) God continues with us while we struggle on with the consequences of our folly.

NEW LIFE. TEXT: Col. 3:1–11. (1) Where we get it—in Christ. (2) What it is like—heavenly rather than earthly. (3) How we live it out—through drastic self-discipline. (4) Who can enjoy this renewal—all, without exception.

Worship Aids

CALL TO WORSHIP. "The Lord is my strength and my shield; my heart trusted in him, and I am helped; therefore my heart greatly rejoiceth; and with my song will I praise him" (Ps. 28:7).

INVOCATION. Lord, stir us up, change us around, reverse our priorities, challenge our assumptions, open us to new truth, that in every way possible we will see what thou hast been trying for so long to tell us, and we will respond in love.—E. Lee Phillips

OFFERTORY SENTENCE. "Set your affection on things above, not on things on the earth" (Col. 3:2).

OFFERTORY PRAYER. Lord, we know that if we love you enough, no earthly love will be able to dim our view of heavenly things. Accept these tokens of our love, and through them bind us ever closer to you and your eternal purposes.

PRAYER.   Eternal God, who art before all, in all, and beyond all, we worship thee. Enlarge our thoughts of thee. Deepen our insight into thy character, revealed in Christ. We stand in awe before this universe in which thou hast housed us. We bow in reverence before its Creator, the heights and depths of whose power and purpose we cannot comprehend. Such knowledge is too wonderful for us; it is high, we cannot attain unto it.

Thanks be to thee for the revelation of thyself in prophets and apostles, saints and martyrs, in all that is excellent and beautiful, and above all in Jesus Christ, our Lord. May some light from thee fall upon our souls today. Search us, O God, and know our hearts! Try us and know our thoughts! And see if there be any wicked way in us, and lead us in the way everlasting.

We pray for thy help in all the innermost relationships of our lives. Guide us in our dealing with ourselves. O thou who hearest the endless conversation wherein we talk with ourselves, give us sincerity, honesty, and candor as we deal with ourselves. Save us from the folly of self-deceit. Grant us grace to see ourselves as we really are, to hate those evil things in us which we ought to hate, and to appraise rightly those powers in us wherewith we can best serve man and thee.

We pray for thy help in our relationships with our fellows. Against all vindictiveness, all malice of heart and unkindness in conduct, we pray. Save us from meanness of spirit and from the love of retaliation. Make us a source of strength and encouragement to those whom we love, and grant us grace to overthrow our enemies by transforming them into our friends. May some human relationships be made radiant and be filled with goodwill because we have worshiped here today.

We pray for thy help in our relationships with thee. Make our Christian faith and life be vital because it is centered in inner fellowship and communion with thy Spirit. May we indeed be thy temples with thy Spirit dwelling in us. From the uproar of the world to the silent sanctuary we have come. Speak to us, O still small voice of calm. Become to us our unseen Friend, our Comrade in life's battles, our Shelter in the time of storm, our Wellspring of courage and steadfastness.—Harry Emerson Fosdick

LECTIONARY MESSAGE

Topic: Being Rich

TEXT: Luke 12:13–21

Some might suppose that materialism is a modern sin. But, *materialism* is just another word for *covetousness* or *selfishness*. This story of the contact of Jesus with a dissatisfied heir emphasizes that selfishness is an ever-present reality. The basic motivation of selfishness is the desire for more and this desire can never be satisfied.

I. *Proper values.* The response of Christ to the request that he adjudicate in the dispute over an inheritance indicates that material possessions are the least of the concerns to which Jesus would give his attention. He made the point that material possessions are not the greatest values one can possess nor to which attention should be given.

There is no intention, obviously, to teach that concern for affairs of everyday life must never have a place. The implication, rather, is that if one places proper emphasis on more significant issues, then resulting attitudes toward possessions will be more correct. Proper spiritual concerns and values instruct on the proper use of the opportunities and possessions one may have.

II. *True relationships.* The expositors of *The Interpreter's Bible* make a significant point on this passage: "Before God we are confessors, not complainants." To complain presupposes that one has adequate understanding of the circumstances and of the general facts to arrive at a conclusion. The refusal to give attention to the request reflects that Jesus considered that the man in the crowd could not even properly evaluate his lack. How deftly Jesus shifted the concern to the need that existed in the life of the one who came to complain.

Obvious physical need often can divert persons from an interest or a concern for spiritual needs. Yet, Jesus warned that eternal values are present and should be sought even by those who have obvious physical needs. It is almost as though he advises that one not be misled by that which appears to be obvious.

III. *Ultimate security.* In this brief passage the Master Teacher has taught the nature both of foolish and of true values.

(a) Here he described the futility of amassing possessions. The things that one may possess have only a transient quality. In addition, the very quality of the things that can be possessed may be marred by that which can happen to them with the passage of time.

(b) He stressed the emptiness of trusting in the wrong kind of "things." Most persons wish to be assured that there is a lasting value in that to which they give attention and energy. "True life" (v. 15, TEV) can never result from "things."

(c) He described the ineffectiveness of human efforts in building ultimate security. The work of God is that which can be most trusted, and the things of God have the greatest value.

(d) He urged that ultimate value is only found in trusting God. To trust God requires that one get beyond dependence on the efforts of oneself or of others.
—Arthur W. Walker, Jr.

SUNDAY: AUGUST NINTH

SERVICE OF WORSHIP

Sermon: The Conflict of Loyalties
TEXT: 2 Kings 5:1–19

Loyalty is one of the royal virtues. He who is without it lacks a quality indispensable to true character. Loyalty is what holds human life together, gives it cohesiveness and solidarity.

I. The problem for many, however, is not how to be loyal but how to deal with conflicting loyalties. Naaman, the Syrian, cleansed of his leprosy, swore that he would thenceforth be loyal to the God of Israel, but he had hardly done so before he realized that when he went back to Syria he would have to go with his master in the line of duty into the temple of Rimmon, and when his master bowed down to worship Rimmon, he would be expected to do likewise. One can sympathize with Naaman's dilemma. There was the duty he owed to the God of Israel and the duty he owed to his monarch, the king of Syria. "Bowing down in the house of Rimmon," has become a proverbial expression to denote the danger and dishonesty associated with compromise. Yet when loyalties conflict, how is compromise to be avoided?

It may be a conflict of loyalties in the course of the day's business. An employee is asked to do something that his conscience does not approve. Dependent on him and his earnings are his wife and children. What is he to do? Register a protest? Give up the job? Tell himself that the employer is responsible, not the employee?

The conflict of loyalties may take place in war time. What a fierce and terrible conflict it is! There was the Christian member of the French Resistance Movement who wrote as he went underground:

I ask God that He now forgive my sins, and the decision which I voluntarily take this day (for I know that recourse to violence has need of pardon). But I am leaving without hate and fully convinced that we Christians have not the right to leave it to non-Christians alone to offer their lives.

If only all that was asked were to offer one's life! Did that French Christian have to do what so many in the Resistance felt obliged to do?

The issue of loyalty to one's country and government poses one of the most poignant and difficult questions in life. For example, what should be the attitude of a Christian when he sees a government in power that denies the spiritual basis upon which he himself interprets life but at the same time is carrying through land reforms which, as a Christian, he has long desired to see? We ought not too quickly come up with dogmatic answers to those pressing questions. We are not living on the spot. We are not familiar with all that is at stake. We do not know at first hand the tension that such conflicting loyalties create, nor are we having to work out the problem as they have to in concrete situations and personal relationships.

II. Thus far I have been doing no more than stating the case. Even so, just to state the problem is to render a service. These are issues about which we should be sensitive and to which we should give careful thought. It is easier, of course, to pose the problem than to come up with solutions. There are no simple solutions. It is hard to be a Christian.

(a) For instance, when should one obey, and when defy, a law which one in soul and conscience believes to be unwise or even morally wrong? It is easy to say that the voice of conscience should be supreme. But is there no difference between an instructed and an uninstructed conscience?

(b) Is it possible to do always what is ideally right? Stanley Gaudin (a student with a hatred of war, who yet, because he loved his country, went on to enlist in the Royal Canadian Air Force, got his wings and was shot down) did not find it possible. And many another has found himself in a position where, through no fault of his own, there seemed no right course open to him but only a choice between evils.

(c) A Christian, however, will not make this an excuse for lowering his standards and conforming to the ways of the world. He will not give up trying to apply his Christianity to everyday life. He will strive to act as nobly as possible in every situation, in wartime, in race relations, in the fiercely competitive world of business, seeking always to select the better of two alternatives. By so doing, he will not only cultivate a worthy character but will do his part in building up a better state of society in the future, so that things impossible for him may be possible for future generations.

Maxims like "One step at a time" and "Half a loaf of bread is better than none" are not necessarily maxims of worldly prudence. Those who by nature are idealistic have no patience with them, are contemptuous of them. But doesn't it often happen that the idealist, after declaiming indignantly about an evil situation, withdraws into an ivory tower? As Christians we shall serve our generation most by seizing on whatever of good the situation of the moment makes possible. By the vigilant detection and the practical use of each concrete opportunity of improvement and reform we can lift society to a higher level.

William Temple was a practical Christian statesman. He believed that Christian principles would be workable if a sufficient number of people would get behind them, but he accepted the fact that people by and large don't get behind them, and he joined hands with them to secure the lesser good they were willing to support. He worked with his fellows for the second best when they were not ready to work for the best. He preferred to achieve in cooperation with them an attainable good, while at the same time he kept pointing them to the supreme good.

(d) Even so, compromise has its limits. What those limits are each of us must find out in each case for himself, keeping before us continually the example and spirit of Christ. We shall be on our guard, prayerfully and constantly, against a lowering of standards and a cowardly compliance with the demands of self-interest and worldliness. We shall be on our guard, prayerfully and constantly, lest a minor loyalty lead us to sacrifice a major one. That is the thing especially to avoid: a little loyalty to one's family, one's profession, one's class, one's race, pressed at the expense of a larger one. Jesus has so much to say about that.

Devoted to our family, but unconcerned about other families. Devoted to our nation, but caring little about other nations. Devoted to our denomination, but isolated from, if not critical of, our brethren in other denominations.

And first, last, always, we must remember that our supreme loyalty is to God. What do you and I believe in most? When the choice of loyalties finally narrows down, in what direction does it point? For that is the real source of power behind us. Is it our family? Is it our profession? Is it our nation? Is it God?—Robert J. McCracken

Illustrations

LOYAL TO WHOM?   I've been accused of being disloyal to the king. I don't know about that. What I do know, however, is that I am loyal to Jesus Christ. If that isn't the same thing as being loyal to the king, then that's something for the king to worry about, not Studdert Kennedy.—Studdert Kennedy, British Army chaplain, World War One, quoted by J. E. Large

LOYALTY, THE BASIC CONDITION OF LIBERTY.   We are so made that liberty without loyalty ruins us. So one young woman who had lived an emancipated life committed suicide and wrote in explanation: "I am killing myself because I have never sincerely loved any human being all my life." Alas what thin fodder, in the end, liberty without loyalty turns out to be!

This is the nub of the matter, is it not: liberty alone is not an organizing principle; it puts nothing together; it is dispersive. Within society it produces autonomous, irresponsible individuals, confusedly following their private whims, and within the individual it sets our various emotions and desires going every which way, doing as they please. Liberty alone is not an organizing principle—it does not draw us together into one-directional, purposeful, integrated living; but loyalty does. "All things are yours"— that by itself alone scatters us. "And ye

are Christ's"—that unifies us.—Harry Emerson Fosdick

Sermon Suggestions

A SECOND CHANCE.   TEXT: Jer. 18:1–11. What was true in the experience of Israel is true also in the experience of a church or an individual. (1) God works to achieve some high purpose in and through us. (2) However, things happen that frustrate the divine purpose. (3) Nevertheless, God graciously renews his efforts to achieve his purpose despite our resistance and self-defeating ways.

FAITH DOES IT!   TEXT: Heb. 11:1–3, 8–19. (1) Faith discovers the approval of God, verse 2. (2) Faith discovers the will of God, verse 8. (3) Faith discovers the vision of a higher and better home, verse 13.

Worship Aids

CALL TO WORSHIP.   "The Lord looked down from heaven upon the children of men, to see if there were any that did understand and seek God" (Ps. 14:2).

INVOCATION.   We seek you, O Lord, because you are seeking us, your erring sheep who have allowed ourselves to be misled through both ignorance and willfulness. Come to us in redeeming mercy and guide us now and always by your gracious counsels.

OFFERTORY SENTENCE.   "Now faith means that we are confident of what we hope for, convinced of what we do not see. It was for this that the men of old won their record. It is by faith we understand that the world was fashioned by the Word of God, and thus the visible was made out of the invisible" (Heb. 11:1–3, Moffatt).

OFFERTORY PRAYER.   Our Father, we now present to you tithes and offerings in faith, the full results of which we may never see in this life. We give them in the confidence that you will use them as you fashion your eternal plan.

PRAYER.	We adore thy name and bless thee, O Lord! most high and holy. We draw near to thee to give thanks. We draw near to thee to render thee tokens of love. We draw near to confess our sin and unworthiness, and to lay hold, by faith, upon all thy promises, and upon thy help. We love to be loved. And those that hold us in dear esteem—how precious to us is their coming, and their words, if they be words of wisdom and of truth! And art not thou glad when we love thee, and behold that in thee which is worthy of love? When we are like little children, and our hearts go out unto thee in trust and in joy, is not this worship? And is not this that which pleases thee? May our hearts make thee glad tonight, O thou abounding Savior! whose word and work and love never cease. Grant that we may see more and more, as the days and years go on, that which makes thee Chief among ten thousand, and the One altogether lovely. Perfect truth thou art. Honor and integrity and righteousness are with thee for evermore. Thou art full of gentleness; and mercy makes its home in thy heart. Thou dost love to give rather than to receive. It is thy nature to joy for evermore in thoughts, and in the power of thy right hand to give forth the reasons of gladness and of joy to all thy creatures. Thou art full of graciousness, and eminent above all in power and in wisdom. Yet more art thou in graciousness and goodness than thou art in wisdom. And love sits crowned upon thy brow. And all thy joys are joys supernal and noble. Oh! that we could catch thy spirit. Oh! that it were given to us to be like thee, even in lower measures, and according to the proportion of our nature. Oh! that we might have thy purity, thy truth, thy justice, thy love, and mercy, and graciousness, and magnanimity, and that we might be like unto our God. Give forth to every one of us that spirit—that gracious, enlightening, and sanctifying spirit—by which, cleansed from all the defilements of the flesh, and all the dominations of the world, we may rise into sympathy with thee, and into thy likeness, so that at last it shall be easy for our thoughts to go forth from ourselves and into thee; and for thy thoughts to issue forth and find a resting place in us. May we be united to God, so that he shall dwell in us, and we shall abide in him.—Henry Ward Beecher

LECTIONARY MESSAGE

Topic: True Rewards

TEXT: Luke 12:32–40

Frequently, a recorded teaching of Jesus has touches that are found in a variety of stories and emphases from differing settings. This collection of wisdom sayings and the allusions to a parable of a bridegroom and a master returning from a journey remind of similar parables in each of the synoptic Gospels. In all such places there is an emphasis on being faithful and that the consequence of faithfulness is the receiving of rewards.

I. *Nature of the rewards of the kingdom of God.* The setting of the chapter implies that the rewards of the kingdom are not material possessions. This truth is further stressed as Jesus reiterates that material values and the actual material objects themselves are destroyed by the natural consequences of life. The treasure to which one commits his/her life must have a durability that is not lost as a result of natural consequences. Even trusting in other individuals who may change or prove untrustworthy must be avoided. Only God is always true and faithful!

The faithfulness of God and the permanence of his kingdom justify the admonition, "Sell your possessions." The recent examples of individuals whose fortunes have changed or whose seemingly secure reputations have been destroyed remind of the importance of the timeless possessions that cannot age, lose their value, or be destroyed.

II. *Delay of rewards.* The parables of the returning master give repeated warnings for those who may lose heart in the delay of expected events or results.

Jesus essentially said that it is a natural human response to lose heart and become lax in response if the expected consequence is repeatedly delayed. He repeats that faithfulness for his follower is not demonstrated by the fulfilling of an expected calendar but in being faithful even when expectation is disappointed.

In fact, the repeated allusions to delay seem to emphasize that delay and disappointment are to be anticipated. One wonders if the question becomes, Will you be faithful when events do not turn out as you may wish?

III. *Joy of the reward.* Jesus also challenges his followers not to succumb to the faithlessness of others. Some have found in the verses on the faithful and unfaithful servants an allusion to recognized church leaders who become untrustworthy. Regardless of these interpretations, the emphasis is obviously on faithfulness that is unaffected by the circumstances that one must face.

Sometimes it is easy for a modern interpreter to forget the significance of the circumstances pictured in a scripture passage. It is particularly important to note that these sayings of Jesus were given as he had "steadfastly set his face toward Jerusalem." He was not speaking of disappointment without an understanding of its impact. He already was facing the apparent frustration of his own efforts and ministry.

Again, Jesus has said that the victorious life is difficult but the result is well worth the effort. He also seems to say that the difficulty of remaining faithful is evidence of faithfulness.—Arthur W. Walker, Jr.

SUNDAY: AUGUST SIXTEENTH

SERVICE OF WORSHIP

Sermon: Living by Grace

TEXT: Rom. 16:24

Our task is not to define "grace" but to experience it. So grace doesn't mean to me first of all a Christian doctrine on which I once passed exams. Grace is the infant at the font whom we commit, as a helpless morsel of humanity launched into the mysterious ocean of life, to the company of Christ forever. Grace is that silence that sometimes falls on us when we receive the food for our souls that comes with that other sacrament of Holy Communion. Grace is in the eyes of one who tells me of being condemned with a terminal disease—and is radiant with faith. Grace is the victory of one we know over drug-addiction, alcoholism, or a messed-up marriage. Grace is the laughter that relieves the tensions. Grace is the spurt of generosity that makes us give beyond the calculations in which we are imprisoned. Grace is the joy of one who has discovered that God accepts us as we are without waiting for some signs of sainthood.

I. Grace can be experienced only by those who are willing to acknowledge our need, only by those who are aware of the full force of the powers of evil with which we have to contend. A genial, optimistic shallow version of Christianity, such as is apt to surface in times of peace and tranquility, knows little of the grace of our Lord Jesus Christ, which flows from the cross on which he died—not with dignity but with defiance.

The only thing that can exclude us from this grace is the assumption that we don't need it. The offer of grace means nothing to the one who is self-sufficient and wants no help from anything or anybody. Grace is for those who are willing to acknowledge their need. That is why, for instance, Alcoholics Anonymous, which has no specific religious affiliations, is based on such a conviction.

II. Grace comes to the heart that is open to receive this power beyond ourselves, to the mind that is not trapped in the prison of pride and self-sufficiency, and to the society that is released from the arrogance of believing that human beings with their cleverness and "many inventions" can save themselves. And grace comes to the Christian believer, not as some vague invisible influence or some magic fluid that flows from a spiritual faucet controlled by the clergy, but in the living person and presence of Jesus Christ. Grace is personal. It is God coming near to meet us, receive us, inspire us, empower us.

Christ was grace incarnate—God's rescuing love translated into human terms. The great revolution that he brought in human history which has spawned the myriad of churches throughout the world is simply his grace. Simply? Let me try to put it simply. We want to have a working belief in God. We want to sense his enfolding presence, his strength and his love. We may think, we may have been told, that the way to him is to do good so that we can deserve his love. He made it clear, by what he said and what he did, that there's nothing whatever we can do to earn this acceptance by God. He loves us just as we are. He accepts us, warts and all. He consults no records to see what our score has been. If we want forgiveness we have no claim except on the love which beckons us in Christ, the humility which says, "Lord Jesus Christ, Son of God, have mercy upon me a sinner." Living by grace is living joyfully in the knowledge that we have been, as Paul beautifully said it, "accepted in the beloved."

III. Does this sound too passive, too lacking in the self-esteem that is commended to us today? On the contrary, it is the most liberating message the world has ever heard. It frees us from the nagging question that sometimes rises to the surface: Am I good enough for heaven? Grace says, "None of us is good enough for heaven." It saves us from grading all our neighbors, near and far, on some moral scale where we hope to be reckoned near the top. "Judge not," says Jesus. We're all the children of his grace, and who knows what the other we criticize has had to cope with by heredity or environment? It frees us from congratulating ourselves when we help a neighbor or raise our pledge to the church. And it frees us from keeping our religion in a special compartment wherein we have worked out what we think are our dues and obligations.

Living by grace means that our religion is not a matter of an occasional prayer and an obligation to come to church. To live by grace is to see the whole world around us, our homes, our families, our friends, our opponents, our ambitions, our delight in the arts, the social and political responsibilities that press on us, our instinct for justice and compassion, as the arena in which we learn to respond with thankfulness and joy. As a working belief grace teaches us that there is no moment of ecstasy or of agony that is without the presence of this Lord who works in all things for good with those who love him.—David H. C. Read

Illustrations

GRACE.   "Grace?" he said. "Grace? Well, that's very difficult to explain, Mrs. Gowan. Many learned men have thought about grace for many centuries. Most of them think it has to do with forgiveness and mercy, but I'm inclined to disagree with them. I rather think grace means just the constant presence of God."—Mary Ellen Chase, *The Lovely Ambition*

"COME TO ME."   We are to come to him even though the world calls us in a hundred different directions. We are to be fools for his sake. We are to take risks for him and be merry for him. We are to work for peace and pray for miracles. We are to go places and do things and speak words that, without him, we wouldn't even dare dream of. We know so much more than we ever let on about what he would have each of us do in our own lives—what door to open, what hand to take. We have within us, each one, so much more of his power than we ever spend—such misers of miracle we are, such pinchpenny guardians of grace.—Frederick Buechner

Sermon Suggestions

WHEN GOD LETS BAD THINGS HAPPEN TO US.   TEXT: Jer. 20:7–13. (1) Then we may be tempted to speak against God, verses 7–8. (2) Then we may try unsuccessfully to ignore God and withhold a faithful testimony, verse 9. (3) Then we may rediscover the justice of God, verses 10–11; and emerge chastened but rejoicing in the Lord, verses 12–13.

HOW TO BE A WINNER.   TEXT: Heb. 12:1–2, 12–17. (1) Consider the heroes of the faith. (2) Consider Jesus Christ who definitively marked out the way for us. (3) Consider yourself and maintain the needed disciplines.

Worship Aids

CALL TO WORSHIP.   "Lord, thou hast heard the desire of the humble: thou wilt prepare their heart, thou wilt cause thine ear to hear: To judge the fatherless and the oppressed, that the man of the earth may no more oppress" (Ps. 10:17–18).

INVOCATION.   Lord, fill our hearts with praise again. Let our prayers rise from humility again. Let our songs be joyous and vibrant again. Let this fellowship be all it can be to us again. Place us in touch with our spiritual moorings again . . . and let us see the Christ.—E. Lee Phillips

OFFERTORY SENTENCE.   "Let us run with patience the race that is set before us, looking unto Jesus the author and finisher of our faith" (Heb. 12:1c–2a).

OFFERTORY PRAYER.   Lord, give us patience in times of discouragement and leanness and help us to be persistent and faithful, too, as we follow our Savior. Bless these offerings, large and small, as they reflect our grateful stewardship.

PRAYER.   Bless, we pray thee, severally, all that are in thy presence and each according to his special want. Accept the confessions of sin which are made. Accept the humiliations of heart which thou dost behold before thee. Accept the faintest purpose of service, the slightest yearnings toward love, the earliest breathings of love, the first returns of conscience, the beginnings of petition, and all the infantile experiences of those that have been men in sin, and must needs be born again, and become little children in holiness. We beseech of thee that art in overmastering power, and yet that art the most gentle of any that is, that thou wilt deal so gently with them that there shall be no petitioner afraid to speak to thee, no suppliant that dare not look up and behold all the hope and promise there is in thy glorious face. And we beseech of thee that there may be those who shall run quickly to the side of every one that is distressed and ready to fall; that thy servants may recall God's grace to them; that they remember the "wormwood" and the "gall" of their own experience and that they be prompt in seeking to save those who are out of the way and are yearning again to be restored to the right path.

And we pray, O Lord our God! that thou wilt bless those who are afar off and yet have some thoughts, at time, they know not whence, that visit them—some experiences of better days; some heart-chidings; some prickings of conscience. Grant, we pray thee, that they may have no rest. Grant that they may be condemned before the bar of their own conscience. And may they know that if their consciences condemn them, God is greater and shall much more condemn them.

We beseech of thee, O Lord our God! that thou wilt grant unto every one in thy presence that is seeking thee, whether afar off or near at hand, the gracious tokens of thy mercy; and may those especially who would this morning renew their covenant obligations and consecrate themselves afresh, find that thou art very near and very precious.—Henry Ward Beecher

LECTIONARY MESSAGE

Topic: The Crucial Time
  TEXT: Luke 12:49–56
  However the allusion to fire may be interpreted, it is obvious that Jesus refers to a great crisis. This crisis would result in intense divisions even among those whose loyalty might usually be expected. The reference to divisions within families probably has as its background his own

separation from those who were dear to him. The allusion to fire and the resultant divisions also remind modern Christians that their commitment to Christ carries requirements with difficult consequences. This picture is a far cry from the promise of comfort and ease that is often made in the name of Christianity in today's world.

I. *Challenge of the time.* The reference to his own circumstances and the intensity with which he faced these certainly seem to imply his death but also justify the interpretation that loyalty to his mission may require ruptures of relationships that are both personal and precious.

Allusion to his own death in verse 50 is seen as a definite expression of his messianic consciousness. His own awareness of his fate caused him to challenge those who would follow him, to accept the consequences of their loyalty. There is little of "meekness" and "mildness" in this challenge.

II. *The present time.* The call to interpret "the present time" has a timeless quality. It is obvious that Jesus primarily meant that the events of his own life marked the dramatic disclosure of the purpose and nature of God. The events to which he referred were most likely those which reached their conclusion in the destruction of Jerusalem in A.D. 70. He clearly, however, had in mind a larger fulfillment of the purpose of God. A new epoch in human experience came with the events by which God "reconciled the world unto himself." Those reconciled are members of a new spiritual community. Jesus also explosively called attention to the blindness and inertness of those of every age who failed to recognize the power of God in their own time. The believers of his own lifetime are not the only ones who fail to understand the nature and purpose of God. In every age those who have missed the meaning of events that are taking place can expect the condemnation "Hypocrites."

III. *Looking to the future.* God continues to stand poised to reconcile the disobedient to himself, to establish a new spiritual community with those who believe and accept his reconciliation. The greatest condemnation may not be for those who did not recognize the significance of the events in his own lifetime but for those who have the evidence of those events and of the work of God in the intervening millennia who still stand on the edge of God's breakthrough in their own life and world and yet fail to recognize the crucial time in which they live and who fail to acknowledge the evidence of the power of God that awaits the opportunity to be expressed in this age! —Arthur W. Walker, Jr.

SUNDAY: AUGUST TWENTY-THIRD

SERVICE OF WORSHIP

Sermon: Sneaking Up on Success
TEXT: Matt. 14:22–33

I. The crowds were intent on sneaking up on success. It is the Evangelist John (6:15) who tells us that they intended to take Jesus by force and make him their king. Jesus would have no part of it. His "kingship was not of this world," he told Pilate (John 18:36). Only an hour or two before, the crowds tasted the fish and bread he had multiplied out of a few loaves and several fish the disciples had with them (Matt. 14:13–21). The crowds wanted him to rule Israel, to be their king . . . and supply more bread! Lots of bread . . . and fish, free fish!

But Jesus was not that kind of messiah. His disciples were elated with the crowd's enthusiasm for their teacher. They would become fuses to explode the issue into something Jesus did not want. Thus he hustled them off in the boat. The RSV says, "Jesus made the disciples get into the boat." Barclay translates the word as "compelled," and J. B. Phillips says it means "insisted," while the King James

Version speaks of having constrained them to depart. Zodhiates says the word means to compel by force. He writes that "apparently, they did not want to go, but the Lord allowed them no choice. They had to. The disciples went because he wanted them to."[1] He literally commanded them, these robust, determined, sometimes impulsive Twelve, to set sail, so that he could dissolve this attempt to sneakily foment a revolution to declare him king.

When the disciples were gone, Jesus dealt with the crowds. He sent them scampering also ... nicely, of course, politely ... but nevertheless they were dismissed, sent away. They would have to get bread elsewhere, unless they wanted what the Bread of Life had to give (John 6:35ff). Jesus then went up the mountain ... alone ... to pray! He needed fortification, encouragement from his Father, and a wearied soul restored.

He forestalled a conspiracy to catapult him into an unwanted arena. He was not a political messiah to apportion bread. He was not a military messiah to annihilate the Romans and win Israel's freedom from their captors. He was not Caesar to offer bread and circuses. He was not an earthly king needing a gilded throne. He could not be sneaked into a successful cabal to uproot the Herodians or supplant the high priests either. He had a grander mission, and he stuck by it. No temptation would be too great, as the sneaky tempter learned in the wilderness, to divert him from the cause (Luke 4:1–13).

But he had to pray, and pray he did. The afternoon passed, and evening came; he was still praying. The evening lapsed into darkened night, and night was alert for the morning sunrise, but Jesus was still praying ... until the fourth watch, about three in the morning.

Then, energized by prayer, confident in his role, Jesus awakened to another need. His disciples were being swept to their deaths by the terror of a ferocious wind storm that was about to capsize the boat. They were far out into the whitecaps, many furlongs from the shore, says Matthew. Neither wind nor waves discouraged him. Jesus walked to the Twelve, eager to be with them, eager to insure their safety, eager to help them in that perilous hour.

They saw him, this apparition on the sea, this mystic figure in glowing, flowing windswept robes, striding toward them. We surmise this was in the spring of the year, because the five thousand men he fed the day before sat on "green grass."[2] Thus it may have been near Passover. The moon would have been full. Its eerie light in the spray of the wind-stirred sea would indeed give to any figure on the water an otherworldly look.

"It is a ghost," they cried. Fear engulfed them anew. This was not Patrick Swayze in blue jeans and a tee shirt. It was no movie fantasy but reality. It was enough to have their boat dashed to splinters by the tireless wind, but now this mysterious, ghostly form seemed to come threateningly upon them. They were afraid. Agony registered in their screams. They were grown men crying like frightened children, howling like scared cats.

"Take heart," said the wondrous Friend, calming their panic, "It is I; have no fear."

"Lord, if it is you, bid me come to you on the water," shouted a reassured, relieved Peter, eager to try this new means of transport.

And the Lord, caring as he was, accommodating as only he can be, responded simply, "Come!"

It was then that the invigorated Peter climbed out of the boat "and walked on the water and came to Jesus." He, too, seemed to be sneaking up on success, bypassing the laws of nature, reinventing human capability ... until, until he saw the action of the wind churning the water, pummeling the boat, whipping his clothing into tatters. Fear seized him

[1]Spiros Zodhiates, *Pulpit Helps*, August 1990, 10.

[2]William Barclay, *The Gospel of Matthew*, Daily Study Bible Series, vol. 2 (Philadelphia: Westminster Press), 105.

anew with a tenacious hold that would not let go, so that he began sinking in the foaming froth of the sea, gasping and crying. He, whose name meant rock, went skipping along the waters like a cleverly thrown stone, only to sink like a rock once he looked at the storm about him.

"Lord, save me," he bellowed.

"Jesus reached out his hand immediately, caught him gently, and chided him, 'O man of little faith, why did you doubt?' "

Here is the key to succeeding; it is never doubting. Success is not something to be stealthily followed and sneakily conquered, for true success—spiritual success—requires but one infinitesimal element. It is faith, genuine and true, never fading, never fouled; faith no bigger than a mustard seed, but faith through and through.

Archbishop Trench says that Jesus' rebuke of Peter was "gracious." He explained to that disciple in a few words how he could do all things through the strengthening Christ gives. "His error lay, not in undertaking too much," writes Trench, "but in relying too little upon that strength which would have triumphantly borne him through all."[3]

Most of us are like Peter. Faith exists, but it pales in a moment of terror. We have it, this thing called faith, but it seems to evaporate in the thick of trouble, flooding us when life is easy but instantly disappearing when times are hard. Jesus, by rebuking Peter, reminds us that the antithesis to faith is not unbelief actually but doubt. Doubt is the corrosive. It is an acid that eats deep into the tenderness of young and growing faith, for it is a negative factor that gnaws through the positive, devouring it wholesale and without reason. Jesus, in his followers, seems to expect a toughened faith, one hardened to realities, and strengthened for moments of fear and hours of danger.

When a group of tourists saw a legless war veteran go to the Shrine of Lourdes, they whispered and laughed, "Does he suppose God will give him back his legs?"

The veteran overheard this remark. Turning to the group, he said, "No, I don't expect God to give me back my legs. I expect him to show me how to live without them." There was no doubt in his voice. Caught in the storm of life, he was not sneaking up on success; he was, however, without doubt.

Like Peter, David MacLennan says, "We are in a similar boat. The wind is contrary. There is the same opposing force which cannot be changed or ordered off. It cannot be climbed over or crawled under. It will not explain its meaning. For an entire generation the night is dark, the sea is rough and the wind is contrary."[4] How are we to master the wind, to endure the storm, to cross to the Lord? It is by having faith, not doubts!

II. There is a secret conveyed in this episode of the life of Peter and the ministry of Jesus that enables us to move toward that very goal. It is prayer, earnest prayer, sincere prayer, deep prayer, prayer that wrestles with doubt and pins it; prayer that volleys uncertainty repeatedly and scores; prayer that races against seemingly faster, more logical engines to push past the checkered flag first. Jesus mastered the wind and the waves, beckoned Peter, and rescued the Twelve, because prayer gave him that doubtless, faithful spark of spiritual energy needed. If something less dramatic for you and me, daily prayer equips us also to face life unafraid and meet our storms, our crises, with the will to master them through Christ.

If Jesus needed to pray, isn't that need even greater for the likes of us?

The word *doubt* Jesus uses in rebuking Peter is *distazo*, which means "to stand in

[3]Richard C. Trench, *Notes on the Miracles of Our Lord* (Grand Rapids: Baker Book House, 1949), 178.

[4]David MacLennan, *Revell's Minister's Annual*, 1966 (Westwood, NJ: Fleming H. Revell, 1965), 88.

two ways."[5] Like the Roman God Janus, when you look longingly to the future, as well as yearningly to the past, you are uncertain. You have doubt. Like a truck jackknifed in the freeway median, you are uncertain which way it wants to go. The kind of doubt Jesus speaks about will not allow you to decide which way to travel. Doubt, of this kind, holds you undetermined. It leaves you in confusion; it makes for hesitation, leading to frustration and immobilizing fear. No wonder Peter sank! He had neutralized his faith, shut off its power, turned off the ignition that kept him going.

When you start to walk on water, you can't afford to doubt!

Friend, the world is full of tactics and techniques to succeed. There's a whole substrata of success books, magazines, videos, training courses, and the like marketed with the intention of motivating you to achievement. They are intent on emphasizing the positive, bent on clearing out the negative, primed to fill you and me with motivational inspiration to send us right to the top. While it revitalizes us temporarily, stimulating our hopes and encouraging our determination, it cannot succeed like prayer, Christian prayer, prayer that goes to the Source of power rather than an alternative resource.

Had Peter spent that night of prayer with Jesus, he could have walked across the whole sea instead of a few feet. Had he kept prayerfully awake in Gethsemane, instead of falling asleep while the Lord prayed that Thursday Judas betrayed him, he would never have denied the Savior nor fled in fright nor found the Resurrection hard to believe.

But Peter did pray, you might argue. It is true that twice he petitioned the Lord. First, he begged, "Bid me come to you on the water," and, second, when he was sinking, "Lord, save me." In both instances the Lord responded affirmatively. "Come," he said. When the big fisherman was about to drown, the Lord "caught him" by the hand. Are not both of these responses indications to us that prayer works, that God has an attentive ear to our needs, and that he personally takes our frightened hand?

But, you might say, there was a rebuke! But what a rebuke! It was a kindly word, one intended to instruct not only that fisherman but all the disciples and not only the disciples of that time but every time. Jesus was battling negativism, doubt, faithlessness, and human weakness with the encouragement to dare to believe.

III. Jesus comes to us in our troubles and our trifles. He comes to calm our fears and show us love. He comes to draw us to himself and encourage us for the future. Jesus comes to save us . . . not only from drowning, as he did Peter, but from eternal death.

The truth is we are more like Peter than we care to admit . . . we as individuals and we as a congregation. In the midst of walking on water, we, too, have our doubts, and fear seizes us! Let us learn the Lord's secret. We can't sneak up on success, but we can believe and pray ourselves into it, for God is the focus of our faith and the power behind prayer.—Richard Andersen

Illustrations

GO FORWARD. A man should orient his will and all his works to God and having only God in view go forward unafraid, not thinking, am I right or am I wrong? One who worked out all the chances ere starting his first fight would never fight at all. And if, going to some place, we must think how to set the front foot down we shall never get there. It is our duty to do the next thing: go straight on, that is the right way.—Meister Eckhart

BACKSTAGE. Often I go behind stages which are all cluttered up. Thus many of us live with outward stages all set, but be-

[5]W. E. Vine, *An Expository Dictionary of Biblical Words*, ed. by Merrill F. Unger and William White (Nashville: Thomas Nelson, 1985), 182.

hind this frontage we are all cluttered up with conflicts and fears and resentments and frustrations. We keep up a brave front, but behind the curtains!

Peter speaks of "illicit idolatry" (1 Pet. 4:3, Moffatt). It was behind-the-scenes idolatry—out on the stage of life apparently seeking altruistic ends, but behind the scenes practicing illicit idolatry, bowing the knee at the shrine of self. Paul speaks of those who "proclaim Christ for their own ends" (Phil. 1:17, Moffatt)—Christ is being proclaimed, but in the service of the self. The pulpit is used as a stage for self-display. Of one politician it was said, "He couldn't use the Lord's Prayer without weighing its political significance—for himself." There are many politically minded people in religious positions using religion as the frontage to backstage political maneuvering for position, place, and power. They are not bad men—they are divided.—E. Stanley Jones

Sermon Suggestions

SPOUTING OFF IN GOD'S NAME.   TEXT: Jer. 28:1–9. (1) *Then*: A prophet foretold prosperity for the Lord's people. (2) *Always*: An alleged message from God is to be judged by its fulfillment and fruits. (3) *Now*: Not everyone who invokes the name of God can be trusted. Judgment as well as prosperity can be the work of God.

LIVING TOWARD AN UNSHAKABLE KINGDOM.   TEXT: Heb. 12:18–29. (1) The experience of the people and Moses at Sinai was awesome, even terrifying. Such is the effect of sheer law and judgment. (2) In contrast to Sinai, the experience of Christian believers is one of acceptance, security, and joy. Such is the effect of the grace of God through Jesus Christ, whose blood, unlike that of Abel's, which cried out for vengeance, offers forgiveness. (3) Nevertheless, to spurn the one who speaks to us from heaven—Jesus Christ—is a greater offense than to refuse "to hear the oracle speaking on earth" (REB).

Worship Aids

CALL TO WORSHIP.   "How amiable are thy tabernacles, O Lord of hosts! My soul longeth, yea, fainteth for the courts of the Lord; my heart and my flesh crieth out for the living God" (Ps. 84:1–2).

INVOCATION.   This morning we open the gates of the temple of our hearts, Father, that Christ may come in. May he find all ready for his coming in this special hour. As we prepare, enable us to remove all false pride that destroys, all superficial pomp, all arrogance that divides, so that only a humble shrine exists in our hearts and lives to give welcome to the Master of life. Create within us the beauty of holiness. May all that transpires in this hour be dedicated as a gift of love for Christ and thus be used to praise him. May every hymn, every prayer, every anthem, every thought truly give honor to his name.

Generate in our weary and sometimes fretful lives a new spirit of expectancy. Create a feeling of excitement in our midst and lead this worshiping congregation to await eagerly the glory of his presence even as did those among whom he walked in that long ago day in Galilee and whom he taught to pray ... [the Lord's Prayer].—Henry Fields

OFFERTORY SENTENCE.   "Let us be thankful, then, because we receive a kingdom that cannot be shaken. Let us be grateful and worship God in a way that will please him, with reverence and fear" (Heb. 12:28, TEV).

OFFERTORY PRAYER.   Our Father, we are thankful that we can offer the perishing fruits of our labor in the service of your kingdom that will remain forever. Raise these gifts as an acted prayer that your kingdom may come and your will be done on earth as it is in heaven.

PRAYER.   O Lord, I know not what to ask of thee. Thou alone knowest what are my true needs. Thou lovest me more than I myself know how to love. Help me to see my real needs which are concealed from me. I dare not ask either a cross or consolation. I can only wait on thee. My heart is open to thee. Visit and help me, for thy great mercy's sake. Strike me and heal me, cast me down and raise me up. I worship in silence thy holy will and thine inscrutable ways. I offer myself as a sacrifice to thee. I put all my trust in thee. I have no other desire than to fulfill thy will. Teach me how to pray. Pray thou thyself in me.—Metropolitan Philaret of Moscow (d. 1867).

LECTIONARY MESSAGE

Topic: The Disciplines of Faith

Text: Luke 13:22–30

There is a consensus that all religious sentiment is good and all religious practices will result in a desired consequence. The sayings of Jesus in this passage bring a very abrupt, grating denial of this. Even the question that caused the response seems to imply that already Jesus had communicated that some responses and actions of his followers are unacceptable or inadequate.

The emphasis on striving, restrictions, and exclusions makes both decision and effort requirements of a relationship with him.

I. *The narrow door (no excuse will be accepted).* The particularism of the Christian gospel is nowhere more clearly expressed than in the statement that even some who "strive to enter" (v. 24) shall be unable. There is no implication that even commitment will be adequate. Matthew adds "the way" to the admonition that the door is narrow. The implication may well be that some continued restriction is to be expected.

The emphasis on God's grace as found in other passages is even more significant in the light of this passage. The attitude of the waiting father who embraces the returning son (Luke 15:20) offers hope for those for whom the door is too narrow.

II. *Time is short (no extension will be made).* Even without the first-century emphasis on Parousia, a reference to the brevity of opportunity is needed. In a day when the prospects of planetary self-destruction are prevalent, the consequences of both personal and societal mistakes and failures must be dealt with. Only old age adequately warns of the brevity of life and the fleeting opportunity, but warnings must be issued of the possible missed experiences.

These verses also stress the prerogative of the householder to shut the door when he pleases. Here, too, the emphasis is placed on God's decision, which results from the indecision and procrastination of those who are shut out.

III. *Judgment without favoritism (no one can slip in).* It is especially human to feel that one falls into a special category or has acceptable excuses. Jesus often warned the religionists of his day that they did not have an exclusive claim to acceptance (Luke 3:8).

Rejection or exclusion result from the failure to meet the challenges of the "narrow door" and the "shortness of time." The words also challenge the hearer to face the question, How do you measure in regard to these? Each life and all religious motive come under scrutiny.

The saying about the reversal of the ultimate outcome for "the first" and "the last" is quoted in the other synoptics (Matt. 20:16 and Mark 10:31). This implies an acceptance of the significance Jesus obviously intended. One can only wonder if the same significance is recognized by the modern hearers.

One can also be encouraged that the inequities and disappointments of life will face a time of balancing. There is tremendous healing in the assurance that disparities and brokenness are not left uncorrected when "the former things are passed away" (Rev. 21:4).—Arthur W. Walker, Jr.

SUNDAY: AUGUST THIRTIETH

SERVICE OF WORSHIP

Sermon: A Fresh Look at Renewal
Text: Ps. 51:1–9

Most churches do extensive planning before a revival or a lay renewal weekend. Why all the fuss and bother? "Who says that *I* need revival?" may be one unspoken question in your congregation. The need for renewal is nothing new. For thousands of years, human beings have been searching for a fresh relationship with God.

One evidence of the need for spiritual renewal may be the presence of personal sin. Five times in these nine verses David referred to his sin, also using such words as *transgressions, iniquity,* and *evil* to describe both his nature and his deeds.

Verses 3 and 4 hint that the psalmist sensed an acute separation from God, which may be another evidence of the need for renewal. Who among us never has felt a great distance between us and God at times?

In verse 6 perhaps David was referring to his attempts to hide his hideous crime before God. His failure to be honest with either God or himself had resulted in his drastic need for renewal. When we either attempt to hide something in our lives from God or refuse to acknowledge our condition, we need renewal.

When we are dry, when our spirits are stale and stagnant, when our prayer lives are powerless and our resistance to temptation, rotten attitudes, and bitterness is at its lowest, how can we receive the renewal desperately needed?

I. *Renewal comes when I confess my sin to God* (vv. 1–2). Never once did David blame his sin on Bathsheba. The transgressions, iniquities, and sins to which David referred in this psalm are "my" transgressions, iniquities, and sins. He accepted responsibility for his evil deeds. David looked at his crimes from three angles.

First, David pleaded with God: "Blot out my transgressions." *Transgression* means "a deliberate violation of a known standard." David realized afresh that sin

is whatever causes a person to willfully disobey God.

The second angle is seen in verse 2: "Wash away all my *iniquity*" (NIV). The Hebrew word for *iniquity* comes from a word which means "to bend" or "to twist." David's fresh perspective on his life caused him to realize that his life had become twisted out of proportion.

At the end of verse 2, the third angle is revealed: "Cleanse me from my sin." The word *sin* David used here means simply "to miss the mark" and is similar to a New Testament word. David realized that sin is anything which causes a person to fall short or miss the goal of God's best.

Without acknowledgment of personal sin, forgiveness has no basis. Without forgiveness, renewal is not possible. We individually must admit, "I have sinned."

II. *Renewal comes when I confess that I have sinned against God* (v. 4). Deep in our hearts we must concede that we have sinned against *someone*, and that someone is almighty God. Some would say that David was attempting to ignore the many people he had hurt when he said, "Against you, you only, have I sinned" (NIV). What about Bathsheba and Uriah? What about the little baby which had resulted from David's illicit union with Bathsheba? What about the anger and turmoil in David's family?

The word *only* in verse 4 also could read *especially*. David wasn't trying to ignore the many people he had hurt. Instead, he was admitting that sin which hurts others is first and foremost against God. If he had not broken the laws of God, the others would not have been hurt.

III. *Renewal comes when I admit that my sin has separated me from God* (v. 3). David began to realize the seriousness of his sin, so he prayed, "My sin is always before me" (NIV). He could not enjoy the sweet fellowship and communion with God that he once did. His brief moments of misdirected pleasure and his previous unwillingness to confess had in effect separated him from God.

The Scriptures are explicit in describing the effects of unconfessed sin (see Ps. 38:18; 66:18; Isa. 59:2; 64:7). Someone once suggested in a group discussion that perhaps the "hell" of hell will be the knowledge that one is eternally separated from God.

Once a Christian sins, he does not become "unborn." He is still a child of God. But as long as that sin is unconfessed, he is cut off from the privileges and riches rightfully his as a child of the king. To receive a renewal of his relationship with his Father, the Christian must confess, "My sins have separated me from God."

IV. *Renewal comes when I admit that God is the only one who can forgive me of my sin* (vv. 1–2). David's plea for forgiveness was grounded in the character of God. "Unfailing love" (v. 1, NIV) is similar to the New Testament concept of unmerited, undeserved grace. God's "great commission" (NIV) is derived from another Hebrew word which means "womb," a vivid description of the loving forgiveness of our heavenly Father.

Based on these characteristics of God, David asked God to "blot out" his transgressions. This accounting term pictures God erasing the tally of wrongdoing from David's account.

David's plea in verse 2 is that God would "wash away" (NIV) all his sin. This Hebrew term describes a woman on wash day grinding the clothes on the rocks at the river bank to remove even the stains which had soaked into the fibers of the cloth. In the same verse, David prayed that God would "cleanse" him from his sin, picturing the process of melting silver or gold to remove the impurities.

In admitting that God was the only One who could forgive him for what he had done, David prayed that God would erase the charges, beat him against the rocks, purify him with fire—that God would do anything necessary to remove the fault and stain of sin.

V. *Renewal comes when we realize that God's forgiveness is thorough and complete* (v. 7). David was not asking God to merely wink at what he had done. He wanted all the forgiveness God had to offer.

That's why David further pleaded: "Cleanse me" (NIV). The King James usage of the word *purge* here is probably closer to David's intention. The word is derived from the word for "sin," so David was praying that God would "de-sin" him.

That David was praying for a complete purging and renewal in his spirit is seen in his request that God purge him with "hyssop." This vivid figure of speech recalled the small, aromatic plant used in Jewish ceremonies for cleansing from leprosy. When God cleanses a man, he is really clean!

David was ruthless in the description of his sin and just as descriptive of the wonderful grace of God in restoration and renewal. He told us why he personally needed renewal and how he received it. If we would obtain renewal today, we must walk the same road as David.—S. M. Henriques, Jr.

Illustrations

WHAT GOD CANNOT DO.   God gives man a "new heart" and a "new life," but he does not render undone what has been done.—Romano Guardini

TRUE CONFESSION.   Real confession is to God who alone is good, with whom alone at last "we have to do." So a condemned man "gets it off his chest" not merely to "level" with the community, for nothing he can do cancels his crime, but to cast his burden on the unseen God whom perchance he has rarely worshiped in life. Only Life, brooding over both our failures and our pretensions of virtue, can forgive us. The Prodigal Son was not so blind as to reckon his guilt merely "antisocial conduct." It was that of course, but such a description is thinner than a coat of varnish. He said to his father, "I have sinned against heaven and before you." Who could doubt that such confession lances the boil which otherwise spreads beneath the skin to issue in worse ills?—George Buttrick

Sermon Suggestions

WHO'S TO BLAME?   TEXT: Ezek. 18:1–9, 25–29. (1) Our parents, in the end, cannot be blamed for what we do. (2) If, after living a good life, we turn to evil ways, we are personally responsible and suffer the consequences. (3) However, if, after living a bad life, we turn and do what is right, we will enjoy the consequences.

SOME BASIC GUIDELINES FOR CHRISTIANS.   TEXT: Heb. 13:1–8. (1) Love your fellow Christians. (2) Keep your conduct in line with the sacredness of marriage. (3) Trust God to take care of you and your needs. (4) Respect and follow in faith and life the good example of your leaders. (5) Therefore, let the unchanging Christ keep you on course for a safe arrival.

Worship Aids

CALL TO WORSHIP.   "Lord, who shall abide in thy tabernacle? Who shall dwell in thy holy hill? He that walketh uprightly, and worketh righteousness, and speaketh the truth in his heart" (Ps. 15:1–2).

INVOCATION.   Lord, we come as we are today: Some are cornered by temptation, others are deep in grief, and many are anxious. Help us to cast our burden on the Lord who knows all about us and longs to hear from us more than we long to be heard. In the Savior's name.—E. Lee Phillips

OFFERTORY SENTENCE.   "Keep your life free from love of money, and be content with what you have; for he has said, 'I will never fail you nor forsake you' " (Heb. 13:5, RSV).

OFFERTORY PRAYER.   Lord, we know that if we love you enough no other love can compete with what is right. So fix our hearts on you, O God, that everything we gain and control will be under your lordship.

PRAYER.   O merciful Lord, enlighten Thou me with a clear shining inward light, and remove away all darkness from the habitation of my heart. Repress Thou my many wandering thoughts, and break in pieces those temptations which vio-

lently assault me. Fight Thou for me, and vanquish the evil beasts; that so peace may be obtained by Thy power, and that Thine abundant praise may resound in Thy holy court, that is, in a pure conscience. Send out Thy light and Thy truth, that they may shine upon the earth; for, until Thou enlighten me, I am but as earth without form and void. Lift Thou up my mind which is pressed down by a load of sins, for no created thing can give full comfort and rest to my desires. Join Thou me to Thyself with an inseparable band of love; for Thou even alone dost satisfy him that loveth Thee.—Thomas à Kempis

LECTIONARY MESSAGE

Topic: Under Scrutiny

TEXT: Luke 14:1, 7–14

A theme of judgment runs through the scripture passages on which this group of sermons is based. The admonitions on achieving spiritual goals all reflect the danger of a wrong emphasis in how to arrive at desired ends. The methods of accomplishing a purpose are important. Even sought-after spiritual goals can become ends in themselves.

In the opening verse of the chapter, the Gospel writer emphasizes, "They watched him closely." The circumstances indicate that the Pharisees were watching to see if Jesus would break any of the religious laws. A secondary meaning may imply that they watched to see if he lived by his own teaching. They could have learned from the fact that he also was concerned for living what is taught.

I. *Practicing humility.* Most of the teaching of Jesus grew out of the immediate setting in which he and his followers found themselves. The writer alludes in a telling way to the fact that Jesus began to teach on humility "when he noticed how the guests picked out the places of honor at the table" (v. 7, NIV). The height of pride is demonstrated by going to the lowest place with the expectation of being called to a higher position. If the original teaching grows out of the events of the life of Jesus and his followers, it would appear that the application must be made to the events of modern life. The modern believer must give special attention lest the practice of "humility" becomes the expression of pride. This parable reiterates the teaching of Prov. 25:7.

II. *True humility.* Genuine humility is practiced only in the lives of those willing truly to occupy the lowest place. There is no intention in true humility in using appearance as a means of achieving status.

Humility is an attitude that affects all that one may do. It becomes the basis for all human relationships. It can only result from the proper relationship with God. Only those who properly understand and accept God's grace can demonstrate it.

Paul incorporated the true nature of humility into his teaching to early believers (see Rom. 12:3).

III. *Judgment of humility.* In both verse 11 and in the teaching on hospitality (vv. 12–14) there is a reference to end-time judgment and rewards. Most persons are sensitive to how others may view them and the rewards to be received as a consequence of one's actions. The emphasis in these verses is on how God will view attitudes. Before God there will be a reversal of most popular values.

The divine judgment of humility will deal only with motive. There will be little concern for appearances or what is generally thought. Service and kindness to those unable to return our actions are the basis for divine rewards.

Concern for those unable to return our service or hospitality is a reflection of the divine attitude. Divine love is given without expectation of the return of like value.—Arthur W. Walker, Jr.

SUNDAY: SEPTEMBER SIXTH

SERVICE OF WORSHIP

Sermon: When Things Do Not Go Well

TEXT: Isa. 40:27–31

If you are a parent, what do you do when your daughter tells you that she is going to marry a man whom you don't like? You don't like him personally and, in your parental love and care, you don't think that he will make her a good husband. Or when your daughter comes to you and tells you that she is going to divorce the husband she already has, or when she comes and says to you that she is going to have a baby with no husband in sight—what do you do then?

What do you do when you lose your job and can't find another, and all the doors of life are suddenly closed, slammed in your face, shut tight? Or when the doctor finds a lump and says that it must be removed *at once?* When someone who has been very close to you dies? When your son goes off to war with nothing but the call of duty? When someone you greatly love is mentally blank, and there is no longer any communication at all between you and that person? What do you do then?

What you do then reveals the kind of person you are. Do you panic? Do you fold up in a state of paralysis? Do you withdraw from the situation in fear and trembling? Do you protest and shake your fist in rage and say, Why does this happen to me? Or do you pray? Do you do what the psalmist did who wrote, "When I was in trouble, I called on the Lord, and he heard me"? Or do you call up someone else and ask him to call upon the Lord?

These are all possibilities, but there is a more excellent way.

I. The first thing to do is to sit down for a half hour and do nothing at all. You can sit still and do nothing if you think something. Say to yourself these four things:

(a) There is nothing that can happen to me that has not happened to millions of others. Say to yourself, I am unique, I am a unique creature. There never before has been one like me and there never will be another. I am unique; but my trouble is not unique. To be sure, it comes to me in different ways, but it comes to everyone. You shed once and for all the idea that you have been selected as a special target for life's worst blows.

(b) Then say this: I knew ahead of time that as a human being I ran the risk of something like this. One of the things that surprises me as I see people going through difficult times is that so many of them seem to be completely surprised that anything like this could happen. Life means exposure to all sorts of things, and among other things, it means exposure to all the four winds of misfortune. Those four winds come from the four corners of the earth: They are disappointment, disease, defeat, and death. The winds do not often blow all the time, and they do not all blow at once.

Adverse winds are a part of life. To be sure, you can never be prepared for them, not in one sense. You are never ready for them; you are never waiting to welcome them, surely not if you are normal. But you can prepare yourself for the possibility that they may one day or another strike you.

(c) Then go further and say to yourself, There are people who did their greatest work when they were blown by all four winds at once.

If you are anything like myself, think of Pablo Casals, the veteran performer, the great musician, now having celebrated his ninetieth birthday. Remember how he said, "Nerves and stage fright before playing have never left me throughout the whole of my career." But it did not stop him from playing. It may have helped him play more magnificently.

You may say, Well, to think of people like that depresses me. They are great, and I am not. They can do it, but I can't. It is impossible. It simply makes me feel more inadequate than I did in the beginning. If thinking of people of that kind does do that to you, then I suppose the best thing is not to think about them, but I do not think it need do that. It doesn't do that to me, even though I recognize their superiority and the greatness which I know I do not have. When I try to enter into their lives and see what they do, I say to myself, "That he overwent; that also may I"—in some way and to some degree. If he can do it so magnificently, then I can do it in my own small way.

(d) The last thing you say to yourself is this: I do not know *how* I am going to handle this, but I know that I *can*. I know that, from sources of which I am not conscious, help will come, not necessarily the help I ask for, but help that I know nothing about will rise up in me, will appear suddenly from all sorts of unexpected places. If I wait quietly, that help will come. I can do all things through Christ who strengtheneth me.

II. Then you are ready to pray. That is the next thing to do. Instead of praying *for* something, pray *about* it. In one sense, you have already been doing it. You have already been thinking about your situation in God's presence before you ask for anything. You have been draining off some of the bitterness in yourself.

Then ask God for what you want. If you want a job, ask him for it. If you want help, ask him for it. If you want to win some battle, perhaps some inner battle fought behind the closed doors of your life, ask him to give you the victory. If you want to get out of a difficult situation, ask him to help you get out of it.

And after you ask him, then go to work on it yourself. If you want to be well, work with the forces of nature that will help to make you well. Don't work against them, let them work in you and with you.

If you want a job, go out and look for one. You probably will not find the one you are looking for, but if you don't look, you won't find any. They don't come looking for you until you go looking for them. If you want a friend, if you feel left alone in life, be a friend to someone. If you want to find the meaning of life (and a great many people now are saying that they do not see any meaning in life at all; this is one of our current moods, the meaninglessness of life), if you don't see any meaning and you want to find the meaning of life, begin to make some little corner of your life mean something.

You will not get what you want just for the asking. If you do nothing about it, nothing will happen. On the other hand, if you pray about it, you may get it, but you may not. You may get something even greater than what you asked for. You may get what I wish all of us could get, myself included, and that is a deeper rootage in things. One of the reasons why we are so likely to snap in heavy storms, the way trees do, is that our roots don't go deep enough. You may get a deeper rootage, and the deeper your rootage is, the greater your lifting power will be; that is, the deeper you go into the very nature of existence, the more realistic you are about life and suffering, joy and sorrow, death and defeat, the greater lifting power you will have when the time comes for you to raise some great burden that you would never choose, but which has been laid upon you.

I wonder if this is what Isaiah meant by "waiting" upon the Lord. I have never been absolutely sure what he meant, but I think that this may be partly what he meant when he wrote the famous lines in the fortieth chapter of his book. "They that wait upon the Lord shall renew their strength; they shall mount up with wings as eagles; they shall run and not be weary, and they shall walk and not faint."

As you have waited upon him, you are more than likely to find that you will not only have the strength to run but to walk, step by step, day by day, and not faint.—Theodore Parker Ferris

Illustrations

BENEFITS OF ADVERSITY.   Think now about John Keats as a young man and to what misfortunes he was exposed. When he was nine years old his father was killed; he fell from a horse. When he was ten his grandfather Jennings, his mother's father, whom he adored, died. When he was fifteen, his mother died. When he was nineteen, his grandmother died. She was the last one to hold the family together and to provide a home. When he was twenty-two, his younger brother, George, married and left for the United States, and when he was twenty-three, his youngest brother, Tom, at the age of nineteen, died of tuberculosis.

Not long after Tom's death, John recognized symptoms of tuberculosis, his

own fatal illness, in himself. At about the same time he fell desperately in love with Fanny Brawne, whom he could never marry because he didn't have the money and had nothing to look forward to but the prospect of almost certain death in the near future. At the same time his reputation among the literary people of the world was ruined by cruel reviews of his second book. Nevertheless, in two months in 1819, after all those things had happened, in two months he produced the five poems, including the great odes, which raised him to the highest ranks of English literature, and in six months of that year produced all the great poetry that he ever wrote.—Theodore Parker Ferris

ADVERSITY.   F. W. Boreham in one of his essays refers to the occasion when the great naturalist Alfred Russell Wallace tried to help an emperor moth and only harmed it by his well-intentioned efforts. He discovered the moth struggling wildly to break its way through the cocoon which covered it. It was a handsome creature of fine proportions, and Wallace was moved by the sight of its severe ordeal. So he split the cocoon and released the moth from further struggle. But that moth never developed; its wings never expanded; the colors and tints that should have adorned them never appeared. In the end it died undeveloped, stunted, ruined. That hard and severe struggle with the cocoon was Nature's method of developing its splendid wings, of bringing forth the glory and beauty of the creature. The moth had been saved from struggle, but the naturalist's ill-considered ministry had ruined and slain it.—J. D. Jones, quoted by A. Gordon Nasby

Sermon Suggestions

URGENCY IS THE MOTHER OF INTERVENTION.   TEXT: Ezek. 33:1–11. (1) God calls his prophet to be a watchman to warn his people, of sin and its consequences. (2) If the prophet fails to warn the people and they are destroyed, the prophet is answerable to God. (3) If the prophet fulfills his duty, and the people do not respond, then those warned are fully responsible for what happens. (4) However, if they mend their ways and make restitution, none of the sins they have committed will be remembered against them (Ezek. 33:14–16, REB).

THE KIND OF CHRISTIAN TO THANK GOD FOR.   TEXT: Philem. 1–12. (1) A believer who loves Jesus Christ and all God's people, verses 4–5. (2) A believer who has a growing understanding of the blessings that are in Christ, verse 6. (3) A believer who refreshes the hearts of other believers, verse 7. (4) A believer who can be counted on to express his or her faith in concrete ethical acts, verses 8–17.

Worship Aids

CALL TO WORSHIP.   "Lord, how happy is the person you instruct, the one to whom you teach your law!" (Ps. 94:12, TEV).

INVOCATION.   Gracious Lord, we thank you for the opportunity to find better lives for ourselves and our families by discovering what you want us to know and do. Let this service of worship be a time of blessed discovery and joyful obedience.

OFFERTORY SENTENCE.   "[I pray] that the communication of thy faith may become effectual by the acknowledging of every good thing which is in you in Christ Jesus" (Philem. 6).

OFFERTORY PRAYER.   Loving Father, you have given us gracious gifts. They are a blessing and make us a blessing. Open our hearts to the purpose that you will to work in and through us. Receive this portion of our material gifts as a token of our larger giving back to you of what we have received.

PRAYER.   A Labor Day prayer.

LEADER: For persons unable to work; for persons with inner turmoil, with self-destructive habits, with destructive friends;

RESPONSE: Hear our prayer, O Lord.

L: For persons taken advantage of by employers: deceived, underpaid, unpaid, lied to, betrayed, for vulnerable persons;

R: *Hear our prayer, O Lord.*

L: For persons taken advantage of by employees: cheated on, lied to, shirked by, undercut, betrayed;

R: *Hear our prayer, O Lord.*

L: For small and family businesses— that each pull his or her oar; that trust be honored; that ordinary civility apply and ordinary expectations;

R: *Hear our prayer, O Lord.*

L: For businesses or jobs in jeopardy— that, if need be, they accept a time to let go, a time to pull down, a time to scatter stones; that they accept the blessing of endings; that they know the new day that night is, and him who watches over it, his spirit on the air all night, talking us down, talking us up, saying with the psalmist, I will lay me down and sleep, for you alone cause me to dwell in safety;

R: *Hear our prayer, O Lord;*

L: For workers who are burned out—by long hours, by dead-end jobs; by greedy families; by pressure; by tedium; by lack of thanks and the dripping faucet of complaint; by unsupportive families or by loneliness; by poor health; and by their own inner compulsions, by the unfurnished rooms of empty lives;

R: *Hear our prayer, O Lord;*

L: For persons burned out by make-work; by self-serving bureaucracies of business and government; by cozy harbors of ships permanently at anchor; mothball fleets fully manned;

R: *Hear our prayer, O Lord.*

L: For workers, employers, and employees who treat each other square, are generous, are not abusive or mean, do not exist for the easy out and the early drive home; are gracious, considerate, elegant, self-critical, open, vulnerable, fair;

R: *We give you thanks, O Lord;*

L: For persons who in the workplace ask how you are, encourage you, pray for you, prod you, challenge you, stick by you;

R: *We give you thanks, O Lord.*

L: For persons who love their work, persons who, with enthusiasm and skill, simply redefine the job;

R: *We give you thanks, O Lord;*

L: For persons with the good fortune to have work that is interesting, demanding, exciting, fulfilling, and who use their good fortune for the public good;

R: *We give you thanks, O Lord;*

L: For the vocation of volunteer, and its leaven in a world of sharp elbows, for its reminder of other rewards;

R: *We give you thanks, O Lord;*

L: For the vocations of parent, caregiver, friend, and for the vocation of prayer;

R: *We give you thanks, O Lord.*

—Peter Fribley

LECTIONARY MESSAGE

Topic: Challenge of Discipleship

TEXTS: Luke 14:25–33

There were never any appeals to popularity in Jesus' promise to those who were called to follow him. Such was not the basis of his call. Reading his discussion of the consequences of being his disciple raises questions about those who offer a success philosophy as a consequence of faith and faithfulness.

I. *Requirements of discipleship.* The leaders of great human movements have consistently pointed to the consequence of involvement with their cause. Most have pictured a result that is worth the cost. This principle in itself negates the requirements of a later interpretation of "cross bearing." Even the contemporaries of Jesus understood the cost of commitment to a cause that challenged the authority of Rome.

Earlier Christian disciples seem to have better understood the requirements of discipleship. These requirements are given as the loss of relationships (v. 25); the loss of physical life (v. 26); the loss of reputation (vv. 28–32); and the loss of possessions (v. 33). Perhaps it is a lack of commitment that makes these requirements more difficult for modern followers rather than the need for additional explanation.

II. *Cost of discipleship.* The acquiring of social acceptance, status, and even governmental support changed the position of Christianity in the general society. Eventually, it was not social suicide, treason, or folly to be a Christian. These changed social, political, or economic conditions did not change the basic requirements of Christian commitment. More recent developments that again place Christians in a minority role, even in Western society and particularly in world relationships, more truly picture the true cost of discipleship.

It may appear that Jesus was discouraging those who might follow him. Yet, this extensive discussion on the cost of discipleship clearly indicated that Jesus was, in fact, encouraging discipleship by his emphasis on the cost. The cross was and has become the symbol of death, but it was also the means of life.

Jesus was claiming that the cost of discipleship was death to self-love, self-trust, and self-assertion. He also was saying that rejecting these was the way to true life.

III. *Counting the cost.* The parables of Jesus were not intended to convince one not to follow him. Jesus, rather, sought to convince all of the nature of the costs involved in following him.

Also he did not intend to say that failure to follow was worse than never trying. Again, he simply explained the nature of the cost.

Understanding the nature of discipleship is as important for believers today as in Jesus' time. True discipleship is still costly. Understanding the cost of discipleship requires equally that one know the cost of failure to be a disciple.

Many may minimize the cost of discipleship in today's society. It is important properly to evaluate the cost so that one is not misled to believe that somehow it is possible to coexist with society in such a way that the cost of discipleship is less than Jesus pictured it.—Arthur W. Walker, Jr.

SUNDAY: SEPTEMBER THIRTEENTH

SERVICE OF WORSHIP

Topic: A Healthy Religion

TEXTS: John 10:1; Mic. 6:8

One often hears remarks like these: "One religion is as good as another. Sincerity in religious beliefs is all that matters. It makes little difference what your religion is so long as you live up to it."

It is certainly true that religious faith is a powerful force in the world. But the object of faith and the expression of faith are just as important as sincerity of belief. Religious faith can be either constructive or destructive. It can bring about good or evil. Is one religion as good as another? Certainly not! Religion can be sick. Religion can be satanic.

I. There are many things involved in a healthy, constructive religious experience. First, a healthy religion promotes a personal relationship between man and God. The uniqueness of Christianity can be summed up in a word—Christ. Christianity focuses on a person, Jesus Christ, who can now be known and experienced as a living person. He is not a character of history; he is not a teacher from the past; he is not a good man who lived once-upon-a-time. He is alive today!

There are many people who come to church Sunday by Sunday, who contribute to the support of the church, who are members in good standing, but who have never had a life-changing experience with Christ. Some inherited their religion from their parents. Others acquired it for business reasons. A few borrowed it from their spouses. Such religion won't stand the test of either time or eternity because it is built upon a secondhand experience with God.

II. A healthy religion stresses grace and plays down guilt. Jesus accused the Pharisees of making heavy loads for the people to bear in their religious life. Their religion had become a petty legalism and a destructive negativism. There are too many people majoring on minors and calling it morality. The end result of this type of religion is needless guilt.

Christianity sounds a highly positive note. Listen to some of Christ's words: "You are loved! Your sins are forgiven! You are a new person! You are salt! You are light!" Christianity is both a life- and a person-affirming religion. It reminds us that we are forgiven by God and can, therefore, forgive ourselves (not an easy task at times). We are acceptable because of God's acceptance.

III. A healthy religion, also, enables one to live victoriously in the pedestrian hours of life. It offers strength and meaning for the regular and the routine. Our fast-paced society has caused many of us to expect our lives to be filled with the novel and the dramatic. This expectation has been fastened to our faith. Many people try to go from one emotional high to another one in their religious pilgrimage. Such an approach to religion is bound to issue in disappointment and sometimes guilt. Emotion is good! It is good to be touched deeply by great music, by people making decisions, by the preaching of the gospel. Emotionalism is bad! It deifies emotion and neglects the fact that we are rational and volitional beings as well as emotional ones. We are much more than feelings. Also, there are times when we cannot trust our feelings. Life was meant to be more like a level plain than a roller coaster. God can reach out to us in the ordinary moments of life. Listen to the prophet Isaiah: "But they who wait for the Lord shall renew their strength, they shall mount up with wings like eagles, they shall run and not be weary, they shall walk and not faint" (Isa. 40:31, RSV). God is not only the God of high emotional peaks but the God of uneventful days and pedestrian hours.

IV. A healthy religion faces forward and forgets much of the past. It unloads yesterday's burdens. Past sins once forgiven are forgotten. Past hurts, former angers, prior insults are cast aside. A healthy religion enables us to cast aside the rubbish of the past; it also equips us to throw aside yesterday's successes. We forget that God is always asking impertinently; "Yes, but what have you done lately?"

V. Next, a healthy religion builds bridges rather than barriers to other people and to other groups. The great theme of Ephesians is that God is a bridge builder who unites his people through the work of his Son. Listen to what Paul says: "For he is our peace who had made us both one, and has broken down the dividing wall of hostility" (Eph. 2:14, rsv). One of the few times when Jesus became angry was when he entered the Temple and saw that it had become a bazaar separating people from God and from each other. A healthy religion creates a warm fellowship.

VI. A healthy religion calls one to serve God and minister to human needs in the real world. The gospel isn't a sedative; it is a stimulant. Christ calls us to minister to the hurting humanity around us. There is no promise of placid seas nor smooth sailing. We are called to discipline our bodies as athletes, to prepare ourselves as soldiers going into combat, and to pick up our wash basins and towels as servants. Ernest Gordon in *Through the Valley of Kwai* tells of his confinement in a Japanese prison camp during World War II. In his agony Gordon turned to God in prayer and through Bible study. Yet he found no release from his agony and his aloneness. He was about to cast off his faith as a useless, unnecessary crutch when something began to happen. He saw one prisoner helping another by sharing his own rations with him. Gordon observed another comrade bathing the hot brow of a soldier being consumed by fever. He beheld a true spiritual awakening as other prisoners began to minister to their comrades. The spirit of sacrifice grew daily. Gordon goes on to say that he found God in a cup of water being shared with a thirsty soldier, that he discovered in the breaking of bread with a hungry comrade a time of communion with God, and that he heard the rustle of the Spirit in the words of encouragement offered a dying soldier. A healthy faith is one that ventures into the world of hurting humanity to offer a helping hand!—James E. Sorrell

Illustrations

SELF-DENIAL.   By words and example, Jesus taught the path of authentic asceticism. He explained why people engage in ascetic excesses. Such excesses can happen because of attachment to the letter rather than the meaning of the law, as in Jesus' hilarious description of religious leaders diligently straining gnats out of their cups only to wind up swallowing camels. Ascetic excesses can also happen because of attachment to pride, a desire to show off one's holiness. Jesus told his disciples to give alms in secret and to pray in private. Excesses can also come from thinking that the real enemy is not attachment but the objects to which one becomes attached. "It is not what goes into a person's mouth that defiles," he said, "but what comes out."—Gerald G. May

PULLED TOGETHER.   Healthy religion binds people together in such a way that their individuality is enabled both to be realized and to be consecrated to the total community of relationships to which they belong. This is a religion of mature and responsible relatedness, which does not interpret disdain for people as the call of God to withdraw from or attack other people. Rather, as an old woman in Kentucky said in a prayer meeting in her home, "Religion is aimed to pull people together and not to wedge 'em apart."—Wayne E. Oates

Sermon Suggestions

WHAT REALLY MATTERS.   TEXT: Hos. 4:1–3; 5:15–6:6. (1) The problem: Sin and crime among the people, and the resulting absence of God, 4:1–3; 5:15. (2)

The solution: Returning to a forgiving God, 6:1–3; giving faithfulness priority over religious formalities, 6:4–6.

ON BEING MADE EQUAL TO THE TASK. TEXT: 1 Tim. 1:12–17. (1) Through the grace of forgiveness. (2) Through the grace of calling for special service. (3) Through recognition and worship of the one for whom and from whom the task receives its dignity.

Worship Aids

CALL TO WORSHIP. "I will remember the works of the Lord: surely I will remember thy wonders of old. I will meditate also on all thy work and talk of thy doings" (Ps. 77:11–12).

INVOCATION. As we meet to worship, O Lord, turn our thoughts to what you have done in our lives, what you are doing at the present moment, and what you promise to do in the days to come. Let our gratitude for your grace rise up in joy and praise and testimony to your goodness.

OFFERTORY SENTENCE. "I thank Christ Jesus our Lord, who hath enabled me, for that he counted me faithful, putting me into the ministry" (1 Tim. 1:12).

OFFERTORY PRAYER. We also thank you, Lord Jesus Christ, for giving us a ministry. Use our talents, our work, and our possessions, we pray, that we may truly serve you. To this end, we bring our tithes and offerings.

PRAYER. O God of light shining in darkness, O God of hope caring in our despair, O God of salvation gracing us beyond our deserving, we laud and magnify thy name, the one true God. We cannot escape from the needs of our world, for hunger and pestilence plague the peoples of the earth: the poor, the refugees, the oppressed. We lift up those whose bodies fail for lack of nourishment and whose spirits are dimmed for lack of faith.

Lord, teach us to bind up the wounds of the sick, to harken to the cry of victims, to listen to the pain of the lonely, to visit the prisoner, and to aid the grieving until they can stand again. In seeking to be good neighbors, we pray for those in whose power it resides to make the Jericho road safe, and for the institutions, the corporations, the governments of this world, who can make changes in society to bring justice, equality, and peace. Guide people of influence in this nation and other nations, that justice may prevail over injustice, reconciliation replace war, and caring replace apathy, through the blessings of our Redeemer and the power of the Holy Spirit, clear to the very end.—E. Lee Phillips

LECTIONARY MESSAGE

Topic: God's Joy
TEXT: Luke 15:1–10

The larger context of this passage includes the familiar stories of the lost sheep, the lost coin, and the lost son. The teaching can be understood only in the setting of the criticism that had been made of the acceptance by Jesus of all who came to him. The critics felt that a truly religious person would recognize that there were unacceptable qualities in some of those gathering around Jesus. The passage teaches that the great joy of Jesus was in the truth that all are acceptable and can be forgiven. In each story the joy results from recovering that which was lost.

I. *The joy of the shepherd* (vv. 3–7). The shepherd could not be satisfied even though ninety-nine of the sheep were safe. He was not willing to rest with either an overwhelming majority or a good percentage. His concern was directed to including all.

The distress over a single loss emphasizes the importance of every one. The large numbers of our society tend to lessen concern for the individual. This passage teaches God's love for any who may stray.

Joy is the result of having all. The shepherd was no less concerned for the sheep safely at home. He was also concerned for each one not yet protected.

The context also teaches that the concern of the shepherd is not dependent on the condition of the sheep. The religionists of Jesus' day spoke of the lessened value of certain kinds of persons, but in the parable the only consideration was that the sheep was lost.

II. *The joy of the diligent woman* (vv. 8–10). The parable presents the same lessons: the value of even one, the search for the lost, the joy at recovery.

Each story emphasizes a basic truth of the Christian religion: God takes the initiative in establishing a relationship with those who are lost, in reaching out to those separated from him. His initiative is the basis of the relationship that any one can have with him.

The diligence of the searcher shows the nature and intensity of need of evangelistic endeavors. Jesus himself spoke of how the woman "scoured" and "searched carefully" until the lost coin was found. Followers of Jesus should exercise the same diligence.

III. *Joy in heaven.* The parables were told in the context of the reaction of those observing the obvious joy of fellowship even with those who were usually considered "unacceptables."

The stories expand the joy to include those who are not a part of the search. This implies that others do and should join in the joy experienced when the lost sheep and coin are found. Jesus expands the joy of the searcher to include all those who may be expected to rejoice with those who search for the lost. The obvious application is to the corporate nature of the friends and neighbors, the church. The expansion of the joy experienced to an eternal group is equally expressed.
—Arthur W. Walker, Jr.

SUNDAY: SEPTEMBER TWENTIETH

SERVICE OF WORSHIP

Sermon: Hindrance or Wings
TEXT: Matt. 16:21–28

I. We find Jesus in Caesarea Philippi. He has just rejoiced in the affirmation made by his disciples that he is the Messiah, and then immediately he is confronted with the temptation to be the kind of messiah that Peter and the rest of the disciples expect him to be.

(a) Jesus has faced this temptation before in the wilderness, but it returns now in the form of Peter. Like so many of our temptations, it comes from those we love: not from our enemies, but from our friends, from our parents. The pressure and the temptation before Jesus is to be the kind of military messiah, to be the conquering hero, to lead the rebels in their triumph over the forces of the empire. The temptation is to allow the human agenda to dictate to God where and how God will act. The temptation is to have our own agenda for what we want God to do and to pray that God will do it.

There is always the temptation for us to try to get God to do our agenda, to use God's power for our purpose. There is the side that sees God as being on the side of changes, of liberation, of casting out the demons, and using his power to make those changes.

(b) But Jesus keeps rejecting that temptation, because he knows that if God made his power and love subject to the whims and wishes of everybody then there would never be any peace. If God used his power and mercy to meet human needs, even God's power and love would be exhausted before our lists of wants and wishes would be finished. But even more important than that is the fact that there are simply situations in life where power does not work. How can the power of God by might and force eliminate the self-destroying habits of a son or daughter who has fallen prey to drugs? How can force or winning ever make for peace?

Jesus knows that whatever conversion, whatever redemption, is to be brought by the Messiah must address the anxiety of the human heart that seeks the security of building "bigger and bigger barns," must speak to the collective fear of the unknown that is always making and projecting images of some great enemy. The work of the Messiah has to deal with the false pride that sets race against race, sex against sex, generation against generation, and must find a solution to the economic greed that tries to find permanence, value, and meaning in the amassing of possessions. But those can't be touched by force, power, or might. They have to be met with a grace that convicts from within and an alternative that invites and commends from without, through love and forgiveness. So Jesus told Peter to get behind him. Peter's temptation to use the power of God to fulfill the expectations and desires of people would not bring about the kind of redemption God sought and humanity needed.

II. If there is a Peter who wants God to use his power in a certain way to bring about Peter's own ideas of paradise, there are always those who like things exactly as they have been, and they do not want any changes. If there is a boyfriend who wants the relationship to change, there are parents who do not want the parent-daughter relationship ever to change. If there are dictators who want to use the power of God on their side to change the balance of power in the world, there are those who like the way things are, and we are asked to sacrifice to preserve our way of life. Jesus and we have to decide. We cannot ever keep it the way it is. There is one thing we cannot ever do with our lives: We cannot keep them. As Jesus discovers, as you and I must always discover, there is no way to keep our lives. That is the limit placed upon us by God's creation of us. We are finite. We do not last forever, and we cannot preserve our lives with any piece of the rock. The one thing we cannot do with our lives is keep them. We either have them snatched away from us, controlled and taken away from us by others, or we decide to what and for whom we will give them away in love and joy.

We will have our lives taken from us, or we will decide to what we will give our lives. I was told of a young man who had been made to go to seminary. He had not wanted to be a minister, but his mother wanted him to be one. He told the committee of presbytery that he did not want to be one, and they tried to refuse to take him under care. But mother was a large contributor to the church, and the church was an important church in presbytery, so the committee accepted him under the pressure and the young man ended up at seminary. Our lives are taken from us by the demands and expectations, or we give them away.

We either have to give our lives away, or they will be taken from us. Even the most health-conscious person will be sick. So we come to the place where we discover that we have to decide to what we will give our lives. We can't keep them. We lose them either by their being taken from us or our giving them away. Jesus said, "No one takes my life from me, but I lay it down for my friends." But to what shall we give it? The Scriptures suggest that we may waste it as well by giving it away to the wrong things. What shall it profit us if we gain the whole world and lose our own souls?

III. Jesus came that we might have life and have it more abundantly. He did not come to be a hindrance but to give our lives wings. He came to give us the grace and power to discover, not only that we had to decide to give our lives away rather than to allow them to be taken from us by the expectations of others, but also to show us what we might give them to in order to discover our real joy and peace. We give them away in service of those who cannot serve themselves. We give them away in sacrificial love for the enrichment of the community. We use them up in the work of making for peace. We wear ourselves out in the labors of bringing and giving hope to those who have no hope. We set our sights on the joy of pursuing the kingdom of God. If you have given in love, you will be given back to in love. If you have given away in joy, it will be returned with great joy. If you have worked for your own prestige and your own importance, then you will get back what you gave, in selfishness and loneliness. It was said of the Queen Victoria of England that she lived unforgiving, she died unforgiven.—Rick Brand

Illustrations

GOD'S WILL.   What is the will of God to me? My answer to that question will determine the tone and purpose of my whole life today. Shall I think of it as primitive savages did, as a hostile power that one must escape? Or, as the serpent suggested to Adam, as a will that meant to cramp and limit life? Shall I dread or fear it?

No, let me not begin the day like that. Let me rather think as Jesus did. God's will is my Father's will. To do his will is the strength of my life. As I follow his Word I shall discover hidden manna to supply my needs for the tasks of the day.—J. B. Weatherspoon

PREPARATION.   On the night of the tenth of May, 1940, Winston Churchill became prime minister of England. His country faced the greatest crisis of her history. Of this significant event in his life, Churchill said, "I felt as if I were walking with Destiny, and that all my past life had been but a preparation for this hour and for this trial."

David was a young man of bright promise, for God had found in his heart the elements of true greatness. But David could have permitted many things to jeopardize his future. He could have forgotten God. He could have turned in callous pride and selfishness from the cries of his fellowmen. He could have completely given way to the desires of the flesh. This has happened to young people of great promise.

But David had a vision of his destiny, and he consciously fitted all of life into harmony with what God intended him to be. God uses the person who is prepared and who will make God's will in little things a part of his preparation. God blesses those who include him in their plans.—James W. Cox

Sermon Suggestions

GOD DOES NOT FULFILL OUR WORST FEARS.   TEXT: Hosea 11:1–11, especially verse 9. (1) God's people are blessed with tender mercies from their earliest days. (2) Nevertheless, they show themselves ungrateful, unworthy, and even ignorant of God's blessings. (3) Judgment seems inevitable. (4) However, God withholds his deserved fury and visits his people with compassion.

ON COMING TO KNOW THE TRUTH.   TEXT: 1 Tim. 2:1–7. (1) What God desires for us: a good life here; salvation, verses 1–4. (2) What God has provided for us: a Savior, the one mediator between us and God, verses 5–7; apostles and preachers to make the truth known to us, verse 7.

Worship Aids

CALL TO WORSHIP.   "He satisfies those who are thirsty and fills the hungry with good things" (Ps. 107:9, TEV).

INVOCATION.   Today, O Lord, may the water of life and the bread of life that come from you satisfy our deepest hungers and thirsts. May we not be content with a cheap, quick fix for our desires but find in you what we truly need.

OFFERTORY SENTENCE.   "I urge that petitions, prayers, requests, and thanksgivings be offered to God for all people" (1 Tim. 2:1, TEV).

OFFERTORY PRAYER.   O God, we pray many prayers for many causes, and we thank you for hearing us. Now we pray one prayer more: that you grant us the grace so to give that these offerings will bless all people.

PRAYER.   Almighty God, high above all, yet in all, we enter your sacred presence this morning through the portal of worship that in this hour we may indeed worship you in spirit and in truth. We cannot fathom your mystery. When we pause to consider the vastness of your created universe, look upon the moon and the star-studded heavens, we join the singer of ages past asking in all humility, "What is man that you are mindful of him or the Son of man that you would visit him?" With questioning difficulty in radical times we ponder the meaning of life, love, and eternity—mysteries originating with you—and then lift up our minds with our fathers before us to declare that before the mountains were brought forth or even before you had formed the earth and the world, even from everlasting to everlasting, you are God.

Knowing that you have opened a vast universe before us, we come now to ask that you will fill the universe within us. For it is in the inner universe that we discover the meaning of truth, that we might walk in its shining light. It is from within that goodness grows glorious and beauty is magnified. Yet, unless you reign within us, truth, goodness, beauty, love, and honor will not be meaningful. So we await with anticipation the coming of your powerful Spirit to fill the inner space of our hearts. In large measure that is why we have gathered here with our troubles, pleading for light, that we might find our faltering way through trouble's darkness until we see the light of relief. That is why we have come expressing joy, feeling fortunate in love, happy in our families, prosperous in our place in life, and wanting our happiness touched with sacredness, that it may be translated into service bringing human good to others. That is why some have come today, buffeted by temptations and sins, seeking wholeness and redemption.

All of us need your abiding presence, that we may not be crushed by failure, that shallow faith may be deepened, that we might have courage to go forth into the world from this hour to live and work so that we shall leave it a fairer place in which coming generations can rear the human family. That such may be, we come to you, seeking the guidance and love given through Christ, who taught all his disciples to pray: [the Lord's Prayer].—Henry Fields

LECTIONARY MESSAGE

Topic: Using What You Have

Text: Luke 16:1–13

Possessions are tyrants. They demand protection. Establishing ownership usually requires that distinctions be established. Lines must be drawn between what is "mine" and the claims that others might make. This difficult parable teaches, above all else, the prudent use of opportunity and possessions. Clearly the most important teaching emphasizes living in a manner that has lasting and eternal consequences. The proper attitude toward possessions is particularly important in proper living.

I. *The eternal home.* The story has a unique quality; it looks to the future. The point of the parable is to instruct on how to "be welcomed in the eternal home" (v. 9, TEV).

The assumption is made that trusting in "mammon" or money and in the friends that this brings into one's experience will fail. The context places the time of failure at death, though application of the truth could be made to any event or time in which true value may be revealed. The eternal home is the ultimate point of true value.

The timelessness of the eternal home also is emphasized. Contrasted to the changing circumstances of life, career, success, and personal acceptance and the possible loss of any or all of these is the permanence of the eternal home.

II. *The present opportunity.* Jesus repeatedly emphasized the importance of the present moment. In this parable, too, he spoke of the importance of the proper use of the available time. The steward was commended for understanding the significance of an opportunity available to him. In fact, this is the only thing for which he was commended.

To understand the significance of the moment—this Jesus encouraged in his followers. He taught them that what one does with the present opportunity affects both this life and the life to come.

III. *Right attitude.* The order of development of these points seems reversed. It would seem most logical to begin with attitude. The Scripture passage itself has reversed the points and concludes with attitude.

The emphasis on attitude probably should be seen as a safeguard against misunderstanding the parable. Certainly the story is open to misunderstanding.

In an age of attention to dimensions, the insistence on faithfulness in small issues takes on special significance.

Faithfulness in the right use of money results in being entrusted with true riches. How one uses or serves possessions becomes the basis for judging one's attitude. The use of temporal things provides a guide for determining what one's attitude is.

The statement, "You cannot serve both God and money" (v. 13c, TEV) is the natural consequence of establishing a right attitude. Only by accepting the sovereignty of God can one overcome the tyranny of material possessions. Since money is the basis for acquiring these possessions, money is the greatest threat to a right attitude. It is also the greatest temptation to directing one's loyalty away from God.—Arthur W. Walker, Jr.

SUNDAY: SEPTEMBER TWENTY-SEVENTH

SERVICE OF WORSHIP

Sermon: The Wealth of Worship
TEXT: Psalm 95

Do you remember the ads that were on radio and television, even billboards, some years ago, urging us to "Go to Worship; You'll be Richer for It"? A commendable public service announcement, but advertisements imply products. So it is natural to assume worship is a product or at least an experience. The truth is that worship *is* important, eternally important. But worship is not a product or an experience or even a noun. It is a verb meaning *to bow down* in the Hebrew Old Testament, *to serve* in the Greek New Testament; two of the hardest things to do by ego-obsessed humanity.

Worship is also more a way of life rather than an event. The key to this understanding of worship is found in the Book of Psalms. The Psalms, or Psalter, served as the worship book of Israel, of the early Church, and the Reformation. So it is here in the Psalms that we can discover the wealth of worship, the reason this day of corporate worship is the foundation on which the other six rest.

I. The first essential element of worship, whether individual or corporate, high church or low, is in the ninety-fifth Psalm's gleeful commitment to "*sing songs of praise.*" The worship of Israel's God, of the God made known in Jesus Christ, is

praise filled. We talk of the needs that are present in any congregation gathered for worship: healing, comfort, guidance. Yet what about a fundamental human need we often neglect? We were made to respond to the highest, that which is totally worthy of devotion, awe and honor. Like a fine-tuned instrument, the strings of our heart are made to resound with praise. Worship was, in early English, "worth-ship," meaning to respond in praise and devotion to that which is ultimately *worthy* of praise. The problem is our aim is off. We miss the mark. We ascribe ultimate worth to something or someone less than God. The *Peanuts* character Linus has been "smitten" by his teacher Miss Othmar. Lucy says to him, "You always *overdo* things. It's all right to *like* a teacher, but it's wrong to *worship* her!" "I never said I *worship* her," responds Linus. "I just said that I'm very fond of the ground on which she walks." Ouch! We place others in the place only God can hold.

Blaise Pascal, mathematician and philosopher whose name now graces a computer language, once said that each person has a God-shaped vacuum. Indeed, I believe much of our misery and spiritual malaise comes from trying to fill that vacuum with people, projects, and possessions that will not fill the void. Because we have forgotten, as a people, how to bow down before God, we fall for most anything. Because we no longer sing without embarrassment the praise of God, we sing the hollow songs of self-importance and join in anthems that praise lesser things. Therein is our emptiness. For only God will fit in the vacuum, only his praise will elevate our souls and liberate our minds.

Some of us say we believe that, but we often are just not in the mood to sing or speak God's praise. I am certainly sympathetic, but I wonder (for myself, too) if we often are not too willing victims of our emotions. Were the apostles in prison or the martyrs in the arena in the mood for praise? Yet did they not "sing songs of praise"? Is our worship *praise filled*?

II. The psalm goes on to say that . . . "he is our God, and we are the people of his pasture and the sheep of his hand." This is a graphic description of the pastoral nature of all worship. In other words, the great God, high and lifted up, enters into a relationship with his people. Like the shepherd of the Old Testament, he guides, guards, feeds, and disciplines his flock. Further, in the Gospel the Shepherd becomes also a Lamb (one of us) and gives up his life for us that we might become new creatures. That same pastoral or shepherding metaphor in the epistles suggests that we are not dumb sheep, but able as undershepherds to give warm, personal care to one another.

That's why the "electronic church" will not replace the local church. It is here and in smaller groups that we act out God's caring, saving relationship with us. The Word is not confined to heaven or the air waves. The Word has become flesh in the bread we eat together, in the handshakes, hugs, and passing of the peace one to another. Indeed, not just the prayer by the pastor but all our prayers are "pastoral" when we lift up the needs of "the people of his pasture." Worship is *pastoral*.

III. This caring aspect is essential, but worship is more than fellowship. For this passage ends with the words, "O that today you would hearken to his voice!" A prophet is one, through no ability or merit of his or her own, who speaks a word from the Lord! Worship is *prophetic*.

By that is meant the possibility of receiving a word from the Lord . . . today. Remember the age-old question, "Is God dumb, that he speaks no more?" Or we might say, "Does God still speak after his 'book' has gone to press?" The pilgrim pastor John Robinson had the answer when he spoke to his stalwart flock, "God hath yet more light to break forth from the Holy Word."

The prophet must sometimes speak against our comfortable idolatries and cherished heresies. Yet he or she is always a shepherd, a pastor, whose arms are around the congregation when speaking. This is the tricky but necessary business of "speaking the truth in love." Reject the idea that the prophetic word is a word of hate, even when it is searing and cutting. It is as a scalpel is to surgery; it is an instrument that must penetrate before it can bring healing. Hosea, Nathan, Esther were reluctant prophets. Even as we worship today, God speaks through the unlikely, the unexpected, the reluctant prophets. Whether the word comes through preacher, anthem, a child's song, or the still, small voice within, worship must be *prophetic*.

Yet we still miss the mark concerning worship if we see this hour of promise and power as an event unto itself. This hour is not exclusive but representative. A certain place is sacred so that all places become holy ground. A certain hour is set aside so that all hours are hallowed. Although in a sense worship to almighty God is an end in itself, it is also rehearsal.

If life in Christ is to be as God intended, our lives are to be *praise-filled* daily. It does not matter whether you use the words "Praise the Lord" but that you pause to give credit to God in all times and seasons. Flowing from this will be an ability to give credit to others who are God's instruments. What would happen if you really praised your son, your spouse? Cardiac arrest? Rehearsal in this hour could help your life to become more *pastoral*: caring and praying for others; seeking out the used, abused, neglected to befriend. And finally, if we worked at it starting here, couldn't we become more attuned to the *prophetic*?

Hearing God's Word in the unexpected places, in unlikely messengers, could become our experience.

Talk about wealth: our lives more filled with praise, more caring, more attuned to God's Word. It can begin here, in this hour of worship.—Gary D. Stratman

Illustrations

CARING.   In caring we aim not at giving birth to something new; we aim at nurturing, protecting, guiding, healing, or empowering something that already has life. The energy behind caring is compassion for others which, in turn, is energized by the knowledge that we are all in this together, that the fate of other beings has implications for our own fate. Caring may take a personal form, for instance, when we comfort a grieving friend. But it can also take form through movements for political and economic justice, in speaking on behalf of strangers whose oppression diminishes us all.— Parker J. Palmer

AS EAGLES FLY.   There is a wisdom that is woe; but there is a woe that is madness. And there is a Catskill eagle in some souls that can alike dive down into the blackest gorges, and soar out of them again and become invisible in the sunny spaces. And even if he forever flies within the gorge, that gorge is in the mountains, so that even in his lowest swoop the mountain eagle is still higher than other birds upon the plain, even though they soar.— Henry Melville, *Moby Dick*

Sermon Suggestions

COMPENSATION.   TEXT: Joel 2:23–30, especially verse 25. (1) Life often brings deprivation and suffering to God's own people. (2) God, however, brings blessings that outweigh our losses, abundant blessings here or hereafter (see John 10:10b).

DO YOU WANT TO BE RICH?   TEXT: 1 Tim. 6:6–19, RSV. (1) To begin with, remember "You can't take it with you." (2)

Remember also: "The love of money is the root of all evils." (3) Remember especially, if you are rich, more or less, "to do good, to be rich in good deeds, liberal and generous."

Worship Aids

CALL TO WORSHIP.   "O give thanks unto the Lord, for he is good: for his mercy endureth forever" (Ps. 107:1).

INVOCATION.   Great and Everlasting God, you have called us from our sundry tasks and ways of life and placed us in this congregation of your followers. Help us to draw strength from each other's presence so that we will want to worship you. But more than anything else, help us to draw strength from your presence among us, so that by feeling your love we might be comforted, by drawing from your strength we might have courage, and by hearing your challenge we might do your will.—James M. King

OFFERTORY SENTENCE.   "But godliness with contentment is great gain. For we brought nothing into this world, and it is certain we can carry nothing out" (1 Tim. 6:6–7).

OFFERTORY PRAYER.   Lord, if by our living on less others might know more of thee, then permit us to ponder such a sacrifice in prayer and let us give as we are able every time.—E. Lee Phillips

PRAYER.   "Holy, holy, holy is the Lord God Almighty, who was and is and is to come." How can we appear before you, O Father, except in the spirit and meaning of praise?

We praise you for the elation of worship when contemplating your power, your otherness, your love, your nearness, we discover ourselves lost in wonder, love, and praise, and heaven does seem very near.

Save us, O Father, from sticking in the literalness of words lest we miss your Word—the wonder, the mystery, the miracle of your coming in creation, in the Incarnation, and in the commonplace of our everyday. Lest we miss the wild creativity of your love by slowness of imagination, give us something more agile than the mind of prose. When you come speaking in lively pictures of an amazing grace, grant us a mystic's insight and a poet's fancy.

Without vision—without the seeing of the prophet, the insight of the poet, the creativity of the artist, we do perish—we never live.

Save us, O God, from the conformity that resists the new thing that you are doing in our day and is quite content with "business as usual," persisting in humanitarian aid that is so inhumane, denying to others the right of self-determination that we have fought for and demanded for ourselves. Grant us such imagination, excited by your love, that we will dream and implement policies that will destroy enemies by making them friends. For our nation and for all nations we pray the vision of the new heaven and the new earth, that your truth and justice inspire. We pray through him who through your creative love is the Lamb slain from the foundation of the world and is present among us now as your eternal Word full of grace and truth and is teaching us to pray and live together: [the Lord's Prayer].—John Thompson

LECTIONARY MESSAGE

Topic: Judgment!

Text: Luke 16:19–31

Interest in judgment and the outcome of living continues in this account, which is found only in the Gospel of Luke. The story of Lazarus and the rich man illustrates man's futile attempt to justify himself.

I. *Judgment of the rich man.* The great sin of the rich man was blind casualness. He simply did not see much of his problem. Both in life and after his death he continued in his self-centeredness. He demonstrated his egocentricity both in his life-style and in the complaint from Hades.

After death the attitude of the rich man was basically unchanged; he still was self-centered, and he still viewed Lazarus

as an inferior. Even as he saw the result of his own life, he thought of Lazarus as a servant (v. 24).

The plea for the brothers also seems to be an effort to justify himself. He implies that if he had been adequately informed he would not have been in Hades. Abraham corrected the mistaken concept by pointing out that the problem was not a matter that the warnings were insufficient but that they were unheeded (v. 31).

II. *Judgment of attitude.* The resulting state of both Lazarus and the rich man reveals that judgment is a matter of attitude and not deeds. The attitude of each is revealed by the circumstances in the life of each.

(a) Lazarus was a man with neither worldly goods nor friends. His only claim was that reflected in his name. The name *Lazarus* means "God helps." The passage reveals nothing that Lazarus had done or was able to do.

(b) The judgment experienced by the rich man shows that one's attitude toward one's fellowman also reflects the relationship that individual has with God. Like the rich farmer (Luke 12:13–21) this man was separated from both God and others by his worship of mammon. It is important to note that the future condition of each was determined by attitude; life after death is not always a reversal of the conditions that existed prior to death.

III. *Additional truths about judgment.* The truths perceived about judgment from this passage are numerous. These include the following: (a) Possessions are trusts from God to be used to help others. (b) The consequences experienced by a person in life are not always what that person deserves. (c) The Gospel writer emphasizes life beyond death. (d) Future life is bodily with physical senses. (e) At death one goes immediately into God's presence (contemporaries of the rich man were yet in this life). (f) In the life after death one will be able to recognize others as individuals. (g) One's destiny is determined in this life. (h) The time for penitence is limited to life. (i) The judgment of each person is pictured in terms of relationships. The joy at the feast is contrasted to the isolation experienced by the rich man. (j) Even miraculous events will not change the hardened heart.—Arthur W. Walker, Jr.

SUNDAY: OCTOBER FOURTH

SERVICE OF WORSHIP

Sermon: He Made Us a Supper
TEXT: John 12:2

I. That's an intriguing sentence in John 12:2. "They made him a supper." It is a verse to kindle the imagination. Suppose we had the opportunity to make him a supper. We'd certainly make careful preparation. We'd want advance notice. No one would want to send out for Kentucky Fried Chicken if Jesus were coming to supper. No one would want to say, "Come on in. You can just take potluck with us." No. We'd want to know as far ahead as possible. We'd want to make careful preparation.

There are so many scriptures about being prepared. We think of Jesus' parable of the ten virgins and of the five who were unprepared. We think of the man without a wedding garment who came to the festivities unprepared. We think of that ringing Old Testament cry, "Prepare to meet thy God!" The Bible has a lot to say about being prepared.

In our own experience of life, we see the need for preparation. The motto of the Boy Scouts is "Be Prepared." We prepare for every major event in our lives. We prepare for marriage. We prepare for the birth of a child. We prepare for the child's education. We prepare for retirement. We prepare for death; we write a will and buy a cemetery lot. If Jesus were coming to supper at our house, we'd want to be prepared.

II. We'd also want to give our best. In the context of this verse is the story of Mary anointing Jesus with precious perfume, the very best. If Jesus came to supper at our house, we'd want to serve the very best food. The lady of the house would plan to serve her specialty—the one dish all the family says that she makes better than anyone else. We'd shop for the very best ingredients: the best cut of meat, the freshest vegetables, the best of everything. When Jesus arrived, we'd offer him the best seat. We wouldn't let him sit on the floor. We wouldn't say, "Just find yourself a seat anywhere." We'd say, "Here. Sit here." We'd give him the best seat in the house. And when he spoke we'd give him our best attention. We'd look him right in the eye and listen attentively to every word.

We'd use our best manners. Have you ever had the experience of finding too many forks and spoons by your plate? Not all of us were "to the manor born." Sometimes we've had to watch to see which fork comes first, and which spoon was intended for what. Have you ever sat at the head table at a banquet and wondered which salad was yours? You wanted to use your very best manners, and you were not sure that even they were good enough. If Jesus came to supper we would not want to do anything that would embarrass us. We'd coach the children on their manners, too.

III. And if Jesus came to supper at our house, we'd cherish the memory. We'd think about it often. We'd talk about it at every opportunity. Sometimes we'd make an opportunity to talk about it. If we wrote our life story there would be a chapter about it in our autobiography. It would not be just experienced and forgotten. We'd cherish the memory.

In the eastern states one often encounters a sign: "George Washington slept here." That may be a town's only claim to fame. It seems that he never went anywhere that the thing was not recorded and remembered. If any monarch ever visited any English village the event is recorded. Maybe he only rode through town and waved, but you will read that "in such and such a year, the king of England passed through this village and waved." Surely if Jesus had supper at our house, the memory of it would be cherished.

IV. It will never happen. We will never make him a supper. However, he has made us a supper: communion. You might suppose that in communion we made him a supper. But such a supposition would be wrong. It's true that we spread the cloth and put the seats in order. But he made the supper. He planned it. He is the reason for it. His presence makes it what it is. The distinction is not just poetical, it is doctrinal and theological. He made us a supper.

(a) We ought to make some preparation before we come to his supper. He has made his preparation. We must make ours. All too often we are out late on Saturday night. That's the night to go out to eat, and maybe take in a movie. So we sleep late on Sunday morning. Then we must eat our breakfast quickly and dress hurriedly. We get the children dressed, and then they get dirty, and we must do it again. We race out to the car and drive hurriedly through the streets. We then must find a place to park. We rush into the service just as the organ begins the prelude and drop breathlessly into a seat. We come to worship totally unprepared and then complain that we got nothing out of it.

Suppose we devoted some time Saturday night to Bible reading, meditation, and prayer. Suppose we got up early on Sunday morning, watched the sunrise, heard the birds sing. Suppose we prayed before we left our houses; prayed that God would bless the services of the morning and bless us through them. Surely we'd get more from our worship if we were prepared.

(b) For communion we must make special preparation. "Let a man examine himself" wrote the Apostle Paul. That takes some time. We don't examine ourselves to see if we're worthy. We know we're not worthy and never will be. We examine ourselves to see what we can do that we have not done and what we can be that we have not become. We examine ourselves during communion to see what resolutions we ought to make. We need

time for preparation before we come to supper.

(c) When we come to his supper we ought to give him our best. He ought to have our best attention. We ought not let our minds wander. We ought to fix them on the events of Calvary so touchingly displayed before us. We ought to wear our best clothes—not to impress others but to express our devotion to the Lord Jesus Christ. If we were going to meet the president, we'd wear our best clothes. It is not necessary that we wear fine clothing. Jesus will be satisfied with the most humble clothing, if it is our best. When we choose to wear our best we express something of our faith and love. I know the Bible says that man looks on the outward appearance but God looks on the heart. Still, we express what is in the heart by what we choose to wear. A young man dresses up to impress his girlfriend, if he is serious about her. People dress up for weddings and funerals. Such actions say something about the importance we attach to the event—and there can be no more important event than going to the supper Jesus prepared.

The preacher ought to preach his best sermon. The choir ought to sing its best anthem. The congregation ought to sing its best songs. Those who pray ought to pray their best prayers. We ought to give him our best.

Certainly we ought to use our best manners. Those who serve ought to do so with quiet dignity. Those who eat and drink ought to do so with quiet reverence and humility. It is not a time to judge others. It is not a time to watch and see if our neighbor partakes nor to wonder if he ought. It is not a time to worry about the manners of another. It is a time to watch our own. I once knew a congregation in which two men disliked each other intensely. If one of them served communion, the other would not partake. What bad manners that was! Communion is a time to speak respectfully, listen attentively, and worship humbly.

I once observed a congregation where some children had learned a secret. After the service they raced to the communion table, and they ate the leftover bread and drank the leftover grape juice. (In this case it was fortunate that they didn't use wine!) But what bad manners that was! One British churchman suggested that the leftover wine should be poured back into the ground from which it came, and the leftover bread put on the ground for the birds, God's creatures, to eat. I thought it was an interesting suggestion. He felt we ought to use our best manners at the Lord's Supper.

V. Certainly we ought to cherish the memory of this supper until the time comes for us to eat it again. I knew a man who had been invited to the inaugural ball when a new president was elected. He didn't go, but he kept the invitation. He framed it and hung it on the wall. He spoke of it often. In Britain every year a few hundred lucky people are invited to tea at Buckingham Palace to have tea with the queen. Of course, most of them never get to speak to her personally. She doesn't pour and ask, "One sugar or two?" They will only see her from a distance. But it's such an honor. People cherish the memory of such an event and talk about it for the rest of their lives. So the memory of the Lord's Supper should bless the coming week. It should fall like a shadow across the days ahead . . . or to use a better illustration, it should fall like a ray of sunshine on the days ahead. But memory fades, and we begin to look forward to the next time when we shall again have the opportunity to have supper with Jesus.

He made us another supper. You can read about it in Revelation, chapter 19. It's called the wedding supper of the Lamb. He's been preparing for it for a long time now. John 14 says that when he left this earth he said, "I go to prepare a place for you." Surely there he will give us his very best. And while we must always depend on grace to cover our bad manners, our Host lived a perfect life to enable us to enjoy this eternal supper. And while there will be no minutes or hours or days in eternity, surely we will cherish every experience of heaven . . . just as our Lord will cherish eternal fellowship with us.

Recently in church I heard a man pray. He thanked God that we could be there that day in God's home. I thought he had misspoken himself. We were in God's house—the church. Someday we will be in heaven—God's home.—Robert C. Shannon

Illustrations

WHO IS WORTHY? Who then dares to ascend the hill of the Lord? And who is worthy to stand in his holy place? You see the question that faces you and me every Sunday morning is basically, Am I ready for church? Clean hands and a pure heart are not so much conditions to worship as they are marks of an inner disposition or state of being that makes real worship possible. It is the mood of him who has tried to do right but who throws himself finally upon God and asks for pardon for doing what he ought not to have done and leaving undone what he ought to have done. In his helplessness he comes to the source of all help and reaches out for the hand of everlasting mercy. Up to the best of his ability he has tried to do the right by his fellowman before bringing his gift to the altar. For him, outside the church are the tyranny of routine, the canker of moral compromise, and the slow cramping of all genuine aspiration, and so he comes into the sanctuary to be captured by a new spiritual adventure under God and to be one in faith and fellowship with those whose aims and ends are good.—Donald Macleod

OTHER WAYS. It is not only prayer that gives God glory but work. Smiting on an anvil, sawing a beam, whitewashing a wall, driving horses, sweeping, scouring, everything gives God some glory if being in his grace you do it as your duty. To go to communion worthily gives God great glory, but to take food in thankfulness and temperance gives him glory, too. To lift up the hands in prayer gives God glory, but a man with a dung fork in his hand, a woman with slop pail, give him glory, too. He is so great that all things give him glory if you mean they should.

So then, my brethren, live.—Gerard Manley Hopkins

Sermon Suggestions

"IF YOU WOULD LIVE." TEXT: Amos 5:6–7, 10–15, REB. (1) *The problem*: practicing injustice, verse 7. (2) *The specifics*: hating "the whistleblower," verse 10; exploiting the poor, verse 11a; intimidating the innocent, verse 12. (3) *The correction*: seeking God and good and hating evil, verses 6a, 14–15.

A YOUNG MAN'S SURVIVAL KIT. TEXT: 2 Tim. 1:1–14. (1) Being an object of intercessory prayer. (2) Living out of a devout and believing heritage. (3) Renewing the inner spirit. (4) Remembering one's salvation and holy calling. (5) Following sound counsel. (6) Keeping safe the treasure of truth.

Worship Aids

CALL TO WORSHIP. "Enter into his gates with thanksgiving and into his courts with praise; be thankful unto him, and bless his name" (Ps. 100:4).

INVOCATION. Lord, let all that is within us praise and magnify thy holy name. Incline thy ear unto us and fill us with thy power, O Lord of hosts.—E. Lee Phillips

OFFERTORY SENTENCE. "He saved us and called us to be his own people, not because of what we have done, but because of his own purpose and grace" (2 Tim. 1:9a, TEV).

OFFERTORY PRAYER. Work your purpose through us, O Lord, so that others also may know your salvation and hear your call to serve you and bless the lives of others in that service.

PRAYER. We celebrate the memorial of our redemption, O Father, in this sacrifice of praise and thanksgiving. Recalling his death, resurrection, and ascension, we offer you these gifts.

Sanctify them by your Holy Spirit to be for your people the Body and Blood of your Son, the holy food and drink of new and unending life in him. Sanctify us also that we may faithfully receive this holy Sacrament and serve you in unity, constancy, and peace; and at the last day bring us with all your saints into the joy of your eternal kingdom.

All this we ask through your Son Jesus Christ. By him, and with him, and in him, in the unity of the Holy Spirit all honor and glory is yours, Almighty Father, now and for ever.—*The Book of Common Prayer*

LECTIONARY MESSAGE

Topic: Faith and Service

TEXT: Luke 17:5–10

The request of the apostles for more faith (v. 5) is a universal appeal. Every person of faith has been aware, at some time, of the need for more faith. Even the person of great faith may face a situation where reassurance is sought.

The apostles made their request because of the requirement for unlimited forgiveness Jesus had made (vv. 3 and 4). They saw this as an impossible demand. Other believers may request more faith as they face requirements that seem impossible.

I. *Kind of faith.* In response to their request Jesus emphasized that the kind of faith is more important than the amount. To place an emphasis on the amount would focus on the person exercising faith. By shifting the emphasis to the kind of faith, Jesus was expressing a greater concern for the power of God and the believer's openness to and commitment to the work of God in one's life. In essence Jesus said, the need is not for the means to do greater things but the need to allow God to do greater things.

Even the exercise of faith can shift the emphasis to the person instead of an emphasis on the power of God. Faith is not a magical charm to be used to accomplish wondrous works. It is, rather, the channel through which God's power can flow.

The way to increase faith is to act on the faith one has. The amount of faith is unimportant; it is the kind of faith that counts. Significant faith is the faith that allows God to work.

II. *Acting in faith.* To act in faith is to be obedient. Disobedience is the assertion of one's own will. The act of faith is the recognition that there is never a way that one can go beyond God.

The person of faith acknowledges that there is never a point where one has done all or more than is required. Those who think only of themselves and their rights lose the joy of service.

The relationship of faith and service are obvious if one sees that both shift one's emphasis away from self and selfish claims to God and what he previously has done. Even the service of God is the return of the strength, the ability, the time, and the grace that he has given the believer.

Both faith and service come as the result of God's equipping. The word *unworthy* (v. 10) emphasizes that the servant can never do more than the master and that the believer who is serving should never expect recognition for simply acting on the power that is a gift of God. Jesus here warns that the sin of pride is possible, especially if one claims special credit for doing that which should be expected.

The dependence on God for all of life is reflected in the awareness that there is no time when his servant has achieved a self-sufficiency or has fulfilled the debt owed to God.—Arthur W. Walker, Jr.

SUNDAY: OCTOBER ELEVENTH

SERVICE OF WORSHIP

Sermon: A Holy Calling

TEXT: Psalm 101; 2 Tim. 1:1–4

What does it mean to say that we are called of God? What does it mean to say that we have a ministry, lay and clergy? I cannot come to this group with accolades of being a great preacher. Yet I can come as one who is a reminder. Together, we are to be reminded of what the Scripture has said this morning. We are called by God with a holy calling.

In Christ there is no Greek or Jew, bond or free, male or female. Therefore, when Paul says "us" he means all those who have been called according to God's purposes. There is, in Jesus Christ, no lay or clergy. We are all ministers. "Minister" means one who services. God has called us with a holy calling. Sometimes we need to have that calling rekindled, because we forget who we are. Things don't seem to be happening the way we want them to, and we begin to question our own calling.

I. *Our call is by grace.* The very first point that the writer of this passage makes is this: Our call has nothing to do with what we have accomplished. It is by grace that you are saved, not by works; it is the gift of God.

Then what do we contribute to our calling? We are called, not because we have greater gifts than anyone else or we are more privileged than anyone else. We are called through the grace of God. God has called us according to his purposes, not according to our works, what we've done or left undone. That is the great foundation of the calling of God. You are called. We have this ministry together.

II. *Our calling is to Christ's power.*

(a) The second great affirmation made clear in this passage is that our calling has everything to do with what God has done in Christ. Remember that the one central assertion of the Christian faith is that Jesus Christ was crucified, dead, buried, and he rose again on the third day. The Resurrection tells us that death does not have the final victory; but Jesus Christ, who is raised from the dead gives us the promise of eternal life. Because of that we can go beyond fear.

(b) Paul says, "Christ has given us, not a spirit of fear, but a spirit of power and of love and of a sound mind." Now hear this: God has given us not a spirit of fear. In Christ death is abolished. God has called us with a holy calling, and the evidence of that, first of all, is that he has given us a spirit of power. God has given us the power to do something. The spirit of fear and powerlessness is replaced with the spirit of power. God has given us something to do, not everything; a place to be, not everywhere; and God has given us gifts to give. This is the mark of ministry, your ministry and mine. God has given us a spirit of power.

III. *Our calling is to a spirit of love.* If we have a spirit only of power it is not enough. I have known people who have had great spiritual power. They had tremendous gifts, but they became "bulldozers" who would roll over other people, not conscious of their needs or hurts. God has given us a spirit of power but also a spirit of love.

The word that is used here is based on *agape*: Love is for those who aren't very lovely at the time. It suggests a kind of practical helpfulness. This is loving in the practical, concrete ways God provides for us. When this spirit of love is let loose in the world it casts out fear.

IV. *Our calling is to faithfulness.*

(a) The description of the spirit that comes last in Paul's list is difficult to translate. God has given us "a spirit of a sound mind" some translations say. Another says "of self-control"; yet another says "of discipline." All of these are a part of this majestic word. We need a spirit, first of all, of self-control, which literally means standing firm in a time of panic or passion. We read about well-known ministers who topple from high peaks of popularity. We know of friends who have drifted away from faith and family. They have fallen into sin and feel that there is no way out. In a moment of panic or passion to have the spirit of self-control can make the difference.

(b) It is also a spirit of discipline: of continuing to be on our knees in prayer when we are tired of being on our knees in prayer, keeping on with the things that we know are right to do, even when the results are not coming. Maintain the discipline, and the results will come.

(c) It is also a spirit of a sound mind. Of course, we face complicated questions that require hard thinking. God can give us the spirit of a sound mind to come up with the answers that are not easy but are possible. This is our ministry. God has given us, not a spirit of fear, but of power and of love and of a sound mind.

We all know the story of the Wizard of Oz and those three who went on the journey with Dorothy of Kansas seeking the missing ingredient for their lives. You remember the end of the story. They didn't get those gifts from any human wizard: They already had those gifts within them. They were ready to be used. In this scripture it says God has already given us a holy calling and God's grace ages ago. It's good doctrine: You already have it by the power of the Holy Spirit. In Jesus Christ let us call forth in each other gifts similar to those the three on the journey needed: power to be courageous and bold, love to really care about others, and a sound mind to think with the mind of Christ. These are a gracious part of our high calling.—Gary D. Stratman

Illustrations

KEPT FAITHFUL.　　African Christians in the Mau Mau country, writing to their fellow-Christians outside, asked simply for one thing. "Pray for us," they said, "not that we may be kept safe but that we may be kept faithful." There is no other safety that a Christian can desire except the safety of his faith, his faith to live and die as a witness of the Name. And where this faith is present, there is present also the power to maintain the unity of that Name.—D. T. Niles

WHY THE CHURCH?　　To the church is committed a threefold responsibility. She stands for the manifestation of God to the world. She exists for the reconciliation of the world to God. She has within her fellowship the living means of grace. Some of you may say that is very high-church doctrine. It is the highest of the high, because it is the New Testament doctrine of the church. She stands first for the manifestation of God. Hear this great word of the New Testament, "Ye are an elect race, a royal priesthood, a holy nation, a people for God's own possession, that ye may show forth the excellencies of Him Who called you" (1 Pet. 2:9). In other words, the church exists to manifest God. Not through the Word alone will the world find the Father, but through the Word incarnate in the lives of people who have been obedient to it. Only through those who share his nature can his name ever be known.—G. Campbell Morgan

Sermon Suggestions

ASKING FOR IT AND NOT WANTING IT!
TEXT: Mic. 1:2; 2:1–10. (1) What ought to be preached against, 2:1–5. (2) The wrong and right ways of preaching, verses 6–10.

REMEMBER JESUS CHIRST. TEXT: 2 Tim. 2:8–15. (1) By being willing to suffer for him. (2) By trusting in the unfettered power of the gospel. (3) By stressing essentials over nonessentials. (4) By trustworthy handling of God's message.

Worship Aids

CALL TO WORSHIP.   "Examine me and test me, Lord; judge my desires and thoughts" (Ps. 26:2, TEV).

INVOCATION.   As we come into your presence, O Lord, we, like Isaiah of old, need to be cleansed of our sins, so that we may speak your wonderful truth with meaning and clarity, to each other here and to our friends and neighbors where we live. Forgive us, and form us into your effective witnesses, we pray.

OFFERTORY SENTENCE.   "The saying is sure: If we have died with him, we shall also live with him; if we endure, we shall also reign with him; if we deny him, he also will deny us; if we are faithless, he remains faithful—for he cannot deny himself" (2 Tim. 2:11–13, RSV).

OFFERTORY PRAYER. Lord Jesus Christ, we believe that you will never fail or forsake us, but we pray that we may never take your love and faithfulness for granted. Teach us and help us to be good stewards of your mysteries and of your many blessings.

PRAYER.   O Thou God of Eternity, how sublime is the religion of thy Son. What marvelous facts are these that come to us so finite, too weak to bear their weight, and yet thou art within us, helping us to bear the superior weight and importance of these majestic ideas. We thank thee for the triumphant soul; we thank thee for the experience of being able in time to so have the relish and taste of eternity, to so have given ourselves to that which is immortal that we do here and now betimes triumph over time. We thank thee for the brave and the true, for the good and the beautiful, for the holy and the wise who scorn time's judgment, who will not permit the dictation of a day or an hour's opinion, but who appeal in their lives to eternity and ask the judgment of the everlasting and so triumph over time. We thank thee for the affection, we thank thee for the inspiration, we thank thee for the instruction that comes out of eternity and, enfolded as our earth is today in all the soft, sweet brilliance of this morning, we move on in the eternal. By and by dates shall cease. O help us, heavenly Father, to be so acquainted with the eternal, to have so accustomed ourselves to breathe in the eternal that when death comes and life opens and all is over with time, we shall live accustomed to the eternal. So let us take to ourselves at the beginning of our prayer and faith, him who is the Life Eternal of all—our Lord and Savior, Jesus Christ.—Frank W. Gunsaulus

LECTIONARY MESSAGE

Topic: The Grace of Gratitude
TEXT: Luke 17:11–19
How easy it is to let our religion degenerate into mere rule-keeping. Our Christian service is so often characterized by joyless obedience, rather than joyous thanksgiving. We methodically do what we have been told. We mindlessly do what we know we should. We mechanically keep the rules. How do we move beyond thoughtless obedience to Christian

복종만이 아니라   감사드리는 종교

gratitude? This story reminds us that we are called to a life marked by gratitude for God's grace. Faith is more than obedience.

I, *Ten needy lepers* (vv. 11–13). All ten of the lepers are needy. They need to be healed of the dread degenerative disease that caused them to be ostracized from society and separated from their loved ones. They are isolated and lonely—pariahs in permanent quarantine. Even when they ask for help from Jesus, they "keep their distance" (v. 12).

Like these lepers, all of us are in need of the Master's mercy (v. 13). We cannot heal ourselves but need a saving word from God.

II. *Ten obedient lepers* (v. 14). Jesus commands the lepers, "Go and show yourselves to the priests." They immediately obey and are healed as they go. There is no questioning of Jesus' command. There are no expressed doubts (in vivid contrast to the story of Naaman the leper and Elisha—1 Kings 5:11–12). All are equally obedient, and all are equally healed.

This ready obedience to Jesus that results in healing is not the point of the story, however. For one can keep all the rules and even receive God's rewards and yet still be far from true faith. Certainly the life of faith calls for obedience, but there is much more to discipleship than just keeping the rules. For obedience comes in two different forms—thoughtless obedience and thoughtful obedience. Nine who are obedient are thoughtless; only one is thankful. Nine just do what they are told; only one stops and reflects.

III. *One grateful leper* (vv. 15–19). Luke observes that the one grateful leper "was a Samaritan" (v. 16). Why are no observant Jews—the chosen people of God, the people of the covenant—among the grateful? No, the grateful leper is the one who is doubly outcast. He is both a leper and a Samaritan. This "untouchable" is the one who stops to praise God in Jesus' healing. Luke has given us a picture of another "good Samaritan" (cf. 10:25–27). The story foreshadows the coming of the kingdom of God to the Gentiles (cf. also "this foreigner" in v. 18), a major theme throughout both Luke and Acts (e.g., 24–47 and Acts 1:8).

In the cleansing of these lepers God was acting *through* Jesus, and so God must be thanked through Jesus. As a form of prayer, Christian gratitude must be offered through Jesus Christ. The salvation of the grateful leper (v. 19) represents more than physical healing. The leper's salvation reflects his awareness through faith of God's gracious presence. As Christians we are called to follow the example of this grateful leper and let the grace of gratitude transform our daily lives.—Charles J. Scalise

SUNDAY: OCTOBER EIGHTEENTH

SERVICE OF WORSHIP

Sermon: Things That Never Wear Out
TEXT: Matt. 6:19–21

I. *Love of natural beauty.* In lines familiar to us all, Wordsworth celebrated his delight in a rainbow:

My heart leaps up when I behold
  A rainbow in the sky;
So was it when my life began;
So is it now I am a man;
So be it when I shall grow old,
  Or let me die!

That is to say, the kind of experience represented in the love of nature with a rainbow in the sky is not spoiled by the attrition of time. A boy can begin it, and an old man can still find there fresh delight.

The wear and tear of time are obvious. If we older ones feel that more poignantly, you younger ones with your eyes open must see it, too. There are experiences peculiar to childhood which, after childhood passes, never will come back again, and ardors and romances in youth which, after youth is gone, will not return. Yet how much of the depth and richness of life lies in this other realm, in experiences like Wordsworth's with nature, which we can start in childhood and then go on with all our life long to the end!

The vicissitudes of the passing decades have been many and sometimes difficult but always the friendship of nature, steadying, healing, comforting, has been there. Why do we not speak of this more often in our churches—this spiritual ministry of nature to those who love her, this literal meaning of the Psalm?

He maketh me to lie down in green pastures;
He leadeth me beside still waters.
He restoreth my soul.

The Bible, for example, the supreme book of religion, is also one of the great books of nature. At its best the Old Testament sprang from the out-of-doors, where

The heavens declare the glory of God;
And the firmament showeth his handiwork.

This fellowship with nature one can begin as a little child. Although one live ever so long it will not wear out.

II. *Love of reading.* Consider another illustrative experience which we can begin in childhood and which never need wear out, the love of reading. Many here remember as one of the earliest reminiscences of home the excitement and fascination of reading. Here was an experience opening before our childhood's astonished eyes, new and strange and marvelous, and with this significance also which then we did not understand—that always books would be our friends.

Why do we not speak of this oftener in the churches? Reading is so influential in our lives! Many a perplexing question about Paul we do not know the answer to, but this we know, that he was a great reader. For in his last imprisonment in Rome, with the end almost at hand, he wrote to his young friend Timothy, "Bring when thou comest . . . the books, especially the parchments."

To be sure, we for whom the printing press has made reading the common

habit of every day often use trivially this great resource. We read to keep up with our professional or business specialties. Or we read to keep up with the swiftly moving times. Or again, we read because other people read and because we are expected to read the books they are talking of.

I celebrate today another and higher kind of experience, the spiritual friendship of great books intently read, deeply pondered, one of the abiding experiences of life which a child begins and an old man still gets his comfort from. So said Charles Kingsley—"Except a living man, there is nothing more wonderful than a book!" So said Milton—"A good book is the precious life-blood of a master spirit."

III. *Love of life's lessons.* Now, with these two illustrations in mind, the love of nature and the friendship of books, consider that the seasonal experiences of life, fitted to one period only of our existence, constitute our foreground, so important that life grows ill if it be not well handled, but that the background of life, its depth and horizon and enduring worth, comes from this other kind of experience which we can begin in childhood and go through with to the very end. I raise the question: How many things do we possess of this enduring kind?

(a) For example, consider a clear conscience as belonging to this category. A child can enter into that experience and an old man deeply needs it. I can remember yet the first time I tried as a boy to cover up a piece of crookedness and felt the appalling inner misery of an accusatory conscience.

When one pleads for a kind of life that leaves the conscience unashamed, one is commonly understood to be talking morals. But today I am thinking rather of the fact that as a man grows older few things so help him to stand up under hardship as does an unashamed conscience. Standing the gaff as the years pass is not in itself easy but if, in addition to the natural gainsayings and limitations of aging life, a man has to live inwardly with a nasty conscience, how does he stand it?

Indeed, we have spoken so far as though only lovely things—delight in nature, the friendship of books, and a good conscience—carried through to the end. But, of course, other things also carry through. As the years pass, as much as any other thing, an unashamed conscience makes life worth living.

(b) Consider also that deep interest in intellectual and social causes belongs to this category. Now as the years pass and age comes on, he who enters ever more deeply into this experience—until he lives not simply in himself but in great interests, intellectual and social, more important than himself—is preparing an enriched old age.

As the years pass, a woman like Jane Addams, for example—interested in everything worth being interested in—though she grew old could not by any one be pitied. The whole background of such a life is steady, the continuous experience of living in and for something more than oneself that begins in childhood and ends only with the grave.

Here again our plea is made, you see, not simply in the name of morals. Selfishness is immoral. Self-centeredness peters out. Time corrodes it. It has no enduring quality. Under it one shrivels up at last. The years do devastating things to the man who lives by it. Only the other day I had a letter from a man who confessed to an absorbingly self-centered life and now at sixty wanted me to tell him how on earth he could make life seem worth going on with.

As we see the years pass over us and old age coming on, do we not all feel one desire? We want something about us that time and tide cannot touch. And here plainly is something—great interests more important than oneself that one lives in and cares for, that were before we came and will be afterwards—treasures, Jesus called them, treasures which neither moth nor rust doth consume, nor thieves break through and steal.

(c) Consider also a deep, interior, spiritual life, grounded in faith in God and sustained by a sense of divine companionship, as belonging to this category. A child can begin that and an old man

deeply needs it. In this regard religion is like music, an experience to which, in ways simple yet profound, a child responds and which, if we are fortunate, lasts and grows through all the years, to be the comfort and sustenance of age.

Today we are trying to get clearly in our view another range of experience, not aristocratic and reserved for the few, not costing much in money, rather the most democratic and accessible of all experiences—the love of nature, the companionship of books, the unashamed conscience of a good character, the great interests of man's common weal, music, the interior resources of a spiritual life, the lasting experiences that are not merely periodic but go with us across all the years from childhood to the grave.

A profound religious experience—"I live; yet not I, but Christ liveth in me"—does belong to that category.

The religious experience itself, the deep and inward sense of a divine companionship is like the love of nature or of music, one of the enduring things. Some of us, remembering back, think we understand at least a little what Jesus meant when he took children in his arms and as the second Gospel says, "laying his hands upon them," he talked to his disciples about the kingdom of God in terms of a child's spirit. There are some of us on whom he laid his hands when we were about as young as seven, and now as older years come on we bear witness to an abiding experience of divine companionship that holds life together, gives it resources of power, and makes sense of it.

So was it when my life began;
So is it now I am a man;
So be it when I shall grow old.

Throughout this sermon I have not been quite sure whether I was talking more to the older people or to the young, but now at the close I know. Now I am not talking about being young; I am talking about growing old. And you may not say that we do not know about that; that is something we do know about.

And we are saying that as the years pass you are going to want the enduring experiences. For your happiness, then, if for no other reason, get them now. All these things we have spoken of, from the love of nature to the inward divine companionship, are easy to possess when one is young. Is it not as natural as breathing for children to know them all if they have half a chance? But when the years have passed and all one's days have been expended on the transient and the merely seasonal in human life, then it is not easy. Then one wakes up to discover how much he needs the abiding treasures of experience, concerning which one can say, "As it was in the beginning, is now, and ever shall be, world without end. Amen."—Harry Emerson Fosdick

Illustrations

A WORTHY CAUSE.   I well remember the fascinated hours in boyhood when my father told me of my grandsire's house with its secret closet where escaping slaves were concealed until they could be rowed on dark nights across the Niagara River to Canada and liberty. There to a small boy's fascinated imagination was a strange new interest—a social cause that had cost danger and sacrifice, not finished even yet, which our fathers served and then handed on to us, as though we too should have a hand in making a freer world. Such are some of the great hours in childhood.—Harry Emerson Fosdick

THESE THINGS REMAIN.   I watched a friend of mine offer to buy a handsome gun from the veteran craftsman who had made it. He was able to pay; he was interested enough to pay—and well.

The gun was a marvel of the builder's art. Many a day had gone into the inletting and chequering of that perfect walnut, the reshaped bolt and polished receiver, the true barrel and keen scope sight, the fine trigger assembly and honed action.

"I'll buy," said my friend. "How much?"

And the old man who had made it for himself, pouring years of skill and enjoyed work into the one perfect creation of his art, cradled the beautiful rifle across his arm, looked down it, and said, "I made it for my own; nobody could buy it; there isn't anything that would buy it. Perhaps my son will want it."

My friend with me smiled and got a good lift from it as he said to me a little wistfully, "Every man ought to have something somewhere that he wouldn't sell for anything." And that is true. Every man ought to have right in the middle of his life something that he wouldn't sell for anything.—Carlyle Marney

Sermon Suggestions

THE WORD FROM THE WATCHTOWER.   TEXT: Hab. 1:1–3; 2:1–4. (1) The human question: the apparent deafness of God to the cry for justice. (2) The divine answer: the ultimate and unfailing justice of God worth waiting for and living toward.

THE IMPORTANCE OF HOLY SCRIPTURE.   TEXT: 2 Tim. 3:14–4:5. (1) For salvation in Jesus Christ. (2) For equipping teachers and preachers for total ministry. (3) For providing hearers with a sure word to steady them in trying times.

Worship Aids

CALL TO WORSHIP.   "The righteousness of thy testimonies is everlasting; give me understanding, and I shall live" (Ps. 119:144).

INVOCATION.   Lord, we open our hearts to thee. Renew us, revitalize us. Bring us to a mighty worship and a joyful praise and commitment that will make the difference for Jesus' sake.—E. Lee Phillips

OFFERTORY SENTENCE.   "Although the fig tree shall not blossom, neither shall fruit be in the vines; the labor of the olive shall fail, and the fields shall yield no meat; the flock shall be cut off from the fold, and there shall be no herd in the stalls; yet I will rejoice in the Lord, I will joy in the God of my salvation" (Hab. 3:17–18).

OFFERTORY PRAYER.   God of mercies, help us to rejoice as readily in the difficult times as in the days when everything runs smoothly. We know that we can rejoice, because you are in final control of all things, and you can make the banes of today the blessings of tomorrow. Keep us from embarrassment or reluctance in our giving, though our gifts be small, and multiply our little, as the loaves and fishes, for the good of others.

PRAYER.   Father, what a privilege to be among your people. In this special place surrounded by the symbols of the faith, we are reminded of your mighty deeds of grace for our salvation. Your Word of grace spoken from the beginning brings order out of chaos. In your Word in Christ in these latter days, we discover order for life on this planet that you have ordained from the beginning. From the early disciples, those who make this discovery enthusiastically confess: Christ is *Lord.*

With crumbling walls and old orders giving way to new, how we need to live life with great expectancy, for eye has not seen, nor hear heard, neither has entered into mind of man what you have prepared for those who love you. Let us not be so unimaginative—so laggard in thought, so slow to believe—that we cannot share the exultation of these days. Let us exult in the insight of the prophet, so boldly apparent in these changing times, when you put it in his mind to declare: "It is not by might, nor by power, but by my Spirit," says the Lord. Never has the weakness of power to bring order out of chaos been more evident in the history of humankind today. When we are being prodded by cataclysmic events to beat swords into plowshares and spears into pruning hooks, grant us the faith, a vision, courage to lead the way. Grant to us imaginative and courageous leadership, that our rich resources may be invested in tools for life rather than implements of death.

Remind us: To whom much is given, of them much is required. For those who have committed their lives to be your instruments in bringing reconciliation to troubled areas we pray. We pray for the people who have suffered and are suffering and rejoice in their victories of faith and courage and hope. We pray for your gift of Shalom and that right soon.

As a family of faith we are very conscious of needs among us. For those broken in health we pray the wholeness of your healing. For those of us lonely in bereavement we pray the companionship of the Good Shepherd to strengthen and encourage. Bless us now as Christ leads us to pray together: [the Lord's Prayer].—John Thompson

LECTIONARY MESSAGE

Topic: On Unjust and Righteous Judges
TEXT: Luke 18:1–8

When was the last time you were in a situation in which you felt powerless? The circumstances may have really been bad, and you knew what you desperately hoped would happen, but you lacked the ability, authority, or opportunity to change things. Perhaps you lacked money. Perhaps you lacked social status. Perhaps you lacked political influence. If so, you were like the widow in this parable. Lacking any power either against her opponent (v. 3) or within the legal system, all she had was her persistence.

I. *A parable about persistent prayer* (vv. 1–5). Jesus told this parable to remind us that, no matter how powerless we may feel, we always have the power of persistent prayer, which rests upon the promise of God's justice. As we struggle to live out our faith as Christians in an unjust world, it is so easy to become discouraged. So Jesus' parable encourages us "not to lose heart" but instead "to pray always" (v. 1).

The widow's situation looks bleak indeed. She has been wronged by her opponent. She is politically, socially, and culturally powerless in a world that grants all authority to married men, particularly in the legal system. To make matters worse, she has the misfortune to be forced to deal with a judge with a terrible reputation ("who neither feared God nor had respect for the people"—v. 2).

Persistence is her only weapon—her last resort—and she uses it with a vengeance! The parable hsows that even an unjust judge may ultimately yield to a persistent cry for vindication. Such an outcome should be empowering to Christians who struggle for justice against powerful systems in our day that "neither fear God nor have respect for people."

II. *A promise about vindicating justice* (vv.6–8). Jesus' comments following the parable offer some explanation and application. If persistence like the widow's is successful with a judge who only cares for his own peace, *how much more* (*a fortiori* argument) will it succeed with God the Righteous Judge, who shows mercy on God's chosen ones? G. B. Caird observes that "if, then, election means favoritism, it is because God has a bias in favour of the innocent victims of persecution."

The parable does not only work by similarity but by dissimilarity. What a dramatic contrast exists between the unjust judge's annoyed listening to the widow who is only a nuisance to him and God's compassionate listening to "his chosen ones who cry to him day and night" (v. 7)!

Jesus was not oblivious to the power of evil in the world in which he lived. He concludes by asking how long the persistent, praying fiath for which this parable pleads can endure on this earth (v. 8b). Yet it should be a comfort to Christians, who continue to struggle with the powers of injustice and iniquity, to realize that the coming of the Son of man heralds God's ultimate vindication of his chosen ones (v. 7).—Charles J. Scalise

SUNDAY: OCTOBER TWENTY-FIFTH

SERVICE OF WORSHIP

Sermon: Facing Life's Temptations
TEXT: James 1:12–18

From one of our college campuses comes the story of a young man who took his semester final and made a zero. More than a little unnerved, he went to his professor and said, "I don't think I deserve a zero." "Neither do I," his professor declared, "but it's the lowest grade I could give you!"

There are times when all of us feel we are failing just as miserably when it comes to facing life's temptations. By the way, how did you do the last time you faced temptation? Did you make an *A* or something less? In James, we find some help.

I. *A bold declaration* (1:12a). James tells us it is a blessing to face temptation. But this is not happiness. In the New Testament, blessedness is an inner assurance or peace that is not dependent on our external circumstances. Whether the days of your life are cloudy or clear you can still experience blessing.

And be sure of this—you will face temptation. As surely as you cannot avoid the undertaker or the IRS, neither can you escape temptation. But are you ready to face it? Winston Churchill speaking to the House of Commons during World War II said, "We must always be ready to meet at our *average* moment anything, that any possible enemy could hurl against us, at his *selected* moment." The Christian life can be hard at times. However, James boldly declares it is worth it all. Why? There are three reasons.

First, facing temptation can help us develop perseverance (1:20). God intends that we learn from our trials, not fall away. Second, facing temptation can mature you (1:4). So often when times get hard for us we may be quick to think that God is punishing us. It could be that he is trying to mature us. Then, third, successfully encountering temptation grants to us the "crown of life" (1:12b). Literally, this is the "crown that consists of life." It is life in the full sense of the term, the consummation of our life in heaven with God.

No wonder James can be so bold as to declare life's temptations a blessing. But just as a good eye doctor will not rest until her patient sees clearly, so James seeks to focus our view of temptation in verses 13 and 14.

II. *A proper perspective* on our temptations. James is confronting the age-old propensity to blame God for our woes. Adam did it when he shouted at God, "The woman *you* put here with me—she gave me some fruit from the tree, and I ate it" (Gen. 3:12, NIV). You may not be so bold as to say this, but have you ever said, "I can't help my temper, I inherited it from my father"? Always blaming others!

While other places in Scripture tell us Satan and other people can tempt us, James puts the burden squarely on us. James would give a hearty "Amen!" to the words one individual had printed on his T-shirt. They read, "Lead me not into temptation—I can find it for myself."

Even God is cleared of any charge of temptation to evil. Because he is holy, it is against God's character to entice anyone to evil. Until we can quit blaming God, the devil, and other people for our temptation to sin we will never have victory over it.

III. *The pathway to victory* over our temptations. In verses 19–22, I see James telling us how we can overcome our temptations instead of being overcome by them. First, we must decide to take control of our situation. Too many people prepare for defeat by thinking along with Oscar Wilde that "I can resist anything but temptation." But we must and we can.

I read that in Colorado a girl appeared in court to ask the judge to put her in jail until after January twentieth. She explained that January twentieth was her wedding day, and that she was engaged to a man much older than herself that she did not want to marry. However, in his presence she could not resist his charm. The judge complied. Did it work? Well, she said so. But talk about deter-

mination! Let us determine we will be strong.

A second avenue on the pathway to victory is to stop living in sin (1:21). The idea here is to make once-for-all the decision to no longer have anything to do with evil. It may sound old-fashioned, but I believe this means we will avoid various movies, reading steamy books and magazines, and having nothing to do with gambling and going to bars. James is saying, When you run from temptation, don't leave a forwarding address. One day after Augustine had been converted, a former lover saw him and began to call out to him. He tried to ignore her and wanted to pass by with only a formal nod. She stopped him and said, "Augustine, do you not know me anymore? See, it is I." "Yes," replied Augustine, "but it is not I." We have died to sin, so how can we live in it any longer?

But James's commands are not just negative. At verse 22 he tells us the third aspect of victory. It is that we must start living in obedience. I wonder how many people would be content to be married to someone who was mostly faithful to them. Probably not too many. Most of us expect 100 percent faithfulness from our spouse. Indeed, can anything less than 100 percent faithfulness even be considered faithfulness at all? Yet in our churches, unfaithfulness to God is viewed as normal, and those who try to be faithful are deemed fanatics.

Someone said, "The best way to get the best of temptation is just to yield to it." I know something better—yield to the Word of God. We must realize that the Bible is not the Christian's crutch, it's his or her iron lung. You will never have victory over temptation, never pass life's tests if all you can say is "I know the Bible." The real ticket to victory comes when we can say, "I am doing the word, not merely listening to it."—Allan Wooters

Illustrations

"THE VANISHING SINNER." Some of our church fathers, prior to the Civil War, defended the institution of human slavery with sincere fervor. Now we believe it to be utmost villainy. At one time dueling was the accepted method of vindication of one's honor. If it were practiced today, someone would be tried for murder. In the Old Testament, God condemned Israel's King Solomon, not because he had many wives, hence was a polygamist, but because he had many gods, hence was a polytheist. Obviously, many of our vices have slipped over in the virtue column and things formerly considered virtuous are now considered vices. So we jump to the conclusion that morals are man-made rather than God ordained. If morals are man-made we are not sinners. We are simply nonconformers. — Gaston Foote

CHRISTIAN EXPERIENCE. Christian experience, when seen from the vantage point of levels of feeling relationships, moves from hearsay about Christ to the level of personal acquaintance with Christ and personal dependence upon Christ, to the level of learning from Christ, to the level of confession to Christ, to the level of healing by Christ, to the level of reconciliation with Christ, and finally achieves spiritual usefulness on the level of comradeship alongside Christ to witness for Christ. — Wayne E. Oates

Sermon Suggestions

THE GIFT OF PURE LIPS. TEXT: Zeph. 3:1–9, REB. (1) Symbolizing forgiveness, Isa. 6:5–7. (2) Removing the curse of Babel, Gen. 11:1–9. (3) Anticipating Pentecost, Acts 2:1–11. (With credit to *The New Oxford Annotated Bible*.)

RESCUE FROM THE LION'S MOUTH. TEXT: 2 Tim. 4:6–8, 16–18. (1) Because of a courageous, persistent faith. (2) Because of a faithful God.

Worship Aids

CALL TO WORSHIP. "Salvation belongeth unto the Lord: thy blessing is upon thy people" (Ps. 3:8).

INVOCATION. For all of us who have wandered to the far country of our own willfulness, the image that gives us assurance of forgiveness is that striking portrait painted by Jesus entitled "The Waiting Father." When the prodigal turns his steps homeward, the father cannot wait until he arrives but runs down the road to meet him with his arms outstretched to embrace him. Such is God's love, mercy, and forgiveness that await each of us as we repent, confess our sins, and turn our steps homeward. Glory be to God! — John Thompson

OFFERTORY SENTENCE. "Set your mind on God's kingdom and his justice before everything else, and all the rest will come to you as well" (Matt. 6:33, NEB).

OFFERTORY PRAYER. O God, our Father, deepen our trust in your will and your purposes and make us your joyous partners in all that you are doing. To that end, receive our tithes and offerings and bless them wherever they go.

PRAYER. Grace—God's amazing grace—through which our sins are forgiven is not easy for us to accept. Our pride gets in the way. We think we can save ourselves. But we cannot. But what we cannot do God is willing and able to do for us. This is the good news of the Gospel. As the Apostle Paul declares, "There is therefore now no condemnation to those who are in Christ Jesus, who walk not after the flesh but after the Spirit." Glory be to God! — John Thompson

LECTIONARY MESSAGE

Topic: A Tale of Two Sinners
TEXT: Luke 18:9–14
This parable holds up a mirror to our religious practices. The story challenges us to face the truth about ourselves. There are two kinds of sinners in the story. They both "went up to the temple to pray," but only one really prayed. The Pharisee thought he was praying, but only the tax collector "went down to his home justified" in the eyes of God (v. 14).

The parable asks each of us, Which kind of sinner are you?

I. *The proud pharisee* (vv. 9–12). The Pharisee comes to the Temple as a *respectable religionist*. He chronicles his religious qualifications (good works) in verse 12. The greatest flaw in the Pharisee's life is that his self-righteousness causes him to look down on others, in particular on despised, good-for-nothing tax collectors (v. 11). Even when he tries to pray, the Pharisee is unable to avoid exalting himself and putting down others. Even his posture in prayer "standing by himself" (v. 11) emphasizes his superiority and distance from others.

The Pharisee thinks he is praying, but really he is only talking to and about himself. His words of prayer are only a pretense for self-congratulation. Notice all of the first-person pronouns and verbs in his words in verses 11 and 12. God only serves as the formal addressee for his self-adulation. As Geroge Caird comments, "the Pharisee was not really interested in God, but only in himself." What a great irony that the Pharisee's religious piety and zeal are the very things separating him from God. The religious practices that should enable the Pharisee to humble himself and draw near to God are instead the obstacles that prevent any real communication with God from occurring.

II. *The penitent publican* (vv. 13–14). The repenting publican has plenty of which he can and should repent. Not only the Pharisee, but most decent Jews of the day viewed the tax collector as a *repugnant rip-off artist*. Their prejudice may not have been far from the truth. Notice how he keeps his distance, "standing far off" (v. 13). One is reminded of the lepers whom Jesus healed in the previous chapter who were "keeping their distance" while crying out for mercy (17:12). Tax collectors were social lepers and religious outcasts (like Zacchaeus in the following chapter (19:1–10).

God is the last and only hope for this sinful tax collector. So he comes in humble and genuine repentance. Instead of lifting his head and hands in the customary posture of prayer, he addresses God without even looking up and "beating his breast" pleads for mercy.

We should come before God in prayer with the attitude of the tax collector. A sense of our own great neediness, rather than a pretense of our own righteousness, should characterize our prayers. Contrition instead of self-congratulation should be the tone of our approach to God. What does God require of us sinners? We are to look into the mirror of Jesus' parable and face the truth about ourselves. Then we are invited to throw ourselves into the arms of the compassionate God.—Charles J. Scalise

SUNDAY: NOVEMBER FIRST

SERVICE OF WORSHIP

Sermon: The Joy of the Christian Life
TEXT: Matt. 5:1–12

These chapters from Matthew continue to inspire, to trouble, and to challenge all of us. Somewhere, Mark Twain commented that the sections of the New Testament giving him the most trouble were not those he couldn't understand but rather the sections he could. The Christian life is not so much a matter of doctrine, dogma, belief systems, ideas and worldviews; it is a matter of character. It handles the pressures, stress, temptations, and necessities of our present age with a serenity and courage unshakable even through the worst life can do to us.

I. Beatitudes describe the Christian life. Where do we begin? What clues do we possess about the depth and joy of the Christian life? The Beatitudes, which we read this morning, provide a crystalline description of life rooted in the grace of the only security that sticks with us through life and death: the all-embracing, undergirding love of God we know through Jesus Christ.

(a) The Beatitudes tell us what shapes character when we are ruled, not by the everyday tyrants of credentials, status, and the bottom line, but by a new sovereignty gained by surrendering our lives to the gracious purpose of Christ.

This surrender to the sovereignty of God creates a new universe for action. Let me offer an analogy. The falling of the Berlin Wall represented a dramatic change in world history. It seems a new world was born. Old allegiances collapsed. Old barriers disappeared. Budgets changed. Prisoners were released. We saw a world where laws altered, nations began to treat one another differently, conversations once forbidden now became the order of the day. The sovereignties altered, the world changed, and human behavior changed with it.

(b) Jesus, as Christ, is not simply a Nazarene stumbling along the dusty roads of Palestine. Jesus represents an event qualitatively changing human existence. He promises a city where race, culture, neighborhood, creed, and gender no longer pit us against one another; but where, rather, they serve as diverse components in the forging of a whole and reconciled community.

In the new world Matthew describes, the Beatitudes become descriptions of the life one lives in this world when one's allegiance shifts from all our current rulers to the outgoing, risky, daring love of Christ.

II. Beatitudes describe our position.

(a) Take that first Beatitude, for instance: "Blessed are the poor in spirit, for theirs is the realm of heaven." That Beatitude describes our posture before God when we surrender our lives to Christ's new world. The poor in spirit come with no claim of success in business, academia, politics, child-rearing, committee memberships, or salary schedules. The poor in spirit come before God with no claim to rectitude, brilliance, fame, or accomplishment. They let go of every claim to special identity except as they are claimed for humble, gracious service. To be poor

in spirit is simply the way it is alongside Jesus Christ.

(b) And incredibly enough, alongside Christ Jesus you will not only be poor in spirit; you will, at the same time, know the realm of heaven. Living in the realm of heaven means we are no longer ruled by the sovereignties of this world tearing us apart, stressing us out, eating us alive, worrying us to death. It means we gain our full humanity. We are saved not by our bank accounts, our reputations, graduate degrees, achievements of our children, the success of our spouse, the connections we have, the books we read, the cars we drive, or the jeans we wear. Nothing this world offers as a key to value and self-worth provides anything but illusion, fraud, and seduction to fruitless striving.

III. Other Beatitudes build on the first. And what about the rest of the Beatitudes? They reflect what life is like when we've surrendered to the sovereignty of Jesus Christ.

(a) Our first loyalty being to Jesus Christ, we mourn for a broken creation riddled with illness, hostility, wars, and rumors of war. We are sickened and saddened by the tragedy of the world. Alongside Christ we are comforted and consoled by One who himself suffers and knows that you suffer, too.

(b) Or again, walking alongside Jesus Christ, we are meek. We possess a serenity impossible to ruffle, embitter, or enrage.

(c) Yet again, committed to Jesus Christ, we hunger and thirst for righteousness. We do not labor under any illusions of our own gifts and talents. We starve for the food of grace and peace, strengthening us to bear up under the worst, granting us courage even as we rest more securely in the everlasting arms.

(d) Walking with Jesus Christ, living under his sovereignty, we discover ourselves merciful. In a world riddled with blowing the enemy out of the water and driving the opposition to the wall—mercy is the order of the day. We offer mercy to others, exercising the very character of God.

(e) And yes, even again, loyal to the realm of Jesus Christ, we are pure in heart. Purity of heart means that we live without dissimulation before, or diversion from, the healing, reconciling will of God. It means we stand with integrity. Standing and surrendering with total integrity enable us to see those healing purposes of God come to fruition.

(f) And those who surrender to the realm of Christ will know the joy of peacemaking. Peacemaking means reaching out, empathizing with, identifying with, and reconciling the alienated, the marginalized, the outsider. It means standing beside those who are afar off and walking with them into a new and healed community.

(g) And one thing more: By surrendering to Christ we incur the disbelief, cynicism, mockery, laughter, and resistance of the world. To encounter the world in the style of Jesus turns the world upside down; and if you press your loyalty to God as far as Jesus did: gone! like Jesus. Fool that he was for God, the world of achievement, success, pride, get-rich-quick, complacent religion, and imperial politics got rid of him; and it will happen every time. Expect it!

Dare we really try it? I guarantee that if we do, Jesus Christ can make your life—Jesus Christ can make my life—nothing less than a courageous, radiant, joyous beatitude.—James W. Crawford

Illustrations

THIS LIFE AND THE NEXT.   We cannot tarry to argue if there is an immortality awaiting us; we must obey the immortality urging and lifting us. We do not move to a possible mirage of a city of God; the citizenship is within us. Ask, Am I living as immortal—not as one who will be immortal? Do not waste time asking if there is a coming eternity; ask, What must I do to give effect to my present eternity; how shall I be loyal to the eternal responsibility in me and on me? Is my faith a life? It must make a great difference to life whether we treat our eternity as a present or a future, as a power or as a possibility, as a duty or as an ideal—whether

our Christ is a Bystander or an Occupant of us.—P. T. Forsyth

WAITING FOR THE LORD.   Maturity is never merely a matter of age but one of development. A mature sentiment has a way of handling doubt, of realizing (as we note in Cardinal Newman's struggle) that personal commitment is possible even without absolute certainty, that a person can be half-sure without being half-hearted.

The mature religious sentiment is dynamic in its desire to be truly comprehensive; it is not called upon only in fear, sorrow, and mystical moments; it saturates one's life. It joins a person's religion, which is deeply solitary, to social living.

Putting away childish things is not easy. We need to respect each individual's unique attempt. It takes tolerance and understanding for us to aid one another in our religious quest, which is our effort to find the supreme context in which our lives rightfully belong.—Gordon W. Allport

Sermon Suggestions

RECOVERING THE GLORY.   TEXT: Hag. 2:1–9. (1) The glory of Solomon's Temple, verse 3. (2) The promise of an even more splendid Temple, verses 4–9. (3) The ultimate Temple in the regenerated heart, John 4:21–24.

ON THAT DAY.   TEXT: 2 Thess. 1:5–12. (1) It will be a day of judgment. (2) It will be a day of reward. (3) It will be a day of glory for Jesus Christ.

Worship Aids

CALL TO WORSHIP.   "O God, it is right for us to praise you in Zion and keep our promises to you, because you answer prayers. People everywhere will come to you on account of their sins. Our faults defeat us, but you forgive them" (Ps. 65:1–3, TEV).

INVOCATION.   Lord, we worship this day in the name of the Father and the

Son and the Holy Ghost, bringing our need to thy filling and our desires to thy leading, sure that at last we are where we belong and then we may go about the duties of our week in thy peace.—E. Lee Phillips

OFFERTORY SENTENCE. "We pray always for you, that our God would count you worthy of this calling and fulfil all the good pleasure of his goodness and the work of faith with power" (2 Thess. 1:11).

OFFERTORY PRAYER. Heavenly Father, in you we live and move and have our being; we humbly pray you so to guide and govern us by your Holy Spirit, that in all the cares and occupations of our life we may not forget you, but may remember that we are ever walking in your sight; through Jesus Christ our Lord.—*The Book of Common Prayer*

PRAYER. In the hushed stillness, ever listening God, hear the presence of our seeking spirits. As you have taught, let us be still and know that you are God, you have made us and not we ourselves, and we belong to you. Free us from all the vain things that charm us most, and turn our hearts toward home into your tender and everlasting arms.

Different as fingerprints, O God, our footsteps have brought us from many places and times in life. But we are here, beggars all, whether we know it or not, longing to hear and hold your still small voice. We who have everything, have nothing without you, so abide with us, fill our emptiness, feed our hunger, and accept our worship and praise.

Master of mercy and forgiveness, in your holy presence our sin is ever between us. Hear our confessions, believe our repentance and sorrow, and restore us to right relationship with you, with others, and with ourselves.

Creator and Redeemer of all time and goodness, we are reminded of how rich and blessed we are. We voice thanks for many gifts: for the simple, deep joys of life; for beautiful music; for sunrises and sunsets that awake and bid farewell to the light of each day; for compassion that lifts us beyond ourselves, closer to you, and into the needs and hurts of others; for good books that capture and become treasures of our minds; for experiences that prompt and release our healing tears.

Generous God, we give thanks for the darkness and pain that reveal unexpected paths to you and nurture deep kinship with your Holy Spirit; for spontaneous gestures of generosity that surprise even ourselves; for our family of faith who believes in and sustains us abidingly; for friends who embody your love and reveal your face; for brooding doubts that lead to better questions and purer faith; and most of all, for your love that will not let us go and from which nothing, no, not anything can separate us in Jesus Christ our Lord. So, our prayer is quietly, Thanks be to God, thanks be to God.—William M. Johnson

LECTIONARY MESSAGE

Topic: Too Little to See Jesus?
TEXT: Luke 19:1–10

The story of the "wee little man" Zacchaeus is a favorite with small children because they know what it is like to be "too little" to see things. Zacchaeus is "too little" to see Jesus in two ways: his stature and his character. The story reminds us that we are all too short to measure up to Jesus. What are the things in our lives that prevent us from seeing the Lord?

I. "*Up a tree*" (vv. 1–4). Zacchaeus's desire to see Jesus was more than mere curiosity. A Jewish "chief tax collector" was held in contempt by his fellow Jews as both a traitor to and an exploiter of his own people. Just to satisfy a passing whim, Zacchaeus would hardly risk ridicule and perhaps even his personal safety in such a large crowd. No, he really wanted "to see who Jesus was" (v. 3). Perhaps Jesus' reputation as a rabbi who was "a friend of tax collectors and sinners" (7:34) was the reason for Zacchaeus's inner urge to see Jesus. Perhaps Zacchaeus climbed the famous "sycamore tree" not only to get a clear view of Jesus but also a safe one.

II. *"Down for dinner"* (vv. 5–7). Jesus uses strong, commanding language when he calls to Zacchaeus: "Hurry and come down; for I *must* stay at your house today" (v. 5). Jesus does not condemn Zacchaeus, but he also does not coax him. Jesus risks the grumbling hostility of "all" the crowd (v. 7) to befriend the despised and notorious sinner. Jesus does not hesitate to do what he knows will be unpopular, in order to reach out to those who seek to see him.

Jesus' action provides a model for the church's mission today to social outcasts, whether they be rich or poor. Who are the outcasts in our church and our community? Luke emphasizes the diversity of this ministry by placing the story of Zacchaeus (the rich outcast) immediately after the story of the blind beggar (the poor outcast—18:35–43).

III. *"Turning over a new leaf"* (vv. 8–10). The story offers a picture in miniature of Jesus' mission to Israel "to seek out and to save the lost" (v. 10). Zacchaeus's promise of fourfold restitution (v. 8) was far more than what the Jewish Law required (Lev. 6:5; Num. 5:7; but cf. Exod. 22:1), not even taking account of his gift of half of his possessions to the poor. Zacchaeus's repentant and self-giving response to Jesus demonstrates that Zacchaeus is truly "a son of Abraham" (v. 9) and mirrors the response that all Israel should give to "the Son of man" (v. 10).

What a contrast Luke offers us between Zacchaeus's response to Jesus and the response of the *rich* ruler in the previous chapter (18:18–25). The repenting Zacchaeus rather than the law-keeping ruler is the true son of Abraham. God's true children are not those who boast about how they have kept all the rules. God's true children are those who earnestly seek to see Jesus and respond in repentance and generosity.—Charles J. Scalise

SUNDAY: NOVEMBER EIGHTH

SERVICE OF WORSHIP

Sermon: The Nearness of God

TEXT: Psalm 34

We all know people who have no apparent problems, families that seem happy, healthy, well-adjusted, and well-heeled. Somewhat wistfully we say, "God has really smiled on them." Indeed, there is an old folk saying that declares, "God may love the poor but he helps the rich." Not just the rich in things, we muse, but the rich in favor, as well. We may not be given to theological reflection, but we figure it just adds up. That's just the way it is: The Lord has his favorites. He is near to those who go blithely on their way.

Or is he? The bold declaration of Psalm 34 is

The Lord is close to those whose heart is broken, He saves those whose spirit is crushed.

Those words convey the "truest truth" I know, yet it is the hardest to communicate. Perhaps because faith of a conventional sort comes easily enough in the sunshine, but saving faith, faith that makes a difference, is not so automatic when we are living in the shadows. Is God near enough to help when we have been betrayed by the person we trusted the most? Is the Lord near at hand when we have betrayed our own best selves and believe forgiveness and joy are words that now have no meaning? Do we dare believe in a God who can betray our confidence by taking his greatest gift to us away?

This may not be everyone's circumstance, but I believe there is someone listening who does not need me to explain what it means to be heartbroken or crushed in spirit. Can it be possible that God has never been nearer, more ready to help? Maybe we cannot believe it because we have believed lies that have masqueraded as the truth.

I. The very first myth that must be rejected, if we are to experience the nearness of God, is the myth that we are exempted by our faith from ever being broken or crushed. Verse 19 of this psalm says that the afflictions of the righteous are many. Despite cultural denial and false teaching, the Scripture is clear: The rain falls on the just and the unjust. Believers and nonbelievers can and do receive the good things in life. The unjust *and* the just also know the sting of pain, disappointment, and loss.

We know this is true. The question that plagues us is not, Is there suffering? or, Why is there suffering? but, Why me and mine? As a friend said recently, if you try to figure out "Why me?" it will only drive you crazy. I have an indelible picture of Tevye from *Fiddler on the Roof* etched in my mind. He who has endured pain, persecution, and apparent rejection by his children speaks to God with his mouth *and* his hands: "I know we are your chosen people, but couldn't you choose someone else once in a while?" In our Christian tradition we know of that refreshingly human saint, Theresa, who cried out in a violent thunderstorm, "O Lord, no wonder you have so few friends if this is how you treat them."

We try to explain God when the Bible does not gives us warrant to do this. Eugenia Price wrote a book called *No Pat Answers* that reveals our proclivity as Christians for putting words in the mouth of God. Are there clearly understandable answers for all broken hearts and crushed spirits? Beware of those modern scholastics who know exactly why we suffer. Jesus would not abide the pat answers (Who sinned, this man or his parents?) and refused to give them.

Beware also of the "health and wealth gospel" in all its current manifestations. Despite its variations, it essentially promises that if we believe it to be so, trust God for it, make positive confession, *we will be healthy and/or wealthy*! By twisting such texts as Deuteronomy 28 and the salutation in Third John, we are told that we now can be freed from pain and poverty. It can all be so sleek, so beguiling. It is a dangerous half truth that can cause great heartache and disillusionment. God can and does heal and save us in so many

ways. But that does not mean that even faithful Christians are immune to pain. Do not believe any false gospel that tells you when pain and suffering comes that God has abandoned you. No, God will not abandon his own. He will not leave you desolate.

II. If we are to experience God's nearness, then we must reject yet another myth: that God is the unmoved mover, high and lifted up, yet uninvolved in the pain of body, mind, and spirit. The Stoics and the Epicureans held that the highest good was serenity. They taught that for God to be serene, he must have *apatheia*, the complete inability to feel anything at all. Isn't that yet our goal—to be cool, uninvolved? Don't we see God as silent, distant, above it all? Maybe God's silence is not necessarily an inability to feel. I do not hear a word from my earthly father; I take his silence to be indifference. But if I continue to watch, I see his shoulder shake from the great sorrow welling up from inside . . . my sorrow shared by him.

For the Christian, Emmanuel is God with us. In Christ we see a God who has "borne our griefs and carried our sorrow." I hear again a woman's ire, "God, do you weep with me? Don't you see the goodness that was thwarted because one man drank too much and hit us with his speeding car, and didn't care?" (*Song of Sarah*, p. 10). I hear a man crushed in spirit saying only that a suffering God can understand—"Nobody knows the trouble I've known except Jesus." These words from the old spiritual are his only comfort as he numbly repeats them over and over.

Yes, it was Jesus who cried out, "My God, my God. Why hast thou forsaken me?" As Donald McCullough graphically paraphrases it, "MY God, where in the hell are you when I need you—where in this hell of godforsaken sin and brokenness?" Without knowing the horror we say, "He descended into hell." He did . . . for you and me.

We have read of the outraged father who stormed into his pastor's study, grabbed him by the arm, and said, "Tell me, where was God when my son was killed?" The other responded with a depth of compassion born of his own suffering, "God was just where he was when his own Son was killed!" He did not abandon his Christ; he will not abandon you. Do you see how near God is to you in your crushed spirit and broken heart?

III. But the final myth that could keep us from the reality of his presence must be smashed. We must reject the myth that God cannot save. It would be the saddest of conclusions to believe suffering can come to anyone, that God suffers with us, but that he is powerless to save us in and through the suffering.

For the end of God's story is not the cross but resurrection. The end of our story, when we are hid with Christ in God, is not guilt and suffering but resurrection. Heartbreak becomes daybreak. It is either too fantastic to be true or too fantastic not to be true. You and I must decide. For it will make all the difference in the world. It did for Iona Henry. Her fourteen-year-old daughter died. The remaining family of three, unable to shake their grief, started on a trip to Iona's parents. They drove in grieving silence. No one saw the train bearing down on them at the crossing. Her son and husband did not survive. She was alone, crushed in body and spirit; she wanted to die. She said she had nothing to live for. Yet even before she could recognize it or pronounce the name, God was near, healing, saving. When she recovered, she wrote a book titled *Through Tragedy to Triumph.*

Through tragedy to triumph—that is the story of the nearness of God to those brokenhearted and crushed in spirit. That is the story of Christ committing his life into those hands. Can we commit our lives into those same hands? He is near the brokenhearted; he will save the crushed in spirit.—Gary D. Stratman

Illustrations

GOD'S NATURE.   God has no nature other than his own personal being. He is not essentially limited "from outside." He does not come into being, nor will he go out of being. He simply is, ultimate and eternal. It is, however, of his essence to love and to impart himself by loving. His eternal being realizes itself in unceasing activity. There is both an eternal fount of love and a continuing expression of love.—Peter Baelz

REAL FAITH.   Faith is real when we can accept his answer to our prayers any way he chooses to give it, like the father who cried out to his three sons above the fury of a storm at sea, "Living or dying God saves his own child." "At twilight," said Alistair MacLean in *High Country*, "four silent men came to harbor. In their hearts was the hush of a great awe."—James W. Cox

Sermon Suggestions

TRUE RELIGION.   TEXT: Zech. 7:1–10. (1) Even the most spectacular religion may be practiced from self-interest, verses 5–6. (2) The better way demonstrates genuine interest in and concern for others, verses 9–10.

FAITH FOR TRYING TIMES.   TEXT: 2 Thess. 2:13–3:5. (1) Reasons for thanks to God, verses 2:13–14. (2) Reasons for hope in God, verses 2:15–3:5.

Worship Aids

CALL TO WORSHIP.   "Sing praises to the Lord, who dwells in Zion! Tell among the peoples his deeds!" (Ps. 9:11, RSV).

INVOCATION.   O Lord, let our songs rise to you from grateful hearts, and let the echoes of our worship be heard throughout the world. Forgive us for only wanting to receive in church without ever giving. Make us generous with love, concern, and witness today and every day.

OFFERTORY SENTENCE.   "May the Lord lead you into a greater understanding of God's love and the endurance that is given by Christ" (2 Thess. 3:5, TEV).

OFFERTORY PRAYER. We bring our money gifts to you, Father. Use this money to reach those we cannot otherwise touch, to speak to those we cannot hear, to bring salvation to those we have never met. Yet, Father, forbid that we should demand immediate rewards for our faithfulness but having given to your kingdom causes, work to make them realities and wait for you to do all things well in your own time and in your own way.—Henry Fields

PRAYER. God of compassion: you watch the ways of men and weave out of terrible happenings wonders of goodness and grace. Surround those who have been shaken by tragedy with a sense of your present love, and hold them in faith. Though they are lost in grief, may they find you and be comforted; through Jesus Christ who was dead, but lives, and rules this world with you.—The Worship Book

LECTIONARY MESSAGE

Topic: The Trick Question
TEXT: Luke 20:27–38

When was the last time someone tried to trip you up in an argument with a trick question? We all know people who have tried to embarrass us or trap us into saying something we didn't want to say by using clever questions. For example, a trick question might take the form, "If x is true, then of course, it is ridiculous to believe that y could be true." Courtroom lawyers and religious debaters are among the most notorious practitioners of the art of the trick question in our culture. This text pictures Jesus in a religious debate with the Sadducees, who are first-century masters of the art of the polemical trick question.

I. *The puzzle* (vv. 27–34). In a discussion about religion when a complex hypothetical question is posed, it is likely that there is a hidden agenda, a "question behind the question." From the beginning, Luke gives us a clue that this is such a

situation, when he introduces the Sadducees with the identifying comment that they are "those who say there is no resurrection" (v. 27).

In this particular case, the hidden agenda is a dispute between the Pharisees and Sadducees on the resurrection of the dead (cf. Acts 23:6–10, where Paul shrewdly utilizes the dispute to get himself temporarily out of trouble, and also Matt. 22:34). The complex puzzle may have been one of the Sadducees' stock arguments to support their position. They denied the existence of a resurrection because there is no mention of any resurrection in the books of the Law (the Torah). This is why Jesus quotes Moses in his response (v. 37).

The specific law of Mosees to which the Sadducees refer in verse 28 is that of levirate marriage (*levir* is Latin for "brother-in-law") set out in Deut. 25:5–10. During Jesus' time this law was not generally observed, which means that the Sadducees' question was purely academic.

II. *The solution* (vv. 34–38). Jesus first solves the Sadducees' puzzle, declaring that there is no marriage in the life to come. Then he turns to the real issue, the "question behind the question" that generated the puzzle in the first place, namely, the Sadducees' denial of the resurrection. Jesus points to the famous story of Moses and the burning bush for justification (from the Torah) of belief in the teaching of the resurrection of the dead. The key to Jesus' argument lies in his interpretation of Exod. 3:6 (Luke 20:37–38), as necessarily implying a belief in life eternal.

Behind the interpretive intricacies of this rabbinic debate lies an important theological concern. What is the basis of our Christian hope that like Jesus we, too, shall be raised from the grave? Our hope for the resurrection does not rest on some quality inherent in the human body or spirit (e.g., some natural immortality of the soul). Rather our hope rests on our relationship of the *living* God. As Jesus declares, "He is God not of the dead but of the living" (v. 38a).—Charles J. Scalise

SUNDAY: NOVEMBER FIFTEENTH

SERVICE OF WORSHIP

Sermon: Surprised by the Future
TEXT: Exod. 10:21–29

Who among us cannot remember those marvelous stories that we heard in Sunday church school? Many of us must be familiar with the old story of little Johnny who came home from church on Sunday, and his mother asked the usual question, "What did you learn in class today?" "Well," replied the boy, "we learned about the children of Israel fleeing from the wicked Pharaoh. They came to the Red Sea and the Pharaoh's soldiers were in hot pursuit. At that point," he said, "Moses got on his walkie-talkie and called in protective air cover, while the Seabees constructed a pontoon bridge across to the other side. Then Moses and his people hurried safely across. But the soldiers were gaining fast, and just as all of them got on the bridge, those timed explosions that the Seabees left behind went off, so the bridge collapsed, and they all drowned in the Red Sea." His astonished mother said, "Johnny, is that what the Sunday school teacher taught you this morning?" "Well, not exactly," admitted the boy. "But, Mom, if I told it the way she did, you'd never believe it!"

It might be that way with the entire story of the miraculous deliverance of the children of Israel from the clutches of the cruel Pharaoh. We focus this morning on a particular portion of the story from Exodus 10, for it seems to have a special relevance to the new decade that lies before us. Pharaoh had reached the place where he was ready to say, in effect, "OK, Moses, I'll let you and your people go, but I want you to leave your flocks behind with me." Moses was not about to leave behind the ingredients of sacrifice unto the Lord, should they be required. So Pharaoh heard the defiant words, "Not a hoof shall be left behind, for we must take of them to serve the Lord our God, and we know not with what we must serve the Lord until we arrive there."

The uncertainty about the future that Moses expressed is not unlike that which we face as we have just crossed over the threshold of the unpredictable decade of the nineties. We know for sure that it will be filled with surprises—new opportunities, new threats, new challenges, new defeats, new victories, new frustrations, new fulfillments. Like Moses, facing the uncertainties of a difficult wilderness journey to the Promised Land, we must take with us those things that will help us face the changed conditions of the new decade.

Speaking of change, here's something to think about: The last sixty years of human history have seen more changes than in all of the generations that went before. According to insurance mortality tables, our average life span is about sixty-two years. Divide this into the last 50,000 years of human existence, and we have about 800 lifetimes, the first 650 of which were lived in caves. In only the last 70 lifetimes did humans know how to transmit culture to the next generation through writing, and the widespread distribution of this knowledge became accessible to the masses through the invention of the movable-type printing press only six lifetimes ago. The flood of technological development that has overloaded our circuits in recent years may be explained by the fact that 90 percent of all the scientists who ever lived on our planet are alive today. It's safe to say that all of us are bound to be "surprised by the future."

The favorite old hymns seem to gather up many of our thoughts and feelings as we contemplate an uncertain future: "Change and decay in all around I see; O Thou who changest not, abide with me." Belief in Jesus Christ, "the same yesterday, today, and forever," becomes the ground of our hope and the unfailing source of our confidence that we do not face the future alone. Here we may take deeper rootage in our biblical faith as it relates to the threats and challenges of daily life and may search together for the often elusive answers to questions of faith and obedience in a changing world.

We must learn to be at peace with ourselves in the midst of ambiguity. We will be on the right track whenever we demonstrate out of our Judeo-Christian inheritance a preference for significance over success, giving over getting, justice over advantage, service over profit, tenderness over toughness, human rights over property rights.

Whenever we are surprised by the future I believe we would do well to follow the advice of the Apostle Paul, which he offered in his first letter to the Christians at Thessalonica. He recommended a somewhat modern, experimental attitude in the presence of uncertainty when he wrote, "Prove [or test] all things. Hold fast to that which is good, and abstain from all forms of evil." Don't accept or reject the new just because of its novelty; test it out by the mind and spirit of Jesus Christ, and act accordingly. Don't idealize or idolize the past just because it is old. And under all circumstances, reject all conscious participation in the world's evil.

Many years ago our family enjoyed a most unusual trip to Skagway, Alaska, where we boarded a little narrow-gauge puffer-billy that struggled valiantly to cross the White Pass, eventually delivering us to Whitehorse in the Yukon Territory. There we took an old-fashioned, wood-burning sternwheeler up the Lewes River into the fabled Yukon and all the way north to Dawson City, made famous by the turbulent gold rush of 1898. The big flat-bottom vessel runs aground frequently on the recently relocated gravel bars, but the captain finds this no great problem. There is always a channel to accommodate the flow of the mighty Yukon. All that is required is the patience and determination to find it. And so it is with the river of life. God will not leave us without a channel to the future.

Of course, we'll be surprised by the future, but never forget that "the eternal God is our refuge and underneath are the everlasting arms." John Greenleaf Whittier lends beauty to this faith when he writes,

I know not what the future hath
Of marvel or surprise,
Assured alone that life and death
His mercy underlies.
I know not where His island lift
Their fronded palms in air;
I only know I cannot drift
Beyond His love and care.

—George W. Hill

Illustrations

UNDIMINISHED HARMONY.   I recognize a numbness—perhaps a diminution. Eyes are less keen; ears duller. . . . The important thing is that this equation between the urging of the soul and the obedience of the body should be maintained. Even while growing old, may I preserve within myself an undiminished harmony! I do not like the Stoic's proud stiffening of the lip; but the horror of death, of old age, of all that cannot be avoided, strikes me as impious. Whatever may be my fate, I should wish to return to God a grateful and enraptured soul.—André Gide

STRENGTH TO STRENGTH.   Going to the Father without fear is a privilege for every minute of the day. More and more knowledge of the Father is the progress for which we crave, since more knowledge of the Father means a fuller view of all that makes up the spiritual universe. Into that knowledge we are advancing every hour we live; into that knowledge we shall still be advancing at the hour when we die. The Father will still be showing us something new; the something new will still be showing us the Father.

It will be something new, as we can receive it. He who can receive little will be given little; he who can receive much will be given much. In growth all is adjusted to capacity; it is not meant to shock, force, or frighten. The next step in growth being always an easy step, I can feel sure of moving onward easily— "from strength to strength," in the words of one of the Songs for the Sons of Korah, "until unto the God of gods appeareth everyone of them in Zion." —Basil King

Sermon Suggestions

THE DAY COMES. TEXT: Mal. 4:1–6. (1) The plight of evildoers, verse 1. (2) The blessings of those who fear God, verses 2–3. (3) The attitude toward God's written and prophetic Word that makes the difference, verses 4–6.

MAINTAINING A CHRISTIAN WORK ETHIC. TEXT: 2 Thess. 3:6–13. (1) By shunning the company of idlers. (2) By imitating the industrious. (3) By motivating slackers. (4) By doing right even when it is difficult.

Worship Aids

CALL TO WORSHIP. "Arise, O God, judge the earth; for to thee belong all the nations!" (Ps. 82:8, RSV).

INVOCATION. Our hope is in you, O God, for the putting right of all things wrong. Open our eyes to see through faith that you are at work even when present circumstances seem to deny it.

OFFERTORY SENTENCE. "But ye, brethren, be not weary in well doing" (2 Thess. 3:13).

OFFERTORY PRAYER. We confess, our Father, that there are times when our words, our deeds, and our gifts seem futile, and we are tempted to give up in discouragement. Make us strong and faithful in our stewardship, we pray, with the assurance that you will cause our efforts in due time or in eternity to succeed.

PRAYER. Most gracious God, by whose knowledge the depths are broken up and the clouds drop down the dew: We yield thee hearty thanks and praise for the return of seedtime and harvest, for the increase of the ground and the gathering in of its fruits, and for all the other blessings and thy merciful providence bestowed upon this nation and people. And, we beseech thee, give us a just sense of these great mercies, such as may appear in our lives by a humble, holy, and obedient walk before thee all our days; through Jesus Christ our Lord, to whom, with thee and the Holy Ghost be all glory and honor, world without end. — *The Book of Common Prayer*

LECTIONARY MESSAGE

Topic: Discipleship during Disaster
TEXT: Luke 21:5–19

"Must we be carried to the skies on flowery beds of ease, / While others fought to win the prize and sailed through bloody seas?" (Isaac Watts). Living the Christian life means honestly confronting struggle and suffering. At times things will get much worse before they get better. How does one live as a disciple of Christ in days of disaster and in times of persecution? In our text Jesus foretells the coming of destruction to Israel and warns his followers of persecution.

I. *Destruction* (vv. 5–6). When Jesus hears some people admiring the beautiful Temple in Jerusalem, he declares that this finely built Temple and all of its adornment will not endure. The Jewish sacrificial system that the Temple represents will become an ancient tradition, rather than a living practice. Admiration of construction will soon become astonishment at destruction. (Verses 20–24 describe signs that this destruction of Jerusalem is coming.) The Romans sacked Jerusalem and destroyed the Temple in C.E. 70.

II. *Deception* (vv. 7–8). In response to the ever-present questions of "When will this happen?" and "How will we know?" Jesus first points to the dangers of false messiahs. One way of knowing that these prophets are false is the way in which they will publicly proclaim themselves to be the Messiah. "I am he!" (v. 8) is a claim to the sacred name of God (cf. John 13:19).

The *false* messiahs will proclaim that the end of the world is at hand when the Temple is destroyed, but Jesus contends that this destruction and all of the other disasters are not the end of the age, but only preliminary signs. As Jesus maintains in verse 9, "the end will *not* follow immediately."

III. *Disasters* (vv.9–11). The Jewish rebellion and the Roman siege of Jerusalem (c.e. 66–70) are the "wars and insurrections" to which verse 9 refers. Political disasters will be followed by natural disasters ("great earthquakes . . . famines and plagues") and "portents and great signs from heaven" (v. 11). For Luke's description of the end of the age, which will follow these signs, see verses 25ff.

IV. *Discipleship* (vv.12–19). Jesus wants his followers to know that being a disciple will mean being persecuted. Our Lord offers no "rose-colored" view of discipleship. As Dietrich Bonhoeffer declared, "When Christ calls a [person], he calls him [or her] to come and die" (*The Cost of Discipleship*).

Verses 14–15 offer the reassuring promise that in the time of testing the presence of the Spirit will prompt the disciples with the right words of testimony (cf. 12:12). Jesus' followers are not promised that they will avoid suffering during the persecution but rather that their final safety is in the hands of God (v. 18). During days of disaster the call to discipleship is a call to perseverance in the faith (v. 19). When things seem to go from bad to worse in our lives, the presence of God can sustain us in hope.— Charles J. Scalise

SUNDAY: NOVEMBER TWENTY-SECOND

SERVICE OF WORSHIP

Sermon: Surprised by Judgment

TEXT: Matt. 25:31–46

I am judged! I am judged by my neighbors, my friends, and my family. I judge myself, often too severely. If I break a natural law, I am judged by nature. If I break a civil law, I am judged by the state, and I am judged by God. Judgment is one of the inescapable realities of life.

Jesus said that history would end with a grand finale of judgment. I never read that judgment scene without being surprised, sometimes shocked. I am surprised by judgment.

I. *The King.*

(a) The New Testament furnishes my mind with several images of Jesus, the chief one being that of servant. Jesus could have been a political king. There was a strong nationalistic tide that would have swept him into that high position. Thousands of people waited for his word. How they wanted the hated Romans driven beyond the boundaries of their little nation and to have freedom and dignity restored. This was the meaning of the temptation when the devil took Jesus to a high mountain and let the kingdoms of the world pass before his vision.

Yet Jesus, with a scepter within his reach, turned from it and asked for a towel and basin of w!ter. He was called to be a servant, so he washed and dried the dirty feet of his disciples.

(b) His followers were to be servants, too. They were not to be too proud to wash the dirty feet of their world nor too squeamish to swab its running sores.

Yet it must be said that the New Testament holds the two images, servant and king, together without there being any conflict.

In the second chapter of Philippians there is a magnificent hymn that the early church sang. It pictures Christ on an equality with God in power and glory. Then he gave it all up, not because he had to, but because he wanted to. Down, down, down he came. He became a man, lower still a servant man, and lowest of all he died the most shameful death in the ancient world. He made his descent as a servant.

(c) Then there is an ascent as precipitous as the descent—up, up, up he went above principalities and powers. He made his ascent as Lord, King, Sovereign.

The New Testament tells us that he is seated at the right hand of God, which is a position of honor and sovereign power.

Some day he will step forth from his exalted position to consummate history. Like a stream that moves to its appointed sea, so history will move to its appointed end.

II. *The witnesses.*

(a) I am surprised by the witnesses. Who are they? They are the poor, hungry, homeless, disadvantaged people of our earth. We cannot escape these people. They are with us now, and Jesus said we will have to face them in the Judgment.

In our shrunken world these disadvantaged people are not far from us. These poor and hungry people are almost at the end of our walkways. It is as if they press their pinched faces against the window panes of our dining rooms, where tables are burdened with rich and delicious food.

(b) We cannot escape these people now or in the Judgment. How often we are almost totally unaware of these destitute people. We who are overfed, overclothed, oversheltered, and overcared, often indulging ourselves in wild excesses, are not moved by their pain and loneliness.

I think of our pattern of giving especially at Christmas. How often we make gifts to those who do not need them, those who will give back to us. In all of this we miss the real joy of giving that we cannot know until we give to those who can never return the gift.

III. *The questions.*

(a) I am more than surprised by the questions that will be asked on that last great day. I am shocked! This is a very hard passage for those of us who have so spiritualized the gospel that we have left no room for the social dimension.

Listen to these questions again: Did you feed the hungry, give drink to the thirsty? Did you clothe the naked and take in the homeless? Did you visit the sick and minister to those in prison?

We hear no such questions as these: Do you believe in God? Do you believe the Bible is the Word of God? Do you believe the Bible is infallible? Are you an inerrantist? Are you a fundamentalist? Are you a liberal?

We are to be just because God is just; we are to be loving because God is love. Ethics grow in a religious soil, and when separated from that soil they became like cut flowers that, no matter how beautiful, wither and die.

(b) A final observation should be made about these questions. It is not suggested that the righteous people were saved because of their humanitarian concern. We may assume that they were saved the way all of us are—by grace. But the grace that saved them had become graciousness in them.

IV. *The identification.*

(a) Before Jesus were the poor, hungry, and homeless people of the world. Yet he does not say that they were hungry and homeless but that he was. Once more I am surprised.

What could be the meaning of this? He was so identified with these unfortunate people that their hunger, thirst, nakedness, homelessness, sickness, and confinement behind prison bars became his own. Jesus had strange powers of identification. Jesus gave the secret away: "Truly I say to you that as you did it to one of the least of these my brethren, you did it to me." He was so identified with these poor people that when they were fed he was fed.

(b) When Paul met the risen Lord along the Damascus road he was greatly surprised that Christ addressed him by name: "Saul, Saul, why do you persecute me?" Paul could have so easily remonstrated, "Lord, why do you say I persecuted you? I don't even know you." To which Christ could have responded, "What you have said is true, but you persecuted my followers. When you put them in jail, you put me behind prison bars. You can never hurt them without hurting me."

St. Francis of Assisi is one of the most saintly people in the history of the church. A few years ago my wife and I were in Assisi for a day. At lunch that day we ate in an open restaurant, and we could see the beautiful hills that surround Assisi. As I looked out I wondered if I were looking at the hill over which one day Francis rode his steed. A legend has it that he came upon a beggar who was a leper. This day, following a powerful impulse, he flung himself from his horse and got down beside the beggar, taking him into his arms. As he did, the face of the beggar became the face of Christ.

Here is great hope! No person walks alone; Christ walks with us. And no person suffers alone; Christ suffers with us.—Chevis F. Horne

Illustrations

TRANSCENDING.   Human beings bear a consciousness of something beyond the immediate. Human life finds itself forever on the thresholds of time, of space, and of the unseen—"reaching up to the gates of Heaven while one foot is slipping off the edge of the Abyss (Philip Wheelwright). In spite of the massive evidence of the mundane and the ugly in our experience, we human beings tenaciously harbor the conviction that we were "made for more." Something more was promised. There is more for us to live into, to embrace, or to be embraced by. We have a sense that we participate in something wider and deeper than we have yet realized—a more inclusive patterning of relation, a more profound ordering of justice, a richer loving of life in its manifold forms. We intuit a unity of the whole. Time, the world-as-it-is, the world of space and sense—all may be lived into and transcended. We human beings harbor a conviction of a "Beyond filled with Holiness" (Suzanne Langer). Having the capacity to intuit the whole, we have the capacity for faith.—Sharon Parks

FRIENDSHIP.   We need to become free souls if we are to be friends with others. When God sets us free from self and from concern with what others think of us, we can relax into real persons who can live with other real persons and help still others to become authentic. Those of us, at least, who worship as Christians should never forget that Jesus was the friend of all who needed him. He set us an example which if followed with simple

and effective trust could do more than anything else to restore sanity and freedom to our fear-ridden world and our fear-tensed communities.—Nels F. S. Ferré

Sermon Suggestion

KING OF KINGS.   TEXTS: 2 Sam. 5:1–5; Col. 1:11–20. (1) The glory of an earthly king, 2 Sam. 5:2b. (2) The glory of the heavenly king, Col. 1:18–20.

Worship Aids

CALL TO WORSHIP.   "O come, let us worship and bow down; let us kneel before the Lord our maker. For he is our God; and we are the people of his pasture and the sheep of his hand" (Ps. 95:6–7a).

INVOCATION.   We come with gratitude and songs of praise, Lord, for the bountiful harvest of blessings we know. Make us wise stewards and a people given to sharing through Jesus Christ our Lord.—E. Lee Phillips

OFFERTORY SENTENCE.   "Do not be anxious about anything, but in everything, by prayer and petition, with thanksgiving, present your requests to God" (Phil. 4:6, NIV).

OFFERTORY PRAYER.   Our daily bread is enough, O God, but you have given us more than enough. As you have blessed us in the past, we trust you for the future. When there is need, help us to pray not only for ourselves but also for one another; and to give from what we have to relieve anxiety, to promote the gospel, and to build your kingdom.

PRAYER.   Holy Father, we come into your presence this morning to look at ourselves as we are and to seek your power that we might become what you would have us be. Through the week we have been preoccupied with schemes that so often have little to do with your will and way for your children. So much that we have done has had nothing to do with right, nor has it been motivated by a strong sense of wrong. Too often we have simply followed the most expedient pathway and allowed ourselves to drift. In the process we have neglected responsibilities demanded by Christ, even as we have neglected the cries of fellow strugglers on this road we are walking through the world.

Father, attune our ears to hear the cries for deliverance that come to us from all corners of life. Open our eyes to see the needs that we can meet in Christ's strength. Lead us to invest our courage and energy in striving for right where wrong among us is so evident. That we may serve the Master with joy, convict us of our sins and cleanse us of our iniquities. Here in this place we pray that you will indeed create in us a clean heart, O God, and renew a right spirit within each of us. Then will we be able to teach transgressors your ways and sinners will be converted unto you.

Today and through the days of this week call us unto yourself that we may be transformed from mere followers into true servants who come to love the Lord with all our minds, hearts, and souls. Speak gently and convincingly to every person who draws near, that souls may be brought into the kingdom and lives changed for time and eternity, even as was done among those whom the Lord taught to pray: [the Lord's Prayer].— Henry Fields

LECTIONARY MESSAGE

Topic: Mixed Motives in the Peanut Gallery
TEXT: John 12:9–19

On this last Sunday of the season of Pentecost we remember Christ the King. So, it is particularly fitting to reflect on John's story of Jesus' royal entry into Jerusalem. Picture yourself as a member of the great crowd that comes to meet Jesus (vv. 12–13) and that stays with him throughout the story (vv. 17 and 18).

I. *Seeking the miracle* (vv. 9–11). John describes the mixed motives of the crowd: "They came not only because of Jesus but also to see Lazarus, whom he had raised from the dead" (v. 9). The crowd easily succumbed to the temptation to idolize the one upon whom the miracle was performed rather than praising God (the source of the miracle) through Jesus (the agent of the miracle).

As a result of this popular acclaim Lazarus soon becomes targeted for elimination by the chief priests (v. 10). Those in power judged Lazarus's witness to Jesus to be too effective and so too dangerous to the religious and political status quo. The idolatry of the miracle-seeking crowd threatens unintentionally to jeopardize the life of the recipient of the miracle. The one raised from the dead is threatened with death because of the very miracle that gave him life again.

II. *Hailing the King* (vv. 12–16). Jesus converts the mixed-motive crowd into a prophetic sign. He acts out the prophecy of Zech. 9:9, entering the city on a donkey's colt. Many patriotic Jews in the crowd would recall the story os Simon Maccabeus's triumphal entry into Jerusalem with waving palm branches (1 Macc. 13:51). The crowd wants a political liberator, but (cf. Greek adversative in v. 14) Jesus reveals the Messiah. How ironic that this messianic king whom the people hoped would deliver them from the Roman legions makes his triumphal entry on a young donkey, rather than a mighty steed. It is a long way from the trumpets of Roman legions to the hosannas of this crowd!

The disciples seem oblivious to the significance of all of these events (v. 16). They fail to understand the radical choice Jesus portrays between a messiah who will follow the way of war and one who will be the Prince of Peace. As John Marsh observes, "The way of humility, peace and death was the only road to a certain future for the people of God."

III. *Following the sign* (vv. 17–19). The crowds reveal again their mixed motives, bearing witness to Jesus (v. 17) and yet once more following the rumor of Jesus' miraculous sign (v. 18). The Pharisees' resigned reaction is certainl ironic. They say they "can do nothing" (v. 19), yet they are plotting Jesus' death. In less than a week they will see Jesus crucified.

Their declaration that "the world has gone after him" foreshadows the Greeks coming to Jesus in the next verse.

As a member of this crowd of mixed motives, how do you resond to the com-

ing of the Prince of Peace? Are you trapped by the limitations of your cultural expectations, or are you liberated to follow Christ the King?—Charles J. Scalise

표적을 보고 좋는 Xn 과 믿음으로 주를 귀세석로믿는 Xn들!

SUNDAY: NOVEMBER TWENTY-NINTH

SERVICE OF WORSHIP

Sermon: We Belong to God
TEXT: John 1:11
READINGS: Gen. 1:27–31; 1 Cor. 6:12–20; Luke 12:13–21

Why are we here? What brings together this mixed group of people at this time and in this place? There are so many things each of us could be doing. So what brings us here? Today in our city there are other circles to move in if it's prestige and reputation you're after, and your neighbors (if you know who they are) don't give a damn whether you go to church or not.

I. *Belonging to a godly community.*

(a) For the most part, I believe, we are here because we belong, or want to belong, to a community that believes in God and tries to act on that belief. A living church stands for a working belief in God. A working belief in God means, in the Christian and Jewish tradition, that God is a real factor in all we think and do, that we seek a relationship with him that is as close and personal as that we have with our dearest friend. In the great circle of belonging, the most powerful truth is that we belong to God. Such a conviction will inevitably alter the way we confront all the great choices that come our way in life, and the ultimate question mark of death.

(b) Psychologists have said that the two most powerful instincts in human beings are religion and sex. That may account for the fact that when religion loses its grip on society, sex is apt to take over as the reigning god. The two great instincts are not necessarily at war, but everything profoundly human is related to our deep sense of belonging to God. It's that working, all-inclusive sense of belonging to God that should be the real reason for allying oneself with a community that seeks above all else to love the Lord our God with heart and mind and all we have, and our neighbor as ourselves.

II. *Belonging to Jesus Christ.*

(a) "He came unto his own." These words are familiar to churchgoers. They come from that perpetually stimulating, illuminating, and puzzling poem we know as the prologue to the Gospel of St. John. I expect that if I asked one familiar with this phrase what was intended by the words "He came unto his own," the answer might be, It means that Jesus was born a Jew. But the context of these words reveals that the author was not speaking about the historic Jesus. He is speaking about the Word—which means God revealing himself to the human race, God communicating with his human family. He is speaking about God's call to the great human family that had wandered away from the Father's home. For him the Incarnation was the supreme act of God's parental love, but from the dawn of history to this very moment, God comes unto his own.

(b) This is one basic belief of a Christian church with which I begin. It is a belief that marks off live church members off from all who, consciously or unconsciously, reject his claim; that marks off a church as a community that proposes another aim in life, another conviction about life's meaning (or lack of meaning) from those that seem to dominate the society in which we live. It is our business now to ponder the implications of such a working belief.

(c) The men and women of the Bible, characters who have left their mark on history as believers, and those who impress and influence us today as examples of faith in action, draw one tremendous conclusion from the fact that we belong to God. For them it is a daily working belief, and what it says is this: Since I belong to God then nothing, not my worries, my pains, my fears, my sense of loneliness or depression, not the worst catastrophe that can happen to me, not death itself, can separate me from his love. Jesus descended into this hell of alienation from man and God that is our deepest fear in the working belief that nothing could break the tie that bound him to that everlasting love. "Father, into thy hands I commend my spirit," were his last earthly words, and when he appeared again his disciples were given for all time their share in this assurance. They knew what he had meant when he said: "I give unto them eternal life; and they shall never perish, neither shall any man pluck them out of my hand."

III. *Belonging wholly to God.*

(a) Belonging to God is then a belief that is lodged in the depth of the soul and begins to shape the direction of our lives. The Bible has much more to say about the body than the soul. A worshiping congregation is a marvelous assembly of bodies which cannot be transformed into some nebulous flotilla of invisible spirits. So when I realize deep down that I belong to God, I should realize that this goes for my body, too. It's a gift from God which I hold in trust for him. And that has practical consequences as a working belief.

In the passage we heard from Paul's letter to the Corinthian church, he dealt with one aspect of our treatment of the body. Corinth was known for its total sexual license. Paul had discovered that some of his young Christians there were interpreting his gospel of the grace of God and freedom from the Law to mean that, so long as their soul had been saved, they could do what they liked with their bodies. Hence his thunderous denunciation of the licentious bed-hoppers of Corinth: "What? Know ye not that your body is the temple of the Holy Ghost, which is in you, which ye have of God, and you are not your own?"

Your body belongs to God, and you are responsible for it as a steward of God's gift. Without giving in to the prevailing hypochondria of the moment, we owe these bodies of ours at least enough care to keep them in repair, as good stewards of this gift of God.

(b) So when we talk about the Christian doctrine of stewardship, we mean much more than the use of our money. Money and possessions do come into the picture, but only because they are such an integral part of the lives that belong to God. The basic belief is what Paul meant when he simply said, "Ye are not your own." The power and glory of the gospel—and the joy—lie not only in the assurance that, since we belong to God, we have a safety net through which we cannot fall but in the discovery that all we have—bodies, homes, talents, ambitions, bank accounts—we hold in trust for the God to whom they belong.

"He came unto his own." What we really are: his own. This is the crucial decision in anyone's life: recognizing that we are "his own" and not "our own" to do what we like. To as many as receive him, the One who became one of us in Jesus Christ, he gives the power to become the sons and daughters of God. To receive him means just saying, "Yes, Lord: I'm not my own. I belong to you. Take the whole of me."

Then it must become as clear as daylight that a community of Christians with this working belief will want to share this discovery with all our neighbors. Evangelism is the joyful invitation to all who are feeling lost or alone to share what Christ has given us. Rejoice with me! "He came unto his own" and "his own" are not the members of a holy club. "His own" includes the entire human family, but there are millions in our world who don't know it. Shouldn't we tell them—by what we say, what we do, and what we are?—David H. C. Read

Illustrations

SERVICE.   In the story "Winnie-the-Pooh and the Honey Tree" Pooh Bear goes to Rabbit's house for lunch and eats every jar of honey in Rabbit's pantry. Upon leaving, he becomes lodged in Rabbit's doorway, where he must wait until he is thin again.

Pooh Bear is like the Christian whose sole desire is to be fed the sweetness of God's Word, gorging himself to the point of being of no use to anyone. Sunday school and worship attendance are good and desirable, but they are not ends in themselves. They are means to a separate and better end—that of being equipped with the Word of God to serve others. Let us not be too much like Pooh Bear, overly intent on filling ourselves that we forget others. Let's be sure that we can make it through the doors of the church on the way out, prepared to minister. After all, having a Pooh Bear stuck in the doorway means that no one else can get in!—Chuck McElhannon

WHAT IS THE BUSINESS OF BUSINESS? I heard of a man who was offered a deal in which there was a chance to make a great deal of money. He looked it over, then at luncheon he explained to the company representative that he could not take it. When pressed for his reason, he said, "I am a Christian man, my company tries to do business by Christian principles, and in the light of that I can see no possible way to handle this." The other businessman looked at him in amazement and said, "Surely you don't try to mix two good things like business and religion." Then from across the table he heard an expression which should be inscribed over every business. "My friend, I have discovered that it is only when we do mix business and religion that we can prove our religion and improve our business."—J. Wallace Hamilton

Sermon Suggestions

A PERENNIAL HOPE.   TEXT: Isa. 2:1–5.
(1) A universal quest for the will and ways of the Lord. (2) A final renunciation of war and embracing of productive living.

"THIS IS THE HOUR OF CRISIS."   TEXT: Rom. 13:11–14, REB.

(1) Day is near. (2) Therefore, our behavior should befit the day. (3) Christ Jesus is our bright armor to protect us against the darkness.

Worship Aids

CALL TO WORSHIP.   "I was glad when they said unto me, let us go into the house of the Lord" (Ps. 122:1).

INVOCATION.   Lord, open us to directives that are divine and options that are righteous, that we may live as we worship as followers of a loving Savior and a mighty Holy Spirit.—E. Lee Phillips

OFFERTORY SENTENCE.   "Clothe yourselves with the Lord Jesus Christ, and do not think about how to gratify the desires of the sinful nature" (Rom. 13:14, NIV).

OFFERTORY PRAYER.   Father, you have put into our hearts and minds the desire to serve you, even as our Lord Jesus Christ went about doing good. We pray that you will use these tithes and offerings as an extension of our very selves for the good things that are close to your heart.

PRAYER.   We come to you, our Father, in this season of preparation to plead for the wakening and renewal of the conscience of our world. Too long have countless people been lonely, hungry, loveless, and disinherited by us and even by their own. Raise up witnesses among us who know and love the Bible, the story of the Christian church, the amazing record of good and miraculous works, and the radiance of that everlasting childhood which Jesus blessed and named forever as his own. O Lamb of God, whose calling was to cleanse us from our sin and make us pure and holy, make this season a time for us to see who we are as we stand again beside the lowly Child, to resolve to love the right that again the world may stare at the works of heaven, and to scatter the seeds of reconciliation and goodwill across this quarrelsome world. Into your hands we commit our frail and bewildered race. Make this Advent a time for us to be drawn closer to yourself. Occupy our hearts and our homes and in them both may your honor dwell.—Donald Macleod (*Sunday Publications*)

LECTIONARY MESSAGE

Topic: The Coming of Christ
TEXT: Matt. 24:36–44

What should our attitude be toward the future coming of Christ? Some Christians ignore this teaching, while others are so preoccupied with it that their chart-laden fanaticism becomes destructive. How did Jesus describe this event? What counsel did he provide his disciples regarding their attitude toward his coming?

Jesus' description of the coming of the Son of man is preceded by and intertwined with a portrayal of the downfall of Jerusalem and the devastating sacrilege of the Temple. The Jewish religious world would be forever altered as a consequence of this event. The old sacrificial system with its legal prescriptions for interceding with God had passed away and new ways of relating to God (rabbinic Judaism and Christianity) were being born. Our text may be understood as presenting three characteristics of Christ's coming. Each characteristic implies an admonition for disciples regarding their attitude toward the coming of the Son of man.

I. *The mystery of Christ's coming* (v. 36). People are always yearning to know about the future. Although this verse plainly says that "no one knows" when Christ will come (cf. also Mark 13:32), the history of Christianity is replete with attempts to bypass the plain meaning of the words of our Lord. The mystery of Christ's coming faces us with the reality of limited human knowledge. We are right to reject the claims of those who profess to know the when and where of the future. If "neither the angels of heaven, nor the Son" knows "about that day and hour," why should we believe the false claims of others? There are many matters concerning Christ's coming about which Christians can and should be unsure, but one thing of which we can be sure is that those who claim complete and certain knowledge are wrong. Confessing the mystery of Christ's coming, we are admonished: Be humble.

II. *The unexpectedness of Christ's coming* (vv. 37–42). The story of Noah (Genesis 6–9) invites its readers to imagine the shock of Noah's neighbors at the unexpected coming of the great Flood. The sudden judgment of the Flood parallels the sudden return of the coming of Christ (vv. 37–39). People will be going about their daily work and suddenly be taken to be with God (vv. 40–41). Acknowledging the unexpectedness of Christ's coming (v. 42), we are admonished: *Be awake.*

III. *The anticipation of Christ's coming* (vv. 43–44). If you knew that your home was going to be broken into and your possessions stolen, you would be prepared. Both you and the police would be carefully watching. Unfortunately, as R. V. G. Tasker wryly observes, "burglars do not advertise beforehand the hour of their arrival." So we neglect to be watchful with the result that we are unexpectedly victimized. The purpose of Jesus' illustration (cf. "therefore" in v. 44) is to dramatize the necessity for watchfulness—expecting the unexpected—in regard to the coming of Christ. Watching in patient anticipation of Christ's coming, we are admonished: *Be ready.*—Charles J. Scalise

SUNDAY: DECEMBER SIXTH

SERVICE OF WORSHIP

Sermon: This Fateful Hour
TEXT: Luke 12:56

Jesus once rebuked religious leaders for their inability to decipher the momentous events that swirled about them. To be sure, they were expert weather prophets who scanned the skies in search of rain, but they were unable to interpret "this fateful hour"(Luke 12:56, NEB).

As a corrective, Jesus set himself steadily against every form of pious Jewish patriotism that sought to wage war with Rome in the name of God. Unless the nation changed its course, he warned, it would come to the same doom that had fallen on the insurrectionists whose blood Pilate had mingled with their sacrifices (Luke 13:1–3). His lament over Jerusalem (Matt. 23:37–38) seared the disciples' hearts as they left the fabulous Temple precincts. They could not help but remind Jesus, perhaps in gentle rebuke, that, whatever else might happen, these impressive stones were sure to stand! (Matt. 24:1). But he would not have it: Even the supreme Jewish sanctuary was certain to be reduced to rubble (Matt. 24:2).

His disciples could make sense of almost anything else but not the toppling of that colossus. It would seem to make nonsense of their Scriptures as well as their entire religious tradition. Now, in the privacy of Olivet, they demanded that he explain this shocking "sign" that would bring life as they knew it to an "end" (Matt. 24:3).

In response, Jesus gave, not one, but two signs. We, like the disciples of old, stand bewildered on the brink of uncertainty. We, too, seek a sign from the Lord.

I. *The sign of tragedy.*

(a) To describe the first sign (Matt. 24:15), Jesus reached for a technical term loaded with religious history. Immediately, the disciples would remember the days of Daniel when the hated Antiochus Epiphanes went out of his way to desecrate the Temple. To this travesty of the Temple, this rape of the religious sensibilities of the people, Daniel gave the name "the abomination of desolation," or, as Moffatt here renders it, "the appalling Horror" (cf. Dan. 9:27; 11:31; 12:11). This phrase came to stand for the detestable triumph of evil in the face of the Almighty.

Jesus knew full well what wicked men could do. In only a few days they would lay ugly hands upon his holiness and impale him on a cross. He would become an "appalling horror" to all who beheld him.

(b) As with the leader, so with the followers. His disciples would reproduce the wretchedness of his Passion in their own experience. Finally, they would behold the sickening "abomination of desolation," the unmistakable sign of the collapse of every cherished value (v. 15).

Before many years had passed, the worst forebodings of Jesus were fully confirmed. Before the Romans were done, the sanctuary was in shambles, never to be rebuilt to this day. Jesus had indeed read the signs of the time aright. This was the promised "abomination of desolation" that would come in their generation (Matt. 24:32–34).

(c) There are striking signs that we, too, may see the kind of sacrilege that leaves life desolate. The remorseless clock of history is ticking fast in our time as Satan nudges the hands toward midnight. We have sown the bitter seeds of suspicion, distrust, and hatred—and it will do no good to pray for a crop failure!

This is nowhere more obvious than in our persistent flirtation with nuclear war. The entire vocabulary of horror has been activated in an effort to describe such a possibility. It is striking that one of the key words used to describe the effects of nuclear war is the very term that Jesus here employed: *desolation.*

The use of nuclear weapons even in the name of national honor would open a Pandora's box of unimaginable demons and unleash a force capable of fracturing the planet itself. Everything would be tarnished and contaminated, even the air that the soul must breathe.

It is still an open question whether any of us could live long with the memory that we had participated in the suicide of civilization. Today events demand that we recover the insistence of Jesus that misguided zealots are capable of profaning everything precious, blaspheming everything beautiful, making a sacrilege of everything sacred! It is urgent that we recognize this first "sign" of our time.

II. *The sign of triumph*

(a) If tragedy was the first word of Jesus, it certainly was not his last. He dared to believe that when man is at his sinning worst, God is at his saving best.

In the first instance, Jesus applied this astonishing paradox to his own destiny. He would indeed "suffer many things." Finally, the full force of human tragedy would wrest from his lips an awful cry of dereliction and all would be over. But in a short while, within the space of "three days," hard on the heels of unmitigated tragedy would follow unqualified triumph: He would rise victorious from the dead.

(b) Again, as with the Master, so with his servants. If the disciples were to feel the full force of that evil that produced his tragedy, they would also experience the full impact of that redemption that promised his triumph. He had faced his Passion with the overriding conviction that earth's darkest moment would provide an opportunity for heaven's finest hour, and to that certainty he pointed his disciples. Just as the painful spasms of travail are the surest sign of the arrival of new life, the disasters of history would herald the dawn of God's new day (vv. 32–33).

Thus, at the very moment when their heads would be bowed in shame and remorse, the disciples were bidden to look up, for their redemption was drawing near (Luke 21:18).

(c) Our problem, like that of the first disciples, lies essentially in the future. Just as they could not bear to face a day in which the Temple would be reduced to shambles, so we recoil from the grim prospects that stare us in the face. We do not know what the future holds, but we know who holds the future! When history proves utterly helpless to redeem itself, our salvation from terror and despair will come from God.

This means, as Paul saw so clearly, that nothing can finally separate us from the love of God (Rom. 8:39). No despair, however binding, is ultimate. Evil cannot create a present that will permanently shackle God's future.

III. *"Redeeming the time"* (Eph. 5:16).

(a) Why are our lips so strangely silent on this urgent theme? Anyone who listens to modern preaching will hear precious little responsible proclamation of the victorious return of Christ.

The reason for this strange silence is not hard to find. Clearly, Jesus was certain that this dramatic pageant would unfold in his own generation (Matt. 24:34–35), that triumph would follow immediately after the tribulation" (v. 29), and we need not explain it away. Unless these promises somehow came true for them in their own generation, they will scarcely come true for us in ours.

(b) We stumble because the application of this truth demands that we relate an eternal event to our transient times. But is that such an impossible task after all? We readily acknowledge that the first coming of Christ on the cross was a unique historical event, yet we follow Paul in personalizing that event by calling on believers today to be "crucified with Christ." Why, then, are we reluctant to follow Paul in the conviction that the final coming of Christ on the clouds is also a unique event that may become part of our contemporary experience as well?

The first coming is no more "true" because it has happened than the final coming is true because it will happen. To affirm the past but deny the future is to imprison God in the time sequence of earth. To make something meaningful that happened two thousand years ago requires the same faith that is needed to make something meaningful that may happen two thousand years hence.

(c) It is simply incredible how carelessly we have allowed the future dimension to fall out of the landscape of life. In so doing, we have forgotten the radical significance of what it means to live by hope.

The final redemption of God is, as the Old Testament prophesied, only one great event. But in the New Testament this single eschatological act is viewed in its several stages as Incarnation, Atonement, Resurrection, exaltation, and return. Thus the end is always near because it is an integral part of something that has already started happening. This means that we, like the first followers of

Christ, are set down in the midst of a total event. Through the indwelling Holy Spirit, the character of every present moment is shaped by the impact of the first coming, which we have made a part of our immediate past, and by the impact of the final coming, which we must make a part of our immediate future.

When we look at life with the vision of Jesus, we shall rediscover for our nuclear generation the truth of that stately hymn:

O God, our help in ages past,
Our hope for years to come,
Our shelter from the stormy blast
And our eternal home.
—William E. Hull

Illustrations

THE JUDGE. Christ's presence in word and sacrament points beyond itself (by virtue of its indwelling logic of identification) to his presence itself, to his identity in the world. The identification of Christ with the poor and his brotherhood with the very least belong, according to Matthew 25, within the framework of the coming judgment. The Judge who is to come actualizes his presence in the least of his brethren, realizing through the judgment what was done to them as something done to him. Without this orientation the least of the brethren lose their eschatological dignity as brethren of the universal judge. Without his anticipatory incarnation in them the universal Judge loses his present significance.—Jürgen Moltmann

THINKING GOD'S WAY. When I believe in my heart that Jesus Christ is Lord, my outlook toward everything will take on a new tone. That may be long in coming. It may happen gradually, but come it will. When I was a teenager, I heard a man say, "There are some things in the Bible that I wish were not in there." When the pressure of temptation is strong upon us and we want to do a particular thing, we too might wish certain commandments in the Bible were not there. But how foolish! To think like that is like thinking that the guardrails on a winding mountain road should be removed; that all stop signs and traffic signals should be removed. The lordship of Jesus Christ, however, changes such thinking. We begin to think God's way about everything. Our work, our recreation, our politics— everything will be affected. As someone put it a long time ago: "He will be Lord of all or he will not be Lord at all."— James W. Cox

Sermon Suggestions

THE IDEAL RULER. TEXT: Isa. 11:1–10. (1) His spirit, verses 2–5. (2) The conditions of his reign, verses 6–9. (3) His ultimate success, verse 10.

GOD'S TRUTHFULNESS. TEXT: Rom. 15:4–13. (1) Foreshadowed in the Scriptures of the Old Testament, verse 4. (2) Confirmed in Jesus Christ, verses 8–12. (3) Made the basis of hope for the future and of the joy and peace that spring from this hope, verse 13.

Worship Aids

CALL TO WORSHIP. "Endow the king with your justice, O God, the royal son with your righteousness. He will judge your people in righteousness, your afflicted ones with justice" (Ps. 72:1–2, NIV).

INVOCATION. Lord, let our lips sing of thee, our souls rejoice in thee, our wills follow thee, because we pause to pray and seek thy face and follow the Christ.—E. Lee Phillips

OFFERTORY SENTENCE. "Now the God of hope fill you with all joy and peace in believing, that ye may abound in hope, through the power of the Holy Ghost" (Rom. 15:13).

OFFERTORY PRAYER. We thank you, Father, for the joy and peace you give us in our Lord Jesus Christ and for the opportunity to share with others the hope that is ours. May these offerings increase the joy and peace that we experience here and bring hope to the hearts of those who have not yet received our Savior.

PRAYER.   Christ, be with me, Christ before me, Christ behind me, Christ in me, Christ beneath me, Christ above me, Christ on my right, Christ on my left, Christ where I lie, Christ where I sit, Christ where I arise, Christ in the heart of every one who thinks of me, Christ in the mouth of every one who speaks of me, Christ in every eye that sees me, Christ in every ear that hears me. Salvation is of the Lord; Salvation is of the Lord; Salvation is of the Christ; May your salvation, O Lord, be ever with us.—St. Patrick (389–461)

LECTIONARY MESSAGE

Topic: Get Ready
TEXT: Matt. 3:1–12
"Prepare ye in the wilderness a highway for our God." The summons was to those in Babylonian exile and called one out as the preparer. Roads were rough and hilly and crooked. Wheeled vehicles were not equipped with comfortable springs. When a monarch planned to visit a part of the kingdom messengers were sent ahead to prepare the way. John the Baptist was such a messenger. He came preaching.

I. *A Word from God.* After all those years when a prophet had not spoken, a Word came from God. There was a drought of spiritual strength, a dearth of the prophetic Word. Where had God been during those years? Why had he not spoken? Was there no one to listen?

John came preaching and baptizing. He is first described as the mere channel for God's Word, "the voice of crying in the wilderness." It is almost as if his own person had been hidden and only the Word shone brightly. Isaiah had spoken the Word, and now John was seized by the Word.

Yet John was a real person. He sounded like a prophet—"Repent ye, for God's reign is at hand." He dressed like a prophet—inexpensive clothing: camel's hair and a leather girdle. He ate like a prophet—inexpensive food: locusts and wild honey. He looked like a prophet, and he spoke a word from God.

II. *A warm response.* The people came to be baptized. They came confessing their sins. They came repenting, turning from their sins to God. They were getting ready to be subjects of the sovereign God. They all came—from Jerusalem, Judea, all the region around the Jordan. How gladly John must have received them. He responded by baptizing them in the Jordan—preparing them as a messenger might have prepared a rough road for the coming king.

III. *A harsh denunciation.* "Snakes in the grass!" What sort of preacher is that? "Sons of snakes" he called them. It was not enough that they should repent, these religious leaders, but they were to bring forth fruit worthy of repentance. He knew them. He sensed their deep need. In a parallel passage in Luke (3:10–14) he spelled out these fruits of repentance.

They were to trust neither in their history nor in their heritage. Their physical descent from Abraham did not make them his spiritual heirs. The tree that does not bear fruit is to be cut down and burned. You—bear fruit!

IV. *The Coming One.* His tone may have softened a bit. His message was one of mercy and God's love. The one for whom he was preparing the way was mightier than he: He was not even worthy to bear his sandals.

And the baptism—why his baptism was in water and the Coming One's was in the Holy Spirit. He baptized with respect to repentance, and the Coming One would baptize in fire.

Yet in the midst of judgment there was redemption: He will gather his wheat even as he rejects the chaff. The wheat would be treasured; the chaff would be burned.

John was preparing God's people. The Advent of God's Son lay just ahead. The next verse (v. 13) announces it: "Then cometh Jesus." Get ready!—J. Estill Jones

SUNDAY: DECEMBER THIRTEENTH

SERVICE OF WORSHIP

Sermon: Journey to Bethlehem
Texts: 1 Sam. 16:1–13 (Mic. 5:2, 4)

Pilgrims are arriving each day in the ancient village of Bethlehem. There, over nineteen hundred years ago, a baby, for whom the name *Jesus* had long been chosen, was born. In this holy place the little groups huddle together to listen to a pastor or a leader read the old, old story from Luke's Gospel. Frequently, you hear them singing a carol written by an American pastor, Phillips Brooks, who visited the village of Bethlehem and was so deeply moved that he went home that night and wrote "O Little Town of Bethlehem."

It is in chapter 16 of First Samuel in our journey of the Old Testament that we hear the word given to Samuel: "Go to Bethlehem." We remember a thousand years later the shepherds said to each other, "Let us go over to Bethlehem and see this thing which has happened, which the Lord has made known to us." Bethlehem was the setting of the Book of Ruth. Ruth was the mother of Obed, who was the father of Jesse, who was the father of David. Today, as we listen to the text of 1 Samuel 16, we focus on the theme, "Journey to Bethlehem."

I. *The journey begins with a question.*

(a) Notice that the story begins with God's action. The greatest single verse of the New Testament, which summarizes the real meaning of Christmas, is John 1:14. Christmas is God's action, not ours. At the heart of everything that surrounds Christmas there is the good news of a God who communicates. "The Lord said to Samuel, 'How long will you grieve over Saul, seeing I rejected him for being king over Israel?'" Underline with me that question: "How long will you grieve?" God never condemns our sorrow. We have, in fact, the unforgettable picture in the New Testament of Jesus standing beside the tomb of a friend weeping. God does raise questions about timing. He simply asks, "How long will you grieve

over that broken marriage? How long will you grieve over that loss of a loved one?" Prolonged grief can be a form of self-punishment.

(b) No doubt Samuel felt a tremendous sense of responsibility and grief over Saul. Saul was the tallest, the most handsome, certainly the brightest prospect in all of Israel to be the first king. Then after he was anointed by Samuel, it was such a short time before he began to rebel, before he began to put his own will and purposes first and to disobey God.

The journey to Bethlehem is the announcement of a new possibility. It is a word of hope about a new life. Bethlehem is the symbol of the surprising future that God now presents before us! This is the day for the journey to Bethlehem!

II. *The journey continues against the resistance of our fears.*

(a) It is very interesting to read that the journey to Bethlehem was a dangerous journey. A thousand years before King Herod had tried to trick the wise men into revealing the location and identity of the newborn king, Samuel was terrified of King Saul. Samuel asked, "How can I go (to Bethlehem)? If Saul hears it, he will kill me" (v. 2). What had fear done to Samuel? It had paralyzed him. He was afraid to move forward. The purposes of evil will be served well enough if we become afraid to the point that we no longer venture forward in commitment and faith, giving our time and talent and resources to the Lord's work.

(b) It is amazing to read in the very next verse that when Samuel arrived at Bethlehem, the elders came out to meet him with trembling and said, "Do you come peaceably?" Why was Bethlehem so frightened? They just assumed that Samuel was Saul's agent for destruction and death. They have wanted a king! Now they have a king. Why aren't they happy? Why is this a city that is caught in the grip of terror?

The journey to Bethlehem really confronts us with the reality and power of fear and anxiety and insecurity. Phillip Brooks wrote, "The hopes and fears of all the years are met in thee tonight." The question is, Which is going to win? Which will ultimately prevail in my life—the hopes or the fears?

III. *The journey moves forward in commitment and sacrifice.*

(a) Samuel told the trembling elders at Bethlehem that he had come peacefully—to sacrifice to the Lord. Then he gave the people a great challenge. He said, "I have come to sacrifice to the Lord; consecrate yourselves and come with me to the sacrifice" (v. 5). Jesse and his sons joined in the act of worship. The authentic journey to Bethlehem is not a sentimental diversion from real life. It is for the good of my own soul that I hear this wise prophet of the Lord as he says, "I have come to sacrifice to the Lord! Consecrate yourselves and come with me to the sacrifice."

(b) That is the word I hear today, "Consecrate yourselves." God doesn't say in the midst of pressures and problems, "Hide yourselves," or "Defend yourselves," or, "Protect yourselves." He says, "Consecrate yourselves." That is the only answer to fear. A young shepherd boy of Bethlehem found that to be true. "Yea, though I walk through the valley of the shadow of death, I will fear no evil, for thou art with me." That is what Christmas really means. "Thou art with me." That is the affirmation from Bethlehem. We are to understand that we are set apart from the world for a purpose that relates to God's ongoing purpose in creation. We believe that personal acts of consecration have tremendous importance. God wants us to discover personally the freedom and joy that surpasses the secular or worldly bondage that we find that comes through complete consecration to the Lord.

IV. *The journey concludes in joy and hope.*

(a) Samuel already knew that he did not have to choose the new king. He had been told that God had chosen the king from among the sons of Jesse. One by one his sons were paraded before Samuel. Finally Samuel told Jesse that not one of his seven sons had been chosen.

He then asked, "Are all your sons here?" Jesse hesitated and then finally said, "There remains yet the youngest, but behold, he is keeping the sheep." That was just a polite way of saying he was no candidate. Samuel insisted, "Go down and fetch him for we will not sit down until he comes here." They went out to get David. Samuel took one look at him and heard an inner confirmation from the Lord in his own heart, saying, "Arise, anoint him; for this is he." Samuel took the horn of oil, anointed him in the midst of his brothers; the Spirit of the Lord came mightily upon David from that day onward.

(b) "Now David, I want to tell you something. Your father, Jesse, didn't see the potential of your life. Your older brothers certainly didn't see the possibilities within you. They regarded you as a nuisance and a pest. Even Samuel didn't see the potential of your life. Only God could see the hidden greatness that was there. It was God who believed in you. It was his Spirit that came upon you that gave you the strength and courage of your life." There is no person here on this earth that knows your full potential. Only God knows the real possibilities of your life. The depth of this confidence is seen, not just in the word of Scripture, but in the cross of Jesus Christ. He believes you can be forgiven of your sins, can live a radically and totally new life of obedience and joy, and can join him in great commitment in the continuation of his creative purposes and plans. He says to this little shepherd, "Your kingdom is going to last forever." Hundreds of years later when the earthly kingdom of David was crumbling and it seemed that there was no hope for the future, the line of David looked like a great tree that had just been sawed off so that there was nothing left but an old stump. But the prophet Isaiah saw a little green shoot appearing from what looked like that lifeless stump (Isa. 11:1–3).

(c) There are going to be times when the future looks as hopeless and as bleak as that old stump. But God is a creative, victorious Lord who is bringing forth new life from the old stumps. He is a

God of new birth, of new possibilities. Do you know that God voted for your humanity and my humanity there in Bethlehem? He entered our human existence. God knows because he has been there, and he will never forget us or abandon us. That baby born in Bethlehem was the fulfillment of that promise that David's kingdom would not end. Through faith in Jesus you are part of that kingdom. I want you to get the feel of knowing your existence as a child of the King of kings and Lord of lords. I want you to feel the exhilaration and the joy and the hope that God wills to flow through your life as a means of blessing to other people—who are really hurting, desperately longing to know that their lives have some meaning and purpose. The journey to Bethlehem has set you free.

See yourself walking over an ancient road. Visualize yourself entering that little cave behind the Bethlehem inn where there are animals. Now see a father and a mother—and a little baby there in the manger. Consider for a moment the miracle of God's gift of himself in this child.

How could this be? In the little town of Bethlehem, in such a humble place in a tiny, helpless little baby—how could this be?—Joe Harding

Illustrations

HUMILITY AND UNDERSTANDING.   The humble, simple souls, who are little enough to see the bigness of God in the littleness of a Babe, are therefore the only ones who will ever understand the reason of His visitation. He came to this poor earth of ours to carry on an exchange; to say to us, as only the Good God could say: "You give me your humanity, and I will give you my Divinity; you give me your time, and I will give you my eternity; you give me your weary body, and I will give you Redemption; you give me your broken heart, and I will give you Love; you give me your nothingness, and I will give you My All."—Fulton J. Sheen

A LITTLE CHILD.   Bret Harte, in his classic short story "The Luck of Roaring Camp," told of the birth of a baby on the American frontier. The woman of the mining camp, Cherokee Sal, a disreputable woman at best, died in childbirth, leaving a healthy young baby boy to be raised by the now all-male camp. These rough, hard men made a decision that would reflect the changes that would come later. They considered hiring a woman nurse to care for the baby but eventually decided not to. Their logic was this: A nice nurse wouldn't come to their camp, and they didn't want any more women who weren't nice hanging around their baby. And so the work of regeneration began in Roaring Camp. The cabin assigned to little "Tommy Luck," as they called him, was kept scrupulously clean and whitewashed. The beautiful rosewood cradle that they purchased for the baby made the rest of the cabin look wretched, so they had to fix up the rest of the furniture in the room. Then a quarantine was imposed on those who wanted to hold little Tommy Luck, so they had to clean up for that privilege. Each act of cleanliness exposed that much more dirt and filth in the vicinity, so that new measures were taken to keep an ever-wider expanse of the camp clean. Since the baby needed rest, the camp became quieter and more dignified, less noisy and boisterous, no longer the "Roaring Camp" of the story's title. The story of the baby of Roaring Camp is the story of the regeneration of a people.

It's a Christmas story, for, you see, when the baby of Bethlehem was escorted into this earth by the legions of angels, he dramatically changed all of those with whom he came in contact.—Marion Aldridge

Sermon Suggestions

THE GLORIOUS DELIVERER.   TEXT: Isa. 35:1–10. (1) God's glory will appear to all creation, verses 1 and 2. (2) God's glory combines judgment and deliverance, verses 3 and 4. (3) God's glory reverses the ordinary state of affairs and course of events, verses 5–10.

THE JUDGE AT THE DOOR. TEXT: James 5:7–10. (1) Guarantees the wisdom of patient waiting for justice. (2) Demands an ethic of patience in dealing with our sometimes unfair and unjust neighbors.

Worship Aids

CALL TO WORSHIP. "Happy is he that hath the God of Jacob for his help, whose hope is in the Lord his God" (Ps. 146:5).

INVOCATION. As your pilgrim people, Lord, we sometimes feel lost in the wilderness of this world. You led your people once by a pillar of cloud through the day and a pillar of fire through the night, and they found their way. In this sacred hour lead us beside the refreshing streams of worship, and send us on our way again, revived, and rejoicing and guided by your word and spirit.—Henry Fields

OFFERTORY SENTENCE. "Be patient therefore, brethren, unto the coming of the Lord. Behold, the husbandman waiteth for the precious fruit of the earth, and hath long patience for it, until he receive the early and latter rain" (James 5:7).

OFFERTORY PRAYER. As sure as the coming of the harvest is your coming, O Lord. Your blessings are unfailing, though we have to wait for the greatest of them. Give us patience, and make us faithful as we wait. As we give our offerings we wait in faith for the harvest of our stewardship in lives made happy in hope.

PRAYER. Almighty God, most holy, in whom we live and dwell and have our being: We adore thee; we praise thee; we lift up our hearts in gratitude to thee. Wonderful have been thy gifts to us, and resplendent have been thy blessings.

Hear our intercessions for those who stand in great need, whatever it may be. So many walk through threadbare hours devoid of faith, unaware that at the heart of things thou dost wait, and hope lifts, and love lives: For them we intercede in prayer.

Draw near to those who cannot come close to others because they were once hurt. Be close to those who are hard on themselves because life is not perfect and neither are they. Help those who toil but do not earn enough to meet expenses. Chastise those who work to degrade others. Call back those who no longer call thy name in prayer but cannot forget that their parents did. Draw those who want to come closer to thee, who are catching a vision, who feel the tug of the Spirit and the call of Christ.

Comfort the bereaved to see beyond the grave to an empty tomb and a place prepared for those who love the Lord.

Allow us, O God, to minister to those who are in such great need. Robe us in Christ's humility to be thy servants, that we might shower on human need thy divine love, sharing again the poured-out life of Christ, in whom we make our prayer.—E. Lee Phillips

LECTIONARY MESSAGE

Topic: John and Jesus

TEXT: Matt. 11:2–11

Perhaps they were cousins, kinsmen at least. They were certainly friends. Surely they were fellow ministers. The ties that bound them together were both physical and spiritual. Both had been doing their work. John had preached and baptized in preparation for the ministry of Jesus. He continued to preach and baptize after Jesus began his ministry, a ministry of preaching and teaching and healing. It was John who first posed the following.

I. *A question of faith.* Do not ascribe the question to deep-seated doubts. It was a question of identity, of clarification. John was in prison because of his faithful and fearless witness. He might well have doubted God's goodness and faithfulness. Instead he doubted the meaning of his own message—but trusted God.

He had spoken of Jesus as working judgment on the sins of his people. Now it seemed that only John himself was experiencing punishment. And Jesus—John had heard reports of his gentleness and mercy. Hence his question—"Are you the Coming One?" That's all—just make it clear.

But there was more: "Or should we look for another?" It is as if John were saying, I know that God is coming through, but how and when and who. Malachi (3:1) had spoken of the messenger and the Lord. Now John asks, Who are you? If you are not the Coming One, then we'll look for another. God will work it out.

II. *A response in works.* The reply of Jesus was an object lesson: Go and tell John what you hear and see. God's grace was at work in healing the blind, the lame, the lepers, the deaf. Even the dead were being raised. What a message of good news! The prophetic word (Isa. 35:5–6; 61:1) was being fulfilled. All were hearing and seeing the gospel.

A word of commendation followed these messengers of John: Blessed is the person who does not stumble at my ministry. How did the disciples of John react? Was their faith strengthened?

III. *A personal commendation.* How about John? Did Jesus ridicule him? Of course not. Did Jesus send a message of sympathy? No. He turned to the crowds. They knew John. What did you expect when you first heard of John preaching and baptizing? You were certainly not disappointed. He was a fiery prophet. He was a great prophet. And at that moment John might have been enshrined in the prophet's hall of fame.

But Jesus returned to his hearers. God's measure of greatness does not verify only the popular and the powerful. For all of John's excellence—no greater prophet has been born—God is able to look as kindly and proudly on "the least of these." One who has subjected himself or herself to the reign of God has all the qualities of God's greatness.—J. Estill Jones

SUNDAY: DECEMBER TWENTIETH

SERVICE OF WORSHIP

Sermon: The Word Made Flesh
TEXT: John 1

Mark Twain, in *Life on the Mississippi*, wrote about a sunset he saw when he had just started steamboating. It was beautiful, captivating. It made him stop and stare until the sun slowly sank and the scene vanished. Later, he says, he could have looked at the sunset on the river, and he would have seen nothing but the marks of the sandbars and the snags.

Study anything closely enough and long enough, and it loses its mystery, its power over us to enchant and to mystify us. Does the same thing hold true for religion? Is it powerful and moving only so long as you keep some distance from it? Does familiarity with God bring boredom?

Think about the risk God took, then, in revealing himself as he did through Jesus. The message of John 1:6–18 is a story of two revealers, two revelations, and two audiences.

I. "There was a man sent from God whose name was John" (1:6–7). John was a very well known person in first-century Palestine. You can picture him in your mind, probably: a big, burly, hairy fellow with wild hair and an unkempt beard, dressed in animal skins, shouting at the top of his lungs that the world would end soon. These days, he'd be on "Oprah" and "Donahue" as sort of a curiosity; those days, people took him more seriously and began to reform their lives.

Why did he come? The text says that he came "as a witness, in order to bear witness concerning the light, so that everyone might believe through him." His sole purpose was to point people in Jesus, direction—to turn their heads toward the light, and that's what he did.

You see the point, don't you? A witness doesn't speak about himself but about something he's seen. John revealed Jesus to as many people as he could, even pointing his own students away from himself and toward Christ. He gives us a pattern for how a witness—a Christian witness—should operate, pointing away from ourselves to Christ.

II. John pointed to Christ, but the text says that Christ also was a revealer, pointing beyond himself (v. 14). How did he do it? By becoming flesh and living among us. "Dwelt" is really "tented," like the glory of God, the Shekinah, which went with the Israelites through the wilderness. In Christ, the true God was truly present; and in Christ, the true God was truly human, truly like us, truly visible. No one has ever seen God, but people saw Jesus and thus saw all of God that could be visible in a human form. In Jesus, God showed his character; he got up in our faces and hid nothing.

So what did he tell us? Jesus showed us the glory of God, full of grace and truth. There were many God-revealers in the first century; lots of folks claimed to show what God truly was like. One story John's readers may have known is the story of Prometheus. In his story, the gods are indifferent to people, vindictive, jealous, and opposed to anyone who would help us. Jesus, on the other hand, came with God's blessings to show us a God full of grace and truth. Grace is God's commitment to us; he chose us and will not abandon us. Truth is the steadfastness of God's character—he will not go back on his word. Jesus shows us, then, a God who is vitally interested and steadfastly committed to us. He will never abandon us.

III. The rest of the story is about the two audiences who received the revelations. "He came to his own" (v. 11), and we might think here of Jesus preaching to the Palestinians but being rejected and crucified by them. If we remember the first five verses, though, the whole world was created through Christ; everything has his mark, his brand on it, and his light shines throughout the whole world. "His own," then, is not just the Jews but the world.

He came to his own, but his own did not receive him. The word *receive* there is a word that means "to receive a tradi-

tion." Perhaps the writer meant that the world should have received Jesus as one receives a tradition: valuing it, passing it on to their children. But they did not. For most, the story fell on deaf ears, and the tradition died before it ever was passed on.

But there is another audience, which the author designates simply "us": "he dwelt among us . . . we beheld him . . . of the fulness of the Father we have all received." He came—we saw—we accepted his revelation of God, and there the story stops in the text, because the author does not say what we have done with it since we have received it.

If we're honest, all of us would say that some of the time, at least, we feel about our knowledge of God as Mark Twain felt about his knowledge of the Mississippi River. We know too much. We've been too close to the truth for too long, so that we've become immune to its majesty. Jesus is the revelation of the true nature of God, sure enough; but we've got a life to lead and bills to pay and sermons to preach, and we just can't stand around and admire the river all the time.

How do you break out of that boredom? You look at the river through someone else's eyes. One of the best ways to get excited about something is to try to explain it to someone else who's really interested; teaching a child how to use a hammer, or explaining your job to somebody who really wants to know about it. Maybe Twain did lose his romance with the river, but he surely has it back again as he describes that sunset over the mighty Mississippi. We need to be John and Jane the Baptists, pointing people in our world to the Light of the world, thereby bringing meaning and life to our own relationship with God and helping to bring others into the circle of us— those who have seen the face of God in Christ, full of grace and truth.—Richard Vinson

Illustrations

AS MANY SAW HIM.　　St. Augustine, walking out of prodigality and shame to write "The Holy City"; St. Francis of Assissi, finding him in poverty and in the song of birds; John Huss, praising his name above the crackling of the flames; John Calvin, discovering him with his legal mind and logic; Wesley, emerging from cold ceremonialism; Martin Luther, finding no peace in penance; Spurgeon, Moody, John Bunyan, Phillips Brooks, Schweitzer—all these have looked into his face and affirmed with Thomas, "My Lord and My God."—Joseph R. Sizoo

THE UNIQUENESS OF CHRIST.   Jesus is unique because he alone of all mankind of whom we have any external evidence or internal experience was truly normal. He was *the* son of man, *the* son of God, the Proper Man, who lived in a relation to God and his fellow men in which we are all called to live but fail to live. This doesn't mean that he had everything or was everything (you mention it, he had it), but that here was a man who uniquely embodied the relationship with God for which man was created. In this man, God was reflected, as John puts it, in a simile from family life, as in an only son of his father—he who had seen him had seen the Father. Or as Paul puts it, he was the image of the invisible God, the perfect reproduction, as opposed to the distorting mirror, of his fullness, his glory.— John A. T. Robinson

Sermon Suggestions

A BLESSED SIGN FROM GOD.   TEXT: Isa. 7:10–16. (1) The immediate fulfillment in the prophet's time. (2) The ultimate fulfillment in Jesus Christ.

THE GOSPEL OF GOD.   TEXT: Rom. 1:1–7. (1) It was promised beforehand. (2) It was fulfilled in Jesus Christ. (3) It was destined for faith and obedience among all nations.

Worship Aids

CALL TO WORSHIP.   "All the ends of the earth have seen the salvation of our God" (Ps. 98:3b).

INVOCATION.   O Lord, who comes in unexpected ways, breaking through ev-

ery barrier, be born again in our hearts this day, that we might humbly praise and magnify the newborn King.—E. Lee Phillips

OFFERTORY SENTENCE.   "The earth is the Lord's, and the fullness thereof; the world, and they that dwell therein" (Ps. 24:1).

OFFERTORY PRAYER.   O Lord, your holy Word and our own good sense tell us that all that we are and all that we call our own belong to you. Help us to find ways of living and sharing with others that will reflect this truth. May your blessing be upon this way to that end.

PRAYER.   O Lord God, high and lifted up, yet in mercy humbling thyself to enter these poor and often perverted hearts of ours, come, we pray thee, as Christ came, with healing and with peace. Thou shalt find us proud, for we have not yet learned what it means to be humble; thou shalt find us guarded and defensive, for we are weak within and full of fear; thou shalt find us irritable and not a little arrogant, for we are uncomfortably guilty and have not been willing to admit our frailty or our sin. While we dress and parade like little Herods and lordly Pilates we know we have deeper need of thee. Come again, thou meekest of all kings, and save us from ourselves, for ourselves, in God's name.—Samuel H. Miller

LECTIONARY MESSAGE

Topic: God with Us—Yet!
   TEXT: Matt. 1:18–25
   Central to the Christian faith is the truth symbolized by all our Christmas toys and tinsels: Emmanuel, God with us. That God came in the person of a baby who grew up to be an adult—a person in whom God lived . . . this is the Incarnation. Is it to be reserved for the pages of history? The familiar story begins with the following.
   I. *A shocking discovery.* Mary was pregnant. She and Joseph were engaged at least, but they had not come together as

husband and wife. Perhaps Joseph believed that the baby was of the Holy Spirit, but how would her family and friends react? How long could she conceal her condition? What was expected of her betrothed husband, under the circumstances?

II. *A compassionate husband.* The first adjective used to describe Joseph is *righteous.* Now a righteous man might have decided to go by the Law. According to the Law, Mary might have been stoned to death. Or a righteous man might have decided to be defensive and merciful. Joseph chose to be a compassionate righteous man. He decided to divorce her secretly.

Joseph was also a sensitive man. God was able to talk with him. Like an earlier Joseph, he heard God speaking in a dream. "Don't be afraid"—that was the message, suggesting something of the state in which Mary and Joseph found themselves. Against all of his fears, he continued his plan to marry Mary. God assured him that it was all right: "That which is conceived in her is of the Holy Spirit."

III. *A welcome promise.* A child was to be born—what a happy hope. That which had terrified both Mary and Joseph was described as a blessing from God. His name was to be *Jesus.* The meaning of the Hebrew equivalent, Joshua, is "the Lord is salvation." The baby was meant for salvation.

The prophetic word was clear. In another time God had spoken through a prophet—in a time of national danger. Your salvation will come through the birth of a baby, a daily occurrence. And before the baby is weaned you will see God's salvation. And the baby was to be named Emmanuel, which means "God with us."

IV. *An obedient servant.* And Joseph obeyed. He cherished Mary as his wife. The baby was born, and Joseph named the son *Jesus*—the Lord is salvation. And every time we hear the name we hear the word "the Lord is salvation."

In the prophet's day the baby was named *Emmanuel,* God with us. In the day of Jesus' birth the baby was named *Emmanuel,* God with us. Back in eternity there stood the principle—God with us. It is a timeless promise—God with us yet!—J. Estill Jones

SUNDAY: DECEMBER TWENTY-SEVENTH

SERVICE OF WORSHIP

Sermon: The Moving Edge of Time

TEXT: 1 Sam. 7:12

That was the key which for Samuel unlocked the meaning of history, which is the basic, prophetic function of all true religion. The scene is laid out on the hills of Canaan, three thousand years ago. Israel was in a desperate situation. Yet Samuel was sure—so the narrator wants us to believe—that what was going on in the teeth of all the odds was a good deal more than met the eye. So he took a stone and set it up and called its name Ebenezer, Stone of Help, for he said, "Hitherto hath the Lord helped us."

I. *Reading God into the past.* "Hitherto hath the Lord helped us." It's like an echo. You can fairly hear it carom off the years. What right has anybody to say it?

(a) There are times when reading anything into the past is hard enough; reading God into it sounds like saying to yourself, "Go to now, I shall put together this picture-puzzle as I choose. I shall make it spell out for me what I want it to spell out." Just deliberately to read God in is nonsense. But then, just deliberately to read him out is nonsense too! One of Camus' characters, after he had looked on at the agonizing death of a little child, said, "I will never love any scheme of things which permits that." Surely it should be of some significance that it isn't a scheme of things the Christian loves. That's why such words make such a strange sort of noise on Calvary. "And when they were come to the place, . . . they crucified him, and the malefactors, one on the right hand, and the other on the left." Now let's try it: "I will never love any scheme of things which permits that." Christianity concerns itself with a Person, not with a pattern.

Besides, what loving a Christian does, he doesn't do because he has scraped together all the evidence he could find in favor of it and chucked out the rest. You don't read God in on "the credibility of Joshua" or on "the edibility of Jonah." And when you read him out, you don't read him out simply on the evidence.

(b) Have you never realized that you can say nothing and do nothing so as to be recognized by anybody who doesn't know you? Neither can God. Samuel could talk about God's help because these wandering tribes long years before had felt that compelling hand on their lives as they struggled up out of their bondage in Egypt. And their past had become his past!

"Samuel took a stone and set it up." He didn't just decide one Tuesday to read things that way in order to make sense out of them. If we find ourselves unable at this point to look back and say "God," it will not be because we haven't heard enough or seen enough or read enough or studied enough or thought enough. It will be because for one reason or another we have never been anywhere in God's company, not anywhere that mattered.

(c) Now let somebody rush in and try to wipe out all that past which has so strangely become your past. Let him tell you it means nothing—it would all have been the same if there had been no God; not one iota, not one jot or tittle or scrap of it would have been different—so that even the language which speaks of God, he presses it upon you, has no factual content. We knew what he knows before he found it out! Faith is response to a person, it is not compulsion by a fact. And our language about persons has another kind of content entirely. It doesn't begin, and it doesn't issue, simply in facts; it both begins and issues in a relationship which interprets the facts. There

is a relationship with God which sees the very hiddenness of his purpose.

"Hitherto hath the Lord helped us." Samuel said that not merely to boast of a fleeting victory over the Philistines. He didn't do it because somebody had nudged him when he was discouraged and reminded him of how it was with Abraham and Isaac and Jacob. He said it to get into words something profounder than any of that, something deep inside of him, at the "very marrow of his being." And he wasn't just thinking about some part of the past that was pretty; he was thinking about all of it, the pretty and the ugly alike—perhaps on the actual spot where Israel had lost to the Philistines the ark of God's covenant, the shining symbol of his presence in the midst of her! You'll not keep a man like that from saying, "God," not even when all of life cries out against him. So he took a stone and set it up.

II. *Reading God into the future.*

(a) But now let's get on. "Hitherto hath the Lord helped us." The "hitherto" left out nothing, and it looked both ways. It read God into the past, and it read him into the future. I do not understand what grounds we have for thinking so comfortably of what lies ahead. Whoever learns as he looks back to say, "God," will gird up his loins when he turns around to look ahead. Because he's moving now in turbulent company, across the frontiers of a strange country where the only "authentic" being is being on the edge of peril and disaster. If only somebody could have persuaded folk that the only peace available is the no-peace where Christ is!

(b) Why is it that in prayers and sermons congregations are still being promised more than God ever has been able on his terms to manage? On a Saturday morning the *New York Times* announced that one visiting divine would preach the next day on "Getting What You Want," which indeed may very well be the risk you run! It isn't a question anymore of getting what we want: It's a question of being able to deal with what we get. And to get God may mean to get hurt—at home or around the corner on a picket line, in the struggle for some decent justice where the only justice there is, is indecent.

It's the kind of double talk that runs all through the Bible: Men can't live without God, and they can't live with him. These chapters of Samuel, I dare say, were not intended to be humorous, but they are. No sooner had the Philistines run off with the ark of the covenant than they wished they hadn't. Wherever they put it down, a plague broke out, and all the lords of the people said, "What shall we do with it?" "How on earth can we get rid of it?" So they sent it back to Israel where it came from; and even there it stirred up trouble.

(c) Holiness does that in our kind of world. When God quits having you on his hands and you start having him on yours, you'll see! He won't let you take much time to count your many blessings: He'll want to know right away what you plan to do with them. You'll not just smile as you read him into the future. We talk so glibly about security, and there is none, except in that peril which he is. "My peace I give unto you," says Jesus and proceeds to heighten the tension in every man's life between what he is and what he could be, though he may never yet have thought of being it. His elect are not the elite: They are the uneasy ones, with the crust broken!

All we may know of the God we have met in Christ is that in every bit of it, sunlight and shadow, he means intensely, and he means good. "Hitherto hath the Lord helped us." Can't we, too, get that into the record now and keep it there against the odds? Samuel did, with nothing to look forward to, you would say, but more of the same that lay behind him: still these scattered tribes in a land of promise where the promise never seemed to come true. A thousand years later Paul got it into the record again—for no reason except that he, too, was a man "scoured on the side facing eternity," thrown out of what God had done into what God was doing, with everything which through the centuries had made God God and kept him God breaking into the world through the sound of the hammers that nailed the hands and feet of Jesus to a cross.

"Hitherto"—with nothing but the face of Christ there in front of you! Can you manage? How on earth, in the strange radiance of all these haunted years, can we leave that "nothing but" standing to make fools and cowards of us? What more do we want than his face? There is a face which I never have to romanticize. It does things to me that hurt and heal.—Paul Scherer

Illustrations

THE SPIRITUAL JOURNEY.   The question of my future confronted me at age nine when I walked alone across the highway at my Uncle John's, near the very spot where my great-grandfather had been hit by an automobile and fatally injured. Suddenly death became very personal. As I walked across that road, the question impacted itself on me: What will happen to me when I die?

I could not deal with it. Though the weather was sultry, I shivered as the chill awareness of my own death paralyzed my mind. Often, after that marker day, the reality of my death confronted me. Because I did not then have a religious background, I had no notion of a loving God who would be with me even in death. My only way of coping with this disturbing reality was to put off thinking about it until I grew older; but try as I might, I could not escape the continuing awareness that I am dependent on another for my life and that one day life as I now know it will end.

The awareness of my life's finiteness has, I suspect, fueled the intensity with which I have asked, Why am I here? I did not ask this question seriously until the third decade of my life. Toward the end of that decade I began to fear that I might live my whole life for naught. What if I should come to the end of life, look back, and discover that I have spent my time to no avail? Since then I have continued to grapple earnestly with the meaning of my life.—Ben Campbell Johnson

HENCEFORTH. And when the other moments come, the moments of depression when you wonder whether there is any use in keeping on trying to be a Christian, and when the part of you that reflected something of the beauty of Jesus seems to die, remember that it can never die. As death could not hold him in Jerusalem, it cannot hold him now. His life in you is mightier than any tomb of discouragement or seeming defeat. And you, you in your own place and in what you might think your common duties, may dare repeat for your own soul the deathless words, "Henceforth I live, yet not I; but Christ liveth in me."—Walter Russell Bowie

Sermon Suggestions

THE LORD'S UNFAILING LOVE.   TEXT: Isa. 63:7–9, REB. (1) He declared us to be his people. (2) He comes in person to deliver us.

THE PIONEER OF OUR SALVATION—JESUS CHRIST.   TEXT: Heb. 2:10–18. (1) He reached his perfection, his maturity, through suffering. (2) Yet he was tempted to go his own way and escape the cross. (3) Therefore, he is able to help those who are tempted to renounce their faith and their Lord in times of stress and persecution.

Worship Aids

CALL TO WORSHIP.   "Praise the Lord! With all my heart I will thank the Lord in the assembly of his people" (Ps. 111:1, TEV).

INVOCATION.   Father as your beloved Son stands at the door knocking and awaiting our summons to enter, help us to fling wide the doors of our individual lives so that his presence may bind us all together in ties of love, fellowship, and ultimate purpose. Break through the noise of our hurried world and bring us to stillness that in the silence we may hear and heed that still small voice of God. In these sacred moments, bathe us in your peace, gird us with your courage, sustain

us by your power, and call us to your purpose as we join disciples through the ages worshiping and praying: [the Lord's Prayer].—Henry Fields

OFFERTORY SENTENCE.   "The Lord does not let us forget his wonderful actions; he is kind and merciful" (Ps. 111:4).

OFFERTORY PRAYER.   Increase all in us that honors thee, O Lord, and multiply the usefulness of this offering beyond our limitations, because thy Spirit is at work and thy Word will not return void, and we proclaim Jesus as Lord.

PRAYER.   O God, I know not what a day may bring forth. In perfect confidence I would place my hand in thine and follow thee this day, whether thou leadest me to joy or sorrow, pleasure or pain, success or failure. I know not what is good for me. Thou knowest. My deepest desire is to love what thou lovest and will what thou willest. Hear my prayer for Jesus Christ my Redeemer's sake.—Samuel McComb

LECTIONARY MESSAGE

Topic: The Hand of Providence

TEXT: Matt. 2:13–15, 19–23

Following the visit of the wise men with their expensive gifts and guiding star, they responded to a dream and went back home by another route. Then Joseph himself had another dream. God was guiding all along. God was concerned not only with the beginning of the child's life but the continuation of life. Providence is not a once-for-always experience.

I. *God guides.* This is the testimony of many Christians. We may trust his guidance because he knows what lies ahead. Past, present, and future are one with him who dwells in eternity.

He loves. This is our experience with God. He desires the best for us. His nature is love. His actions reveal love. Almost any young family—father, mother, and baby—provokes love. How much more God's love. How much more this family.

But to Egypt? Surely there were more attractive places to go. Egypt had been the site of slavery, and God had redeemed his people out of Egypt. And how could anyone hate or fear a child enough to threaten its life?

II. *God's people follow.* Joseph was a believer in dreams. He had heard God speak on a previous occasion. Now he listened again. God's people hear his voice. There are many voices that command attention, but Joseph singled out God's voice.

God's people believe. As incredible as it might have seemed Joseph believed God was leading to Egypt. What might have happened if Joseph had not believed?

God's people obey. Obedience is closely related to faith. Indeed, it is doubtful if faith is ever expressed in disobedience. Faith is active not passive.

And the prophet was called to testify (Hos. 11:1).

III. *God leads through suffering.* Providence does not guarantee comfort. God does not always lead around suffering.

He is with his people in suffering. There was a light at the end of the tunnel for Joseph and his family.

The cruelty of Herod was widely known and feared. He had murdered his own sons and his beloved wife. He became angry at the wise men and took his spite out on the children of Bethlehem. It was a terrible act of vengeance. The Herods of this world are a part of reality.

Herod died. This should have been the end of danger. Joseph obeyed the voice of God. He followed the leadership of Providence through suffering.

IV. *God works through human good sense.* Had Joseph been less than sensible he would have returned to the region of Jesus' birth. He knew that Archelaus ruled instead of his father, Herod. He took his family into Galilee, into Nazareth.

And the prophet was called to testify. We do not know the source of that prophecy, but the hand of Providence is clear. Joseph and Mary and Jesus followed. Do not despise common sense where Providence is concerned!—J. Estill Jones

SECTION III.
Messages for Communion Services

SERMON SUGGESTIONS

Topic: God's Vineyard

TEXT: Matt. 21:33–43

I. I have a friend who says that if you like the parables of Jesus then you haven't heard them. What he is suggesting is that Jesus tells us the parables to reveal to us the nature and character of God, and if we don't find the stories disturbing, perplexing, somewhat strange, then we haven't heard them correctly. The parables of Jesus so often begin, "The kingdom of God is like. . . ," and that suggests that where God is, these different qualities apply that are different from the way you and I normally do things. Jesus is revealing to us the mystery and power of God who is other than we are. His thoughts are not our thoughts. His ways are not our ways. So the parables will only reveal to us something about God when they strike us as strange.

If that is the case, then we have no problem with this parable about the vineyard and the dishonest tenants. When you hear this story, there is in most of us an immediate response of how stupid of the owner. Where have you or I ever met an owner who has had that much trouble trying to collect his just obligations who would send in his own son or go himself to try to collect the rent after all that trouble. In the kingdoms of this world, if the prince who owns the land had not received his fair share, if his agents had been beaten and abused, the immediate

response would be to call in the law. Send the sheriff and his deputies. Get a warrant and send in the police. Now there may be a few cases where if you haven't been paid, if the rent check had not come in the mail, after a couple of letters, we might send someone in the family around personally to find out what is the problem. But if our servants have been sent two or three times, and one is beaten, one dragged out of town tarred and feathered, and the third killed, we certainly would not send our own flesh and blood in to get the rent. We would turn to the law.

P. D. James has a scene in one of her mystery novels, *Unnatural Causes*, where her hero Adam Dalgliesh is talking with a bar owner named Luker, and Luker says that both he and Adam had the disadvantage of being raised in minister's homes. "The Superintendent of Police and I," says Luker to an employee, "have a common misfortune. We both had a parson for dad. It's an unhappy start for a boy. If their fathers are sincere, you despise them as a fool; if they're not sincere you write them off as a hypocrite. Either way, they can't win." And when we hear this parable, I suggest that we all find ourselves in the same boat. If Jesus says God sends his Son into that kind of situation and is sincere, God's a fool. If God is pulling some kind of trick, like sending his Son so God has the right to punish them all the more, then he's a hypocrite. This story is really strange, so that if strangeness is necessary to be hearing this story correctly, we are off to a good start.

II. There is always our expectation that behind the goodness and graciousness of God there is the law. We continue to believe that somewhere the kindness, the love, and the compassion, the redemptive activities of God will run out and when we get to the end of gentleness, to the end of mercy, to the end of meekness, then God will bring in the legions of angels, the heavenly missiles, the secret weapons of destruction, the divinely engineered torture chambers, and God will clean house. He will run off those tenants who will not pay. He will bring in good guys who will cooperate. For most of us think that there are just so many second chances, and then you get it in the neck.

That is what the people were convinced would happen at the end of this story, when Jesus asks them what they would expect to happen after the death of the son. You and I would have brought in the police after the servant got killed, and maybe we think Jesus says that God goes the next step, gives them one more chance, and sends his Son, and we shake our heads at his foolishness. When the Son gets killed, we are sure that the vineyard will be taken away from those lawless tenants and given to others.

But Jesus meant what he said about the rejected stone being the foundation stone for a new community. What I think Jesus was saying is that this love of God that made him choose to send his Son when we would have called in the police is still the only way he will seek us. There is no end to his loving kindness. There is no hammer hidden behind the wooing handkerchief of love. W. H. Auden, in "Friday's Child," understands that we keep thinking there will be force in the last resort to correct those who are too bumptious to repent, and yet Jesus suggests that this wooing love of a broken God will continue to be the way God deals with his wayward tenants. It is this rejected and slain Son who will be the very foundation and center of the new community of God's people.

III. For in many ways you and I are those wayward tenants. We have been ones blessed with the fully operational vineyard. We have been blessed by creation and orderliness. We are ones who have been left to care for and benefit from the vineyard, and yet we have not loved justice, done mercy, or walked humbly with God. This is how we have dealt with God who has entrusted his creation to our care, who has shown his patience with us, who has given us freedom and responsibility, who has sent his servants to teach us and show us a new kingdom. We have hushed and abused, arrested and ridiculed the servants of God.

And yet it is still by this slain God that God continues to woo us back. It is still by the story of this merciful God who has come in flesh and blood to seek us once more, to call us home; it is still by this celebration of communion that we are being sought, we are being invited into this new community of mercy and love. At a great number of points in the story, we would have thrown in the towel. We would have said, "Enough of Mr. Nice Guy, now we will play hard ball." We could have understood that story. But this story and this sacrament of communion says that God has no other means, God will never come to the end of his love, God will not stop being gracious. He sent his Son to bring the lawless tenants back—there is no end to the second chances he will provide for us. In celebration of this sacrament of communion we are affirming that in the dying Christ we hear once again the whispering voice of God saying, "Come home, ye who are weary, come home. Softly and tenderly Jesus is calling, 'O sinner, come home.'" The kingdom of God, God's vineyard, is still being offered to those who will be faithful servants of the Son who was slain.—Rick Brand

Communion Meditation: Pentecost— Unity in Diversity

In his account of that first Pentecost, Luke lifts up two things: first, the amazing *diversity*—that was a motley congregation the Apostle Peter addressed. Luke takes great pains in noting some nineteen or twenty different peoples or nationalities: Parthians, Medes, Elamites, Mesopotamians, and on and on. The second feature the author notes is the strange *unity* that these diverse peoples experienced: They exclaimed in amazement, even in perplexity, "*We hear* them telling in our own tongues the mighty works of God."

The same elements are present in our celebration of Pentecost: What diversity among *us*! How many different nationalities, how varied our religious backgrounds—to say nothing of our educational and cultural diversities—how different the roads we have traveled. What strange diversity, but what glorious unity created by God's own Spirit—holy in wholeness, fullness, completeness.

Here the one bread, the one cup translates in language in which we can all understand the mighty deeds of God for our salvation, and these meager elements mediate to us the grace of our Lord Jesus Christ—the fullness of the Father's love according to our diverse needs.

Let us pray in their consecration: O God, may the strange images that Luke used in describing that first Pentecost excite in us a sense of mystery and wonder that we may be open in imagination to receive the fullness of your coming symbolized in the bread and the cup. These are gifts you have given for our physical sustenance that we return to you now that you may consecrate them that they may become—the spiritual bread and drink—the means of grace that Christ intended when he said: "Do this in remembrance of me." In his name we pray.

Prayer of thanksgiving: O Father, we thank you for this occasion that reminds us of the good news that diversity is not to be eradicated by man's machinations in attempting uniformity but is to be celebrated in all of its richness as the *gift* of your creative Spirit. You have come in the fullness of your grace filling up our emptiness; you have come in the wholeness of your Spirit healing our brokenness; you have come in your persevering love overcoming our every estrangement. To all of us in all of our uniqueness you are present as we have touched your broken body and your shed blood so appropriately symbolized in the sacrament. Thank you, God.—John Thompson

Communion Meditation: Holy Ground

Surely goodness and mercy shall follow me all the days of my life: And I will dwell in the house of the Lord forever.

The concluding affirmation of the beloved Twenty-third Psalm, "I will dwell in the house of the Lord forever," is to take off one's shoes and approach all of life barefoot—in awe and with reverence. It is not that the believer set up residence in the Temple. But having worshiped the living God in the sanctuary, he is convinced of his livingness in all of life—there is no place where God is not; wherever he is, God is. Every day is the Lord's Day and every place is the Lord's house, "the dwelling place of the Most High."

To commune at this table with the Creator of the worlds and all that in them is, the Father of our Lord Jesus Christ and our Father, is to discover that there is no longer any sacred or secular as we try to divide life, but all of life is holy unto the Lord. There is nothing that is not touched by his grace. Every bit of bread, every cup is a means of grace. To so believe and live is to dwell in the house of the Lord forever. With these meanings let us pray in consecration.

—John Thompson

Topic: The Impossible Possibility

TEXT: Luke 16:19–31

Sometimes it is so tempting to take a teaching of Jesus, roll it up in self-righteous, moral indignation, and begin beating up on those we are sure Jesus was condemning. For instance, this morning's parable. On the surface this parable appears to give every pastor a golden opportunity to take a shot at the filthy rich. The parable also provides a perfect soap box for the pastor who wishes to shake a finger of fault at the captive members of the congregation. Why not use this story to warn people about the wickedness of wealth? After all, it's the high-rollers Jesus is taking to task, isn't it?

Well, yes and no! I've no doubt Jesus saw the potential danger in our desire to live high off the hog. But that's not the issue in this parable. Perhaps because *wealth* is a relative term. Here's what I mean. When two homeless people are hungry, and only one has a loaf of bread, the one without will surely think her counterpart "rich." And I know that to us there's a recognizable difference between one worth hundreds of millions and any one here. Still, I'm no longer sure that God sees things that way. Because this parable told by Jesus could apply to anyone! How?

By virtue of one simple fact. Every human being I've ever met is capable of being or becoming indifferent to the needs of others. That's right. This parable is about indifference. And when it comes to indifference, you needn't be a fat cat to be guilty as charged. In fact, I'd go so far as to say that "indifference" is the "common cold" of bad attitudes! Sooner or later, under some foreseeable circumstance, we all come down with a severe case of indifference. And once we find ourselves sniffling with selfishness, the sickness can be hard to shake! Indifference—that's the real culprit!

Just take a moment and consider the characters in the parable. Here's this guy who wears Brooks Brothers suits and silk underwear. His chateau is stocked with the best imported wines, and he dines every day, at five, on the finest French cooking. He has an outstanding reputation at the local country club, and his son attends the finest rabbinic school in all Israel. Just the kind of person we would admire. No doubt, if he and his family moved into our community, we'd be falling all over ourselves to get them to join our congregation!

And then, of course, there's that other character. You know the kind. He spends most of his time in the gutter only because he has no home. But hey, who's fault is that? He's probably a good-for-nothing lazy bum. His clothing smells; his teeth are green. And the last time he saw the inside of a doctor's office, he was in diapers. So you can just imagine the condition of his health. Well, perhaps it's best not to imagine. You might get sick! Around five in the evening you'll find this guy rummaging through the local dumpsters for his "lean cuisine." If he should cross our path, we'll simply turn a cold shoulder. And who would dare suggest that this street-slime become a member of our congregation.

Now, of course, that was exactly the attitude of the rich man in the parable! He could not have cared less that this poor beggar needed some attention. Maybe this rich fellow was a pretty decent neighbor to his neighbors. I've no doubt he was a real good citizen who paid his taxes on time, attended the local PTA, and contributed his fair share to the "Fraternal Order of Temple Guards." The problem is he was completely indifferent to the needy soul lying at his very doorstep.

Well, maybe you want to give this guy the benefit of the doubt. After all, isn't it at least possible that he didn't even know the bleeding beggar was there? It sure would be convenient for us if that were true. At least maybe then we too could muster up an excuse for ignoring the obvious! But I'm sorry to inform you that's not possible. To be honest with you, the truth is pretty painful. Not only did the rich fellow know the starveling was there, he knew the wretch by name! That's right. I'm telling you that the banker and the beggar were buddy-buddy on a first name basis! How do we know that?

Do you recall the scene from hell, where the tables were turned, and the banker was now the beggar? Do you remember what he said? He was playing out his cards with "Father Abraham" — hoping that no one could possibly be as indifferent to human suffering as he had been. And in the midst of his misery he cried out, "Please send Lazarus to comfort me!" Whoops! The cat was out of the bag! Forget all his good deeds through the local Lion's Club. This guy had a neighbor in need perched on his doorstep, and yet he chose to remain hopelessly out of touch with a helpless soul he knew by name. Now that's sad!

But not nearly as sad as the fact that even though this parable has been in circulation for well over two thousand years, little seems to have changed—even with the church! Just look at us. The number of homeless persons in this country alone is simply appalling. Not to mention the countless number of children who go to bed each evening, without so much as a lick and a promise. Companies leave areas in which workers have been faithful for years, and no one seems to care. And while the motto of our contemporary society appears to be "Fend for Yourselves," judging by the response of the Christian church to such needs, you might think her to be blind as a bat!

And yet the problem of "indifference" is more than just another "social issue." It would appear that, whether rich or poor, people are becoming increasingly more insensitive to each other. And the church is no exception to the rule! Even in this community where compassion is to be the order of the day you'll discover people facing hardship, heartache, and personal problems without so much as a wink and a nod from another. It might not hurt us to begin asking ourselves questions like these: Whose troubles have I shared? Whose heartaches have I eased? Whose loneliness have I lifted?

Then again, maybe we suffer from the same infection plaguing the rich fellow in the parable. It's the unspoken conviction that this life is the whole ball of wax. So we might as well grab for the gusto! Each day is a fleeting moment filled with opportunities to increase our own personal pleasures. Besides, if we get all hung-up helping some unfortunate soul, we're liable to end up making him dependent on us. And you know what happens when you open that can of worms. Help one beggar, and before you can drop a dime, the whole clan will be pounding down your door looking for some handout! Perhaps if we ignore them they'll simply go away—or die. Regardless, at least when we die we won't have to fret about all this stuff any more, right?

Wrong! That's the mistake made by the rich fellow. Jesus made it quite clear where indifference will land us. He placed the rich rogue in hell! Now before we get our hackles up, let me tell you that Jesus isn't giving us an agenda for getting to heaven and escaping hell. He is, however, telling us in no uncertain terms that this life we live each day has eternal significance. And while we might think that our indifference is weaving us a net of protection from those in need, in the end we could find that we have forged our own ball and chain!

Jesus had three great words—the last, the least, and the lost. He said, "The last shall be first, the least shall be greatest, and the lost shall be found!" The descendants of Lazarus are all around us every day. We must choose. We can step over them or help them take their next step. We can reach over them or reach out to them. We can give them the back of our hand, or we can hand them back their lives. With the strength Christ gives, we can take their pain, problems, and perplexities to heart. Or we can become indifferent. But if we fail to care in this life, perhaps in God's will and wisdom the tables will one day turn—and then who will we turn to?

You see, living well and fostering indifference may be the world's idea of the best revenge and the world's criterion for distinguishing the winners from the losers. But in the mystery of Christ's kingdom that's not the way things are to be done. Here we win by losing and become first by being last. In this kingdom, indifference is deadly because we worship and serve a Lord who was anything but indifferent to our loathsome wounds and wretched condition. In fact, he stepped into the gutter and lifted us to our feet. He made his palace our home. And he put his riches in our pockets.—Albert J. D. Walsh

ILLUSTRATIONS

BY ROBERT C. SHANNON

GOD'S LOVE IS REAL! In December 1989, *Newsweek* magazine carried a story about a little-known mental illness called erotomania. Erotomania describes a condition in which the patient imagines love affairs that never happened. Often there is nothing erotic in erotomania but rather an idealized romantic love that the patient believes to exist even though in actual fact it does not. The title of the article was "The Delusions of Love." Communion exists to reassure us that the love of God for us is no delusion. The cross was a harsh reality and the ultimate expression of God's love. That cross and that love are displayed before us in the bread and in the cup.

WORLD'S BEST MEMORIAL.   In June 1885, the French steamship *Isere* from Rouen, France, docked at New York harbor. The principal cargo was 210 enormous crates. It took sixteen months to put together the parts inside those crates. When it was finished, a 225-ton statue stood overlooking New York harbor: the Statue of Liberty. Committees in 180 French towns and cities raised the money for that memorial to Franco-American friendship and to freedom. It was a lot of effort, but people have always believed that memorials were important. They built the Sphinx three thousand years before Christ. The memorial of the Lord's Supper seems small compared to the Sphinx or the Statue of Liberty. In fact, simple and plain though it is, the Lord's Supper is the world's greatest memorial, the world's best memorial. It is a memorial to freedom, to love, to grace, to forgiveness. And the cost was borne by one man alone—a penniless carpenter from Nazareth.

A SPIRITUAL FEAST.   Ivan the Terrible once gave a feast that lasted for three entire days! Such extravagances were not uncommon among the rich and powerful in those days. By comparison, our communion table with only a bit of bread and wine hardly seems a feast at all. And its duration is measured in minutes, not in hours or days. But surely those are the wrong measuring sticks. The importance of communion is measured by its depth not its length. It is a feast, not for the body, but for the mind and for the soul.

QUESTION OR STATEMENT.   At the first communion on the night before the crucifixion, Jesus spoke of his betrayal. Those at the table all asked the same question: "Lord, is it I?" Whenever we come to the Lord's table we always say those same words—but in a different order and not as a question but as a statement. We say, "Lord, it *is* I!"

SECTION IV.
Messages for Funeral Services

SERMON SUGGESTIONS

Topic: The Way Home
TEXT: John 14:1–14

Modern, sophisticated people think little (if at all) of heaven. It is, for them, a throwback to more superstitious days of parents and grandparents who may have had few of this world's goods and, therefore, were highly expectant of having the situation reversed in the heavenly realm. And we might argue on their behalf that there has been in evangelical Christianity too great an emphasis on "pie in the sky bye and bye" theology. It has tended to underrate the importance of living in these days.

On the other hand, however, our sophisticated friends do not have much to offer as an acceptable alternative. What do you have without any meaningful existence beyond earth's days? A very fatalistic approach to life, I think. "Eat, drink, and be merry, for tomorrow we die" is about the only philosophy one could propose.

Our text comes from the words of Jesus to his disciples in preparation for his departure from them. He describes not only what he will do but also what his followers might expect. In describing life beyond death, he draws on one of the noblest images of relationship, security, and joy we know—the home. Jesus speaks of his "Father's house." For the disciples, this will be their future home. In an hour when they are distraught and unsure, our Lord gives them assurance of the reality of *home*.

Not ignoring the problems of a too materialistic idea of heaven, one might in all sincerity seek to know about this home of which Jesus spoke and how to find the way to it.

I. Of first importance is identifying a *home worth finding*. Unfortunately, not every home is one that we would want to find. We know of homes that if heaven were to be an eternity of them, we would beg pardon and kindly excuse ourselves from the premises. How tragic that for some people home is a place to escape from rather than run to. The increased number of runaway teens points a condemning finger at much home life. They have not found home worth their staying. If the Father's house is synonymous with a tyrant parental figure who knows only how to issue orders and expects everyone to "toe the mark," that is not likely a home worth finding.

Then, to respond to the sophisticated friends mentioned a moment ago who are turned off by the material reward idea of heaven, we might remind them that much in our society knows only this way of putting value on life. The very one who might question such a view of heaven is probably engaged in the same quest, only for this life instead of the one to come. In either case, whether on earth or in heaven, materialism is not equal to successful life. The word Jesus used to describe his Father's house is translated in the King James Version as "mansions."

233

This is unfortunate, for it contributes to the idea of heaven being a place of elegant homes, gold, and leisure. There seems to be a significant number of cases documenting persons who have had these things in this life and still came up wanting, thereby proving they were hardly worth finding.

And by the way, what a boring idea of heaven! Who wants only to sit in a mansion in a state of leisure. Those workaholics among us might say quickly, "I think I could go for that." But could you really? A home worth finding would have to be more.

Indeed, the home Jesus described is more, much more! To begin with, it is identified as *prepared*. There is no note of haphazard, slipshod, anything-will-do in the home his followers are called to. This is something Jesus has taken vital interest in. One always senses the welcome involved in adequate preparation. It says, "We really want you here." Everything is to be well suited, appropriate, all needs cared for. Preparation requires personal attention to detail. This responsibility our Lord takes upon himself: "I go to prepare . . ."

In addition to the emphasis on preparation is the promise of "a place" for each one. The familiar translation "mansions" is better rendered "dwelling places" ("rooms," RSV). In other words, the disciples, each of them, had a place; they *belonged*. How important to the idea of home is a sense of belonging. Robert Frost states the truth well: "Home is the place where, when you have to go there, they have to take you in" ("The Death of the Hired Man"). A home worth finding is a place where you really belong, where you are made to feel at home. The Father's house is such a home.

Furthermore, there is an emphasis on relationships in this heavenly home. Jesus prepares such a home, he says, "that where I am you may be also." This home is in the Father's house where one is vitally related to him. God is not pictured as some benevolent landlord who allows us the use of his house with little or no personal contact, much like Daddy Warbucks initially related to Little Orphan Annie. Rather, he is lovingly involved in relationship with us, more like Daddy Warbucks giving his heart to Annie. What an overpowering thought, that God wants to relate to each of us. A home worth finding is one of loving relationships.

One additional characteristic of a home worth finding may be hinted at in Jesus' reference to "greater works." A home worth finding is one that provides opportunity for growth. This is just the opposite of the view of luxuriant leisure presented by some. Methodist missionary E. Stanley Jones expressed every intention of growing and finding work to do in heaven. He asks, "Will there be tasks in heaven? If not, how could we grow . . . ? Give me twenty-four hours for rest in heaven, and I'll ask for an assignment . . ." (*Growing Spiritually*, p. 364). Heaven is not a celestial retirement home but an unrestricted laboratory of personal growth.

Such a home as Jesus has prepared is the kind of place we surely want to find. But how to find it? The preparer has provided that as well.

II. Not only is heaven a home worth finding, there is a *way worth following* to get there. Such a noble home ought to have a worthy means of arrival. Just as we would not expect a cow path to take us to the White House, we cannot expect a low road to a high life.

There have been those who attempted various shortcuts to find access to a happy and easy existence. These, without exception, fail. There are always the briars, potholes, fallen bridges, and unknown dangers on these short cuts. Tranquility ultimately cannot be found in what are known as recreational drugs. Nor can it be found through material gain. Home is not made with easy and noncommittal relationships. All these shortcuts to a supposed "heaven" are fraught with tragedies and lead ultimately, if not literally, to a dead end.

For a home with God where we can enjoy his fellowship, love, and a secure place of belonging, Jesus made the way. He said, "I go to prepare a place for you." But, oh, how he went! The way home is the way of the cross. Even as he was speaking, Jesus was aware of his destiny. He would be arrested on false charges, convicted by lying witnesses, and crucified on a Roman cross between two thieves.

Since heaven represents the eternal presence of God, we need to be fitted for such a place. Our sin makes us unfit. There is no deodorant bar effective enough to wash off the stench of sin. Cleansing must be done by a greater cleansing agent. Jesus going the *via dolorosa*, the way of the cross, has made it possible for us to go to the Father through him. He cleanses us of all unrighteousness and presents us holy and altogether righteous before God.

In response to Thomas's question, "How can we know the way?" Jesus answers, "I am the way and the truth and the life." God's only Son has come the distance from the presence of God to presence with humankind that he might become the representation of all truth and real life before us. And then through the offering of his life, he has made the way for us to join him in the presence of God.

Furthermore, Jesus says, "No one comes to the Father but by me." Interpretations of this have been many. Some of the subtleties of meaning will probably be debated until the Lord returns. Nevertheless, we must take what he said very seriously. Not only is Jesus the way worth following, he presents the only way by which we might come to the "Father's house."

The way home worth following is Jesus Christ, and we join ourselves to that way by faith. Note the emphasis on faith: "Believe in God, believe also in me"; "He who has seen me has seen the Father"; "Do you not believe that I am in the Father and the Father in me?" "He who believes in me will also do the works that I do"; "Whatever you ask in my name, I will do it, that the Father may be glorified in the Son." Jesus has provided the way; he asks us to take his hand in faith and follow him all the way home.—C. Kenny Cooper

Topic: Into Thy Hands
Texts: Luke 23:44–46; Phil. 1:6

As I reflected on this message, I thought about how many times we have joined to mark the death of one of our loved ones and how much we have talked about death and life. We have thought about the meaning of life, the meaning of death, the Resurrection, and grace; we have celebrated lives, mourned our own losses, sung our thanksgiving, recited our hopes, prayed our needs, cried our pains, and laughed our courage.

What shall we say this time? What can we do, except tell again the old, old story that we have loved so well?

Listen to Jesus' last words in life, as told by Luke. These words, "Into thy hands I commit my spirit," were from a bedtime prayer little Jewish children learned as soon as they could form the words.

When Jesus made this great prayer of faith his life had hit its roughest point. He was nailed to the cross, the sky was dark, his friends were gone, his body was broken, and he was dying by degrees. He was fully conscious and aware of death stealing upon him.

We may learn from him how to go on in faith when our lives feel as if they are being crushed. The more I see of life the more I realize that no one has it easy in life, and faith does not come easy either. Faith is hammered out on the anvil of crisis; it is wrung out of the struggles of life; it is a courageous act of the will; and it is the gift of God working in us to bring faith to life.

You know how faith can sustain you. I know many of your stories. Some of you have had dreams in life that never came true. Some of you have problems with your health; some have been acquainted with grief before it was time.

By the time we reach adulthood we don't need anyone to tell us that life doesn't go as we plan it. Being Christian doesn't prevent things going wrong. So where does it leave us? It leaves us with faith in God. Faith that our lives have not been in vain, faith that we have touched others, faith that one day we will find complete fulfillment, faith that our bodies will not wear out again, that loved ones will welcome us one day, that God is Lord over death and all the forces that have harmed us.

We can trust our loved ones to God. That is what the example of Jesus tells us today. We can trust the love of God, the mercy and compassion of God, and the power of God, in the same way Jesus trusted.

God's assurance and power allow us to live out the journey of our lives without worrying about the conclusion. More than that, we can live boldly and fearlessly, not slinking back from dangers or trials, but meeting life head-on, because the last chapter of our lives has been written already.

Paul gave words to this faith when he said, "What God has begun in us, God will complete." He was in prison, no doubt reflecting on the uncertainty of the future and feeling his weakness and helplessness. But he kept coming back to faith that God does not start a good work without finishing it. What God began in Jesus, God finished with the glorious Resurrection, no matter the pain and darkness in between.

I spoke with a woman recently who wondered if her faith was strong enough to carry her through death, and I assured her that her faith did not have to be that strong, because the strength was in God, and God's power would carry her through. It is like the hymn has it, "Nothing in my hand I bring, simply to the cross I cling."

After all, faith in God is all we have, isn't it? The question is, is it enough? The witness of Jesus on the cross and Paul in the prison is that, yes, it is enough. That is how Horatio Spafford, after the drowning of his four daughters in a shipwreck at sea, could write the great hymn "It Is Well With My Soul," which says, "Whatever my lot, Thou has taught me to say, 'It is well, it is well with my soul.' "
—Stuart G. Collier

Topic: We Do Not Lose Heart

Text: 2 Cor. 4:16–18

Burying someone we love is not a new experience for most of us. The pain of heart and emptiness of spirit have visited us before when we buried our mother or father, brother or sister, child or friend, and we are reminded again that all life is fleeting.

This death is especially hard for us.

It is hard because she was so young in spirit. We forgot her age. We weren't ready.

It is hard because she left us unexpectedly, and we didn't have time to tell her all those things we can think of now that we wish we had said to her. We would like to tell her that we loved her; that she was a treasure of a daughter, a wonderful sister to grow up with, all a child could want in a mother, a wife beyond compare; that even if our relationship was brief, with few words spoken, or if we had only known each other on the surface, we still loved her.

We would like to tell her that she touched us, down deep under our crusty exteriors. We would like to tell her we appreciated her smile, that she blessed us when we were around her, that she showed us a way to live with goodness in the rocky places of life, and that we will miss her.

For all that we left undone, we ask God's forgiveness and comfort, and we leave all those cares in God's healing hands. In fact, we may even smile a little bit, because we know she would wave us off with a smile, and we would feel forgiven. She would remind us of all the things we did for her, whether it was saying a cheerful word or helping with her wheelchair or being her loving family and friends in life. She was one of those delightful people who could be thoroughly happy with what she had, without missing what she didn't have.

Each of us has basic attitudes toward life that give color to how we live. When someone dies, we reflect on what underlay that life, what shaped it, what gave it meaning. For this life, I believe I found a good expression of it written on an inside cover of one of her books. On the back page she had copied these lines from the poet Tennyson: "Live pure, speak true, right wrong, follow the King—Else, wherefor born?"

Our lives can say eloquently, more eloquently than words, the values that we hold dear. Paul spoke of fruits of the Spirit—not words, but tangible expressions of the Spirit's life within us. We can be witnesses to the work of God within us. People can see sermons in us that need no pulpits. We have been in the presence of one whose life preached wonderful sermons that enriched us and nourished us and touched us and changed us. We thank God for her.

For us the living, we have guidance to living beautifully through whatever conditions life brings us. "We do not lose heart," Paul wrote. "Though our outer nature is wasting away, our inner nature is being renewed every day" (v. 16). Paul did not overlook the frustrations and suffering of the body, and by his own account his own thorn and his bodily appearance brought him severe hardships, but when he put those and all his other afflictions in the balance opposite the eternal glory beyond these days, he found no comparison at all.

That kept Paul going. He could be fully in the world and still live in the light of heaven's radiance, so that a little of that light gave beauty and worth to his struggles, and he could keep going even in the most trying times.

In our difficulties we often forget the activity of God. We do not face life alone, in our own strength. We don't face our sorrow alone; we don't try to rebuild life's temples alone; we don't do anything alone. God is always re-creating, rebuilding, renewing us. There is an old proverb: "God comes to us without a bell." In other words, God's renewal is promised, but it comes silent, unseen, without fanfare, but in many ways.

The complete renewal has come, silently, unseen, without fanfare, but surely and wonderfully. While we are in the presence of the things that are seen, we rejoice to renew our faith in the things that are not seen but are of glory beyond all comparison.—Stuart G. Collier

Topic: Imperishable

TEXT: 1 Cor. 15:42–44

I would take nothing away from the grief we feel today. I would not say everything is all right. It is not. We hurt. We know we will hurt for a long time, and our grief is a dark valley we have to trudge through before we feel the warmth of the sunshine again. God made us so that we can feel the pain of grief, and it only means that we loved the way we were meant to love. We pay the price of love and courageously go on loving because the ones we love are worth it. We have loved. Now we hurt.

I say to you, grieve, long and deeply. Do not run away from it, do not treat your grief as if it were a stranger you can send away, or deny it because someone who doesn't know better thinks it makes your faith look weak. Grieve what is lost, honestly, lovingly, patiently, until the cup is emptied. There is no other way back to wholeness but by facing what life brings.

Yet, I would speak a word of comfort. Christians don't need to fear death as pure evil. We know those fears well enough. I would point you now toward the promise of death, the pearl within the cold, hard exterior.

Paul said that we are not like those who have no hope, for we know death as the doorway to the Promised Land, a rest from our labors, a reunion time with those we have loved. More than that, it is the time when we see our Lord as he is, and we can only dream of such a wonderful thing. We can lay down the struggles of faith. Faith will have completed its work, we won't be assailed by doubts and questions any longer, and we will know the glories of God in ways we cannot even imagine.

Wouldn't it seem wrong if life were all for nothing; if all the struggle, the overcoming, the loving, the development of character and goodness and beauty and heroism here were all for nothing; if nothing so precious lasted but were obliterated forever? We know in our hearts that we shall live, that eternity has been placed in our spirits, and that in another world we will continue what we have begun here.

Paul tells us that our bodies of flesh and blood are perishable, and we can let them go. Truly, dust to dust, ashes to ashes. But he finishes triumphantly: "What is raised is imperishable . . . it is raised in glory . . . it is raised in power . . . it is raised a spiritual body."

Why should we doubt this? We have been changing all our lives! Who can recognize the adult from looking at the infant's picture? In the plant and animal world a small round acorn perishes in the ground and a towering oak tree is raised, an egg perishes and little yellow chick is raised, a caterpillar is raised from its tomb in the cocoon as a beautiful butterfly, and so may we expect the same.

We are like babies in the womb. An unborn baby has no idea what life outside the mother is like and could never describe a rainbow or love or a puppy. Nor can we describe the next life beyond the hints the Bible gives us.

But we know that this life has prepared us for the next phase, and we know that we shall be where God is, and we have nothing more we can ask. Thanks be to God for this inexpressible gift through Jesus Christ!—Stuart G. Collier

ILLUSTRATIONS

BY ROBERT C. SHANNON

THE OBVIOUS DIFFERENCE.   In summer most trees look alike, uniform in their green color with only some slight variations in shade and some variations in shape. But in autumn as the leaves begin to die they reveal a great variety of colors and are seen at their loveliest. So people's lives sometimes appear much the same, but when death approaches we can see at once the difference between the person who has faith and the person who has none.

OUR POTENTIAL.   An eggshell is a marvel of structure and design. It protects the developing chick. But there comes a time when it must be broken. If it is not, the chicken will never live. So our life here is pleasant and satisfying but must eventually be broken before we can reach our full potential, the potential for which we were created.

THE GREAT ADVENTURE.   Frohman said, "Why fear death? It is the most beautiful adventure of life." Whitman wrote, "Nothing can happen more beautiful than death." Scott's comment was "Death is not the last sleep but the first real awakening." James Drummond Burns said, "I have been dying for twenty years. Now I am going to live." Paul said, "Christ has brought life and immortality to light through the gospel." And in another place he wrote, "The last enemy that shall be destroyed is death."

THE RESURRECTION.   The Babylonian Talmud, written about A.D. 600, gives three hundred arguments for the resurrection of the dead. Paul's half dozen in 1 Corinthians 15 are more convincing. Most often the apostles offered no arguments at all. They simply said that God had raised up Jesus from the dead, and they were witnesses of it. The Resurrection of Jesus Christ is the one best argument.

A BUILDING OF GOD.   Ralph Waldo Emerson wrote, "It is the secret of the world that all things subsist and do not die but only retire from sight and afterwards return again." It's a beautiful sentiment but is it true? Certainly we know of one thing that retires from sight and then returns again: the human body. "We know," said Paul, "that if our house of this tabernacle were dissolved we have a building of God, a house not made with hands."

SECTION V.
Lenten and Easter Preaching

SERMON SUGGESTIONS

BY RICHARD B. VINSON

Topic: Leadership
TEXT: John 13:1–20

On this night, someone needed to do something. The text says that Jesus knew perfectly well that his hour was close at hand. He would die soon and his disciples would be without his leadership to hold them together. If there was to be a church, then he had to do something that night—take some leadership, some initiative, and do something to make things turn out all right. Will he arm the Twelve and himself, grit his teeth, and yelling "Follow me!" over his shoulder, charge the temple complex? Will he lead them out of the city quietly and hole up until the crisis is past? What will he do? He washes the disciples' feet. It's a night for heroic deeds, for leadership, for action—he washes their feet.

That's the act of a slave, not a hero. Yet he who does it is no slave. The narrator reminds us in the introduction to this scene that Jesus is in complete control. He knew that his hour had come; he knew about Judas's intentions to betray him; he knew that he had come from God and that when they killed him he was going to God. A slave does things because he has to. Jesus does this because he wants to. He was not controlled by circumstances, but he chose carefully and deliberately to do what he did. And he did it, the text says, as "Lord and Teacher," not as a slave.

When you think of it this way, you begin to realize just how radical an act it was. Jesus is redefining what it means to be his follower, his disciple. Everyone respected him and acted with appropriate humility. We can all do that, can't we? We know who our superiors are, and we can act with proper respect and humility when we need to—that's no great virtue. The humility that Jesus called for went far beyond this, however. "If I, your Lord and Teacher, washed your feet, you ought to do this for each other." This is a discipleship without status, without pride, and that was a radical idea.

We have ways to put people in slots. "He's nothing but poor white trash, and he'll never amount to anything." "She's one of those ivory tower intellectuals—probably hasn't worked an honest day's labor in her whole life." "Just another welfare family, sponging off my hard work." We know how to put people in their proper places, don't we?

What if we took our leader seriously here? Jesus is plunging into the fray, opposing the whole world system of dividing people up into more important and less important: "I've washed your feet—now you follow me!" If we ever really stopped trying to make ourselves better than someone else and concentrated on improving everyone's lot in life, what a world this would be! He washed their feet—what an act of leadership!

Foot washing could be an act of love in Jesus' world. A popular romance from his day had a scene in it where the husband was uncertain of his wife's devotion, so she washed his feet to show her true love. Jesus loved his disciples throughout the ministry, but now he would show them just how much by one specific act of love: "He loved them to the end."

John likes to use words that can mean more than one thing. Here he does it in the phrase "to the end." It can mean completely—that he would give them all his love. Surely the foot washing showed them that, by demonstrating how far he was willing to go to prove his love. "To the end" can also mean "all the way," and with his death approaching, somehow the foot washing was also a symbol to them of that act of love, in which he would sacrifice his life for his own.

So the foot washing is a symbol of Jesus' sacrifice. Look how John draws out this comparison. He laid aside his garment, just as he had already said he would lay aside his own life voluntarily. After it was over, he took up his garments again, just as he told Pilate he had the power to do with his life. He poured out water onto them to make them clean, just as he would pour out his life to make them clean in his death. So it is a picture of sacrifice.

Jesus will say just a little later that the mark of his disciples was their love for each other. "By this shall all men know that you are my disciples, if you love one another, even as I have loved you." This is discipleship without limits—a love that does not stop, even for death, to sacrifice what is needed for the benefit of the other. Jesus did it, and he calls us to follow his lead. "We're going in," he says, and then instead of filling his hands with guns, he dies for the life of the world—and we have to follow him.

There is a vivid, almost funny scene in the first part of this section where Jesus and Peter have their conversation. You have to imagine all the disciples stretched out on pillows around a low table, leaning on their elbows with their feet out away from the table. Jesus begins to wash their feet one by one, finally winding up with Peter, who as the leader of the Twelve was saved until last. Peter draws his feet up a little and says, "You aren't really going to do this, are you, Lord?" Jesus responds, "I know you don't understand what I'm doing, but you will later." Peter replies, "I know this much—you'll never wash *my* feet!" Jesus has just told him he won't understand, but he makes up his mind anyway; just like Peter, jumping before he looks.

Jesus then says something puzzling: "If I don't wash you, then you have no share in me," and he uses a word for "share" that was the Old Testament word for the share the tribes of Israel had in the Promised Land. He's talking about salvation, then: The washing is a symbol for Jesus' offer of grace and forgiveness, which we must accept. The conversation continues. Peter says, "If I must be washed to be a part of you, then don't stop with my feet. Do my hands and head!" Jesus again says something a little odd. We can paraphrase verse 10 as "he who has washed does not need to wash again, but he is clean all over." In other words, Jesus says that his salvation, represented by the washing, is a permanent remedy for sin. Once you have participated in Christ's washing, there is no need for any further cure.

Jesus washed their feet. His was the act of a slave, going over the top to show us discipleship without pride, without arguments over status. His was an act of sacrifice, showing us discipleship without limits, love that doesn't stop even for death. His was an act of salvation, and here we have to say that we as his disciples cannot directly participate in salvation. We cannot save others or ourselves. We can, however, tell the story of what Christ has done. We can follow him into the world, into the fray, not with guns blazing but with Bibles open and words of hope on our tongues. We can tell the story, and Jesus promises that when we do and when they receive our message they have received him as well.

Topic: No Small Comfort

TEXT: John 14:1–3

"Let not your hearts be troubled." The first ears to hear those words belonged to the apostles, sitting around the supper table on the night Jesus died. You can bet they were troubled, though, no matter what Jesus said, after it sank in that he was serious about dying. How many ears have heard those words in the two millennia since the time of Christ! We Christians have grown to associate them with funerals, when they are read to the bereaved sitting on the front rows of the chapels. They, too, are troubled no matter how sincerely the minister reads the text. It is some small comfort to know that Jesus cares, but at the moment the loss drowns out the sensation. Just where is Jesus, that my heart should be less troubled?

Gone, the text says: "In my father's house are many rooms; if it were not so, would I have told you that I go to prepare a place for you?" Jesus is in heaven, then, in his father's house, preparing our future dwelling places, building me "just a cabin in the corner of glory land." Some small comfort, maybe, to know that he is there getting things ready for us. You can think of it as slogging through a workday, kept going by the promise of the loving response you will get when you get home. I don't mean to belittle this, because looking forward to good times can certainly keep you going sometimes when nothing else will.

But if that's all there is, then it is comfort but only small comfort. "Suffer through it, because you'll go to heaven when you die" is not an adequate reason to live. In the first place, it is entirely self-centered; if the world blows up, if half of Ethiopia starves, at least I'll go to heaven. Somehow, that's not Christian, not Jesus talking. In the second place, it makes most of our life irrelevant. A preacher once said, "This life is only the dressing room for eternity." Why not end it now, then, and go on to the part that really matters? If this is only marking time until the real living starts, why wait?

No, there's more here than we might see at first glance. Jesus is going to prepare our place, he said, rooms within the Father's house. He is speaking of heaven, but of more than heaven. In verse 23, the picture changes from Jesus leaving earth to reserve rooms for us in heaven to Jesus and his Father moving in with each one of us who loves him and obeys him. Jesus left to prepare our place by bringing God's presence within the reach of every human being. This life is not just the dressing room for eternity; eternity began the day you gave yourself to Jesus. That's no small comfort, I think, because it means that we are not waiting through this life to finally gain the blessings of God in heaven, but we should be enjoying his presence with us now.

Does that comfort our hearts? Perhaps it doesn't, because we have not experienced the full presence of God in our lives. I saw a movie recently where at one point a man said, "It's a sad, crazy day when you wake up and discover that your whole life is built on nothing." His wife responded angrily, "Your life is not built on nothing. I love you." Those Christians we call saints have realized that their lives were built on God's love, God's nearness; to them, God's presence was as real as this pulpit. They talked to God, listened to God, walked next to God. "Believe in God, believe in me," said Jesus; the place he went to prepare for you is here with you now, and if you and I believed that, it would be no small comfort to us.

Where is Jesus? Gone but coming back, says the text: "And when I go and prepare a place for you, I will come again and will take you to myself, that where I am you may be also." Coming again, they believed, and they looked forward to his return as a rescue from the evils of a world that tried hard to put them to death. They were impatient for it, longing for it to happen within their lifetimes. Paul once even urged people who were engaged to stay single if they could, because he believed the time of Christ's return was so close. Believing that he was coming again was a comfort, because they could see an end to their suffering and a vindication for their faith.

We, too, believe that Jesus is coming again. I say that with no apologies—he will come again, to close out this era, to judge the wicked, to reward the righteous. That is most important, I think. It means that our salvation is about more than just our own individual happiness. Jesus died, not just to make me feel better, but to one day restore all things to God. It also means that we're heading somewhere, not just spinning our way through the universe with no particular place to go. Jesus is the goal of all things. But once again, as important as it is, the future return of Jesus is not an adequate reason to live, if that's all we have. We can't spend our lives sitting on rooftops waiting for the clouds to part. Despite Paul's advice, we have gotten married, and there are children to raise and educate. I do believe that Jesus is returning, but what about now?

Jesus answers, "I will pray the Father, and he will give you another Counselor, to be with you forever, even the Spirit of Truth." In a sense, Jesus has returned already, in the person of the Holy Spirit. "I will not leave you desolate; I will come to you," he says, and in a real sense he has. Jesus explained that the Holy Spirit would teach us about Jesus, would remind us of what Jesus taught us. He will be the representative we need—a "counselor," a lawyer or advocate. Just as Jesus went before us to prepare the way, so the Holy Spirit will go before us in the world to assist us in our task of living as Christ's disciples.

Does that comfort our hearts? It should. Each time we feel the Spirit tugging at our conscience, warning us that something is not right, we know that we are not alone or abandoned. Each time we are led to try harder to live like Jesus, we know that God still believes there is hope for us. Every time we note an answer to prayer or we feel the encouragement of God in something our brothers or sisters say to us—every little touch should remind us that we are not orphans, abandoned by our Lord, but that the Spirit is with us. We hope for Christ's return, but in the meantime we are not alone.

Let your hearts be comforted, says Christ. He is gone, but he left to prepare a place with the Father, and that place is here. He will return, but he has already returned through the Spirit. No small comfort, indeed.

Topic: Jesus at Prayer
Text: John 17

He was saying good-bye to his friends, to students who had depended on him to tell them where to go and what to think for three years. He knew what was about to happen. He'd be arrested and executed, and they would have to grieve and be scared out of their wits at the same time. So Jesus paused to pray for his friends; how perfectly natural it seems, when you think of it that way. He knew how the coming tragedy would nearly kill them, so he prayed for them.

But of course, Jesus was no ordinary pray-er. He addressed God as "Dad" and taught his followers to do the same. He told outrageous parables about prayer. "Keep on praying," he said. "It's just like an old woman who bothered a judge until he was sick of hearing her complain. You just keep on asking God, and you know God will hear you." Jesus was no ordinary pray-er, and this prayer is not ordinary, either. It was a real prayer, I'm convinced, but it is as if Jesus had one eye toward heaven, just like the text says, and the other one cocked toward his disciples. This is as much a sermon as a prayer; it is, in fact, both a prayer and a sermon on prayer all rolled into one. The question we need to ask ourselves as we think about it this morning is, Can I pray like this?

In the first part, Jesus prays for himself. "Father, the hour has come; glorify thy son that the son may glorify thee" (v. 1). That is Gospel of John code language and sounds a little like Jesus is asking for fame: "Glorify thy son" sounds like Jesus wants his name in lights over Jerusalem. The "hour" that he says has come is the hour of his death, however: "Dad, the time has come for me to be killed" is what he really says. "Glory" then means nothing like fame and fortune; "glory" is the way Jesus in this Gospel talks about the true nature of God. God's glory is God's inner being, the straight line, the inside scoop on who God really is. "Glorify your son, that the son may glorify you" is a request to let God's true character shine through what is about to happen. "Dad, the time has come for me to be killed; please let people see you in what is about to happen to me."

"Let others see Jesus in you," we sing, and that is the first part of our lesson on prayer today. Christ's first request was that others be able to see God's character on the worst day of his life. Can we really pray that? Are we really that dedicated to looking like Christians that we can say with honesty, "Dad, tomorrow is going to be a rough day; let others see you in what happens to me"? That was Jesus' number one task, according to what he said in the Gospel of John; that was the first item on his prayer list here, as he was about to go to his death; it should be our number-one task and our number-one prayer item, too. Let others see Jesus in me, no matter what I'm saying or doing.

But we can't do it all alone. Jesus was unique; he could reveal God to the world, and even if no one else ever did, his life would stand on its own. Mine is different, though. Even on my best days, when God is most at work in me, I will not let people see all of God. There are others, because of the kind of persons they are, who can let the world see God's creativity, God's patience, or God's compassion more clearly than I ever could. So we need a group of committed people, people who have made up their minds that the world will see God in them. That's the Church, our brothers and sisters, and that is what Jesus prays for next. Can we pray for each other like this?

"Unify them in your name" is his first request (v. 11); "Holy Father, keep them in thy name, that they may be one, even as we are one." That was a prayer for the Twelve, but later, in verse 20, he repeats the same request for all Christians of all time. Now that's a nice thought, isn't it? Jesus is about to leave them, about to die, so he prays that they won't fight with each other, like the scene from the mov-

ies where the dying mother makes the two sons swear to make up. Often that kind of unity is in name only; the sons agree not to make a scene at the funeral, but there is no real love between them and no real unity. Jesus wants the real thing, however. He continues: "I pray . . . that they may all be one; even as you are in me, Dad, and I am in you; I want them in us in the same way, so that the world may believe that my mission was really from you."

Unity—real unity—unity like that between the Father and Son. Not just in name, but visible unity, unity so real that the world can see it and know that Jesus wasn't just a flash-in-the-pan idealist. He didn't want people coming along later and saying, "Yes, Jesus had some fine-sounding advice, but it was totally impractical; look, his followers can't even get along with each other." So unity—real, visible unity—among all of Jesus' followers is absolutely essential to the success of what Jesus wanted to do. He wanted his disciples to show God to the world, and to do that they would need to be united in God's name.

Can we pray this? Jesus knew we might have some trouble with this, so he prayed not just for our unity but for our holiness. "Sanctify them in the Truth," he said (v. 17). Make them holy; unite them, but shape their unity so that it is a true unity. It is like a platoon of soldiers on parade. When they first assemble, they are a group, but they are not organized around anything. But then the man who carries the flag puts himself in the proper place, and the squad leaders line up on him, and then the command goes out to dress up the ranks—to get everyone else to line up on the leaders. "Sanctify them" is Jesus' prayer that we will form an organized unity, that we will have a place for everyone in Jesus' name.

What is the guide for our unity? Jesus suggests two things: his Word and his Spirit. The Bible ought to shape our unity. We are supposed to be trying to show God to the world by all we do and all we say, and the Bible teaches us who God is. But people can read the Bible in lots of different ways. People used the Bible to justify slavery; people continue to use it to justify their own greed and pride. That's why there is the guide of the Spirit also. Can we really imagine Jesus owning slaves or having a million bucks in the bank while people starve or keeping any person of either sex or any race out of a place of ministry? That is not the Spirit of Jesus. So our goal is to make God known, and we join with other believers to do a better job of it. And to make sure we are heading in the right direction, we check ourselves against the Bible and against the Spirit of Jesus. Can we really pray this? Can we pray that God will line us up where he wants us?

Once we are lined up properly, then comes the time to move out, and Jesus prays for us again. "I do not pray for you to take them out of the world, but that you should keep them safe from Satan. . . . As you sent me into the world, so I have sent them into the world" (vv. 15, 18). Can we pray this for each other? This is a missionary's prayer, offered by one missionary for another; "keep us all safe, Lord, because you are the one who sent us all out here." Can we pray that? Can we pray as one missionary for another? The problem is not that we aren't out there ourselves; the problem is that we are, but we just don't think of it that way. Put it another way: God has sent every follower of Jesus Christ into the world. We are in the world, unless we are in a monastery or in outer space somewhere. You rub shoulders with the world every day. You are out there, but do they know that you are a missionary?

Jesus' last act before his arrest in the Gospel of John was to pray for his friends. "Dad, the time has come for me to die. Please let me show you to the world through what is about to happen to me. For my friends, I ask that you give them the unity that will continue to show you to the world; shape them up where they need it, Dad, and keep them safe while they are out there in the world." Can we pray that ourselves, for ourselves and for each other? That prayer—that sermon on prayer—could be a great checklist for us to follow every day.

Topic: Pilate's Trial
TEXT: John 18:28–19:16

"All I'm trying to do is my job," Pilate thought, as he got up to start the day's work. "Just trying to keep these fanatics in line in this godforsaken place. Terrible climate, unreasonable people, none of the comforts of Rome—I'll be glad when my term as governor is up and I can go back to a civilized place. All I have to do is keep things in line just a little longer, and then someone else can have my spot." A servant came to tell him that a delegation from the Temple was waiting to see him. Exasperated, he snarled, "Why won't they wait inside the receiving area like everyone else?" "They say they can't. Passover begins at sundown tonight, and they have to keep pure to kill the lambs this afternoon," replied the servant. "Pure! What does that make me? These are the most bigoted people in the world! They think they have the only religion and the only God; they won't even eat our food. Well, I suppose I must see them, if only to keep them from complaining. I must keep things in line."

You almost feel sorry for Pontius Pilate, a second-rank noble in the Roman aristocracy, working in what was considered one of the worst jobs in the Roman civil service. One writer pictures him in a dreary office, an electric fan stirring the air over him, cigarette hanging out of his mouth, glaring out at the world through lidded eyes. Early on the morning described in the selection he received the leaders of the Jews, the chief priests from the Temple. They had a prisoner for him, someone he had already heard a little about—Jesus of Nazareth. Pilate had heard that he and a band of followers had been going around in Palestine and that some people thought this Jesus was to be the Jewish king who would deliver the Jews from the Romans. "Maybe the Jews have done me a favor this time in bringing this troublemaker to me," he thought. Then he asked the priests, "What's the charge for this one?" Typically, the priests failed to give him a straight answer: "Charge? Don't you worry about a charge. If he wasn't guilty of something we wouldn't be turning him over to you."

"Look at them," Pilate thought. "They won't come in my palace or touch me, so that they can stay pure, yet they hate this man so much that they will turn him over to me to kill for any reason at all." With contempt in his voice, he told them, "You want him dead—you kill him yourselves." "You know we can't do that—only you Romans have the right to put people to death." Technically, they were correct here. Although the Jewish courts occasionally did execute people, they were not permitted to do so legally, and they certainly wouldn't have tried to get away with a lynching with the procurator in town.

So Pilate brought Jesus in for interrogation. "Are you the king of the Jews?" he asked—no beating around the bush, but straight to the point. The prisoner might have been expected to beg for mercy or to claim that he was innocent of the charge. Instead he asked, "Who told you to ask that? Did you think I claimed to be king, or did someone else tell you?" "What difference does that make? I'm no Jew—I talk to your kind as little as possible. All I know is that the leadership of your own Temple surrendered you to me voluntarily, and I want to know what you've done." The prisoner spoke slowly, "I don't rule over anything in this age. If I had an ordinary kingdom, I'd have soldiers to take up for me. I rule over the age to come." "Now we're getting somewhere," thought Pilate. "So you are a king, are you? You are claiming to be a king?" "No, those are your words. This is what I am: I am a witness to the truth, and everyone who belongs to the truth understands what I'm talking about." "Truth? What is truth?" asked Pilate.

Commentators have drawn Pilate at this moment with several different expressions on his face. Some see him laughing at Jesus: "You can't really expect me to believe that you are chasing around the country after truth, do you? Come on, what are you really in this for?" Some see him looking off into the distance, remembering his schoolboy lessons in Plato, trying to think again of that definition he once knew by heart: "What is truth, really?" I see him genuinely puzzled—he's heard the word before, of course, but he doesn't see the point. Picture this: A man really loves fishing and tries to take his friend along with him, someone who has never been before. Picture them both sitting on the banks of a clear lake, the warm sun on their backs, birds singing in the branches across the water, bass jumping after the early morning bugs, no phones ringing, no deadlines to meet—and the friend leans over to him and says, "I don't get it. What's so great about fishing?" That's the expression on Pilate's face—he really doesn't see what's so great about the truth. Think of it—he's going to judge Jesus guilty or innocent, but he doesn't recognize even the idea of truth!

Pilate has heard enough and goes back out to the priests. "This man is innocent. He's no threat to anyone but himself. I'll release him as my token of goodwill for Passover." The priests cry out angrily, "No, you can't release him! If you want to release anyone, release Barabbas." If Pilate is a judge who doesn't know truth, then these men are members of a jury who prefer a known criminal to an innocent man. That's the way of things, isn't it? The world always prefers sin, given the choice.

Pilate is caught in the middle. He knows Jesus is innocent—he can see that much truth—but what he wants to do more than anything else is just to keep things in line. So he tries to compromise. He has Jesus flogged. That is, he had soldiers take the skin off his back with heavy leather whips. They dressed him up as a mock king and then presented him to the crowd. "Look at him, poor schnook! He's not dangerous, and I'll bet after this he'll never try to preach in public again!" But you can't compromise with the world. You can go along with them, or you can stand up to them, but many times you can't do both things at once. If Pilate was going to make a stand, he should have released Jesus, period; the priests see that he's waffling by beating Jesus, and they won't let him off the hook. "Crucify him! Crucify him!" "I told you before, if you want him dead, you kill him yourselves!" "He has to die, and we can't kill him. He has to die because he thinks he is equal to God."

He can't compromise with the world, so he tries to compromise with Jesus. Back inside the palace one more time, one last chance to talk to this prisoner who is wrecking his day so completely. "Where do you come from?" Pilate asks. Now, this is rich, brothers and sisters. That is the central question in the whole gospel. The correct answer is that Jesus comes from God, to bring the world the clearest picture of God ever. Pilate is finally asking the right question, but there's no way he's going to understand the correct answer. So Jesus doesn't answer, which makes Pilate furious. "Don't you get it? I'm trying to save your life here. I can let you go, but you have to work with me a little bit." The prisoner raised his head to speak for the last time: "No, you are powerless. I am here because God has set it up that way. You're not even the worst of the criminals here—the high priests are more guilty of my death than you are."

"I'll show him," Pilate thought. "I can release or kill anyone I want to." So out he goes, all ready to set him free, but then the priests hit his weak spot. "If you let this man go, then you are betraying your emperor. He thinks he's a king. He's guilty of treason. What would Caesar think if you let him go?" All Pilate really wanted to do was to keep things in line; he never wanted to get into this situation. But now he has to choose between Christ and Caesar. Will he be Caesar's friend or Christ's friend? If he does follow that little bit of truth he knows—that this man is innocent—then he has to run the risk of his boss's anger. If he wants to stay in good with Caesar, then he has to kill this man.

In the end, there's no real choice at all. But Pilate gets a measure of revenge at the end. "Shall I kill the king of the Jews?" "We have no king but Caesar," they reply. "The hypocrites think they belong only to their God. They go to all this trouble to avoid touching me because I'm impure, because this evening they will celebrate the time when God chose their people out of all the families of the earth. Yet they have no king but Caesar. Their hands are in this as much as mine."

Pilate's trial ends here. He tried to stay in the middle between Christ and the world, but he couldn't. He tried to avoid a choice, but he couldn't. Neither can we, in the trials we face daily. You can't lie just a little or cheat just a little, or deny your faith in other ways without choosing for the world and against Jesus. That's our trial. We who sit here on the Lord's Day in God's house, moving toward the celebration of Christ's death and Resurrection—that's our choice. What do we do with it?

Topic: Jesus' Death

Text: John 19:17–42

Christ on the cross: When we look, what do we see? We know what a crucifix looks like, with the outstretched arms, the legs crossed at the ankles, the face laid to one side, and even in polished wood or gold that looks awful enough. But for a minute, imagine standing on the hill looking up at the cross, Jerusalem the Holy City at your back and a crowd of spectators on either side of you. The man you see on the central cross looks like the other two and like every other criminal you have ever seen die this way, except that the fake wreath on his head makes him look a bit more pitiful. Words like *criminal* and *wretched* come to mind, but not in your wildest dreams would you call him *Messiah* or *Son of God* on that day.

Jump forward almost three quarters of a century and look up at the cross again, as John tells the story; what do we see? An amazing transformation has taken place. The cross is still the cross, and the man on it is still dying, but the story is told from a different point of view. We hear no cries of anguish, no thud of hammers, not even the shouted taunts of the crowd. All is more serene, and the man on the central cross looks more divine.

Now the cross is a throne, and the man on it looks like a king. Pilate had tried to ridicule Jesus in his trial by putting the crown of thorns on his head and by draping a purple robe around his body still bleeding from the beating he got from the soldiers. Yet when it came time to put him on the cross, Pilate wrote the sign out: "Jesus of Nazareth, the King of the Jews." The Jews saw the irony in this and wanted the sign changed, but Pilate would not budge. Nope, it stays just as it was written: "Jesus, the King of the Jews." Later, at the end of the story, he gets a king's burial. Criminals who died for their crimes were not permitted an honorable burial by Jewish law but were dumped unceremonially into a common grave. Jesus, on the other hand, got a private tomb. In a normal burial, the preparer would mix a little of the pungent burial spices with oil and smear it on the corpse before they wrapped it in the burial cloth. Joseph and Nicodemus used an incredible amount of spices: one hundred pounds, enough for a whole town or for the gaudy funerals of an emperor. Jesus died as a king dies: with a king's inscription over his head and a king's burial at the end.

The cross is a throne, and Jesus hangs upon it as a king. Isn't that appropriate. This man, as future Lord of Israel, rode in triumph into Jerusalem six days before—on a donkey, a pack animal. This man, as Lord and Teacher of the Twelve, washed their feet only the night before. If you want to be Lord, be a slave, he said, and so it is fitting that his throne is a cross. As you look up at it, remember that he is your king and his cross is your throne. There is no gold on it, there are no armies to protect it, and it is unsupported by any territory. Turn aside from the cross, and look back to Jerusalem or across the sea to Rome; they have armies and swords and money. They scrap because the strongest survive, and the king is the one who can claw to the top and hang on the longest. But if you are to belong to the one on the cross, it shall not be so among you. In this kingdom, the only way to rule is from the cross.

Scene change: As we watch John's drama progress, the throne is moved away for a little while, and a stone table moved onto center stage. The cross is an altar, and Jesus is dying on it as the Passover lamb.

Jesus died on the afternoon before the Passover meal, according to John. If you and I had been in Jerusalem that afternoon, we would have seen lots of fathers and husbands walking toward the Temple, crowding around the door that separated the big open area where any male Jew could stand from the smaller area in which only the priests could go. Inside the priests' court was a huge stone altar, and on this afternoon countless priests would be working steadily. Their bright knives flash in the sun, their robes are already stained and splattered, as they work steadily killing lambs, draining their blood into small golden bowls, and splashing them around the altar. Outside the city on the hill on the central cross another Lamb is dying, and soon his side is pierced by a bright spear and his blood is drained out. "Behold the Lamb of God, who takes away the sins of the world." John the Baptist said it first, when Jesus began to preach and heal; now the Evangelist says it again with the words he writes.

Jesus died as God's Passover, God's lamb. In the original Passover, God rescued a bunch of slaves and made them his people. In the new Passover, he did it again, rescuing us from all the powers of evil. He rescues us—not out of the world, of course, for death is still death and temptation is still temptation. But we don't have to be afraid of them. Today, can we sing of our victory over greed, over prejudice, over despair? Look up at the cross, beloved; the man dying on it has rescued you from all that.

The set changes again, and the prop men move away the altar, replacing it with a canopy: a big sheet of cloth held up at the four corners to make a tent open on all four sides. The cross is a canopy, and in it Jesus stretches open his arms to welcome his newly made family.

Sometimes all it takes to make a collection of individuals into a group is a canopy. Once a bunch of Boy Scouts on an overnight hike, sleeping out under the stars, woke up in the middle of a drenching rain storm. One boy found a large piece of plastic from a refuse pile, and it was quickly stretched and nailed to some nearby trees. We had to scrunch, but we all got under it and had a great time telling stories until the rain quit.

Under the cross, looking up on this day were several people who felt like they had gone to sleep under the stars and woke up in a torrent. What must Mary have felt, to watch her son suffer so? How must John, "the disciple whom he loved," have wished he could do something to make his pain less? How could things have turned out so badly after they started out so well? From the cross Jesus looked down at them and said, "You are family now; he is your son, and she is your mother." She would lose her son Jesus, but she would gain as a son a man who was closer to Jesus than anyone else. He would lose his friend, but from this day on he would be a member of his friend's earthly family. Jesus' death created the opportunity for a relationship that never would have existed otherwise.

What keeps us coming back to this place? There are other ways to find friends, you know. We could join a club for companionship. This place offers more than that; it offers the family of God. Jesus died to make us into a family that cares about and cares for each other. Brother, she is your sister; he is your brother; love each other, because you are family now.

John's Passion play is complete. The stage is empty now—the cross has been taken down, and the man on it is in the garden tomb. All is quiet, and yet you know that the story cannot end there. The king must return to reign, the Passover must be celebrated, and the community that he created must survive. Isn't it something how even a death such as this can be the sign of a happy ending yet to come?

Topic: The Resurrection and the Life
Text: John 11

We've all been there, or we'll all be there someday, where Martha and Mary are in this story; having prayed as hard as we can for the recovery of someone we love, we find ourselves grieving their loss, wondering what we'll do now. Or we'll find ourselves where Jesus is, trying to comfort a grieving family member, wondering what we can say to make it easier. Common human experience, that, and it was inevitable that Jesus would face it sooner or later. What would he do, and what can we learn from this uncommon story that will help us as we grieve or as we help others who grieve?

Let's take a walk through the story. Jesus "was good friends" with Lazarus and his two sisters, staying at their house in Bethany on occasion. They trusted him and knew his power, for when Lazarus grew ill, they called for Jesus to come the fifty miles or so—this despite the plot against his life—to heal him. It is strange, then, when Jesus seems so unconcerned. "This sickness is not unto death," he says, but as it turns out, Lazarus dies. "Jesus loved them," the narrator tells us, but then Jesus deliberately waits too late to heal his friend. The conversation between the master and the disciples, odd as it is, tells us that he hasn't delayed because he is afraid of death but so that the miracle that is coming will be resurrection rather than a healing.

Why do we need one sort of miracle more than another? This one is a preview of another one coming toward the end of the Gospel; it is for the sake of the disciples and the world, to show them the power of God and to give a hint of what is to come.

The raising of Lazarus is supposed to remind us of Jesus' Resurrection. The similarities are superficial, but they are there: the rock tomb with the stone over the door, the women who visit the tomb, the grave clothes and face wrap, and even the comments of Thomas. You are supposed to think of Jesus as you read these details and think ahead to the happy ending on the other side of the terrible details of the trial and death.

When Jesus arrived at Bethany, Lazarus had been dead for four days. The Jews believed that a person's death was not final until after the third day, so he was legally, truly dead. Since Palestine's climate was hot and since the Jews did not embalm the dead like the Egyptians, they buried the person immediately and then mourned for thirty days. Many people, family and friends, had therefore gathered to pay their respects to the sisters when Jesus arrived. Martha broke custom by leaving the house and running to greet Jesus. You can hear the hurt and hope commingled in her words to him: "Had you come sooner, my brother would still be alive; yet even now God will give you whatever you ask." Jesus tries to reassure her: "Your brother will live again." That's not what she has in mind. "I know he'll live again—at Judgment Day," as if to say, "What good does that do me now?" Jesus has more to say, though, and his words are not only the climax of this story, but of the first half of the Gospel: "I am the Resurrection and the Life."

The Resurrection: Jesus claims to be the one who will bring the dead to life. "He who believes in me, though he dies, yet shall he live." How important is this to Martha? It is the central Christian claim. Christ's own Resurrection and his power to raise others is absolutely critical for Christianity. If it isn't true, then Christianity is meaningless, and if it is true, only then do we have hope for the future.

In my first year at seminary, I took a course called "The Resurrection Narratives" in which we studied all those stories. We read scholarly books and essays about what we could prove and what we should believe. Then one day our teacher came in rather shaken. He had played tennis the afternoon before with a friend of his who had a heart attack in the middle of their game and then died at the hospital. "Brothers and sisters," he said to us, "after all the arguments and debates are over, I believe in the Resurrection because without it life makes no sense."

Why do people die horrible deaths with cancer and heart disease and AIDS? Why do natural disasters take the lives of people without distinction to their morality or status in life? "Why wouldn't God answer my prayers?" Martha thought. "Why didn't Jesus have mercy on my suffering?" We can't answer those questions, either for ourselves when we grieve or for others who ask them of us. And while

we are in despair, it doesn't help us to know that God has a purpose in mind too big for us to understand. But we can hold onto the fact that Jesus is the Resurrection and that he will bring back to life all those who fall asleep in him. No matter how long the world will last or how long my name has been forgotten, Christ will remember and will raise me to life. You and I matter to him forever.

I am the Life: Being the Resurrection was a claim big enough, and it was what Martha wanted to hear. But Jesus went further: "I am the Life: he that lives and believes in me will never die." This life and death is not physical but spiritual. He that lives and believes in me, that is, in Christ, will never die.

What does it mean to be alive in Christ? The New Testament uses lots of different figures of speech for it. Matthew talks about seeking the kingdom of God; Paul, about being crucified and buried and raised with Christ; and John, a little later, about abiding in Christ like a branch in a vine. It seems to me that to come alive in Christ is to be awakened to his presence in your life, in such a way that your life is never again the same.

What would Jesus say to a grieving sister? "I am the Resurrection and the Life." The promise is that, for those who believe in him, he will be with them in all their moments now and forever and will raise them to stand with him at the last day. We have all stood, or still stand, where Martha stood, grieving over the loss of someone we love very much; or we'll stand where Jesus stood, trying to comfort a Martha close to us. We will stand, and Christ will whisper the same words to us: "I am the Resurrection and the Life; he that believes in me, though he were dead, yet shall he live; and he that lives and believes in me shall never die." Do you believe this? Do you believe that you are of eternal consequence to God? That's a promise that can carry us through life and death and everything in between.

ILLUSTRATIONS

BY ROBERT C. SHANNON

REDEEMER HOSTAGE.   Returning from the Crusades, Richard the Lion-Hearted was captured and held hostage by the Babenberger king Leopold. Later, Leopold gave the prisoner to the emperor Henry VI. According to the poet Ulrich von Zataikhoven, in the transfer Richard's place was taken by a knight, Hugo de Morville, who became the hostage instead of the king. Of course, in Christ we have just the opposite. The king takes our place as a hostage to sin and dies for us on the cross.

CRUCIFIED, DEAD AND BURIED.   Some Orthodox Muslims believe Jesus didn't die on the cross but rather ascended to heaven. The Ad Admadi sect believes rather that he was taken down from the cross before death, revived with a special ointment, and then went to Kashmir, where he died at the age of 120. But suppose for a moment that Christ had escaped the cross. Suppose he had lived to be a senile old man and died peacefully in his sleep. Would there by any such thing as the Christian religion? Of course not. Could we rejoice in the assurance of forgiveness? Never! That's why Paul in 1 Corinthians 15 emphasizes that Jesus truly died and was buried. Our faith depends on it.

HE IS NOT HERE, HE IS RISEN.   Despite his difficulties with the government Boris Pasternak was beloved by thousands as a great Russian writer. Who can ever forget his *Doctor Zhivago*? He died in isolation in 1960 at the age of seventy, but every year since, his admirers have made a pilgrimage to his grave. Thank God we cannot do that with Jesus Christ. We can make pilgrimages to Jerusalem. We can visit the Church of the Holy Sepulchre and the Garden Tomb. But we can never go to the place where Jesus lies buried. He rose again!

NO REMAINS TO SEE.   Lenin's tomb in Moscow was closed for two months in 1989 and early 1990 so that they could "touch up" the body of Lenin. Then it was reopened, and once again long lines formed, and people filed by to see the glass-topped coffin and to view the body of Lenin. How sad it would be if we had the body of Christ preserved somewhere under glass. Of course, thousands would go to see it. He was, after all, the most famous man of history. But the power would be gone. Christ would be a curiosity but not a Savior.

TODAY IS DIFFERENT—ALWAYS.   In Santiago, Cuba, you can see signs, "IT'S ALWAYS THE 26TH." They refer to the day the Communist revolution began in Cuba. In a sense, for Christians it is always Good Friday and always Easter. Every day of life is lived in the light of the cross and the empty tomb. Every day is different for the believer because of what happened at Golgotha on Good Friday and because of what happened in the garden on Easter.

SECTION VI.
Advent and Christmas Preaching

SERMON SUGGESTIONS

Topic: A Love for All Seasons

(Christmas Eve Communion)

Every year we don't think we are going to make it. We get so caught up in the Christmas celebration with all of the things that we have to do, and it gets us so tired. We don't think we're going to make it.

But we always do. We need these moments to give time for our souls to catch up with our bodies, to try to get everything in proper perspective. What I want us to remember is the song that Christ sang at Christmas. It is about a love that's for all seasons, a love that meets all of our needs forever.

I. The first stanza begins with a birth. A baby was born in Bethlehem in a stable. What was the big deal about that baby's birth? The big deal had to do with who he was.

Christmas is a reminder that God has come to be where we are. Into the midst of all of our lives, our confusion, our suffering, the trouble of this world, God has come to pitch his tent right next to us. He has come to look us, as it were, in the face to say, "I know you. I know who you are and what you need. I have not forgotten you."

Under the Christmas tree at your house, there are presents with names on them.

At Christmas, God has sent us a gift, wrapped with our names on it, addressed just to you or to me. As we open it, it is Christ. As I see him, the angels sing what God wants me to know. "I love you and I will love you forever."

II. The second stanza is a song about a death. Babies do grow up. Christ left the cradle and became a man. As he went about doing God's will, he got into trouble with the religious leaders. They would not fellowship with sinners; he ate with them. They were judgmental of sinners; he forgave them. They lived hypocritically, playing at religion; Christ was the man who had integrity of word and deed. He was what he said. They loved only a few; he loved them all. They asked for a cheap price to pay; keeping the rules. He came calling for total commitment of life; it was the only way to live.

It's no wonder that, finally, a cross had to be lifted up. All along he told them that he knew what they needed for life: "Follow my way. Do it my way, and you will have life abundant." They did not want to follow. Instead they nailed the nails through his hands and hung him there and turned and walked away.

There is nothing in the world that you and I can face that Christ has not already faced himself. At times we may wonder if there is a God who does understand us. But God is not a God living in some faraway heaven oblivious to what goes on down here where we dwell. He is a God who understands because he faced it all even to the point of throwing himself on a cross to help us know how much he did understand.

251

He dwells where we are. We can know that each step of the way we go, there is a God who understands the pain and the struggles as well as the joy. He so loved us that he went through it all himself so we would know we are understood.

III. Stanza three is a song about resurrection! You know that if Christ had not been raised from the dead, we would not have Christmas to celebrate. If he had not been raised, he would have just been another good man who died, a memory but not a Savior. Sin is so powerful; it drags us down and destroys us. It can even cause us to crucify the Son of God. But he defeated that. And death! We don't like to think of that. It seems to be so final. We all have a date with death, but how we fear it. But he conquered that! This is the joy of Christmas: Easter. We can't have Christmas without Easter. Easter and now Christmas mean that those who face suffering, who face difficulty, who are struggling under insurmountable burdens have a Savior that knows the way to help us triumph over it. Easter and now Christmas mean that death is not our end but a door that leads to that which is beyond. What is beyond we do not know. Who is beyond we do know. This Christ who came is there. He is a Christ who sets us free. Nothing can stop us because nothing could stop him.—Hugh Litchfield

Topic: Don't Forget the Baby
TEXT: Heb. 1:1–9

A family was going home for Christmas. It was a journey they had been anticipating for some time. Indeed, they had talked about little else at dinner for weeks. Everything was now in the car and in readiness. As they were getting ready to back out of the drive, they were doing a verbal inventory to be sure they had everything. They had stopped the newspaper and milk delivery. They had arranged for a neighbor to feed their dog, to take in the mail, and to check the furnace periodically. They had packed their clothes, their gifts for other family members. They had a marked map. The thermostat had been turned back low enough to keep the pipes from freezing. They had packed their lunch for the trip. They had their traveler's checks and motel reservations. Everything was in order. Just as the husband eased the car out of the driveway, his wife let out an agonized wail. She said, "Oh, Jim, we forgot the baby!" It can happen. We left one of ours asleep on a church pew one Sunday night.

Christmas is a busy time. A time of cards and cooking and candy . . . a time of gifts and parties. Don't forget the baby . . . that's what it's all about.

Strange, isn't it? God's way of coming into his world . . . coming not as some towering intellect, to dazzle us with his brilliance; coming not as some triumphant general returning from battles won and nations conquered; coming not as some suave politician or statesman, leaving us aghast at his wit and wisdom. But he came as a baby, helpless and dependent, a warm, cuddly baby. Everyone can understand that. It doesn't really require a lot of explanation. What does it mean . . . this baby at Christmas time?

I. It means we must think small. That was once the motto of imported little automobiles. It sort of went against the grain of America's mania for everything to be bigger and better. And of course, we assume that if anything is bigger, it will be better. But what can you think of a baby, except small?

Christmas means that God has come into our commonplace world. God has invaded the ordinary. God is here with us in the person of the Christ, in a cobweb cave and a cow's trough, in our ordinary, everyday world. You see, God is in the little matters of life, as well as in the great cosmic concerns. Why, God opened the wall of China with nothing any bigger than a ping-pong ball! And the Berlin wall is tumbling down without a shot being fired. Yes, he works in common and extraordinary events.

He comes incognito into our lives. Suddenly he is there, laying his claim upon us. It is so easy for us to become blasé . . . so easy for us to live in the commonplace and never have a catch in our throat or a tear come unbidden to our eyes. It is easy for us to live, taking it all for granted, like the woman who said, "Well, that's a rather lovely sunset for such a little town!" We're like that aren't we? We don't expect deity in the midst of the ordinary. Think small. He came into his world in a little baby. Don't despise the baby.

II. It means God stooped to save us. God took upon himself our humanity. The great deity who spoke the universe into existence; the great Mind behind everything that is; who gave us the return of the seasons; who gave the beauty and wonder of this earth; who gave us the wonderful possibility of life and love—came into this world at Bethlehem. Oliver Goldsmith wrote a play entitled *She Stoops to Conquer.* This is a sense in which that phrase can be said of God. He stooped and came into our world as a baby. "He became what we are," said one of the church fathers, "in order that he might make us what he is." God didn't come slumming. He became one of us, taking our humanity upon himself. God became man, and the miracle of miracles is the Incarnation, God in flesh. He never pulled rank on us; he was one of us. He knew what it was to be sleepy and tired and hungry. He knew what it was to be elated and to be disappointed. He knew what it was to have a close friend die, to stand in the cemetery and weep. He knew what it was to be tempted in all points just as we are, yet without sinning. He knows and understands our heartache, our pain, our disappointment, our joy, our ecstasy, our thrill. God stooped to win us to himself. That's what the babe means. Don't forget the baby.

III. It means God spoke by his Son. "In old time," said the author of Hebrews, "God spoke in many wonderful ways through the prophets, but in these latter days, he has spoken to us by his Son." He speaks of our worth. Look at the trouble God went to for our salvation. Look at the price he paid that we might be saved. You are somebody. You matter. You count. You have great worth because the Lord God of glory loves you that much. Christmas speaks of his limitless love, of his joy, and of his peace.—Alton H. McEachern

Topic: When the Angels Stop Singing

TEXT: Luke 2:15

I. Someone once told me that loneliness and depression are more intense at Christmas than at any other time of the year. I believe that's true. Because somewhere amid all the gaiety, the tinsel, and the colored lights, there is the awareness of an empty chair. Somewhere, in some aged face, the memory of a loved one—lost to death—clings to the heart like wet snow. On this night so filled with marvel and mystery, someone, somewhere is crying.

Loneliness and desperation. Even on this night so filled with wonder. Somewhere in some smoke-filled dive, a solitary soul takes another shot of whiskey, trying to drown the memory of love—lost long ago. And somewhere, huddled beneath a cardboard split-level a mother fails to keep her child's hands warm and hopes alive. Somewhere—in a thousand names and faces—this night of mystery holds nothing but misery. And yet maybe that's what happens in life when the angels stop singing!

II. You see, most of us are fortunate. For us, Christmas is a time of life and laughter. Smiles seem wider and steps lighter. People decorate the streets like characters from a Dickens novel. Colored lights twinkle in the cold night air with the warmth of a starlike sparkle. And our children's eyes are wide and wild with expectation.

And so we give little or no thought to the other side. That place where hunger lays waste to happiness. The house in which loneliness will silence the voice of laughter. The nursing home where aged eyes watch for someone who will never come. The hospital patient whose tears glisten in the darkness, like tinsel on a dying tree. It is painful to think about those whose lives are broken, even on this most blessed night.

Maybe we want to believe that the rest of the world feels as we do on this holy night. Perhaps it would spoil our evening if we were to remember all those unfortunate souls who are out there straining to hear the song of angels above the cries of their homeless and hungry children.

Can we be blamed if we want to forget? After all, we are only asking for one night and one day to forget. And maybe that's possible, when the angels stop singing.

I suppose our request is all right. Don't you? After all, we have a right to some joy, don't we? Why should this night—of all nights—be squandered on dark and dreary thoughts? On this night there is beauty and fun and family. And besides, we've had our shattered buildings and battered lives! So maybe our request for a little time to ourselves and our joy isn't so extreme or selfish.

Three hundred and sixty-four days of the year our eyes are assaulted by misery and our ears by moaning. Now we want to bask in the light of this holy and peaceful night. This evening we simply want to wrap our hearts in the warm glow of that gentle story of Mary and Joseph. Away with all this talk of the lost and the lonely. But of course, for the destitute and deserted, that will be the case anyway—once the angels stop singing. Or so I've been told. By those less fortunate than myself.

III. She had spent most of her life alone. A hermit of sorts. Certainly not by choice or design. I suppose you could say she had fallen through the cracks of compassion. She had no family—no friends. And yet for years she had faithfully contributed to the church I had been serving. I'll never forget. How could I forget?

It was Christmas Eve, and she was scheduled for a visit. I had never met the woman. But I had been told. Actually, I had been warned. "She's a bitter old bat," they'd say. "She's mean-spirited and spiteful," said others. And as I drove down her winding driveway, my wandering mind was filled with foolish thoughts of bat wings and broomsticks!

She was nothing of the kind. No contemporary Scrooge—humbugging Christmas cheer. But she was lonely and alone with her thoughts. A woman tormented by a troubled life. A person scarred by sadness and bruised by the bad faith of others she once held dear. Let me tell you about this lady.

Her husband beat her without mercy until the night he drove into a pole. She had one son in prison and a daughter walking the streets of New York City. And in ten years no one from the church had expressed a lick of interest in her welfare!

Eventually, the conversation turned from pain to pleasure, as I spoke of Christmas and the promise of joy. With one deep sigh she said, "Pastor, Christmas is for brightly wrapped presents and parents with pleasant children—and not for the poor and lonely." I said, "But the angels first sang to lowly shepherds." And smiling, she said in return, "Sure. But when the angels stopped singing—the poor were still poor and the lonely, alone. Nothing had changed. Nothing!"

Well, I don't mind telling you I was stunned into silence. I made my way to the car—and through the remaining afternoon—haunted by her words. Was it the bitterness talking? Were her wounds so deep that even the warmth of a Christmas wonder could not melt her icy emotions? Or did she speak on behalf of life's losers? Maybe the reason isn't important to us. And yet her words trouble me. So here's something to think about.

IV. Sooner or later, the decorations will find their way back into the attic. The once gaily dressed tree—now stripped—will gradually turn brown in some open field. And we'll pull the plug on all those bright colored lights. Then what?

Then life returns to its usual hectic and hassled pace. Smiles are no longer wholesale. Holiday cheer gets short-circuited. And sad but true, we all become a tad more self-centered. But maybe that's the most we can hope for when the angels stop singing! Or is it?

I certainly hope not! I prefer to believe that this night will make a difference. A difference in you and me, that is. But the mystery and wonder of Christ cannot be confined to one night. Even a night filled with the voices of angels. The real wonder of Christ can be experienced only by those who worship and follow—long after the tinsel has tarnished and the presents are packed away. But that takes ✳ courage and commitment. Because when we turn from the crib, we face the cross!

And when the angels stop singing—we are summoned to begin serving.

"Sure," she said, "but when the angels stopped singing, the poor were still poor, and nothing had changed." I couldn't disagree more! In fact, everything had changed—and has continued to change wherever the Spirit of the Savior born in a stable has been active.

And Christ is active still, wherever his followers plant their feet. With those who are lonely. With those who are hungry. With those who are homeless. With those who are heartless.

So when the wonder of this night has worn thin and the enchantment has ended—Christ will be waiting. Waiting for you and for me to commit to his ministry of mercy and compassion.

And you know, if you listen with care above the voices of angels singing, you'll hear Christ asking, "Isn't there someone whose loneliness you can lighten? Isn't there someone whose burden you can bear? Isn't there someone whose sorrow you can share?"—The Rev. Albert J. D. Walsh

Topic: I Came That They Might Have Life

TEXT: John 10:7–15

What if Christmas had happened in modern times? What if some of the technological capabilities of our time had been available that night? Can't you just see it now? CNN is on the scene filing a report hours after the hallowed moment of birth. Mike Greenspan reports from Israel:

"Just inside this cave behind me a young woman and her husband have just welcomed into the world their first child. It's a boy. The father is Joseph, a carpenter from Nazareth. The baby's mother is Mary, a young maiden also from Nazareth. Both mother and son are doing fine.

"So why am I telling you this? Because there are aspects of this birth that set it apart from the ordinary. One unusual occurrence with this birth has been the sudden appearance of nearby shepherds who came to pay their respects to the newborn. The shepherds said something

about an angel's message, but how they knew about it is a mystery we have yet to unravel.

"When I interviewed the parents, Mary hinted that she had been told months ago that she would have a son and that he would be the Savior of the world. Attempts to get more details concerning a divine destiny have failed. Like any new mother, I suppose Mary just wants to savor the beauty of the moment. She appears embarrassed by all this attention.

"So another child is born, a common event with uncommon trappings. Will this night prove to be a benchmark in history, or will it fade into oblivion like the births of all the other babies born this night? Will this new Jewish baby grow up to be more than a mere man or will his life blend into the sea of humanity? Only time will tell. Mike Greenspan reporting from Bethlehem."

Time indeed has told the outcome of that common-yet-uncommon birth. What became of that peasant child is a matter of record now. Not only do we know what happened to Jesus, a man born in Bethlehem among cattle to lowly parents, but also we know what God was up to that night.

Jesus was constantly explaining himself . . . to the disciples, to the throngs, and especially to the Pharisees. Because Jesus didn't always conform to their expectations, they made it their business to monitor his movements. In one of those times when the Pharisees had questioned something Jesus had done, he gave the third "I came" statement.

He said, "I came that they might have life and have it abundantly." When one considers the context, it becomes obvious that Jesus wanted to distance himself from those who masqueraded as shepherds of the flock. He exposed them as the thieves and charlatans they were. At the same time, he pointed to himself as the true shepherd who cares for the sheep even more than he cares for himself. He said, "They are false. I am true. They are fake. I am authentic."

Who were these thieves? In the immediate situation of John 10, they were probably those leaders among the Jews who used their political connections with the Herods and Rome to their own profit and security. For a long time the people had suffered under many such tyrants. To them, the common folk were a flock of sheep valued as so much flesh and fleece.

Or Jesus may have had in mind the insurrectionists, rebel leaders, and self-proclaimed messiahs who became as oppressive as the oppressors they would overthrow. They cared little for the people. And their rebellious ways often brought death and destruction to the masses. So Jesus said, "I am not like these. I have come to bring life."

What was God up to at Christmas? Upgrading life, that's what. What appeared to almost everyone as an insignificant event in a shepherd's village of unsurpassed humility turned out to be the beginning of abundant life according to the creator God.

It's not hard to see that Jesus is for us and that many who would have us believe they are for us are, in fact, out for themselves. But this is not all Jesus meant by abundant life. How does Jesus bring life?

A special relationship exists between a shepherd and his sheep. Part of the answer is there, and the more we know about that pastoral relationship the better we can understand what Jesus said about himself.

For example, he said, "I am the door of the sheep" (John 10:7). Sounds peculiar, doesn't it. It stretches the imagination to think of a person acting as a door. But that's just what a shepherd does, particularly one who is devoted to his sheep.

One day George Adam Smith, an Englishman who traveled extensively in the Middle East, came across a sheepfold and said to the shepherd, "That is where they go at night?" "Yes," said the shepherd, "and when they are in there, they are perfectly safe." "But there is no door," said the Englishman. "I am the door," replied the shepherd. Sir George looked at him and asked, "What do you mean by the door?" The shepherd answered, "When the light has gone, and all the sheep are inside, I lie in that open space,

and no sheep ever goes out but across my body, and no wolf comes in unless he crosses my body; I am the door."[1]

When Jesus said he is the door of the sheep, he meant that the fold has only one entrance; abundant life has one source; spiritual nourishment is obtained one way; heaven can be entered one way. And the single means of access to all that is good is Jesus.

When we read the Bible, we interpret it according to what we see of Jesus. When we pray, we do it in the name of Jesus. When we minister to persons in need, we do it as unto Jesus.

If we suffer from the burden of guilt, we take it to Jesus. If fear gets the best of us, we lean on the everlasting arms of Jesus. If hatred becomes as a millstone around our neck, taking us down with it, we let Jesus teach us how to forgive. If we are held down by self-pity or low self-esteem, we turn to Jesus to lift us up.

This is what Christmas is about. Jesus came into this world to bring light because darkness is everywhere, to bring truth because lies are abundant, to bring life because death abounds.

In the Frank Capra movie *It's a Wonderful Life*, the main character, George Bailey, is facing a very dismal Christmas. His business has failed because of the deceitfulness of one of the town's most influential citizens. George, believing he is ruined, determines to take his own life. He is prevented from suicide by an angel who gives George a chance to see what life would have been like if he had never been born. George's hope is restored as he finds out that his acts of kindness have made a difference. He determines to go back into the real world and face with courage whatever problems he has.[2]

And what would life be like if Jesus had never been born?—David Crocker

[1]G. Campbell Morgan, *The Gospel According to John* (Westwood, N.J.: Fleming H. Revell, n.d.), 177.
[2]J. Michael Shannon and Robert C. Shannon, *Celebrating the Birth of Christ* (Cincinnati: Standard Publishing, 1985), 44.

ILLUSTRATIONS

BY ROBERT SHANNON

THE BEST WAY.   Marshall Tito is still venerated in Yugoslavia as the founder of the nation. March 25 is his birthday. About two weeks before, runners start from remote villages bringing messages to Belgrade, all arriving on March 25. We observe Christmas best, not by bringing messages to a central place but by sending out in all directions to the entire world. The message is "Unto you is born this day a Savior."

PROMISE AND PERFORMANCE.   In his poem, "Well, so that is that," W. H. Auden reflects the old complimentary close the English used to put at the end of their letters: "Your obedient servant." Auden says of Christ, "Once again we have sent him away, / Begging to remain His disobedient servant, / The promising child who cannot keep his word for long."

THE REAL ST. NICHOLAS.   In 1507 the Florentine Renaissance painter Mainardi painted a picture of the Virgin and the Christ child, flanked by St. Justin and St. Nicholas. St. Nicholas is tall and thin, not fat and round like our Santa Claus. He is red-robed, like ours, and red-gloved. He doesn't carry a sack of toys but four loaves of bread. He is not the "jolly old elf" of Clement Clarke Moore's poem, but a man profoundly sad. Over the years we have changed the image of the man who was visibly saddened by the world's need into that of a man whose "Ho, ho, ho" suggests that he is always merry and jolly. Is it because the world is now a happier place than it was in 1507? Or is it because we prefer the world of fantasy to the real world of human need and human suffering?

THE TOTAL GIFT.   Stuart E. Jacobson has published a book entitled *Only the Best: A Celebration of Gift Giving in America*. In it he relates some of the more unusual gifts that rich and famous people have given. But the title is intriguing. At Christmas some of us may have to give less than the best. Our financial condition will not permit us to do otherwise. But we remember that at Christmas God gave us his very best, and that is what makes it truly Christmas.

CHRISTMAS KINDLINESS.   David Grayson wrote, "I sometimes think we expect too much of Christmas Day. We try to crowd into it the long arrears of kindliness and humanity of the whole year. As for me, I like to take my Christmas a little at a time, all through the year."

SECTION VII.
Evangelism and World Missions

SERMON SUGGESTIONS

Topic: The Quest
TEXT: Matt. 2:1–12

We have heard Matthew's account of the wise men who came to find and worship Jesus. I want to say four things about this story.

I. *God longs for us.* God longs for your love and your salvation and to be in fellowship with you.

Many clouds can obscure that truth to our vision. Even in this passage we may be a little put off because the prophet said Jesus would come to be a ruler over us. We don't like rulers so much, because we haven't found many good ones. Rulers don't always have our best interests at heart.

We read that Jesus is our judge, and we don't like that because we haven't found many judges we can trust. Judges have hurt us, and we have a hard time trusting that Jesus' judgment is redemptive and for our benefit.

Jesus says we have to take up a cross, too, and we secretly wish he didn't require that, because we don't want to get involved in things that aren't pleasant. We have our lives to live as best and as happily as we can, and we don't see how a cross helps us.

We hear Jesus say that in this world we will have troubles because of him and in spite of believing in him, and we can't understand how God would let things happen to us or lead us into harm's way. We can't get very excited about a Jesus who doesn't shield his followers from pain and disappointments.

Those, and other objections, are like thick cataracts over our eyes, and we stumble along in life, half angry at God, half afraid, half believing, half committing ourselves—two people, a Christian and a non-Christian—because we can't see clearly that God has done all this for us, and it all is a vision of beauty.

We are like a hiker along the rim of the Grand Canyon at dusk, having a sense of what is there but not seeing until lightning flashes and, for a precious moment, he can see reality as it is, and he can go on in the twilight and even darkness because he has seen and knows the truth. The truth is that God longs for us and has gone to all extremes because of it. Christmas is a flash of light that reveals it.

II. *We long for God.* The wise men symbolize the longing of every human being for God. Of course, not everyone knows this longing for what it is. The debris of life, the wants, the idols, obscure the object of human longing. People go in quest of substitutes.

One task of evangelism is to uncover this longing, to help a person understand the hungers of the heart. The wise men knew what they wanted. They wanted to see Jesus more than they wanted to keep their gold and treasures, more than they wanted to play it safe with their lives, more than they feared the difficulties of the journey.

You have journeyed this far. You are here. Why? In hopes that you will be touched by God in some way that will meet a need that you can't describe or explain or take care of yourself. You journey into this place to hear the sacred story again and to sing from your heart, to pray and be prayed for and to listen and look and feel and hope that you are touched and you can go home healed and whole for a little while because you have grabbed onto the hem of his garment.

Don't you need to be something of a gambler to be a Christian? Of course, the scarier gamble is to gamble against Christ, but I don't think Christians who play their lives and faith close to the vest do very much for Christ. Those who make a difference are the Abrahams and the wise men who bet their lives on their faith and give everything they have for what they believe, whose longing for God is more powerful than their longing for gold or comfort or respectability.

There's something beautiful about that. There is something beautiful about a Messiah who gives everything for the God he believes in and for the people he believes in. The wise men did it, too. And you can do that beautiful thing with your life.

III. Unfortunately, there is a problem. *Your spirit will resist you.*

In the story, we see it in Herod. He is the king. He has a lot of what the world offers: It has its own sweetness. He was troubled. The chief priests and the scribes were troubled, too. They were threatened by this Jesus.

You are threatened by Jesus. I am threatened by Jesus. Everything I have collected in life, everything I am or hope to be someday, all my dreams, all my talents, resources—everything—is threatened by Jesus. Your lives, your time, your wants in life, your money, your respectability in the community and among your friends are threatened by Jesus.

For all our desire to grow spiritually, we are afraid to, because we don't want to lose anything we are attached to. We want to be good Christians, for God to be pleased with us. But we are afraid that growing spiritually would mean our lives would change. We might have to teach Sunday school if we really gave in to this one from Bethlehem. What if we grew

spiritually and really gave him our hearts, what would happen with everything in our lives that we like the way it is? We might become missionaries. We might open our treasures and give gifts the way the wise men did.

Herod is no wicked man of the past; he is us. We just do different things to keep Jesus from getting too close to us. We resist even while we want to mature as Christians.

IV. *There is another obstacle: It is evil.* Evil will resist our growth spiritually, even as Herod tried to intervene in the wise men's mission of adoration and worship.

Just try to grow spiritually. Try to devote yourself more to God. Try to take a greater role in the church's work. See how many obstacles there are.

Perhaps you work in the business world, and you find yourself enmeshed in systematized dishonesty, profiteering, or greed. Perhaps an attorney finds herself caught between the demands of a client and the demands of Christ. Or opposition may come from tragedy that seems to destroy any trust in the goodness of God or in the form of internal weaknesses that bedevil our best efforts to reform or in subtle ways in which the powers of evil seduce us into turning aside from the quest. Whatever the source, evil opposes God and opposes us and tries to turn our faces away from God.

What may we say in conclusion? Three cheers for the wise men, who were not defeated in their quest by inner resistances or external oppositions but felt their longings, went, worshiped, opened their treasures, and not only went home by another way but went home in another way!

What about you? Have you begun your quest? Are you walking with determination and direction? Are you satisfied with where you are, or would you like to make a new start today?*—Stuart G. Collier

*For the four major points, I am indebted to the thought of Gerald G. May, M.D., *Care of Mind, Care of Spirit: Psychiatric Dimensions of Spiritual Direction* (San Francisco: Harper & Row, 1982), 20–21.

Topic: Remembering Salvation

TEXT: Rom. 10:9–17

We all are conditioned by the world in which we live. Music is an example of shaping our responses and thought patterns. The "William Tell Overture" may not make us think of a great musical age but of the Lone Ranger. Another song sounds like "I've Been Working on the Railroad," but it also can be "The Eyes of Texas." "Sweet Georgia Brown" makes me think of the Harlem Globetrotters. Southern pride swells when "Dixie" is played. Did you know it was written by a Northerner?

Just as we often are shaped by our environmental setting, an evangelistic zeal should be shaped by the Scriptures.

I. *Remember how personal salvation became public salvation* (10:9–10). The Lord is clear that, if we possess a personal relationship with Jesus, our faith will be expressed publicly. The key to our salvation showing on the outside is the presence of the Holy Spirit on the inside. We should be so full of love for Jesus that we cannot wait to share it and shout it.

The summer of 1988 brought tragedy to the Texas border town of Brownsville. On a hot, seemingly uneventful day, a downtown department store collapsed without warning. Many shoppers and employees were caught beneath the rubble of twisted steel and concrete that the crashing roof created. Rescue workers began immediately. They worked around the clock for many days.

At first the rescue teams made many exciting discoveries of victims who were alive and OK once freed from the debris. Yet as time went on and on, many dead bodies were discovered.

One of those grim discoveries was a young Hispanic man. As the workers slowly dug their way to the man, their fears of the worst became true. There in the dust and rubble was another victim. It wasn't until they were taking his lifeless body from the tragic scene that they were startled at what the man had scrawled on the wall beside him.

There in cryptic letters was written in Spanish, "Jesus es el camino." Translated in English, the man had written "Jesus is the way"!

When we have some important news, we can't help but share it. We must tell others about what Jesus means to us. That's when we first become a light, a testifier, a soul-winner. The zeal that takes an intimate salvation experience and shares it publicly with excitement is the outreach spirit that comes from the heart of our Savior Jesus.

II. *Remember how a Savior for me became a Savior for all* (10:13). An evangelistic spirit reminds us that we are not any more special than others. The difference between us and our neighbors is that we have realized God's love in Jesus and have responded to him.

Nadia Comaneci was the first gymnast to ever score a perfect 10 in the Olympic games. She collected three perfect scores in the Olympics. When one judge was questioned about it, he said: "A 9.7 or 9.8 is a technically perfect routine or score, but to receive a 10, a competitor has to stir the soul of the judge! Nadia did that."

Birds, animals, insects—none of these stir the soul of God our Judge like a human being. We are created in his image!

God is so stirred by us that the death of his Son tells everyone how precious humanity is to him. Yet we must find new and creative ways of going to the masses with the gospel.

Can you make a commitment today to share your Jesus with those with whom you come in contact? To accomplish that goal, we must allow the Lord to stir us with the power of heaven to propel us into a life-style of witnessing.

We must remember how a Savior for us became a Savior for all—all are precious in his sight!

III. *Remember how a Savior's mission became a sinner's message* (10:14–17). Sometimes we forget, with all the billions of people in the world, that the Scripture is the message of God's love to individuals. "This is good and acceptable in the sight of God our Savior, who desires all men to be saved and to come to the knowledge of the truth" (1 Tim. 2:3–4, NASB).

We must surrender everything to become the messengers God wants us to be. What keeps you from committing today to become a trained soul-winner? Lay every hindrance before the foot of the cross and witness for Jesus. You will have no regrets.

Jesus warned the church in Laodicea not to be lukewarm in Christian commitment. At the crossroads of two highways in Bartlesville, Oklahoma, stand three water towers. Each tower has only one word on it. On one tower you can see the word *hot*; on another, *cold*; on another, *warm.*

The discernment of God labels each of us as hot, cold, or lukewarm. We all must rise above the mediocre landscapes around us to glorify Jesus, sharing the message of his mission with those who need him so desperately.—Bruce Kelley Edwards

Topic: Lost in Your Own Backyard

Text: Luke 15:11–32

Most of us can immerse ourselves so deeply in a good book that we lose count of the passage of time. If you are one of the unfortunate persons who has lost the art of reading, similar experiences arise as you fight the enemy with John Wayne, face up to the boss with Debbie Reynolds, or solve an intriguing murder mystery with Peter Falk. The allure of all movies, television, and fiction lies in the identification we feel with the characters presented in life situations that hold our interest and entertain us.

This may be why Charles Dickens, England's greatest novelist, once described the parable of the prodigal son as "the finest short story ever told." He may have been thinking of narrative, plot, characters, or description; but mostly, I suppose, he liked it because it is so true to life. The prodigal was a young man, like young men in every age, who felt he had some rights, was permitted to exercise his independence, and spent all to find himself facing a famine without resources. Then he came to himself, repented, returned, and was received, forgiven, and

restored by his earthly father. Certainly every Christian can see himself in the parabolic picture as one who was away from his heavenly Father but is now restored and in the family.

I want to suggest to you that this is not the story of *one* but of *two* prodigal sons. One went to a far country and one stayed home; but both were away from their father. In the background, Jesus sketched in the figure of the angry elder brother, refusing to come to the welcome-home party. I believe Jesus put him there to show us how easy it can be for a faithful servant of the Father to be a child lost in his own backyard.

Two major evidences arise in this story that prove that the elder son was as much a prodigal as his younger brother. First, it is obvious that the elder son was . . .

I. *Away from faith in his father.* Certainly he remained very busy on the farm, but his actions upon returning from the fields suggest that he sent the servant to inquire and to confirm what he largely suspected—that his father was acting unjustly (Luke 15:25–26). He was angry at the information discovered. His resentment and criticism of his father showed a hurt spirit and a son who felt he could not trust his father's love as being equal for both of his children (vv. 29–30).

One attitude forming this mistrust appears to be pride. Verse 29 includes *I, I, me, I, my.* "You gave my brother a special calf, but not even a goat for me!" He was proud of his service. He claimed the right to some rewards. He saw the welcome-home party as unfair in the light of all that he felt was due him and had not been paid.

The elder brother saw his father's treatment of the prodigal as unfair and unjust, but his father corrected him, insisting that their relationship was not a master-and-servant one of service and reward but a father-and-son one of love. The party given for the younger son was not given because it had been deserved or earned but because he was lost and now found (vv. 31–32).

I am sure that a gathering of the finest persons in any particular district, those whose ethics, morals, and community concern was the highest in any particular community, would be a group almost identical with the Christian congregation that meets in this district. Christians develop a life-style of this character as a norm. But we forget that these values have nothing whatsoever to do with our acceptance before God. They arise as results of our faith, not first as qualities that secure our approval in his kingdom.

We are saved by the cross-work of God's Son, who created a way of salvation by grace. Yet often when we begin to question the dealings of our heavenly Father, we tell him that we deserve better than we are having; and we do it so often on the master-servant model. We talk about our loyalties, our rights, our sacrifices. We discuss what we deserve, how faithfully we serve, and what our rewards should be. Like the elder brother we, too, get away from faith in our Father, and we do so often from the attitude of pride, forgetting that all we have is from his mercy and grace.

A second attitude the elder brother had was obviously envy, which formed mistrust for his father. It is hard to keep on working when you have all the responsibility and others get the parties. Jealousy, envy, anger, and hate may all be marked in verses 28–30.

Psalm 73 tells a similar story. Here one of God's people scrambled for a foothold on faith in his Father but had almost slipped back because he was "envious at the foolish, when I saw the prosperity of the wicked" (Ps. 73:3). He thought they had less trouble than the righteous and a far easier time (vv. 4–5). This made his faithfulness seem all the more pointless (v. 13). He continued, "it was too painful for me; until I went into the sanctuary of God; then understood I their end" (vv. 16–17).

Envy takes us away from faith in our Father. Looking too much at others affects our own balance, leads us to self-pity, and destroys our faith. We can be confident in God's love for us, but only as we look to him and not to others for comparisons. Our judgments are always wrong about every situation and relationship except our own. We can never know others as we know ourselves.

Pride and envy made this elder brother just as much a prodigal son as any because he was away from faith in his father. He had lost affection and distorted situations because he had allowed this sin to control.

A second major evidence that he was a child lost in his own backyard can be seen in the truth that he was . . .

II. *Away from fellowship with his father.* His words do reveal an amazing selfishness. He was obviously not close enough to share the love and joy his father felt at his brother's return and thought only of his own selfish needs. The contrast between descriptive terms in verses 17, 30, and 32 reads as if an argument proceeds between father and son. The elder son refers to the prodigal contemptuously as "this thy son," although the father calls him "this thy brother." In selfish bitterness he seems to be saying, "Father, he may be your son, but he is no brother of mine! I refuse to call him that or acknowledge him as that!"

The elder son's family relationship appears to be solely for what *he* could get out of it. Like so many Christians today, he endeavored to live the life of faith in isolation. But when you become a child of God, sonship also means brotherhood! So many backslide because they never become involved with the family or care to be identified as loving them. Many in the church remain unmoved by Christ's compassion for the lost. They shed no tears for the vacant pew or the missing member. Their faith means coming to church for a spiritual feast for themselves but shows no care or responsibility to reach others or even to care for their fellow believers in the local congregation.

Many a prodigal never leaves home. He just sits there, taking everything he can get from the Father, often working hard at his own responsibilities, knowing other sons are in the family but insisting that they cannot be brothers of his. Selfishness destroys fellowship. It crushes the family spirit and causes the child of God to be lost in his own backyard, unable to share his Father's love and falling more and more from his fellowship.

A further element in his drawing away from fellowship with his father seems to be neglect. Jewish law required two-thirds of the father's estate to be the elder son's portion and one-third the younger son's portion. As the prodigal had already taken all that was due him, the father's statement that "all that I have is thine" (v. 31) has significance. The elder brother ought to have known this, but it would appear that he was so busy with the farm that he never got to spend enough time with his father to straighten out even as simple a matter as this.

Can you see that scene in the farm-house at the end of a heavy and tiring day? Supper is barely finished when the elder son quickly scrapes the chair from the table and leaves the room. "Going so soon, son? Can't you wait a while with me and talk by the fire?" "No, Father, the sheep must be counted in the western pasture and brought into shelter, for a storm is coming."

The same scene plays each evening. "Can you stay and visit with me a while tonight, son?" "No, Father. Books must be balanced; seed must be ordered—not tonight!" And an old man sits by the fire with his head in his hands and groans, "Oh, my son, you share nothing with me; you spend no time with me; you do not care for my loneliness. I have one son away in a far country, but my other son is just as far away. You work hard, and I am thankful for your service, but most of all I need your love and fellowship. Yet you are so busy with the farm you are neglecting your father."—Craig Skinner

Topic: Reason to Believe

TEXT: Matt. 28:1–20

Think of what we just sang: "Ours the cross, the grave, the skies, Alleluia!" How can we sing about a cross? About the grave? How can we ask people to believe in Jesus Christ when our faith has such morose elements in it? Isn't our faith something dreary and burdensome that we have to manipulate people into ac-cepting? What can we say to the nonbe-liever?

Let's try to understand what Matthew wanted to get across to the people of his day concerning the Resurrection of our Lord. In a way, it is Matthew's final word; it will help us with our witness. We look at the end of the Gospel as the beginning of life for us as Christians. What may we tell our friends who don't know or care about being a Christian?

I. *Life begins with joy.* Despite what some non-Christians and Christians believe, being a Christian is not dark and de-pressing. Joy brackets the entire Bible, from the Genesis account of God's de-light in creation to Revelation's joyful an-ticipation of Jesus' Second Coming.

Then, within the joy of the beginning and the end, was the joyful welcome of Jesus into Jerusalem, with the stones ready to shout for joy if the people did not recognize their king.

There followed the violence, tragedy, betrayal, and execution of Jesus. This darkness is not of God. We can't look around us and say that the world is too cruel to allow us to believe in God. Too much of the darkness is our own doing. We can read the day's newspaper and know that it is ours, and the death of Je-sus by betrayal and violence is only telling it the way it is.

But, is that the last word? Does God leave us in the darkness of our own mak-ing? Not at all. God redeems our vio-lence, and in Matthew 28 we have the closing of brackets of joy around Christ's victorious death. If there is any room for joy in life it is because of God, not in spite of God.

Some people don't like Easter egg hunts for children because it has some borrowed features from other religious beliefs. But I think if there were not laughing children running around in God's green grass, looking for these Res-urrection Day surprises, those God-created chicken eggs, enhanced in color a little bit by God's people, hidden by God's bunnies—if the children didn't do this on Easter Day, the eggs themselves would cry out!

It is so good to see unrestrained joy like that!

I would not be surprised if a part of the reason we adults enjoy Easter so much is that as children we learned in that simple, childish way that it is a day of surprises, gifts, serendipities, and joy. Matthew's Gospel ends with joy, but we need to remember that only the believers are joyful. Jesus appeared only to those who claimed him, and the others had no reason for joy.

II. *Life begins with hope.* We hope in the Resurrection. I have tended to think of the Resurrection first in terms of my own personal resurrection. That may not be surprising or all wrong, since I do see myself as worth preserving beyond the altogether too few years I will be allotted. I would like to see myself go on living, and I think that is a delightful opinion for God to share and to see to.

I feel that way about some people I know. I have a lot of family I want to see again. Especially to see them in their purest form, without all the messed up brokenness that besets our lives and relationships here. I believe there is a sense in every one of us that we are not who we are meant to be—yet.

Our relationships are just as imperfect. Wasn't that wonderful news when Jesus told the Sadducees, who asked about marriage in heaven, that there won't be marrying in heaven; we will really be family—one family, without the diminishment our humanness causes in relationships here.

There is hope for all people who stand between their own Good Friday and the Resurrection. A great part of the world is there. We find ourselves there sometimes, and then there are the ones for whom there is not enough justice, not enough freedom, not enough food, not enough medicine or clean water or opportunity or education.

III. *Life begins with grace.* In our society we know about winners—the people who are first, who meet the world's standard of success. They are the few who write autobiographies that the rest of the world reads. Most of us form the middle of the pack, at best. Our lives are filled with disappointments and wasted talents. We struggle to get by and look forward to the rest of retirement. We need a lot of understanding from people around us because we are so imperfect.

Good news! Mary Magdalene and "the other Mary" were about like most of us. One had no reputation, and the other had no identity. They went to the tomb first, in Matthew's account. Did you hear that? Two nobodies were the first to see the greatest event in the history of the world. *Grace is big, isn't it?*

Christians are children of grace. We can tell that to our friends. There are no losers in God's kingdom, only winners by grace.

But anyway, the two women, this prostitute and this "other Mary," got up while the disciples were still asleep and went to see about Jesus. Did you catch what Matthew said about this—they just went to look at the tomb!

What was in their hearts? Have you ever stood in the presence of something precious that has died in your life? Then you know what was in their hearts. Something too painful for words. With all that is in our hearts when we stand at the tomb of what was precious to us, we don't need to hear mere words. We need real help.

We get it. There was no impersonal note, "Gone to heaven" left in the door explaining it all. *There was an earthquake.* And the angel, the messenger of God, said to them exactly what you hear today: "He is not here, he has been raised from death, and before long you are going to see him!"

The Gospel of John recalls many of Jesus' words about the resurrection of believers. The immortal fourteenth chapter recalls the words of Jesus to the disciples: "I go to prepare a place for you, so that where I am you may be also. And I will come for you."

And one of the most worn pages in my Bible is 1 Corinthians 15 where Paul says, "Lo! I tell you a mystery. We shall not all sleep, but we shall all be changed, in a moment, in the twinkling of an eye, at the last trumpet. For the trumpet shall sound, and the dead shall be raised incorruptible, and we shall be changed. For this perishable nature must put on the imperishable, and this mortal nature must put on immortality. Death is swallowed up in victory. O death, where is thy victory? O death, where is thy sting? So then, my dear friends, stand firm and steady."

IV. *Life begins with a personal Christ.* As risen Lord, Jesus was still the Good Shepherd. "Peace be with you," he said to them. It is a greeting from Jesus who cares for them and also the conveying of a blessing. I wish we could all hear it more clearly every day and believe it more deeply. It is for all those who take his name on their lips and his cross on their backs.

But we can't stop with the personal touch and care of Jesus for us. He was not interested in merely "feel-good" religion. He said to the two women, "Go tell my brothers . . ."—what a wonderful expression of community—"go tell my brothers to go to Galilee. They will see me there."

V. *Life begins with a mission.* What will Jesus do when he sees the disciples again? What is the resurrection meaning for Jesus and for them? In other words, what does Matthew most want us to see about the resurrection appearance to the disciples?

They go and meet Jesus, and even the delirious delight of that reunion, which was a preliminary to the great and final one, is covered with a hurried note that they worshiped him and some doubted. Fully one-third of this account takes note of doubting but without judging it. It seems that doubts are expected and do not disqualify anyone for service.

The emphasis is on something else, something that the entire Gospel crescendos with, and that is the Great Commission.

Here is the point of every one of the resurrection accounts: "Go, then, to all peoples everywhere and make them my disciples: Baptize them in the name of the Father, the Son, and the Holy Spirit, and teach them to obey everything I have commanded you."

Mark ends by saying, "The disciples went and preached everywhere. . . ." In Luke, Jesus says, ". . . the message about repentance and the forgiveness of sins must be preached . . . I myself will send you. . . ."

John ends with the encounter between Jesus and Peter in which Jesus recommissions Peter: "Feed my sheep!" Jesus ends the exchange and the Gospel with the words with which he began his work: "Follow me! and I will make you fishers of men!" Follow me, even if you have doubts and fears; follow me even if your loyalties are divided right now. But follow me! And I will send you into the world, even as lambs among wolves, baptizing and teaching.

And lo! I will always be with you as you go! Invite everyone to know me. I commission you. I will be with you. Go in joy! That is the resurrection faith.—Stuart G. Collier

ILLUSTRATIONS

BY ROBERT C SHANNON

THE "GREAT ATTRACTOR." In January 1990, the newspapers reported that astronomers had found the "great attractor." It is one of the largest concentrations of galaxies and matter ever found. One hundred and fifty million light-years from earth, it exerts a steady gravitational pull on the Milky Way and millions of other galaxies. The finding may bring great changes in the way astronomers think about the structure of the universe. The term *great attractor* fascinates us. Spiritually, the great attractor is the cross of Christ. "If I be lifted up," said Jesus, "I will draw all men unto me." He was lifted up upon a cross, and ever since the magnetism of his sacrificial love has been felt. He has done what he said he would do. He has drawn people to himself.

SIGNIFICANT LOSS. In London there is a warehouse where all the items left on the city's buses or subways are taken. They've collected 17,000 umbrellas, 19,000 books, and 100 sets of false teeth.

All these and scores of other items were left on buses and subway trains by forgetful passengers. How easily we forget. How lightly we take some of our losses. But the loss of a soul can never be taken lightly.

THE IMPORTANCE OF ONE.   As far as the biblical record goes, Andrew led one person to Christ. Without doubt he led many, many more, but only one is recorded. That one was his brother Simon Peter, who won thousands! So far as we know, Joel Stratton led only one person to Christ, but that one person won by the waiter Joel Stratton became the great missionary John Gouge. Ezra Kimball was a Sunday school teacher. His class of boys was small and unruly, but one of them was Dwight L. Moody, whose life touched two continents for Christ. Frank C. Laubach has spread literacy among millions of people by his picture lessons for adults learning to read and by his slogan, "Each one teach one." If Christians had a similar slogan, "Each one reach one," the world would soon be won to Christ.

THE DIMENSION OF HEIGHT.   When Herbert Billings was serving as a missionary in Guatemala, the nearly seven-foot-tall minister was called "the tallest man in Guatemala." Every missionary, man or woman, big or little, stands tall. The missionaries may not stand tall financially or socially or politically, but they stand tall spiritually. They come very close to "the fullness of the stature of Christ."

CREATIVE WITNESS.   It has been estimated that 60 percent of the world cannot be reached by traditional missionary methods. These places are the focus of a new effort to be led by self-supporting missionaries who will work in nontraditional ways. Taking their name from the life of the Apostle Paul, they are called tentmakers.

SECTION VIII.
Preaching from The Book of Isaiah

BY JOHN D. W. WATTS

Isaiah is known as the prince of prophets. The Book of Isaiah is a virtual treasure trove of preaching resources because it so perfectly captures genuinely biblical insights on God's relation to his people, both as sinners and as elect, potential saints.

The main prophetic teaching of the book, as it interprets three centuries of Israel's history that straddle the fateful destruction of Jerusalem in 587 B.C., turns on two poles. God exercises his duty in covenant to pass judgment on his people's sin, pride, and apostasy. He exercises his grace in opening the way to renewal of covenant. God's judgment extends to the "nations" who share residence in Canaan, God's own land. And he extends grace by inviting "all who will" to participate in covenant and worship.

Isaiah is complex, much more so than this outline would suggest. There is no pure "age of judgment." God's continued will to maintain and protect the institutions of covenant is depicted in the very moments when disaster looms. And there is no pure "age of grace." The strange reluctance of Israel to respond to his Word is pictured graphically. And continued paganism is judged harshly at the very moment when the new Temple for all peoples is being inaugurated. God's idealism is pictured repeatedly. His realistic appraisal of his apostate and rebellious people is equally apparent. All this makes Isaiah very much our contemporary. How like us those generations were!

Topic: **Useless Worship, Useful Goals**
TEXT: Isa. 1:10–20
After nine verses dealing with judgment on northern Israel, the Word of God turns to Jerusalem, proud city of David, home of the Temple. The text identifies the city's false faith in formal worship and its need for simple justice and worship of the heart. The depth of the city's plight is shown in being called "Sodom and Gomorrah" (see Genesis 19).

I. *Useless worship*. God finds their sacrifices (worship) revolting (1:10–15).

(a) Where does the Law call for sacrifice without repentance (1:10–11)?

(b) Who authorized this disorderly conduct (1:12)?

(c) Stop doing meaningless worship (1:13–14)!

(d) God doesn't heed such prayer (1:15).

II. *Useful actions* (1:16).

(a) Clean up your act.

(b) Remove dirty actions from God's sight, at least out of God's Temple and God's city.

(c) Turn your life around! Stop doing wrong.

III. *Useful service* (1:17).

(a) Learn how to do right.

(b) Actively seek justice. Encourage the oppressed.

(c) Defend and plead for the helpless.

IV. *God will make this possible* (1:18–20).

(a) God's invitation: Cleansing is offered (1:18).

(b) God's conditions: Be willing and obedient (1:19).

267

(c) God's threat: If one resists and rebels . . . (1:20).

This is God's own sermon. He is the speaker from beginning to end. He speaks as one who has a right to do so. He is creator of this people. He has saved them from Egypt. He has entered into covenant with them. They are in his land, indeed in his city, even in his Temple. Yet they act like pagans and worse. They are lucky that he has not already wiped them out as he did Sodom and Gomorrah (1:9). How much of these accusations might apply to our church life today? Jesus cleansed the Temple and pronounced doom on it for his day.

Topic: The Church God Builds

TEXT: Isa. 2:1–5

This text is placed at the beginning of the Book of Isaiah, in the mid–eighth century B.C. It stands in contrast to the picture of temple worship in chapter 1 and in contrast to the monarchy in Judah, so filled with violence and war. It is mirrored in the vision of a restored Temple for the people after the Exile in chapter 66. It states God's goal, the kind of worship community he wants to have.

I. *God's time* (after the days of judgment).

II. *God's place* (2:2).

(a) The place of God's house will be firm.

(b) It will be higher than anything.

(c) But all kinds of people will flow to it like water flowing downstream.

III. *The people's expectations* (2:3).

(a) They know it is the Lord's house.

(b) They know he is the God of Jacob.

(c) They want to be taught his ways.

(d) They want to walk in his paths. (All of this in contrast to Israel and Judah as portrayed in chap. 1.)

IV. *The product and purpose of the new city* (2:3c).

(a) To propagate the Law (the Torah).

(b) To proclaim the Word of the Lord. (In contrast to the useless sacrifices of chap. 1.)

V. *The political and social effect* (2:4).

(a) God's function in the new city: to judge between the nations; to decide (disputes) for many peoples.

(b) The results: They can turn arms into tools. They can dispense with military preparation.

VI. *The invitation to Israel* (2:5).

(a) To join the nations in these goals and actions.

(b) To walk in the light of the Lord. (The "light of the Lord" may well be the vision that has just been revealed. It would include the Law and God's ways, which they already knew but seldom followed.)

Topic: God's Loyalty in the Time of Judgment

TEXT: Isaiah 4, 7, 9, 11, 12, 36–39

There is no question but that the decision of full destruction has fallen on Israel and on Judah through Isaiah's prophecies in the eighth century. But the Book of Isaiah portrays God's remarkable continuation of loyalty to Zion and the house of David through the eighth century.

I. *The Lord's loyalty to Zion* (4:2–6).

(a) Grace beyond judgment for king and land.

(b) A remnant in Jerusalem: holy, separate and alive, cleansed and protected.

II. *The Lord's loyalty to David's son* (7:1–9; 9:6–7; 11:1–5; 36–39).

(a) The Lord sends Isaiah to assure Ahaz (7:1–9).

(b) A son is to ascend the throne (9:6–7).

(c) The Lord's Spirit is to equip him to reign (11:1–5).

(d) The Lord intervenes to protect both city and king (chaps. 36–39).

Both the city and the dynasty will eventually fall. They are under judgment (chap. 6). But the Lord shows remarkable faithfulness to both in the meantime. Justice must be served. But faithfulness to promise and relationships is repeatedly revealed, even under the pressure of required justice.

Here are more preaching resources listed by topic only—Isa. 5:1–7: God's Garden; Isa. 6:1–13: Preaching without Hope of Response; Isa. 12:1–6: A Song for a Saved People; Isa. 30:15–18: The

Blessings of Faith; Isa. 34:16–17: Our Place in God's Future.

Topic: Good News: God is Coming
TEXT: Isa. 40:1–11

The obvious turn from judgment to restoration appears in chapter 40. Isaiah 40:1–9 is often considered the counterpart to 6:1–13. It announces the divine decision to change the direction of God's attitude toward Israel.

The background for this text is the destruction of Jerusalem in 587 B.C. and the subsequent Exile of the people of Judah. The city, with its few remaining residents living among the ruins, seemed abandoned by God and by their exiled compatriots.

I. *Good news for the defeated and abandoned* (40:1–2).
(a) Your struggles are over.
(b) Your sins are pardoned.
(c) You have suffered enough.
II. *God is coming* (40:3–5).
(a) God is ready. Prepare the way.
(b) God's glory is about to be revealed.
(c) Everybody will see his glory.
(d) God himself says so.
III. *A skeptic is answered* (40:6–8).
(a) "It is no use. We are all going to die."
(b) "That is true. But God's Word is forever."
IV. *God is coming* (40:9–11).
(a) Tell your neighbors: See your God!
(b) He is strong.
(c) He is well financed.
(d) Like a shepherd for his sheep, (1) he will feed, (2) he will nurture, (3) he will carry, and (4) he will lead.

Topic: God is Able
TEXT: Isa. 40:26–31

The skepticism about human nature's fragile and temporary existence apparently carries over to doubt that God is able to do what is announced. God defends his ability by reminding the readers that he has created the world and its universe. He is able to care for every believer's needs.

I. *Look at the stars and think of God* (40:26).
(a) Who created these?

(b) Who keeps up with all of them?
II. *Why do you think God doesn't know and care* (40:27–28)?
(a) Don't you know? God takes the long view.
(b) He never grows tired or weak.
(c) You cannot understand his reasons.
III. *Power to overcome comes from God* (40:29–31).
(a) God gives power to the powerless.
(b) Human resources are limited.
(c) Those who "wait on the Lord" (1) have their strength renewed, (2) fly on the wind, (3) run but do not tire, and (4) walk but do not faint.

Topic: God Has Power to Redeem
TEXT: Isa. 44:24–28

God's resources are found in history as well as in nature. God's announced goals include restoration of Jerusalem. How can this be accomplished when pagan rulers control the entire region? God answers: These, too, belong to me.

Israel is in exile. Jerusalem is in ruins. Pessimism is rife. Yet God has promised "good news" for Jerusalem. How can he do anything when pagan empires remain in control?

I. *This is the Lord, your God, speaking* (44:24a):
(a) "I am your redeemer."
(b) "I am the same one who cared for you from conception."
(c) It is the same God throughout.
II. *I am the Lord* (44:24b–25).
(a) "Who stretched out the heavens by myself."
(b) "Who formed the earth."
(c) "Who confounds predictions and knowledge."
III. *I, the Lord* (44:26).
(a) Confirm prophecy.
(b) Command Jerusalem to be built.
(c) Command Judah to be rebuilt.
IV. *I, the Lord* (44:27–28).
(a) Dried up the sea and parted the river (see Exodus 14–15 and Joshua 3).
(b) Command Cyrus to do my work: (1) to build Jerusalem, (2) to found the Temple (see Ezra 1:1–4 and the rest of Ezra-Nehemiah).

Topic: What Animal Sacrifice Could Not Do
TEXT: Isa. 53

Thus God uses emperors to do his work. He calls his own people to fulfill their destiny as his servants. But more is needed for the redemption of his people and believers from all mankind. A servant who suffers and dies accomplishes atonement.

I. *The unbelievable truth confessed* (53:1–6).

(a) We thought nothing of him (vv. 1–3).

(b) Yet now we know he died for us (vv. 4–6): (1) It was our sins, not his own (v. 4); (2) yet his death brought us peace and healing (v. 5); (3) God put our sins on him (v. 6).

II. *The event described* (40:7–9).

(a) He accepted affliction without protest (v. 7).

(b) He was executed for the people's sin (v. 8).

(c) The innocent was assigned a criminal's grave (v. 9).

III. *What God accomplishes* (40:10–12).

(a) God's will is accomplished when this is seen as a sin-offering for the people (v. 10).

(b) Forgiveness and justification is achieved (v. 11).

(c) Therefore this death is honored (v. 12): (1) He accepted death, (2) he bore the sins of many.

The model for this chapter in the prophet's time remains a mystery. Gospel writers found an unmistakable likeness to the crucifixion of Jesus and patterned their treatments on the prophetic interpretation.

Topic: God's Open House
TEXT: Isa. 54:17b–56:8

God's gracious restoration of Israel and Jerusalem is not exclusively theirs but fits God's intention to offer redemption to everyone. This invitation is especially clear in chapter 55 but is also shown to be fulfilled in the new Temple by chapter 66.

The passage defines the congregation being invited to God's new Temple in Jerusalem. It defines the new Israel.

I. *The Lord's servants are heirs* (54:17a).

(a) Of spiritual food and drink that satisfies (55:1–2).

(b) Of life in covenant like David's (55:3).

(c) Of joy without end (55:12–13).

(d) Of a place in God's house (56:7).

II. *The Lord's servants are secured.*

(a) In the devotions of David (55:3).

(b) By a mighty nation chosen to help (55:4–5).

(c) By God's unbreakable Word (55:1–11).

III. *The Lord's servants are required . . .*

(a) To seek the Lord (55:1, 6).

(b) To repent, for the Lord is different (55:7–9).

(c) To keep justice, do right (56:1).

(d) To keep Sabbath (56:2).

IV. *God's purpose is . . .*

(a) To beautify Jerusalem (55:5d).

(b) To fill his new Temple (56:7a).

(c) To make it a house of prayer for all nations (56:7b).

(d) To gather Israel's outcasts and many more (56:8).

V. *Invitations are out.*

(a) To everyone who yearns for God (55:1–3).

(b) To foreigners who join the Lord's people (56:3, 6).

(c) To eunuchs who choose God's ways (56:4–5).

This means that a place in Israel, heir to all the privileges of the elect, is to be offered to anyone who sincerely wants to be with God and do his will, a condition that many Israelites by birth did not fulfill. The groundwork is laid for Paul's definition of the Israel of God. Most of the Book of Isaiah deals with punishment or salvation for Israel as a whole. But from chapter 55 on to the end, the book recognizes that part of Israel will never be reconciled to the Lord. They want no part in his new plans. They are pagan and want to stay that way. Chapter 55 called for those who yearn for the Lord to step forward.

Topic: God and the Lonely Believer
TEXT: Isa. 57 (vv. 1–2, 15)

Chapter 57 speaks of the lonely believer's lot in an unbelieving and violent community.

I. *God's recognition and judgment of the profligate rebels* (57:3–13a).

II. *The isolated righteous one* (57:1–3).

(a) If he dies, no one notices (57:1a).

(b) If he is arrested, no one pays attention (57:1b-c).

(c) Afterward, his uprightness stands firm while others are to be punished (57:2ff.).

III. *The status of the believer* (57:13b, 15).

(a) He will possess the land (57:13a).

(b) He will have a place in God's holy mountain (57:13b).

(c) He will dwell with God (57:15).

When the humble righteous perish, no one seems to notice. But God does. This is the one with whom God chooses to dwell eternally. This one may appear dispirited and lifeless in death. But God will revive the spirits of his humble ones.

Topic: God's Idea of Proper Worship

TEXT: Isa. 58:3–14

The nature of acceptable worship is an issue throughout Isaiah. Jerusalem's worship was condemned in chapter 1. Chapters 55 and 57 have spoken about the participants in worship. Chapter 66 will have no place for sacrifice in the new Temple. Chapter 58 asks about the usefulness of fasting and defines God's idea of a proper fast.

I. *Why doesn't God reward our worship* (58:3)?

II. *You worship for your own pleasure* (58:2 and 3a).

III. *Worship for strife and contention is unacceptable* (58:4).

IV. *God's choice for worship* (58:5–8).

(a) Does God rejoice in self-humiliation (58:5)?

(b) No! God likes (58:6) this: (1) Opening bonds of wickedness, (2) breaking bonds that bind, (3) setting the oppressed free.

(c) God's favorite worship (58:7): (1) Sharing bread with the poor, (2) sharing your home with the homeless, (3) providing clothes for the naked, and (4) not avoiding the need of your kin.

V. *Such worship gets divine response* (58:8–11).

(a) Your light will shine.

(b) Your righteousness will be recognized.

(c) God will answer your prayers.

(d) This will happen when you remove the yoke of oppression and the critic and troublemaker; when you give yourself to the needy.

VI. *The blessings reserved for such worshipers* (58:10b–12).

(a) Your light will shine in darkness (v. 10b).

(b) The Lord will guide, satisfy, and strengthen you.

(c) You will flourish like a watered garden (v. 11b).

(d) You will rebuild the ruined city (v. 12).

VII. *Those are blessed in keeping Sabbath* (58:13–14).

(a) If such keep Sabbath (58:13a), not doing what you want, but what God wants (v. 13b),

(b) then you may delight in the Lord (v. 14a);

(c) then he will make you ride high and eat well (v. 14bc).

Topic: God's Anointed Agent

TEXT: Isa. 61:1–7

The Book of Isaiah describes several persons who lead in making her new salvation a reality. Cyrus is introduced in chapters 44 and 45. A key role is played by the suffering and death of one person in chapters 50 and 53. A person anointed by God's own Spirit is introduced in chapter 61. Jesus read this passage and saw his own role portrayed in it (Luke 4:14–21).

I. *The Spirit-anointed bearer of good news is sent* (61:1–2):

(a) To bring good news to the poor.

(b) To bandage broken hearts.

(c) To proclaim liberty to captives.

(d) To announce the day of favor and of vengeance.

II. *The grieving people are served* (61:3–7).

(a) They will have gladness for mourning.

(b) They are to be called oaks of God's planting.

(c) They will build the ancient ruins.

(d) They will have flocks and vineyards.

(e) They are to be called priests of the Lord.

(f) They will not be shamed but blessed with the heritage of Jacob.

Topic: Why the Apostates Are Excluded
TEXT: Isa. 65:1–16

The separation of the believing and loyal people of God from the unbelieving rebels, which began in chapter 55 and 58, reaches its peak in chapter 65. They will not be allowed to spoil God's celebration in the new Temple.

I. *God's patience* (65:1–8).

(a) God was open, but these did not seek him (65:1–2).

(b) These provoked God with pagan practices (65:3–4).

(c) They wanted no part of God (65:5–7).

(d) "I was patient, so as not to destroy the whole" (v. 8).

II. *God's determination* (65:9–10).

(a) To have a worthy heir for Jacob.

(b) To have an heir for Judah in Jerusalem.

(c) To have genuine elect heirs living there.

(d) To have a beautiful land for those who seek him.

III. *Patience now ended* (65:11–12). Apostates are assigned to slaughter.

(a) Because God called, but they did not answer.

(b) Because they chose what God did not like.

IV. *A necessary separation* (65:13–15).

(a) God's servants will eat, but they will go hungry.

(b) God's servants will drink, but they will be thirsty.

(c) God's servants rejoice, but they are shamed.

(d) God's servants sing, but they cry.

(e) They leave their name as a curse for the chosen.

V. *The new unspoiled age* (65:15b).

(a) God's servants are to get a new name.

(b) Therefore, the former troubles may be forgotten.

Topic: God's New City on His Mountain
TEXT: Isa. 66:6–24

The Book of Isaiah had defined God's goal of a new and different Temple in 2:2–5. It pictures the fulfillment of the vision in the new Temple to which seeking and believing worshipers, Israelites and Gentiles alike, come. There are still problems with unbelieving opposition, and the book ends on a sour note that not all Jews believed and sought the Lord.

I. *God's new city*

(a) It suddenly appears (66:6–9).

(b) There is a reason for rejoicing (66:10–11).

(c) It is blessed by God (1) with peace like a river (66:12a), (2) with the glory of nations (66:12b), (3) with comfort and support for his people (66:13).

(d) This is a sign that the Lord is with his servants (66:14b) and against his enemies (66:14c–17).

II. *The Lord is coming to his new city* (66:18).

(a) To gather everyone to come and see his glory (66:18).

(b) To establish a sign among them (66:19).

(c) To send witness of his glory to the nations (66:19b).

(d) The witness will bring Israel's brothers (1) as an offering to the Lord, (2) to come to the Lord's mountain, (3) for some to become priests to the Lord (66:20).

(e) This will continue permanently (66:22–23). (1) All kinds of people will come to worship. (2) As they leave, they will witness the signs of Israel's apostasy.

The Book of Isaiah ends with the triumphant fulfillment of Isaiah's vision of a new Temple and city on God's mountain. But it continues to the end to witness to Israel's failure to recognize and follow God in his triumphant march. Only believers, some descendants of Abraham and some Gentiles, fill the house of prayer for all nations on that glorious day.

SECTION IX.
Resources for Preaching on Family Issues

BY WADE ROWATT AND MARY JO BROCK ROWATT

The Scriptures describe a wide variety of family situations. Family enters at the creation story with God creating male and female for the twin purpose of procreation and companionship. We sometimes shy away from preaching on family issues because of the controversial nature of certain texts. For example, "Wives be subject to your husbands."

While the cultural context of the Old and New Testament needs to be taken into account, this does not mean that principles in the Scriptures don't apply directly to family living. For example, we would not take a wayward child out to the edge of town and stone him to death. Nevertheless, it seems apparent that *all* principles for relationships in the church and in society would at least be principles for family living.

These resources develop an understanding of the Scripture and then seek applications for Christian family life. The resources are provided as guidelines to stimulate the readers' thoughts in preparation for their own messages.

Topic: The Energy Crisis Comes Home
TEXT: Isa. 40:27–31

The text seems to be addressing the nation Israel in a time of doubt and despair. They are asking, "Where is God when we need him?" The prophet reminds them that the God of creation, the everlasting God, is never without resources. God is sufficient for needs. Those who trust in their own strength,

even though they might be a youth, are not sufficient in and of themselves. Nevertheless, persons who place their trust in God find renewed strength to soar, run, and walk.

In one way or another, families in crisis repeat the question, "Where is God when we need him? It seems as though I can't go on." While the presence of God may not radically alter the dimensions of the crisis, the presence of God certainly sustains individuals as they face the crisis. Although persons can experience crises in many contexts, family life is perhaps the most frequent area of crisis, if not the most critical.

Crises that bring intrusions into our family life (like illness or death of a loved one, family conflicts and broken relationships that might end in divorce, and generational conflicts between a rebellious child and a hysterical parent) can leave family members wondering if God is sufficient for the hour. When crises place heavy demands on the family, it seems that resources for coping with the distress can fail to suffice. When it appears that an energy crisis has come home, calling upon personal reserves and strengths seldom suffices. The power of God is a promised resource.

Just as God's power is sufficient for life's critical situations, God's power can also be of assistance when little things create big hurts. Frequently, families are not torn apart by catastrophes, but family ties are gnawed by little mouselike problems such as a word hastily spoken, a mis-

273

"어디에 숨어 계십니까?"　　"어떠한 연료를 쓰고 계십니까?"

understanding in scheduling of time, a difference of opinion regarding discipline, or a variety of interests in clothing styles. These can all be sparks that start a major fire in the family. As one writer put it, "It's the little things that irritate and put you on a rack, you can sit upon a mountain but not upon a tack." When family ties seemed frayed and little things threaten to tear apart the family fabric, we must remember that God the Creator of all the earth is sufficient.

Verse 31 may be referring to three levels of God's response or three levels of personal crises. God certainly is sufficient to supply our needs at the level of soaring like an eagle, but it appears that certain family crises are such that even as we experience the full power of the presence of God we do not soar like an eagle. While there are mountaintop experiences in family life, more often God's presence keeps our family well grounded and running smoothly. However, there are times when family burdens are so heavy that it is all that we can do to walk (perhaps stumble) and not fall. Leaving the grave of one's child seems to be more of a time of walking without falling than a time of soaring like an eagle.

In conclusion, families are challenged in times of large, critical, and small irritating crises to turn to God for their strength. Rather than trying to paddle our own canoe, we need to lift our life before God and let the presence of God blow fresh through our lives like the wind catching a sail. God's strength, which undergirds the universe, provides power for facing family crises!

Topic: Where Is This Family Headed?
TEXT: Matt. 16:24–28

As Jesus clarifies his mission for the disciples, a new paradox unfolds. Those who seek to find themselves will lose themselves, but those who lose themselves for Christ's sake will find themselves. Those who desire an easy way seek a life that brings personal satisfaction and reward with a minimum amount of sacrifice. While rejecting that alternative, Jesus sets forth a higher vision. He offers a vision of sacrificial love. Most certainly, Jesus is not even hinting at earthly rewards as a promise to those who take up their cross. The life-changing principle of verse 25 is not a principle of "making Jesus your choice to drive a Rolls Royce." Rather, it is a principle of following Jesus and finding life's ultimate meaning.

As the Viennese psychiatrist Victor Frankl has put it, those who have the *why* of life can endure any *how*. When the why of life is following Jesus, any circumstance in life can bring meaning.

More than a few families mistakenly pursue goals of selfish fulfillment. They direct their family resources, energies, and even themselves toward the pursuit of power, of praise, or pleasure.

Seeking power for families can mean pursuing political power, that is, the ability to impact the decisions of others. Others devote their attention to seeking praise from community leaders. Some families use their resources in pursuit of pleasure. They acquire "gizmos," gadgets, and giveaways, hoping beyond hope to satisfy the unsatisfying desire for the ultimate emotional high. The pursuit of power and praise and pleasure are void as providers of meaning in life because of their addictive nature. It takes a little more power and a little more praise and a little more pleasure to bring this sense of satisfaction the next time. One does not have to look far in any community to find examples of families that have lost themselves in the process of trying to find themselves on the road to power, praise, or pleasure.

Individuals in families can find direction in Jesus. Losing themselves for Christ's sake means finding the unique call of Christ for their family. Each family is an uncommon package of gifts and relationships. When this package is dedicated to the service of others in the name of Jesus, it can provide a new depth to life. *A call of Christ* serves as a sense of direction for families, and as such is especially helpful in a pluralistic society where value questions rewards. Families can have a fine commitment to losing themselves for Christ's sake and have a clear sense of direction when making ethical decisions. Losing self for Christ's sake becomes the foundation stone for use of resources of time, relationships, and finances.

Likewise, families who lose themselves for Christ's sake have following Jesus as a plumbline for value clarification. Whatever the situation, the family's decision to take up the cross serves as a direct true line from whence to make the decision.

Children habitually ask, "Daddy, Mommy, where are we going?" and "How much farther?" when taking a trip or family vacation. They ask in similar ways where is this family headed as they call into question value conflicts for their parents. Children and adolescents who observe their parents spending economic and time resources in the pursuit of power and pleasure have a sense of confusion as to their own direction in life.

While following Jesus may be in full-time Christian service for some families, it will more likely mean the pursuit of a vocation within the context of the church. Not all may be called to be missionaries, evangelists, pastors, or teachers. Many may be called to be of service in the choir, teaching church school, or working in missions as a volunteer. Picking up the cross and following Jesus may mean being the best Christian physician, attorney, teacher, truck driver, retail sales person, or homemaker that one can be.

Picking up one's cross does not mean living a life without power, praise, or pleasure. But it means making your calling, not the receiving of these rewards, the goal of life. It seems that those who live their lives for Christ's sake do find a new kind of power and praise and pleasure—a kind of pleasure that is the by-product of losing themselves.

The new age of exploding options brings conflict. This calls for families to place priority on finding a sense of direction. That sense of direction is losing self for Christ's sake and taking up the cross to follow Jesus.

Topic: A Christian Family Feud
TEXT: Matt. 18:15–22
The story of the brother who sins

against you provides Christians with attitudes and specific guidelines for resolving conflicts. Jesus appears to be addressing the disciples—perhaps in context of one of their "who-is-the-greatest" conflicts. Verses 21 and 22 fit well with the story, although they perhaps serve as a transition to the parable of the unmerciful servant. The parable also serves as an illustration of the reciprocal nature of forgiveness and conflict resolution.

Conflict is perhaps the most intense within the family. Intimacy increases the intensity of differentness. While we can easily tolerate different behavior in the lives of new acquaintances, such behavior in the lives of those within the family circle produce frustration, irritation, and perhaps even anger.

A slight injustice might be brushed off with a brief apology. Someone bumps up against you in the line at the grocery store and says, "Excuse me," and you smile acknowledgingly and accept their apology. But when sisters, brothers, spouses, parents, or children behave in uncaring, unjust ways, the hurt feels much deeper.

Whether a large or small injustice, these words from Jesus provide attitudes and behaviors for resolving the difference. Consider the following. First, the one feeling offended is to take the initiative. Though it might feel natural to wait, expecting the initiative from the offender, it is more in keeping with God's ways for the one being offended to take the initiative. Consider the Incarnation: God entered in to our world of sin. When we are sinned against by one in the family, we take the initiative. If you are hurt, tell the offender!

Second, the purpose for resolving the conflict is "gaining the person." The passage realistically acknowledges that unresolved, conflicting anger creates a barrier between family members. Christians do not fight to defeat one another but fight to defeat their differences or learn to accept them in regaining their relationship. The focus for Christian family feuds needs to be resolving the difference and preserving the unity as the Body of Christ.

Third, the context of resolving differences needs to be private. We are to go alone and discuss our differences as the first line of recourse. Gossip, ventilating with friends, or even spreading conflict among other family members can escalate the conflict beyond reasonable hope for resolution. Before spreading rumors and marshaling persons to take our side, we need to go privately and discuss the difference in ways that can be resolved.

Fourth, when person-to-person resolution fails, we are to seek a peacemaker. That is, we are to take one or two witnesses with us that our words might be established. These witnesses are individuals who can hear both sides of our conflict and assist us in winning back the relationship. Rather than wallow in self-pity, a second attempt to resolve the conflict must be taken.

Fifth, when person-to-person and personal-peacemaker attempts to resolve the conflict fail, it is suggested that we take it before the church. The use of *church* is an interesting term, since this has been a preresurrection statement. This was referring to the synagogue or to the family of disciples. Whichever, it seems that the intention is clear, for it involved that group of persons that we would call church—those with whom we pray and worship and study. While certainly this did not suggest airing of our family differences in the official business session of the church, I think it does suggest that some concerns are large enough to be taken public. It seems that the Qumran community practiced this literally, and after public discussion persons were expelled.

Sixth, when person-to-person, peacemaker, and public forums fail, there is a time to back off. The analogy of treating one like a publican and tax collector could mean many different things. Perhaps it means to break the relationship. Perhaps it means to maintain a distance but to continue to pray for the other family members. Whatever the specific intent, the content is obvious. Broken relationships from an unresolved conflict seem to have eternal consequences.

Seventh, Peter's reflection in questioning "How often shall I forgive my brother?" obviously is designed to show his wisdom of his own answer of seven. Jesus seems to indicate an unlimited response in the offering of forgiveness among family members. Caution should be taken with this verse that it is not used out of context to support the codependent habit of some family members or to force a family member to remain in an abusive, potentially dangerous situation.

Practical reflections upon family feuds are in order. It seems that many families have difficulty with communication and the inability to communicate effectively makes this above-mentioned process difficult. Families who can follow a simple process of negotiation resolve conflicts more quickly.

The process in negotiation involves several phases, such as definition of the problem, brainstorming the alternatives, evaluating the alternatives, selecting a mutually agreed upon alternative, and planning its implementation. Reevaluating the decision can help prevent future conflicts.

Topic: Home: Where Love Is Spoken
TEXT: 1 Cor. 13:1–13

Long before Steven Spielberg's touching words in *E.T.*, "come home" had made a message at the heart of humankind. Home conjures up romantic images, unselfish love distributed in abundance by idealized persons.

Few homes measure up to the reality of the romanticized dreams dancing across our minds. Our homes, while not perfect, nevertheless should be centers of love.

Paul had been addressing the disunity in the church at Corinth. He elevates love above dissension as a better way of relationships. Paul reminds the readers that no matter how great the talents they might have, if we lack love we are as nothing. In modern slang Paul might have said, "What's the big whoop, if you don't have love."

In his familiar list of the characteristics of love, Paul holds out a standard that few families can ever attain. Nonetheless, love is something we do, and home should be the place where love is spoken. Consider the following list in light of family relationships.

Love is patient. Does this mean waiting for slower family members to be ready to go to church? Does this mean not pushing children to grow up faster than they should?

Love is kind. Could this mean curtailing cutting remarks so popular on sitcoms? Could this mean a total reapproach to the discipline of hard-to-manage children?

Love is not jealous. Could this mean an end to sibling conflict? Could this bring new definition to the way family members relate to each other's success?

Love is not boastful. Could this mean mothers transform their comparisons by calling off "see what my kid can do"? Would put-downs in relationship soon become terms with little meaning?

Love is not arrogant. Could this mean husbands and wives do not respond in self-righteous affirmation when they prove a point? Could this change the attitude of parents who want so much to say to their wayward children, "I told you so"? Love does not jump in line ahead of a family member. Love does not point out the mistakes of another (certainly not publicly).

Love does not insist on its own way. Can this bring a new level of cooperation to relationships? Can this transform the process of breaking loose from the way Mom and Dad used to do it to the trying of new methods?

Love is not irritable. When love is spoken at home, minor injustices can often go unnoted. Love knows when to speak up in irritation but also when to shut up.

Love does not rejoice in wrongdoing but in right. Could this mean that siblings could actually celebrate for each other's report cards? Could this mean that the generations would stop putting down the mistakes of those that follow them?

Love bears all things. Could this literally be an end to the demands for "I've got to have it my way"? Could this transform those irritating moments into opportunities for growth? This certainly would not demand that one be abused, however.

Love believes, hopes, and endures all things. Love does not give up on one another. Families broken by injustice and wrongdoing can mend their relationships. This *agape* love is a love with mutual forgiveness and respect as its foundation.

Love never ends. Love is complete. Can this mean that although a marriage ends in divorce, Christian love would not give up on each other? That divorced couples might still in love learn to cooperate for their children's sake? Does this mean that parents and children will never completely give up on a broken relationship? Can it be that grandparents will never be cut off and that wayward family members might always have a place at home?

Indeed, the kind of love that transforms family relationships is the greatest of these. Home is where love is spoken, if it is spoken any place with authenticity.

Topic: The Trouble with You Is . . .
Text: 1 Cor. 12:4–13

Paul addressing the adversity in the church at Corinth speaks directly to the differences that arise from a variety of gifts by calling attention to the fact that it is the same God who inspires all. We are all part of one body. To a church member using different gifts as a symbol of status and power, Paul says remember that we are all interdependent. We cannot hold it over each other but need to rejoice in our differentness.

Differentness in the family frequently results in unresolvable conflict. In romantic bliss a newly married couple may gloss over their differences. As their love matures they can discover the power in their differences. These differences all too frequently result in separation and/or divorce. Likewise, family members will point to the gifts of one child to the exclusion of another and alienate the child whose gift may be different.

If Christian families can take seriously Paul's statement that all gifts are inspired by one and the same spirit and that we are all one body, then we can accept family differences with a new attitude. Differences provide the family with expanded talents when the family as a whole minimizes the uniquenesses of the individuals as a source for conflict.

Some family members may have the gift of wisdom, while others have the capacity to organize and administrate, and still others are talented at hospitality and warm relationships. Rather than working to force each person into a common mold, families grow stronger and maintain happiness when they can accept the gifts as of equal value.

When families can stop using roles and ascribed power that comes with the roles as a means of their decision making and divisions of labor, then new possibilities unfold. Thus, families can discover the gifts of family members and make decisions about how the family will operate on the basis of the gifts. For example, the person who is better at retail work might keep the books. A person gifted in the area of interpersonal relationships will be the primary person responsible for maintaining the social calendar.

Whatever the gift, Paul seems to indicate that a gift is from God, can be used for the glory of God, and is to be accepted as a part of the one body. Families who can accept each other's uniqueness as a gift minimize the potential for anger and conflict while they maximize the family's overall talent pool.

Topic: Covenant Makers, Covenant Keepers

Text: Jer. 31:31–34

God gives Jesus and forgiveness as a means of keeping the new covenant with people and as our means of keeping covenants with each other.

I. In the Old Testament, God made covenants with the people.

(a) God gave the Ten Commandments, but people sinned. Many of our children know the story about God choosing Moses to lead the people out of slavery in Egypt. After the water parted and allowed them to cross the Red Sea, the people came into the wilderness of Sinai. Moses went up the mountain at Sinai and

returned with God's commandments, which we call the Ten Commandments. Exod. 20:20 says, "And Moses said to the people, 'Do not fear, for God has come to prove you and that the fear of him may be before your eyes that you may not sin' " (RSV). God gave rules about how to live without sin. Soon, though, the people did sin. Even though God was patient with them, the people broke the covenant with God.

(b) Jeremiah and the other prophets tried to call the people back into a relationship with God. Through the prophets, God kept trying to bring the people of the Old Testament into a close relationship of God and people. Repeatedly, Jeremiah urged his people to stop their sinning and return to God. Through Jeremiah, God tried to bring the people back into relationship.

(c) God promised the new covenant. Then God promised a new covenant with the people. Many people considered this the high point of the Old Testament. Jeremiah knew this new covenant would be personal, internal, and intimate with God. God would write the Law on human hearts. God would put the Law inside humans, in their minds. God wants everybody to know and to experience this relationship from the least to the greatest, from the low to the high; God wants everyone to experience this relationship. God will be God. The people will belong to God. "They will be my people."

(d) The new covenant is unbreakable because of forgiveness. The new covenant doesn't depend on our ability to be faithful to God. Keeping the new covenant does depend on God's faithfulness. God is faithful. The new covenant is based on God's nature. God will forgive the sins of the people and will not remember the sins.

(e) Jeremiah did not know that Jesus would fulfill the new covenant. Jeremiah did not know just how God would do all of this. He didn't know the details. He didn't know that Jesus Christ would fulfill the promise. He didn't know the cost of this new covenant, that Jesus would die on the cross and be resurrected on what we call Easter. We have a different

viewpoint than Jeremiah had then. Today we know Jesus' death on the cross
and Resurrection has made all of this
possible for us.

II. In the New Testament, Jesus sacri-
ficed for our sins. The writer of Hebrews
considers this Jeremiah passage so important that it is quoted in Heb. 10:16–
17. Verse 18 continues, "Where there is
forgiveness of these [sins]), there is no
longer any offering for sin." Jesus was
the offering for our sin. We no longer
offer sacrifices on altars. We can accept
Jesus' sacrifice on the cross for us and
our sins.

III. People today can make current
covenants.

(a) We can accept God's gift of salvation through Jesus. The most important
action we can do is to accept Jesus, God's
gift to us, to each one of us as an individual. Each one of us has wrongdoings
and sin. Each one of us can believe with
our own mind and our own heart that
Jesus died on a cross for our own sins.
We can believe this in knowledge and in
feelings. Jesus was resurrected and offers
forgiveness for our sins. Each one of us
can be a part of the new covenant that
was mentioned in Jeremiah. Even though
we sin, we can have forgiveness. Each
one of us can know and experience God
because of what Jesus did for us.

(b) In human relationships, despite
failures and disappointments, forgiveness is the key to keeping covenants. God
promises a faithful and durable relationship with us. We can be faithful in our
human relationships also. We can determine to stay in covenant with others
through good and bad, for better and
worse, through thick and thin. At times
each one of us fails and disappoints God.
Also, in our human relationships, failures
and disappointments will come. Forgiveness is the key to the new covenant in
Jeremiah's prophecy. Forgiveness is the
key to keeping our human covenants. We
make several covenants in our lives.
When we marry, we make a marriage
covenant. We can make covenants with
friends. We can have covenants within
our church family. We may make a covenant to parent our children.

(c) We make (and break) covenants in
marriage. In a marriage ceremony, people often covenant to remain together for
better and for worse. Some of us have
been able to keep these promises; others
of us have not.

(1) Sometimes in a marriage a really
tragic event happens and the end result
is divorce. The husband may commit a
felony and be imprisoned. The marriage
cannot stand the strain. The wife may be
able to steal the stocks from in-laws, and
the marriage cannot withstand the pressures. Something big can happen that results in the marriage blowing up.

(2) Sometimes in marriages we let little
things continue to pile up and the marriage doesn't blow up; it fizzles out. Such
marriages are like dropping grains of
sand on fire until the flame of love is ex-
tinguished. Divorce may be the result.

(3) Forgiveness can come within the
marriage or forgiveness may come after a
divorce. Either way, God is able to forgive.

(d) We can make covenants with
friends. Some of us have been married
and are now divorced. Some of us are
widowed. Some of us have never been
married. In the Old Testament, Ruth
stated a pledge of loyalty to her mother-
in-law, Naomi, after they were both widowed. In Ruth 1:16–17, she states, "En-
treat me not to leave you or to return
from following you. For where you go, I
will go, and where you lodge, I will lodge.
Your people shall be my people, and
your God, my God. Where you die, I will
die, and there will I be buried. May the
Lord do so to me and more also if even
death parts me from you."

Jonathan and David are examples of a
covenant between friends. First Samuel
18:3 says, "Then Jonathan made a covenant with David because he loved him as
his own soul." Jonathan and David chose
to make a covenant with each other because of their friendship. Ruth chose to
express her love to Naomi. We may
choose to state our loyalty or make a covenant with a friend. As in other relationships when disappointments and failures
may come, forgiveness is the key to keeping the friendship, the relationship. In

the New Testament, Paul mentions several relationships.

(e) We can make covenants within the church. In Eph. 5:12–33, Paul compares the mutual subjection relationship of husband and wife to the mutual subjection relationship of Christ and the Church. Sometimes, though not always, our close friends will be church members with us. Sometimes we work hard to have a right relationship with others in our church.

When we call a pastor to minister in our local congregation, we covenant to work together as pastor and people. As in other relationships, disappointments and failures can come. Forgiveness again is the key to keeping the covenant. Rather than a church firing a pastor or rather than a pastor resigning over disappointments and failures of one another, we can work toward a durable, long-term relationship.

(f) We can make covenants with our children in God's way. We try to work toward durable, long-term relationships with our children. As well as covenants in our church families, we can have covenants in our biological and blended (step) families. Often in parent dedication services, parents and church members will both covenant to rear the children in God's ways.

IV. While God gives commandments and covenants, forgiveness is the means of keeping covenants. Remember, forgiveness is the way God keeps renewed covenant with us. Throughout the Old and New Testament, God has given commandments and covenants. Moses received the Ten Commandments, yet the people sinned. When God made covenants, the people sinned. Jeremiah prophesied about a new covenant. On the cross, Jesus made this new covenant possible. When asked about the greatest commandment of all, Jesus answered, " 'Love your God with all your heart and with all your soul and with all your mind.' This is the first and greatest commandment. And the second is like it: 'Love your neighbor as yourself.' " (Matt. 22:37–40, NIV).

God has given us commandments and covenants. God has given us Jesus as an example of loving and forgiving. Although we are sometimes covenant breakers, God forgives. In our marriages, friendships, churches, and families, God has given us forgiveness as a way to be not only covenant makers but also covenant keepers—as God has done for us.

Topic: Like Parent, Like Child—Like Christ

TEXT: Eph. 5:21; 6:1–4

Parents are to love in mutual subjection with children so that they honor and obey the parents, while the parents rear them in the discipline and instruction of Christ. Children can often make our world happy. We have some good experiences with our families, and some not so good. Each of us has been a child.

I. Mutual subjection is for Christ's sake.

(a) Children are instructed to obey their parents in the Lord. Children are to honor both father and mother. Often these verses have been separated from the other verses surrounding them.

(b) In Ephesians, Paul emphasizes how we are to walk or live as Christians. He continues this overarching idea as he applies his theme to family relationships.

(c) Recall writing a theme or essay at school. Very likely in an English class a teacher taught you about using a thesis sentence to introduce an overall or central idea. Paul states a central idea in Eph. 5:21. "Being subject" is in a sense of voluntarily yielding in love. Paul clarifies his thought with the phrase "to one another." This subjection is to be mutual. A mutual subjection is not because of the worth of either person. Reverence for Christ is the reason. Evelyn and Frank Stagg state, "Any submission or service rendered another is to be expressive of one's submission to Christ" (*Women in the World of Jesus*, p. 193). We as Christians are to model Christ's love for the world.

(d) Paul then applies the general thought to three areas of life. The first is wives and husbands. He compares this relationship to that of the Church and

Christ. The second is the relationship of children and parents. The third is that between slaves and earthly masters. Paul does not expect this small band of Christians to change their entire social system overnight. He does expect them to help change individuals because of Christ.

(e) Paul urges a shared responsibility. In New Testament times, men had the power. Women, children, and slaves were property. Christ's words and actions were revolutionary for the culture in which he spoke. Here Paul is revolutionary. He thinks wives, children, and slaves have responsibility to make changes and progress. Paul encourages them to share with the men the responsibility of modeling Christ's love to their world. Their relationships with each other are to reflect Christ's love.

II. Parent/child relationships are the next focus. Paul addresses the children and then the fathers. Remember, Paul says we are to be subject to one another.

(a) Children. Should parents be subject to their children? At first it seems the answer is a definite no. Some kids have too little respect for grown-ups as it is, and then they are to be subject to them? However, when a parent cares for a little child, a little dependent infant, they voluntarily subject themselves to that child. With each caring act of feeding or diapering, they subject themselves to that child and the needs of the child. As children grow toward adulthood, the parents respect the child's movement toward their becoming their own person. We are to subject ourselves to our children for Christ's sake. They, in turn, are to subject themselves to their parents out of respect and reverence for Christ.

(b) Regarding parents, Paul gives instruction to the men as husbands, fathers, and masters. In all those verses he addresses the fathers. Surely this instruction can apply to mothers in our society. The fathers are not to bring the children to anger. Are the mothers supposed to bring them to anger? No. Are the mothers to do nothing at all and yet be obeyed and honored? No. Without distorting we can say that we as parents are not to

bring our children to anger. What a task! What are we to do? Be so permissive they can do just anything they want?

(c) Are we to be permissive? If we let them do anything they want, surely then they won't get angry. Not true. Children need limits. They need to know we care enough about them to train them.

(d) Training a child takes time. Proverbs 22:6 states, "Train up a child in the way he should go and when he is old he will not depart from it." How nice it would be if it stated, "and when they are teenagers they will not depart from it either." However, this scripture does not say tell them what is right. It says to train them, which does take time.

(e) How strict should parents be? In some families we seem to hold on too tightly. The children feel that in order to be a person they must rebel in a strong way or they will simply be a person with no thoughts or feelings of their own.

(f) Anger sometimes is outward and shows for all to see. Sometimes anger is turned inward and becomes hurt and depression and suicide. Either way the anger is there. How hard it is to be parents day after day without bringing our children to anger! We usually do not intend to bring them to anger.

(g) Our intention usually is to be effective parents, to be good enough. We try to bring up these children in the discipline and instruction of the Lord. Sometimes it is easy to instruct children in the Lord. We teach Bible stories and even what they mean for our day.

(h) What about discipline? The word can be translated discipline, upbringing, correction, instruction, or training. Parents can learn about discipline—natural consequences, logical consequences, age-appropriateness, how to listen, ways to respond, and discipline that teaches. Parents can learn ways to model the love of Christ for children.

III. Remember, Paul is telling Christians to be models for the world, to witness for Christ by the way they walk or live. Jesus is a model of love for the world. We are to be models in our world, in our families, for our children.

Whether we like it or not, our children learn by the models that we live before them.

IV. Forgiveness.

(a) Sometimes people have regrets. At times we have modeled what we did not intend to teach our children, and we have regrets about this. They can bring an angry response.

(b) What are we to do in our anger or when we bring our children to anger? Psalm 4:4 says, "In your anger do not sin" (NIV).

(c) But sin so often follows the anger—the child's anger or the parent's anger. We are not to bring the child to that situation, yet we fail. We sin by what we do and by what we don't do—by what we commit and omit both. We all fail at this ideal. Sometimes we need to excuse ourselves. We expected too much. Sometimes we need forgiveness.

(d) Col. 3:13 says, "As the Lord has forgiven you, so you also must forgive" (RSV). Sometimes parents are to forgive children; sometimes children are to forgive parents. At times we need to forgive ourselves and accept God's forgiveness of us. Those regrets may cause us to go to our child to ask for forgiveness. Sometimes we cannot go to the person; they refuse to listen or they may be dead. We can go directly to God for forgiveness. God forgives us. We forgive our children. They learn from our modeling to forgive us. One part of our modeling is asking for and granting forgiveness from our families.

V. Therefore, with mutual subjection children obey and honor, while parents instruct and discipline without arousing anger. When anger is aroused and sin follows, we forgive. We can put aside any negative patterns of parenting that we have as models from the past. We can learn new ways. Remember: like parent, like child. Models make our parent/child relationships to be loving models—like Christ's.

SECTION X.
Children's Stories and Sermons

January 5. Plan Now!
TEXT: "So teach us to number our days / that we may get a heart of wisdom" Ps. 90:12

Visual introduction: Appointment book or calendar.

Sentence summary: Plan your time to include the best things.

Here is a new calendar to remind us that we are beginning a new year with many new opportunities. It will likely be another busy year.

Have you ever noticed that every day becomes filled with too many things to do? We stay busy all the time, yet we cannot do it all. We can be in only one place at a time. That is why this little book or calendar is so helpful. It has every day of the week and month listed in plain sight. We have room to write down all the important things we want to do for each day. This is called an appointment book. Most people use a regular calendar for the same purpose.

A calendar helps us to realize that we have only seven days a week. If we want to do something important, like take a vacation or go visit grandparents, we must plan in advance. So we write it down on this calendar for the new year.

Perhaps your parents want you to keep your room clean. To remind you of this duty, they ask you to schedule it on your calendar. So you write a note on each Saturday. "Clean my room!" That helps you plan your time for chores and still have time for fun.

Long ago Moses realized how important good planning is. We must count our days carefully. Here is what Moses said in a poem which became Ps. 90:12: "So teach us to number our days / that we may get a heart of wisdom."

We won't live forever here on earth. Best count your days carefully. Be wise in your heart, and plan all the best things that you want done. That will help make a new year happy.—C. W. Bess

January 12. The Super Bowl
A special event is shown every year on television. Not everyone watches, but people who are interested in football probably do. Do you know what it is called? [Super Bowl] That is a rather strange name. I guess it refers to the fact that the stadium is shaped like a bowl, with people sitting around the bowl to watch what happens on the field of the floor of the bowl. It is called super because the team that wins is supposed to be the best team in the country for this year.

One of the most important parts of the game of football is that each team has eleven people who must all work together to make anything happen. What they do together is called teamwork.

You are showing good teamwork when all of you come up here on Sunday morning and let me talk to you. Those people out there, in the sanctuary, are showing good teamwork when they come to church to worship with others and when they do their part in helping to make our worship experience meaningful. They are showing good teamwork when they do their share in supporting our ministry together. You show good teamwork when you help your parents do what needs to be done around the house.

Whenever we have to do things with other people, we have a super opportunity to show good teamwork. Part of being a good Christian is to love other people and part of our loving is to help one another. Whenever we do that, we are playing in our own super bowl.—Kenneth Mortonson

January 19. The Prodigal's Brother

[You may prefer to have a children's class come up with the following two lists ahead of time.]

Have you ever thought about what you don't like about having a brother or sister? Have you ever thought that the way your brother or sister was treated just wasn't fair to you? What is it you don't like? [Allow time for children to read their answers or respond to the question.] Now that we've aired these complaints, tell me what you love about having a brother or a sister in your family. [Listen to responses.] Which was easier—thinking of what you don't like about your brother or sister, or thinking about what you do like?

You may know the story of the prodigal son. In that story there are two brothers. The younger one runs away, but he comes back. The older one never leaves home. But while the father is so excited when the younger son returns, the older son is just plain jealous. In fact, he is mad that his dad is throwing a party for the runaway son. After all, that's not fair. The older brother isn't happy with his dad or his brother. Actually, he doesn't seem like a happy person. The older brother may miss out on a lot of things—the party, the fun he could have with his family, the good relationship he could have with his dad and his brother. He may spend so much time being jealous and feeling sorry for himself that he misses out on the love and joy he could have.

Maybe Jesus told us this story to warn us that we are a lot like the older brother sometimes. We can be so jealous of others that we forget how lucky we are, and how many good gifts we already have. Let's pray that we see and enjoy the good gifts around us—gifts like those people who are our brothers and sisters.—Carol Younger

January 26. What Other People Think about Us

TEXT: Rom. 12:17–21

Do you know what a "reputation" is? *Reputation* is a word that means "what others think of you." To have a good reputation means that people are glad to see us and be with us and will listen to us. To have a bad reputation means that people are not glad to see us and do not want to be with us and will not listen to us.

The Bible tells us that we need to be careful about what others think of us, that we need to be sure that we have a good reputation. Only if people want to be with us and listen to us will we be able to tell them about Jesus and how much he loves them and how much we love them. If we have a bad reputation, they won't listen to us; they won't believe us. So let's be sure that people think we are good people by doing the right things and saying good things. Let's tell God that is what we will do.—Michael Lanway

February 2. Shoes

Object: A pair of my shoes.

Have you ever heard the song, "All God's Children Got Shoes"? What do you think it means?

Let me tell you how that song came to be written. You remember that we had slavery in this country until about one hundred and fifty years ago. Many of the slaves were also Christians. Their owners were Christians, usually, but they still did not treat the slaves right.

The slaves didn't have their freedom, and they didn't own much. Often they didn't have decent shoes. They just didn't have the bare necessities of life in this world. So they made up this song about heaven. They said things would finally be right in heaven. People could treat them wrong on earth and make them feel that they weren't as good as white people, but in heaven it would be different. *All* God's children would have shoes in heaven.

What does that mean to you? Doesn't it mean that God will make things right one day for all people? People who are not fair to others will not really get away with it. That also means you and I should be trying to be fair in our lives. We can dedicate ourselves to seeing that people are not mistreated. Sometimes we may really need to help people have shoes, but more than that, we need to help God see that people around us get treated fairly in every way.—Stuart G. Collier

February 9. Using Questions

Who can tell me what this sign means? [? on a piece of paper] Have you ever asked a question? What do you use questions for? [To find out things.]

This morning I would like each of you to answer a very simple question for me. What is your name? [Give each child a chance to tell his or her name.]

A name is a very important thing. When you know someone's name, you can then identify that person from all the other people around you. And as you get to know more and more about that person, when you hear their name, you remember all the things you know.

Who is [name the current president of the United States]? Who is [name your choir director and/or your organist, etc.]? See how important a name is.

The same thing applies to Jesus. When we hear the name of Jesus, when we pray in his name, when we say we believe in his name, we are saying that we remember who he is and what he did for us. So the more you know about Jesus, the more you can remember when you hear or use his name.

That is what we all need to do. We all need to learn as much as we can about Jesus and his ways.—Kenneth Mortonson

February 16. What Does God Sound Like?

Preparation: On a tape, record several items. Have two or three members of the church that the children would know

(i.e., Sunday school teachers, etc.) speak to them. Next, record someone reading Scripture. Finally, record the accompaniment for a familiar hymn.

Sometimes you will hear people say that God spoke to them. If you ask them what God sounded like, they may not describe the sound of his voice, but they might tell you what they were doing or what they were listening to when they heard him. Listen to a few sounds and tell me what you hear. [Play the first set of voices—those members who are greeting the children. Pause between each voice and ask who they heard.] How can other people help you hear something God wants to say to you? [Listen for responses. Suggest that teachers and church workers can help us grow and learn more that God wants us to know. Play the Scripture reading.] What did you hear? How can the Bible help us hear God's voice? [Play the music.] What did you hear? How can the music we hear and the songs we sing in church help us hear God's voice?

God uses many different ways to get his message across to us. That's one of the reasons we need to pay attention to the things around us so we don't miss what he is trying to tell us. When you are in Sunday school listening to a lesson, you might hear something you hadn't heard before or think about something in a new way, and God might teach you something new through that. When you are sitting in church listening to the Bible being read, you might hear God speaking to you, showing you something about him that you hadn't seen before. When you are singing in a worship service or listening to special music, you might feel that God is trying to get a message across to you through the song.

It's good to know that God speaks in many different ways to people. Let's pray that he'll help us pay attention to what he's trying to tell us.—Brett Younger

February 23. Is Anyone Better than You?

TEXT: Matthew 7

I want to tell you a story. It is about Billy Bob and Suzy Q. Billy Bob is the biggest boy in school. Because he is the biggest boy in school, he thinks he is better than everybody. He says to the other boys and girls, "I am bigger than you, and I can do more things than you. That means I am better than you." Is he right? Is Billy Bob better than everyone? No, he is not. He is the same as everyone else. Just because he is bigger does not mean that he is better.

Now Suzy Q thinks she is better than everyone, too. She has beautiful brown hair and pretty teeth. She wears pretty clothes and has nice shoes. And she is very pretty. She says to the other boys and girls, "My clothes are nicer than yours and so are my shoes. That means I am better than you." Is she right? Is Suzy Q better than everyone else? No, she is not. She is the same as everyone else. Clothes and shoes and hair have nothing to do with being better than others.

No one is better than anyone else. You are not any better than anyone else. No one else is better than you. We all are the same. Let's thank God that we are the same and that he loves us all the same.—Michael Lanway

March 1. Snap Your Fingers
What do you usually do when you meet someone? [Say hello or shake hands.] That is the way we greet people. But there is a country, far away from here, called the Sudan where the people greet one another in a different way. They snap their finger, like this. In that country, a group of people greeting each other would sound like this. [Ask the congregation to reply to your snap by snapping back.]

As these people translated the Bible into their own language, they had to find a way of expressing what the Bible says in a way they could understand. Our word *reconciliation* means being united with God again as a friend. And so they translated that idea as "Meet, snapping fingers together again."

This is a very important idea for us to remember. God wants to be our friend. He wants to snap fingers with us. He wants to love us and help us, if we will let him.

So let us snap our fingers once more to show God that we want to be friends with him.—Kenneth Mortonson

March 8. Why Do We Pray?
TEXT: Matt. 6:9–13
Take one minute to talk with someone you know who is sitting here with us. I will call time. Now take a minute to let your friend talk to you. Again, I will call time. That was hard, wasn't it. Because you did not know you were going to have to say something, it was difficult just to make up some words when you were being timed. But I have noticed you at other times, when you are playing and coming to Sunday school, you talk together and have a great deal to say.

Now we want to talk to God. So let us bow our heads and close our eyes. If you know the Lord's Prayer, repeat it with me. [Pray slowly the Lord's Prayer.] Now that was both easy and hard. It was easy if you knew the words. It may have seemed difficult because we had our eyes closed and heads bowed. We likewise did not have a time for God to talk to us. Sometimes prayer may seem strange to us. So I would like to tell you why we pray and why we do what we do when we pray.

Why do you think we pray? [Receive and respond to the various answers of the children.] Well, these are good answers. We pray because God is our friend. We pray because God asks us to pray, and we pray because we need to talk to one who loves us and one whom we can trust.

It is important to pray at certain times. What are some of the times you think we should pray? [Receive and respond to the various answers of the children.] Yes, these are important times, such times as before meals and before bedtime. Might it even be a good time to pray before we get out of bed in the morning or before we start our day? It often helps to know when we are going to pray. When we know we are going to talk to God we can say prayers we remember, like the Lord's Prayer. This makes prayer easier because we do not have to wonder what we are going to say. There are also mealtime prayers and bedtime prayers we can learn as well.

Why do you suppose we close our eyes and bow our heads when we pray? [Receive and respond to the various answers of children.] Yes, we bow our heads as a sign of respect to God. We close our eyes because we do not want anything around us to distract us when we are talking to our special friend.

Now, let me ask you one last and very important question. Do we have to pray to God only at special times, with words we have memorized, with heads bowed and our eyes closed? [Receive and respond to the children's answers.] You were right; we can pray to God anytime. We can pray in our own words. We can talk to our friend with our eyes open, and even while we are doing other things, we can think about God. There are two kinds of prayer: formal prayer, like the Lord's Prayer, and informal prayer, when you let your mind and your own words go to God.

Thank you for helping me to answer the important question, Why do we pray? You may go back to your places now. Remember what we have talked about today, because I will want to ask you about it next Sunday when we will ask another important question about why we do what we do.—William Hendricks

March 15. Why Do We Come to Church?

Welcome boys and girls to the house of God. I have a special treat for you today. [Have an autoharp or some such simple instrument, play a child's hymn, "I Was Glad When They Said unto Me Let Us Go into the House of the Lord." Then lead the children or have someone lead the children in singing that song.] That is a special song, and it tells about our happiness in coming to church. That song also answers one of our important questions. Remember we began asking our important questions last Sunday. The first question was, Why do we pray? In a moment I will see what we can remember about that question; but just now I want to ask the question, Why do we come to church? Did you know that you have already given one answer? The church is

God's house, and God invites us to God's house. [Read Ps. 122:1.] Recall how much happiness you have when you visit a friend's house. It is a special privilege. It means you have a friend who likes you very much. What does your mother tell you when you go to a friend's house? [Receive and acknowledge the answers of the children.] Well, one of the things you always do when you visit a friend's house is to be on your best behavior and remember to thank your friend for her kindness. We should also remember those rules when we go to the house of God, our friend.

There is another reason we should come to church. Why do you go to school? [Receive and acknowledge the children's answers.] Among the important reasons we go to school is to learn about things that will help us in life. This is also a reason we should come to church—to help us learn about things that will help us in life. In church we learn about what is right and what is wrong. We hear and tell stories of people who loved God and who helped other people. We greet our friends. We have picnics and social times with our church groups. But most of all we learn about God, and we learn about Jesus, God's Son.

We come to church because we do things here that we do not always do in school. We do special things in church, which help us to enjoy life. We sing, just as you sang a moment ago. We hear about God just as you will hear about God in the sermon a moment later. And we pray. Now, that reminds me about last Sunday's question, Why do we pray? Does anybody remember when we pray? [Receive and acknowledge the answers of the children about prayer.] Yes, we pray because God is our friend. We pray because God asks us to pray. We pray because we need to talk to someone who loves us and whom we can trust. These are very much the same as our reasons for coming to church. These reasons are (1) because this is God's house, and God invites us to come; (2) because we want to learn about God and God's son, Jesus; and (3) because we do special things in church that will help us enjoy life. It is a good thing to come to church, and I am especially glad to see you when you come to church.

Now let me tell you one final important word. The Church is really the people who come to worship God. The building is God's house; and we often call it the church. But we really know that *the* Church is the people of God, and the church building is God's house. Let me show you something I learned when I was a little boy that helped me to remember that the Church is really the people of God and that the building is God's house. [Make the steeple with the index fingers while the other fingers are bunched inside one another, then reverse.] Here is the poem that goes with that action: Here is the church / Here is the steeple / Open the door / See all the people.

Now, you practice that with your hands while we say the poem together. [The children imitate the hand positions and recite the poem.] Now let us pray before you go back to your places.—William L. Hendricks

March 22. Why Do We Read the Bible?
Welcome to God's house. Welcome to worship. Worship is recognizing God's Word and giving honor to God. How do we know about God? [Receive and acknowledge the children's answers.] That is right! The most important way we know about God is through the Bible. [Show the children your Bible.] Let me tell you what the words *Holy Bible* mean. The word *Bible* means a collection of books. This is one book, but it is also a collection of sixty-six books. [Open the Bible to the contents page.] See, here are the names of the books that are found in the book we call the Bible.

The word *Holy* means that this is a special book, different from all other books. The word *Holy* means that this is God's very special book. So the Holy Bible is a collection or set of very special books that tell us about God.

[Show the children a letter.] What is this? You are right, it is a letter from my mother who lives in____. This letter is full of news about my family and my friends. It makes me very happy to hear from people who love me. I showed you this letter because it will help us to answer the question, Why do we read the Bible? We read the Bible because it is like a letter from someone who loves us. The Bible tells us that we are part of the family of God. God is the heavenly Father of us all. Jesus is a good and loving brother. The Bible gives us this good news.

There is a second reason we read the Bible. [Show the children a volume of *Child Craft* or the *World Book.*] What is this? [Receive and acknowledge the children's responses.] Yes, this is a sourcebook. It is a good place to find out what we need to know about many things. I showed you this book because it will help us with the second answer, why we read the Bible. The Bible is our best sourcebook to find out what we need to know about God. The Bible gives us stories about the fact that God made the world, about the fact that God guided the people of Israel in the Old Testament days, and about the fact that God sent Jesus to be our friend. The Bible is our very best sourcebook about God. So we read the Bible when we want to know about God.

What is this? [Hold up an atlas or a map.] Yes, it is a map. When do you use a map? [Receive and respond to the answers of the children.] You are right! You use a map when you are going on a trip or a journey. We use maps as a guide to help us find our way to where we want to go. I showed you the map because it helps us with the third reason we should read the Bible. We should read the Bible because it will help us find where we need to go in our trip or journey of life. Other people have gone through life before us. God knows all of the roads that people travel. Life is like a journey. The Bible is like a guide. We read the Bible to help us find the right direction, the direction toward God.

We have found out a lot about the Bible today. Let us see how well you remember what we have learned. [Hold up each item in turn asking the appropriate question.] This is the Bible. Does it have one book or many? [Many.] The Bible is like a _____? [letter]. The Bible is like _____? [sourcebook]. The Bible is like a _____? [map]. I am very pleased that you are learning so much about important questions this month. We have talked together about why we pray, about why we come to church, about why we read the Bible. [Kim], will you thank God for prayer? [Erika], will you thank God for our church? [Pamela], will you thank God for our Bible? —William L. Hendricks

March 29. Why Do We Help People?

[If there are puppeteers in your church, ask them to present the story of the good Samaritan, Luke 10:29–37. If you do not have puppets, briefly and dramatically tell this parable in the fashion children can understand.]

In this story, which Jesus told his followers, there are many kinds of people. There is a man going about his own business. There are thieves who take the man's money and beat him up. There are two people who are too busy to help the injured man. There is a hero, who is a foreigner to that country. Why do you suppose the Samaritan helped the man? [Receive and reply to the children's responses.] Well, these are very good answers. I must tell you honestly the Bible does not tell us why the Samaritan did his good deed. But we certainly know that Jesus approved of what he did.

When you are hurt or are in trouble, what do you need? That is right. You need help. At one time or another does everybody need help? Yes, everyone needs help at some time or another. One of the important things we learn at church is to help other people. Today we ask that final question: Why do we help other people?

One reason we help others is because Jesus asked us to help others. The Bible says, "Be ye kind one to another." Repeat that request with me. [Lead the children in repeating this request found in Eph. 4:32.] Jesus was certainly kind to people, especially to children. We know that Jesus loves us. We want to love Jesus also. One important sign of friendship and

love is to do what those who love us ask us to do. We help other people because Jesus, our friend, asks us to help them.

We also help others because others have helped us. Jesus tells us that we need to help others in the way we would like for them to help us. Jesus said: "Whatever you would that people do to you, do you to them." Let us repeat that together. [It is found in Matt. 7:12.] Name some people who have helped you. [Receive and acknowledge replies of the children.]

There is still another reason we should help other people. We should help others because it is the right thing to do. The Bible also tells us that if we know what is good we should do it, because if we do not do what we know is right, we are doing a very bad thing. We should do the right thing when we know it is the right thing. It is good to help other people. So we must help them.

For four Sundays we have asked very important questions. We have answered why we pray, why we come to church, why we read the Bible, and why we help others. It has been a very important month. I want to thank you for sharing these questions. I hope you remember what we have talked about together. Now let us have prayer and then you may return to your seats.—William L. Hendricks

April 5. Pictures and God

Object: A photograph of someone the children know and like.

Look at this picture. Do you know who it is? That's right, it is our children's minister.

You can tell a lot about her from this picture, can't you? Let's pretend you didn't know her. What can you tell about her from the picture?

Her face is pretty. Her clothes are nice. She is young. All that is right. But there is so much more to her than that, isn't there? You just have to know her! She is so much more than the picture, and the only way you find out is to be around her, talk to her, and be her friend.

That is the same way with God. Some people know some things about God. But the best part is knowing God in person. We can read about God and find out things about God, but that is about as much fun as knowing your children's minister just by her picture. You miss the best part.

The best part of God is knowing God personally.—Stuart G. Collier

April 12. Palm Sunday

Have you ever been standing in a crowd waiting to see an honored guest or someone famous? Sometimes before you see that person, you see or hear something that lets you know someone special is coming. Have you ever heard this? [Have the pianist or organist play "Pomp and Circumstance."] When you hear it, who are the people you are about to see? You'll usually see people who are about to graduate. If you hear this [have the pianist or organist play "The Wedding March"], who is it you are about to see? You'll also see people stand up as the bride walks down the aisle. At some weddings you may see a "runner," a piece of cloth that covers the aisle that the bride comes down. Whenever you see a runner, that's a sign that someone important will come that way. Maybe a bride, maybe a king or queen, maybe a president. One way to honor someone special is to celebrate that person's arrival in a special way, with a song or with special preparations.

When Jesus entered Jerusalem, his followers made his arrival special. They covered the colt he was riding with their coats. Some spread their coats on the road before him. Others covered the road with branches. Some walked ahead of him, announcing his arrival with shouts and praises to God. Some said, "God bless him who comes in the name of the Lord." They were telling everyone who Jesus was, how special this one was. They understood how important it was to do something special for him.

As we think about Jesus during this Holy Week, we need to find special things that we can do for him, just as his followers did long ago. Maybe you know someone you could talk to about your friend Jesus. Maybe you'll see someone who needs a friend, and you'll know that Jesus wants you to be that person's friend. Maybe you could spend a certain time each day thinking about how much Jesus loves you. These are ways that you can celebrate Jesus right now.—Carol Younger

April 19. The Easter Lily

There are many symbols around us in the church. Do you know what a symbol is? It is something that reminds us of something else. The decorated evergreen trees remind us of Christmas, and the lilies remind us of Easter.

What is important about a symbol is to remember what it stands for. The Easter egg is a symbol of Easter because, at the right time, an egg can break open, and we have new life in the chick that is born.

Let's look at the Easter lily and see what symbols are here. The flower is like a trumpet that proclaims this great day. White is the color of maximum light and reminds us of Jesus, who said, "I am the light of the world." Inside the flower we see little specks of gold. Jesus said that he came so that we might have abundant life. Gold is a symbol of richness and abundance.

See this little thing in the center of the flower that has three bumps on it? This reminds us that we know God in three ways as Father, Son, and Holy Spirit. Jesus came to show us the true nature of God.

Green is the color of things growing. The green leaves remind us that we are to grow into true life with Jesus.

The lily grows from a bulb, which is like a tomb, and bursts forth with new life at Easter. So the lily is a good symbol to help us to remember what we celebrate today. In Jesus we have a new, rich, beautiful life.—Kenneth Mortonson

April 26. Sowing Seeds

Objects: Strips of paper with a Bible verse written on them and a seed of some type glued or taped to the paper. [Have one for each child.]

Have you ever heard of Johnny Appleseed? Johnny Appleseed loved apples so much that he decided the best thing he could do with his life was to plant apple seeds. That way apple trees would grow, and people would never run out of his favorite fruit. In fact, people tell lots of stories and legends about Johnny Appleseed, who was always sowing seeds. When pioneers in the United States decided to move west, Johnny decided he should move with them and show them how to plant apple seeds. Otherwise, he thought, their lives would be terrible: no apples for treats, no apple pies, no apple juice. No one knows how many apple seeds Johnny planted. He was so busy doing it his whole life, he probably lost count.

Jesus tells the story of a farmer who sowed seeds everywhere. He was so busy planting seeds that he lost track of how many seeds he planted or where he planted them. Some seeds got lost, some were eaten by birds, some fell among thorns and died, some fell on rocks and didn't grow very long. But some fell on good soil and grew and produced lots of fruit.

[Hand out seeds and verses.] In your hands you have two seeds. One is a seed you bury in the ground. The other one is a Bible verse. After Jesus told this story, he said that God's Word is like the seed the farmer planted. We plant God's Word by giving it to people, by finding ways to show it to them, by inviting them to read it, by teaching it to them. We need to plant it everywhere. We need to be like Johnny Appleseed and like that crazy farmer and try to plant those seeds everywhere we go: not just in a few careful places, but everywhere. Think about what you're going to do with the seeds in your hand. Let's ask God to teach us about sowing seeds.—Carol Younger

May 3. Worshiping at Home

Preparation: Carefully study this sermon. Become familiar with the various feasts the Jewish nation observed.

Think about the things that are in your house. Is there anything in your house that helps you think about God? [Response.] Think about the things your family does. What does your family do that helps you think about God? [Response.]

Today we will learn about some things that families did during Bible times that helped family members think about God. Listen to what those things were.

Pretend that you are living during the time Jesus lived. Many things that happened at your house will make you think about God.

Each time you go into your house you will think about God. A small box called a *mezuzah* is attached to your doorpost. Inside the box there is a small piece of paper rolled up with these words written on it: "Hear, O Israel: The Lord our God is one Lord: And thou shalt love the Lord thy God with all thine heart, with all thy soul, with all thy might." Each time you go through your door, you touch that little box to show your love for the words that are written on the paper in the box.

You will also think about God during the three times each day your family prays. Prayer times are at 9:00 A.M., at noon, and at 3:00 P.M.

During the main meal of the day—the evening meal—you are reminded of God. Your mother will have baked bread and cooked vegetable stew and will have put them on the floor or on a low table. Before you eat, each family member carefully washes his or her hands. You and your family take your places around the food. However, before you start eating, your father thanks God for the food. Then he passes the bread and each family member breaks a piece of bread and uses it to scoop up the stew that you will eat. During the meal you listen as your father tells about things God has done for your family and nation.

On the Sabbath, you and your family attend the synagogue service. The remaining part of the day is used for resting and talking and thinking about God.

Throughout the year your family has special meals called feasts that help you think about God. One of those meals is Passover. At this meal your family hears the story about the night that God freed his people from being slaves in Egypt. Sometimes your family even travels all the way to Jerusalem to celebrate this feast.

Another feast you celebrate is Pentecost. At this feast you thank God for the harvest and think about the time when God gave Moses the Ten Commandments on Mount Sinai.

And another feast your family observes is the Feast of Booths. This thanksgiving celebration lasts for eight days. You and your family live in little booths. During this time your family thanks God for his gifts of food, family, and shelter.

There are other feasts and celebrations. All of them are done to help you and your family think about God.

After Jesus lived and went back to heaven, many of his followers used their homes in which to worship. Those who loved Jesus gathered in homes and talked about Jesus and sang about him. They prayed, gave offerings, and listened to a preacher explain the Scriptures and tell them how to live.—Leon W. Castle

May 10. Mother's Day.
This morning I would like you to line up facing the congregation. I want you to be able to see some special people who are here today.

Do you have any idea who those special people might be? I would like everyone who is a mother to stand. Now while they are standing, I want to ask you children a few quick questions.

How many of you know how to cook? If you get sick, can you take care of yourself? Can you sew on a button? Can you drive yourself to school or to a friend's house?

Well, these mothers that are standing before you know how to take care of children like you. In fact, some of them are your mothers. I think it would be nice for you children to say thank you to these mothers for all the love and care they have given to you and other children. [Make it loud!] —Kenneth Mortonson

May 17. The Lesson from a Broken Arm
This is what is known as a sling. Does anyone know what it is used for? Right. To hold your arm still after you have injured it.

Have any of you ever had a broken arm? When that happens, you have to keep your arm still for a long time.

Then, when you can finally use your arm again, you find it is rather weak. Because the muscles have not been used regularly, they got weak, and you have to start exercising that arm to make it strong.

This reminds us of an important lesson in life. What you do not use, you tend to lose. If you sit at home all day—day after day—watching television, you could get weak. If you do not try to learn new things, you soon have difficulty remembering things. Great athletes and musicians practice all the time so that they can keep their skills. If you do not spend time with a friend, pretty soon, that person is no longer a friend.

The same things apply to our knowledge of God. When people fail to spend time thinking about God and learning about God, soon God is not important in their life, and they lose that sense of fellowship with him. So if you don't want to lose your ability to walk or play an instrument or read or have a friend or know God, then be sure to spend time doing what is important to you and don't let just one thing take up all your time.—Kenneth Mortonson

May 24. Following Through
Objects: A baseball, a golf ball, and a tennis ball.

With the nice weather that we have been having, many people are beginning to think about the special outdoor activities of spring.

I have three different kinds of balls here that are used in those special spring games. Can you name them? [Golf ball, tennis ball, baseball.]

Now, all three of these balls are used in the same way. To play the game, you have to hit the ball. But when you hit it, you have to do something that is very important. It is called "follow through." That means when you hit the ball, you do not stop your swing at that moment, but you keep on with the swing.

This is also an important lesson for life. It is not good enough to simply say, "I will go up front on Sunday morning." You have to follow through and do it. It is not good enough simply to say, "I will clean my room." You have to follow through and do it. Whenever you say you will do something, you must follow through with it.

Now, I have a little treat for you this morning in the shape of a ball, and I will follow through by giving you one. [The object to give can be a piece of hard, ball-shaped candy or a popcorn ball.]—Kenneth Mortonson

May 31. Lost Sheep and Hide-and-Seek

Have you ever played hide-and-seek? Are you good at the game? Hide-and-seek pros usually hide in the sneakiest places, and whoever is "it" has a tough time finding them. In fact, if you're really good at hide-and-seek, you may not get found. After awhile that could feel terrible. Especially after the game is over, everyone goes home for dinner, and there you are, waiting to be found.

Maybe that's the reason I'd rather play "Sardines," instead of hide-and-seek. Sardines is hide-and-seek backwards. One person hides, then everyone else looks for that person. Everyone keeps looking until finally one person is left trying to find where everybody else is hiding. Sardines isn't over until everyone is all together. That way, one person out hiding somewhere won't be forgotten.

In the Bible, Jesus says that he doesn't want you to feel lost and forgotten. He feels like a person who has one hundred sheep, and one gets lost. That shepherd, he says, will leave the ninety-nine just to find that one. When that sheep is found, the shepherd feels more joy than ever before. The shepherd is happier about finding the one lost sheep than he was about the ninety-nine who weren't lost.

You may have times when you feel sad or disappointed or angry. You may feel that God is far away from you. You may feel like you're being forgotten. Jesus wants you to know that he loves you so much that he won't be happy until you're close to him again. You may know some people who feel like nobody cares about them. Maybe Jesus is trying to teach us that part of our job is to go find those people and love them. Maybe it's something we have to keep working at—just

like Sardines—until everyone knows God's love.—Carol Younger

June 7. The Strength of Togetherness

This morning I would like to do a little experiment with you. I would like each one of you to take a piece of paper and see if you can tear it in half. That was easy, wasn't it?

Now let me have the two pieces of paper and put them all together. Can anyone tear them all in half? [Repeat, if needed.]

Soon we get to the place where all the paper together is too strong for us, and we cannot tear it. There is a special strength in togetherness.

Plywood is another example of this truth. This is a piece of plywood, and as you see, it has three layers, which make it stronger than each layer alone.

This is an important lesson for life. People together can do many things that people alone could not do. But for that to happen, people need to be close to one another and to share life together if they are to strengthen each other. And the more people who are willing to work together, the better. This applies to the home as well as to the church.

So, once again, we see how important you are, for you are part of our togetherness.—Kenneth Mortonson

June 14. You Are Important to Your Family

Text: Gen. 2:20–24

Who is the most important member of your family? Is it your brother? Your sister? Your mother? Your father? Is it you? You know what the answer is? The most important member of your family is you—and your brother and sister and mother and father. Every member of your family is important, because without them, your family would not be as special as it is.

The Bible tells us that we need each person in our family to be with and help us. We need each other to talk with each other and hug each other and play together. So that makes everyone special and very important. That makes you special and important, too. Let's thank God for every member of your family and ask God to help us remember that everyone in our families is special and important.—Michael Lanway

June 21. A Father's Guidance

TEXT: Eph. 6:1–2.

Main truth: We should honor our fathers because God gave them to guide us through life.

Interest Object: A compass.

Memory maker: A small, inexpensive compass for each child. These are available through vending suppliers or retail stores.

One way not to get lost in the world is to have a compass. You see on this compass that it has north, south, east, and west. It also has a magnetized needle that always points north. You line up the needle with the *N*, and you can tell which direction you need to go. Then you won't get lost in the world.

There are other ways to keep from getting lost in the world. We have fathers to guide us through life.

One is our heavenly Father: God. He guides us through life. When we feel sad, alone, helpless, God is there. God's job is guiding us through life. He helps us so we don't get lost in sorrow, don't get lost in our problems, don't get lost in sin and stay lost. God helps and guides us through life. Like a compass always points north, God always guides us in the right direction.

Most of us also have an earthly father to guide us. God gave us daddies to help us in life. When you have a problem, when you're hurting or have a need, your dads will help you. They will guide you. Like God, they love you, care for you, and want only the best for you. God gave them to us to see that we are pointed in the right direction and guided through life.

This is Father's Day. We should honor our fathers because God gave them to guide us through life. Be thankful for your heavenly Father and your earthly father. Tell them you're thankful for them. Tell them you love them.

Ephesians 6:1–2 says, "Children, obey your parents in the Lord, for this is right. 'Honor your father and your mother.' "

On this Father's Day, let's honor these God has given us to guide us through life.—Roy E. DeBrand

June 28. Learning to Like People

I know of [a] way of learning to like people, and that is to think about Jesus. He loves us and wants to help us with everything but especially with forgiving—that is, learning to like people. He is very good at that. He had to be when He was on earth, for people were not always nice to Him at all. Here He came, out of God's great world of heaven where everyone is happy and good, in order to tell us that God loves us and wants us to be happy and good, too. But although some people loved Him very much, others did not understand Him. And they were mad because He told them to be kinder to others than they wanted to be. But He still loved them and asked God to forgive them because they did not know what they were doing. So He is very good at loving even the people who are mean, and if you ask Him to help you do it, He certainly can.

Then if you think, "But I just can't like that boy because he was terribly mean to me," you can remember Jesus. People treated Him much worse than anyone has ever treated you. And He did not say that those bad people were good. But He asked God to make them good—and so can you, with Him to help you do it.

Now you may say, "But how can He help me do it when He isn't here any more?"

But He is here, even though you can't see Him. If you wake in the night and you are frightened, don't you know it when your mother is in the house? You do not always go and climb into her bed, though sometimes when you are very frightened you may do so. Most of the time you just remember Mother and Dad asleep in their own room, and you know they are there even though you don't see them. You can feel them right there. So you are comforted and go to sleep again.

Jesus is here now, in a way that is something like that. And it is a very comforting way. If we think about Him with loving thoughts, we can feel Him here, and we are happier. And if we ask Him to help us, He can certainly do it. He can help us in learning to like people and He can help us in lots of ways.—Agnes Sanford

July 5. What Do You Do With Dust?

This morning I have something I want to show you. [A dust-laden object.] Do you know what we call this material that is on this [whatever your dusty object is]? Dust! What do your mother or father do with it? They wipe it away. Dust is always in the air around us. That is why we have little hairs in our nose so that the dust will be caught there and not enter our lungs. Since dust is always in the air, it will land on the surfaces around us, and they will become dusty unless someone takes the time to clean them off.

The dust reminds us of all the things that can mess up life. When something needs to be corrected or cleaned up or put away, someone has to do it, or it will not get done. Can you imagine what a mess we would have here in church if every Sunday the people here just threw the bulletins on the floor, and then no one picked them up during the week, and this happened week after week?

The same thing applies at home or out of doors. If we want things to look nice, if we want to be able to move about, we need to do our part to remove the "dust" of life. And you can help. When you see something that needs to be put away or picked up, do it. Don't expect someone else to take care of it. When each person does his or her part, we will all live in a cleaner, nicer church and home and world.

Now as you go back to your family, see if you can remember what I have just said. [Throw out pieces of paper to see if any of the children will pick them up.] —Kenneth Mortonson

July 12. When Rocks Talk

Object: A handful of small, bright stones.

Purpose: To help the children see God in creation.

Do you remember what Jesus said when he was entering Jerusalem the last time before he was crucified? He said that if the people did not recognize him as their king, the very stones would cry out and tell it! The stones, and everything else in the world, can teach us about God.

I want you to help me understand God. Look at these stones in my hands and tell me what they say to you about God. [Let the children answer first.]

These stones tell us that God loves beauty. Have you ever thought about that? Look at the colors here. God thought them up and put them into the world. You can look around God's world and see how much beauty there is in trees, grass, mountains, oceans, animals. We don't have time to list it all.

They tell us God loves things to be different. None of these rocks are the same shape or size or color. Now that you think about it, can you think of anything God makes by mass production so they are all alike?

I believe God likes variety, in the world and in people. God doesn't want these rocks to be just like each other, and God doesn't want you to be like anybody else. God made you just to be you. So you don't have to feel bad because you are not like someone else. You are you, and that is the way God wants you to be.

There is a little song with the words "Everything is beautiful, in its own way." I believe that, don't you? If we believe that, it will help you get along with people who are different from you and with all the beautiful things God has made in the world.—Stuart G. Collier

July 19. Rules to Grow By

Why do you think babies need rules? [Allow for response.] Rules can show that someone cares for you. When you were a one-year-old, you had lots of rules and restrictions. You always heard "Don't touch!" You slept in what looked like a cage with bars. Doors were shut to keep you out. Someone always held your hand, so you wouldn't run in the street or pull the strange dog's tail. Babies need rules so they won't get hurt, so they can grow up to be everything they can be.

People your age don't need the same rules as toddlers do. You know not to run in front of cars or touch something too hot. Now you have other rules to follow. The rules you have now show that someone cares for you. Your rules may be about doing your homework or eating right or getting enough sleep. [You may want to have the children tell some of their rules.] You need those rules so that you can grow up to be everything you can be.

No matter how old you become, you always need some rules to follow. The Bible shows us many different kinds of things, but some of the things it gives us are rules or guidelines to follow. The guidelines we have show that God cares for us. We need them so that we can grow to be the people he wants us to be. In John 8, Jesus said, "If you continue to obey my teaching, you are truly my followers. Then you will know the truth, and the truth will make you free." Let's thank God that he cares for us enough to guide and teach us, so that we can grow and be what we need to be.—Carol Younger

July 26. Knock, Knock, Who's There?

This morning I want to ask you a question. If you met me on the street this week, would you remember me? When you come to church next Sunday, will you still remember me? If you don't see me for a month, will you forget me?

Now, let's play the "knock, knock" game. Knock, knock. [The children should respond with "Who's there?"] I thought you said you wouldn't forget me.

Sometimes we see people we have met before, but we forget their name. Sometimes you may hear your grandparents say, "I know that person, but I just cannot remember her name." This happens to a lot of people; but we believe it does not happen to God. This morning I want you to hear and remember a very important statement: God will never forget who you are.

Today I'd like you to do something special for us all. I am going to give you a name tag, and I want you to take it back to where you were sitting and take the pencil from the pew rack and put your name on this tag. You may need help from your parents. Then put the name tag on yourself, like this [show how the name tag works]. Then I want all the people here to look for you after church and to see your name and say hello to you.

Just as God does not forget us, we do not want to forget one another in the church. Thank you for coming up here this morning.—Kenneth Mortonson

August 2. How Strong Are You?
Text: 1 John 3:4–10

Who is the strongest person here? Let me see your muscles. Wow! Want to see my muscles? We are pretty strong, aren't we?

Let's find out how strong you all are. Can you all pick up a book? Two books? How about a suitcase? How about a bag of groceries? Wow, you all are strong!

Can you pick up a car? A house? You can't? I can't either. We are pretty strong, but there are some things that you and I cannot pick up.

How about God? Is he strong? Can he pick up anything? A suitcase? A house? A car? God is so strong he can pick up anything. And he is strong enough to help you and me. So when we find out that we need God to help us do something, we can be sure that God can help and he will, just ask him. Let's thank God for our muscles and for his muscles, and that he is strong enough to help us.—Michael Lanway

August 9. How Much Are You Worth?
Text: Matt. 12:1–14
Materials: Coins.

I want to find out how valuable you are. I have some money in my pocket. I have a nickel. Could I buy you for five cents? How about for ten cents? I have this quarter; could I buy you for twenty-five cents? What if I gave your parents all this money? Could I buy you for that? No, I couldn't.

Do you know what? I couldn't buy you from your parents if I had all the money in the world. You are worth more than all the money in the world. Your parents love you very much, and there isn't anything or anyone they would rather have than you.

Let's thank God for who you are and for how valuable you are.—Michael Lanway

August 16. What Can You Do?
TEXT: Matt. 14:22–36

I want to find out what you are able to do. How many of you can brush your teeth by yourselves? How many of you can get dressed by yourselves? How many of you can ride a bike? Wow! You all can do so many things!

God is the one who gives us the abilities to do all these things. God wants us to know that we can do anything that he asks. So we must obey him when we find out what God wants. We find out what God wants by reading the Bible. In the Bible, God and Jesus tell us that God wants us to tell others about them, that God wants us to love others. How many of you can do that?

Let's remember that we can do anything that God tells us to do. Let's thank God for the things we can do and promise we will do anything he wants.—Michael Lanway

August 23. You Can Choose What You Want to Be
TEXT: Rev. 3:14–22

What do you want to be when you grow up? [Let the children answer.] Some of you want to be firemen. Others want to be a doctor. Others want to be stars in the movies. All those things are good things, and God would be happy if you became any one of those things.

God says that whatever we choose to be when we grow up, we need to be the best that we can. He doesn't want us to be just an "OK" fireman or doctor or movie star. He wants us to be the best fireman or doctor or movie star. In that way, when we do our best, we make God very happy.

So whatever you become when you grow up, be the best you can. Let's promise God that.—Michael Lanway

August 30. What's So Bad about Hate?
TEXT: 1 John 2:1–7

Have you ever heard someone say, "I hate you"? Do you think it is good or bad to say that? Why is it bad? Because of the way that it makes people feel.

Has anyone ever said to you, "I hate you"? How did you feel? God felt sad about it, too. God doesn't want anyone to say that to us, and God doesn't want us to say, "I hate you" to anyone else.

God wants us to love each other and to say nice things to each other. Things like "I like you"; "You are nice"; "I am glad you are my friend." Saying those things makes people feel good, and it makes God feel good, too. Let's pray to God and tell him that we will say nice things to others, not mean things, and try to make people feel good.—Michael Lanway

September 6. What Day Is This?
[This sermonette should be used at a time when the children will know that it is not the date you say—in winter or at the start of the new year.]

Good morning. Today is the third of July. Right? It's not July third? Well, what am I going to do? You think I made a mistake? Maybe I should just go home? You must think I am dumb, since I don't know what day it is.

Sometimes boys and girls want to run and hide when they say or do something wrong, but that doesn't solve the problem. What else can I do?

I could refuse to admit that I was wrong and say you are wrong if you think this is not July third. But that would just be stubbornness on my part, and nothing would get corrected that way.

What else can I do? I can ask you to help me and tell me what day this is. That is a good thing to do when you discover you made a mistake. We all make mistakes and need to learn from others. All of us like to be happy in life, and one of the best ways to find happiness is to learn what to do when you make a mistake.

Now, what day is this? Right. Thank you for coming up here this morning and setting me straight.—Kenneth Mortonson

September 13. The Things You Say

All of us say a lot of silly things, don't we? Most of the time it is just harmless fun—it doesn't hurt anyone.

But words are powerful. The right words said by the right people can make other people feel good. These right words can help people know that we love them, that we believe in them. These right words can also help people know that God loves them, that God can forgive them when they have done wrong things, that God has wonderful things for them to do.

Have you said something to someone to let that person know that you love them? Have you said something as a friend to someone who was feeling sad and discouraged and brightened their day?

I said that words are powerful, and they are. How long has it been since someone said something to you that made you feel good or bad because of what they said?

You may not know how much power you have. You may not be able to lift a car or a piano, but you can say something to lift someone's spirits, and that is a lot more important. I hate to say it, but you can also say words that will crush other people and make them sad and discouraged.

Jesus said that he wanted the people he met to share his joy. He told the people who followed him to be of good cheer. He took little children into his arms and blessed them. And he gave his disciples the encouraging words that we know as the Beatitudes, words of blessing that told the disciples and tell us how to be truly happy. Yes, those words themselves have power to make us happy if we listen to them.

If you can say words, you have power, because your words can help or hurt.—James W. Cox

September 20. The Things You Remember

Do you ever forget things? Do you ever forget to wash your hands before meals? Do you ever forget to put away your toys when you have played long enough? Do you ever forget to say please and thank you? Of course, all of us have forgotten to do some things that we were supposed to do.

But suppose your mother or father forgot to wake you up to get ready for school in the morning or forgot to make breakfast, lunch, or dinner. It's pretty important, isn't it, for people to remember a lot of things.

What can we do to be sure that we remember what we should do? Well, in the first place, we have to pay attention and know what we are supposed to do. Then it helps us to understand why we are supposed to do this or that. We don't often forget to do something that is really, really important to us or to someone else.

There is a wonderful verse in the Bible that says, "Remember your Creator while you are young" (Eccl. 12:1, *The Everyday Bible*). Who is our Creator? Yes, God is our Creator, the One who made us; the One who created the whole world. Now, that ought to be really, really important—to remember God. Why is it important to remember God? Because he loves us. Because he wants our lives to be good and kind and helpful to other people.

What helps us to remember God and what he wants us to be and do? The church, the Bible, saying our prayers, and singing hymns—all of these things help us to remember God. What makes you think of God today? —James W. Cox

September 27. What's Your Name?

What's your name? [Let each child respond.] Do you know what your name means? [Have a book of definitions of names ready to tell several children what their name means. Nathan, for example, means "Gift of God."]

I'm sure you remember some well-known fairy tales with characters whose names described them, such as Little Red Riding Hood, the Big Bad Wolf, Tom

Thumb, and Goldilocks. Think of other names like Johnny Appleseed, the Wizard of Oz, and Mighty Mouse. Their names say something about them.

Do you know some names in the Bible? [Let several children respond.]

In the Bible a person's name represents one's personality, who he was, and what he was really like. For example, *Adam* meant "man"; *Jacob* stood for "trickster" or "rascal"; and *Jesus* was "Immanuel" or "God with us." The longest name in the Bible is *Mahershalalhashbaz.*

Also, in the Bible when God changed a person inside and he started living for God (conversion as we sometimes call it), his name was changed. When Jacob finally wrestled with God until he gave in to God, his name changed from Jacob to Israel, or "He who strives with God." Saul used to hurt Christians, but when God took control of him, his name was changed to Paul. Simon the fisherman was transformed by Christ into Peter the "Rock," who eventually became the leader of the twelve apostles.

God knows your name, who you are, and what he has in store for your life. When you come to God in prayer, he knows your personality. He never forgets your name or anything about you.

God wants you always to remember the name of Jesus Christ and follow him every day. There is no greater name than God's Son, Jesus Christ.—Ron R. Blankenship

October 4. Sharing in a Meal

I have a little treat for you this morning. It is not a full meal, because we do not have time to share in a full meal. But I do have a cookie for each one of you, and as you eat it this morning, I'd like you to think about what happens when you share a meal with someone.

There are three things that are present at every meal. First, when you come to a meal, you expect the food to be all right for you to eat. You have faith in the people who provided what you were eating. If you did not trust them, you would not eat the food. Second, when you come to a meal, you have a personal responsibility to accept what is placed before you. If you refuse to eat, then you cannot share in the meal. Finally, when you have faith in the one providing the meal and you are willing to accept what they offer to you, you know you are living with a friend.

These three things are present in every meal, and they are present here today as our church family celebrates communion together. We have faith in God's love for us. We show our willingness to accept God's love and forgiveness by taking what is offered. In that act, in that shared symbolic meal, we know that we have fellowship with God.

I hope that all your meals are happy times that help you to know that you are loved and that you love your parents and the other people seated around your table. When we share a meal it should help us to feel closer to friends and loved ones.—Kenneth Mortonson

October 11. World Hunger

[Select a person to help you act out these two situations. Have this person sit with the other children.]

Imagine being as hungry as you've ever been. Maybe you haven't eaten for a whole day. Your stomach hurts. You have a headache. Your stomach is making loud noises. If you are that hungry, what would you spend your time thinking about? [Listen for responses.] You think about foods that would taste good. You think about ways to get food—any food will do. Suppose I come to visit one of you while you're so hungry. [Have the person you've asked to help stand up.]

"Hello, _____. How are you?" [Let the person begin to tell you about how hungry he or she is feeling, then ignore it.]

"That's too bad. Anyway, the reason I came by is to tell you that you really need to come to church. We haven't seen you for a long time. In fact, have you ever been to church?" [Let the person respond with an answer about how hungry he or she is.]

"Well, I am sorry that you don't feel well. But I think that the first thing I can do to help is to pick you up for Sunday school next week. You should be feeling better by then, right? I'd be glad to do it. We'd love to see you there."

Was that a good visit? Why not? Would you want me to visit if you felt like _____ did? What would you want me to talk about instead? [Listen to their suggestions.]

Maybe I've learned something from what you told me. Let's try it one more time.

"Hello, _____. I just stopped by to see how you're doing." [Have the person tell you how hungry he or she is and why, etc.]

"I'm sorry to hear that. What can I do to help you?" [Exchange a few ideas about how you might help this person.]

"You know, _____, I first came by to invite you to our church. But I understand that when you're hungry, it's hard to think about too much besides food until you get to eat. Jesus tells us that we should feed people who are hungry and take care of their needs. I want to help you and your family, because I care about you."

Was that a better visit? Why? Jesus knew that taking care of the physical needs that people have is an important way to show that we love them. That's why he told us to do it. People also need to know that Jesus loves them. Sometimes, especially when they are hungry or hurting, it may be hard for them to believe that God cares. If we can take care of their needs for food and also help them understand God's love, then we're doing what God commands us to do. World Hunger Day is our opportunity to do both these things. When we as a church give food or money to help people who are hungry, we are telling them that Jesus cares for them. Let's say a prayer about that.—Carol Younger

October 18. Nuts

This morning I want to show you something that we can find on certain trees at this time of the year. They are called nuts.

A nut is an interesting thing. It is a seed with a hard shell, and what is inside the shell is usually good to eat. The nut is a symbol of something we face all the time in life.

We sometimes call a difficult person a nut because the reason for their behavior is hidden from us. Or we say that a problem is a hard nut to crack. The nut is a reminder that there are a lot of good things in life that we have to work at to get.

For example, learning how to read is a wonderful thing to be able to do, but you have to work at it in order to learn. Learning to play a musical instrument is very enjoyable, but you have to practice to learn to play.

The important thing is to remember that what you are seeking on the other side of that shell requires work on your part, and you must be willing to do it to get the fruit of your labors.

Now I'd like to share the fruit of my labors by giving you a homemade cookie this morning. And, of course, the cookie has nuts in it. Thank you for coming up here today.—Kenneth Mortonson

October 25. Protecting Our Families

TEXT: Gen. 14:11–16

Has anyone in your family ever been in a fight? Have you ever been in a fight? I have. I remember one time that a boy told me he was going to beat me up. You know what? He did! He grabbed me by my shirt and threw me down on the ground and began to hit me in the face. It hurt really bad! I thought I was going to die! But suddenly the boy went flying off of me and onto the ground. You know what happened? My sister pushed him off and started to hit him. She told him never to hit me again, because if he did, she would get him. My sister protected me when I needed her.

It is not good to fight, but when someone is beating us up, we need help. Our families are to help us and protect us when we are in danger. That's what my sisters and brothers did for me, and what I did for them.

Your family is there to protect you, and you are there to protect them. God wants us to help each other and help keep each other safe. Let's thank God for our families and for the ways that they protect us, and promise to protect them.—Michael Lanway

November 1. Revenge vs. Forgiveness

TEXT: Matt. 18:21–22

Imagine that the story of Cinderella was told this way. There she was scrubbing the floors, spending all her hours thinking up all kinds of ways to get even with her mean family. With every scrub, she pictured how one day she'd be dressed up while they wore rags. Every time she cleaned out the fireplace, she thought of terrible jobs she'd make them do. Then suddenly she gets her chance. Enter fairy godmother, dashing prince, and all the stuff of which great fairy tales are made. Cindy turns into a princess, lives in a palace, and no longer dusts or does dishes. Now suppose that once she's there, sitting on her throne, she decides it's now time to get even. Suppose she orders her family to be slaves in the palace, working as hard as she did in their house. Do you think we'd like the new Cinderella, the revenge-getter, very much? Would we be as glad when she turned into a princess the next time the story was told?

Revenge has a way of hurting the person who wants it. We like to think that Cinderella didn't seek revenge, because she didn't need to. Everything turned out for her, and to want revenge on her family would have made her a different kind of character.

The Bible tells us not to seek revenge but to learn how to forgive. In Matthew 18, Peter asked Jesus if he should forgive someone as many as seven times. Do you know what Jesus said? Forgive that person over seventy-seven times! Because God forgives us for all the times we do wrong, he wants us to forgive others. When we don't forgive, it hurts us, just as it hurts the other person. This is a hard lesson to learn. Let's pray that God will help us learn it.—Carol Younger

November 8. Why We Rest

TEXT: Matt. 11:28

Materials: Pillow.

[Hold the pillow out so the children can see it.]

What do I have in my hand? Do you have one of these on your bed? I have a pillow of my very own; it makes me feel just right when I go to bed so I can fall asleep.

What time do you go to bed? I go to bed about _____. We go to bed to get our rest. God tells us that we should be sure to get enough sleep so that we will feel good and strong in the morning. If we don't get our sleep, our bodies will hurt and feel tired. Then we won't be able to do things like play with our friends or color pictures or even talk on the telephone.

Rest is one way that God takes care of us. Let's thank God for giving us rest.—Michael Lanway

November 15. Surprises

Do you like surprises? Most girls and boys do. And so do grownups.

The Bible tells us about some wonderful surprises. When Mary and Joseph heard that they were going to have a baby in their home, it came to them as a surprise. And later, when Jesus was born, it was a surprise to the shepherds in the fields who were looking after their sheep. Also, after Jesus grew up, it must have been a surprise to many people that he was the Messiah, the Christ. In fact, the people were looking for a different kind of Christ. They were looking for a powerful man, a king with armies and all the rest. What a surprise it must have been to find out that the Christ was someone like Jesus—not a powerful king with armies! I am sure that some people did not like the kind of surprise God gave them. Others could not have been more pleased. They thanked God for Jesus and loved him. He made life better for them than they had ever known it before. He healed many sick people. He fed the hungry. He forgave people their sins. And he helped bad people to be good people. What wonderful surprises they found in Jesus!

Many times something especially good will happen to you when you did not expect it at all. Someone said something especially nice to you. Someone gave you a present. Someone came to visit you. And you were not looking for any of this. How wonderful! Let's thank God for surprises.—James W. Cox

November 22. Thanksgetting or Thanksgiving?

[Begin the children's sermon talking about Thanksgiving, but say the word *Thanksgetting* instead. Keep asking children questions about *Thanksgetting*—i.e., how their families celebrate, etc.—until one of the children points out that you're using the wrong word. If no one mentions it, call attention to the word yourself.]

Ask: How would a *Thanksgetting* holiday be different from *Thanksgiving*? During Thanksgetting you could spend your time congratulating yourself on how many nice things you had or how sweet you were or how much you did for other people. Thanksgetting would be a time for you to get things, like compliments. If you celebrate Thanksgiving, you'll spend your time finding ways to give thanks to God and to other people for the things that they do. Thanksgiving is a time when you give rather than get. You spend your time looking around to see how you could say thank you.

Many times our Thanksgivings become Thanksgettings. We get lots of good food to eat. We get time off from school to do things we want to do. We might get to spend time with people we love. Those are all great things. But if we're not careful, we can forget to celebrate Thanksgiving. We need to remember, as we eat, that some people need good food and don't have any. There are ways we could give thanks by giving food. We need to remember, as we spend time with the people we love, that some people are lonely, without families to care for them. There are ways we can give thanks for the people who love us, by loving others. This week, I hope we'll celebrate Thanksgiving in a great way. Let's thank God for teaching us to celebrate by giving.—Carol Younger

November 29. God Is Light

TEXT: John 1:1–5

Objects: A collection of night-lights (optional).

Tell me the truth. Does any one of you sleep with a night-light? Did you when you were little? Since children are supposed to be experts on night-lights, I want to ask you a question. What is it about a night-light that makes people feel better? [Listen for responses.] These days you can find night-lights in all kinds of shapes and characters, some even play music when it gets dark. But the best thing about a night-light, the thing that makes it a night-light, is that it brings light to a dark room.

Children aren't the only ones who feel better when there's a light around. Did you ever hear a radio commercial for a motel that said they'd "leave the light on" for you if you'd come stay there? And have you ever seen houses, especially at Christmas, that have candles in the windows? Long ago, when travelers saw a candle in the window of a house that meant that they were welcome to stay there. People have always needed light.

Maybe that's why the Bible says that God is light and in him is no darkness at all. We've all been in the dark before. When we can't see, when things are dark, we may get scared. But if we ask God to be with us when we're afraid, he'll help us. He'll help us feel safe like that night-light does. If you're sitting in a dark room, and you have a flashlight or a night-light in your hand, it would be silly not to use them if you wanted to see. In the same way, when you're afraid or unsure, it would be silly not to ask Jesus to be your light. Let's ask him to be our light right now.—Carol Younger

December 6. A Special Book

TEXT: 1 John 1:1–4

Materials: Several different books.

I brought some books with me this morning. Let me show you what they are. [Show and explain.] Books are important and special because they tell us things about the world and about other people.

I have a very special book right here. Do you know what it is called? This is the Bible. The Bible is a special book because it tells us about a very special person. His name is Jesus. Jesus is God's son, and the Bible tells us that he loves us very much. There are a lot of things about Jesus in the Bible. Ask your mom and dad to read some stories to you. Then you will learn all about what Jesus wants you to know about him.

Let's thank God for the Bible and for the stories it tells us about Jesus.—Michael Lanway

December 13. What Do You Give a Baby?

I have an assignment for you. I want to plan a wonderful Christmas for a baby who is not yet one year old. What do I need to make? What should I buy? What should be on the baby's Christmas list? How should I decorate the house so the baby will like it? What special Christmas activities should we plan to do? [Listen for ideas from the children.]

Those are great ideas! There's just one problem. Many of the things that we love at Christmas don't mean too much to a small baby. Some of the things we might do for a baby, we're really doing because they are important to us. After all, infants don't care how many packages they have under the tree, do they? They won't really appreciate Christmas goodies yet. They might like some of the sights and sounds, but they won't understand what everything means.

But even though the baby may not realize what's going on, a baby's first Christmas is extra special. Parents realize that the baby gives them more than they can give the baby. The new life that baby shares with them is the real present. The best they can do is to love and be thankful for the gift.

On that first Christmas celebration, when visitors came to see the baby Jesus, they brought gifts. Some of their gifts seem like silly things to give to a baby. Babies smell good—why would they need perfume? Maybe when they got there, the people who wanted to bring Jesus something realized that he was giving them more than they could ever give to him. He was the real present. Maybe as they laid their gifts by him, they realized that the best thing they could give was their love and their thanks to God for sending his Son.

Maybe the best Christmas present we could give any baby is the promise of love and care. Maybe the best gift we could give Jesus this year is that same promise of love and care.—Carol Younger

December 20. The Shepherd's Staff

Objects: A candy cane and a staff cut out of plywood or cardboard, with a hook at one end.

Do any of you know what this is called? [Show the staff.] This is a representation of a shepherd's staff. The shepherd had a stick, like this, that he used to help him care for the sheep. With the hook, he could pull a little lamb out of the bushes or out of a hole in the ground, if it should happen to fall in. At night, the shepherd would bring the sheep back home to the place where they would sleep. It was called a *fold*. As the sheep entered the fold, the shepherd would use his staff to block the doorway into the fold. He wanted to stop each sheep and look it over to see if it had any cuts that needed to be treated.

The shepherd's staff is a symbol for caring, and Christmas is one time when we show we care for other people, and we give good gifts to them. So a symbol of Christmas is the candy cane, which is a reminder of the shepherd's staff. I have a candy cane for each one of you, and I hope you will remember that part of the spirit of Christmas is to care for one another—not only today, but all the time.—Kenneth Mortonson

December 27. How Big Is Your Family?

How many people are in your family? [Allow time for each person to answer.] The older you get, the bigger your family may become. For example, one day you may fall in love and decide to get married. Then your family would grow by one. And the person you marry may have brothers and sisters and a father and a mother. And they become part of your family. Then after awhile you may add a little boy or girl to your family, maybe even twins. And then there will be nieces and nephews and cousins, aunts, uncles, and grandparents. Before too long, your family is huge. What's really fun is to get all these family members together for a meal. All ages, all sizes, all there because they're part of the family.

The same thing happens when the church has the Lord's Supper. We're a big family. We're sisters and brothers. All ages, all sizes, all here because we have one Father, and we're all part of the same family. It would be impossible to know how many are in our family. But the larger God's family is, the more joy there is. As we celebrate the Lord's Supper, think about the fact that this is a family celebration, and we need to love and care for each other just as a good family loves each other.—Brett Younger

SECTION XI.
A Little Treasury of Sermon Illustrations

BY ROBERT C. SHANNON

ATTITUDES. There is a restaurant in Bern, Switzerland, in a house where Einstein once lived. His picture is on the wall, and under it a quotation: "Die Welt is ein Narrenhaus; nur der Humor retten Uns." The world is a madhouse; only humor can save us.

ATTITUDES. They have a saying in Vienna, Austria: "The situation is hopeless, but not serious." It's an interesting contradiction in terms, isn't it? Yet life is truly a mixture of optimism and pessimism, of hope and despair, of sunshine and shadow. Sometimes the same situation can have both elements in it at the same time. But faith is finer than optimism. It has none of the distortions of optimism. It is less fragile. It is more lasting. It has a solid base in the character of God. It's fine for us to be optimists, but far better for us to be believers.

ATTITUDES. A traveler swears he overheard this conversation between a British couple visiting France. "What a marvelous sunset," she said. "Yes," replied her husband, "most impressive for such a small village." All of us sometimes judge everything by its size and sometimes forget that God sends some of his blessings uniformly; the sun rising on the evil and the good; the rain falling on the just and the unjust.

ATTITUDES. In Mort Walker's *Beetle Bailey* comic strip, the sergeant is talking to the army psychiatrist. He says, "I'm ir-ritable all the time." The psychiatrist, Dr. Bonkus, says, "That's no problem. We'll try to cure that." "No," says the sergeant, "the problem is I like being irritable."

ATTITUDES. It was Frederick Langdridge who wrote that "two men look out through the same bars: One sees the mud and one the stars."

BIBLE. When Alexander Solzhenitsyn received the Nobel prize, he spoke of the power of literature to enable us to taste the joys and sorrows of men and women in other times and places as though we were with them. Literature, he said, has the capacity to "overcome the human being's liability of learning only from personal experience, so that the experience of others bypasses him with no effect. From human being to human being, filling up their brief time on Earth, art communicated entire the freight of someone else's long life-experience, with all its burdens, colors, juices, recreating the experience endured by another human being in the flesh—permitting it to be absorbed and made one's own as if it had actually been." What Solzhenitsyn said of literature may be said emphatically of biblical literature. It enables us to enter into the experiences of others, long dead, and learn from those experiences.

BIBLE. At one time Muslim scholars memorized all the words of the Koran. No one tries to memorize all of the Bible, but David advises us to commit it to memory, for the word hidden in the heart will keep us from sin. Still, it is never how much Scripture we know, how much Scripture we can quote, but how much Scripture we obey that counts.

BIBLE.   Melville said that to produce a mighty book you must choose a mighty theme. By that definition the Bible towers above all other books. There are no greater themes than sin and forgiveness, hope and despair, life, death, and beyond death, heaven and hell, God and man. The Bible deals with all the great themes of human life and human history. For that reason alone it deserves our attention.

BIBLE.   There is a tradition that the so-called Black Madonna at Czestochowa, Poland, was painted by Luke. The fact is, we already have a picture painted by Luke. It is painted in words, not oils. It was done with a pen and not a brush. It is the Gospel of Luke, and it deserves our careful attention.

BIBLE.   Jonathan Swift is best known for his book *Gulliver's Travels*, but he also wrote a satire published in 1704 entitled "The Battle of the Books." The story is about a pitched battle between the ancient literature of Greece and Rome and the modern literature of Swift's day. Of course, if there should ever be a true battle of the books we are confident that one book and only one would be the winner.

CHARACTER.   When sculptor Albin Polasek died, he left his last work on the lawn of his home in Winter Park, Florida. It is a statue of Christ, overlooking Lake Osceola. He created it with one hand. The other had become useless. Someone who knew him said, "Talking with him was like listening to a sermon." The need today is for walking sermons—Christians whose life is such a blessing that just being in their presence is like listening to a sermon.

CHARACTER.   Some people are like gold: soft enough to be shaped, durable enough to last, rare enough to be valuable.

CHRIST.   At the gate leading into the old walled city of Dubrovnik, Yugoslavia, there is a bas relief of St. Blaise, holding in his hand a stone model of the city. It's a copy of a silver one that is among the treasures of the church of St. Blaise. It was that silver model of the city that enabled the rebuilding of the city after the 1667 earthquake. Because they had the model, men knew exactly how to reconstruct the city. We have a model for living in Jesus Christ. Because of him, we know how life ought to be lived.

CHRIST.   The Celts left eastern Europe long ago, moving ever westward until they reached the farthest limits of Europe in Britain and Ireland. Those who remained melted into and merged with other peoples coming into the region. But the Celts left something behind that remains to this day—their language. In the Slovenian Alps there are still Celtic words that remain a part of the Slovenian language, long after the Celts themselves have disappeared. What did Jesus leave behind? Some words; some very wise words with some very wise ideas embodied in those words. But the words he left behind changed the world.

CHRIST.   In Glastonbury, England, there is a thorn tree said to have grown from a cutting from the original Glastonbury thorn—and it is said to have sprung from the staff of Joseph of Arimathea, who brought the Holy Grail to England. Such relics are greeted with skepticism today. It is recognized that what we need are not objects from the life of Jesus but rather to follow the truth he taught and accept the power he offers through the Spirit.

CHRIST.   In India in 1537 the emperor Humayon nearly drowned in the Ganges River. He was saved by a lowly water-bearer named Nizam. The grateful emperor briefly seated his savior on the throne and even allowed him to issue decrees. But Christ is on the throne eternally, not by the will of some other, but because of his own nature and being. "And he shall reign forever and ever."

CHRISTIANITY. T. S. Eliot once said that "the world is attempting to form a civilized but non-Christian mentality. The experiment will fail." And are not the signs of that failed experiment all around us? Because of them, people are turning back to God and to Christian faith. They recognize that there can be no civilization without moral and ethical standards, and there can be no moral or ethical standards that do not have a base in religious faith.

CHRISTIANITY. The February 3, 1947, issue of *Time* magazine offered this interesting comment: "That strange force called Christianity, despite all its marble monuments and pursed lips, demonstrates again and again that it is still a living thing." What a tribute to Christianity! Some only view Christianity superficially and see its blemishes. Others take the trouble to study it more deeply and see beneath the blemishes a strong, healthy, living thing that has made our world better—and continues to make it better.

CHRISTIANS. Painter and teacher of artists Thomas Cole told his students, "An artist should be in the world but not of it; its cares, its duties he must share with his contemporaries, but he must keep an eye steadfastly fixed on his polar star and steer by it, whatever wind may blow." Precisely the same words can be applied to Christians.

CHRISTIANS. Carrie Nation is famed for her fight against saloons at the beginning of the twentieth century. An interesting sidelight to her life is the fact that she grew up in a very unusual home. Her mother suffered from mental illness and believed she was Queen Victoria. Her family found it easier to go along with the idea, so the family servants were dressed as palace guards, local farmers were knighted, and her husband answered to the name Prince Albert. Is it a delusion when Christians believe that they are the children of a king? No! The Bible says, "He has made us kings and priests," and, "You are a royal priesthood."

CHURCH. Years and years ago a gypsy was hanged in the churchyard at Odstock, Salisbury, England. Annually, gypsies came to his grave. They became a drunken nuisance. The rector locked the doors against them. Then the gypsy queen put a curse on all who locked those doors. After several violent deaths, it became the policy never to lock those church doors. They remain unlocked to this day. Of course, there was nothing to the curse, and many churches in modern times must be locked. But in the spiritual sense the church doors must always be open—open to every honest seeker after God and open to every person in need.

COMMUNION. The gospel is always paradoxical. It turns things upside down and inside out. Blood stains, but the gospel teaches that it cleanses. Death is the opposite of life, but the gospel teaches that it is the door to life. A cross is an ugly thing, but the gospel teaches us that it is a lovely thing. We hold in our hands a crumb of bread and the gospel tells us it is a feast. Yet our experience in worship confirms what the gospel teaches. All these paradoxes, and more, are true. They are the very substance of our faith. So we do not blush to take a bit of bread and wine and say, "All things are ready! Come to the *feast!*"

CONSISTENCY. Pioneers in the hill country of Texas lived on ranches far from town. So they built tiny houses in the town, came in on Saturday to shop, stayed for church services on Sunday, and then made the long journey back to the ranch. They called those little houses "Sunday houses." Do we create intangible but very real Sunday houses? Is our character better on Sunday than it is the rest of the week? Is our disposition better on Sunday than it is the rest of the week? Do we live only in Sunday houses?

COURAGE. A newspaper reporter filed a story concerning a small group of soldiers during the Spanish Civil War. They were surrounded, and some wished to surrender. One man said, "It is better to die on our feet than to live on our knees!"

COURAGE. An old Athenian was teased by his fellow soldiers because he was lame. His reply was, "I came here to fight, not to run." In the cosmic battle between light and darkness, good and evil, God and Satan, we must be certain that we came to fight not to run.

CROSS. At the time of Stephen V, the Hungarian royal seal bore a crown of thorns and a cross with these words: "Crown and cross should warrant this seal's force." Christians are sealed by the same things. The cross is the seal of our forgiveness; the crown is the seal of our future.

CROSS. The cross on the top of the water tower in St. Cloud, Florida, serves as a handy navigational aid for private pilots landing at St. Cloud's tiny airport and for boaters on Lake Tohopekaliga. There was a lawsuit to have it removed, but the complainant didn't live in St. Cloud, and it was successfully argued that he had no right to sue. The cross is still a stumbling-block to some but a spiritual navigational aid to others.

CROSS. Mayans in the Yucatán peninsula were not happy with the new republic of Mexico, and so in 1858 they rallied to a man named Berrera and his ventriloquist friend, Manuel Nahuat. Nahuat created a talking cross, and the resulting Cruzob cult attracted many. Pushed back to the coast by the Mexican government, the Cruzob continued to rule over the area until 1901, calling it the Empire of the Cross. We are drawn not to a talking cross but rather to a man who talked from a cross. And we believe that the empire of the cross is, as Jesus said, "not of this world."

CROWN. Popes and emperors were concerned that kings be crowned with the authentic crown of that particular realm. Much attention was given to the safekeeping of the crown and other regalia. There was a general opinion that the validity of the king's coronation depended on its being done with the true and proper crown. On earth, Christ's only crown was the crown of thorns, but none of his subjects has any doubt about his right to rule.

CROWN. At the end of World War II, the Hungarian crown was secretly buried and the chest in which it was supposedly kept turned over to the U.S. Army. For weeks the Army guarded that empty chest. Finally someone looked inside and saw that the crown was missing. Eventually, one of the men who helped bury it disclosed the hiding place. The crown was taken to the United States and kept at Fort Knox, Kentucky. Finally on January 6, 1978, it was returned to Hungary. Isn't it fascinating to think about the U.S. Army guarding that empty box? Isn't it true that "crowns and thrones perish, kingdoms rise and wane"?

DEATH. Francis Bacon wrote, "Men fear death as children fear to go in the dark; and as that natural fear in children is increased with tales, so is the other." People do fear death and even if that fear is overcome there is a reluctance to die. We ought not feel guilt over being reluctant to die. Jesus in Gethsemane prayed that the cup might pass from him. It is human and natural to want to cling to life, but Christian faith teaches us that we really have nothing to fear in death, except, of course, fear itself. Christ has conquered death. Death has no more dominion.

ECOLOGY. In Parker's *Wizard of Id* comic strip, the little king asks his wizard what he's working on. The reply is, "An air freshener that smells like the great outdoors." "What's in it?" asks the little king. "Carbon monoxide, diesel fumes . . ." says the wizard. It's true that the great outdoors no longer smells fresh and is no longer fresh and clean. God has given us the responsibility for the earth (Gen. 1:26–28). We must suffer the penalty for abusing it, and we must work responsibly to renew and restore it. It's a very real part of our stewardship before God—our stewardship of the earth itself.

ENEMIES.   In the old city of Sibenik along the Dalmatian coast of Yugoslavia, one can see a lovely little cathedral built between 1431 and 1555. The church is adorned with gargoyle faces in medieval headdresses. It is said that some closely resemble the friends of the builder, Juraj Dalmatinac, and that others closely resemble his enemies. It's fairly easy to tell which is which! We do something better than caricature our enemies in stone. We love them. We pray for them . . . and we forgive them.

EQUALITY.   There is a legend that says that Alexander the Great asked Diogenes what he was looking for, when he found him studying human bones. Diogenes replied, "That which I cannot find: the difference between your father's bones and those of his slaves." Death is indeed a great equalizer.

FAITH.   The holiest city in the religion of Islam is Mecca. The center of Mecca is the Kaaba, a plain rectangular building that houses the Sacred Black Stone. It is said to have come down from heaven. It's quite likely that it did! It is probably a meteorite. The stone is embedded in the wall of the Kaaba five feet above the ground in the eastern corner. The Kaaba has no windows and only one door. Some Arabs believe it was built by angels before the creation of man! Christian faith is never tied to any one place or any one building. Christian faith rests upon fact, not fiction. It's based on historical events and is expressed not in holy places but in holy people; not in stones and buildings, but in hearts and lives.

FAITH.   John Stuart Mill said of the nineteenth century that it was "destitute of faith, but terrified of skepticism." How will the twentieth century be character-ized? Are there not still people who are destitute of faith? Some of them are living on the memory of a faith they once had. Some of them are living on an inherited faith their parents had. Yet most of them are reluctant to let go of faith altogether. Like those Mill described in the century before, they are at the least uncomfortable with skepticism and possibly terrified by it.

FAITH.   Brother Lawrence once said that all things are possible to him who believes, that they are less difficult to him who hopes, that they are easy to him who loves, and that they are simple to him who does all three. It may be a slight exaggeration to say that all things are possible for us, but it is certainly no exaggeration to say that faith and hope and love working together can accomplish far, far more than any one of them can do working separately.

FAITH.   William Jennings Bryan said, "Some skeptics say, 'Oh, the miracles. I can't accept the miracles.' One may drop a brown seed in the black soil and up comes a green shoot. You let it grow and by and by you pull up its root and find it red. You cut the red root and find it has a white heart. Can anyone tell how this comes about—how brown cast into black results in green and then red and white? Yet you eat your radish without troubling your mind over miracles. Men are not distressed by miracles in the dining room; they reserve them all for religion."

FAITH.   E. Frenkel was a faith healer in the Soviet Union. He claimed that by faith he had stopped a bicycle, cars, and a street car. He tried it on a train and was killed. But then faith has never lent itself to showmanship. Even Jesus refused to cast himself off the pinnacle of the Temple in a show of faith.

FAITH.   Iturbide once had himself crowned emperor of Mexico in a lavish and self-flattering ceremony. Simon Bolivar described him as "emperor by the grace of God and of bayonets." The kingdom of our Lord Jesus Christ is different.

For not with swords' loud clashing
Nor roll of stirring drums
With deeds of love and mercy
The Heavenly kingdom comes.
—Ernest W. Shurtleff

FAITH.   Madalyn Murray O'Hair must surely have expected more attention than she got at the Moscow International Book Fair of 1989. A reporter noted that seventy-five people waited in line to look at Jewish religious books, but no one even stopped by to see O'Hair's antireligious literature. She was quoted as saying, "I am completely stunned to find out the USSR is absolutely indifferent to atheism."

FEAR.   A man said that he consulted his doctor about chest pains, fearful that he was having a heart attack. The doctor gave him this odd prescription: "The most devastating of all diseases is fear. You are a victim of fear. Go to church at least once a Sunday for three months—and go as a participant, rather than as a spectator."

FORGIVENESS.   Along the Welsh border, spring flowers called snowdrops were often brought into the house for purification. The purification of life, however, can never be accomplished by anything except the grace of God. No object, no matter how beautiful it may be, no matter how pure or white it may appear, can ever purify us from sin. "What can wash away my sin? Nothing but the blood of Jesus."

FORGIVENESS.   The Italian secretary to Mary Queen of Scots, David Rizzio, was murdered in Edinburgh's Holyrood House. There is a tradition that the bloodstain on the palace floor was indelible and could never be removed. Visitors today, however, will see no bloodstain. Only a brass tablet marks the spot. The stains of sin sometimes seem indelible, too, but "there is power in the blood."

FORGIVENESS.   Queen Elizabeth I once said to the Countess of Nottingham, "God may pardon you, but I never can." Perhaps we also sometimes feel such an unforgiving hatred, but the Bible assures us that only those who forgive their debtors will have their own debts forgiven. If we fail to forgive others, we cannot expect to find forgiveness for ourselves.

FREEDOM.   In the German language the words for freedom, for peace, and for joy all sound much alike (*Freiheit, Friede, Freude*). It suggests that without freedom it's hard to find peace and joy, but when we have freedom, we are more likely to have both. It is certainly true that only when we have freedom from the guilt of sin can we have true peace and true joy.

FRIENDLINESS.   In Serbia in central Yugoslavia, there is a time-honored custom that is still followed to this day. When a guest comes to a house, he is offered a tray on which there is something sweet (usually preserved fruit), a glass of water, and a spoon. The guest takes a spoonful of fruit, eats it, drinks part of the water, and then puts the spoon in the glass. The point is plain. You greet your guest with something sweet. What if daily we greeted people with something sweet: a smile, a kind word, a thoughtful act, a gracious gesture? How different their lives would be! How different *our* lives would be!

GOD.   Only a few houses in Northampton, England, survived the great fire of 1675. One of them was the so-called Welsh house built in 1595. Over the main window is a Welsh motto: "Without God without anything. With God—enough." We often sing that lovely chorus, "He's all I need," but someone remarked that it is only when God is all you have that you really understand that God is all you need.

GOD.   Industrial air pollution is causing problems even in the Arctic. Paul Lavalle studied the situation from a hot air balloon and could see a yellow fog on the

European side of the North Pole. Lavalle commented, "It used to be said that the North Pole was somewhere God goes to escape mankind, but he may have to change his destination in the light of what we've discovered so far." Of course, Christians know God doesn't want to go anywhere to escape mankind. God is with us in all our problems and difficulties.

GOD.   A speaker meant to say that he was reading from the Emphasized Version of the Bible. What he said was, "I'm reading from the *Empathized* Version of the Bible." The Bible is, of course, inanimate and can neither sympathize nor empathize with us. But every version of the Bible reveals a God who does sympathize with us and who does empathize with us.

GIVING.   We all understand that the Lord's Supper is a memorial. First Corinthians 10:4 suggests that our giving is also a memorial. The offerings of Cornelius had come up as a memorial before God. We write, "This Do in Remembrance of Me" on the communion table. We might also write it on the offering basket. We remember the Lord by the things on that table. He remembers us by the things in that basket.

GRACE.   The songwriter for *The Sound of Music* really didn't understand grace, for in that classic film the leading lady sings, "Nothing comes from nothing. Nothing ever could. Somewhere in my youth or childhood, I must have done something good." But the good things that happen to us do not happen because we are being rewarded for doing something good. They come to us because God is good. It is his character, not ours, that is the basis for all our blessings. He answers our prayers because he is good, not because we are good. He forgives our sins by his grace, not by our goodness.

HEAVEN.   There is a lovely legend in western Yugoslavia. Near Maribor is a place called *Jeruzalem* (sic). The story is that pilgrims were traveling across Europe on their way to the Holy Land. They rested in this beautiful place. It was so appealing and satisfying a place they decided to stay and not go on to the Holy Land. So they called their new home *Jeruzalem*. On our way to heaven's New Jerusalem we must never be distracted by anything earthly, no matter how pleasant or fair.

HEAVEN.   When the Serbian king Lazar was killed in battle in 1395, Queen Milica took the royal crown with her to the convent where she spent the rest of her life. Eventually it "disappeared" from history. When Peter Karadjorjevic came to the throne in 1903 he wanted to wear that crown. Certain that it had been buried with Queen Milica centuries before, he had her body disinterred, but the crown was not in her coffin. He didn't know that the Turks had taken it years before. Today it is on display in Istanbul's Topkapi Palace museum. His crown was in another place! So is ours! "Henceforth there is laid up for me a crown," wrote Paul.

HEAVEN.   David Hackett Fischer has written a book, *Albion's Seed*, in which he shows that cultural diversity in America can be traced to that part of England from which the original settlers came. The Puritans of Massachusetts, the Quakers of Pennsylvania, the aristocratic settlers of Virginia, and the Scotch-Irish of Appalachia all brought distinctive cultural traits with them that can still be identified in that region. With Christians it is different. Our traits are determined not by the place from which we came but by the place to which we are going.

HEAVEN.   The stone in the doorway to the United Nations building in New York comes from the Adriatic island of Brac. So does stone in the White House in Washington, D.C. So does the stone that forms the altar of the Liverpool Cathedral in England. So does the stone that forms the Church of Sacre Coeur in Paris. Brac stone is famous all over the world, and there is a bit of that island in many, many places. Can we not detect, here and there, a little bit of heaven on earth? Can we not find it in the Christian home? Can we not find it in the fellowship of the church? Can we not find it in acts of benevolence and kindness? All over the world you can find little bits of heaven.

HOLY LIVING.　Thomas Merton wrote that "sanctity does not consist merely in *doing* the will of God. It consists in *willing* the will of God." That's much more difficult. It's hard enough to obey, but what a challenge it is for us to come to the place where we *want* to do what God wants us to do. Perhaps that person was right who said that a true saint of God could do anything he wanted to do!

HOLY LIVING.　In the heart of the old city of Dubrovnik, Yugoslavia, there is a statue of Orlando with his sword. During the Middle Ages, his right forearm was used as a standard of measure called a *lakat*, or elbow. Where is the standard of measure for living? It is to be found in Jesus Christ. No better standard has ever been discovered.

HONESTY.　The legend that Diogenes lit a lamp in the daytime and went about looking for an honest man is probably just that—a legend. It is a fact, though, that he came to Athens because he was exiled from his native state for counterfeiting! We are often disappointed in our models, and dishonesty is common enough! But that should never tempt *us* to be dishonest. We follow Christ who "did no sin, neither was guile found in his mouth." He is the only reliable example, the only reliable model.

HUMILITY.　When reporters interviewed Mother Teresa, world famous for her work among the poorest of the poor in Calcutta, India, she said, "I am a little pencil in the hand of God. He does the writing. The pencil has nothing to do with it."

HUMOR.　When Gene Shalit compiled his recent anthology of modern American humor, he entitled the book *Laughing Matters*. It is, of course, possible to take the phrase in two ways. One is to take the word *matters* as a noun. That is obviously what Shalit intended. It is also possible to understand the word as a verb: laughing *matters*. It *is* true that laughing matters. It makes a difference in our health. Norman Cousins believed that he laughed himself back to good health after a serious illness. He even wrote a book about it. And the Bible says that "a merry heart doeth good, like a medicine."

INFLUENCE.　The coat of arms of George Washington's ancestors in England had two bars and three stars. It is thought that that is the basis of the stars and stripes in the American flag. Wouldn't it be nice to think that some part of your family's heritage had become the symbol of a nation? For most of us such a possibility is quite remote. But for all of us there is the possibility to do something far more significant. We can influence a life—for all eternity.

INFLUENCE.　The name of Alexander Graham Bell, the inventor of the telephone, lives in the language of science. All over the world, sound is measured in decibels, and the *bel* in *decibel* is from the man's name. So Christ's name has been imprinted indelibly in our language. The word *Christian* describes all that is best of faith and morality, of courage and kindness. Perhaps it is too much to hope that our names might thus be enshrined. There is something better for which we can hope. It is that some bit of our character will be implanted in some other life; that some person in a succeeding generation will pick up a good and wholesome trait from us and make it a part of his or her life.

LIFE.　The mineral baths at Sokobanja, Yugoslavia, still draw sick people just as they did in Roman times. There is, in fact, a saying: "Sokobanja, Soko-grad! Dodjes mator, odes mlad," which means, "Sokobanja, Soko town! Arrive old and depart young!" They didn't find the fountain of youth in Florida, and it cannot be found in Yugoslavia.

LIFE.   Bittersweet is a lovely plant common in both Europe and North America. It's a member of the nightshade family. It got its name from this interesting fact. When the leaves are chewed they first taste bitter, then sweet. There are experiences in life that are like that. Some seem so bitter to us at first taste, but turn out to be the sweetest moments of life. The opposite is also true. Our sins seem so sweet at the first, but soon become so bitter.

LIFE.   The Czechoslovakian national anthem is unusual in two ways. First it is partly in the Czech language and partly in the Slovak language, since both are spoken in the country. It is also unusual in this: The first half is a gentle Czech melody, the second an exuberant Slovak dance. Life is like that: gentle and hectic, joyful and sad, sunlight and shadow, pleasure and pain.

LIFE.   Paul's home town of Tarsus was founded by Sardanapalus. In the neighboring town was a statue of Sardanapalus that showed him snapping his fingers, and under it was written: "Eat! Drink! Enjoy yourself! The Rest is Nothing!" That's reflected in Paul's words in 1 Cor. 15:32: "If the dead rise not let us eat and drink; for tomorrow we die." Paul, however, believed in the resurrection of the dead, and so his philosophy was just the opposite of the philosophy of Sardanapalus. Paul's philosophy was that eating and drinking were nothing, and that the significant things were unseen, spiritual and eternal.

LIFE.   "Life is a jest" wrote John Gay, "and all things show it. I thought so once; but now I know it." Most of us would disagree. We would side rather with Longfellow: "Life is real! Life is earnest! And the grave is not its goal. Dust thou art to dust returnest, Was not spoken of the soul."

LIFE.   Sometimes the pressures of life seem too much for us. We long to be free from them. We forget that a diamond is just a lump of coal that has been under pressure! Both coal and diamonds consist of carbon. The difference is due to the situation in which each is found. So if you feel that you are under great pressure, it may be that God wants to make a diamond out of you.

LOST.   Daniel Boone explored the great wilderness of Tennessee and Kentucky. It was Boone who marked the Wilderness Road that brought settlers into the new land. He often wandered over vast areas of forest, living off the land and dodging Indian arrows. Once he was asked if he had ever been lost. He replied, "No." He said that he had never been lost, but he did admit that he was "a mite confused once for about three or four days!" Perhaps it matters but little that Boone's pride would not allow him to admit that he'd ever been lost. It matters much if our pride keeps us from admitting that without Christ we're lost. People will readily admit to being "a mite confused." They will readily admit to mistakes and blunders, but it's very hard to get people to realize that they are lost, and only Christ can save them.

LOVE.   Ljubostinija is a large convent in Yugoslavia. The name comes from two Slavic words that, put together, mean "Love on the Rocks." The convent is located near the spot where Serbian king Lazar later first met the young woman who became his Queen Milica. After his death she spent the rest of her life there. What a romantic name: "Love on the Rocks!" In a far less romantic sense we often encounter "love on the rocks." The rocks of selfishness, thoughtlessness, unkindness, greed, and lust often prove to be the undoing of love and the wrecking of romance.

LOVE.   Christopher Morley once said that if we discovered we had only five minutes left to say all we wanted to say, every telephone booth would be occupied by people calling other people to stammer that they loved them. Why wait until the last five minutes? Many a person has suffered the loss of a loved one and grieved that it was so sudden there was no opportunity to say the things they wanted to say. Because life is uncertain, we ought to say now what we want to say. There is an even better reason. Let people have the rest of their lives to bask in the knowledge that we love them, that we are proud of them, that we forgive them . . . or whatever else it is that needs saying but has thus far gone unsaid.

LOVE.   King Mathias was one of the revered kings of Hungarian history. There is a legend that he once went hunting disguised as a commoner. A lovely peasant girl saw him and fell in love. When she learned who the handsome hunter was, she knew that her love was a hopeless love. She died soon afterward. There is a statue of her in front of a Budapest museum where she waits forever for her lover. Of course, such romantic legends intrigue us. We are even more intrigued by the phrase "a hopeless love." God says in Jeremiah, "I have loved you with an everlasting love." All who experience it know that it is never a hopeless love but ever a hope-giving love.

MEDITATION.   The visitor to the lovely gardens of Florida's Bok Tower soon comes across a sign along a garden path. It reads, "I come here often to find myself. It's so easy to get lost in the world." It is, in fact, easy to get lost in the world, and sometimes the hardest thing we have to do is to find ourselves. To set aside moments for meditation, pauses for prayer, times to think is wise indeed. To fail to do that is foolish and often destructive.

MEMORIALS.   The oldest example of Slavic writing is on a tombstone, erected by Macedonian king Samuel over the graves of his mother and his brothers. If you are researching your genealogy you will eventually end up in a cemetery somewhere reading tombstones. We learn so much from memorials. We learn the most from the memorial Christ chose for himself: the Lord's Supper.

MONEY.   The average life of a U.S. one-dollar bill is eighteen months. After

that it must be replaced. It's worn out. That was not quite what the Apostle Peter had in mind when he wrote of "gold that perishes." It's not exactly what Jesus had in mind when he spoke of earthly treasures that moth and rust corrupt. It's not precisely what Paul had in mind when he wrote of "uncertain riches." It's not exactly what James had in mind when he wrote of gold and silver corroding. But it certainly illustrates the truth behind all those verses.

MONEY.   Many people think that money brings security. Money doesn't bring security. Money *needs* security. Money requires a bank, a safe, a lock, a burglar alarm, a watchdog, and insurance. If you are looking for security, you will never find it in money.

MORALITY.   Justin Martyr eloquently defended Christianity against its attackers. Writing in the second century after Christ, he defended the faith by pointing to the superior moral conduct of Christians. He said that they proved they possessed the truth upon which life could be successfully built. Can we make the same appeal today? Sadly, sometimes the answer is no. But often the answer really is yes! In general it *is* true that believers lead better lives, show greater love, demonstrate more compassion. It will not do to compare the worst example of Christianity with the best example from the world. We must instead compare the world's best with Christianity's best . . . and then we will clearly see what Justin saw.

OPTIMISM.   "Errors, like straws, upon the surface flow; He who would search for pearls must dive below." So wrote Dryden. The pearl divers of Japan are famous for their ability to dive so deeply without air hoses or tanks to sustain them. Dryden's lesson, though, is for all of us. We look at life so superficially, and we look at people so superficially. When we look deeply, we find that there is so much good in the world and so much good in others.

PERFECTION.   There is a town in Georgia named Ideal. Those who live there say it's an ideal place to live. They say that all the citizens are ideal people. No doubt it is a pleasant place, but there is no truly ideal place, no utopia, no paradise on this earth. It is a part of living that we are subject to accident and injury, to disease and death. Everyone must face the possibilities of bad neighbors and bad neighborhoods, of unpleasant events and unpleasant people and unpleasant places, of danger and death. The only perfect place we shall know is heaven.

PRAYER.   The *American* magazine for March 1, 1950, carried an interview with nuclear physicist Harold Urey in which Urey is quoted as saying of the hydrogen bomb, "Frankly, I am scared to death. I wish I had a direct line to the Almighty to ask Him for guidance." Certainly nuclear weapons are a legitimate cause for fear. It is also certain that all who believe really do have a direct line to the Almighty.

PRAYER.   "The gift of prayer," wrote Lessing, "is not always in our power; in Heaven's sight to wish to pray is prayer." Isn't that what the Scripture means when it teaches that we cannot always find words for our prayers? Surely Paul expressed it better when he wrote, "We do not know what we ought to pray for, but the Spirit himself intercedes for us with groans that words cannot express" (Rom. 8:26).

PREACHING.   Stephen Sondheim won the Pulitzer prize for drama and wrote such hits as *West Side Story*, *Gypsy*, and *A Funny Thing Happened on the Way to the Forum*. He once said, "There is nothing more frightening than to look at a blank sheet of paper and wonder how you are going to fill it." That's what every preacher faces every week. It's a most demanding task!

PRIDE.   The state of Illinois gets its name from an Indian word, to which a French suffix has been added. It means "tribe of superior men." Certainly modern-day residents of Illinois do not ordinarily boast of themselves as superior men. But throughout history there have been those who regarded themselves as superior to others. The most extreme example is in Nazi Germany, where Hitler taught people that they were a super race. The Bible urges us not to think more highly of ourselves than we ought to think. Humility is a virtue, and while pride may not be a sin, it can be the root of many sins.

PROCRASTINATION.   In the well-known *Shoe* comic strip, the leading character says, "I try to set aside one day each week and devote it entirely to my work." "That's a good idea," responds his friend. "What day of the week is that for you?" "Tomorrow," is his answer.

PROVIDENCE.   When the Turks conquered eastern Europe they took over the churches and turned them into mosques. Many of them were decorated with frescoes depicting Christian scenes. The Turks plastered over them. Years later the Turks left and those old buildings became churches again. Then it was discovered that the plaster meant to obliterate the frescoes had, in fact, preserved them. Some of them were painted in a particular shade of blue that cannot be duplicated today. The secret has been lost, but the paintings were not lost. The very thing that was intended to obliterate them preserved them! Thus, once again God made "the wrath of men to praise him."

POWER.   They say that one person cannot affect events or effect change. They say that one person has no power. But in 1962 the state of Maine elected a governor by a margin of just one vote per precinct! In the same year the same thing happened in the states of Rhode Island and North Dakota. One person is important. One person has power.

REPENTANCE.   In the Old Testament, people signified repentance by wearing the roughest of clothing and putting dust or ashes on their heads. In India, grasping one's ears is a sign of repentance.

Surely the best sign of repentance is not symbolic but practical. It is a real change in life and conduct.

REPENTANCE. Protestant churches in the USSR almost always paint Bible verses on the inside walls of their church. Orthodox churches usually have pictures from the Bible or church history, but Protestant churches use Bible verses or slogans that reflect biblical ideas. One Russian church had these slogans on its walls: "Every Evangelical Christian is a Missionary." "The Only Enemy—Sin; the Only Fear—God." "Without Repentance No Revival."

RESPONSIBILITY. Van Wyck Brooks said, "Every day I begin my work with the same old feeling that I am on trial for my life and will probably not be acquitted." What a sense of responsibility! Jesus said we'd give account for every idle word. Surely we'll also give account for every idle hour. That doesn't mean we shouldn't rest nor have leisure time, but it does mean that life is serious business, and we should use our time wisely and well.

RESURRECTION. Canaanites worshiped the idol god Baal, who was responsible for the fertility of the soil and for all growing things. But there is no rain in Palestine between April and October, and nothing grows then without irrigation. So they said Baal had been killed. Then in the autumn, rain began and crops grew. So they said that the sun had brought Baal back to life again. Thus every year he kept dying, and every year he was raised again from the dead. What a stark contrast to the gospel, where Jesus is reported to have died once for all of the sins of men and raised again once for all for their eternal redemption.

RESURRECTION. When Fyodor inherited the Russian throne he was so weak and incompetent that his brother-in-law, Boris Godunov, took power. He killed Dmitri, the heir to the throne. But Poland advanced the cause of a man who claimed to be the murdered Dmitri.

When he failed, a second pretender made the same claim. Though his followers actually managed to occupy Moscow, they failed to secure for him the Russian throne. The resurrected Christ, by contrast, had no problem securing his throne. After the Resurrection, God exalted him and set him at his own right hand. "He *must* reign," wrote Paul, "until he has put all enemies under his feet."

RESURRECTION. An Australian tradition among some aborigines is that Wiyaki kept meeting her lover, Japara. Purukupali decided to kill Japara, but when he died, his sister, Wuriuprenala, lit a fire and brought him back to life. Then Purukupali gave firesticks to Japara and to his sister, Wuriuprenala, and Japara became the man in the moon, while Wuriuprenala was changed into the sun. How utterly different is the return of Christ from the dead. He ate and drank as before. He taught as before. Then he returned to the heaven from whence he'd come, with the promise to return to reward his followers.

RESURRECTION. One period of the Iron Age is called the Hallstatt period, because of the many objects found at Hallstatt, Austria. The most important find, however, was lost to science. On April 1, 1734, there was found in a salt mine the perfectly preserved body of a man, dressed in skins. He had been preserved by the salt for a thousand years! It was supposed that he had been killed in a mine accident. The people of that time were very superstitious and quickly buried him. There was no opportunity to study the body. There is so much we might have learned. It's an interesting contrast between Hallstatt and Jerusalem. Hallstatt gets its fame from a man whose body was found there. Jerusalem gets its fame from a man whose body has never been found, the resurrected Christ.

REVERENCE. In 1932 *Time* magazine put a picture of Japanese emperor Hirohito on its cover and printed with it this request: "Let copies of the present issue lie face upward on all tables; let no object be placed upon the likeness of the Emperor." It was a concession to the Japanese who, at that time, regarded the emperor as a deity. After World War II he disavowed divine status. How much reverence, how much respect, do we show for the true and living God? We make no picture of him, for he has strictly forbidden it. But we must hold in reverence his name, his book, his Church, his person, and his character.

RIGHT AND WRONG.   In Stephen Sondheim's great musical *West Side Story*, there is a line of a song that goes something like this: "When loves comes so strong, there is no right and wrong. Your love is your life." Certainly that captures the common philosophy of our day, but it's not correct. No matter how strong romantic love may be, there is still right, and there is still wrong.

SACRIFICE.   The angry clouds of World War I were plainly visible on the horizon. Pope Pius X offered to give up his own life to avert the conflict. No one accepted the offer. No one believed that the death of the pope could really avert the war. Besides, the pope was incurably ill. But it was a noble gesture no matter how futile. Christ offered himself for the sins of the whole world. The offer was accepted. The sacrifice was made, and that sacrifice did accomplish its purpose.

SALVATION.   It was Alexandre Vinet who defined saving faith as being not the conviction that we are saved, but the conviction that we are loved. It's an interesting distinction, and the implications of it might leave room for lots of discussion. Still, it is certainly true that salvation begins and ends with the conviction that we are loved.

SECURITY.   Justin Martyr knew the danger he was facing when he wrote his famous defense of the gospel, and eventually he did die for his faith. But years before he had written, "You can kill us but not hurt us." That's still true. Christians can be killed, but they cannot be hurt. Beyond this life there is a better life. Beyond this world there is a better world. Death is the beginning, not the end. The protection of God is certain even though it may not take the form we would choose. We can be injured. We can suffer illness. We can experience accidents. We can be killed. But we cannot be hurt!

SELF.   Most visitors to France go to Versailles to see the great palace of the Sun King. The centerpiece of the palace of Versailles is the famed Hall of Mirrors. In that room, wherever one looks, he sees himself! Some people *live* in such a room. All they ever see is themselves. All they ever think about is themselves. All they really care about is themselves. But outside their little hall of mirrors there is a big, wide, wonderful world filled with opportunity and need. Let's go outside!

SIN.   In some European countries a house of prostitution is called a Freudenhaus—a house of joy. Solomon would disagree with such a term. In Prov. 2:18 he calls it a house of death. Perhaps we use too mild a term when we call it a house of shame. Sin always tries to fool us by changing the labels!

SIN.   Some cynic said that by the time a person is wise enough to watch his steps, he's too old to go anywhere. Another said that old age did for her what the church never could! We make a great mistake if we assume that youth has a monopoly on sin. The sins of old age are different from the sins of youth, but they are sins nonetheless. There is never a time when we are not subject to temptation. It is only that the form of the temptation changes.

SIN.   Travel writer Bruce Chatwin described a visit to Brazil. He stayed at the Charm Hotel, except that the letter *C* had been blown away. How often in life there are things that seem at first to charm but eventually turn out to harm us!

SIN.   In the summer of 1989, newspapers reported that trees growing near the Chernobyl nuclear power plant that malfunctioned three years earlier were showing signs of serious abnormalities. They also found genetic defects in rodents in the area. Radiation can deform plants and animals. Sin deforms the soul.

SIN.   Forks first appeared in the eleventh century. Preachers preached against them. They said that since food comes from God, it should only be eaten with the instruments created by God, namely, the fingers. Men have often disagreed about what is and what is not sin, but biblical morality is unchanged since Eden, the same in both Testaments, the same in all generations.

SMILE.   The Parker Pen Company has published a guide to international behavior entitled "Do's and Taboos Around the World." It lists all the things one needs to be careful about when traveling abroad. The postscript reads, "There is one universal action, one signal, one form of communication that is used and understood by every culture and in every country, no matter how remote. It can help you with every relationship— business or personal—and become the single most useful form of communication. It is . . . the smile."

STEWARDSHIP.   Since the arrival of Europeans on the North American continent, 75 percent of the topsoil has been lost. Every year six billion tons of it are lost. Good farming land typically has only six inches of topsoil. It takes ten thousand years to produce one inch! On the first page of the Bible, mankind was put in charge of the earth. We are the trustees of the earth. "The earth is the Lord's," but we manage it for him. We haven't managed it very well. Now we call concerns for the environment "ecology," but that's only a synonym for stewardship. When you add to the loss of topsoil the pollution of water and air, the destruction of forests, you can readily see that we need to repent of our mismanagement and then find new ways to stop

the destruction of the only world we know.

SYMBOLS.   Everybody recognizes the tall, thin man with the chin whiskers, top hat, and swallow-tail coat. He's Uncle Sam, the symbol of the United States. Many may not know that there was a real Uncle Sam. His name was Sam Wilson, and he supplied meat to the U.S. Army during the War of 1812. He stamped the cases of beef and pork "U.S.," but his nephew said it stood for Uncle Sam, not for United States. The man himself is a mere footnote in history. The symbol he inadvertently created has almost taken on a life of its own. Symbols are important. Some say that the only way religious truth can ever be communicated is by means of symbols! Whether that's accurate or not, the fact remains that without our symbolic acts, our symbolic designs, our symbolic meanings, Christianity would be poor indeed.

TEMPTATION.   In Bulgaria a nod of the head doesn't mean, yes. It means no. And a shake of the head doesn't mean no. It means yes. That's very confusing to the traveler. Imagine someone saying no, and all the time he is nodding his head. You'd wonder if he really meant it! Isn't that what we do when temptation comes? Sometimes we say no, but we really mean yes. We want our friends and neighbors to hear us saying a very loud no, but in our hearts we are saying yes.

TIME.   When Borglum carved the faces of four presidents on the side of Mount Rushmore, he made their noses over-size. He knew that over the years erosion would reduce them to the proper proportion! What has time eroded in your life and mine? It may have eroded our strength, our health, our idealism, even our optimism. Let us be certain that time is never allowed to erode our faith, our confidence, our convictions, our love.

TIME.   Peter Altenberg wrote once of "people who need to kill time before time kills them." It is true that time will kill us all. It is also true that if we never find the leisure to kill a little time, then time will kill us all the sooner! We need to use our time wisely. One of the ways we need to use it is in quiet contemplation. We try so hard to fill every waking minute that we may one day die without ever having really lived. It's fine to be aggressive and energetic. God has no brief for laziness, but it's also good to take time to think and pray.

TIME.   Richard M. Ketchum has an interesting title for his new book on America between 1938 and 1941. He calls those years "the borrowed years." He uses the term in its common proverbial sense of borrowed time, delineating American innocence and complacency, as war clouds gathered in Europe. We have long used the term *borrowed time* for one who has lived beyond the biblical "threescore years and ten" or who has lived beyond his normal life expectancy. Of course, there is no such thing as borrowed time, and there are no borrowed years. All we really have to use is today.

TIME.   At the end of a causeway in Wiltshire, England, four sun dials decorate an obelisk. These words are written there:

"O early passenger / Look up, be wise / And think how night and day / Time onward flies."

TRUTH.   Chuck Woodbury travels western America gathering material for his quarterly publication, *Out West*. Woodbury is the reporter, editor, and publisher. In fact, he's the entire staff of the magazine. He passes by the cities of the West and gathers his material from the small towns, from places like Nothing, Arizona, and Boring, Oregon. One place he visited was Congress, Arizona. He wrote, "We should all leave our earthly existence with something to show for our years. I only stayed fifteen minutes, but that was long enough. Now when someone asks me what I have accomplished in my lifetime, I can answer with all honesty that I spent some time in Congress." Don't we all, at times, find a

way to lie by telling the truth? And is it really no less a lie?

UNITY.   The country of Panama once had a motto: "The land divided, the world united." It was at least geographically true. The Panama Canal divided North and South America, yet that same canal united the whole world in transport and commerce. The church may be something like that. At one level of observation the church appears to be sadly divided. At a deeper level the church is seen as a great unifying force, uniting people to God and to one another.

VICTORY.   Two fingers lifted to form a V stand for victory both in the United States and in Europe. But in England it must be done with the palm facing outward. Otherwise it's an insulting gesture. Everyone thinks of those pictures from World War II showing a defiant Winston Churchill lifting his hand in a V for victory. The sign, however, didn't begin in World War II, and it began not with an Englishman but with a Belgian. For Christians, however, the cross is ever and always the sign of victory.

VICTORY.   For five hundred years the Turks ruled Ohrid, Yugoslavia, and for five hundred years every day at sunset the gates enclosing the old walled fortress above the town were closed. Every day at dawn they were opened again. But in 1912, the Turks left at last, and ever since the gates have remained open, night and day. Isn't that what was symbolized by the tearing of the temple veil when Christ died? The gates are now open. God may be approached directly. No intermediary is needed. The gates are open . . . and they will never be closed again!

WEAPONS.   The mammoth was an enormous animal that once roamed across great stretches of North America. He was hunted by the Indians but now is long extinct. However, skeletons of mammoths have been found. One, estimated to be twelve thousand years old, still held the spear point that brought death. The weapon remains! Whatever lessons there may be here for nations, there is certainly a lesson for individuals. If the good we do lives on after us, can it not also be said that the evil we do will live on after us? Can it not be added that the evil words we speak may live on after us? When we use words as weapons, we may be leaving behind us a legacy we never intended to leave.

ACKNOWLEDGMENTS

Acknowledgment and gratitude are hereby expressed to the following for kind permission to reprint material from the books and periodicals listed below:

HARPERCOLLINS PUBLISHERS, INC.: Excerpts from Robert A. Raines, *Reshaping the Christian Life*, © 1964, HarperCollins; Excerpts from Robert J. McCracken, *Putting Faith to Work*, © 1960, HarperCollins; Excerpts from Harry Emerson Fosdick, *What is Vital in Religion*, Copyright 1955, Harper & Brothers; Excerpts from Charles R. Brown, *Being Made Over*, Copyright 1939, 1967, HarperCollins; Excerpts from Harry Emerson Fosdick, *A Book of Public Prayers*, © 1959, Harper-Collins; Excerpts from Paul Scherer, *The Place Where Thou Standest*, Copyright 1942, Harper & Brothers; Excerpts from Paul Scherer, *The Word God Sent*, © 1965, HarperCollins; Excerpts from Samuel H. Miller, *Prayers For Daily Use*, © 1957, 1985, HarperCollins; Excerpts from Agnes Sanford, *Let's Believe*, Copyright 1954, 1982, HarperCollins.

SUNDAY SCHOOL BOARD OF THE SOUTHERN BAPTIST CONVENTION: Excerpts from Ralph L. Murray, "The Potter and the Preacher," in *Plumb Lines and Fruit Baskets*, (Nashville: Broadman Press, 1966), pp. 82–89. © Copyright 1966 Broadman Press. Excerpts from Robert W. Bailey, "Our Universal Mission," in *Award Winning Sermons, Vol I*, (Nashville: Broadman Press, 1977), pp. 101–8. © Copyright 1977 Broadman Press. Excerpts from S. M. Henriques, Jr., "A Fresh Look at Renewal," in *Proclaim*, July-September 1990, pp. 22–23. Broadman Press © 1990; Excerpts from Marion Aldridge, an illustration "Christian," in *Proclaim*, October-December 1990, pp. 28–29. Broadman Press © 1990; Excerpts from Hugh Litchfield, *Preaching the Christmas Story*, Broadman Press © 1984; Excerpts from Alton McEachern, "Don't Forget the Baby," *Sermons and Services for Special Days*, Broadman Press © 1979; Excerpts from Bruce Kelley Edwards, "Remembering Salvation," *Proclaim*, January-March 1991, p. 35; Broadman Press © 1991; Excerpts from C. W. Bess, *Children's Sermons for Special Times*, Broadman Press © 1988; Excerpts from Leon W. Castle, *Fifty-Two Children's Sermons*, Broadman Press © 1988; Excerpts from Roy de Brand, *Children's Sermons for Special Occasions*, Broadman Press © 1983. Excerpts from Brian L. Harbour, "And This Is Love," *From Cover to Cover*. Broadman Press and Convention Press Books (Nashville: Broadman Press 1982) pp. 92–94. *All rights reserved. Used by permission.*

TYNDALE HOUSE PUBLISHERS: Excerpts from *The Living Bible*, Tyndale House © 1971 (Wheaton, Illinois, Tyndale House Publishers).

INDEX OF CONTRIBUTORS

SERMON TITLE INDEX

(Children's stories and sermons are identified as **cs***; sermon suggestions as* **ss***)*

SCRIPTURAL INDEX

330

INDEX OF PRAYERS

INDEX OF MATERIALS USEFUL AS CHILDREN'S STORIES AND SERMONS NOT INCLUDED IN SECTION X

INDEX OF MATERIALS USEFUL FOR SMALL GROUPS

TOPICAL INDEX